INTROD
TO
ACCOUNTANCY

T.S. GREWAL, M.A., (COM)
Ex-Director of Studies,
Coaching Board,
Institute of Chartered Accountants of India
New Delhi

S. CHAND & COMPANY LTD.
RAM NAGAR, NEW DELHI-110 055

S. CHAND & COMPANY LTD.

(An ISO 9001 : 2000 Company)

Head Office : 7361, RAM NAGAR, NEW DELHI - 110 055
Phones : 23672080-81-82, 9899107446, 9911310888;
Fax : 91-11-23677446
Shop at: **schandgroup.com**
E-mail: **schand@vsnl.com**

Branches :

- 1st Floor, Heritage, Near Gujarat Vidhyapeeth, Ashram Road, **Ahmedabad-**380 014. Ph. 27541965, 27542369. ahmedabad@schandgroup.com
- No. 6, Ahuja Chambers, 1st Cross, Kumara Krupa Road, **Bangalore**-560 001. Ph : 22268048, 22354008, bangalore@schandgroup.com
- 238-A M.P. Nagar, Zone 1, **Bhopal** - 462 011. Ph : 4274723, bhopal@schandgroup.com
- 152, Anna Salai, **Chennai**-600 002. Ph : 28460026, chennai@schandgroup.com
- S.C.O. 6, 7 & 8, Sector 9D, **Chandigarh**-160017, Ph-2749376, 2749377, chandigarh@schandgroup.com
- 1st Floor, Bhartia Tower, Badambadi, **Cuttack**-753 009, Ph-2332580; 2332581, cuttack@schandgroup.com
- 1st Floor, 52-A, Rajpur Road, **Dehradun**-248 001. Ph : 2740889, 2740861, dehradun@schandgroup.com
- Pan Bazar, **Guwahati**-781 001. Ph : 2514155, guwahati@schandgroup.com
- Sultan Bazar, **Hyderabad**-500 195. Ph : 24651135, 24744815, hyderabad@schandgroup.com
- Mai Hiran Gate, **Jalandhar** - 144008 . Ph. 2401630, jalandhar@schandgroup.com
- A-14 Janta Store Shopping Complex, University Marg, Bapu Nagar, **Jaipur** - 302 015, Phone : 2719126, jaipur@schandgroup.com
- 613-7, M.G. Road, Ernakulam, **Kochi**-682 035. Ph : 2381740, cochin@schandgroup.com
- 285/J, Bipin Bihari Ganguli Street, **Kolkata**-700 012. Ph : 22367459, 22373914, kolkata@schandgroup.com
- Mahabeer Market, 25 Gwynne Road, Aminabad, **Lucknow**-226 018. Ph : 2626801, 2284815, lucknow@schandgroup.com
- Blackie House, 103/5, Walchand Hirachand Marg , Opp. G.P.O., **Mumbai**-400 001. Ph : 22690881, 22610885, mumbai@schandgroup.com
- Karnal Bag, Model Mill Chowk, Umrer Road, **Nagpur**-440 032 Ph : 2723901, 2777666 nagpur@schandgroup.com
- 104, Citicentre Ashok, Govind Mitra Road, **Patna**-800 004. Ph : 2300489, 2302100, patna@schandgroup.com

First Edition 1964
Subsequent Editions and Reprints 1964, 71, 73 (Twice), 74, 75, 76, 77 78, 79, 80, 82, 83, 85, 86, 88, 89, 90, 91, 92, 93, 94, 95, 96, 97, 98, 99, 2000, 2001, 2002, 2003, 2004, 2006
Reprint 2007

ISBN : 81-219-0569-9
Code : 07 007

PRINTED IN INDIA

By Rajendra Ravindra Printers (Pvt.) Ltd., Ram Nagar, New Delhi-110 055 and published by S. Chand & Company Ltd., 7361, Ram Nagar, New Delhi-110 055

This book is respectfully dedicated
to my parents
Sardar Bhagwan Singh
and
Shrimati Inder Kaur

PREFACE TO THE SEVENTH EDITION

I sincerely and gratefully thank my readers, students and teachers alike, for their continued patronage extended to this book on Accountancy, so much so that a thoroughly revised and enlarged edition is in your hands.

In this revised edition, some new topics like "Accounting policies", new concepts of *Income* and *Gain*, "Joint Ventures and Consignments", accounting of Donations and Receipts for Special Purposes, etc. have been added at appropriate points in the text. Latest questions from various Boards and Universitie's Examinations have been included, to make the book more useful and uptodate. Besides, some of the old topics have been further amplified to make the concept more understandable. With all these modifications etc., it is hoped that the book, in its new format, will prove as a true guide to B.Com. students in general and of 'Pass Course" in particular.

Errors and deficiencies are likely to be there. I apologise, in advance, for the same. Suggestions for improvement will be gratefully received.

October 1987

T.S. GREWAL

PREFACE TO THE FIRST EDITION

The reception given to Advanced Accounts, a book written by me in co-authorship with Prof. M.C. Shukla, encouraged me (and doubtless the publishers) to write this Introduction to Accountancy. The book is meant for the beginners. But it will carry the beginner quite some distance—to the Intermediate level. Since I believe that my knowledge of Accountancy is based on a firm grasp of the significance of "debit" and "credit" (for which I am grateful to my teachers, Prof. M.L. Shandilya and Principal J.N. Vaish), I have tried to write this book from the same standpoint. The beginner will do well to spend some time on knowing what exactly debit and credit mean. This book should help him to do so.

Undoubtedly there are mistakes and deficiencies. I will be deeply grateful to those who point them out and to those who make suggestions for improvement.

August 8, 1964

T.S. GREWAL

TABLE OF CONTENTS

CHAPTER I
INTRODUCTION

The dictionary meaning of Book-keeping is "the art of keeping accounts in a regular and systematic manner." This means that a firm (or an individual) has to record the events affecting it in such a way that a correct picture can emerge whenever needed. "Events" in a firm need not be very big ; usually they are small but, sometimes, they are big. Purchase of machinery worth Rs. 5 lakhs and stationery worth Rs. 5 are both events. A systematic record of all events, big and small, is essential. If the firm is involved with outsiders in an event, the event becomes a transaction ; by far the largest number of events to be recorded are of this nature. That is to say, the bulk of the records of a firm will be with reference to transactions with others—buying and selling goods, taking a loan, paying interest, etc. But the records of a firm will not be concerned only with outsiders. There is a number of events that do not concern outsiders, for instance, loss due to fire, wear and tear of equipment and tools, etc. Such events must also be recorded. Book-keeping, therefore, may be defined as a systematic and regular record of events affecting a firm with a view to obtaining a clear picture of the financial state of affairs of the firm and of its performance in monetary terms over a period of time.

Book-keeping and Accountancy practically mean the same thing although the term Accountancy is usually used for accounting work of a higher order. A skilful accountant will prepare accounts in such a way as to show up all the deficiencies and good points of the firm concerned. Thus he will help management to know not only how strong or weak the firm is financially but also to take action to remove shortcomings and inefficiencies—now a special branch of Accountancy has emerged, known as Management Accounting. Even Economists have found a use for accounting techniques. There is such a thing as National Income Accounting. Accounting is now developing into an almost exact science of measurement. Therefore, those who study Book-keeping and Accountancy may hope to play a significant and important role in the affairs of the firms they serve or in the affairs of the country. A committee of the American Institute of Certified Public Accountants has defined Accounting as follows :

> "Accounting is the art of recording, classifying and summarising in a significant manner and in terms of money, transactions and events which are, in part at least, of a financial character, and interpreting the results thereof."

As already said, the object of Book-keeping and Accountancy is to present a clear picture of the financial state of affairs of a firm and of the results of operations carried out during a period. This picture consists of two statements mainly. One statement summarises the incomes and expenses, showing how much profit the firm has earned in a particular period or how much has been the loss during the period. The other statement sets out what the firm possesses (assets), how much the firm owes to others (liabilities) and how much belongs to the proprietors (capital). The first statement is known as "Profit and Loss Account" or "Income Statement" and the second one is called "Balance Sheet". If transactions are recorded properly, the preparation of these two is easy. It should not be thought that Accounting can be useful only for firms or business houses, where the profit motive operates. In fact most institutions, even if their aim is to render social service and not to earn a profit, will find Accounting is very useful, nay essential, since then only with the institution be able to keep track if its financial resources.

Concepts *

The affairs of a firm are generally well reflected in the two statements mentioned above. Hence it is said that Accounting is the language of business. Affairs of a business unit are made understood to others as well as to those who own or manage it through accounting information which has to be suitably recorded, classified, summarised and presented. To make the language convey the same meaning to all people, as far as practicable, and to make it full of meaning, accountants have agreed on a number of concepts which they try to follow. These are briefly given below :

(*i*) **Business Entity Concept.** Accountants treat a business as distinct from the persons who own it ; it then becomes possible to record transactions of the business with the proprietor also. Without such a distinction, the affairs of the firm will be all mixed up with the private affairs of the proprietor and the true picture of the firm will not be available.

This concept has now been extended to accounting separately for various divisions of a firm in order to ascertain the results for each division separately. It has been of immense value in determining results by each responsibility centre—Responsibility Accounting.

(*ii*) **Money Measurement Concept.** Accounting records only those transactions which are being expressed in monetary terms though quantitative records are also kept. For example, a quarrel between the production manager and the sales manager, will not be recorded since its monetary effect cannot be measured with a fair degree of accuracy. If should be remembered that money enables various things of diverse nature to be added up together and dealt with. The use of a building and the use of clerical services can be aggregated only through money values and not otherwise.

(*iii*) **Cost Concept.** Transactions are entered in the books of account at the amounts actually involved. Suppose a firm purchases a piece of land for Rs. 1,50,000 but considers it as worth Rs. 3,00,000. The purchase of land will be

**N.B.* The terms concept, convention and doctrine are sometimes used interchangeably.

recorded at Rs. 1,50,000 and not any more. This is one of the most important concepts—it prevents arbitrary values being put on transactions, chiefly those rosulting in acquisition of assets. Another way of saying the same thing would be that the amount to be recorded is objectively arrived at—as a result of the mutual agreement of the two parties involved.

Of course, sometimes accountants have necessarily to be satisfied with an estimate only—the amount of depreciation to be charged to accounts each year in respect of machinery is an example ; the amount has to be an estimate since the future life of the machinery cannot be known precisely.

(*iv*) **Going Concern Concept.** It is assumed that the business will exist for the foreseeable future and transactions are recorded from this point of view. It is this that necessitates distinction between expenditure that will render benefit over a long period and that whose benefit will be exhausted quickly, say, within the year. Of course, if it is certain that the business will exist only for a limited time, the accounting record will keep the expected life in view.

A firm is said to be a going concern when there is neither the intention nor the necessity to wind up its affairs or curtail substantially the scale of its operations. In other words, it should continue to operate at its present scale in the foreseeable future.

(*v*) **Dual-Aspect Concept.** Each transaction has two aspects : if a business has acquired an asset, it must have resulted in one of the following :—

(*i*) some other asset has been given up ;

(*ii*) the obligation to pay for it has arisen ;

(*iii*) there has been a profit, leading to an increase in the amount that the business owes to the proprietor ; or

(*iv*) the proprietor has contributed money for the acquisition of the asset.

The reverse is also true. If, for instance, there is an increase in the amount owed to others, there must have been an increase in assets or a loss. At any time :

Assets = Liabilities + Capital ; or

Capital = Assets − Liabilities.

In other words, capital, i.e., the owner's share of the assets of the firm, is always what is left out of assets after paying off outsiders. A transaction must affect one of the three things mentioned above.

Income or profit arises only when there has been an increase in the owner's share of the assets of the firm (called owner's equity) but not if the increase has resulted from money contributed by the owner himself. Any increase in the owner's equity is called revenue and anything that reduees the owner's equity is expense (or loss) ; profit results only when the total of revenues exceeds the total of expenses of losses.

(*vi*) **Realisation Concept.** Accounting is a historical record of transactions ; it records what has happened. It does not anticipate events, though anticipated adverse effects of events that have already occurred are usually recorded. This is of great importance in stopping business firms from inflating their profits by recording sales and incomes that are only likely to accrue. Unless money has been realised—either cash has been received or a legal obligation to pay has been assumed by the customer—no sale can be said to have taken place and no profit or income can be said to have arisen.

(*vii*) **Accrual Concept**. When an event takes place or a transaction is entered into, its consequences are bound to follow. For example, if one borrows Rs 1,00,000 @ 15% p.a., at the end of the year Rs. 15,000 will become due as interest. If the amount is paid, the record will certainly show it. If, however, the amount is not yet paid, there is the liability to pay the amount and, there being no corresponding increase in the total assets, the capital will stand reduced. This must be brought into the accounting ; otherwise the accounts will not reflect the true picture. The accrual concept or principle requires that all transactions or events, not yet settled in cash, must be taken into account.

In addition to the above-mentioned concepts, the following should also be noted :—

(*i*) Transactions should be recorded in such a manner as to reflect the true legal position as far as practicable. For instance, it is not proper to treat goods sent on approval as sales and to treat the customer as a debtor since he can always return the goods without any obligation.

(*ii*) Even though it is assumed that business will continue for a long time it is necessary to keep accounts in such a manner as to permit results being ascertained and presented for each financial period, usually a year.

Conventions regarding Financial Statements. In order to make the message contained in the financial statements—the income statement (Profit and Loss Account) and the statement showing the financial position (Balance Sheet)—clear and meaningful, these are drawn up according to the under-mentioned conventions :

(*i*) **Consistency.** Various accounting practices should remain the same from one year to another—for instance it would not be proper to value stock in trade according to one method one year and according to another method next year. If a change becomes necessary, the change and its effect should be stated clearly.

(*ii*) **Disclosure**. Apart from legal requirements, good accounting practice also demands that all significant information should be disclosed. Not only various assets, for example, have to be stated but also the mode of valuation should be disclosed. Various types of revenues and expenses must also be stated separately. Whether someting should be disclosed or not will depend on whether it is material or not. Materiality depends on the amounts involved in relation to the asset-group involved or profits.

(*iii*) **Conservatism**. Financial statements are usually drawn up on rather a conservative basis. Window-dressing, i.e., showing a position better than what it is, is not permitted. It is also not proper to show a position substantially worse than what it is. In other words, secret reserves also are not permitted.

(Discussed again in Chapters VIII and XIII).

It is worth noting that the International Accounting Standards Committee and the Institute of Chartered Accountants of India regard *Going Concern, Accrual and Consistency* as fundamental to the preparation of financial statements. These three are termed as Fundamental Accounting Assumptions. If the firm concerned is silent, it will be assumed that these assumptions are valid. It is the firm's duty to disclose the fact if any of the assumptions is not valid. For example, if there is a change in any accounting practice, say in computing depreciation (involving a departure from the consistency concept), there should be an appropriate note on the financial statements disclosing the departure and effect on profits of the year.

Accounting Policies. The broad difference between Fundamental Accounting Assumptions and Accounting Policies should be noted. Accounting Policies refer to the choice made, one of two or moer alternatives, for dealing with an accounting matter or question. For example, depreciation of assets may be computed in many ways and the management has to choose one method. Similarly the cost of the closing stock may be arrived at in many ways; again the management has to make a choice as to which method should be adopted. There are quite a few other questions where management will have to decide upon the method to follow. The choice made by the management has an important effect on the profit/loss shown, as will be clear when the student studies Final Accounts. The important point is that one firm may choose one method and another firm may choose a different method. This is what is meant by "Accounting Policies." All firms, however, will generally adopt the basis of Going Concern, Consistency and Accural, the three fundamental accounting assumptions. (see page 546).

Cash and Mercantile Systems. Professional people normally prepare their accounts on cash basis only, that is, they do not recognise a transaction (specially income) till it is settled in cash. Such a system is called 'cash system.' Government accounts are also on cash basis only. If the transactions not yet settled in cash are also considered and brought into the books, the system is called the 'Mercantile System'. This is demanded by the 'Accrual' concept and is the normal practice.

Two Systems of Book-keeping. There are two systems of Book-keeping—the Single Entry System and the Double Entry System. The Single Entry System is not really a system because, under this method, there may be no record of some of the transactions and only partial record of some others. We shall discuss the system in greater detail later, but suffice it to say here that proper results cannot be obtained by its use. The other system—Double Entry System—makes a proper and full record of all transactions. Every transaction has a double or dual aspect. If, for instance, goods are purchased, the stock of goods will increase but either cash in hand (or at bank) will be reduced (due to payment) or an obligation to pay the price of the goods at a later date will arise. Thus, all transactions will have two aspects and record of the transactions must recognise both the aspects if it is to be proper. This is what is done under the Double Entry System. This book is, naturally, concerned mostly with this system.

Some Definitions. Before we start discussing the rules followed under the Double Entry System, it will be better to clarify some of the terms that will have to be used again and again.

Account or A/c means a statement setting out for a period all the trasactions relating to a person, a thing or any other subject, the benefits received being on one side and benefits given being on the other. Thus, if a statement is prepared for a customer, showing on one side the various credit sales made to him and, on the other, the various payments received from him, thus showing the amount still due from him, the statement will be known as an account. The "Bank Pass Book" is a good example of an account—it is a copy of the client's account in the bank's books. Accounts are of various types, as shown below.

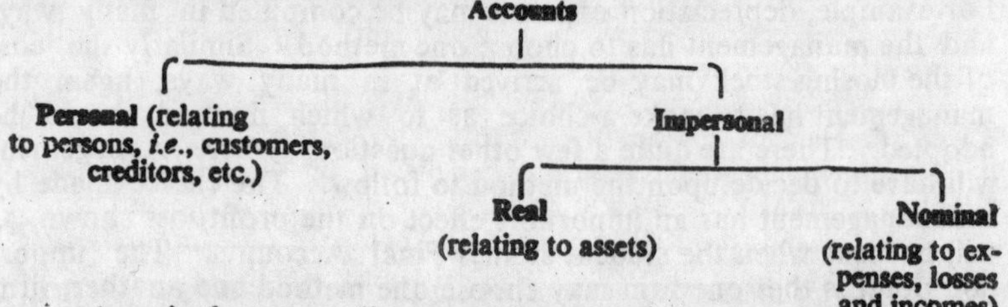

Asset is that expenditure which results in the acquiring of some property or benefit of a lasting nature or something that can be converted into cash. The chief characteristic of an asset in that *either* it can be converted into cash again *or* the firm (or the institution) concerned will derive some benefit from it in the future. For example, when a firm pays for a building or for a motor truck, it acquires assets ; also when it pays for a patent. There are various types of assets :

(*a*) *Fixed Assets* are those assets which are acquired only for use and not for resale, for instance, plant and machinery, land and buildings.

(*b*) *Current or Floating Assets* are those that are meant to be converted into cash as soon as possible. Stock of goods, amounts due from customers (book debts), balance at bank, etc., are examples.

(c) *Liquids Assets* are those current assets which are already in cash form or which can be readily converted into cash, such as government securities.

(d) *Wasting Assets* are those fixed assets which will surely lose their value because of use. Mines are a very good example because when the minerals are taken out, a mine will become useless.

(e) *Intangible Assets* are those fixed assets which cannot be seen or touched or felt. Goodwill (the value of one's name) is an intangible asset because there is no physical form to show for it. Intangible assets are not necessarily valueless.

(f) *Fictitious Assets* are valueless assets *e.g.*, useless trade marks), or expenses treated as assets (such as expenses incurred to establish a oompany, known as Preliminary Expenses).

Liability means an amount owing to outsiders.

Transaction means transfer of money or money's worth from one party to another, for example, purchase of furniture, sale of goods, etc. Kohler defines it as "An event (1) or condition (2) the recognition of which gives rise to an entry in accounting records."

Expenditure means spending of money or incurring an obligation to pay at a later date. For instance, expenditure will include both payment of Rs. 10,000 immediately and a promise to pay the sum after, say, one year.

Expense means an expenditure whose benefit is enjoyed and finished immediately or almost immediately. Examples are : payment of wages. rent, etc.

Losses are usually taken to include expenses also. But strictly speaking, 'losses' should be used for money (or money's worth) given up without any benefit. Examples are : loss due to fire, payment of damages to others, etc.

Income means receipt of cash or equivalent without it having to be returned to any one *e,g.*, receipt of proceeds on sale of goods.

Gain means acquisition of some asset or the extinguishing of liability without any effort, *e.g.*, increase in the value of land.

Voucher is the written record and evidence of a transaction.

Capital means the amount which the proprietor has invested in the firm or can claim from the firm.

Branches of Accounting. Accounting has three main branches :

(*i*) **Financial Accounting** which s concerned with recording and processing all transactions with outsiders and events affecting the financial position of the firm. This leads to the preparation of the annual profit and loss account (or similar statement) and the balance sheet.

(*ii*) **Cost Accounting** seeks to ascertain the cost of each product or job produced or undertaken by the firm. In financial accounting, expenditure incurred is recorded as such but, in Cost Accounting, it will be analysed job-wise or product-wise. Unlike financial accounting, cost accounting has to depend a great deal on estimation.

(*iii*) **Management Accounting** has the objective of collecting systematically and regularly all such information as will help management in discharging its functions of planning, control, decision-making, etc. It draws both on financial accounting and cost accounting.

In this book we shall deal only with Financial Accounting.

Objectives of Financial Accounting. The following are the chief objectives of Financial Accounting :—

(*i*) **Ascertaining the results of operations during a period.** A firm produces goods and sells them and in the process, incurs all sorts of expenses and costs and receives revenue. Naturally it is interested in knowing whether it has made any money or not i.e., whether it has earned a profit or suffered a loss. An institution like a college or hospital, which is not seeking to earn profit will also be interested in knowing whether its current income is sufficient to meet its current expenditure. Financial accounting serves this objective well through preparation of the Profit and Loss Account or the Income and Exyenditure Account.

(*ii*) **Ascertaining the financial position.** All organisations, whether seeking to earn a profit or not, would like to know periodically the financial position, i.e. its assets and liabilities. Financial accounting leads to the preparation of the Balance Sheet which is the statement setting out the assets, liabilities and capital of the concerned firm or institution.

(*iii*) **Maintaining control over assets.** It is absolutely important to see that all assets and properties of an organisation should be used only in its own interest and should be disposed of only in an authorised manner. Frauds and misappropriations as well as unnecessary losses have to be avoided. By keeping an account in respect of individual assets and liabilities, financial accounting helps in achieving this objective.

(*iv*) **Plannning in respect of cash.** Cash budgets are very popular these days : they enable the concerned firm or institution to estimate in advance the requirements of cash by estimating the receipts and expenditure of all types. Financial accounting, being concerned with cash, is of great help in this regard.

(*v*) **Providing information to tax authorities and other government agencies.** Both incomc-tax and sales tax authorities require good deal of information for a proper assessment. It is one of the objectives of financial accounting to provide the required information without delay.

Advantages of Book-keeping. A number of advantages will be available if a proper system of Book-keeping is followed. It will be understood that these advantages will accrue only if the Double Entry System is adopted. The student will be in a better position to grasp the advantages after he has fully followed the system and, therefore, he is advised to read this section again when he himself can prepare the Profit and Loss Account and Balance Sheet. The advantages are :

1. A firm can know, whenever it wants, how much profit it has earned or how much loss it has incurred in a particular period. This knowledge is naturally essential in order to know whether one is on the right path or not ; otherwise one will merely grope in the dark.
2. The exact reasons leading to the profit or loss can also be ascertained. This knowledge will enable the firm to take the necessary action to increase profits and to convert losses into profits.
3. At the end of every trading period (usually a year), the Balance Sheet can be prepared which will disclose the financial state of affairs. Thus it will be known whether the firm is fully solvent or not. A comparative study of the balance sheets for various years shows a firm's progress.
4. Through accounts properly kept, losses of assets will be apparent without delay. This will help in avoiding such losses.
5. Reminders can be sent regularly to those customers who fail to pay in time. This will reduce bad debts.
6. A strict watch can be kept on the amounts owing to outsiders, so that the firm will know what amounts are to be paid and when.
7. Accurate recording of transactions can be assured under the Double Entry System. Existence of errors is revealed by the preparation of what is known as "Trial Balance"—a statement containing balances in various accounts.
8. Proper accounting not only prevents and discovers errors, it also prevents and discovers frauds.
9. Management derives good guidance from accounts properly kept for the purpose of making decisions.
10. From the income tax and sales tax points of view, it is essential to follow a good accounting system, otherwise the authorities may impose heavy tax liabilities.

It should be noted that the advantages stated above are also available, with suitable changes. to non-profit institutions like schools, clubs, etc.

The Accounting Process. Normally, the accounting process covers the following :—

(*i*) Copying details from original vouchers, say, cash

memos, in a modified manner into suitable books and registers ;

(*ii*) anylysing and consolidating the figures which is done through preparation of various accounts ;

(*iii*) proving the accuracy of the work ; and

(*iv*) preparation of the final statements that may be required.

Exercises

1. Ram Lal carries on business as a cloth dealer. State which of the following are transactions to be recorded in his business books :—

(*a*) He purchases a perambulator for his son.

(*b*) He employes a typist for official correspondence and pays him Rs. 450 p.m.

(*c*) He buys a showcase for Rs. 350.

(*d*) He sells old domestic furniture for Rs. 300.

(*e*) He purchases cloth for Rs. 15,000.

(*f*) He buys a Cash Register Machine for Rs. 15,000.

(*g*) He purchases domestic utensils for Rs. 200 for which he gives cloth from the shop.

(*h*) He takes cloth worth Rs. 250 for use at home.

(*i*) He pays salary to his domestic servant, Rs. 50, from private funds.

(*j*) He takes a loan of Rs. 10,000 from a friend for the marriage of his daughter.

2. Following are a number of accounts. Classify them. (Use P for Personal Accounts, R for Real Accounts and N for Nominal Accounts).

(*a*) Rent Account.

(*b*) Buildings Account.

(*c*) Machinery Account.

(*d*) Furniture Account.

(*e*) Mohan's Account.

(*f*) Salaries Account.

(*g*) Interest Account.

(*h*) Sham's Account.

(*i*) Ali's Account.

(*j*) Capital Account.

(*k*) Bank Loan Account.

(*l*) Cash Account.

3. A firm spends money for—

(*a*) Purchasing typewriters.

(*b*) Acquiring trade marks.

(*c*) Paying salaries.

(*d*) Compensation to injured workers.

(*e*) Paying interest.

(*f*) Acquiring a lease of land for 20 years.

(*g*) Paying rent.

(*h*) Advertising.

(*i*) Stationery.

(*j*) Patents.

(*k*) 'Theft of cash'.

Which of the payments are assets, which expenses and which are losses ?

4. A firm receives money for :

(*a*) Interest on loans.

(*b*) Repayment of a loan.

(*c*) Sale of Building.

(*d*) Rent for premises sublet.

(*e*) A loan taken from a bank.

Which of the above receipts are incomes ?

5. The following are the names of assets. Classify them.

(*a*) Leasehold Premises.

(*b*) Accounting Machines.

(*c*) Stone Quarries

(*d*) Goodwill.

(*e*) Stock of Raw Materials.

(*f*) Motor vehicles.

(*g*) Cash in hand.

(*h*) Government securities.

(*i*) Copyright of books (no longer in demand).

(*j*) Amounts due from customers.

(*k*) Loose Tools.

(*l*) Cost of floating a company.

6. Which of the following statements are correct ?

(*i*) Conservatism demands that the declared profit should be substantially less than the real profit.

(*ii*) The Mercantile System adopts the Accrual concept.

(*iii*) A tangible asset may also be valueless.

(*iv*) Consistency demands that the profit declared from year to year should be the same.

(*v*) The going concern concept is not followed when the venture concerned has a short life.

(*vi*) The cost concept demands an absolutely strict measurement in terms of money.

(*vii*) Out of the total assets the amount contributed by the proprietors is deducted ; what remains is due to the outsiders.

(*viii*) Profit increases capital.

(*ix*) Sale of the goods produced is essential for realising a profit.

(*x*) In the financial statements, all information, material or immaterial, should be disclosed ; that is required by the Disclosure Convention.

Answers

1. Transactions *a*, *d*, *i* and j are not business transactions. Others will have to be recorded.

2. P—*e*, *h*, *i*, *j*, *k*.
R—*b*, *c*, *d*, *l*.
N—*a*, *f*, *g*.

3. *c*, *e*, *g*, *h*, and *i* are expenses : *d* and *k* are losses. Others are assets.

4. *a* and *d* are incomes.

5. Fixed—*a*, *b*, *c*, *d*, *f*, *k*.
Wasting—*c*.
Intangible—*d*
Fictitious—*i* and *l*.
Current—*e*, *g*, *h* and *j*.
Liquid—*g* and *h*.

6. Correct : (*ii*), (*iii*), (*v*), (*viii*), (*ix*).

CHAPTER II

RECORD OF TRANSACTIONS—JOURNAL

A firm may first record its transactions in what is known as a waste book. This is only a rough record and, after it, a systematic record is prepared. The rough book or the waste book may look like the following :—

August 5	Purchase of stationery	Rs. 50
August 6	Old newspapers sold	Rs. 20
	Cash sales	Rs. 130
August 7	Purchase of typewriter on credit from Remington Rand Inc.	Rs. 3,500
	Purchase of goods on credit from M/s. Universal Trading Co.	Rs. 2,500
August 8	Paid telephone bill	Rs. 285
	Purchased postage stamps	Rs. 15

Some firms adopt another practice. They record the receipts of cash and payments of cash in a rough book and the relevant papers are filed in a serial order. For other transactions also the papers are properly arranged and filed. The papers, which support a transaction, are known as vouchers. The vouchers which will usually be found in a firm are the following :—

1. Vouchers in support of payments out of the till (office cash) or out of the bank.
2. Vouchers in support of receipts of cash or cheques. This may usually be in the form of counterfoils of the receipts issued by the firm or letters accompanying remittances.
3. Bills received from suppliers of goods.
4. Invoices made out for goods sold to customers or cash memos.
5. Other documents not covering transactions listed above, for instance, bills received for services rendered or a note received intimating that a particular customer has become insolvent, etc.

The above constitutes only a very rough sort of record and for the purpose of making proper entries in the books, it is necessary to classify all transactions methodically and to record them in a chronological order. This record is taken up a little later. First of all, let us discuss the rules regarding the record of the various transactions.

Rules for recording transactions

We have noted the undermentioned accounting equation :

Assets—liabilities=owner's equity (or capital)

From this, we can develop the rules for recording the effects of various transactions and events that occur in an undertaking. We can do this by a process of addition and subtraction as shown below :—

Transaction	*Total Assets Rs.*	*Owing to Outsiders Rs.*	*Capital or Owner's Equity. Rs.*
(1) Commenced business with Rs. 10,000	10,000		10,000
(2) Borrowed Rs. 5,000	5,000	5,000	
	15,000	5,000	10,000
(3) Paid Expenses, Rs. 1,000	−1,000		−1,000
	14,000		9,000
(4) Returned Rs. 2,000 to the lender	−2,000	−2,000	
	12,000	3,000	9,000
(5) Made a profit of Rs. 2,500	2,500		2,500
	14,500		11,500
(6) Withdrew Rs. 1,000 for domestic use	--1,000		−1,000
	13,500	3,000	10,500

It will be seen that the method indicated above will be cumbersome if the number of transactions or events to be recorded is large. Also it is necessary to have information not only about total assets and total liabilities, and therefore the net amount of owner's equity, but also information about individual assets, amounts owing to various creditors, various types of expenses incurred and various revenues earned, etc. Unless such detailed information is kept, the whole purpose of keeping aeccounts will be defeated.

Therefore, another method has to be adopted for recording events and transactions of an undertaking. This method also uses addition and subtraction but does it in a systematic way by having two sides—one to record increases and the other to record decreases in respect of an item. The two sides together are known as an account which would be defined as a statement, showing for a period, various changes which have occurred in relation to a particular item of information, say, dealings with a person, stock of a particular asset or a particular type of expenses incurred. For instance, A's account means a statement which will show all transactions with 'A' foi a particular period.

The manner of recording transactions in an account is shown below :

Asset Account

Dr.	Cr.
Increases	Decreases

Liability Account

Dr.	Cr.
Decreases	Increases

Expense Account

Dr.	Cr
Increases	Decreases

Income Account

Dr	Cr.
Decreases	Increases

Capital Account

Dr.	Cr.
Decreases	Increases

The left hand side is called the debit side (Dr.) and the right hand side is the credit side (Cr.).

Increases in an asset are recorded on the left hand (debit) side and decreases are recorded on the right hand side. In case of liabilities, *i.e.*, amount owing to others and owner's equity, increases are recorded on the right hand side, *i.e.*, credit side and decreases on the other side, namely, the debit or left hand side. In a way, this is arbitrary but it has proved to be extremely convenient. If there is an increase in total assets, it will be either because money is provided by outsiders as loan or by owners as capital. Therefore, it either means an increase in the amount owing to creditors or in the amount of owner's equity. Therefore, when an increase is recorded on the left hand side of assets, a corresponding increase has to be recorded either in the account of the proprietor or that of the creditor ; and it has been found that the two sides *i.e.*, showing the decrease in the amount of assets and that showing the increase in the amount owing to creditors or as owner's equity should be opposite. From this the following rule can be developed :

An increase in any asset should be recorded on the left hand or the debit side and increase in the amount of liabilities should be recorded on the right hand or the credit side ; so also an increase in the owner's equity. Conversely, if there is reduction in the value of any asset it should be recorded on the right hand or the credit side and if there is a reduction in the amount of liabilities or the owner's equity, it is on the debit or the left hand side that the record should be made.

In other words, in case of assets, debit the account concerned for an increase and credit it for a reduction. In case of liabilities or owner's equity (capital) credit the account concerned for any increase and debit it for any reduction.

Instead of having accounts for total assets or total liabilities, there should naturally be an account for each asset, each liability, etc. Thus, there will be separate accounts for cash, stock of goods, furniture, various credit customers etc. and in the same manner there will be separate accounts for all persons to whom money is owing. If 'A' purchases goods on credit, it would mean that he becomes liable to pay and to that extent he becomes an asset for the firm ; but it would also mean that the stock of goods would be reduced. Therefore, for this the entry would be to debit A's account and credit the stock account. If later 'A' pays cash, it would mean that the balance of cash in hand will increase ; therefore, cash account will be debited. It would also mean that the asset in the form of amount owing from 'A' no longer exists ; therefore, A's account will be credited. If money is borrowed from Bank, it means that the amount of cash in hand increases ; and, therefore, cash account will be debited. Since this also means that an amount now becomes payable to the Bank, the Bank account must be credited.

It is now necessary to consider another class of transactions relating to expenses and revenues. Suppose, the clerk is paid a salary of Rs. 500 p.m. On payment, following the rule given above, the clerk's account will be debited and naturally cash account will be credited. In the same way, when rent is paid to the landlord, his account can be debited and cash account credited. But if there are accounts in the name of the clerk or the landlord, it would convey a wrong meaning. It would, perhaps, convey that these amounts are owing by the clerk and by the landlord, whereas it is not so. The amounts paid to them are not returnable since they have already rendered service. Therefore, it is advisable and proper to style these accounts differently and indicate the nature of service for which payment has been made. In case of the clerk, it should be styled as salaries account and in case of the landlord, it should be styled as rent account. From this, a rule can be developed to the effect that when any expense has been incurred, the relevant account should be debited.

A similar reasoning will also show that when an income has been earned, then the relevant account should be credited. For example, if an investment of Rs. one lakh is made in the debentures of 'X' Limited, at 15% p a., then at the end of six months Rs. 7,500 will be received. As per the first rule, the entry would be to debit cash since cash balance has increased and to credit 'X' Limited with Rs. 7,500 since this company has paid the money. But this amount is not at all returnable to 'X' Limited and, therefore, a credit to 'X' Limited would be wrong—it would indicate that the amount is payable to the company. The proper thing would be to credit

"Interest Received Account". Hence the rule is to debit all expenses and losses and to credit all incomes and gains.

If these rules are followed, it would enable all transactions and events to be recorded properly. One should note in this respect that it is not necessary that the record should be made only when actual accounts or goods or something tangible moves. A record is set up when an obligation has arisen. Suppose, the firm borrows Rs. 20,000 at 16%; at the end of the year interest, Rs. 3,200, will become payable. If the interest is actually paid, the entry will be to debit "Interest Account" and credit "Cash Account". But suppose cash has not yet been paid. Since an obligation to pay interest has definitely arisen, it would be proper to recognise it and credit the person to whom the amount is due and debit the the interest account. Therefore, in such a case, the entry would be to debit "Interest Account" and credit the lender. This entry will show that the amount owing the lender is not only Rs. 20,000, which he originally lent to the firm, but also another sum of Rs. 3,200 or Rs. 23,200 in all. Of course, when payment is actually made, cash will be credited, since the amount of balance in hand is reduced and the lender's account will be debited since the amount owing to him now will be less.

Another view of Debit and Credit. We shall now look at the rules regarding debit and credit from another angle and arrive at the same results.

If we try to give ordinary meanings to these two terms, *debits* and *credits*, we shall realise their significance. Suppose two friends—Sohan and Mohan—go to a restaurant. There the entire bill is paid by Sohan. This means that Mohan has been placed under a sort of debt or an obligation (although he may be under no legal obligation to return the hospitality of his friend). Sohan, on the other hand, has done a creditable thing and, therefore, entitled to something in return. In accountancy also debits and credits have more or less the same meaning for persons. A person who receives a benefit or who is placed under an obligation is debited and a person who gives the benefit and who, therefore, is entitled to a return of the obligation is credited. We shall refer to these words again and again. At the moment, let it be clear that when an account is debited it means that particular account has been obliged by someone or on account of something. When an account is credited, it means that an obligation has passed from this particular account—Sohan in our example.

Fundamentally, an account is either debited or credited, and the crux of Accounting lies in finding out which accounts are to be debited and which accounts are to be credited: Here a word of warning may not be out of place. In Book-keeping, every transaction has to be recorded separately even if one transaction is merely in cancellation of another. For instance, Ram buys goods on credit from Sham. This transaction will be recorded naturally. Later Ram pays the necessary sum to Sham. This trasaction must also be recorded and must not be ignored simply on the ground that Ram has done nothing more than what was expected of him. All transactions are recorded and, later, summarised to arrive at the net result.

The rules for recording the transactions are three.

1. The first is : **Debit the receiver and Credit the giver.** In the example given above, Ram has bought goods from Sham. Ram has received goods and Sham has given the goods. Ram, therefore, is under an obligation to pay the price of the goods. Sham is entitled to a credit because he has given up the goods to Ram. In an accountant's language, Ram will be debited and Sham will be credited. Suppose, later Ram does pay the amount to Sham. In this case, Ram has done a creditable thing by giving up a sum of money and Sham has been placed under an obligation because he has received the money. The entry will be : Debit Sham and credit Ram. Thus the first rule is : Debit the receiver and Credit the giver.

2. From the above rule, the second rule can be developed. Suppose Mr. Rao pays cash to the firm's cashier. Mr. Rao has paid and Mr. Cashier has received the amount. Therefore, according to Rule No. 1, Mr. Cashier should be debited and Mr. Rao should be credited. In the same way when Mr. Cashier pays an amount, which he will according to instructions from management, he will be credited. Other similar transactions are for recording goods. Goods are received by the Godown Keeper and are issued by him according to instructions. One can say, therefore, that when goods are received Mr. Godown Keeper should be debited and when goods are issued Mr. Godown Keeper should be credited. Such accounts, like those of Mr. Cashier and Mr. Godown Keeper, however, cannot work well because these two persons, and others like them, work only on behalf of the firm and they do not enter into these transactions personally. Mr. Cashier may be personally liable for any shortage of cash but he will not be allowed to keep any surplus cash. Mr. Godown Keeper, in any case, cannot say, for example, that he received goods worth Rs. 10,000 and he issued goods according to sale invoices equalling Rs. 15,000 and that, therefore, he should be paid Rs. 5,000 (the difference) because he has given more goods than he received. This argument will be fallacious because the amount of Rs. 15,000 is due to higher prices and represents profit which certainly does not belong to the Godown Keeper. Therefore, it is not convenient to open accounts in the names of the cashier and the godown keeper. It is more convenient to open accounts in the name of the articles handled. Therefore, in place of Mr. Cashier, Cash Account should be debited or credited. When cash is received, cash should be debited. When cash is given, it should be credited. Similarly, in place of the Godown Keeper's Account, there should be Goods Account. This account should be debited when goods are received and credited when goods are issued. Of course, the persons who give goods or pay cash will be credited and those persons who receive the goods or receive cash will be debited. From this a general rule can be formulated and that is : **Debit what comes in and Credit what goes out.** If buildings are purchased, buildings

will be debited. If machinery is purchased, Machinery Account will be debited. If old furniture is sold, Furniture Account will be credited. If goods are sold for cash, then cash comes in and goods go out. The proper entry, therefore, is : Debit cash, Credit goods. If goods are sold on credit, say, to Basu, then Basu has received the goods. Therefore, he will be debited and Goods Account will be credited because goods have gone out.

3. Payments are often made on account of expenses. Following the Rule Nos. 1 and 2 we can, for instance, debit the account of the landlord whenever we pay rent to him because the landlord receives the money. The landlord's account will show all the money which has been paid to him. But if we do this, it will be a misleading picture. We will think that the landlord owes us something, whereas he owes us nothing. We have already enjoyed the use of his building and it is on account of rent that he has been paid the amount. In a somewhat lose language, the amount has been lost ; it will not be recovered again. It is much better to recognise this fact and to debit Rent Account and not the Landlord's Account. Thus when expenses are incurred or losses are suffered, the relevant account is debited. The credit, of course, goes either to cash (if cash is paid out) or to the person to whom the necessary payment is due.

Incomes are credited. If, for instance, we as agents earn a commission and receive it in cash, we will, of course, debit cash because cash has come in. It will not be proper to credit the account of the person from whom we have earned the commission. We will not return the amount to him because we have already rendered him service and the amount is remuneration for the service. Therefore, the entry in our books will record this fact and that will be by credting Commission Account. Similarly, when money is received on account of other incomes, for instance, interest on loans given by us or rents for premises sublet by us, these accounts will be credited. The third rule, therefore, is : **Debit all losses (and expenses) and Credit all gains.** If, for instance, cash is received on account of interest, Cash Account will be debited and Interest Account credited. If we pay cash to somebody as interest, then Interest Account will be debited and Cash Account will be credited. If we have earned interest but if we have not yet received the amount, we can make a record of it by debiting the person from whom the interest is due and crediting Interest Account. This will make it clear that the borrower owes us so much money. Care will have to be taken when the borrower actually pays the amount. In that case, he is discharging his obligation and then cash will be debited and his account will be credited.

Significance of debits and credits. The significance of debits and credits will now be clear. In case of debits, the following should be remembered :

(*a*) If some person's account is debited, it means that either that person owes the firm the relevant amount or some obligation to him has been discharged. Such a debit may also mean that the person has become liable to do something for the firm.

(*b*) If an account relating to some asset or property is debited, it means that either the physical stock of that asset or property has increased or there is an increase in the value. For instance, if Furniture Account is debited, this shows that the firm has got more furniture now than before, in terms of rupees.

(*c*) If accounts other than those listed above in (*a*) and (*b*) are debited, it means that either the money has been lost or some benefit for the money spent has been received. Hence, if Advertising Account is debited, it shows that money has been spent for advertising.

In case of credits, the following should be noted :—

(*a*) If Personal Accounts are credited, it means that those persons have either discharged some of their obligations or are entitled to some obligation in future from the firm. A person who becomes entitled to a benefit from the firm is credited.

(*b*) If accounts relating to assets and properties are credited, it means that the value of the stock of such assets or properties has gone down. If, for instance, Machinery Account is credited, it means that the firm has so much less machinery in terms of rupees.

(*c*) If impersonal accounts are credited, it means that there is an income in the sense that the firm has already rendered service for money received or yet to be received.

After the accounts are prepared, the net result of debits and credits of each account will be ascertained. If the debits are more, the balance is known as debit balance ; in the other case the balance will be known as credit balance. A debit balance always denotes *one* of the following :

(*a*) That money is owing to the firm by a person.

(*b*) That the firm owns property or asset totalling the relevant amount.

(*c*) That the firm has incurred so much loss or expense.

Similarly, a credit balance will show *one* of the following :—

(*a*) That money is owing to the person concerned.

(*b*) That the firm has earned an income.

A student will do well to carefully realise the meanings of debits and credits. To repeat, debits will indicate benefits received by the account which is being debited and credits will mean benefits given by the account which is being credited. By themselves debits or credits do not indicate good or bad—a debit may mean something good (like an asset) or bad (like a loss); similarly a credit may indicate something good (such as an income) or bad (*e.g.*, liability).

Journal. On the basis of the entries made in the waste book or on the basis of the vouchers, the accounts to be debited and credited are noted carefully in a systematic manner. This is done in a book which is known as the Journal. The ruling of the Journal is as under :—

Journal

Date (1)	*Particulars* (2)	*L.F.* (3)	*Dr. Amount* (4) Rs.	P.	*Cr. Amount* (5) Rs.	P.

A *B*

This is a chronological record of all the transactions that occur in a firm. In other words, transactions will be recorded as and when they occur and in the order in which they occur. It will be wrong to record transactions of 7th August first and of 6th August later.

The account to be debited is written first. It is written close to the line starting the particulars column, line marked A*. The word Dr. is written close to the line marked B. The amount is written in column No. 4. Then in the next line the account to be credited is written. It is always preceded by the word 'To' and must be written about five spaces away from line marked A. The amount is written in the credit column, *i.e.*, column No. 5. A full explanation of why the entry has been made is given just below the entry. This explanation is known as 'narration'. A journal entry without narration will not be meaningful. To separate one entry from another, a line is drawn below every entry to cover particulars column only; the line does not extend to amount columns.

Suppose a cash amount of Rs. 1,000 was received from Mr. Krishna on May 15, 1985. The entry will be made as follows :—

Date		*Particulars*	*L.F.*	*Dr. Amount* Rs.	P.	*Cr. Amount* Rs.	P.
1985 May	15	Cash Account ... ...Dr. To Krishna Being the amount received from Mr. Krishna as per receipt No...		1,000	—	1,000	—

*In actual practice, the lines or columns are not numbered or marked.
L.F. stands for Ledger Folio, *i.e.*, the number of the page where the relevant account is maintained.

Now we give entries for a number of transactions which often take place in a firm.

1. I start business with Rs. 15,000 as my capital. The entry is :—

		Rs.	Rs.
Cash Account	Dr.	15,000	
To Capital Account*			15,000

2. Out of Rs. 15,000, Rs. 12,000 is deposited in the bank. The entry is :—

Bank Account	Dr.	12,000	
To Cash Account			12,000

3. Goods are purchased on credit from M/s Ram Lal and Sons for Rs. 6,000. The entry is :—

Goods Account	Dr.	6,000	
To M/s. Ram Lal & Sons			6,000

4. A typewriter is purchased for cash for Rs. 3,450. The entry is :—

Office Equipment (or Typewriter) A/c	Dr.	3,450	
To Cash Account			3,450

5. Goods are sold on credit to. M/s Ali Brothers, Rs. 1,000. The entry will be :—

Ali Brothers	Dr.	1,000	
To Goods Account			1,000

6. Goods are purchased for cash, Rs. 500. The entry is :—

Goods Account	Dr.	500	
To Cash Account			500

7. Cash is received for sale of goods to M/s. Rao and Brothers, Rs. 700. The entry is :—

Cash Account	Dr.	700	
To Goods Account			700

8. Rent is paid to the landlord, Rs. 200. The entry is :—

Rent Account	Dr.	200	
To Cash Account			200

9. A machinery is received and payment is made by cheque, Rs. 26,000. The entry is :—

Machinery Account	Dr.	26,000	
To Bank Account			26,000

10. Borrowed, Rs. Rs. 5,000, from a friend, Mr. K. Lal. The entry is :—

Cash Account	Dr.	5,000	
To K. Lal's Loan A/c			5,000

*Capital Account is the proprietor's account ; it shows how much money he has invested in the firm.

11. Interest paid to Mr. K. Lal, Rs. 600. The entry is :—

Interest Account	Dr.	600	
To Cash Account			600

12. Interest, Rs. 600, is due to Mr. K. Lal but not yet paid. The entry is :—

Interest Account	Dr.	.600	
To K. Lal			600

13. There is a fire and certain goods are destroyed ; the value is Rs. 1,000. The entry ts :—

Fire Loss Account	Dr.	1,000	
To Goods Account			1,000

Illustration. Journalise the transactions given below in the books of Kohli.

1985

April
1. Kohli starts business with Rs. 20,000. Kohli opens account with bank and deposits Rs. 18,000.
2. Kohli purchases furniture, Rs. 850, and typewriter, Rs. 1,500. Payment made by cheque.
3. Goods purchased from M/s. Rao and Murty on credit, Rs. 5,600.
4. Goods purchased from M/s. Khan & Singh for cash, Rs. 1,100.
5. Goods sold on credit to M/s. Mohan Lal & Co., Rs. 1,500.
6. Goods sold on credit to M/s. Basu & Co., Rs. 2,800.
7. Paid for office stationery, Rs. 250.
8. Paid rent for April, Rs. 200.
9. Installed neon sign at a cost of Rs. 1,000.
   Paid for postage stamps, Rs. 10.
10. Received cash from M/s. Mohanlal & Co., Rs. 1,470 ; allowed them discount, Rs. 30.
11. Issued cheque for Rs. 5,500 in full settlement (*i.e.*, nothing more is due them) to M/s. Rao & Murty.
12. Deposited Rs. 1,200 in bank.
13. Received bill for two table fans, Rs. 300, from M/s. Electrician Bros.
15. One electric fan stolen.
16. Paid insurance premimum, Rs. 450, by cheque.

Solution :

Journal

Date		Particulars	L.F.	Dr. Amount Rs.	P.	Cr. Amount Rs.	P.
1985 April	1	Cash Account ... Dr. To Capital Account Business commenced with Rs. 20,000		20,000	—	20,000	—
	1	Bank Account ... Dr. To Cash Account Cash deposited in bank.		18,000	—	18,000	—
April	2*	Furniture Account ... Dr. To Bank Account Furniture purchased for Rs. 850 against cheque.		850	—	850	—
	2*	Typewriter Account ... Dr. To Bank Account Typewriter purchased for Rs. 1,500 against cheque.		1,500	—	1,500	—
	3	Goods Account ... Dr. To M/s. Rao and Murty. Goods purchased on credit from M/s. Rao & Murty, *vide* Bill No...		5,600	—	5,600	—
	4	Goods Account ... Dr. To Cash Account Goods purchased from M/s. Khan & Singh for Cash, *vide* Cash Memo No...		1,100	—	1,100	—
	5	Mohan Lal & Co. ... Dr. To Goods Account Goods sold to M/s. Mohan Lal & Co., on credit *vide* Invoice No...		1,500	—	1,500	—
	6	M/s. Basu & Co. ... Dr. To Goods Account Goods sold on credit to M/s. Basu & Co., *vide* Invoice No...		2,800	—	2,800	—
	7	Stationery Account ... Dr. To Cash Acaount Paid for Stationery, *vide* Cash Memo No...		250	—	250	—
	8	Rent Account ... Dr. To Cash Account Paid rent for April, *vide* Landlord's receipt No...		200	—	200	—
	9	Fixtures Account ... Dr. (or Neonsign Account) To cash Account Amount paid for neon sign.		1,000	—	1,000	—
		Total Carried Forward		52,800	—	2,800	—

*Entries for *similar transactions on the same date* may be combined, thus—

Date		Particulars	L.F.	Dr. Amount Rs.	P.	Cr. Amount Rs.	P.
April	2	Furniture Account ... Dr. Typewriter Account ... Dr. To Bank Account Purchase of furniture and typewriter against cheque.		850 1,500	— —	2,350	—

				Rs.		Rs.	
		Total Brought Forward		52,800	—	52,800	—
April	9	Postage Account ... Dr. To Cash Account Postage stamps worth Rs. 10 purchased.		10	—	10	—
*	10	Cash Account ... Dr. To M/s. Mohan Lal & Co. Cash received from M/s. Mohan Lal & Co. *vide* receipt No...		1,470	—	1,470	—
*	10	Discount Account ... Dr. To M/s. Mohan Lal & Co. The amount given up in favour of M/s. Mohan Lal on their prompt payment of amount due.		30	—	30	—
	11	M/s. Rao & Murty ... Dr. To Bank Account To Discount Account The amount paid to M/s. Rao & Murty by cheque to clear the amount due to them (Rs. 5,600—see transaction on 3rd April) : Rs. 100 waived by them credited to Discount Account. (See entries on April 10 if you find it difficult to follow this entry).		5,600	—	5,500 100	— —
	12	Bank Account ... Dr. To Cash Account Amount deposited in Bank.		1,200	—	1,200	—
	13	Furniture Account ... Dr. To M/s. Electrician Bros. Two table fans purchased *vide* bill No...		300	—	300	
	15	Loss by Theft Account ... Dr. To Furniture Account Loss of one table fan by theft.		150	—	150	—
	16	Insurance Premium A/c ... Dr. To Bank Account Insurance Premium paid by cheque.		450	—	450	—
		Total		62,010	—	62,010	—

* It is better to combine such entries. Thus—

April	10	Cash Account ... Dr. Discount Account ... Dr. To M/s. Mohan Lal & Co. Amount received from and discount allowed to M/s. Mohan Lal & Co. *vide* receipt No...		1,470 30	— —	1,500	—

Note : The two columns of the journal should be totalled to ensure that the amounts entered in the debit column and those entered in the credit column are not different.

Opening Entry. The above illustration assumed the starting of a new business. After the first year of its working, a firm will start new books of account. The entry to start the new books is known as Opening Entry. The method is to debit the respective accounts with the opening balances of various assets and to credit the relevant accounts with the opening amounts due to creditors and to credit Capital Account with the amount of capital in the beginning. If the amount of capital in the beginning is not known, it can readily be ascertained by deducting the total of liabilities from the total of assets.* Suppose, the amounts of various assets of a firm total up to Rs. 26,000 and amounts owing to various creditors total Rs, 7,500. The capital, that is, the amount invested by the proprietor or the amount owed by the firm to the proprietor, will then be Rs. 18,500, *i.e.*, 26,000 minus Rs. 7,500. The opening entry is illustrated below. Suppose on 1st January, 1985, Ghosh's assets and liabilities are as under :

Assets	Rs.	*Liabilities*	Rs.
Stock of goods	11,000	Amount owing to	
Cash at Bank	6,000	Shastri	1,800
Cash in hand	500	Amount owing to	
Furniture	1,000	Gupta	1,200
Bannerji (amount due)	1,600		
Sinha (")	900		

The opening entry in the books of Ghosh on 1st January, 1985 will be as under :

			Rs.	Rs.
Stock Account	...	Dr.	11,000	
Cash at Bank	...	Dr	6,000	
Cash in hand	...	Dr	500	
Furniture Account	...	Dr.	1,000	
Bannerji	...	Dr.	1,600	
Sinha	...	Dr.	900	
To Shastri				1,800
To Gupta				1,200
To Capital Account				18,000

Being the various assets and liabilities on 1st Jan., 1985, Capital ascertained by deducting liabilities from assets.

---

* It is worth remembering always that :

Assets = Liabilities plus Capital ; or
Capital = Assets minus Liabilities.

Illustration. Rolly Polly was carrying on business as a cloth dealer. On 1st July, 1985 his assets were : Furniture and Office Equipment, Rs. 2,500 ; Stock of Cloth, Rs. 25,000 ; Cash in hand, Rs. 450 ; Bank balance, Rs. 8,500 ; amount due from Bittoo, Rs. 1,200 ; amount due from Gopan, Rs. 1,500. On that date he owed Rs. 2,000 to Minoo and Rs. 1,450 to Pappu. His transactions during July, 1978 were as follows :

			Rs.
July	1.	Sold cloth on credit to Gifloo	500
	2.	Purchased cloth from Amboo on credit	2,000
	3.	Paid rent for July by cheque	300
	4.	Cash purchase of cloth (paid by cheque)	800
		Cash Sales	450
	5.	Received cheque from Bitto	1,180
		Allowed him discount	20
	6.	Paid for stationery and postage	50
	8.	Drawn cash for private use	250
	10.	Drawn cash from Bank for office	1,500
	12.	Bittoo's cheque returned dishonoured by Bank which charges Rs. 5 for expenses.	
	13.	Purchased goods on credit from Minoo	2,500
	15.	Sent cheque to Minoo in full settlement of amount due on July 1	1,950
		Sent cheque to Pappu	1,450
	16.	Sold goods on credit to Gopan	1,800
	17.	Paid Telephone Charges	80
	18.	Cash Sales	300
		Paid for advertising	350
	20.	Paid income tax	1,900
		Received letter from Pappu saying that he has not received the cheque ; cancelled that cheque and paid cash.	
	21.	Bittoo becomes insolvent ; only 50% received from his estate.	
	22.	Cash purchases	900
	24.	Purchased filing cabinet and paid by cheque	500
	27.	Purchased Government Securities	3,000
	31.	Paid Salaries for the month	800

Journalise the transactions. Note that cheques received are immediately sent to the Bank.

Solution :

Journal

Date		Particulars		Dr. Rs.	Cr. Rs.
1985 July	1	Stock Account ... Dr.		25,000 —	
		Bank Account ... Dr.		8,500 —	
		Cash Account ... Dr.		450 —	
		Furniture & Office Equipment A/c ... Dr.		2,500 —	
		Bitto ... Dr.		1,200 —	
		Gopan ... Dr.		1,500 —	
		To Minoo			2,000 —
		To Pappu			1,450 —
		To Capital Account			35,700 —
		The assets and liabilities brought into new books on July 1, 1985. Capital ascertained by deducting liabilities from assets.			
	1	Gifloo ... Dr.		500 —	
		To Goods Account			500 —
		Sale of goods on credit to Gifloo *vide* invoice No...			
	2	Goods Account ... Dr.		2,000 —	
		To Amboo			2,000 —
		Purchase of goods credit from Amboo *vide* bill No...			
	3	Rent Account ... Dr.		300 —	
		To Bank Account			300 —
		Rent for July paid by issue of cheque No...			
	4	Goods Account ... Dr.		800 —	
		To Bank Account			800 —
		Goods purchased by issue of cheque No...			
	4	Cash Account ... Dr.		450 —	
		To Goods Account			450 —
		Sale of goods for cash, cash memos from no...to no...			
	5	Bank Account ... Dr.		1,180 —	
		Discount Account ... Dr.		20 —	
		To Bitto			1,200 —
		Receipt of cheque from Bitto to clear his account of Rs. 1,200—cheque no... for Rs. 1,180; discount allowed Rs. 20.			
	6	Stationery and Postage A/c ... Dr.		50 —	
		To Cash Account			50 —
		Amount paid for stationery and postage.			
		Total carried forward		44,450 —	44,450 —

			Rs.	Rs.
		Total Brought Forward	44,450 —	44,450 —
July	8	Capital Account ... Dr. (or Drawings Account) To Cash Account Amount withdrawn for private use.	250 —	250 —
	10	Cash Account ... Dr. To Bank Account Amount drawn from Bank for use in office *vide* cheque no...	1,500 —	1,500 —
	12	Bittoo ... Dr. To Bank Account Bittoo's cheque for Rs. 1,180 returned dishonoured : hence his account debited with the amount plus Rs. 5 for expenses charged by bank.	1,185 —	1,185 —
	12	Bittoo ... Dr. To Discount Account Discount allowed to Bittoo on receipt of cheque from him now disallowed on dishonour of his cheque.	20 —	20 —
	13	Goods Account ... Dr. To Minoo Goods purchased on credit from Minoo *vide* bill no...	2,500 —	2,500 —
	15	Minoo Dr. To Bank Account To Discount Account Cheque no...for Rs. 1,950 sent to Minoo to clear his balance of Rs. 2,000 on 1st July—discount earned Rs. 50.	2,000	1,950 — 50 —
	15	Pappu ... Dr. To Bank Account Cheque no...for Rs. 1,450 sent to Pappu.	1,450 —	1,450 —
	16	Gopan ... Dr. To Goods Account Goods sold on credit to Gopan *vide* invoice no...	1,800 —	1,800 —
	17	Telephone Charges A/c ... Dr. To Cash Account Telephone charges paid *vide* bill no...	80 —	80 —
	18	Cash Account ... Dr. To Goods Account Cash sales *vide* Cash memos from no...to no...	300 —	300 —
		Total carried forward	55,535 —	55,535 —

Date		Particulars		Dr. Rs.		Cr. Rs.	
		Total Brought Forward		55,535	—	55,535	—
July	18	Advertising Account ... Dr. To Cash Account Paid for Advertising *vide* bill no...		350	—	350	—
	20	Capital Account ... Dr. To Cash Account Income tax paid *vide* receipt dated......and debited to Capital A/c because it is charged on personal income.		1,900	—	1,900	—
	20	Bank Account ... Dr. To Pappu Cheque issued to Pappu on 15th July cancelled because of loss in transit.		1,450	—	1,450	—
	20	Pappu ... Dr. To Cash Account Cash paid to Pappu for cheque not received by him.		1,450	—	1,450	—
	21	Cash Account ... Dr. Bad Debts Account ... Dr. To Bittoo Bittoo having become insolvent, only 50% of Rs. 1,205 due from him received; the remaining amount written off as bad debt.		602 602	50 50	1,205	—
	22	Goods Account ... Dr. To Cash Account Goods purchased for cash, *vide* cash memo no...		900	—	900	—
	24	Furniture and Office Equipment A/c ... Dr. To Bank Account Filing cabinet purchased against cheque *vide* bill no...		500	—	500	—
	27	Government Securities A/c ... Dr. To Bank Account Purchase of investments *vide* broker's Bought Note dated......		3,000	—	3,000	—
	31	Salaries Account ... Dr. To Cash Account Salaries paid to staff *vide* Salary Register.		800	—	800	—
		Total		67,090	—	67,090	—

Exercises

1. The following transactions have taken place in a firm :

(*a*) Mohan pays cash.
(*b*) Cash is paid to Ram, the landlord, as rent.
(*c*) Goods are purchased from Shyam.
(*d*) Goods are sold to Khurshid for cash.
(*e*) Goods are taken for domestic use.
(*f*) Goods are given to a firm which did an advertising job.
(*g*) Cash is paid for stationery purchased.
(*h*) Cheque issued for purchase of machinery.
(*i*) Cheque issued for damages for late supply of goods.
(*j*) Amount received as rent from sub-tenant.

The two aspects of the above noted transactions are given below without arrangement. Pair the numbers that indicate the two aspects ; a number may be used many times.

(1) Cash balance reduced.
(2) Balance at bank reduced.
(3) Stock of stationery increased.
(4) Cash balance increased.
(5) Stock of goods increased.
(6) Stock of goods reduced
(7) Amount spent as rent.
(8) Proprietor's investment reduced.
(9) Loss.
(10) Income.
(11) Bank balance increases.
(12) Machinery acquired.
(13) Mohan discharges obligation.
(14) Obligation towards Shyam arises.
(15) Amount expended as advertising.

Answers : (*a*) 4 and 13 ; (*b*) 1 and 7 ; (*c*) 5 and 14 ; (*d*) 4 and 6 ; (*e*) 6 and 8 ; (*f*) 15 and 6 ; (*g*) 1 and 3 ; (*h*) 2 and 12 ; (*i*) 2 and 9 ; and (*j*) 4 and 10.

2. Some of the transactions of a firm are given below. Against each transaction the accounts to be debited and credited are given. There are some obvious errors. Point out the errors and give correct answers.

(*i*)	Cash received from Ali :	Debit Cash : Credit Ali
(*ii*)	Purchased goods from Rao for Cash :	Debit Goods ; Credit Rao
(*iii*)	Money sent from office to Bank :	Debit Bank ; Credit Cash
(*iv*)	Paid Salary to Krishna :	Debit Krishna ; Credit Cash
(*v*)	Cash Sales :	Debit Cash ; Credit Goods
(*vi*)	Purchased Furniture for cheque :	Debit Goods ; Credit Bank
(*vii*)	Received Cash as damages from a supplier :	Debit Cash ; Credit Supplier
(*viii*)	Sold old machinery to Khan on credit :	Debit Khan ; Credit Goods
(*ix*)	Mohan the proprietor takes goods for private use :	Debit Mohan ; Credit Goods
(*x*)	Bill for stationery received ; bill not yet paid :	Debit Stationery ; Credit Cash

Answers : Wrong entries : (*ii*) Credit Cash ; (*iv*) Debit Salaries ; (*vi*) Debit Furniture ; (*vii*) Credit Damages Received ; (*viii*) Credit Machinery ; (*ix*) Debit Drawings or Capital ; (*xi*) Credit Supplier.

3. For the transactions given below one of the accounts involved is given. State the other account and say whether the account mentioned by you will be debited or credited.

(a)	Issar starts business with Rs. 10,000	Capital
(b)	Discount allowed by Gopal.	Gopal
(c)	Discount allowed to Madan.	Discount
(d)	Repairs effected to machinery, payment by cheque.	Bank
(e)	Furniture sold for Cash.	Cash
(f)	Amount due from Singh irrecoverable.	Singh
(g)	Amount previously written off as a bad debt now received from Ali.	Cash
(h)	Railway freight paid for machinery.	Cash
(i)	Repair to second-hand machinery	Cash
(j)	Amount charged by bank as bank charges	Bank charges

Answers : (a) Debit Cash ; (b) Credit Discount ; (c) Credit Madan ; (d) Debit Repairs ; (e) Credit Furniture ; (f) Debit Bad Debts ; (g) Credit Bad Debits Recovered; (h) Debit Machinery; (i) Debit Machinery and (j) Credit Bank.

4. You are given a number of accounts below. State which of them will show a debit balance and which credit balance.

(a) Buildings Account
(b) Rent Account
(c) Railway Freight
(d) Cash Account
(e) Ram Mohan & Co. (a customer)
(f) Discount Allowed Account
(g) Prem Sobti & Co. (Suppliers)
(h) Discount Received Account
(i) Capital Account
(j) Repairs to Machinery A/c.

Answers : (g), (h) and (i) will be credit balances.

5. The following transactions take place in the firm of Iqbal & Sons. Give journal entries.

1978 July
1. Rao, a customer, pays Rs. 450.
2. Goods are sold to Ganguli, Rs. 560, on credit.
3. Goods are purchased from Bose, Rs. 850, for cash.
4. Cash sales, Rs. 150.
5. Purchased Office Furniture, Rs. 980, payment made by cheque.
6. Received cheque from Ganguli, Rs. 545.
   Allowed him discount, Rs. 15.
7. Paid Rent for June, 1978, Rs. 200.
   Paid Salaries & Wages for June, 1978, Rs. 250.
8. Drawn cash from bank for office use, Rs. 600.
   Withdrawn Rs. 300 for domestic use.
   Goods taken from firm for domestic use, Rs. 50.

6. Som Datt commences business on 1st October, 1977 with Rs. 10,000. He opened a bank account with Rs. 9,500. His other transactions were as follows :—

		Rs.
October	1. Purchased Stationery	75
	2. Purchased Furniture and Typewriter, paid by cheque	2.000
	Purchased goods on credit from M/s Khurshid Ali & Sons	1,100
	3. Purchased goods from M/s. Mohan & Co. for cash	300
	Sold goods for cash	250
	4. Paid rent by cheque	350
	Purchased goods from M/s. Vasant Brothers on credit	1,500

		Rs.
5.	Sold goods to M/s. Ram Lal & Sons on credit	800
	Paid for advertising in cash	150
6.	Issued cheque in favour of M/s Khurshid Ali & Sons on account	600
	Cash Sales	200
	Cash sent to Bank	100
8.	Received cheque from M/s Ram Lal & Sons, Rs. 780 ; Allowed them Discount	20
	Issued cheque in favour of M/s Vasant Bros. Rs. 1,470 ; Discount allowed by them Rs.	30
10.	Cheque of M/s. Ram Lal & Sons returned dishonoured by Bank	
11.	Withdrew cash for domestic use	150

7. R. Andley possessed the following assets and liabilities on 1st January, 1979 :

Assets	Rs.	Liabilities	Rs.
Furniture	2,600	Due to : Basu	900
Stock	16,000	Rao	600
		Total	1,500
Cash in Hand	200	Andley's Capital	23,500
Cash at Bank	4,100		
Due from : Dutt	1,300		
More	800		
Total	25,000		25,000

Give the opening entry to start the books for 1979.

8. Chadha is doing business in shoes. On 1st January, 1979 his assets were :

Stock, Rs. 31,000 ; Furniture & Fixtures, Rs. 5,600 ; Cash at Bank, Rs. 800; Cash in Hand, Rs. 100 ; Due from Puri, Rs. 1,500 ; Due from Gopi, Rs. 600. His liabilities were : Due to Krishna, Rs. 1,600 ; Mrs. Chandra's Loan, Rs. 5,000.

The transactions for January, 1979 were as under :

			Rs.
Jan.	1.	Sold old furniture for cash	350
		Purchased new furniture on credit from M/s. Ravi & Co.	900
	2.	Purchased goods from Dimpi on credit	1,100
	3.	Cash Sales	500
		Paid Rent for January	200
	4.	Cash Purchases, payment by cheque	600
		Received cheque from Gopi in full settlement	585
	5.	Issued cheque in favour of Krishna in full settlement	1,550
		Purchased goods from Krishna on credit	900
	6.	Puri pays cash on account	600
	7.	Paid income tax	300
		Withdrawn for domestic use	250
	10.	Gopi's cheque returned dishonoured ; Bank charges Rs. 5 as expenses	
	11.	Sold goods on credit to Puri	1,000

	Rs.
13. Shose taken for domestic use	50
15. Issued cheque in favour of Dimpi	1,100
Purchased goods from Mathur & Co., payment by cheque.	700
18. Dimpi returns cheque because it has been dishonoured by Bank	
20. Gopi declared insolvent ; only 40% received from his estate.	
22. Amount received from Pinki against a debt written off in 1976	200
24. Puri sends cheque to clear the amount due on 1st January, 1979	
26. Purchased Stationery	75
Paid for Telephone Charges	15
Paid for Postage and Telegrams	50
31. Paid Interest to Mrs. Chadha	100
Puri returns goods, not being up to the mark	150

9. Give journal entries for the following :

(*a*) Interest, Rs. 250, charged by the bank.

(*b*) Interest, Rs. 600, due but not paid on a loan taken by the firm.

(*c*) Goods, worth Rs. 1,500, lost by theft ; Insurance company admits claim in full.

(*d*) Delivery van repaired at a cost of Rs. 600.

(*e*) Cash stolen by the peon, Rs. 400 ; insurance company admits claim for Rs. 350 only.

(*f*) Goods, worth Rs. 600, lost by accident. Insurance company does not admit claim.

(*g*) Furniture purchased for Rs. 2,000 on 1st January, 1977 is valued at Rs. 1,800 on 31st December, 1977.*

(*h*) Salaries paid to clerks, Rs. 250.

(*i*) Received claim for Rs. 1,000 from a customer for late supply of goods ; claim admitted for Rs. 600.

(*j*) Purchased Machinery for Rs. 15,000 from M/s. Machine Makers; payment to be made by monthly instalments of Rs. 1,000 each.

10. Journalise the transactions given below :—

(*a*) Ram Krishan who owes Rs. 1,850 pays Rs. 1,775 in full settlement.

(*b*) A cheque for Rs. 950 is sent to Mohan Ram & Co., a creditor, in full settlement of the amount due, Rs. 975.

(*c*) Amount due from Puri & Co., Rs. 450, written off as a bad debt.

(*d*) M/s. Sohan & Co. who owe Rs. 900 become insolvent. Only 30% of the amount due is received.

(*e*) A sum of Rs. 200 is received from Khan & Co., against a debt previously written off.

11. The following accounts show the balances shown against them. What is the significrnce of these accounts and figures.

	Rs.
(*i*) Plant and Machinery Account (Dr)	3,60,000
(*ii*) Mrs. Proprietor's Account (Cr)	50,000
(*iii*) Interest Account (Cr)	5,000
(*iv*) Staff Loans Account (Dr)	20,000
(*v*) Octroi Duty Account (Dr)	3,000
(*vi*) Bad Debts Account (Dr)	1,100
(*vii*) Discount Account (Cr)	350
(*viii*) Freight Account (Dr)	1,750
(*ix*) Bank Account (Dr)	8,750
(*x*) Capital Account (Dr)	6,200

*Reduction in value is called depreciation if it is because of wear and tear.

CHAPTER III

THE LEDGER

In the journal each transaction is dealt with separately. On perusing the journal one cannot form any idea of the net effect of the transactions since it records only which account is to be debited and which to be credited. The record is made datewise. Transactions of a similar nature will be recorded in different places if they occur on different dates. Transactions on one day will be rather diverse in character, *e.g.*, purchase of furniture, sale of goods, payment of expenses, etc.

To get the picture as a whole, the entries recorded in the journal have to be processed further. All similar transactions must be brought together. For instance, all transactions relating to cash must be put in one place. Similarly, all transactions with a customer or a supplier must be assembled. Further, the transactions must be arranged, debits on one side and credits on the other. The statement which contains all transactions relating to a particular subject for a particular period and in which the transactions are neatly arranged into debits and credits is known as an account. In other words, an account is a statement which contains all benefits received by the subject concerned on one side and all benefits given by it on the other. The usual form of a ledger account is as under:

Dr. *Cr.*

Date	*Particulars*	*Folio*	*Amount* Rs. P.	*Date*	*Particulars*	*Folio*	*Amount* Rs. P.

An alternative ruling is as follows :

Date	Particulars	Folio	Dr. Amount Rs.	P.	Cr. Amount Rs.	P.	Dr. or Cr.	Balance Amount Rs.	P.

The column for folio is meant to record the number of the page on which the relevant transaction has been journalised in the journal.

Preparation of ledger accounts or Posting. The task of preparing ledger accounts on the basis of the journal is known as "posting". The student should note at this stage that a transaction is first journalised and then, on the basis of the journal, it is recorded in the ledger (that is, the book which contains accounts). Journalising is more important because there it is decided which account is to be debited and which to be credited. It calls for judgment. Posting is comparatively easy and more or less routine work.

Posting consists in (1) recording the relevant amount on the left hand side of the account which, according to the journal, is to be debit ed and (2) recording the amount on the right hand side of the account which, according to the journal, is to be credited (accounts preceded by the word "To").In the ledger account, it is customary to write "To" on the debit side and "By" on the credit side. In the particulars column, reference is made *to the other* account involved, to provide easy cross referring. In the particulars column of the account to be debited, the name of the account which furnished the 'benefit' has to be mentioned; the nam of the account receiving the benefit is similarly stated in the account to be credited. The student should note that a new account is *not* opened for *every* transaction. Transactions will be recorded in the account already opened. Of course, a new account will be opened, if not already there. The opposite sheet illustrates posting (assuming the journal entries are on page 39 and ledger account on page 17).

Posting the Opening Entry. The opening entry is always for balances of assets, liabilities and capital in the beginning. As the student knows, an opening entry looks like the following :

				Rs.	Rs.
July 1	Stock Account	...	Dr.	20,100	
	Furniture Account	...	Dr.	2,000	
	Bank Account	...	Dr.	3,400	
	To Loan Account				10,000
	To Capital Account				15,500

In the ledger, an account will be opened for each one of the above. The amounts are written on the debit side in case of assets. In the particulars column, the words "To Balance b/d" are written. In case of liabilities and the Capital Account, the amounts are written on the credit side. "By Balance b/d" is written in the column for particulars (b/d stands for brought down). The posting or the opening entry given above will be as follows :

Ledger Accounts

Dr. Stock Account Cr.

Date	*Particulars*	*Folio*	*Amount* Rs.	P.	*Date*	*Particulars*	*Folio*	*Amount* Rs.	P.
July 1	To Balance b/d		20,100	—					

Furniture Account

Date	*Particulars*	*Folio*	*Amount* Rs.	P.	*Date*	*Particulars*	*Folio*	*Amount* Rs.	P.
July 1	To Balance b/d		2,000	—					

Bank Account

Date	*Particulars*	*Folio*	*Amount* Rs.	P.	*Date*	*Particulars*	*Folio*	*Amount* Rs.	P.
July 1	To Balance b/d		3,400	—					

Loan Account

Date	*Particulars*	*Folio*	*Amount* Rs.	P.	*Date*	*Particulars*	*Folio*	*Amount* Rs.	P.
					July 1	By Balance b/d		10,000	—

Capital Account

Date	*Particulars*	*Folio*	*Amount* Rs.	P.	*Date*	*Particulars*	*Folio*	*Amount* Rs.	P.
					July 1	By Balance b/d		15,500	—

The student will note that the debits placed in the first three accounts, named above, total Rs. 25,500 which is also the total of the credits placed in the two accounts named last.

Balancing an account. After all transactions have been posted and thus various accounts prepared, the balances of real and personal accounts are ascertained. This is done by totalling the two sides of an account and by noting the difference. This difference is put on the *shorter* side, thus making the two sides equal. Against the difference the words "To (or By) Balance c/d"* are written. The account is then ruled off, *i.e.*, the totals are written in the two columns opposite each other. A single line is drawn across the amount columns before totalling and two lines are drawn below the figures of totals. The balance is written on the opposite side as balance brought down for the next period. This is illustrated with a Bank Account with imaginary figures for a week.

Dr. **Bank Account** **Cr.**

Date		*Particulars*	*Folio*	*Amount Rs.*	*P.*	*Date*		*Particulars*	*Folio*	*Amount Rs.*	*P.*
1978						1978					
July	1	To Balance b/d		4,100	—	July	1	By Murty & Sons		900	—
	2	To Kohli & Co.,		1,500	—		4	By Furniture Account		650	—
	4	To Cash A/c		600	—		6	By Wages A/c		1,200	—
	6	To Ali Bros.		750	—		7	By Kohli & Co. (cheque dishonoured)		1,500	—
								By Balance c/d		2,700	—
				6,950	—					6,950	—
July	8	To Balance b/d		2,700	—						

The total of the debit entries is Rs. 6,950. The total of credit entries is Rs. 4,250. The difference is Rs. 2,700. This is put on the credit side because it is short ; then totals are written and after that the balance is again written, but now on the debit side (the opposite side) to signify the balance at bank in the beginning of the next week.

We now work out a comprehensive example showing the journal entries and ledger accounts.

Illustration. Pearey Lal was carrying on business as a stationery merchant. On 1st January, 1978 his assets and liabilities were as under :

Assets : Furniture and Fixtures, Rs. 2,400 ; Stock of Stationery Rs. 35,600 ; Cash at Bank Rs. 3,500 ; Cash in Hand Rs. 400 ; Due from Bimal, Rs. 1,600 ; Due from Kewal Rs. 800.

Liabilities : Due to Landlord (December's rent), Rs. 150 ; Due to Sharma Bros., Rs. 1,400 ; Due to Verma Sons, Rs. 550.

The transactions during January, 1978 were :

			Rs.
Jan.	2	Cash Sales	150
	2	Sales to J. P. Stores on credit	450
	3	Purchases from Verma Sons	380

* denotes carried down.

Jan.	4	Paid rent to Landlord (for December 1977)	150
		Used Stationery for office	60
		Used Stationery for domestic purposes	20
	6	Sold Stationery to I.P. College on credit	250
		Bought Postage Stamps	15
	7	Paid Insurance premium by cheque	350
		Received cheque from Kewal in full settlement	780
	9	Issued cheque in favour of Verma Sons in full settlement of the amount due on Jan. 1	540
	10	Cash Sales	600
		Sent Cash to Bank	500
	11	Received cheque from Bimal on account	1,000
		Cash received from J.P. Stores	430
		Goods received back from J.P. Stores	20
	13	Bimal's cheque returned dishonoured.	
		Issued cheque in favour of Sharma Bros. in full settlement	1,350
	15	Sales on credit to Kewal	500
	16	Cheque in favour of Sharma Bros. returned dishonoured because of improper rubber stamp.	
	17	Incurred advertising, Rs. 250 ; paid cash Rs. 100 and stationery given for balance.	
	20	Exchanged old furniture for new : Price of new furniture Rs. 600; value of old furniture Rs. 200 (cost Rs. 350); balance paid in cash.	
	22	Bimal declared insolvent ; 40% received against amount due from him.	
		Sent cheque to Sharma Bros., Rs. 1,400.	
	23	Kewal claims Rs. 50 as special allowance because of defect in goods ; allowance agreed to.	
	25	Borrowed Rs. 10,000 from Mrs. Pearey Lal @ 9% pa. Money put in bank.	
		Installed a small printing machine at a cost of Rs. 9,500 ; paid by cheque.	
		Repairs to furniture Rs. 100.	
	28	Cash Sales Rs. 400	
		Paid Income Tax, Rs. 550.	
	30	Withdrawn for domestic use, Rs. 200	
		Amount drawn from bank for office use, Rs. 600.	
	31	Paid Salaries, Rs. 250.	
		Amount due to Landlord as rent for January, Rs. 150.	

Write up the journal and ledger accounts of Pearey Lal for January, 1978.

Solution:

Journal of Pearey Lal

Date		Particulars		L.F.	Dr. Rs.	Cr. Rs.
1978 Jan.	1	Furniture & Fixture A/c ...	Dr.		2,400 —	
		Goods A/c	Dr.		35,600 —	
		Bank A/c	Dr.		3,500 —	
		Cash A/c	Dr.		400 —	
		Bimal	Dr.		1,600 —	
		Kewal	Dr.		800 —	
		To Landlord				150 —
		To Sharma Bros.				1,400 —
		To Verma Sons				550 —
		To Capital Account				42,200 —
		The opening entry to record assets and liabilities on January 1, 1978 ; Capital ascertained by deducting liabilities (Rs. 2,100) from assets (total Rs. 44,300).				
	2	Cash Account ...	Dr.		150 —	
		To Goods A/c				150 —
		Sale of goods cash, cash memo nos...				
	2	J.P. Stores ...	Dr.		450 —	
		To Goods Account				450 —
		Sale of goods on credit to J.P. Stores *vide* invoice no...				
	3	Goods Account	Dr.		380 —	
		To Verma Sons				380 —
		Goods purchased from Verma Sons *vide* their invoice no...				
	4	Landlord ...	Dr.		150 —	
		To Cash Account				150 —
		Rent paid for December, 1977; debited to him because the Landlord's A/c already stands credited by the amount.				
	5	Office Stationery A/c ...	Dr.		60 —	
		Capital Account	Dr.		20 —	
		To Goods Account				80 —
		Stationery used in office and at home out of stock.				
	6	I.P. College	Dr.		250 —	
		To Goods Account				250 —
		Sale of stationery (or goods) to I.P. College, *vide* invoice no...				
	6	Postage Account ...	Dr.		15 —	
		To Cash Account				15 —
		Postage stamps purchased.				
		Total carried orward			45,775 —	45,775 —

Date		Particulars		L.F.	Rs.		Rs.	
1978		Total Brought Forward			45,775	—	45,775	—
Jan.	7	Insurance Account	Dr.		350	—		
		To Bank Account					350	—
		Insurance premium paid by cheque no...						
	7	Bank Account	Dr.		780	—		
		Discount Account	Dr.		20	—		
		To Kewal					800	—
		Cheque for Rs. 780 received from Kewal to clear his account for Rs. 800 ; Rs. 20 allowed as discount, *i.e.*, Rs. 800—780.						
	9	Verma Sons	Dr.		550	—		
		To Bank A/c					540	—
		To Discount A/c					10	—
		Cheque no...for Rs. 540 issued to Verma Sons to clear the amount of Rs. 550 due to them.						
	10	Cash Account	Dr		600	—		
		To Goods Account					600	—
		Sale of goods for cash, cash memos no...						
	10	Bank Account	Dr.		500	—		
		To Cash Account					500	—
		Cash sent to bank.						
	11	Bank Account	Dr.		1,000	—		
		To Bimal					1,000	—
		Cheque no......for Rs. 1,000 received from Bimal in partial payment of the amount due from him.						
	12	Cash Account	Dr.		430	—		
		Goods Account	Dr.		20	—		
		To J.P. Stores					450	—
		Cash Rs. 430, and goods Rs. 20, received from M/s. J.P. Stores.						
	13	Bimal	Dr.		1,000	—		
		To Bank Account					1,000	—
		Dishonour of Bimal's cheque.						
	14	Sharma Bros	Dr.		1,400	—		
		To Bank A/c					1,350	—
		To Discount A/c					50	—
		Cheque no......for Rs. 1,350 issued in favour of M/s. Sharma Bros in full payment of Rs. 1,400 due to them.						
	15	Kewal	Dr.		500	—		
		To Goods A/c					500	—
		Sale of goods on credit to Kewal, *vide* invoice no......						
		Total carried forward			52,925	—	52,925	—

Date		Particulars		L.F.	Rs	Rs
1978		Total Brought Forward			52,925	52,925
Jan.	16	Bank Account	Dr.		1,350	
		Discount Account	Dr.		50	
		To Sharma Bros				1,400
		Cheque no...cancelled because of dishonour ; Sharma Bros. credited with full amount of Rs. 1,400; discount previously allowed by them now disallowed.				
	17	Advertising A/c	Dr.		250	
		To Cash Account				100
		To Goods Account				150
		Advertisement, Rs. 250, paid for in cash, Rs. 100 and in the form of goods, Rs. 150.				
	20	Furniture Account*	Dr.		250	
		Loss on Sale of Furniture A/c	Dr.		150	
		To Cash Account				400
		Cash paid for new furniture (Rs. 600 Rs. 200). Loss on sale of old furniture being Rs. 150 (*i.e.*, Rs. 350 minus Rs. 200) [see footnote below]*				
	22	Cash A/c	Dr.		640	
		Bad Debts A/c	Dr.		960	
		To Bimal (40% on Rs. 1,600, *i.e.*, Rs. 640) received from Bimal's estate, the remaining amount written off as bad.				1,600
	22	Sharma Bros	Dr.		1,400	
		To Bank A/c				1,400
		Cheque sent to Sharma Bros to clear their account of Rs. 1,400				
	23	Goods Account	Dr.		50	
		To Kewal				50
		Special allowance credited to Kewal, debited to Goods A/c as it reduces sale.				
		Total carried forward			58,025	58,025

*The entry on January 20 can be more readily understood if we assume that the transaction takes place with A. For purchase of furniture, the entry is :

Particulars		Dr. Rs	Cr. Rs
Furniture A/c	Dr.	600	
To A			600

For sale of old furniture, the entry is :

Particulars		Dr. Rs	Cr. Rs
A	Dr.	200	
Loss on Furniture A/c	Dr.	150	
To Furniture A/c			350

For payment to A, the entry is :

Particulars		Dr. Rs	Cr. Rs
A	Dr.	400	
To Cash A/c			400

The entry already made is the net effect of these three entries.

Date		Particulars		L.F.	Rs.		Rs.	
1978 Jan.		Total Brought Forward			58,025	—	58,025	—
	25	Bank Account To Mrs. Pearey Lal's Loan A/c Loan taken from Mrs. Pearey Lal @ 9% p. a.	Dr.		10,000	—	10,000	—
	25	Machinery Account To Bank Account Cheque no...issued for Rs. 9,500 to acquire printing machine.	Dr.		9,500	—	9.500	—
	25	Repairs to Furniture A/c To Cash Account Repairs affected to furniture.	Dr.		100	—	100	
	28	Cash Account To Goods Account Rent paid by issue of cheque no...	Dr.		400	—	400	—
	28	Capital Account To Cash Account Income Tax, Rs. 550, paid on behalf of the proprietor.	Dr.		550	—	550	—
	30	Capital Account To Cash Account Amount taken for domestic use.	Dr.		200	—	200	—
	30	Cash Account To Bank Account Amount withdrawn from bank, *vide* cheque no......for use in office.	Dr.		600	—	600	—
	31	Salaries Account To Cash Account Salaries paid in cash.	Dr.		250	—	250	—
	31	Rent Account To Landlord The amount due to Landlord for January, 1978.	Dr.		150	—	150	—
		Total			79,775	—	79,775	—

LEDGER ACCOUNTS

Dr. **Furniture and Fixtures Account** **Cr.**

Date		Particulars	L.F.	Amount Rs.	Date		Particulars	L.F.	Amount Rs.
1978									
Jan.	1	To Balance b/d		2,400 —	1978				
	20	To Cash Account		250 —	Jan.	31	By Balance c/d		2,650 —
				2,650 —					2,650 —
Feb.	1	To Balance b/d		2,650 —					

Goods Account

Date		Particulars	L.F.	Amount Rs.	Date		Particulars	L.F.	Amount Rs.
1978					1978				
Jan.	1	To Balance b/d		35,600 —	Jan.	2	By Cash A/c		150 —
	3	To Verma Sons		380 —		2	By J. P. Stores		450 —
	11	To J. P. Stores		20 —		2	By Sundries		80 —
	23	To Kewal		50 —					
						6	By I. P. College		250 —
						10	By Cash A/c		600 —
						15	By Kewal		500 —
						17	By Advertising A/c		150 —
						28	By Cash Account		400 —

Bank Account

Date		Particulars	L.F.	Amount Rs.	Date		Particulars	L.F.	Amount Rs.
1978					1978				
Jan.	1	To Balance b/d		3,500 —	Jan.	7	By Insurance A/c		350 —
	7	To Kewal		780 —		9	By Verma Sons		540 —
	10	To Cash A/c		500 —		13	By Bimal		1,000 —
	11	To Bimal		1,000 —		13	By Sharma Bros.		1,350 —
	16	To Sharma Bros.		1,350 —		22	By Sharma Bros.		1,400 —
	25	To Mrs. Pearey Lal's Loan A/c		10,000 —		25	By Machinery A/c		9,500 —
						30	By Cash Account		600 —
						31	By Balance c/d		2,390 —
				17,130 —					17,130 —
Feb.	1	To Balance b/d		2,390 —					

Cash Account

Date		Particulars	L.F.	Amount Rs.	Date		Particulars	L.F.	Amount Rs.
1978					1978				
Jan.	1	To Balance c/d		400 —	Jan.	4	By Landlord		150 —
	2	To Goods A/c		150 —		6	By Postage A/c		15 —
	10	To Goods A/c		600 —		10	By Bank A/c		500 —
	11	To J. P. Stores		430 —		17	By Advertising A/c		100 —
	22	To Bimal		640 —					
	28	To Goods A/c		400 —		20	By Sundries— Furniture		250 —
	30	To Bank A/c		600 —			Loss on Furniture		150 —
						25	By Repairs to Furniture A/c		100 —
						25	By Capital A/c		550 —
						30	By Capital A/c		200 —
						31	By Salaries A/c		250 —
						31	By Balance c/d		955 —
				3,220 —					3,220 —
Feb.	1	To Balance b/d		955 —					

Bimal

Date		Particulars	L.F.	Amount		Date		Particulars	L.F.	Amount Rs.	
1978						1978					
Jan.	1	To Balance b/d		1,600	—	Jan.	11	By Bank A/c.		1,000	—
	13	To Bank A/c		1,000	—		22	By Sundries—			
								Cash A/c		640	—
								Bad Debts A/c		960	—
				2,600	—					2,600	—

Kewal

Date		Particulars	L.F.	Amount		Date		Particulars	L.F.	Amount	
1978						1978					
Jan.	1	To Balance b/d		800	—	Jan.	7	By Sundries—			
	15	To Goods A/c		500	—			Bank A/c		780	—
								Discount A/c		20	—
							23	By Goods A/c		50	—
							31	By Balance c/d		450	—
				1,300	—					1,300	—
Feb.	1	To Balance b/d		450	—						

Landlord

Date		Particulars	L.F.	Amount		Date		Particulars	L.F.	Amount	
1978						1978					
Jan.	4	To Cash A/c		150	—	Jan.	1	By Balance b/d		150	—
"	31	To Balance c/d		150	—		31	By Rent A/c		150	—
				300	—					300	—
						Feb.	1	By Balance b/d		150	—

Sharma Bros.

Date		Particulars	L.F.	Amount		Date		Particulars	L.F.	Amount	
1978						1978					
Jan.	13	To Sundries—				Jan.	1	By Balance b/d		1,400	—
		Bank A/c		1,350	—		16	By Sundries—			
		Discount A/c		50	—			Bank A/c		1,350	—
	22	To Bank A/c		1,400	—			Discount A/c		50	—
				2,800	—					2,800	—

Verma Sons

Date		Particulars	L.F.	Amount		Date		Particulars	L.F.	Amount	
1978						1978					
Jan.	9	To Sundries—				Jan.	1	By Balance b/d		550	—
		Bank A/c		540	—		3	By Goods A/c		380	—
		Discount A/c		10	—						
	31	To Balance c/d		380	—						
				930	—					930	—
						Feb.	1	By Balance b/d		380	—

Capital Account

Date		Particulars	L.F.	Amount Rs.		Date		Particulars	L.F.	Amount Rs.	
1978 Jan.	1	To Goods A/c		20	—	1978 Jan.	1	By Balance b/d		42,200	—
	28	To Cash A/c		550	—						
	30	To Cash A/c		200	—						

J. P. Stores

Date		Particulars	L.F.	Amount Rs.		Date		Particulars	L.F.	Amount Rs.	
1978 Jan.	2	To Goods A/c		450	—	1978 Jan.	11	By Sundries—			
								Cash A/c		430	—
								Goods A/c		20	—
				450	—					450	—

Office Stationery Account

Date		Particulars	L.F.	Amount Rs.		Date		Particulars	L.F.	Amount Rs.	
1978 Jan.	4	To Goods A/c		60	—						

I. P. College

Date		Particulars	L.F.	Amount Rs.		Date		Particulars	L.F.	Amount Rs.	
1978 Jan.	6	To Goods A/c		250	—	1978 Jan.	31	By Balance c/d		250	—
Feb.	1	To Balance b/d		250	—						

Postage Account

Date		Particulars	L.F.	Amount Rs.		Date		Particulars	L.F.	Amount Rs.	
1968 Jan.	6	To Cash A/c		15	—						

Insurance Account

Date		Particulars	L.F.	Amount Rs.		Date		Particulars	L.F.	Amount Rs.	
1978 Jan.	7	To Bank A/c		350	—						

Discount Account

Date		Particulars	L.F.	Amount Rs.		Date		Particulars	L.F.	Amount Rs.	
1978 Jan.	7	To Kewal		20	—	1978 Jan.	9	By Verma Sons		10	—
	16	To Sharma Bros.		50	—		13	By Sharma Bros.		50	—

Advertising Account

Date		Particulars	L.F.	Amount Rs.		Date		Particulars	L.F.	Amount Rs.	
1978 Jan.	17	To Sundries—									
		Cash A/c		100	—						
		Goods A/c		150	—						

Loss on Sale of Furniture Account

Date		Particulars	L.F.	Amount Rs.		Date		Particulars	L.F.	Amount Rs.	
1978 Jan.	22	To Cash A/c		150	—						

Bed Debts Account

Date		Particulars	L.F.	Amount Rs.		Date		Particulars	L.F.	Amount Rs.	
1978 Jan.	22	To Bimal		960	—						

Mrs. Pearey Lal's Loan Account

Date		Particulars	L.F.	Amount Rs.		Date		Particulars	L.F.	Amount Rs.	
1978 Jan.	31	To Balance c/d		10,000	—	1978 Jan.	25	By Bank A/c		10,000	—
					—	Feb.	1	By Balance b/d		10,000	—

Machinery Account

Date		Particulars	L.F.	Amount Rs.		Date		Particulars	L.F.	Amount Rs.	
1978 Jan.	25	To Bank A/c		9,500	—	1978 Jan.	31	By Balance b/d		9,500	—
Feb.	1	To Balance b/d		9,500	—						

Repairs to Furniture Account

Date		Particulars	L.F.	Amount Rs.		Date		Particulars	L.F.	Amount Rs.	
1978 Jan.	25	To Cash Account		100	—						

Salaries Account

Date		Particulars	L.F.	Amount Rs.		Date		Particulars	L.F.	Amount Rs.	
1978 Jan.	31	To Cash Account		250	—						

Rent Account

Date		Particulars	L.F.	Amount Rs.		Date		Particulars	L.F.	Amount Rs.	
1978 Jan.		To Landlord		150	—						

The student will have noted that a number of accounts have not been balanced in the working shown above. With the exception of the Capital Account, accounts that have not been balanced, pertain to profit or loss of the firm. The information contained in these accounts will be used to ascertain how much profit the firm has earned. This task will be discussed in a later chapter. Capital Account has also not been balanced because the account will be credited with the profit when ascertained or debited with the loss.

Arrangement of Accounts. In the illustration given above, accounts have been opened as and when they arise and no thought has been given to the order in which they should be opened. However, the accounts should be opened in some order. The order suggested is :

Capital Account
Real Accounts
Personal Accounts—Debtors
—Creditors
Nominal Accounts.

A Test. Some of the accounts worked out above have debit balances and others have credit balances. Let us list these two sets of accounts separately. Thus :

Debit Balances	Rs.	*Credit Balances*	Rs.
Furniture Account	2,650	Landlord	150
Goods Account (debit side, Rs. 36,050 minus credit side, Rs. 2,580)	33,470	Verma Sons	380
		Capital Account (Rs. 42,200—Rs. 770	41,430
Bank Account	2,390	Mrs. Pearey Lal's Loan Account	10,000
Cash Account	955		
Kewal	450		
Office Stationery Account	60		
I.P. College	250		
Postage Account	15		
Insurance Account	350		
Discount Account	10		
Advertising Account	250		
Loss on Sale of Furniture A/c.	150		
Bad Debts Account	960		
Machinery Account	9,500		
Repairs to Furniture A/c.	100		
Salaries Account	250		
Rent Account	150		
Total Rs.	51,960	Total Rs.	51,960

The student notes that the total of the two lists is the same. This should be so since for every debit entry there is a credit entry and *vice versa*. We can ascertain the accuracy of our work by preparing a list of debit balances and another of credit balances and seeing whether the totals of the two lists agree. If the totals do not agree, there is definitely some mistake. The lists, if put in one statement, are known as a Trial Balance. This will be discussed in a later chapter.

Exercises

1. Are the following journal entries correctly made ? If not, give the correct entries.

				Rs.
	(*a*) Cash Account To Goods Account Sale of goods for cash.	Dr.	350	530
	(*b*) Cash Account To Mohan Amount received from Mohan against a debt written off last year as a bad debt.	Dr.	150	150
	(*c*) Goods Account To Ravi and Sons Purchase of office furniture from Ravi and Sons on credit.	Dr.	650	650
	(*d*) Rent Account To Cash Account Payment of rent.	Dr.	200	200
	(*e*) Furniture Account To Cash Account Repairs to furniture paid for in cash.	Dr.	100	100

(All entries except (d) are wrong)

2. Prepare Accounts from the journal entries already made by you for exercise nos. 7 and 8 of the previous chapter.

3. Distinguish the ledger from the journal.

4. Are the following accounts correctly prepared ? If not, prepare them properly.

Cash Account

	Rs.		Rs.
To Balance b/d	1,800	By Typewriter	1,250
To Ram (amount paid to him)	600	By Repairs to Furniture	70
To Goods Account (cash sales)	500	By Ganapathy & Co. (goods purchased for cash)	250
To Karim			
Cash Received	650		
Discount allowed	30		

Goods Account

	Rs.		Rs.
To Balance b/d	16,200	By Cash Account	500

Discount Account

		By Karim	30

Ganapathy & Co.

To Cash Account	250		

Office Furniture & Equipment A/c

To Balance b/d	1,700		
To Cash—Typewriter	1,250		
To Cash—Repairs to Furniture	70		

Ram

To Cash Account	600		

Karim

		By Cash Account	680

5. William Jones commenced a business on the 1st January. The following were his transactions for the first month :—

			Rs.
Jan.	1	Commenced business with	25,000
		Paid to bank	23,500
		Purchased Furniture, paid by cheque	2 000
	3	Bought goods from James Harrison and Co.	5 400
		Sold goods to William Adams	4,800
		Installed Telephone under Own Your Own Telephone Scheme, paid by cheque	2,000
	7	Bought goods from James Harrison and Co.	6,450
	8	Paid for office stationery in cash	80
		Sold goods to H. Allan & Co.	5,350
	10	Received cheque from William Adam (discount allowed Rs. 120)	4,680
	11	Paid James Harrison & Co. by cheque (discount received Rs. 270)	5,130
	12	Paid 3 months' rent to 31st March, in cash	400
	13	Bought goods from H. Kershaw	7,400
	15	Paid wages in cash	80
		Paid office expenses in cash	70
	17	Bought goods of W. Smith & Co.	6 250
		Sold goods to H. Hobson	3,200

			Rs.
Jan.	19	Sold goods to Wm. Adams	1,600
	21	Sold goods to H. Allan & Co.	2,500
		Received from H. Hobson's cheque	1,000
	22	Paid wages in cash	80
		Paid office expenses in cash	50
	25	Paid W. Smith & Co. by cheque in full settlement	6,130
	26	Received cheque from H. Allan & Co. in full settlement	5,200
		H. Hobson's cheque returned dishonoured	
	27	H. Allan & Co. returned goods, not up to sample	200
	29	Paid wages in cash	80
		Paid for newspapers and periodicals	30
		Paid office expenses in cash	40
		Sold old newspapers	5
		Received from W. Adams' cheque	1,600
		Drawings out of bank for personal use	750

Prepare Journal entries and ledger accounts. Test your working by taking out a Trial Balance.

CHAPTER IV

THE PRACTICAL SYSTEM (I)

The Cash Book and Banking Transactions

So far we have thought of only one way of recording the transactions, *viz.*, journalising and then posting. There is another way of doing this work. This method is known as the Practical System or, even, the English System. It consists of keeping various registers (or books as they are called by accountants) to record various types of transactions and then preparing ledger accounts. In one book only one type of transactions are recorded. The transactions of a firm will fall into three main categories, *viz.*,

(1) Receipts and Payments of Cash, including payments into and withdrawals from the Bank Account ;

(2) Purchase of goods, materials and stores ; and

(3) Sale of goods.

There will be one book to record cash (and bank) transactions, another to record purchases of goods, and a third to record sale of goods. If any other class of transactions is numerous, a book can be maintained for that class also, for example, to record return of goods from customers or to suppliers. The journal will also be maintained but only to record such transactions as cannot be recorded in other books. In this chapter we will consider the cash transactions. The next chapter will be devoted to other classes of transactions.

THE CASH BOOK

In any business house there will be numerous transactions relating to cash—receipts and payments of it. The student now realises that on receipt, cash account is debited and on payment, cash account is credited. On this basis, the Cash Account can be prepared straightaway *without* the transactions being first journalised. When cash is received, the Cash Account can be directly debited and when cash is paid, it can be directly credited. A short explanation should be given with each entry. Thus the clerical labour in first making the journal entry is saved. Since cash transactions will be numerous, it is better to keep a separate book to contain only the Cash Account. The book is known as Cash Book.

Simple Cash Book. The Simple Cash Book is ruled exactly like a ledger account. Thus :—

Cash Book

RECEIPTS				PAYMENTS			
Dr.							*Cr.*
Date	*Particulars*	*L.F.*	*Amount* Rs. P.	*Date*	*Particulars*	*L.F.*	*Amount* Rs. P.

The above type of Cash Book is also known as Single Column Cash Book.

Illustration. Enter the following transactions of Akbar in Single Column Cash Book :—

1979			Rs.
Jan.	1	Commenced business with	15,000
	2	Paid into Bank	13,000
	3	Purchased goods for cash	1,500
	4	Sold goods for cash	1,100
	5	Paid for Stationery	60
	6	Received from Nariman	1,500
	7	Paid to Gupta	80
	7	Purchased Office Furniture	60

Solution :

Cash Book*

RECEIPTS *Dr.*					PAYMENTS				*Cr.*
Date		*Particulars*	*L.F.*	*Amount* Rs. P.	*Date*		*Particulars*	*L.F.*	*Amount* Rs. P.
1979					1979				
Jan.	1	To Capital A/c. (Business commenced with Rs. 15,000)		15,000 —	Jan.	2	By Bank A/c. (A/c. opened with Rs. 13,000)		13,000 —
	4	To Goods A/c. (Goods sold for cash)		1,100 —		3	By Goods A/c. (goods purchased)		1,500 —
	6	To Nariman (amount received)		1,500 —		5	By Stationery Account (Office Stationery purchased)		60 —
						7	By Gupta (amount paid)		800 —
						7	By Office Furniture A/c. (Furniture purchased)		600 —
							By Balance c/d.		1,640 —
				17,600 —					17,600 —
Jan.	8	To Balance b/d		1,640					

The Cash Book is balanced just like an ordinary ledger account. The two sides are totalled and the difference put on the shorter side. In the above case the total of the receipts (or debit) side is Rs. 17,600 and the total of payments made is Rs. 15,960. The difference is Rs. 1,640. This is put on the credit side as "By Balance carried down". The two columns are then totalled. On the debit side, the balance is written as "To Balance brought down", showing the cash balance on hand in the beginning of the next period.

Double Column Cash Book. Usually cash discount is allowed to customers who pay promptly—in any case, there will be no question of cash discount unless payment is received from the customer. Similarly, no cash discount is received unless payment is made to suppliers. Cash discounts accompany cash receipts from customers

*The student who finds difficulty in following the Cash Book entries will do well to mentally journalise the transactions and then prepare the Cash A/c. on the basis of the journal entries.

and payments to suppliers. Therefore, it is convenient to record discount allowed or received along with cash receipt or cash payment. The method to do this is to add one amount column on each side to record discount. The column on the debit side will record discount allowed to customers and the one on the credit side will record discount received from suppliers. The Cash Book which contains columns for discount in addition to cash columns, is known as a Double Column Cash Book. The ruling is shown in the solution to illustration given below. Note that the discount columns are not balanced but merely totalled.

Illustration. Enter the following transactions of Prakash in Double Column Cash Book :

1978			Rs.
July	1	Balance of Cash in hand	1,600
	2	Paid to Mohan (discount allowed Rs. 20)	780
	3	Cash Sales	400
	4	Sale of old newspapers	20
	4	Paid for Duplicator	1,000
	4	Withdrawn from Bank	400
	5	Received from Anand (in full settlement of his debt of Rs. 600)	570
	6	Sale of old furniture	300
	7	Received from Ram (discount allowed Rs. 15)	400
	7	Paid Wages	500
	7	Received from Raja against debt previously written off	150

Date	Particulars	L.F.	Discount Rs. P.	Amount Rs. P.	Date	Particulars	L.F.	Discount Rs. P.	Amount Rs. P.
1978 July 1	To Balance b/d			1,600	1978 July 2	By Mohan (amount paid, discount Rs. 20 received)		20	780
3	To Goods Account (cash sales)			400	4	By Duplicator A/c. (Duplicator purchased)			1,000
4	To Miscellaneous Sales A/c. (sale of old papers)			20	7	By Wages A/c. (amount paid as wages)			500
4	To Bank A/c. (amount withdrawn from bank)			400	7	By Balance c/d.			1,560
5	To Anand (Amount received from Anand, discount allowed, Rs. 30)		30	570					
6	To Furniture A/c. (sale of old furniture)			300					
7	To Ram (amount received; discount Rs. 15).		15	400					
7	To Bad Debts A/c. (amount received against debt previously written off)			150					
			45	3,840				20	3,840
8	To Balance b/d.			1,560					

Triple Column Cash Book. In modern business houses transactions with a bank are even more numerous than cash transactions. Money at bank is as good as cash. Hence, it is advantageous to have a column for bank transactions also on each side of the Cash Book. This column will record payments into the bank and payments out of the bank just as the cash columns record receipts of cash and payments of cash. The addition of the bank column will mean that on each side of the Cash Book, there will be three columns for amount—for Discount, Cash and Bank. Entries are made as explained above. Receipts of cash will be entered in the Cash Column (debit side) and payments in cash will be entered in the cash column on the credit side. Cheques issued by the firm represents payments out of bank and hence the amounts will be entered in the bank column on the credit side. When cash or cheques are paid into the bank account, the amounts will be entered in the bank column on the debit side. Cheques received by the firm should be entered in the bank column straightaway because the cheques will have to be sent to the bank.

If cash is withdrawn from the bank for use in office, it should be entered in the Cash Column (debit side), saying 'To Bank...', and it must also be entered in the bank column on the credit side, saying "By Cash...". If cash is deposited in the bank, the amount is entered in the bank column on the debit side and in the cash column on the credit side. These are known as *contra* transactions and in the column for Ledger Folio the letter 'C' should be written to indicate the fact. 'C' will mean that the double entry is complete in the Cash Book itself—it stands for 'contra'.

The Discount Columns are merely totalled and not balanced. The other two columns should be balanced separately. The total of cash column on the debit side will always be bigger than the total of the cash column on the credit side. The difference represents cash in hand and must tally with actual cash with the cashier. The difference is written in the cash column on the credit side. Usually, the total of the bank column on the debit side is also bigger than the total of the bank column on the credit side. The difference represents cash at bank and it should be written in the bank column on the credit side. However, the total of the bank column on the credit side may sometimes be more than the total of the bank column on the debit side. This means that the payments exceed the amount put into bank. The difference represents money overdrawn, that is, loan from bank or bank overdraft. This amount is written on the debit side of the Cash Book in the bank column. After writing the closing balances, the various columns are totalled. The closing balances are the opening balances of the next period and are written as "To Balance brought down...". If there is a bank overdraft, the opening balance will be written on the credit side (in the bank column) as "By Balance b/d..."

Posting the Cash Book. The particulars column on the debit side of the Cash Book will indicate the account on whose account the money has been received. Such accounts will be credited. Similarly, the particulars column on the credit side will indicate the account on whose account payment has been made. Such accounts will be debited. In case a person has paid some money and has been allowed some discount (as shown by the Discount Column), his account must be credited with the total of the amount received from him and the discount allowed to him. Similarly, if an amount has been paid to a person and some discount has been received from him, his account must be debited with the amount paid to him and the discount received from him. Items marked with 'C' do not require any posting because the double entry is already complete in the Cash Book itself. The total of the Discount Column on the debit side is *debited* to the Discount Account because this amount is the loss suffered by the firm by way of discounts allowed to customers. The total of the Discount Column on the credit side is *credited* to the Discount Account since this amount is the gain made by the firm because of Discounts allowed by the creditors. Posting is shown in the working of the following illustration.

Illustration. Ram and Alam had on 1st January, 1978 cash in hand, Rs. 450 and cash at bank, Rs. 6,500. The cash transactions for the first fortnight were as follows :—

			Rs.
Jan.	2	Received cheque from Alam (in full settlement of debt of Rs. 650)	620
		Paid for Advertising by Cheque	350
	3	Cash Sales	250
		Paid Salaries & Wages	435
	4	Amount withdrawn from bank for use in office	600
	5	Drawn Cash for domestic use by Ram	200
	6	Issued cheque in favour of Rao & Sons (Discount received Rs. 25)	1,000
	8	Received cheque from Mehta Bros. (Discount allowed Rs. 20)	800
	10	Sale of Machinery, payment received in cheque	2,500
	12	Bank returns cheque of Mehta Bros. dishonoured	
	15	New Machinery purchased, and cheque issued	10,000
		Paid installation expenses in cash	500
		Bank charges as per pass book	10

Write up the Triple Column Cash Book and illustrate how the accounts will be posted.

The solution is presented on the attached sheet, coloured lines showing how the various items are posted into the ledger.

BANKING TRANSACTIONS

A bank is an institution which deals in money. It receives money on deposit from people and pays it back to them or according to their instructions. In all countries where commerce and industry has developed, banks will be found. A bank has become a vital necessity for modern business houses because they have to deal in large sums of money. We will take up the services rendered by banks to businessmen a little later.

Types of Account. Money can be deposited with a bank in quite a few ways. But three types of accounts that can be opened with a bank are very common. These are : current accounts, savings bank accounts and fixed deposit accounts. In the current accounts, money can be deposited as often as desired and, also, it can be withdrawn without notice and as often as necessary. But the bank may insist upon a certain minimum balance to be maintained. No interest is allowed by good banks. On the other hand, a charge is made by the bank, known as bank charges, every six months or every year. In savings bank accounts, money can be deposited as often as desired but restrictions are placed on withdrawals either in respect of the amount or in respect of the number of withdrawals. Interest is allowed by banks at 5 per cent* per annum on the lowest monthly balances. In fixed deposit accounts, money is deposited only once and cannot be withdrawn before the stipulated period is over. The fixed deposit is evidenced by a receipt which has to be surrendered on withdrawal. For a businessman, a current account is the most suitable. It is not known how many withdrawals will have to be made and when. Savings bank accounts are meant only for individuals who wish to save and for institutions which do not need withdrawals very often. Banks generally insist on a current account for business houses: Saving's Bank Account is not allowed.

How to open an account. For opening an account, the bank will require an introduction. In case of fixed deposits, money is tendered at the counter along with a properly filled in form, and the bank will then issue a receipt. The client will have only the receipt and nothing else. In its own books, the bank will maintain an account in the name of the client. In case of savings bank and current accounts an application form has to be filled in, in which the client has to give all particulars about himself. Specimen signatures have also to be provided. In the case of an individual no further documents are necessary. In case of a partnership firm, the bank will require a certified copy of the partnership deed, that is to say, the agreement among the various partners. In case of a company, the bank will require a copy of the Memorandum of Association and Articles of Association, the two documents governing the establishment and running of the company. Also copies of the appropriate resolutions will be required. Savings bank accounts are not opened for firms or companies—for them only current accounts are allowed for day-to-day operations.

When the first deposit is made, the account is opened. The bank will give a pass book to the client. This is a sort of small note book in which the bank will record all deposits and withdrawals of money. This pass book is an evidence of the balance held at the bank in the name of the client. Many banks do not give a pass book; they send a statement to the client at the end of every month. This statement contains all transactions which the client has had with the bank in respect of the account concerned during the month.

---

*The rate is often changed ; but usually all banks allow the same interest.

Deposits and Withdrawals. The deposits are made by filling up a pay-in-slip. The form of the pay-in-slip is given below :

FOR CASH ONLY.

UNITED COMMERCIAL BANK

Ajmere Gate Extn.

A/C. No./Folio............Ledger Keeper.............. NEW DELHI.......................19

PAID in to the credit of ....

Particulars of Payment.			
Notes :			
x 100			
x 50			
x 20			
x 10			
x 5			
x 2			
x 1			
Whole Rs.			
Small Coins			
Total Rs			

....

The Sum of Rupees..

....

....

In Current Deposit Account.

By..

Receiving Cashier. Chief Cashier

There is a counterfoil which is stamped by the bank's cashier signed by him and returned to the client. This is evidence that money has been duly received by the bank. Usually, separate pay-in-slips have to be filled in for cash and for cheques. Also cheques which are on local Banks have to be filled in one pay-in-slip and cheques on out station banks in another slip.

Withdrawal of money is always through a cheque. The form of the cheque is given below :

No G 26630 15-10-1959

Allahabad Bank Limited,

AFFILIATED TO THE CHARTERED BANK OF INDIA, AUSTRALIA & CHINA

JULLUNDUR CITY

A cheque is an unconditional order on the bank made by the client instructing the bank to pay a certain sum of money to the person named in the cheque or his order or the bearer. If properly made out and if the balance at the bank permits, the bank must pay the amount whenever the cheque is presented. For making out a cheque the following points should be noted :—

1. A cheque must be properly dated. It should be remembered that a bank will refuse to pay a cheque if it is more than six months old. Such a cheque is known as a stale cheque. Also, a bank will not pay a cheque which is dated in advance (ante-dated) until the date arrives.

2. A cheque must be made out in the name of a proper party. It must not be vague. But cheques can be made out, for instance, in the name of "wages" when it really means that the money has to be paid to the client himself.

3. The amount must be written in words and also in figures. The two amounts must agree. The bank, however, is at liberty to pay the amount written in words but, in practice, the bank will refuse to pay if the two amounts differ.

4. If there are any alterations, these must be attested by the full signatures of the drawer (the client).

5. A cheque must be properly signed—the signatures tallying with the specimen signatures with the bank.

While drawing a cheque, the following options are available to the client.

1. The cheque can be made payable to the bearer. In this case, the bank will pay the amount to whosoever presents the cheque without inquiring into the identity of the payee.

2. It may be made payable to order. In such a case, the payee must sign at the back of the cheque and prove to the satisfaction of the bank that he is the right person. If the payee wants that somebody else should receive the money he will have to write at the back of the cheque 'Pay to.........' and sign his name. The bank will require the identity of both the first payee, the second payee, and so on, to be established.

3. It may be crossed. This is done by drawing two parallel lines on one corner of the cheque. The effect of this is that the cheque will not be paid across the counter. The bank will pay the amount to another bank only. Hence, the payee must give the cheque to his own banker who will then, in turn, collect the amount from the paying bank.

Crossings. These are many types of crossings. The types are given below :—

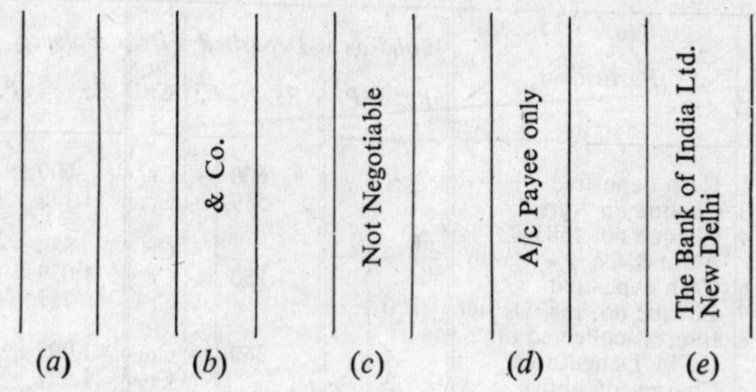

Types (*a*), (*b*), (*c*) and (*d*) are known as general crossings and type (*e*) is known as a special crossing. In case of special crossing, the name of the collecting bank is entered and it is the duty of the paying bank to pay the amount only to the bank mentioned and not to any other bank. In case of other crossings, the amount can be paid to any bank which presents the cheque. In case of crossing (*d*), the effect is that the cheque cannot be passed on further. The payee must send the cheque to his bank who will collect the amount. In case of (*a*), (*b*) and (*c*) the cheque can be passed on to other parties. The effect of crossing (*c*) is that of a warning. The person who is taking a cheque must enquire into the *bona fides* of the person who is giving him the cheque. If the person who gives him the cheque does not have a good title, then he also will have a defective title and if he collects the money, he will have to return it to the rightful owner. In other cases, a person who takes a cheque in good faith and for a valuable consideration, will have a good title even if the title of the transferer is bad or defective.

Pass Book. The pass book, as already stated, records the transactions between the client and the bank. It is issued to the client and it is his duty to send it to the bank at intervals so that transactions can be entered up-to-date. The client is entitled to rely upon the entries made in the pass book unless the bank notifies the mistakes within a reasonable time. The pass book looks like the following :—

M/s Black and White in Current Account with United Commercial Bank, Connaught Place. New Delhi.

Date		Particulars	Withdrawn Rs.	P.	Deposited Rs.	P.	Dr. or Cr.	Balance Rs.	P.	Signatures
1978										
Jan.	1	Cash deposited			600	—	Cr.	600	—	
	3	Cheque on Agra			539	—	Cr.	1,139	—	
	4	Cheque no. 158349, Alam & Co.	250	—			Cr.	889	—	
	6	Cash deposited			150	—	Cr.	1,039	—	
	7	Cheque no. 158351, self	300	—			Cr.	739	—	
	8	Interest collected on DCM Debentures			360	—	Cr.	1,099	—	
		Charges on above	2	—			Cr.	1,097	—	
	10	Amount paid to L.I.C. as per instructions	200	—			Cr.	897	—	

Endorsement. The act of passing on a cheque is known as endorsement. If a cheque is made payable to 'A' and he wishes to pass it on to 'B', he will have to write at the back of the cheque the following :—

Pay to 'B'
'A'.

An endorsement means writing the order to pay the amount to somebody else, signing it and handing over the cheque to the person named. If the cheque is not handed over, it is not an endorsement. An endorsement has to be made properly. The person must sign his name with the same spellings as written on the face of the cheque although he can, then, give his correct spellings. If a person endorses the cheque on behalf of somebody else, then he must make it clear. For instance, if 'X' (managing director of XY & Co. Ltd.) endorses the cheque on behalf of the XY & Co. Ltd., he must give the endorsement as follows :—

For XY & Co. Ltd.
X
Managing Director.

An endorsement like the following means that 'X' himself is endorsing and not the company :—

X
Managing Director,
XY & Co. Ltd.

A cheque can be endorsed a number of times (unless the cheque is crossed 'Account payee only'). If the back of the cheque is full, a slip known as "Allonge" is attached. The last endorsement on the cheque must be made partly on the cheque and partly on the slip to establish the previous endorsements. An endorser is liable to all subsequent endorsees so that if the cheque is dishonoured, the person holding the cheque can claim the amount from any of the previous parties, that is to say, all of the previous endorsers including the payee and also the person who issued the cheque originally. An endorser may escape liability by writing the words 'Sans Recourse' after endorsement. Sans Recourse means without recourse. Of course, it is open to an endorsee not to accept a cheque thus endorsed.

Dishonouring of a cheque. A bank will dishonour a cheque in the following cricumstances :

1. If the drawer has stopped payment of the cheque.
2. If the bank has learnt of the death of the drawer.
3. If the bank has learnt of the drawer becoming insolvent.
4. If the bank has received notice of the drawer becoming of unsound mind.
5. When the court has issued an order to the bank stopping payments out of the account. Such an order is known as Garnishee Order.

If the cheque is made out defectively, then also the bank will refuse payment. In the following cases the bank may refuse payment :—

1. When the drawer does not have sufficient amount in his account.
2. If the cheque is not dated or is dated in advance or the cheque is more than six months old.
3. If the payee is not certain. For example, pay Ram or Sham means uncertainty of the payee and the bank will refuse to pay to either party.
4. When the amounts in words and figures differ.
5. When the cheque is not properly signed.

If a cheque issued by a party is dishonoured, it affects the reputation of the party. For a business house this is serious. Therefore, if a bank wrongly dishonours a cheque issued by a firm, it will be liable to compensate the firm for the damage to its reputation.

Services which a bank renders to a business house.

1. A bank saves a business house from handling large sums of money. This avoids mistakes and also possibilities of misappropriation or fraud.

2. Payments can be made by cheques. This constitutes a permanent proof of payment.

3. A bank lends money to business houses in various ways. Businessmen are able to carry on business even when they are short of funds.

4. A bank discounts hundies or bills of exchange, thus enabling the seller of goods to receive payment promptly without forcing the buyer to pay immediately.

5. A bank offers facilities for remittance of large sums of money at a very low cost.

6. A bank handles papers relating to import and export of goods so that those who purchase goods from foreign countries can rest assured that no money will be paid unless proper documents are received. Similarly, those who export goods can rest assured that documents will not pass hands unless payment has been received. Within India also, a bank renders the same sort of service. For instance, goods can be sold by a party in Delhi to another party in Madras. The railway receipt can be handed over to the bank who will then send it to Madras asking the buyer to make payment and then get the railway receipt. Thus the rights or interests of both the buyer and the seller are safeguarded.

7. A bank is always willing to advise a client regarding investments in the form of shares, debentures or government securities and is also willing to act as an agent of the client for this very purpose.

8. A bank is also willing to keep in safe custody valuable articles and investments. It is also willing to collect, on due dates, interest on debentures and government securities. It also collects dividends on behalf of the client.

9. A bank can be instructed to make payments at regular intervals to specified parties. Thus the client can be free from the worry of making payments at the right time.

10. A bank issues circular letters of credit by which a person, who has to go to a number of places, need not carry cash with him. By taking the letter of credit, he will be able to receive the money from the bank's representative wherever he goes.

11. A bank renders guarantee service. That is to say a bank is willing to stand as surety for its client. This enables the client to enter into business transactions with others and for payment to be made later.

Bank Reconciliation Statement. The Bank Pass Book and the Cash Book (bank columns) record the same transactions. Hence the balance shown in the Pass Book and that in the Cash Book should agree. However, in actual practice this is rarely so because of the time lag of a few days between entries made by a firm in its books and by the bank. For example, a firm enters the amount in the bank column on the credit side of the Cash Book as soon as a cheque is issued. The bank will not pass an entry until the cheque is presented and paid. The following are the reasons for the difference between the balances shown by the Cash Book and by the Pass Book :—

(*a*) Cheques may have been entered in the Cash Book and sent to the bank but the bank may not have, as yet, credited the client's account. This is because the bank usually credits the client only when the amount has been collected.

(*b*) Cheques issued by the firm may not, as yet, have been presented for payment. These cheques must have been entered in the bank column on the credit side of the

Cash Book, thus reducing the balance at bank (or increasing the overdraft). In the books of the bank, entries will be made only on payment. Due to this fact, the balance, according to the Pass Book, appears more than that shown in the Cash Book.

(*c*) Entries regarding bank charges, interest on overdraft, or payments made according to the standing instructions of the client, are made in the Pass Book first and in the Cash Book later (on the client coming to know of them). This reduces the balance as per Pass Book and, therefore, it is less than that shown by the Cash Book.

(*d*) The bank may have collected certain sums on behalf of the client, for example, interest on securities. The bank will make entries straightaway but the client will pass entries only on coming to know of the fact. Till entries are made in the Cash Book, the balance as per Pass Book will appear to be more than that according to the Cash Book.

(*e*) Mistakes will obviously make for a difference in the balance shown by the Pass Book and that shown by the Cash Book.

How to prepare Bank Reconciliation Statement. The Bank Reconciliation Statement is prepared on common sense basis. Start is made with one of the balances—the Pass Book balance or the Cash Book balance. Then the causes that lead to the difference are classified into :—

(*a*) entries that have been made in the Cash Book but not in the Pass Book ; and

(*b*) entries that have been made in the Pass Book but not in the Cash Book.

(The student should note that entries that have been made both in the Cash Book and the Pass Book will *not* be the cause of the difference).

The starting balance is then adjusted by noting how the balance would have changed if the same entries are made in the two books and none other. Suppose we start with the Pass Book balance. We should see how this balance would have changed if (1) the entries made in the Cash Book but not in the Pass Book had also been made by the bank and (2) if entries made in the Pass Book but not in the Cash Book had been omitted from the Pass Book also. The result should be the balance as per Cash Book.

Illustration 7. On 31st December, 1977, the Cash Book of a firm showed a balance at bank of Rs. 1,729. From the information given below prepare the Bank Reconciliation Statement, showing the balance as per Pass Book :—

(*a*) Cheques issued for Rs. 600 had not yet been presented at the bank for payment.

(*b*) Cheques amounting to Rs. 750 were paid in on 29th December but had not been credited by the bank. One cheque, for Rs. 230, was entered in the Cash Book on 31st Dec., but was banked on 2nd January, 1968.

(*c*) A cheque from Vinod, for Rs. 150, paid in on 27th December was dishonoured but the advice of dishonour was received only on the 2nd January, 1968.

(*d*) Pass Book shows bank charges, Rs. 15, debited by the bank. It also shows Rs. 350 collected by the bank as interest on securities.

Solution :

Explanation : (*a*) Had the cheques for Rs. 600 not have entered in the Cash Book just as in Pass Book, the balance at bank would have increased to Rs. 2,329, *i.e.*, Rs. 1,729 + Rs. 600.

(*b*) Cash Book shows a total debit of Rs. 980 in respect of cheques paid into the bank or not yet sent to the bank. The Pass Book has not yet made entries for these. If these are omitted from the Cash Book also, the Cash Book balance will be reduced to Rs. 1,349, *i.e.*, Rs. 2,329 – Rs. 980.

(*c*) The Pass book will not credit the client in respect of Vinod's cheque because it has been dishonoured. Had the Cash Book recorded the dishonour the balance would have been reduced. Hence the balance is now reduced to Rs. 1,199, *i.e.*, Rs. 1,349—Rs. 150.

(*d*) If the two entries are made in the Cash Book also, the Cash Book balance will be reduced on account of bank charges, to Rs. 1,184, but increased because of the interest on securities, to Rs. 1,534.

Presentation :

Bank Reconciliation Statement as at Dec. 31, 1977.

		Rs.	Rs.
	Balance as per Cash Book		1,729
Add :	Cheques issued but not yet presented	600	
	Interest collected by the bank but not yet entered in the Cash Book	350	950
			2,679
Less :	Cheques paid in but not yet collected	750	
	Cheques entered in Cash Book but not yet paid in	230	
	Cheque dishonoured but not yet entered in Cash Book	150	
	Bank charges not yet entered in Cash Book	15	1,145
	Balance as per Pass Book		1,534

[The student is advised to prepare this Reconciliation Statement again, now starting with the Pass Book balance of Rs. 1,534].

Alternative Presentation. The Reconciliation Statement can be shown as above, but another way of presentation is possible. Two columns are given, one to record items that increase the balance (plus column) and the other to record items that reduce the balance (minus column). The opening balance is put down in the plus column (overdraft is put down in the minus column). The two columns are then balanced and the difference is the desired figure. This is shown in the following illustration.

Illustration The Pass Book of a company showed an overdraft of Rs. 2,560. Comparison of the Pass Book with the Cash Book showed the following :

(*a*) The company had sent to the bank three cheques on 28th December, 1978. The cheques were for Rs. 1,100, Rs. 1,560 and Rs. 930. Of these only the cheque for Rs. 1,100 was credited by the bank before 31st December, 1978.

(*b*) The company had issued, on 27th December, cheques for Rs. 820, Rs. 530 and Rs. 760. The cheque for Rs. 760 was paid before the 31st December. The other cheques were paid on 3rd January, 1979

(*c*) The Bank had debited the company with Rs. 20 as bank charges and Rs. 120 as interest. Entries in the Cash Book had not yet been made.

(*d*) The Bank had collected Rs. 500 from a customer against a bill but the fact was not yet recorded in the Cash Book.

Prepare the Bank Reconciliation Statement as on 31st December, 1978.

Solution :

Bank Reconciliation Statement as on December 31, 1978.

	Rs. +	Rs. —
Overdraft as per Pass Book		2,560
Cheques sent to the bank but not yet collected	2,490	
Cheques issued but not yet presented		1,350
Bank charges and Interest not yet entered in Cash Book	140	
Amount collected by the bank but not yet recorded in the Cash Book		500
Total	2,630	4,410
Overdraft as per Cash Book	1,780	
	4,410	4,410

How to ascertain items for reconciliation. Items that make for difference between the balance as per Cash Book and as per Pass Book can be ascertained only by comparing the two. Entries that appear *in both in the same period* do not make for the difference and hence do not enter the Reconciliation Statement. The items that appear in the Pass Book but not in the Cash Book in the same period and *vice versa* cause the difference. These are noted. Consider the following Pass Book and Bank Column of Cash Book of Alam for June, 1968.

The Ideal Bank Ltd.

Alam in Current Account

Date		*Particulars*	*Withdrawn* Rs.		*Deposited* Rs.		*Dr. or Cr.*	*Balance* Rs.	
1978 June	1	Balance					Cr.	1,650	—
	5	Wages cheque No....	450	—			Cr.	1,200	—
	8	Cash deposited			300	—	Cr.	1,500	—
	9	Cheque on Agra (Less Re. 1 charges)			619	—	Cr.	2,119	—
	15	Cheque favouring Ali Bros. No....	700	—			Cr.	1,419	—
	26	Cheque favouring Goel & Co., No. ..	430	—			Cr.	989	—
	30	Payment of Premium as per instructions	200	—			Cr.	789	—
	30	Bank Charges	10	—			Cr.	779	—

Alam's Cash Book (Bank Columns only)

Dr. *Cr.*

Date		*Particulars*	*L.F.*	*Amount* Rs.		*Date*		*Particulars*	*L.F.*	*Amount* Rs.	
1978 June	1	To Balance b/d		1,650	—	1978 June	5	By Wages		450	—
	5	To Akbar—cheque on Agra		620	—		9	By Ali Bros.		700	—
	8	To Cash		300	—		15	By Gupta & Sons		350	—
	15	To Mohan—cheque		710	—		25	By Goel & Co.		430	—
	28	To Ram—cheque on Kanpur		580	—		30	By Balance c/d.		1,930	-
				3,860	—					3,860	—
July	1	To Balance b/d		1,930	—						

If the debit side of the Cash Book is compared with the 'Deposited' column of the Pass Book, it will be found that :

(*a*) cheques received from Mohan (Rs. 710) and from Ram (Rs. 580) have not yet been credited by the Bank ; and

(*b*) the Bank has charged Re. 1 for collecting the cheque on Agra. This amount has not been entered in the Cash Book as yet.

Similarly, by comparing the credit side of the Cash Book and the withdrawals column of the Pass Book, it is found that :

(*i*) cheque issued in favour of Gupta & Sons has not yet been paid ; and

(*ii*) the Bank has debited Rs. 200 in respect of premium and Rs. 10 in respect of charges. These amounts have not yet been entered in the Cash Book.

The Reconciliation Statement can now be prepared, as under :

Bank Reconciliation Statement as on June 30, 1978.

		Rs.
Balance as per Cash Book		1,930
Less cheques paid in but not yet collected :	Rs.	
Mohan	710	
Ram	580	1,290
		640
Add cheque issued to Gupta & Sons but not yet presented		350
		990
Less : Premium paid, entered in the Pass Book but not in the Cash Book	200	
Bank charges entered in the Pass Book but not in the Cash Book	11	211
Balance as per Pass Book		779

The Real Balance at the Bank. In the example given above Alam has, on 30th June, 1978, Rs. 1,930 at the bank according to his books. A comparison with the Pass Book shows that the following relate to the period prior to June 30, 1978 :—

(*i*) Bank charges, Rs. 11 in all ; and

(*ii*) Premium, Rs. 200.

Strictly speaking, entries for these should have been passed before the Cash Book for June is ruled off. Such entries would have reduced the Cash Book balance to Rs. 1,719.

But it should be noted that there is no need to again pass entries for :

(*i*) Cheques paid into the bank but not yet collected ; and

(*ii*) Cheques issued but not yet presented for payment.

This is because these have already been entered in the Cash Book. Except for these two items, entries for other items appearing in the Bank Reconciliation Statement should be passed to arrive at the proper balance at the bank. It is obviously wrong to say that one has so much money at the bank when interest, bank charges, dishonoured cheques, etc. have still to be recorded.

Illustration. M/s. Shah and Akbar close their books on 31st December each year. When they received the bank statement for December 1981, they found that the bank showed an overdraft of Rs.45,600 against the firm. On comparison with the Cash Book it was found that:

(*i*) the Bank had charged interest, Rs.810, and bank charges, of Rs.40;

(*ii*) a cheque for Rs.1,150, received from a customer on 26th December and banked the next day was returned as dishonoured, the bank charging Rs.5 for expenses;

(*iii*) cheques issued in the last week of December, totalling Rs.3,570, were not yet presented for payment;

(*iv*) cheques paid in on the 29th and the 30th December, Rs. 4,120 in all, had not yet been cleared; and

(*v*) the total of one page in the Cash Book (Debit side), Rs.15,690, was carried forward as Rs.16,950 to the next page.

Ascertain the balance shown by the Cash Book as at present and prepare the Bank Reconciliation Statement assuming items (*i*) and (*ii*) had not yet been recorded in the Cash Book.

Solution :

Statement Showing the Balance as per Cash Book as on 31-12-81.		Rs.
Overdraft as per Bank Statement		45,600
Less : Debits by the Bank, not yet recorded in Cash Book :	Rs.	
Interest and Bank Charges	850	
Cheque dishonoured and charges	1,155	
Mistake in Cash Book to reduce O/D (16,950—15,690)	1,260	
Cheques paid in, not yet collected	4,120	7,385
		38,215
Add : Cheques issued, not yet presented		3,570
Overdraft shown by the Cash Book		41,785

Overdraft after the necessary corrections are made :

	Rs.
Amount of Overdraft as shown above	41,785
Add : Interest and Bank charges	850
Debit to customer for dishonoured cheque	1,155
Correction of error in carry over	1,260
Correct amount of Overdraft as on 31-12-81	45,050

Bank Reconciliations Statement as on Dec., 31, 1981.

	Rs.
Overdraft (corrected) as per Cash Book	45,050
Less : Cheques issued, not yet presented	3,570
	41,480
Add : Cheques paid in, not yet collected	4,120
Overdraft as per Bank Statement	45,600

Illustration. M/s. Iyer and Sons close their books on 30th June every year. Their Cash Book showed a balance at Bank on 30-6-81 to the extent of Rs.7,570. On comparing the Cash Book and the Pass Book, the following items came to notice :

(*i*) A cheque issued by the firm in favour of Singh and Khan on 10-12-80 for Rs.850 had not yet been presented.

(*ii*) Of the cheques paid into the bank on the 28th and 29th June, 1981, totalling Rs.10,500, only cheques for Rs.3,560 were credited.

(*iii*) The bank had made a payment of Rs.650 as premium on the policy of the senior partner in accordance with standing instructions.

(*iv*) Cheques issued in June 1981 had totalled Rs.4,520, including one cheque for Rs.750 in replacement of a cheque reported lost—the Cash Book showed Rs.4,520 on the credit side—of these cheques, those for Rs.2,100 had not yet been paid.

(*v*) There was a debit in the Pass Book for Rs. 1,870; it was found that a cheque issued by M/s. Aiyer and Sons had been charged by mistake to the account of M/s. Iyer and Sons.

(*vi*) The bank had made a charge of Rs.30 for bank charges.

Ascertain the balance shown in the Pass Book and prepare the Bank Reconciliation Statement as on June 30, 1981.

Solution :

Statement Showing Balance as per Pass Book as on June 30, 1981

		Rs.
Balance as per Cash Book		7,570
Add : Cheques issued not yet present	Rs.	
Singh & Khan	850	
Lost cheque	750	
Others	2,100	3,700
		11,270
Less : Cheques paid in but not yet collected (10,500—3,560)	6,940	
Premium paid	650	
Wrong debit	1,870	
Bank Charges	30	9,490
Balance as per Pass Book		1,780

Corrected balance as per Cash Book :

		Rs.
Balance as per Cash Book at present		7,570
Add : Cheque to Singh & Khan to be written back, being stale	850	
Cheque, entered twice in Cash Book	750	1,600
		9,170
Less : Premium paid	650	
Bank charges	30	680
Correct Cash Book Balance		8,490

Bank Reconciliation Statement as on June 30, 1981

	Rs.
Balance as per Pass Book	1,780
Add : Cheques paid in not yet collected	6,940
Wrong entry in Pass Book to be corrected	1,870
	10,590
Less : Cheques issued, not yet presented	2,100
Balance as per Cash Book	8,490

Petty Cash

A firm has to make a large number of small payments, like bus fare, cartage, cooliage, etc. If all these payments are entered in the Cash Book, it will become very bulky. Usually, these payments are made by the Petty Cashier, a person other than the main cashier. The Petty Cashier is given a certain sum of money and then all small payments, say below Rs. 20, are made by him. At intervals, the Petty Cashier produces the vouchers before the cashier. The cashier checks the vouchers and hands over the necessary cash to the Petty Cashier again.

Imprest System. The best system of Petty Cash is the imprest system. In the beginning, a fixed sum of money is given to the Petty Cashier who makes payments out of it. At the end of the week (or fortnight or month), the vouchers are checked and an amount equal to the amount spent is again given to the Petty Cashier. Thus the next period (week, fortnight or month) is again begun with the fixed sum of money. Whenever payment is made to the Petty Cashier, Petty Cash Account is debited and Cash Book is credited. The Petty Cash Account shows the total petty expenses—only the amount actually in the hands of the Petty Cashier is deducted. This amount in hand is, of course, an asset.

Analytical Petty Cash Book. If the Petty Cashier is asked to analyse the Petty Cash payments, it will be known how the money has been spent and then the relevant accounts can be debited (instead of just one Petty Expenses A/c). The Petty Cashier will be given a Petty Cash Book. It has two sides. The left hand side records receipts of cash from the main Cashier. The right hand side records payments and analysis of payments. There are a number of columns to record payments for, say, wages, cartage, postage, stationery, etc. (For ruling see the working of the following illustration). The Petty Cash Book is balanced periodically. The various expenses (according to the analysis) are debited and Petty Cash Account is credited. The Petty Cash Account will then show balance equal to cash in the hands of the Petty Cashier.

Illustration A Petty Cashier received Rs. 100 as the Petty Cash imprest on Monday, the 2nd December, 1978. During the week his expenses were as under :

			Rs.
Dec.	2	Taxi fare for manager	5·20
		Wages to casual workers	10·00
	3	Stationery	8·00
		Bus fare	0.80
	4	Postage stamps purchased	15·00
		Telegram	2·50
	5	Repairs to furniture	6·00
		Taxi fare to salesman	3·00
		Telegrams to suppliers	3·50

6	Electricity bill for November	18·00
	Stationery	4·00
7	Refreshments to customers	6·00
	Cartage for goods purchased	4·00

Prepare Petty Cash Book, give the necessary journal entry and show the Petty Cash Account.

Solution :

(See Petty Cash Book on the next page).

Journal Entry :

1978			Dr. Rs.	Cr. Rs.
Dec. 7	Conveyance Account ...	Dr.	9.00	
	Stationery Account ...	Dr.	12.00	
	Postage and Telegrams A/c ...	Dr.	21.00	
	Cartage and Cooliage A/c ...	Dr.	4.00	
	Wages Account ...	Dr.	10.00	
	Repairs Account ...	Dr.	6.00	
	Electricity Account ...	Dr.	18.00	
	Entertainment Account ...	Dr.	6.00	
	To Petty Cash Account			86·00
	Being the various expenses as per Petty Cash Book analysis.			

Petty Cash Account

Dr.		Rs.	P.		Cr.	Rs.	P.
1978 Dec. 2	To Cash	100	00	1978 Dec. 7	By Sundries—		
					Conveyance	9	00
					Stationery	12	00
					Postage & Telegrams	21	00
					Cartage & Cooliage	4	00
					Wages	10	00
					Repairs	6	00
					Electricity	18	00
					Entertainment	6	00
					By Balance c/d.	14	00
		100	00			100	00
9	To Balance b/d.	14	00				
	To Cash	86	00				

Petty Cash Book

Dr. | *Cr.*

Amount Received Rs.	P.	*Date*	*Voucher No.*	*Particulars*	*Amount paid* Rs.	P.	*Conveyance* Rs.	P.	*Stationery* Rs.	P.	*Postage & Telegrams* Rs.	P.	*Cartage & Cooliage* Rs.	P.	*Miscel-laneous* Rs.	P.	*Remarks*
		1978															
100	00	Dec. 2		Cash Received													
		2	1	Taxi fare (manager)	5	20	5	20									
			2	Wages to casual workers	10	00									10	00	Wages A/c.
		3	3	Stationery	8	00			8	00							
			4	Bus fare	0	80	00	80									
		4	5	Postage stamps	15	00					15	00					
			6	Telegram	2	50					2	50					
		5	7	Repairs to furniture	6	00									6	00	Repairs A/c.
			8	Taxi fare for salesman	3	00	3	00									
		6	9	Telegrams	3	50					3	50					
			10	Electricity bill for November	18	00									18	00	Electricity A/c.
			11	Stationery	4	00			4	00							
		7	12	Refreshments to customers	6	00									6	00	Entertainment A/c.
			13	Cartage for goods	4	00							4	00			
					86	00	9	00	12	00	21	00	4	00	40	00	
				Balance c/d.	14	00											
100	00				100	00											
14	00	9		Balance b/d.													
86	00			Cash Received													

Exercises

1. Anand starts business with Rs. 10,000 on 1st July, 1978. Of this he pays Rs. 9,000 into his bank account. His cash transactions during the first week were :

			Rs.
July	1	Purchased stationery, paid cash	40.00
		Purchased goods for cash	650.00
		Purchased Office Table and Chair	200.00
	2	Cash Sale	150.00
	3	Received from Gopal, cash as advance	200.00
	4	Paid to Sethi & Sons, cash	140.00
	5	Paid for signboard	130.00
	6	Cash Sales	160.00
		Purchased old Typewriter	300.00

Make out the Cash Book (Single Column).

(*Balance in hand, Rs. 50*).

2. On 1st January, 1979 Kumar had Rs. 140 in hand. During the first week of January, his cash transactions were as follows :

			Rs.
Jan.	2	Drew from bank for use is office	800
		Paid Salaries and Wages	540
		Paid Rent for December, 1968	150
		Received from Wahid	530
		Discount allowed to him	20
		Cash Sales	200
		Sent to Bank	400
		Paid to Ram (in full settlement of amount due to him of Rs. 410)	395
		Goods purchased for cash	150
		Postage stamps purchased	15
		Purchased two chairs	40
	4	Received from Lohia against a debt previously written off as bad	250
		Paid travelling expenses to salesman	150
	7	Received from Akbar (in full settlement of his debt of Rs. 450)	430

Prepare (1) Single Column Cash Book and then

(2) Double Column Cash book.

Post the ledger accounts in each case. [Note the time taken by you]

(*Cash Balance in hand, Rs. 510*)

3. What purpose does a Cash Book serve ? Take Question No. 2 and journalise the transactions and then prepare ledger accounts. Note the time taken by you. Compare it with the time taken previously for solving Question No. 2.

4. Enter the following transactions in the Cash Book, assuming that receipts are paid daily into the bank and all payments are made by cheque :

Jan.	2	Balance at bank, Rs. 2,500.
	2	Received from George Rs. 950 in full discharge of his account for Rs. 1,000.
	3	Paid F. Manton's account of Rs. 400, less discount at 2 per cent.
	4	Drew cheque for Rs. 900, of which Rs. 800 was for payment of wages and Rs. 100 for petty cash.
	5	Received from W. Bentley a cheque for Rs. 1,000 and allowed him Rs. 50 discount.

5 Received Rs. 450 from William Henson in full discharge of his debt of Rs. 470.

6 Paid Rs. 650 to J. Browning in full settlement of his account for Rs. 680.

Rule off the Cash Book and show the balance at bank.

(**Hint :** Have Cash Book with bank column and discount column only ; all receipts and payments should be entered in bank columns).

(Balance at bank, Rs. 2,958)

5. The Cash Book of Robert Arthur was framed to deal with cash and bank transactions, and the following are the transactions which took place during January :

Jan. 2 Balance of Cash in hand Rs. 400, at bank Rs. 1,600.

3 Paid to J. Jones by cheque Rs. 950 in full settlement of his account for Rs. 1,000.

5 Bought goods for cash Rs. 80 and for cheque Rs. 300.

6 Drew cash from Bank for office use Rs. 300.
Paid Wages in Cash Rs. 250.
Paid Woods & Co. Rs. 120 by cheque.

8 Sold Goods for cash, Rs. 800.
Received cheque from J. Robinson Rs. 320 in full settlement of account for Rs. 340.

9 Paid Rs. 920 into Bank.

10 Received cheque from A. Williams Rs. 4,200 on account.

11 Paid John Beecroft Rs. 4,750 in full settlement of his account of Rs. 5,000.
Received cheque from C. Stevenson in full settlement of his account of Rs. 600, he having deducted cash discount of 2½ per cent.
Robinson's cheque returned dishonoured.

Balance the Cash Book and bring down the balances of cash in hand and at bank.

(Balance in hand Rs. 250 ; at Bank Rs. 885)

6. Enter the following transactions in a three column cash book of M/s. Barkat & Co. :

April 1 Cash in hand Rs. 237 ; balance at bank Rs. 6,594.

2 Received from K. Agarwalla cash Rs. 590, allowed him discount Rs. 10.

4 Paid salaries for March by cash Rs. 200.
Cash Sales, Rs. 134.

5 Paid B.K. Bose by cheque Rs. 300. Cash Purchases Rs. 60.

7 Paid Q. Ahmad by cheque Rs. 585 ; discount received 2½%.

8 Cash Sales Rs. 112. Paid cartage and coolie Rs. 6.

10 Paid rent in cash Rs. 50.

14 Cash Sales Rs. 212.
Received from G.C. Dhar Rs. 194 by cheque, discount 3%.

16 Deposited into Bank Rs. 600.
Purchased a motor car for Rs. 5,800 and draw a cheque for the amount.

23 Received a cheque from Robert & Co. for Rs. 291 ; discount received 3%.

28 Cash Sales Rs. 298.

29 Bank notifies that Robert & Co's cheque has been dishonoured.

30 Deposited with Bank Rs. 300. Paid wages Rs. 72. Bank charges as shown in Pass Book Rs. 5.

[Cash at Bank. Rs. 295 ; at Bank Rs. 998 ; Discount Re. 1 (Dr.), net]

7. Agarwal owed Rs. 1,400 to the Bank and had cash in hand Rs. 230 on 1st June, 1978. During the month his cash transactions were as under :

June 5 Drew cash for office use Rs. 800.
Paid wages Rs. 500 ; paid rent Rs. 100.
Drew for domestic use cash Rs. 150.

6 Cash Sales Rs. 200.
Cash purchases Rs. 250.

7 Received cheque from Anand Rs. 650 in full settlement of his debt of Rs. 700.

8 Issued cheque in favour of Handa and Sethi in settlement of the amount due to them of Rs. 400 less 2½% discount.

9 Received by sale of old packing cases etc. Rs. 100. Received from Sethi Bros. cheque for Rs. 400 ; discount allowed Rs. 10.

10 Purchased one bicycle, paid by cheque Rs. 250.
Paid municipal taxes in cash Rs. 100.

11 Cheque from Sethi Bros. returned dishonoured by bank. The bank charges Rs. 5 as expenses.

12 Issued cheque in favour of Ahmed & Co. for Rs. 480 ; discount received 4%.

13 Received from the estate of Bapat against debt previously written off, Rs. 250.

14 Own cheque to Ahmed & Co. returned dishonoured because of wrong stamping.

15 Issued new cheque to Ahmed & Co. for full amount of original debt.

Prepare triple column cash book from the above particulars. Also post the ledger accounts.

[*Cash Balance, Rs. 480 ; Bank Balance, Rs. 2,695 (Cr.); Discounts column totals, Rs. 80 (Dr.) and Rs. 40 (Cr.)*]

8. The cash book of Swami showed a balance of Rs. 1,580 at the bank. This did not agree with the Pass Book. From the following particulars ascertain the balance as per Pass Book :

Cheque paid in but not yet credited by bank Rs. 430.

Cheque issued but not yet presented for payment Rs. 510.

Bank charges made by bank not yet entered in cash book Rs. 10.

Interest charged by bank not yet entered in cash book Rs. 20.

Amount collected as interest by the bank on Government securities not yet entered in cash book, Rs. 300.

(*Balance as per Pass Book, Rs. 1,930*)

9. From the following particulars, prepare a Bank Reconciliation Statement showing the Balance as per Bank Pass Book on 31st March, 1979.

The following cheques were paid into the firm's Current Account in March, 1969 but were credited by the bank in April, 1979.

Shri Morarji Dalal Rs. 2,500, Shri Dinker Tepase Rs. 3,000 and Shri Baliram Gidwani Rs. 2,400.

The following cheques were issued by the firm in March 1969 but were cashed in April, 1979.

Shri Manishanker Kher Rs. 3,000, Shri Natverlal Mehta Rs. 5,000 and Shri Dayabhai Desai Rs. 3,000.

A cheque for Rs. 1,000 which was received from a customer was entered in the Bank Column of the Cash Book in March, 1969 but the same was paid into Bank in April, 1969.

The Pass Book shows a credit of Rs. 2,500 for Interest and a debit of Rs. 500 for Bank Charges.

The Balance as per Cash Book was Rs. 1,80,000 on 31st March, 1979.

(*Balance as per Pass Book, Rs. 1,84,100*)

10. From the following particulars ascertain the Balance that would appear in the Cash Book of A on 31st December, 1978 when the books were closed.

(1) The Bank Overdraft as per Pass Book on 31st December, 1978, Rs. 6,340.

(2) Interest on Overdraft for 6 months ending 31st December, 1968, Rs. 160, is debited in the Pass Book.

(3) Bank charges of Rs. 30 for the above period is also debited in the Pass Book.

(4) Cheque issued but not cashed prior to 31st December, 1968 amounted to Rs. 1,168.

(5) Cheque paid into Bank but not cleared before 31st December, 1978 were for Rs. 2,170.

(6) Interest on investments collected by the Bankers and credited in the Pass Book, Rs. 1,200. (*Overdraft as per Cash Book, Rs. 6,348*)

State what the balance in the cash book should be. [*Rs. 5,338 (Cr.)*]

11. Prepare a Bank Reconciliation Statement from the following particulars :

On 31st December, 1978, the Cash Book of a merchant showed a Bank Overdraft of Rs. 1,729 ; the Pass Book differed. On comparing the two books, the following discrepancies were noted :

(*a*) Cheques drawn for Rs. 600 were entered in the Cash Book but were not presented at the bank till first week of January, 1979.

(*b*) Cheques amounting to Rs. 1,680 were deposited in the bank but of these those for Rs. 930 were collected by December 31.

(*c*) A cheque for Rs. 150 received from Mahesh Chander and deposited in the bank in December was dishonoured but advice of non-payment was received from the bank on January 3, 1979.

(*d*) Rs. 2,500 being the proceeds of a bill receivable collected appear in Pass Book but not in Cash Book.

(*e*) Bank charges Rs. 15 and interest on Overdraft Rs. 85 appear in the Pass Book but not in the Cash Book.

Ascertain the balance appearing in the Pass Book. [*Rs. 371 (Cr.)*]

What should be the balance in the Cash Book ? [*Rs. 521 (Dr.)*]

12. On 30th June, 1979, the Balance as per the Bank Pass Book of K. Krishna was an overdraft of Rs. 3,300 and his balance did not agree with the balance as per the Bank Account in the Books of K. Krishna.

You find that Krishna had issued three cheques for Rs. 6,000, Rs. 9,000 and Rs. 12,000 on 25th June, but the cheque for Rs. 6,000 was presented to the Bank for payment on 4th July. Krishna had deposited into his Bank Account on 26th June cheques for Rs. 15,000 ; Rs. 18,000 ; Rs. 10,000 and Rs. 6,000. Of these, the cheque for Rs. 10,000 was credited by the Bank on 2nd July. You also find that the Bank had debited Krishna's Account with Rs. 1,200 for interest and Rs. 100 for charges, but these had not yet been recorded in his books.

You are required to prepare a Bank Reconciliation Statement as on 30th June, 1969, showing the Balance as per the Bank Account in the books of K. Krishna. (*Balance as per Cash Book, Rs. 2,000*)

13. M/s Ali and Ispahani found the following on comparing their Cash Book and thePass Book, on 30th September 1981, when the books were to be closed; the Pass Book showed a balance of Rs.3,170.

(*i*) While carrying forward a total in the Cash Book on one page (Cr. side), it was written as Rs.19,410 instead of Rs.14,910.

(*ii*) A cheque issued by the firm in February 1981 for Rs.1,250 was not yet presented.

(*iii*) The bank had charged Rs.40 as bank charges and Rs.260 for other services rendered in respect of sale of shares.

(*iv*) The firm had sent cheques, totalling Rs.6,610 to the bank for collection. Of these, cheques for Rs. 1,530 had not yet been collected.

(*v*) Of the cheques issued in September 1981, totalling Rs.4,570 only those for Rs.2,890 had been paid.

Prepare the Bank Reconciliation Statement, using the balance to be entered in the Balance Sheet. (*Balance as per Cash Book* for **B/S** *Rs.*3,020).

14. From the following particulars prepare a Bank Reconciliation Statement of A.E. Company as at 30th September, 1977, the date of closing of the books :

(*a*) Overdraft balance on 30th September, 1977 as per Bank Pass Book, Rs.13,095.

(*b*) Cheque deposited in bank not recorded in Cash Book, Rs.105.

(*c*) Cheques received and recorded in the bank column but not sent to bank for collection, Rs.1,015.

(*d*) Several cheques were drawn in late September totalling Rs.15,075. Of these, cheques totalling Rs.9,074 were cashed.

(*e*) On 11th September, 1977 the credit side of bank column of the Cash Book was cast Rs.1,000 short and on 15th September, 1977 the credit balance of Rs.2,600 was brought forward on 16th September, 1977 as debit balance of Rs.2,600.

(*f*) Trade Association fee of Rs.250 was paid by the Bank but was not recorded in the Cash Book.

(*g*) In the Cash Book, a bank charge of Rs. 30 was recorded twice while another bank charge of Rs.45 was not recorded at all.

(*h*) Interest of Rs.1,400 was charged by the bank but was not recorded in the Cash Book. (*Adapted from B.Com., Madras*)

(*Correct O/D as per Cash Book Rs.*18,081)

15. From the following information, prepare a Bank reconciliation statement, as at 31st December, 1983 for Messrs New Steel Limited :—

	(Rs.)
(1) Bank overdraft, as per Cash Book, on 31st December, 1983.	2,49,900
(2) Interest debited by Bank on 26th December, 1983 but no advice received.	27,870
(3) Cheque issued before 31st December 1983 but not yet presented to Bank	66,000
(4) Transport subsidiary received from the State Government directly by the Bank but not advised to the Company	42 500
(5) Draft deposited in the Bank, but not credited till 31st Deeember, 1983	13,500
(6) Bills for collection credited by the Bank, till 31st December, 1983 but no advice receiued by the Company	83,600
(7) Amount wrongly debited to company's account by the Bank, for whieh no details are available.	7,400

What is the amount for bank balance that should be shown in the balance sheet of the company, as at 31st December 1983 ?

(*Adapted from C.A. Entrance*)

[*O/D as per Pass Book Rs. 1,06,570 ; to be shown in B/S Rs. 1,51,670*]

16. A petty cashier in a firm received Rs. 150 as the petty cash imprest on Monday, the 3rd June, 1978. During the week, his expenses were as follows :

1978			Rs.
June	3	Tonga charges for manager's trip to the city	5
		Wages to casual labourers	15
June	4	Bus fare to workmen sent to customer's premises	2
		Stationery purchased	10
	5	Sent telegram to Head Office	4
		Postage stamps purchased	10
		Revenue stamps for payment of wages	5
	6	Repair to typewriter	4
		Paid electric lighting charges	17
	7	Wages paid to coolies for shifting furniture, etc.	4
		Taxi fare to assistant manager	5
		Telegrams sent to different suppliers	10
	8	Locks purchased	8
		Stationery purchased	4
		Refreshments to customers	2

Write up the Petty Cash Book and draft the necessary journal entry for the payments made.

17. Prepare a Petty Cash Book on the Imprest System from the following :

1978			Rs.
January	1	Received Rs. 100 for Petty Cash	
	2	Paid bus fare	0·50
		Poid cartage	2·50
	3	Paid for postage & telegrams	5·00
		Paid wages to casual labourers	6·00
	4	Paid for stationery	4·00
		Paid tonga charges	2·00
	5	Paid for repairs to chairs	15·00
		Bus fare	1·00
		Cartage	4·00
	6	Postage and telegrams	7·00
		Tonga charges	3·00
		Cartage	3·00
		Stationery	2·00
		Refreshments to customers	5·00

CHAPTER V

THE PRACTICAL SYSTEM (II)

Sale & Purchase of Goods

In the previous chapter we have dealt with one main class of transactions, namely cash (and bank) receipts and payments. In this chapter we shall deal with purchase and sale of goods. The student can readily realise that in almost any firm purchases and sales of goods will form the bulk of transactions It will save clerical labour if such transactions are not journalised but are entered in suitable registers or books. Transactions relating to goods may be classified as under :

(1) Purchase of goods ;

(2) Return of goods purchased ;

(3) Sale of goods ; and

(4) Returns from customers.

The ruling for recording all the above named transactions is the same. It is :

Date	Particulars	L.F.	Details		Amount	
			Rs.	P.	Rs.	P.

The particulars column is meant to give, in all cases, the name of the party concerned and details of the goods involved. In the "Details" column amounts for various items are entered and the total is extended into the "Amount" column.

Purchase of Goods. To record purchases of goods, a register, named the Purchase Book, Purchase Day Book or Purchase Journal, is kept. The ruling is as given above. *Only credit purchases of goods dealt in the firm or raw materials and stores used by the firm are entered in the Purchase Book*. The student must note this. Cash purchases will not be entered in this book because entries in respect of cash purchases must have been made in the Cash Book. Credit purchases of things other than goods and materials have to be dealt with specially in accounts and hence these must not be entered in the Purchase Book. For instance, purchase of furniture by a bookseller will not be entered in the Purchase Book but purchase of furniture by a furniture dealer will be recorded in the Purchase Book.

At the end of each month, the Purchase Book is totalled. The total shows the total amount of goods or materials purchased on credit.

Posting the Purchase Book. The total of the Purchase Book is posted to the debit of Purchases Account. [Goods Account may be debited if it is not desired to keep Purchases Account, but it is advantageous to keep a Purchases Account to show total purchases made]. Names of suppliers appear in the Purchase Book. These parties have supplied the goods. They are, therefore, credited with the amount appearing against their respective names. The double entry will thus be completed—the total debit placed in the Purchases Account equals the total of various credits given to suppliers. This is illustrated below.

Illustration From the following transactions prepare the Purchase Book of Adams for July, 1978 and prepare ledger accounts connected with this book.

July 5 Purchased on credit from Paul & Co :
50 Electric Irons @ Rs. 25
10 Toasters @ Rs. 30

6 Purchased for Cash from John & Bros. :
25 Table Lamps @ Rs. 15

10 Purchased from Harsha & Sons on credit :
20 Electric stoves @ Rs. 20
10 Heaters @ Rs. 30

15 Purchased on credit from More & Co. :
15 Heaters @ Rs. 20

20 Purchased, on credit, one typewriter from Remington Rand Inc. for Rs. 1,500.

[For solution, please see sheet facing p. 84]

Sale of Goods. The book to record sale of goods is called Sales Book, Sales Day Book or Sales Journal. *Only credit sales of goods dealt in or produced by the firm are recorded in the Sales Book.* Cash sales are recorded in the Cash Book and credit sale of things other than goods dealt in are entered in the journal. The total of the Sales Book shows the total credit sale of goods during the period concerned. Usually, the Sales Book is totalled every month.

Posting. The total of the Sales Book is credited to Sales Account (Goods Account, if that is maintained). Customers whose names appear in the Sales Book are debited with the amount appearing against their names. Double entry is thus completed—the total of the debits placed in the accounts of customers will be equal to the amount credited to the Sales Account.

Illustration From the transactions given below prepare the Sales Book of Amin Chand, a furniture dealer :

June 5 Sold on credit to Ideal College :
10 tables @ Rs. 25 } less 10%
10 chairs @ Rs. 15 }
8 Sold to Mohan Bros. :
5 stools @ Rs. 10
10 chairs @ Rs. 15
10 Sold on credit M/s. Golchand & Co.
3 tables @ Rs. 75
5 chairs @ Rs. 30
20 Sold to M/s. Ram Lal & Sons for cash :
5 tables @ Rs. 40
27 Sold on credit to Anand Pal & Co. old typewriter for Rs. 400.

[For solution, please see reverse of the sheet facing this page]

Purchase Returns. If goods are returned to suppliers only now and then, a journal entry should suffice to record the return. But if goods are returned frequently, it will be better to keep a separate book to record the returns. The name of the book in which these returns are entered is called Purchase Returns Books or Returns Outwards Book. The ruling is absolutely the same as shown above.

Posting. The total of the Returns Outwards Book is credited to Returns Outwards Account (being the total of goods sent out). Individual suppliers to whom goods are returned are debited (because they receive the goods).

Debit Note. When goods are returned to suppliers, an intimation is sent to them through what is known as a Debit Note. It may appear as follows :

Debit Note

New Delhi,
Nov. 19, 1968

M/s. Kohli & Sons
Park Street,
Calcutta.

	Rs.	P.	Rs.	P.
To Goods returned :				
10 shirts @ Rs. 15	150	—		
10 pairs trousers @ Rs. 20	200	—	350	—
Goods Returned as per R/R No .... dated.....................against goods purchased as per Invoice No...........dated.................				
Rs. Three hundred and fifty only.				

E. & O.E. *For* **Goodluck & Co.**

Partner

E. & O. E. stands for Errors and Omissions Excepted, that is to say, clerical errors can be rectified later.

Purchase Book of Adam

Date		Particulars	L.F.	Details Rs.	P.	Amount Rs.	P.
1978 July	5	*Paul & Co.* 50 Electric Irons @ Rs. 25 10 Toasters @ Rs. 30 Goods purchased vide their Bill No... dated...		1,250 300	— — —	1,550	—
	10	*Harsha & Sons* 20 Electric Stoves @ Rs. 20 10 Heaters @ Rs. 30 Goods purchased vide Bill No ... dated ...		400 300	— — —	700	—
	15	*More & Co.* 15 Heaters @ Rs. 20 Goods purchased vide Bill No.... dated ...				300	—
		Total				2,550	

[Transaction on July 6th will be entered in the Cash Book and that on July 20th will be journalised].

Ledger Accounts

Purchases Account

Dr.		Rs.				Rs.	Cr.
1978 July 31	To Purchases as per Purchase Book	2,550					

Paul & Co.

			1978 July 5	By Purchases	1,550	—

Harsha & Sons

			1978 July 10	By Purchases	700	—

More & Co.

			1978 July 15	By Purchases	300	—

Sales Book of Amin Chand

Date		Particulars	L.F.	Details Rs.	P	Amount Rs.	P.
June	5	*Ideal College* :					
		10 tables @ Rs. 25		250	—		
		10 chairs @ Rs. 15		150	—		
				400	—		
		Less 10% Discount		40	—	360	—
		Sales to Ideal College, invoice no...					
	8	*Mohan Bros.*					
		5 stools @ Rs. 10		50	—		
		10 chairs @ Rs. 15		150	—	200	—
		Sales as per invoice no...					
	10	*Golechand & Co.*					
		3 tables @ Rs. 75		225	—		
		5 chairs @ Rs. 30		150	—	575	—
		Sales as per invoice no...					
		Total				935	—

Will the student say why the last two transactions have not been entered in the Sales Book?

Ledger Accounts

Sales Account

Dr. *Cr.*

		Rs.		June 30	By Sales as per Sales Book	Rs. 935	—

Ideal College

June 5	To Sales	360	—				

Mohan Bros.

June 8	To Sales	200	—				

Golechand & Co.

June 10	To Sales	375	—				

Debit notes are prepared and sent to customers also when they have to be charged with an extra amount, say, when price charged is less than the right one. In fact, the invoice made out against customers is a debit note.

Sales Returns. Against sales there can be returns. If the returns are only a few, they can be recorded through the journal. But if the returns are numerous, a separate book should be maintained to record them. The name of such a book is Sales Returns Book or Returns Inwards Book. The ruling is exactly as given above for Sales Book.

Posting. The total of the Returns Inwards Book is debited to Returns Inwards Account. The customers who have returned the goods are credited with the amount shown against their names.

Credit Note. Customers who return goods should be sent a Credit Note. Credit Notes are also sent whenever any party is to be given a credit, say for prices overcharged. The form is as under :

Credit Note

New Delhi,
Nov. 19, 1978

M/s. Ideal Traders, Agra
Cr. in account with
M/s. Goodluck & Co., Delhi.

	Rs.	Rs.
By 10 shirts @ Rs. 20 Price overcharged in Invoice No............ dated............... Rs. Two hundred only.		200.00

E. & O. E. *For* **Goodluck & Co.**

Partner.

A credit note is usually printed in red ink.

Role of Journal. The student will have noted that transactions relating to cash, bank, sale of goods, purchase of goods or materials, returns inwards and returns outwards are *not* entered in the journal because for each class of such transactions a separate book is maintained. *But* a journal will be still maintained. The purpose of the journal in such a case will be only to record such transactions as do not find a place in the special books maintained. Following are examples of transactions that will be recorded in the journal under the Practical System of Book-keeping :—

(*a*) Opening entry—the entry to record the opening balances of assets and liabilities. [*See* page [illegible] of Chapter II].

(*b*) Credit sales and purchases of :

(*i*) fixed assets ;
(*ii*) investments ; and
(*iii*) anything else that is not usually dealt in by the firm.

(*c*) Special discounts or allowances given to customers or received from suppliers.

(*d*) Writing off of bad debts.

(*e*) Recording diminution in value of assets.

(*f*) Receipts of and issue of bills of exchange, hundis, etc. and their dishonour.

(*g*) Incomes earned but not yet received and expenses not yet paid for in cash.

(*h*) Losses such as due to fire, earthquakes, etc.

If a class of transactions becomes numerous, a book can be started for recording such transactions. In that case, these transactions will be no longer journalised. In Chapter VII we shall discuss one such class of transactions—relating to Bills of Exchange, Promissory Notes, etc.

Subsidiary and Principal Books. The ledger is known as the Principal Book because it contains the accounts showing the results of various transactions. The accounts are prepared on the basis of the Cash Book, the Purchase Book, the Sales Book, the Journal, etc. Transactions are first entered in these books and then, on their basis, ledger accounts are written up. These books are known as Subsidiary Books. They are also known as Books of Primary Entry. Subsidiary books, therefore, may be defined as books where transactions are first entered and properly classified. The Cash Book is a subsidiary book because cash transactions are first entered here. But it is also a Principal Book because it shows the balance at bank and the cash in hand. Final results of carrying on business cannot be ascertained without considering cash in hand and at bank.

Illustration Sundharam was carrying on business in ready made clothes. On 1st January, 1978 his assets were :

Cash at bank, Rs. 3,500 ; Cash in hand, Rs. 370 ; furniture, Rs. 4,530 ; Stock of goods, Rs. 35,100 ; Amount due from Andley, Rs. 1,500 ; from Gupta, Rs. 1,600.

He owed Rs. 10,000 to Mrs. Sundharam and Rs. 2,600 to Kadam. During January, his transactions were :—

			Rs.
Jan.	2	Paid wages and salaries by cheque drawn for the purpose	600
	3	Purchased on credit from Kadam : 10 shirts @ Rs. 15 20 neckties @ Rs. 5	
	4	Sold goods for cash to Mehta	500
		Drawn cash for private use	300
	6	Paid Telephone rent, cash	180
		Issued cheque in favour of Kadam	2,500
		Discount allowed by him	100

		Rs.
Jan. 8	Received cheque from Gupta in full settlement	1,550
10	Sold to Andley on credit : 20 prs. trousers @ Rs. 20 10 neckties @ Rs. 6	
11	Gupta's cheque returned dishonoured by bank	
12	Sold to Apte on credit : 10 shirts @ Rs. 20 5 prs. trousers @ Rs. 20	
15	Cash Sales to Anand	600
	Cash sent to Bank	500
20	Purchased one Scooter Rickshaw on credit from Delhi Motor Co.	3,500
	Issued cheque in part payment	1,000
22	Gupta declared insolvent, a dividend of 60% is received from his estate	
23	Old newspapers sold for cash	25
25	Old furniture sold (cost Rs. 400)	250
27	Purchased from Kulkarni 100 Shirts @ Rs. 11	
	Apte returns 2 shirts as defective	
28	Received from Andley cheque in full settlement of the amount due on 1st January	1,450
	Sent cash to Bank	1,100
31	Interest due to Mrs. Sundharam @ 9% p. a. for one month :	
	Goods taken for domestic use	50

Enter the transactions in the books of Sundharam.

[*Note* : **In the working some mistakes have been deliberately committed. Let us see whether the student can spot them. There are six errors.**]

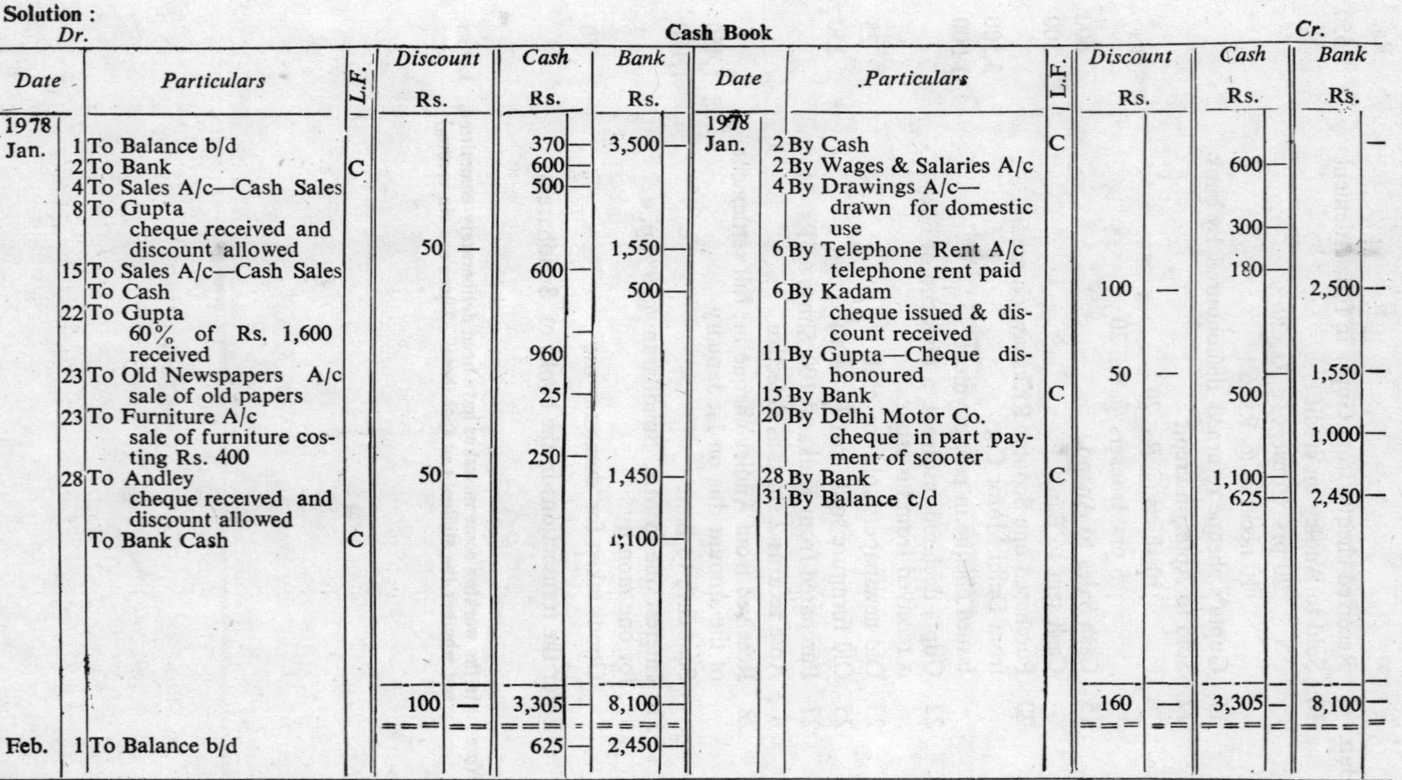

Solution :

Cash Book

Dr.

Date	Particulars	L.F.	Discount Rs.	Cash Rs.	Bank Rs.
1978 Jan. 1	To Balance b/d			370	3,500
2	To Bank	C		600	
4	To Sales A/c—Cash Sales			500	
8	To Gupta cheque received and discount allowed		50		1,550
15	To Sales A/c—Cash Sales			600	
	To Cash				500
22	To Gupta 60% of Rs. 1,600 received			960	
23	To Old Newspapers A/c sale of old papers			25	
23	To Furniture A/c sale of furniture costing Rs. 400			250	
28	To Andley cheque received and discount allowed		50		1,450
	To Bank Cash	C			1,100
			100	3,305	8,100
Feb. 1	To Balance b/d			625	2,450

Cr.

Date	Particulars	L.F.	Discount Rs.	Cash Rs.	Bank Rs.
1978 Jan. 2	By Cash	C			—
2	By Wages & Salaries A/c			600	
4	By Drawings A/c—drawn for domestic use			300	
6	By Telephone Rent A/c telephone rent paid			180	
6	By Kadam cheque issued & discount received		100		2,500
11	By Gupta—Cheque dishonoured		50		1,550
15	By Bank	C		500	
20	By Delhi Motor Co. cheque in part payment of scooter				1,000
28	By Bank	C		1,100	
31	By Balance c/d			625	2,450
			160	3,305	8,100

Purchase Book

Date		Particulars	L.F.	Details Rs.	Amount Rs.
1978 Jan.	3	Kadam			
		10 shirts @ Rs. 15		150 —	
		20 neckties @ Rs. 5		100 —	
		Purchases as per invoice on.........of...........			250 —
	27	Kulkarni			
		100 Shirts @ Rs. 11			1,100 —
		Purchase as per invoice on .....dated			
		Total			1,350 —

Sales Book

Date		Particulars	L.F.	Details Rs.	Amount Rs.
1978 Jan.	10	Andley			
		20 prs. trousers @ Rs. 20		400 —	
		10 neckties @ Rs. 6		60 —	
		Sale as per invoice no...........dated............			460 —
	12	Apte			
		10 shirts @ Rs 20		200 —	
		5 prs. trousers @ Rs. 20		100 —	
		Sale as per invoice no...............dated........			300 —
		Total			860 —

Returns Inward Book

Date		Particulars	L.F.	Details Rs.	Amount Rs.
1978	27	Apte			
		2 Shirts @ Rs. 20			0 —
		Goods returned : Credit Note no			
		Total			40

Journal

Date		Particulars		L.F.	Dr. Rs.	Cr. Rs.
1978 Jan.	1	Bank A/c.	Dr.		3,500 —	
		Cash A/c.	Dr.		370	
		Furniture A/c.	Dr.		4,530 —	
		Stock A/c.	Dr.		35,100 —	
		Andley	Dr.		1,500 —	
		Gupta	Dr.		1,600 —	
		To Mrs. Sundharam's Loan A/c				10,000 —
		To Kadam				2,600 —
		To Capital A/c.				34,000 —
		The opening assets and liabilities—Capital ascertained by deducting liabilities from assets.				
	20	Scooter Rickshaw A/c.	Dr.		3,500 —	
		To Delhi Motor Co.				3,500 —
		Purchase of Scooter Rickshaw from Delhi Motor Co. as per invoice no...				
	22	Bad Debts A/c.	Dr.		640 —	
		To Gupta				640 —
		The amount to be written off because of insolvency of Gupta—40% of Rs. 1,600.				
	25	Loss on Sale of Furniture A/c	Dr.		150 —	
		To Furniture A/c.				150 —
		The entry to record loss on sale of furniture—furniture costing Rs. 400 sold for Rs. 250.				
	31	Interest A/c.	Dr.		75 —	
		To Mrs. Sundharam's Loan A/c.				75 —
		Interest on Rs. 10,000 @ 9% for one month due but unpaid.				
	31	Drawings A/c.	Dr.		50 —	
		To Sale A/c.*				50 —
		Goods used by the proprietor for domestic purposes.				
			Total		51,015 —	51,015 —

* It is better if the credit is given to Purchase Account because, usually, the proprietor values such goods at cost and not at selling price.

Ledger

Dr. **Capital Account** **Cr.**

Date	Particulars	L.F.	Amount Rs.	Date	Particulars	L.F.	Amount Rs.
				1978 Jan. 1	By Balance b/d		34,000—

Mr. Sundharam's Loan A/c

Date	Particulars	L.F.	Amount Rs.	Date	Particulars	L.F.	Amount Rs.
1978 Jan. 31	To Balance c/d		10,075—	1978 Jan. 1	By Balance b/d		10,000—
				31	By Interest A/c		75—
			10,075—				10,075—
				Feb. 1	By Balance b/d		10,075—

Kadam

Date	Particulars	L.F.	Amount Rs.	Date	Particulars	L.F.	Amount Rs.
1978 Jan. 6	To Cash & Discount		2,600—	1978 Jan. 1	By Balance b/d		2,600—
31	To Balance c/d		250—	3	By Purchases		250—
			2,850—				2,850—
				Feb. 1	By Balance b/d		250—

Andley

Date	Particulars	L.F.	Amount Rs.	Date	Particulars	L.F.	Amount Rs.
1978 Jan. 1	To Balance b/d		1,500—	1978 Jan. 28	By Cash		1,450—
10	To Sales		640—	31	By Balance c/d		690—
			2,140—				2,140—
Feb. 1	To Balance b/d		690—				

Gupta

Date	Particulars	L.F.	Amount Rs.	Date	Particulars	L.F.	Amount Rs.
1978 Jan. 1	To Balance b/d		1,600—	1978 Jan. 8	By Cash & Discount		1,600—
11	To Cash—cheque dishonoured		1,600—	22	By Cash		960—
				22	By Bad Debts A/c		640—
			3,200—				3,200—

Apte

Date	Particulars	L.F.	Amount Rs.	Date	Particulars	L.F.	Amount Rs.
1978 Jan. 12	To Sales		300—	1978 Jan. 27	By Returns Inwards		40—
				31	By Balance c/d		260—
			300—				300—
Feb. 1	To Balance b/d		260—				

Delhi Motor Co.

Date		Particulars	L.F.	Amount Rs.	Date		Particulars	L.F.	Amount
1978					1978				
Jan.	20	To Cash		1,000—	Jan.	20	By Scooter Rick-shaw		3,500—
	31	To Balance c/d		2,500—					
				3,500—					3,500—
					Feb.	1	By Balance b/d		3,500—

Kulkarni

Date		Particulars	L.F.	Amount	Date		Particulars	L.F.	Amount
1978					1978				
Jan.	31	To Balance c/d		1,100—	Jan.	27	By Purchases		1,100—
					Feb.	1	By Balance c/d		1,100—

Drawings Account

Date		Particulars	L.F.	Amount	Date		Particulars	L.F.	Amount
1978									
Jan.	4	To Cash		300—					
	31	To Sales A/c		50—					

Stock Account

Date		Particulars	L.F.	Amount	Date		Particulars	L.F.	Amount
1978									
Jan.	1	To Balance b/d		35,100—					

Furniture Account

Date		Particulars	L.F.	Amount	Date		Particulars	L.F.	Amount
1978					1978				
Jan.	1	To Balance b/d		4,530—	Jan.	25	By Cash		250—
						25	By Loss on Furniture A/c.		150—
						31	By Balance c/d		4,130—
				4,530—					4,530—
Feb.	1	To Balance b/d		4,130—					

Scooter Rickshaw Account

Date		Particulars	L.F.	Amount	Date		Particulars	L.F.	Amount
1978					1978				
Jan.	20	To Delhi Motor Co.		3,500—	Jan.	31	By Balance c/d		3,500—
Feb.	1	To Balance b/d		3,500—					

Purchases Account

Date		Particulars	L.F.	Amount	Date		Particulars	L.F.	Amount
1978									
Jan.	31	To Purchases as per Purchase Book		1,350—					

Sale Account

Date		Particulars	L.F.	Amount Rs.	Date		Particulars	L.F.	Amount Rs.
					1978 Jan.	2	By Cash		500—
						15	By Cash		600—
						31	By Sales as per Sales Book		860—
						31	By Drawings A/c		50—

Wages & Salaries Account

Date		Particulars	L.F.	Amount Rs.	Date		Particulars	L.F.	Amount Rs.
1978 Jan.	2	To Cash		600—					

Telephone Rent Account

Date		Particulars	L.F.	Amount Rs.	Date		Particulars	L.F.	Amount Rs.
1978 Jan	6	To Cash		180—					

Old Newspapers Account

Date		Particulars	L.F.	Amount Rs.	Date		Particulars	L.F.	Amount Rs.
1978 Jan.	23	To Cash		25—					

Bad Debts Account

Date		Particulars	L.F.	Amount Rs.	Date		Particulars	L.F.	Amount Rs.
1978 Jan.	22	To Gupta		640—					

Loss on Sale of Furniture Account

Date		Particulars	L.F.	Amount Rs.	Date		Particulars	L.F.	Amount Rs.
1978 Jan.	25	To Furniture A/c		150—					

Interest Account

Date		Particulars	L.F.	Amount Rs.	Date		Particulars	L.F.	Amount Rs.
1978 Jan.	31	To Mrs. Sundharam's Loan A/c		75					

Discount Account

Date		Particulars	L.F.	Amount Rs.	Date		Particulars	L.F.	Amount Rs.
1978 Jan.	31	To Discount Allowed as per Cash Book		100—	1978 Jan.	31	By Discount as per Cash Book		160

Exercises

1. R. P. Bros. carry on business as wholesale cloth dealers. From the following write up their Purchase Book for January, 1969 :—

Jan. 3 Purchased on credit from Ambika Mills :
100 pieces long cloth @ Rs. 30
50 pieces Shirting @ Rs. 50

8 Purchased for cash from Arvind Mills :
50 pieces muslin @ Rs. 40

15 Purchased on credit from India Textiles Ltd.
20 pieccs coating @ Rs. 100
10 pieces shirting @ Rs. 60

20 Purchased 5 typewriters on credit from Bharat Type writers Ltd. @ Rs. 1,400 each.

Write up the ledger accounts also.

(*Total of Purchases Book*, *Rs. 8,100*)

2. From the following particulars prepare the Sales Book of Akbar & Co. who deal in furniture :

June 5 Sold on credit to Anand & Co :
10 tables @ Rs. 30
20 ehairs @ Rs. 15

10 Sold to Bannerji & Co. on credit :
5 almirahs @ Rs. 150
5 stools @ Rs. 10

20 Sold old typewriter for Rs. 600 to Mohan & Co. on credit.

25 Sold to Ram Lal & Bros. on credit :
5 tables @ Rs. 50
1 revolving chair @ Rs. 60

Write up the ledger accounts.

(*Total Sales Book*, *Rs. 1,710.*)

3. Enter the following transactions of P.C. Lal & Co. in the proper books :

July 5 Sold on credit to Sethi & Co. :
10 electric Irons @ Rs. 25
5 electric Stoves @ Rs. 15

8 Purchased on credit from Hari & Bros :
25 Heaters @ Rs. 40
10 Water Heatess @ Rs. 20

10 Purchased for cash from Mohan & Co :
10 Electric Kettles @ Rs. 30

15 Sold to Gopal Bros on credit :
10 Heaters @ Rs. 50
5 Water Heaters @ Rs. 25

18 Returned to Hari & Bros :
5 Heaters being defective.

20 Purchased from Kohli & Co. :
10 Toasters @ Rs. 20
10 Toasters @ Rs. 30

26 Gopal Bros. return one Water Heater as defective.

(*Total of Sales Book*, *Rs. 950 : Purchases Book*, *Rs. 1,700 Returns Outwards Book*, *Rs. 200 ; Returns Inwards Book*, *Rs. 25.*)

4. Krishan Kumar commences business on 1st July, 1978 with Rs. 25,000 out of which he pays Rs. 24,000 into bank. His transactions in July were as under :

			Rs.
July	1	Purchased furniture, against cheque	600
		,, typewriter ,, ,,	1,450
		Paid rent in advance, cash	250
	2	Purchased goods on credit from Ahmed	4,100
	4	Cash Sales	250
	5	Sold goods on credit to Kohli	1,500
	10	Purchased goods on credit from Nair	2,500
	15	Issued cheque in favour of Ahmed in full settlement	4,000
	16	Received cheque from Kohli on account	1,100
	18	Cash Sales	300
		Paid into Bank	700
	20	Issued cheque for advertising	450
	21	Paid for Stationery	250
	23	Purchased goods against cheque	1,500
	23	Sold goods on credit to Som Dutt	900
	25	Issued cheque in favour of Nair for amount due less discount @ 2%	
	26	Received cheque from Som Dutt in full settlement	880
	31	Paid wages	200

Nair notfies that the cheque is dishonoured. Enter the above mentioned transactions in the proper books (under Practical System) ; post the ledger accounts and test the accuracy of your work.

5. On 1st April, 1967, the Books of John Alvey showed the following Dr. Balances :— Cash at Bank, Rs. 9,600 ; at Office, Rs. 480 ; Stock of goods, Rs. 7,000 ; Walter Bell, Rs. 500 ; John Taylor, Rs. 450 ; Office Furniture & Fittings, Rs. 800.

			Rs.
April	1	Bought of J. Gray, Tea, Rs. 200 ; Sugar Rs. 400 ; Coffee, Rs. 200	800
	2	Purchased of Wm. Wilson, Tea Rs. 800 ; Coffee, Rs. 450	1,250
	3	Received from John Taylor on A/c.	200
	3	Paid into Bank	600
	3	Sold to Thos. Mason : Tea, Rs. 400 : Sugar, Rs. 560	960
	5	Bought of James Gray : Tea, Rs. 200 ; Sugar, Rs. 270	470
	6	Sold Chas. Jones : Sugar, Rs. 270 ; Tea, Rs. 200	470
	7	Cash Sales, Tea, Rs. 160 ; Sugar, Rs. 190 ; Coffee, Rs. 120	470
	8	Sold to Thomas Mason on credit : Tea, Rs. 890 ; Sugar, Rs. 200 ; Coffee, Rs. 200	1,290
	9	Paid Cash for Repairs	60
	8	Paid Fire Insurance Premium	10

			Rs.
April	9	Paid Cheque to James Gray, Rs. 800 ; Discount Rs. 40	840
	10	Recd. from T. Mason : Cash Rs. 900 ; Discount Rs. 70	970
	12	Paid Cash to James Gray	500
	12	Paid into Bank	800
	14	Bought of J. Gray, Tea, Rs. 400, Sugar, Rs. 260 ; Coffee. Rs, 350	1,010
	14	Sold for Cash : Tea, Rs. 100 ; Sugar, Rs. 120 ; Coffee Rs. 80	300
	15	Reed. Cheque of Charles, Jones, Rs. 410 ; Discount Rs. 60	470
	15	Deposited in Bank	700
	16	Bought of William Wilson : Tea, Rs. 800 ; Sugar, Rs. 200 ; Coffee, Rs. 400	1,400
	16	Paid him an A/c. by cheque Rs. 950 ; Discount Rs. 50	1,000
	17	Withdrew from Bank	200
	17	Pd. Cash for Office Files & Copying Press	120
	19	Recd. of John Taylor, Cheque in settlement	250
	20	Sold to Charles Jones : Tea, Rs. 1,000; Coffee, Rs. 200	1,200
	21	Cash Recd. for Tea, Rs. 190 ; Sugar, Rs. 230 ; Coffee Rs. 200	620
	22	Recd. of C. Jones, Cheque, Rs. 1,110 ; Discount Rs. 100	1,210
	22	Paid in Bank	1,400
	24	Sold Thomas Mason : Tea, Rs. 350 ; Sugar, Rs. 270 ; Coffee, Rs. 120	740
	26	Walter Bell pays a first and final dividend of 60 P. in the rupee	
	27	Tea of the value of Rs. 500 destroyed by fire Insurance Co. admits claim	250
		Insurance Co. Dr. Rs. 250 Loss by Fire A/c. Dr. Rs. 250, Cr. Sales Rr. 500)	
	27	Paid into Bank	400
	28	Cash Sales : Tea, Rs. 110 ; Sugar Rs. 90	200
	29	Recd. Cheque from the Insurance Co.	250
	29	Paid into Bank	500
	30	Drew for Private Expenses by cheque	100
	30	Paid Sundry Expenses in Cash	160
	30	Paid Wages by Cheque	110
	30	Rent due to James Shaw	40
	30	Depreciation of Office Furniture, etc.	60
	35	Charge Interest on Capital	100

Prepare the various books of account including ledger accounts.

6. Jackson carries on business as Tobacco Merchant.

On 1st Oct., 1977 his position was : Assets :—Stock of goods. Rs. 8,430 ; Cash, Rs. 200. Bank, Rs. 26,000. Furniture & Fittings, Rs. 3,800. Edward Wade, Rs. 2,120, Thos, Elliott, Rs. 1.130 Liabilities :—Ogden & Co., Rs. 1,900. Bell & Sons, Rs. 2,500. Wills & Co., Rs. 8,000. Hignett & Co. Rs. 5,050. Martin Bros, Rs. 6,060.

			Rs.
Oct.	1	Sold to Edward Wade :— Tobacco, Rs. 200, Cigars Rs. 500 ; Cigarettes, 150	850
	1	Recd. from him cheque, Rs. 20,20. Discount Rs. 100	2,120
	2	Paid Cash for Stationery	50
	4	Bought of Hignett & Co. : Tobacco Rs. 420 ; Cigars Rs. 960 ; Cigarettes Rs. 190	1,570
	4	Paid them cheq., Rs. 4,800, Discount Rs. 250	5,050
	5	Paid Wills & Co., cheque on A/c.	4,000
	5	Sold Jone Parson : Tobacco. Rs. 300 ; Cigars, Rs. 800 ; Cigarettes, Rs. 200	1,300
	6	Recd. from him, cheque Rs. 1,210. Discount Rs. 90	
	7	Invoiced to Albert Kershaw, Cigars	880
	7	Received cheque from him	500
	8	Bought Cigars from Martin Bros.	1,500
	8	Paid them cheque Rs. 2,850. Discount Rs. 150	3,000
	8	Received cheque from Joe Parson on A/c	430
	8	Paid Ogden & Co., cheque Rs. 1,800, Discount Rs. 90	1,890
	9	Sold Cigarettes to Thomas Elliot	180
	9	Paid into Bank	930
	9	Sold to Henry Hirst :—Tobacco, Rs. 630, Cigars. Rs. 360 ; Cigarettes, Rs. 210	
	11	Edward Wade paid cheque on A/c. (not banked)	500
	11	Endorsed Wade's cheque and sent it to Bell & Sons	
	11	Bought of Ogdon & Co. : Tobacco Rs. 1,300 ; Cigars, Rs. 160 ; Cigaretts, Rs. 320	
	12	Parsons' cheque returned by Bank dishonoured	430
	14	Sent io Thomas Elliot : Tobacco Rs. 890 ; Cigars Rs. 1,130 ; Cigarettes, Rs. 450	
	16	Withdrew from Bank	200
	16	Paid Wages in Cash	80
	15	Paid for Postage	50
	18	Bought of Bell & Sons : Tobacco, Rs. 830 ; Cigars, Rs. 540 : Rigarette Rs. 270	
	20	Recd. cheque from Henry Hirst (not banked)	1,000
	20	Endorsed Hirst's cheque and sent it to Martin Bros.	1,000
	21	Paid Municipal Taxes in Cash	110
	21	Sold Edward Wade : Tobacco, Rs. 530 ; Cigars, Rs. 480 ; Cigarettes, Rs. 270	
	21	Recd. from him cheque Rs. 320. Discount Rs. 40	360
	22	Sold Henry Hirst : Tobacco, Rs. 680 ; Cigars, Rs. 1,000 ; Cigarettes, Rs. 280	
	22	Recd. from him cheque Rs. 1,240 Discount Rs. 60	1,300
	22	Drew cheques for cash	200
	23	Paid Wages in cash	80
	25	Parson absconded, left no assets.	
	25	Paid cheque for new Show Case	230

			Rs.
Oct.	26	Bought of Wills & Co. : Tobacco. Rs. 1,300 ; Cigars, Rs. 1,800 ; Cigarettes, Rs. 630	
	26	Paid them Cheque Rs. 3,600. Discount Rs. 400	4000
	27	Bought Cigars from Martin Bros.	1,230
	27	Paid them Cheque Rs. 2,750, Discount Rs. 300	3,050
	27	Paid Cash for Fire Insurance Premium	40
	28	Recd. from T. Elliott, cheque Rs. 1,240, Discount Rs. 60	
	28	Sent Elliott's cheque to Wills & Co. on A/c.	
	28	Paid rent by cheque	100
	30	Withdrew from Bank for domestic use	400
	30	Cash Sales—Tobacco, Rs. 190, Cigars, Rs. 230 ; Cigarettes. Rs. 80	
	30	Paid Wages in Cash	80
	30	Depreciation of Furniture, etc.	220
	30	Bank Interest credited	80

Enter the above transactions in the various books, prepare ledger accounts and test their accuracy.

CHAPTER VI

TRIAL BALANCE AND ERRORS

Trial Balance

The student has now seen how ledger accounts are prepared on the basis of the journal or other subsidiary books, namely, the Cash Book, the Purchase Book, the Sales Book, etc. He has also seen how the two aspects of every transaction are given effect to while making entries. This means that if an amount has been placed on the debit side of any account, then a corresponding amount, or amounts totalling to the same figure, is also placed on the credit side of some other account or accounts. Thus for every debit entry there is a credit entry and *vice versa*. For instance, when the total of the Sales Book is credited to Sales Account, the accounts of customers are debited. The total of all these debits is equal to the single credit placed in the Sales Account. For amounts received, the entry is made on the debit side of the Cash Book ; but various accounts are credited on the basis of the entries made in this book. To state it again, in Book-keeping and Accountancy there will be no entry which is not accompanied by a corresponding entry or entries on the other side but, of course, in different accounts.

This helps us to check the accuracy of our work. If the total of debit entries made in various accounts are listed and, similarly, if another list is prepared of all accounts, but this time with the total of credit entries made, then the total of these two lists must be equal. If it is not equal, it means that there is some error. If it is equal then it indicates that it can be taken to be correct, although with certain reservations which we will see later. These two lists if combined in one statement, would be known as a trial balance.

Another method of preparing the trial balance is to, first of all, find out the difference of the two sides of every account. As has been pointed out already, if the debit side is bigger, it is known as a debit balance and if the credit side is bigger, it is known as a credit balance. One statement can be prepared with the names of all accounts ; there will be two columns in the statement for amounts—one for debit balances and the other for credit balances. The total of these two columns must also be the same. This statement is also known as trial balance and this is the usual way in which a trial balance is prepared these days. The following is the specimen of trial balances prepared according to the above two systems. The student is referred to illustration on p. 86 on the basis of which the trial balance has been prepared

Trial Balance (Illustration

Serial No.	*Name of Account*	*L.F.*	*Totals*				*Balances*			
			Debit		*Credit*		*Debit*		*Credit*	
			Rs.		Rs.		Rs.		Rs.	
1.	Cash in hand		3,305	—	2,680	—	625	—		
2.	Cash at Bank		8,100	—	5,650	—	2,450	—		
3.	Capital Account		—	—	34,000	—			34,000	—
4.	Mrs. Sundharam's Loan A/c.		—	—	10,075	—			10,075	—
5.	Kadam		2,600	—	2,850	—			250	—
6.	Andley		2,140	—	1,450	—	690			
7.	Gupta		3,200	—	3,200	—	—	—		
8.	Apte		300	—	40	—	260	—		
9.	Delhi Motor Co.		1,000	—	3,500	—			2,500	—
10.	Kulkarni		—	—	1,100	—			1,100	—
11.	Drawings Account		350	—	—	—	350	—		
12.	Stock Account		35,100	—	—	—	35,100	—		
13.	Furniture Account		4,530	—	400	—	4,130	—		
14.	Scooter Rickshaw A/c.		3,500	—	—	—	3,500	—		
15.	Purchases Account		1,350	—	—	—	1,350	—		
16.	Sales Account		—	—	2,010	—			2,010	—
17.	Wages and Salaries A/c.		600	—	—	—	600	—		
18.	Telephone Rent A/c.		180	—			180	—		
19.	Old Newspapers A/c.		25	—	—	—	25	—		
20.	Bad Debts Account		640	—	—	—	640	—		
21.	Loss on Sale of Furniture A/c.		150	—	—	—	150	—		
22.	Interest Account		75	—	—	—	75	—		
23.	Discount Account		100	—	160	—			60	—
	Total		67,245	—	67,115	—	50,125	—	49,995	—

The student notes that in each case the total of credits is less than that of debits by Rs. 130. This shows definitely that there are some mistakes. The careful student must have noted the following errors in the working of Illustration referred to above :-

(*a*) The total of the Discount column on the credit side of the Cash Book is Rs. 160 ; it should be Rs. 150. The effect of this error is that the Discount Account has been credited by Rs. 10 excess. This will have to be corrected by debiting the amount :

"To Mistake in casting of Discount

Column (cr.) Rs. 10."

This correction will reduce the credit balance of the Discount Account to Rs. 50.

(*b*) On January 28, a discount of Rs. 50 has been allowed to Andley on his paying Rs. 1,450. He has been credited with only Rs. 1,450 instead of Rs. 1,500, *i.e.*, Rs. 1,450 plus Rs. 50. This will now be corrected by crediting Rs. 50 to his account, thus—

"By Omission of Posting of

Discount on Jan. 28 Rs. 50."

This will reduce the amount due from Andley to Rs. 640.

(*c*) While posting Andley's Account with credit sales to him on January 10, the amount has been written as Rs. 640 instead of Rs. 460. This means he has been debited with Rs. 180 extra. This will be corrected by placing the amount on the credit side, thus—

"By Excess amount debited
on Jan. 10. Rs. 180."

This correction will reduce the amount due from him to Rs. 460.

(*d*) While posting the Old Newspapers Account from the debit side of the Cash Book, the amount has been placed to the debit of the Old Newspaper A/c. ; this account should have been credited. This will be corrected by putting Rs. 50 on the credit side (Rs. 25 to remove the wrong debit and Rs. 25 for the correct credit). The entry is :

"By Mistake in posting
on Jan. 23 Rs. 50."

This will convert the debit balance into a credit one.

(*e*) The total of the Sales Book is wrong ; it should be Rs. 760. The effect of the mistake is that the Sales Account has been credited with Rs. 100 extra. To correct the error, Rs. 100 must be debited, thus—

"To Mistake casting
the Sales Book Rs. 100."

The Sales Account will now show a credit balance of Rs. 1,910.

(*f*) There is an omission in posting the total of the Returns Inwards Book. The total of the book should be debited to Returns Inwards Account. This has not been done. It will now be done by opening Returns Inwards Account and placing a debit in it, thus—

"To Returns Inwards as
per Returns Inwards Book Rs. 40."

We can see now that with the corrections suggested above, the trial balance will agree. The trial balance with correct balances is given below :

Trial Balance

Ser. No.	Name of Account	L.F.	Debit Rs.		Credit Rs.	
1.	Cash in hand		625	—		
2.	Cash in Bank		2,450	—		
3.	Capital Account				34,000	—
4.	Mrs. Sundharam's Loan Account				10,075	—
5.	Kadam				250	—
6.	Andley		460	—		
7.	Apte		260	—		
8.	Delhi Motor Co.				2,500	—
9.	Kulkarni				1,100	—
10.	Drawings Account		350	—		
11.	Stock Account		35,100	—		
12.	Furniture Account		4,130	—		
13.	Scooter Rickshaw Account		3,500	—		
14.	Purchases Account		1,350	—		
15.	Sales Account				1,910	—
16.	Wages & Salaries Account		600	—		
17.	Telephone Rent Account		180	—		
18.	Old Newspapers Account				25	—
19.	Bad Debts Account		640	—		
20.	Loss on Sale of Furniture Account		150	—		
21.	Interest Account		75	—		
22.	Discount Account				50	—
23.	Returns Inwards Account		40	—		
	Total		49,910	—	49,910	—

The importance of trial balance. As has been pointed out, the trial balance is prepared to check the arithmetic accuracy of the work done in preparing ledger accounts. Since the amount of work to be done in a business firm is always fairly large, there is always the possibility of some mistakes being committed. A trial balance is a very good way of giving a clear indications of some mistakes that may be there. This will be shown immediately if the totals of the two columns of the trial balance differ. Thus the trial balance is essential to ensure that mistakes do not remain unearthed. Further, the aim of Book-Keeping and Accounts is to present a final picture of the profit earned or loss incurred and of the financial state of affairs. This work is much facilitated if, first of all, a trial balance is prepared. However, the student must note that agreement of a trial balance does not show conclusively that no mistakes have remained undetected. Some errors wlll not be disclosed by the trial balance whereas some will be. An agreed trial balance, therefore, is only a reasonable proof of arithmetic accuracy of books.

Errors disclosed by a trial balance. There are a number of errors which, if committed, will lead to the disagreement of a trial balance. These are stated below :

1. *Wrong totalling or casting of the subsidiary books.* Suppose, the Sales Book is under cast by Rs. 1,000.

This will mean that the Sales Account will be credited with an amount of Rs. 1,000 less than the right one. Since individual customers' accounts are debited with their individual purchases, their accounts will be correctly posted. In this case, therefore, the debits will exceed the credits by Rs. 1,000. In the same way the casting of any of the subsidiary books, the total of which is debited or credited in the ledger, will throw the trial balance out.

2. *Posting of the wrong amount.* Suppose a supplier has supplied goods worth Rs. 540. This amount is entered in the Purchase Book. But when his account is credited the amount written may be Rs. 450. In such a case the credits will be less by Rs. 90. There will be no mistake on the debit side because the amount has been correctly entered in the Purchase Book and the Purchase Account is debited only with the total of the Purchase Book.

3. *Posting an amount on the wrong side.* Suppose goods, Rs. 250, have been returned to the supplier. This amount will be naturally entered in the Returns Outwards Book. The total of this will be credited to Returns Outwards Account. Suppose, the Supplier's Account is credited with Rs. 250 instead of being debited with this amount. This means that the amount has been placed on the wrong side, *i.e.*, on the credit side instead of the debit side. This will mean that the credits will increase by Rs. 500.

4. *Omission of an amount from ledger accounts.* Suppose Rs. 900 is paid to a supplier. The entry is made in the Cash Book on the credit side but, by a mistake, the Supplier's Account is not debited by Rs. 900 as it should be. In such a case the trial balance will be out ; the debit side will be short by Rs. 900.

5. *Omission of an amount from the trial balance.* Obviusly, if some balance has been omitted from the trial balance, the trial balance will not agree.

These five types of errors will throw the trial balance out. The student has already had an exercise in locating and correcting such errors, committed in the working of Illustration

Errors which do not affect the agreement of the trial balance :

1. *Omission of an entry altogether from subsidiary books.* For instance, if goods worth Rs. 150 have been received back from a customer and the entry has not at all been made in the Returns Inwards Book. In that case, the Customer's Account will not be credited and the Returns Inwards Account also will not be debited (because the

amount of Rs. 150 has not been entered in the book and, therefore, could not have been included in the total). Thus there is no debit and no credit and the trial balance will still agree.

2. *Writing the wrong amount in the subsidiary books.* If a wrong amount is written in subsidary books, then entries on both the debit and credit sides will be on the basis of the wrong amount and then the trial balance will naturally agree. For instance, if an invoice for Rs. 640 is entered in the Sales Book as Rs. 460, then the customer's account will be debited with Rs. 460. Also,the total of the Sales Book will be on the basis of this very amount and hence the credit in the Sales Accouni will also be short by Rs. 180. Thus, both debits and credits will be less by Rs. 180 and the trial balance will agree.

3. *Posting an amount on the correct side but in the wrong account.* Goods have been supplied by R. Murty & Sons but, while posting, the amount is put on the credit side of the account of S. Murty & Sons. In that case, the trial balance will still agree. This is because the account of S. Murty & Sons will show a higher credit and that of R. Murty & Sons will be correspondingly less.

4. If there is an error involving principles, the trial balance will still agree. An error of principle takes place in the following cases :—

   (*a*) *Treating an expense as an asset.* For instance, repair to machinery may be debited to Machinery Account instead of Repairs Account. Since the amount has been placed on the debit side, the trial balance will not show up the mistake.

   (*b*) *Treating an asset as an expense.* Suppose furniture worth Rs. 5,000 has been purchased. If this amount is debited to Office Expense Account, the trial balance will not disclose the error since, again, there is a correct amount on the correct side.

   (*c*) *Treating an income as a liability or* vice versa. Suppose Rs. 10,000 are received by a firm as commission earned. If this amount is placed to the credit of the party which paid the amount, the trial balance will conceal this mistake because there is, again, a correct amount on the correct side although in the wrong account. Similarly, when a liability is treated as an income it will not be shown up by the trial balance. If Rs. 10,000 received as a loan is credited to Sales Account instead of the personal account of the lender, the trial balance will still agree.

5. *Compensating errors are also not shown up by the trial balance.* Compensating errors are those which cancel out one another and thus enable the trial balance to agree. Suppose the following four mistakes are committed :—

(*i*) The total of the Purchase Book is Rs. 1,000 excess.

(*ii*) An amount of Rs. 400 paid to a supplier is credited to his account.

(*iii*) The total of the Returns Inwards Account is Rs. 100 excess.

(*iv*) A sale of Rs. 300 to a customers has been omitted to be posed to his account.

The student will see that the net effect of the above four errors is precisely nil. The effect of errors (i) and (iii) is to increase debits unnecessarily by Rs. 1,100 but error (iv) reduces the debits by Rs. 300. Error (ii) has increased the credits by Rs. 800 because the amount of Rs. 400 has been put on the credit side instead of the debit side. These errors together are "compensating errors."

Types of errors. Errors can be classified as :

1. Clerical errors (*e.g.*, the errrors (i) to (iv) above) ; or
2. Errors of principle (*e.g.*, errors (a) to (c) above).

Clerical errors may be of the following nature :

(*a*) *Errors of omission* which may mean either a complete omission of an entry from subsidiary books or partial omission in the sense that posting from subsidiary books to the ledger accounts has not been made.

(*b*) *Errors of Commission.* When a wrong amount is entered either in the subsidiary books or in the ledger accounts or when totals are wrongly made or when a wrong account is involved or when amount is posted on the wrong side, it is a case of errors of commission.

(*c*) *Compensating errors* which cancel themselves out.

Errors of principle always mean that a rule of accountancy has been violated. This involves wrong distinction between expenses and assets and between incomes and liabilities, that is between revenue and capital items.

The following chart gives the various types of errors :

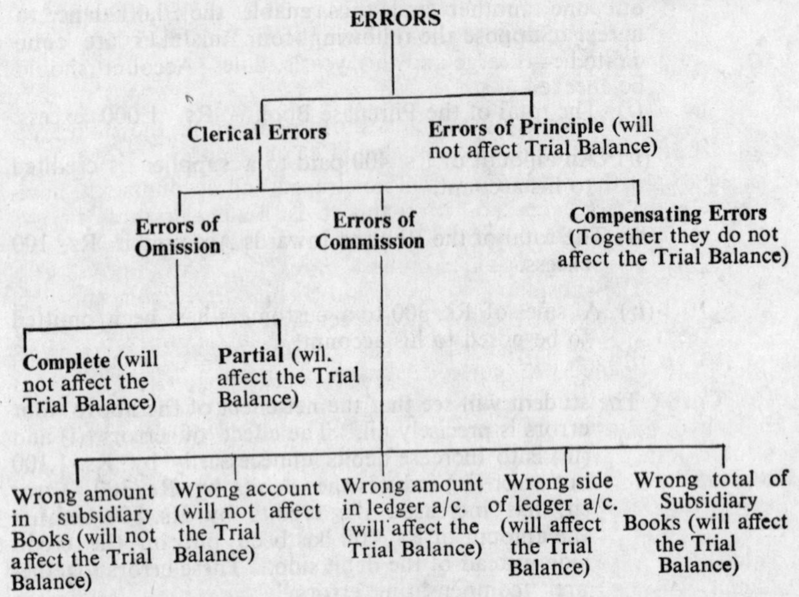

Steps to locate errors. When the trial balance does not agree, the accountant must immediately try to spot the errors and correct them. The following steps can be suggested for speedy location of errors :—

1. Total the Dr. and Cr. columns of the trial balance. If one amount has been shown for a group of accounts (for example, in place of all customers individually, only one amount against "Sundry Debtors" is shown), recheck the total of the list of such accounts.
4. See that the balances of all accounts, including the Cash and Bank balances, have been written in the trial balance.
3. See that there is no mistake in the balancing of the various accounts.
4. Find out the exact difference in the trial balance. Look for such accounts as show the same amount. It is possible that the balances of the particular account has been omitted from being entered in the Trial Balance. Accounts showing a balance equal to half the difference should also be checked ; the amount may have been written on the wrong side of the trial balance.
5. Recheck the totals of the subsidiary books—specially if the mistake is of Rs. 1, 10, 100, 1,000, and so on.
6, If the difference is a large one, compare the figures with the trial balance of the corresponding date of the previous year. Any account showing rather large diffierence

over the figure in the corresponding trial balance of the previous year should be rechecked. For example, Sales Account this year may be Rs. 25,30,000 whereas last year's figures may have been Rs. 36,45,000. The difference is large and this year's Sales Account should be checked again.

7. Postings of all amounts corresponding to the difference or half the difference shouid be checked.
8. If the difference is still not traced, all accounts will have to be checked. For this it is better, first of all, to check the posting of the totals of subsidiary books such as Sales Book, Purchase Book, Returns Books, etc. The subsidiary books should then be again gone through to see if any items have been left unposted. It should also be seen whether the various accounts have been opened with correct balances.

Correcting the errors. Errors are always corrected in accounts books by a suitable additional entry. If correction involves transfer of an amount from one account to another, a journal entry should be made ; otherwise, the concerned account may be corrected by debiting or crediting the correcting amount. Of course, a complete explanation for the correction made should be given so that no difficulty is experienced later when accounts are checked. [The student will do well to first see what should have been the correct entry, compare it with the entry actually made and then see how the correct position can be restored.]

Illustration Correct the following errors :—

(*a*) The total of the Purchase Book is Rs. 1,000 short.

(*b*) While posting the account of Ghosh from the Sales Book, the sale of Rs. 360 has been credited to him.

(*c*) Goods received back from Ali, a customer, Rs. 150, have not been entered in the Returns Inwards Book at all.

(*d*) The total of the Discount Column of the Cash Book (Cr.) is Rs. 10 short.

(*e*) Furniture for office purchased from Ravi, Rs. 800, has been entered in the Purchases Book.

(*f*) Discount of Rs. 25 allowed by Anand has not been entered in the Cash Book although debited to him cocrectly in the ledger.

(*g*) A sale of Rs. 159 to Kohli has been debited to his account as Rs. 195.

(*h*) A purchase of Rs. 251 from Gopal & Co. has been entered in the Purchases Book as Rs. 215.

(*i*) Repairs to Motor Van, Rs. 374, have been debited to Motor Van Account as Rs. 174.

(*j*) A sporting gun, costing Rs. 300, purchased for the proprietor has been debited to General Expenses A/c.

(*k*) A cheque for Rs. 75 issued to the petty cashier has not been posted to the Petty Cash Account.

(*l*) Rs. 150 received from C. Dass has been debited to G. Dass. (Cash Book correctly posted).

(*m*) Rs. 130 received from Krishen against a debt previously written off has been credited to his account.

(*n*) Carriage on machinery, Rs. 510, has been debited to Carriage Account.

(*o*) A purchase of Rs. 158 from Soni has been debited to his account as Rs. 185.

Solution :

(*a*) The total of the Purchase Book is debited to Purchases Account. If the tota is less, the debit will be less. No other account is involved since accounts of individual parties **are** posted with individual amounts. Hence the correction is to debit Purchases Account by Rs. 1,000 saying "To correction of wrong totalling for the month of Rs. 1,000".

(*b*) Ghosh should be debited and not credited. Hence to convert credit into debit, he should be debited with Rs. 720, Rs. 360 to remove the wrong credit and Rs. 360 for the correct debit.

(*c*) Wilh the complete omission, there has been no debit and no credit. Hence a journal entry should now be passed :

		Rs.	Rs.
Returns Inwards Account	... Dr.	150	
To Ali			150
Goods returned by him on...not entered in the Returns Inwards A/c.			

(*d*) The total of the Discount Column (Cr.) in the Cash Book is credited to Discount Account. If the total is less, the credit is less. Hence Discount Account should be credited by Rs. 10.

(*e*) Office furniture should not be entered in the Purchases Book, the total of which is debited to Purchases Account. Due to the mistake, Purchases Account has been debited (wrongly) but Ravi has been correctly credited; and the debit to furniture Account has been omitted. Hence, the debt should be transferred from Purchases Account to Furniture Account. The entry is :

		Rs.	Rs.
Furniture Account	... Dr.	800	
To Purchases Account			800
The (wrong) debit to Purchases A/c transferred to Furniture Account.			

(*f*) Discount of Rs. 25 should have been entered in the Discount Column (Cr.) in the Cash Book. By this omission the total of this column is less and hence the credit to the Discount Account is also less. Anand's Account is already correctly posted. Hence the correction is to credit Discount Account by Rs. 25.

(*g*) Kohli has been debited Rs. 36 excess (Rs. 195 instead of Rs. 159). Hence he should be credited by Rs. 36.

(*h*) Entry in the Purchases Book is Rs. 215 instead of Rs. 251, that is, Rs. 36 less. The effect is that Purchases Account has been debited (since the total of the Purchases Book is also affected) and Gopal & Co. have been credited with Rs. 36 less. This should be corrected by the entry :

		Rs.	Rs.
Purchases Account	... Dr.	36	
To Gopal & Co.			36
Correction of the mistake by which Rs. 215 were entered in the Purchases Book instead of Rs. 251.			

(*i*) There are two mistakes. The amount is wrong and the account is wrong. Rapairs should be debited to Repairs Account and not to Motor Van Account. To correct the errors :
Credit Motor Van Account, Rs. 174 ; and
Debit Repairs Account. Rs. 374.

(*j*) Sporting gun purchased for the proprietor should be debited to Drawings Account and not to General Expenses Account. Hence the debit should be transferred by the entry :

		Rs.	Rs.
Drawings Account	... Dr.	300	
To General Expenses A/c			300
Transfer of wrong debit to General Expenses in respect of sporting gun for the proprietor.			

(*k*) The Petty Cash Account is debited when a cheque is issued to the Petty Cashier. Hence the omission should be corrected by debiting Petty Cash Account.

(*l*) There are two mistakes—wrong account and wrong side. Hence G. Dass should be credited by Rs. 150 (to remove wrong debit) and C. Dass should be credited by Rs. 150 (because he has paid the amount and thus to be credited.)

(*m*) When an amount is received against a debt previously written off, Bad Debts Recovered Account is credited and not the party which pays (because the party's account was closed by a credit entry when the bad debt arose originally). Hence the credit to Krishen should be transferred to Bad Debts Recovered Account by the entry :

		Rs.	Rs.
Krishen	... Dr.	130	
To Bad Debts Recovered Account			130
Wrong credit to Krishen in respect of amount received against a debt written off now transferred.			

(*n*) Carriage on machinery should be debited to Machinery Account. Hence the entry :

		Rs.	Rs.
Machinery Account	... Dr.	510	
To Carriage Account			510
Transfer of wrong debit to Carriage A/c. in respect of carriage on machinery.			

(*o*) Soni should have been credited by Rs. 158. He has been debited with Rs. 185. Hence he should be credited with Rs. 343 (Rs. 185 to remove the wrong debit and Rs. 158 for the correct credit).

Will the student (*i*) say which errors will affect the trial balance and (*ii*) classify the errors ?*

Suspense Account. Some accountants put the difference in the trial balance to a newly opened account. The name of the account is Suspense Account. If the credit side is short, the Suspense Account will be credited and if the credit side is bigger, this account will be debited. With the inclusion of this account in the trial balance, it will appear to be agreed. However, the errors which have led to the difference in the trial balance still remain and have to be found out. The opening of the Suspense Account does not mean that the errors may be forgotten.

The student will realise that the difference in trial balance is caused only by "one sided" errors, like errors a, b, d, f, g, i, k, l and (o) in the illustration given above. The other errors do not lead to a difference in the trial balance. They are not reflected in the Suspense Account. The amount standing to the debit or credit of

**Key* : (*i*) a, b, d, f, g, i, k, l, o.

(*ii*) Errors of Omission c, f, k.

Errors of Commission a, b, d, g, h, i, l, o.

Errors of Principle e, i, j, m, n.

the Suspense Account represents the net effect of one sided errors. Therefore, when such errors are corrected, by placing the correct amount to say, the debit of the proper account, the credit is placed in the Suspense Account. Similarly, when the proper account is credited with the correct amount, the debit is placed in the Suspense Account. For example, error (*a*) in the above illustration will be rectified (if a Suspense Account has been opened) as under :

		Rs.	Rs.
Purchases Account	... Dr.	1,000	
To Suspense Account			1,000
Rectification of the effect of undercasting of the Purchase Book for the month of....			

Error (*e*), for example, does not affect the trial balance and hence will be corrected as shown already, *i.e.*,

Furniture Account	... Dr.	800	
To Purchases Account			800

This correction does not concern the Suspense Account.

When all one-sided errors are corrected, there should be no balance left in the Suspense Account. Errors which do not affect the trial balance, are corrected as already shown. If the Suspense Account continues to show a balance, it means that there are still some mistakes which remain unearthed.

[Sometimes, in the examination, the balance of the Suspense Account is not given. The student should post the Suspense Account in the process of rectification and put the difference of the two sides at the *top of the shorter* side as "Difference in Trial Balance."]

Illustration The books of A. Vikram did not agree. The accountant put the difference in a Suspense Account. Rectify the following errors and prepare the Suspense Account.

(*a*) The total of the Returns Outwards Book, Rs. 210, has not been posted in the ledger.

(*b*) A purchase of Rs. 400 from Saran has been entered in the Sales Book. However, Saran's account has been correctly credited.

(*c*) A sale of Rs. 430 to Ramakant has been credited in his account as Rs. 340.

(*d*) A sale of Rs. 296 to Krishen has been entered in the Sales Book as Rs. 269.

(*e*) Old furniture sold for Rs. 540 has been entered in the Sales Account as Rs. 450.

(*f*) Goods taken by proprietor, Rs. 100, have not been entered in the books at all.

Solution :

	Journal		*Dr.* Rs.	*Cr.* Rs.
(*a*)	Suspense Account ...Dr. To Returns Outwards Account Rectification of the error by which Returns Ourwards A/c was not posted		210 —	210 —
(*b*)	Purchase Account ...Dr. Sales Account ...Dr. To Suspense Account Removal of the wrong credit to Sales A/c and placing the correct debit to Purchases Account. [Rectification necessary because of entry in Sales Book in place of Purchase Book]. Saran's account already credited.		400 — 400 —	800 —
(*c*)	Ramakant ...Dr. To Suspense Account Conversion of credit of Rs. 340 into a debit of Rs. 430 in Ramakant's Account.		770 —	770 —
(*d*)	Krishen ...Dr. To Sales Account The effect of entry of Rs. 269 instead of Rs. 296 now rectified		27 —	27 —
(*e*)	Sales Account ...Dr. Suspense Account ...Dr. To Furniture Account Rectification of error by which Sales A/c was credited by Rs. 450 instead of Furniture Account by Rs. 540.		450 — 90 —	540 —
(*f*)	Drawing Account ...Dr. To Purchases Account Omission of taking of Rs. 100 worth of goods by the proprietor rectified.		100 —	100 —

Dr.	Suspense Account			Cr.
	Rs.			Rs.
To Difference in Trial Balance (balancing figure)	1,270	By Sundries— Purchase	400	
		Sales	400	800
To Returns Outwards Account	210	By Ramakant		770
To Furniture	90			
	1,570			1,570

In the Suspense Account Rs. 1,570 have been credited and Rs. 300 debited. Since the Suspense Account shows no balance after all errors have been rectified, there must have been a debit of Rs. 1,270 in the Suspense Account as difference in trial balance.

Correction in the next trading period. Rectification of errors discussed so far assumes that it was carried out before the books were closed for the concerned year. However, sometimes, the rectification is carried out in the next year, carrying forward the balance in the Suspense Account (or even transferring it to the Capital Account). In this case, it should be noted that there should be no violation of the principle that the Profit and Loss Account should reflect amounts relating to the year for which the account is being prepared—amounts relating to the previous years, if they are substantial, should be shown separately. Suppose, the Purchase Book was cast Rs.1,000 short in Dec., 1979 and a Suspense Account was opened with the difference in the trial balance. If the error is rectified next year and the entry passed is to debit Purchases Account (and credit Suspense Account), it will mean that the Purchases Account for 1980 will be Rs.1,000 more than the amount relating to 1980 and thus the profit for 1980 will be less than the actual for that year. Thus, correction of errors in this manner will "falsify" the Profit and Loss Account. To avoid this, correction of all amounts concerning nominal accounts, *i.e.*, expenses and incomes, should be through a special account styled as Profit and Loss Adjustment Account. The balance in this account should be transferred to the Capital Account. The Profit and Loss Account will then remain unaffected. It is to be noted that the correction in respect of real or personal accounts should be made as stated already.

Illustration : The books of Meher were closed on Dec. 31, 1980 with a Suspense Account showing a credit balance of Rs.410. In 1981 the following errors were located :—

(*i*) In November, 1980 the total of the Sales Book on one page was carried forward to the next page as Rs.26,130 instead of Rs.21,630.

(*ii*) Furniture of the book value of Rs.3,500 was sold for Rs.4,100 to Lalwani but the amount was entered in the Sales Book. In 1980 10% depreciation was charged on the closing balance of all asset accounts.

(*iii*) The total of the Discount Column (Cr.) for December, 1980, Rs.240, was not posted in the ledger.

(*iv*) Goods returned to Mehta in October 1980, costing Rs.650, were not recorded in the books at all.

(*v*) Rs.3,100, goods purchased from G. Sorabjee, a supplier, were debited to the account of C. Sorabjee, a customer—the amount was correctly entered in the Purchases Book.

Pass journal entries to rectify the errors and make any comments that you may have to make.

Solution :

		Dr. Rs.	Cr. Rs.
(*i*) Profit and Loss Adjustment A/c.	Dr.	4,500	
To Suspense Account			4,500
Rectification of excess amount credited to Sales Account in 1980 because of wrong carry forward (Rs.26,130—21,630).			
(*ii*) Profit and Loss Adjustment A/c.	Dr.	3,150	
To Furniture Account			3,150
urniture A/c for Rs.3,150, *i.e.*, Rs.3,500 (book value) *less* 10% Depreciation. (No need for taking note of the remaining amount since it was profit of the previous year and, in effect, has been so treated).			
(*iii*) Suspense Account	Dr.	240	
To Profit and Loss Adjustment A/c			240
Rectification of the omission to post the Discount Column (Cr) in December.			
(*iv*) Mehta	Dr.	650	
To Profit & Loss Adjustment A/c			650
Rectification of the omission of goods returned to Mehta in October, 1980.			
(*v*) Suspense Account	Dr.	6,200	
To C. Sorabjee			3,100
To G. Sorabjee			3,100
Entry to remove the wrong debit to C. Sorabjee and to give credit to G. Sorabjee in respect of goods purchased on			
Capital Account	Dr.	6,760	
To Profit and Loss Adjustment A/c			6,760
Transfer of the balance in the P. & L. Adjustment A/c, representing the net effect of errors affecting profit last year.			

Comment :

The Suspense Account will now appear as shown below :

Suspense Account

	Rs.	1981		Rs.
To Profit & Loss Adjustment A/c	240	Jan. 1	By Balance b/d	410
To Sundries—			By Profit & Loss Adjustment A/c	4,500
C. Sorabjee	3,100		By Balance c/d	1,530
G. Sorabjee	3,100			
	6,440			6,440
To Balance b/d	1,530			

Since the Suspense Account still shows a balance, it is obvious that there are still some errors left in the books.

Illustration. Lee closed his books on June 30, 1980 and prepared the final accounts. However, the books had shown a difference which was transferred to the Capital Account. Later the following errors were found :

(*i*) Repairs to the delivery van, Rs.2,500 were debited to the Van Account as Rs.3,500. Depreciation @ 20% was provided on the closing balance.

(*ii*) In the Cash Book, the total of the bank column on one page (Dr.), Rs.5,120 was carried forward to the next page as Rs. 5,210.

(*iii*) Goods returned by Chopra, Rs. 1,100, were not

(*iv*) The total of the inventory sheets as on 30-6-80 was found to be Rs.1,000 short.

(*v*) The total of the Discount Column (Cr.) for April, 1980, Rs.160 was found posted to the debit of the Discount A/c.

(*vi*) A dividend of Rs.410 received from the estate of Singh, an insolvent, was found posted to the credit of his account.

Give journal entries to rectify the errors given above.

Solution :

			Dr Rs.	Cr Rs.
i)	Profit & Loss Adjustment A/c	Dr.	2,500	
	Suspense Account	Dr.	300	
	To Van Account			2,800
	Credit to Van Account to remove the wrong debit (now Rs.2,800 i.e. 3,500 *less* 20% Depreciation), debit to P. & L. Adj. A/c for repairs and the balance put to Suspense A/c			
(*ii*)	Suspense Account	Dr.	90	
	To Bank			90
	Correction of the wrong carry forward (Rs.5,210 instead of Rs.5,120) which must have increased the bank balance shown in the books.			
(*iii*)	Profit and Loss Adjustment Account	Dr.	1,100	
	To Chopra			1,100
	Entry to rectify the omission of goods returned by Chopra.			
(*iv*)	Opening Stock	Dr.	1,000	
	To Profit & Loss Adjustment A/c			1,000
	Correction of the figure in respect of opening stock—last year the profit shown was less because of the error.			
(*v*)	Suspense Account ...	Dr.	320	
	To Profit and Loss Adjustment A/c			320
	Correction of the error by which Discount A/c was debited instead of credited in April, 1980.			
(*vi*)	Singh	Dr.	410	
	To Profit & Loss Adjustment A/c			410
	Correction of the errors by which Singh was wrongly credited instead of Bad Debts Recovered A/c for the dividend from his estate.			
	Capital Account	Dr.	710	
	To Suspense Account			710
	Transfer of the balance in the Suspense A/c to the Capital A/c since last year it was so done.			
	Capital Account	Dr.	1,870	
	To Profit and Loss Adjustment A/c			1,870
	Transfer of the balance in the P. & L. Adj. A/c to the Capital Account, being the net amount by which profit was affected last year.			

Exercises

1. Which of the following statements are true ?
   - (*i*) Errors of principle do not affect the trial balance.
   - (*ii*) All errors of commission will cause a difference in the trial balance.
   - (*iii*) All clerical errors lead to a difference in the trial balance.
   - (*iv*) Trial Balance is left unaffected by compensating errors.
   - (*v*) Compensating errors comprise an error of principle and a clerical error.
   - (*vi*) A small balance in the Suspense Account, representing difference in the trial balance, may be ignored since the amount is not substantial.
   - (*vii*) An agreed trial balance is absolute proof that there are no errors in the books of account.
   - (*viii*) It does not matter when the errors are corrected—in the current year or the next year.
   - (*ix*) The Suspense Account shows the effect of only those errors that affect the trial balance.
   - (*x*) The agreement of the trial balance is due to the recording of both aspects of a transaction or event. [*True* : (*i*), (*iv*), (*ix*) & (*x*)]

2. State what is wrong, if any, with the following entries :—

			Rs.	Rs.
(*i*)	Akbar and Sons	Dr.	2,000	
	To Sales			2,000
	Cash Sale of goods to M/s Akbar & Sons.			
(*ii*)	Purchases Account	Dr.	7,500	
	To Machinery Mart			7,500
	Purchase of equipment for use in office.			
(*iii*)	Cash Account	Dr.	510	
	To Bad Debts Recovered A/c			510
	Amount received from the estate of Mohanrao, an insolvent.			
(*iv*)	Cash Account	Dr.	440	
	To Gupta			450
	To Discount			10
	Settlement of Gupta's account of Rs.450.			
(*v*)	Desai & Co. ...	Dr.	570	
	To Cash			370
	Amount paid to Desai & Co.			
(*vi*)	Freight Account	Dr.	2,300	
	To Bank			2,300
	Freight paid on machinery purchases for the factory.			

[(*iii*) *is correct*]

3. Out of the following correct the errors without opening a Suspense Account.

- **(*a*) Total of the Purchase Book is Rs. 1,000 excess.**
- **(*b*) A discount allowed by Atma Ram, Rs. 15, correctly entered in Cash Book, has not been posted to his account.**
- **(*c*) Sales of goods, Rs. 200, to Suri has not been entered in the Sales Book.**
- **(*d*) Purchase of furniture, Rs. 600, has been entered in the Purchases Book.**
- **(*e*) While posting a sale of Rs. 350 to Ram, his account has been debited.**
- **(*f*) A sale to Gopal of Rs. 320 has been entered in the Sales Book as Rs. 230.**

(*g*) Returns to Rao, Rs. 150, have not been posted to his account.

4. Point out which of the following are errors. Pass correcting entries where necessary and classify the errors :—

(*a*) Sale of old machinery, Rs. 1,000, has been entered in the Sales Book.

(*b*) Gupta & Bros. pay Rs. 300 and discount of Rs. 20 is allowed to them. Their account is credited by Rs. 320.

(*c*) Cash sale of old newspapers, Rs. 40, has been entered in the Cash Book and from this Old Newspapers Account has been credited.

(*d*) The total of the discount column, debit side, of the Cash Book is Rs. 10 short.

(*e*) A sale of Rs. 250 to Murti & Co. has been debited to them as Rs. 520.

(*f*) Haridas pays Rs. 200. This amount has been credited to Hariram.

(*g*) Old machinery was purchased for Rs. 5,000. This is debited to the Machinery Account. The machinery was overhauled by own workmen to whom Rs. 500 were paid as wages for the time. This amount stands debited to Wages Account.

(*h*) A purchase of typewriter on credit for Rs. 1,200 has not been entered in books at all.

(*i*) Returns Inwards, Rs. 140, from Bose & Co. have not been posted to their account.

(*j*) Rs. 210 received from the estate of Gopi have been credited to his account. His account was written off last year as bad.

[(*b*) *and* (*c*) *are not errors*]

5. Correct the following errors :—

(*a*) Salary, Rs. 200, paid to Anand has been debited to his account.

(*b*) Repairs, Rs. 180, to furniture has been debited to Furniture Account.

(*c*) Railway freight, Rs. 780, on machinery has been debited to Railway Freight Account.

(*d*) A cheque for Rs. 450 received from Chatterjee has been entered in the Cash Book but not posted to his account.

(*e*) A sale of Rs. 510 to Mathur and Co. has been entered in the Returns Outwards Book.

(*f*) A purchase of Rs. 800 from Gopal & Co. has been entered in the Sales Book.

6. The following two entries have been made in the books of Ideal Sugar Co., Ltd. :—

(1) T.P. Soni	Dr.	4,760	
To Sales Account			4,760

Being the sale of 40 bags of sugar at Rs. 120, less freight to be paid by the customer, Rs. 40, sale being f.o.r. destination.

(2) Railway Freight Account	Dr.	40	
To T.P. Soni			40

Being the railway freight to be paid by the customer because the sale is on f.o.r. destination basis.

If there is anything wrong with the above two entries, pass the correcting entry.

7. In taking out a Trial Balance, a book-keeper finds that he is out, Rs. 127·89 excess debit. Being desirous of closing his books, he places the difference to a newly-opened Suspense Account which is carried forward. In the next period he discovers that (*a*) a credit item of Rs. 97·27 has been debited to a personal account as Rs. 79·72 ; (*b*) a sum of Rs. 85 written off fixtures as depreciation has not been posted in the Fixture Account ; (*c*) Rs. 1,500, paid for Furniture purchasad has been charged to the ordinary Purchases Account ; (*d*) a discount of Rs. 37·69 allowed to a customer has been credited to him as Rs. 36·79 ; (*e*) the total of the Inward Returns has been added Rs. 99 short ; and (*f*) an item of sale for Rs. 59 was posted as Rs. 95 in the Sales Account.

Give the correcting entries and prepare the Suspense Account.

8. A book-keeper while balancing his books finds that he is out, excess credit, by Rs. 91·80. Being required to prepare the final accounts, he places the difference to a newly opened Suspense Account which he carries forward to the next year. In the next year the following mistakes were discovered :—

(*a*) Goods bought from a merchant amounting to Rs. 5.50 had been posted to the credit side of his account as Rs. 55.

(*b*) A dishonoured cheque for Rs. 200 returned by the firm's bank had been credited to the Bank Account and debited to General Expenses Account.

(*c*) An item of Rs. 10.10 entered in the Sales Returns Book had been posted to the debit of the customer who return the goods.

(*d*) Sundry items of plant sold amounting to Rs. 260 had been entered in the Sales Day Book ;

(*e*) An amount of Rs. 60 owing by a customer had been omitted from the Schedule of Sundry Debtors.

(*f*) Discount amounting to Rs. 2.50 allowed to a customer had been duly entered in his account but not entered in the Discount Column of the Cash Book.

Draft the journal entries necessary for rectifying the above mistakes. Prepare the Suspense Account.

9. The following mistakes were located in the books of concern after its books were closed and "Suspense" Account was created in order to get the Trial Balance agree :—

(*a*) Sales Day Book totalled Rs. 6,450. While posting Sales Account, the amount was written as Rs. 6,540.

(*b*) A sale of Rs. 50 to X was wrongly debited to the account of Y.

(*c*) General Expenses, Rs. 18.25, was posted in the General Ledger as Rs. 1·82.

(*d*) A Bills Receivable for Rs. 155 was passed through Bills Payabie Day Book. This bill was given by D.

(*e*) Legal Expenses, Rs. 199, paid to Mr. Law was debited to his personal account.

Find out the nature and amount of the Suspense" Account and pass entries for the rectification of the above errors in the subsequent year's books.

[*Suspense Account opened with a debit of Rs. 106·43*]

10. There was an error in the Trial Balance of Ram Gopal on 31st December, 1961, and the difference in books was carried to a Suspense Account. On going through the books you find that :—

(*a*) Rs. 540 received from M. Mehta was posted to the debit of his account.

(*b*) Rs. 100 being purchase returns were posted to the debit of Purchases Account.

(*c*) Discounts Rs. 200 received were posted to the debit of Discount Account.

(*d*) Rs. 374 paid for repairs to Motor Car was debited to Motor Car Account as Rs. 174.

(*e*) Rs. 400 paid to C. Das was debited to the Account of G. Dass.

Give journal entries to rectify the above errors and state what amount was carried to the Suspense Account.

[*Suspense Account opened with a credit of Rs. 1,480*]

11. The Trial Balance of P. Mohan did not agree and the difference in books was carried to a Suspense Account which was opened with a credit of Rs. 9,340. Pass the entries required to rectify the following errors and state any difference that may be drawn.

(*a*) A Sales Invoice for Rs. 1,000 for goods sold on credit to Lele was entered in the Purchases Book.

(*b*) Goods bought on credit from Ram Lal for Rs. 4,500 were wrongly debited to his account as Rs. 5,400.

(*c*) A Cash Discount of Rs. 50 allowed to G. Gupta remained unposted to his account in the Ledger from the Cash Book.

(*d*) The Sales Book for the month of April undercast by Rs. 100.

(*e*) Rs. 460 paid for repairs to Building was debited to Building Account as Rs. 640.

(*f*) Purchase of Rs. 600 from Gopi & Co. was entered in the Purchase Returns Book. However, the account of Gopi & Co. stands credited by the account.

[*As the Suspense Account still shows a balance, some errors still remain untraced*]

12. Yousaf closed his books of account on September 30, 1980 inspite of a difference in the trial balance. The difference was Rs.830, the credits being short; it was carried forward in a Suspense Account. Later the following errors were located:—

(*i*) A sale of Rs.2,300 to Lala was posted to the credit of Mala.

(*ii*) The total of the Returns Inward Book for July, 1980, Rs.1,240 was not posted in the ledger.

(*iii*) Freight paid on a machine, Rs.5,600 was posted to the Freight Account as Rs.6,500.

(*iv*) While carrying forward the total in the Purchases Account to the next page, Rs.65,590 was written instead of Rs.56,950.

(*v*) A sale of machine on credit to Nanda, for Rs.9,000 was not entered in the books at all. The book value of the machine was Rs.7,500. The firm has the practice of writing off Depreciation @10% on the balance at the end of the year.

Pass journal entries to rectify the errors. Have you any comment to make?

(*Suspense A/c now Rs.* 2,870 (*Dr.*)—*all errors not yet located*; *P. & L. Adj. A/c* (*Cr.*) *Rs.*15,590)

13. Nitish closes his books on 31st December, in 1980, his books showed a difference which he transferred to the debit of his Capital Account and prepared the Profit and Loss Account and Balance Sheet. After doing so he found that the undermentioned errors had been committed in 1980:—

(*i*) A machine, book value Rs.8,200 was sold on credit to Mehtani for Rs. 7,500. The amount was posted to the credit of Mehta.

(*ii*) A cheque for Rs.2,100 was received from Kapoor and was correctly dealt with. It was, however, returned dishonoured and was then posted to the debit of Trade Expenses Account.

(*iii*) The closing stock sheets for 1980 were found to be totalled Rs.10,000 in excess.

(*iv*) The income-tax paid on behalf of the proprietor, Rs.2,370 was debited to Income-Tax Account as Rs.3,720.

(*v*) A steel cupboard was purchased for Rs.1,250; it was debited to General Expenses Account as 2,150.

Give journal entries to carry out the corrections required. How much was the difference in the books on December 31, 1980?

(*Difference*; *Rs.*12,750 (*excess credit*); *P. & L Adjustment A/c* (*Dr.*) *Rs.* 4,400)

CHAPTER VII

BILLS OF EXCHANGE OR HUNDIES

When exchange of goods takes place, either the payment will be made immediately or it will be made later. Often when goods are sold on credit, the party which has sold the goods will like that the purchaser should give a definite promise in writing to pay the amount of the goods on a certain date. Commercial practice has developed these written promises into valuable instruments of credit so much so that when such a written promise is made in proper form and is properly stamped, it is supposed that the buyer has discharged his debt and that the seller has received payment. This is because these written promises are often accepted by banks and money advanced against them. Otherwise also they can be passed on from person to person. The written promise is either in the form of bill of exchange or in the form of a promissory note.

A bill of exchange has been defined as an "instrument in writing containing an unconditional order signed by the maker directing a certain person to pay a certain sum of money only to or to the order of a certain person or to the bearer of the instrument." When such an order is accepted by writing on the face of the order itself, it becomes a valid bill of exchange. Suppose A orders B to pay Rs. 500 three months after date and B accepts this order by signing his name, then it will be a bill of exchange. The following is a specimen of a properly drawn bill of exchange :—

Delhi,
October 28, 1978.

Rs. 1,000

Stamp

Three months after date pay M/s. Mohan Lal & Sons or order the sum of Rs. 1,000 for value received.

G. Nanda

To

M/s. Gulab Singh & Co.,
Sadar Bazar,
Delhi-6.

This is known as a draft. This will be sent to M/s. Gulab Singh & Co. If the order is acceptable to them, they will write across the order as under :—

Accepted
Payable at
Punjab
National Bank,
Sadar Bazar,
Delhi.*

for M/s. Gulab Singh & Co.

Gulab Singh
Partner.

After acceptance it becomes a proper bill of exchange.

The following points should be noted :—

1. A bill of exchange must be in writing.

2. It must be dated.

3. It must contain an order to pay a certain sum of money (not a vague sum of money).

4. The money must be payable to a definite person or to his order or to the bearer.

5. The draft must be accepted for payment by the party on whom the order is made.

The party which makes the order is known as the drawer ; the party which accepts the order is known as the acceptor and the party to whom the amount has to be paid is known as the payee. The drawer and the payee can be the same.

A bill of exchange can be passed on to other persons by endorsement. Endorsement on a bill of exchange is made exactly as it is done in the case of cheques. This has already been discussed in the chapter on banks and the students are advised to refer to Chapter IV. The primary liability on the bill of exchange is that of the acceptor. If he does not pay, a holder can recover the amount from any of the previous endorsers or the drawer.

A foreign bill of exchange is generally drawn up in triplicate. Each copy is sent by separate post so that at least one copy reaches the intended party. Of course, payment will be made only on one of the copies and when such a payment is made, the other

*It is not essential to mention the name of a bank.

copies become useless. A foreign bill of exchange is usually drawn like the following :—

New Delhi,
October 28, 1978.

Rs. 5,000

Stamp

Ninety days after sight of this First of Exchange (Second and third of the same tenor and date being unpaid), pay to the order of M/s Ghosh and Sons, London, the sum of Rs. 5,000 only, value received.

Wallis & Sons.

To

M/s. Black & White,
Hardsworth, Birmingham, U.K.

Section 12 of the Negotiable Instruments Act provides that all instruments which are not inland are foreign. The following are examples of foreign bills :—

1. A bill drawn in India on a person resident outside India and made payable outside India.
2. A bill drawn outside India on a person resident outside India.
3. A bill drawn outside India and made payable in India.
4. A bill drawn outside India and made payable outside India.

Promissory Notes.

A promissory note is an instrument in writing, not being a bank note or a currency note, containing an unconditional undertaking signed by the maker to pay a certain sum of money only to or to the order of a certain person. Under Section 31 (2) of the Reserve Bank of India Act a promissory note cannot be made payable to bearer. A promissory note has the following characteristics :—

1. It must be in writing.
2. It must contain a clear promise to pay. Mere acknowledgement of debt is not a promise.
3. The promise to pay must be unconditional. "I promise to pay Rs. 500 as soon as I can" is not an unconditional promise.
4. The promisor or maker must sign the promissory note.
5. The maker must be a certain person.
6. The payee (the person to whom payment is promised) must also be certain.

7. The sum payable must be certain. "I promise to pay Rs. 500 plus all fines" is not certain.
8. Payment must be in legal money of the country.
9. It should not be made payable to bearer.
10. It should be properly stamped.

Specimen of a Promissory Note :

New Delhi,
September 5, 1978.

Rs. 1,000

Three months after date we promise to pay M/s. C. Lal & Co. or order the sum of one thousand rupees with interest at six per cent per annum for value received.

Stamp

Ram Lal & Sons.

Ram Lal & Sons are the promisors while M/s. C. Lal & Co. are the payee.

Hundies. Instruments drawn in Indian languages and made payable according to the custom prevailing in the local markets are known as hundies. The practical effect of hundies is the same as that of bills of exchange and promissory notes.

Negotiability. As has already been pointed out, promissory notes and bills of exchange are readily accepted by banks and other parties. This is because for every instrument there will be at least two parties. For instance, in case of a bill of exchange, if the acceptor does not pay, the amount can be recovered from the drawer or from any of the endorsers. In the same way, in case of a promissory note, the primary liability is that of the promisor. But if it has been endorsed, the endorser is also liable to subsequent endorsees. Thus every instrument has a minimum of two parties responsible for payment. This is the reason why banks readily accept bills of exchange and advance money against them and also why other parties are willing to accept proper bills of exchange and promissory notes in discharge of their debts. The act of handing over a bill of exchange or a promissory note to another party is known as negotiation. Proper negotiation can only be made by endorsement and delivery. A person who holds the bill becomes a holder in due course if he fulfils the following three conditions :—

1. He has taken the bill without notice of defect in the title of the transferer.
2. He has taken it before the date of maturity.
3. He has taken it for a valuable consideration.

If all these three conditions are fulfilled, the holder in due course will have a good title even if the title of transferer was bad or defective. This means that a person who takes the bill in good faith, before maturity and for consideration will be entitled to recover the amount of it irrespective of any defect in the title of the previous parties. Further, when a bill of exchange or a promissory note passes through the hands of a holder in due course, it is purged of all defects and subsequent holders will also have a good title to the bill. This is another factor why bills of exchange can be readily negotiated. (The only exception to the above is that of forgery. If signatures of any of the parties are forged, then there is no negotiation or endorsement). Negotiability is the main reason why a debt is supposed to be discharged if the debtor has given a bill of exchange properly accepted. Bills of exchange have become the most reliable, useful and easy form of credit.

Date of Maturity. The date of maturity will be determined according to the tenor of the bill adding three days for grace. Thus, if on 25th May a bill is accepted for three months, it will be due for payment on 28th August, *i.e.*, 25th August plus three days. If the date of maturity falls on a holiday, the bill will be due for payment on the preceeding day.

Discounting of Bills. When the bill is taken to a bank and the necessary cash is received, the act is known as discounting. The bank will always deduct a small sum depending upon the rate of interest and the period of maturity. If, for instance. a bill for Rs. 5,000 payable after three months is discounted at 16 per cent, the amount of discount will be Rs. 200, *i.e.*, $\frac{5000\times16\times3}{100\times12}$. The student must always be careful to calculate the discount with reference to the period still to be run. If the bill has been discounted after one month of its receipt, that is to say, if the bill has to run only for two months, the discount will also be for period of two months. In that case it would be Rs.133 in the above example.

Record of Bills of Exchange and Promissory Notes. A party which receives a promissory note or receives an accepted bill of exchange will treat these as a new asset under the name of Bills Receivable. A party which issues a promissory note or accepts a bill of exchange will treat it as a new liability under the heading of Bills Payable. We shall first deal with entries in the books of the party which receives promissory notes or bills. (When we talk of bills, we include promissory notes also.)

I. On Receipt of a bill :

Bills Receivable Account Dr.

To the party irom whom
the bill has been received.

Examples. 1. A accepts a bill of exchange drawn on him by B. In the book of B the entry will be :—

Bills Receivable Account Dr.
To A.

2. A sends to B the acceptance of D. In this case also, the entry in the books of B will be :—

Bills Receivable Account Dr.
To A.

II. The person who receives the bill has three options. These are :

(*i*) He can hold the bill till maturity.
(Naturally, in this case no further entry is necessary until the date of maturity arrives) ;

(*ii*) The bill can be endorsed in favour of another party. In that case the entry will be to debit the party which now receives the bill and to credit the Bills Receivable Account. Suppose B sends to A the acceptance of C; the entry will be (in the books of B) :

A. Dr.
To Bills Receivable A/c.

(*iii*) The bill of exchange can be discounted with a bank. The bank will deduct a small sum of money as discount and pay the rest of the money to the client. In this case cash is received, the bill receivable is given up and, in the bargain, there is a small loss. The entry will, therefore, be :—

Cash Account	Dr.	(with the amount actually received.
Discount Account	Dr.	(with the amount of loss or discount)
To Bills Receivable Account		(with the amount of the bill).

III. On the date of maturity there will be two possibilities. The first is that the bill will be paid, that is to say, met or honoured. The entries for this will depend upon what was done to the bill during the period of maturity. If the bill was kept, the cash will be received by the party which originally received the bill. In his books, therefore, the entry will be :—

Cash Account Dr.

To Bills Receivable Account.

But if he has already endorsed the bill in favour of his creditor or if the bill has been discounted with the bank, he will not get the amount; it will be the creditor or the bank which will receive the money. Therefore, in these two cases, no entry will be made in the books of the party which originally received the bill.

The second possibility is that the bill will be dishonoured, that is to say, the bill will not be paid. If the bill is not honoured, the bill becomes useless and the party from whom the bill was received will be liable to pay the amount (as also the expenses incurred by the wronged party). Therefore, the following entries will be made :—

1. If the bill was kept till maturity, then—

The party giving the bill Dr.

To Bills Receivable A/c.

2. If the bill was endorsed in favour of a creditor, the entry is :

The party giving the bill Dr.

To the Creditor.

3. If the bill was discounted with a bank :

The party giving the bill Dr.

To the Bank.

Thus it will be seen that in case of dishonour, the party which gave the bill has to be debited (because it has become liable to pay the amount). The credit entry is in the Bills Receivable Account (if it was retained) or the creditor or the bank (if it was endorsed in their favour).

Noting Charges. It is necessary that the fact of dishonour and the causes of dishonour should be established. If the acceptor can prove that the bill was not properly presented to him for payment, he may escape liability. Therefore, if there is dishonour or fear of dishonour, the bill will be given to a public official known as "notary public". These officials present the bills for payment and if the money is received, they will hand over the money to the original party. But if the bill is dishonoured, they will note the fact of dishonour and the reasons given and give the bill back to their client. For this service they charge a small fee. This fee is known as noting charges. The amount of noting charges is recoverable from the party which is responsible for dishonour.

Suppose X received from Y a bill for Rs. 1,000. On maturity the bill is dishonoured and Rs. 10 is paid as noting charges. The entry in that case will be :—

		Rs.	Rs.
Y	... Dr.	1,010	
To Bills Receiveable A/c			1,000
To Cash			10

Suppose X had endorsed this bill in favour of Z. In that case the entry for dishonour would have been :—

Y	... Dr.	1,010	
To Z			1,010

This is because Z will claim Rs. 1,010 from X and X has the right of recovering Rs. 1,010 from Y. Similarly, if the bill has been discounted with a bank, the entry will be :—

Y	... Dr.	1,010	
To Bank Account			1,010

Renewal of a Bill. Sometimes the acceptor is unable to pay the amount and he himself moves that he should be given an extension of time. In such a case, a new bill will be drawn and the old bill will be cancelled. If this happens, entries should be passed for cancellation of the old bill. This is done exactly as already explained for dishonour. When the new bill is received, entries for receipt of bill will be repeated. These have already been given above.

Illustration Amrit sells goods worth Rs. 1,500 to Anand on 15th April, 1978. On the same date Anand accepts a bill for two months drawn on him by Amrit for the amount. Give journal entries in the books of Amrit in the following cases and show the Bills Receivabile Account.

(*a*) The bill is retained till maturity.

(*b*) The bill is endrosed in favour of Sudesh.

(*c*) The bill is immediately discounted with bank @ 16% per annuam.

Assume that the bill is met on maturity.

Solution :

Journal

Date		Particulars	L.F.	Dr.	Cr.
		All cases		Rs.	Rs.
1978 April	15	Anand ...Dr.		1,500 —	
		To Sales Account			1,500 —
		Goods sold to Anand as per invoice no...			
	15	Bills Receivable Account ...Dr.		1.500 —	
		To Anand			1,500 —
		Bill of Exchange received from Anand in settlement of his debt.			
		Case (*a*) No entry			
		Case (*b*)			
April	15	Sudesh ...Dr.		1,500 —	
		To Bills Received Account			1,500 —
		Anand's acceptance endorsed in favour of Sudesh			
		Case (*c*)			
April	15	Bank Account ...Dr.		1,460 —	
		Discount Account ...Dr.		40 —	
		To Bills Receivable Account			1,500 —
		Anand's acceptance discounted at bank @ 6% discount being $\frac{1500\times6}{100\times12}\times2=$Rs. 15.			
		On Maturity : Case (*a*)			
June	18	Cash Account ...Dr.		1,500 —	
		To Bills Receivable Account			1,500 —
		Anand's acceptance met on the due date and cash received			

Cases (*b*) & (*c*) : No entry.

Bills Receivable Account (Case a)

Dr.				Rs.					Cr. Rs.
1978 April	15	To Anand		1500	1978 April	18	By Cash		1,500

Bills Receivable Account (Case b)

				Rs.					Rs.
1978 April	15	To Anand		1500	1978 April	15	By Sudesh		1500

Bills Receivable Account (Case c)

				Rs.					Rs.
1978 April	15	To Anand		1500	1978 April	15	By Bank A/c		1,460
							By Discount A/c		40
				1,500					1,540

Illustration Ram Saran owes Rs. 2,000 to Ganpat. On 1st June, 1978 he sent his promissory note for the amount for 3 months. Assuming that the bill was dishonoured on maturity and that Rs. 10 had to be paid as noting charges, give journal entries in each of the following cases:—

(*a*) This bill is retained by Ganpat.

(*b*) It is endorsed in favour of Wahid.

(*c*) It is immediately discounted @ 5% with the bank.

Also give the accounts of Ram Saran and Bills Receivable.

Journal

Date	*All Cases*	Particulars		Dr. Rs.	Cr. Rs.
1978 June	1	Bills Receivable Account To Ram Saran Promissory note at 3 months' received from Ram Saran to settle his debt.	Dr.	2,000 —	2,000 —
Case	(*a*)	—No entry			
Case June	(*b*) 1	Wahid To Bills Receivable Account Ram Saran's acceptance endorsed in favour of Wahid.	Dr.	2,000 —	2,000 —
Case June	(*c*) 1	Bank Account Discount Account To Bills Receivable Account Ram Saran's acceptance discounted at bank @ 5%-discount being Rs. 25 *i.e.*, $2{,}000 \times \frac{3}{12} \times \frac{5}{100}$	Dr. Dr.	1,900 100	2,000 —
		On Maturity : *Case (a)*—			
Sept.	4	Ram Saran To Bills Receivable Account To Cash Account Ram Saran's acceptance dishonoured, Rs. 10 paid as noting charges.	Dr.	2,010 —	2,000 — 10 —

				Dr.	Cr.
Case	(b)			Rs.	Rs.
Sept.	4	Ram Saran Dr. To Wahid Ram Saran's acceptance endorsed in favour of Wahid dishonoured, Wahid having had to pay Rs. 10 as noting charges.		2,010 —	2,010 —
Case	(c)				
Sept.	4	Ram Saran Dr. To Bank Account Ram Saran's acceptance discounted with bank, now dishonoured, the Bank having had to pay Rs. 10 as noting charges.		2,010 —	2,010 —

Ram Saran

Dr.				Rs.				Cr. Rs.
1978					1978			
Case	(a)							
June	1	To Balance b/d		2,000 —	June 1	By Bills Receivable A/c		2,000 —
Sept.	4	To Bills Receivable A/c	Rs. 2,000			By Balance c/d		2,010 —
		To Cash	10	2,010 —	?			
		or	Rs.					
Case	(b)	To Wahid	2,010					
		or						
Case	(c)	To Bank	2,010					
				4,010 —				4,010 —
		To Balance b/d		2,010 —				

Bills Receivable Account (Case a)

1978 June	1	To Ram Saran	2,000 —	1978 Sept. 4	By Ram Saran	2,000

Bills Receivable Account (Case b)

1978 Jnne 1	1	To Ram Saran	2,000 —	1978 June 1	By Wahid	2,000 —

Bills Receivable Account (Case c)

1978 June	1	To Ram Saran	2,000 —	1978 June 1	By Bank A/c	1,975 —
					By Discount	25 —
			2,000 —			2,000 —

Illustration Ghosh sold goods to Gupta on 1st September, 1978 for Rs. 1,600. Gupta immediately accepted a 3 months' bill. On the due date Gupta requested that the bill be renewed for a further period of 2 months. Ghosh agreed provided interest @15% was paid immediately in cash. To this Gupta was agreeable. The second bill was met on the due date. Give journal entries and ledger accounts in the books of Ghosh.

Solution

Journal

Date		Particulars		Dr. Rs.	Cr. Rs.
1978 Sept.	1	Gupta To Sales Account Sale of goods to Gupta as per invoice no......	Dr.	1,600 —	1,600 —
"	"	Bill Receivable Account To Gupta 3 months' acceptance received from Gupta for the amount due from him.	Dr.	1,600 —	1,600 —
Dec.	4	Gupta To Bill Receivable Account Gupta's acceptance cancelled because of renewal.	Dr.	1,600 —	1,600 —
"	"	Gupta To Interest Account Interest @ 15% on Rs. 1,600 due from Gupta for 2 months because of renewal of bill.	Dr.	40 —	40
"	"	Bills Receivable Account Cash Account To Gupta New acceptance for 2 months for Rs. 1,600 and cash (for interest) received from Gupta.	Dr. Dr.	1,600 — 40 —	1,640
1979 Feb.	7	Cash Account To Bills Receivable Account Cash received against Gupta's second acceptance	Dr.	1,600 —	1,600 —

Ledger Accounts

Gupta

Dr. Cr.

Date		Particulars	Rs.	Date		Particulars	Rs.
1978 Sept.	1	To Sales Account	1,600 —	1978 Sept.	1	By Bills Receivable Account	1,600 —
Dec.	4	To Bills Receivable A/c	1,600 —	Dec.	4	By Cash	40 —
		To Interest A/c	40 —	"	"	By Bills Receivable Account	1,600 —
			3,240 —				3,240 —

Bills Receivable Account

Dr.			Rs.				Cr. Rs.
1978				1978			
Sept.	1	To Gupta	1,600	Dec.	4	By Gupta	1,600
Dec.	4	To Gupta	1,600	1979			
				Feb.	7	By Cash A/c	1,600
			3,200				3,200

Sales Account

				1978			
				Sept.	4	By Gupta	1,600

Interest Account

				1978			
				Dec.	4	By Gupta	40

Cash Account

1978							
Dec.	4	To Gupta	40				
1979							
Feb.	7	To Bills Receivable Account	1,600				

Books of the Acceptor. The party which accepts a bill of exchange or signs a promissory note creates a liability for itself. The party on whose request the bill is accepted is supposed to have received satisfaction. Suppose, a bill of exchange is drawn by A on B and B accepts it. B will pass the following entry in his books :—

A Dr.

To Bills Payable A/c

The party on whose request the bill has been accepted should be debited and the Bills Payable Account should be credited. Suppose, a bill of exchange is accepted by Ali at the request of Ram but is payable to Sham. Ali will debit Ram (and not Sham) and credit Bills Payable Account.

The acceptor of the bill is not concerned with what happens to the bill during its currency. It is only on the date of maturity that the acceptor will be concerned again. If the bill is met, the entry to be passed is:—

Bills Payable Account Dr.

To Cash (or Bank) Account

One should note carefully that the party which receives the payment is not to be debited ; the debit must always be to the Bills Payable Account. Sometimes our own acceptance may be discharged by giving some body else's acceptance which may have received. In this case the entry will be :—

Bills Payable Account Dr.
To Bills Receivable Account

Suppose, our own promissory note for Rs. 5,000 in favour of Rao becomes due for payment. We persuade Rao to take the bill of exchange accepted by Nanda (this bill of exchange was received by us from him earlier). In this case the liability against Bill Payable has been discharged by giving up an asset in the form of a Bill Receivable. Therefore, the entry is:—

Bills Payable Account Dr. Rs. 5,000
To Bills Receivable Account Rs. 5,000

Dishonour. If at the date of maturity the bill is not met, it means that we become liable to the party which was originally given the bill. The old bill payable, so to say, becomes useless. This fact should now be recorded. This is done by the following entry :—

Bills Payable Account Dr.
To the party at whose request the bill was accepted.

In other words, the entry passed at the time of issuing the bill should now be reversed. Thus, if a Bill Payable issued in favour of A is presented by C and is dishonoured, the entry will be :—

Bills Payable Account Dr.
To A

As has already been pointed out, there may be charges incurred as noting charges on the dishonour of the bill. The acceptor is liable for these charges also. Hence noting charges account should be debited and the party concerned (to whom the bill was given originally) should be credited. In the above example the entry will be:—

Noting Charges Account Dr.
To A

The two entries in respect of dishonour of the bill and of noting charges can be combined as under :—

Bills Payable Account Dr.
Noting Charges Account Dr.
To A

Renewal. If we wish that our acceptance should be renewed for another period, the entries for dishonour should first be passed, because the old acceptance becomes useless. In addition, interest will have to be paid. This interest must be calculated with reference to the period for the new proposed bill. Thus if a bill for Rs. 5,000 has to be renewed for two months and if the interest to be charged is at 6% the interest will come to Rs. 50. The entry for interest is :—

Interest Account Dr.
To the party to whom the bill was given.

Illustration White accepts a bill of exchange at 3 months on 1st May, 1968 in favour of Green in settlement of the amount of Rs. 900 due to him. Green endorses the bill in favour of Black. Give journal entries and ledger accounts in the books of White in the following cases :—

(*a*) The bill is met on maturity.
(*b*) The bill is dishonoured, the noting charges being Rs. 10.
(*c*) The bill is renewed for a further period of 2 months together with interest at 16% p.a.

Solution :

Journal

Date		Particulars		Dr. Rs.		Cr. Rs.	
		All Cases					
1978 May	1	Green To Bill Payable Account Acceptance given to Green to settle amount due to him	Dr.	900	—	900	—
		(*Case a*)					
Aug.	4	Bill Payable Account To Cash Account Acceptance given to Green met.	Dr.	900	—	900	—
		(*Case b*)					
"		Bills Payable Account Noting Charges Account To Green Acceptance given to Green dishonoured, hence cancelled ; Rs. 10 credited to Green in respect of noting charges.	Dr. Dr.	900 10	— —	910	—
		(*Case c*)					
"		Bills Payable Account To Green Acceptance given to Green cancelled for purposes of renewal.	Dr.	900	—	900	—
"		Interest Account To Green Interest due to Green for 2 months @16% on Rs. 900 for renewing the bill.	Dr.	24	—	24	—

				Rs.	Rs.
Aug.	4	Green To Bills Payable Account New acceptance given to Green to settle the amount due to him.	Dr.	924 —	924 —

Note : White is not concerned with the endorsement of the bill in favour of Black. Hence he will pass no entry for this.

LEDGER ACCOUNTS

Case (a)

Green

Dr. *Cr.*

			Rs.	1978			Rs.
1978 May	4	To Bills Payable A/c	900 —			By Balance b/d	900 —

Bills Payable Account

			Rs.				Rs.
1978 Aug.	4	To Cash Account	900 —	1978 May	1	By Green	900 —

Cash Account

							Rs.
				1978 Aug.	4	By Bills Payable A/c	900 —

Case (b)

Green

Dr. *Cr.*

			Rs.	1978			Rs.
1978 May	1	To Bills Payable A/c	900 —			By Balance b/d	900 —
	?	To Balance c d	910 —	Aug.	4	By Bills Payable A/c	900 —
						By Noting Charges A/c	10 —
			1,810 —				1,810 —
						By Balance b/d	910 —

Bills Payable Account

			Rs.				Rs.
1978 Aug.	4	To Green	900 —	1978 May	1	By Green	900 —

Noting Charges Account

Dr.			Rs.					Cr. Rs.
1978 Aug.	4	To Green	10					

Case (c)

Green

			Rs.				Rs.
1978 May	1	To Bills Payable A/c	900	1978	?	By Balance b/d	900
Aug.	4	To Bills Payable A/c	924	Aug.	4	By Bills Payable A/c	900
						By Interest A/c	24
			1,824				1,824

Bills Payable Account

			Rs.				Rs.
1978 Aug.	4	To Green	900	1978 May	1	By Green	900
	?	To Balance c/d	924	Aug.	4	By Green	909
			1,824				1,824
					?	By Balance b/d	924

Interest Account

			Rs.				
1978 Aug.	4	To Green	9				

Accommodation Bills. Bills of exchange are usualy drawn to facilitate trade transactions. That is to say that bills of exchange are meant to finance actual purchase and sale of goods. But the mechanism of bills can be utilised to raise finance also. Suppose, Bhalla needs finance for three months. In that case he may persuade his friend Kohli to accept his draft. This bill of exchange will then be taken by Bhalla to his bank and get it discounted there. Thus Bhalla will be able to have the use of funds. When the three months' period draws to a close, Bhalla will send the requisite amount to Kohli and Kohli will meet the bill. Thus Bhalla is able to raise money for his use. If both Bhalla and Kohli need money, the same device can be used. Either Bhalla accepts a bill of exchange or Kohli does. In either case, the bill will be discounted with the bank and the proceeds divided between the two parties according to mutual agreement. The discounting charges must also be borne by the two parties in the same ratio in which the proceeds are divided. On the due date the acceptor will receive from the other party his share. The bill will then be met. **When bills are used for such a purpose, they are known as accommodation bills.** It should be noted that such bills in the hands of a holder in due course or subsequent endorsees are fully valid. Entries are passed in the books of the two parties exactly in the way already pointed out for ordinary bills. The only additional entry to be passed is for sending the remittance to the other party and also debiting the other party with the requisite amount of discount. The entry to be passed is : Debit the party concerned and credit Cash Account and Discount Account. The party which reeeives the amount will debit Cash Account and Discount Account and will credit the party from whom the money has been received.

Entries are passed in the books of the two parties exactly in the way already pointed out for ordinary bills. The only additional entry to be passed is for sending the remittance to the other party and also debiting the other party with the requisite amount of discount. The entry to be passed is : Debit the party concerned and credit Cash Account and Discount Account. The party which receives the amount will debit Cash Account and Discount Account and will credit the party from whom the money has been received.

Insolvency. Insolvency of a person means that he is unable to pay his liabilities. This will mean that bills accepted by him will be dishonoured. Therefore, when it is known that a person has become insolvent, entry for dishonour of his acceptance should be passed. Later something may be received from his estate. When and if an amount is received, Cash Account will be debited and the personal account of the debtor will be credited. The remaining amount will be irrecoverable and, therefore, should be written off as a bad debt. The student should be careful to calculate the amount actually received from an insolvent's estate and the amount to be written off only after preparing his account.

Illustration Rose, being in need of funds, persuaded Lily to accept his draft for Rs. 1,000 on 1st January, 1968 for 4 months. Lily agreed. The bill was discounted at 6%. On the due date Rose sent the necessary sum to Lily who met the bill. Give journal entries in the books of both the parties.

Solution :

Books of Rose

Journal

Date		Particulars		Dr. Rs.	Cr. Rs.
1978 Jan.	1	Bills Receivable Account To Lily Bill received from Lily as requested.	Dr.	1,000 —	1,000 —
	1	Bank Account Discount Account To Bills Receivable Account Lily's acceptance discounted with bank @ 15%, discount being Rs. 50, *i.e.*, 15% on Rs. 1,000 for 4 months.	Dr. Dr.	950 — 50 —	1,000 —
May	4	Lily To Bank Account Amount remitted to Lily, the amount being due to him for his acceptance.	Dr.	1,000 —	1,000 —

Books of Lily

Journal

Date		Particulars		Dr. Rs.		Cr. Rs.	
1978 Jan.	1	Rose To Bills Payable Account Amount of acceptance sent to Rose on his request.	Dr.	1.000	—	1,000	—
May	4	Bank Account To Rose Amount received from Rose against amount due from him.	Dr.	1,000	—	1,000	—
"	"	Bills Payable Account To Bank Account The acceptance to Rose met.	Dr.	1,000	—	1,000	—

Illustration Mota and Chhota were both in need of funds temporarily. On 1st April 1978 Mota accepted Chhota's draft for Rs. 1,500 for three months. On the same date Chhota accepted a bill of exchange payable to Mota for Rs. 1,500 for three months. Both the bills were discounted at 15%. On the due date both parties met their acceptances. Give journal entries in the books of both the parties.

Solution : **Books of Mota**

Journal

Date		Particulars		Dr. Rs.		Cr. Rs.	
1978 April	1	Bills Receivable Account To Chhota Acceptance received from Chhota for Rs. 1,500 for 3 months.	Dr.	1,500	—	1,500	—
"	"	Chhota To Bills Payable Account Acceptance given to Chhota for Rs. 1,500 for 3 months.	Dr.	1,500	—	1,500	—
"	"	Bank Account Discount Account To Bills Receivable Account Chhota's acceptance discounted at 6%.	Dr. Dr.	1,425 75	— —	1,500	—
July	4	Bills Payable Account To Bank Account The acceptance given to Chhota met.	Dr.	1.500	—	1,500	—

Books of Chhota
Journal

				Dr.		Cr.	
				Rs.		Rs.	
April	1	Bills Receivable Account To Mota Mota's acceptance for Rs. 1,500 received.	Dr.	1,500	—	1,500	—
,,	,,	Mota To Bills Payable Account Acceptance given to Mota for Rs. 1,500 for 3 months.	Dr.	1,500	—	1,500	—
,,	,,	Bank Account Discount Account To Bill Receivable Account Mota's acceptance discounted at 6%.	Dr. Dr.	1,425 75	50 50	1,500	—
July	4	Bills Payable Account To Bank Account Acceptance given to Mota met.	Dr.	1,500	—	1,500	—

Illustration Mohan accepted on 1st June, 1978 Ali's draft for Rs. 2,000 at 3 months for that mutual accommodation. Ali got the bill discounted at16% and remitted half the proceeds to Mohan. On the due date Ali sent to Mohan the amount due to him and Mohan met the bill. Give journal entries in the books of both the parties.

Solution :

Books of Ali
Journal

				Dr.		Cr.	
1978				Rs.		Rs.	
June	1	Bills Receivable Account To Mohan Mohan's acceptance for Rs. 2,000 received for mutual accommodation.	Dr.	2,000	—	2,000	—
,,	,,	Bank Account Discount Account To Bills Receivable Account Mohan's acceptance discounted at16% for 3 months	Dr. Dr.	1,920 80	— —	2,000	—
,,	,,	Mohan To Bank Account To Discount Account Half the proceeds of the bill remitted to Mohan who is also debited with half the discount.	Dr.	1,000	—	960 40	— —
Sept.	4	Mohan To Bank Account The amount due to Mohan to enable him to meet the bill sent to him.	Dr.	1,000	—	1,000	—

Books of Mohan

Journal

Date		Particulars		Dr. Rs.	Cr. Rs.
1978 June	1	Ali To Bills Payable Account Acceptance given to Ali for mutual accommodation.	Dr.	2,000 —	2,000 —
,,	,,	Bank Account Discount Account To Ali Half the proceeds after discounting received from Ali who is also credited with half the discount.	Dr.	960 — 40 —	1,000 —
Sept.	4	Bank Account To Ali Amount retained by Ali from the proceeds of the bill now received from him.	Dr.	1,000 —	1,000 —
,,	,,	Bills Payable Account To Bank Account The acceptance to Ali met.	Dr.	2,000 —	2,000 —

Illustration Bose and Mitra were in need of funds. On 1st May, 1978 Bose accepted Mitra's draft for Rs. 6,000 at 3 months. Mitra got it discounted at 15% and remitted one-third of the proceeds to Bose. On the due date Mitra was not able to send the amount. Instead, he accepted Bose's bill for Rs. 4,500 at 2 months. Bose got it discounted for Rs. 4,330. Out of this Rs. 220 was sent to Mitra. Early in October Mitra became insolvent. His estate paid 40%. Give journal entries in the books of both the parties and give Mitra's account in the books of Bose.

Solution :

Books of Bose

Journal

Date		Particulars		Dr. Rs.	Cr. Rs.
1978 May	1	Mitra To Bills Payable Account Mitra's draft for Rs. 6 000 accepted for mutual accommodation.	Dr.	6,000 —	6,000 —
,,	,,	Bank Account Discount Account To Mitra One-third of the proceeds of the bill after discounting received from Mitra.	Dr. Dr.	1,925 — 75 —	2,000 —

Date		Particulars		Dr. Rs.		Cr. Rs.	
1978 Aug.	4	Bills Receivable Account	Dr.	4,500	—		
		To Mitra				4,500	—
		Acceptance received from Mitra to cover the amount due from him.					
,,	,,	Bank Account	Dr.	4,330	—		
		Discount Account	Dr.	170	—		
		To Bills Receivable Account				4,500	—
		Mitra's acceptance discounted for Rs. 4,320.					
,,	,,	Bills Payable Account	Dr.	6,000	—		
		To Bank Account				6,000	—
		Own acceptance due this day met.					
,,	,,	Mitra	Dr.	333	33		
		To Bank Account				220	—
		To Discount Account				113	33
		Rs. 280 (which is ⅔ of the amount remaining after deducting amount due from Mitra *i.e.*, 4,330 – 4,000) remitted to him. He is also charged with ⅔ of discount.					
Oct.	7	Mitra	Dr.	4,500	—		
		To Bank Account				4,500	—
		Mitra's acceptance dishonoured because of his insolvency.					
		Bank account	Dr.	1,733	33		
		Bad Debts Account	Dr.	2,600	—		
		To Mitra				4,333	33
		Amount received and bad debt written off in respect of amount due from Mitra. (*See* account below).					

Dr. Mitra Cr.

1978		Rs.		1978		Rs.	
May 1	To Bills Payable A/c	6,000	—	May 1	By Bank A/c	1,970	—
Aug. 4	To Bank A/c	220	—	,,	By Discount A/c	30	—
	To Discount	113	33	Aug. 4	By Bills Receivable Account	4,500	—
Dec. 7	To Bank A/c (Dishonour)	4,500	—	?	By Bank A/c 40% of Rs. 4,333.33 *	1,733	33
					By Bad Debts A/c 60% of Rs. 4,333.33 *	2,600	—
		10,833	33			10,833	33

*The difference of the two sides without these two entries is Rs. 4,333.33. This is the amount due from Mitra.

Books of Mitra

Journal

Date		Particulars		Dr. Rs.		Cr. Rs.	
1978 May	1	Bills Receivable Account To Bose Acceptance received from Bose for mutual accommodation.	Dr.	6,000	—	6,000	
”	”	Bank Account Discount Account To Bills Receivable Account Bose's acceptance discounted at bank at 6%.	Dr. Dr.	5,910 90	— —	6,000	—
”	”	Bose To Bank Account To Discount Account One-third of the proceeds remitted to Bose.	Dr.	2,000	—	1,970 30	— —
Aug.	4	Bose To Bills Payable Account Acceptance forwarded to Bose towards amount due to him.	Dr.	4,500	—	4,500	—
”	”	Bank Account Discount Account To Bose Amount received from and discount credited to Bose.	Dr. Dr.	220 113	— 33	333	33
Oct.	7	Bills Payable Account To Bose Acceptance to Bose dishonoured because of insolvency.	Dr.	4,500	—	4,500	—
”	?	Bose To Bank Account To Deficiency Account Amount paid (40%) and the balance credited to P. & L A/c as being unable to pay.	Dr.	4,333	33	1,733 2,600	33 —

Illustration Journalise the following in the books of Harpal :—

(i) Harpal's acceptance to Govind for Rs. 2,000 renewed at 3 months together with interest @ 9%.

(ii) Hari requests Harpal to renew his acceptance for Rs. 1,500 for two months. Harpal agrees to it provided interest is paid at 10% in cash.

(iii) Jose informs Harpal that Mike's acceptance for Rs. 1,300, endorsed in favour of Jose by Harpal, has been dishonoured, noting charges Rs. 20. Jose agrees to accept Rs. 300 in cash and an acceptance at 3 months together with interest at 12 per cent.

(iv) Harpal's own acceptance in favour of Chung for Rs. 3,100 received from Tai in settlement of his debt for the like amount.

(v) Harpal sends Henry's acceptance for Rs. 1,600 to Bun to meet his acceptance for the like amount in favour of Bun.

(vi) Harpal retires his own acceptance for Rs. 2,000 in favour of Sekiya 20 days before the due date; the agreed rate of interest is 9%

Solution :

Journal of Harpal

		Dr. Rs.	*Cr.* Rs.
(i) Bills Payable Account To Govind Cancellation of acceptance in favour of Govind for purposes of renewal.	Dr.	2,000 —	2,000 —
Interest Account To Govind Interest due to Govind @ 9% for 3 months on Rs. 2,000.	Dr.	45 —	45 —
Govind To Bills Payable Account New bill accepted in favour of Govind to cover interest and the amount of the old bill.	Dr.	2,045 —	2,045 —
(ii) Hari To Bills Receivable Account Cancellation of Hari's acceptance for purposes of renewal.	Dr.	1,500 —	1,500 —
Hari To Interest Account Interest due from Hari @ 10% for 2 months, the period of the new bill.	Dr.	25 —	25 —
Bills Receivable Account Cash To Hari Cash, Rs. 25, and new bill for Rs. 1,500 received from Hari.	Dr. Dr.	1,500 — 25 —	1,525 —
(iii) Mike To Jose Amount due to Jose because of dishonour of Mike's acceptance, including Rs. 20 for noting charges.	Dr.	1,320 —	1,320 —

Particulars		Dr. Rs.		Cr. Rs.	
Interest Account Dr. To Jose Interest due to Jose on Rs. 1,020 (Rs. 300 to be paid in cash immediately) @ 12% for 3 months.		30	60	30	60
Jose Dr. To Cash To Bills Receivable Account Cash Rs. 300 and new acceptance for Rs. 1,050.60 (the balance due to him) sent to Jose.		1,350	60	300 1,050	— 60
(iv) Bills Payable Account Dr. To Tai Receipt of own acceptance (in favour of Chung) received from Tai—acceptance stands cancelled.		3,100	—	3,100	—
(v) Bills Payable Account Dr. To Bills Receivable Account Acceptance in favour of Bun met by endorsing Henry's acceptance in favour of Bun.		1,600	—	1,600	—
(vi) Bills Payable Account Dr. To Cash To Discount Account Own acceptance retired 20 days before time discount being earned at 9% for 20 days.		2,000	—	1,990 10	— —

Note : The student should note that in questions like the above, entries for the original issue or receipt of bills should not be passed. For example in (i) there should be no entry for Harpal's acceptance of Rs. 2,000 in favour of Govind since the entry must already have been made.

Bills for Collection. When a person receives a bill of exchange he may decide to receive the total amount by keeping it till the date of maturity. But in order to ensure safety, he may send it to his bank with instructions that the bill should be retained till maturity and should be realised on that date. This does not mean discounting because the bank will not credit the client until the amount is actually realised. If the bill is sent to the bank with such instructions it is known as "bills sent for collection". It is better to make a record of this also in books by passing the following entry :—

Bank for Collection Account Dr.
To Bills Receivable Account.

When the amount is realised the entry will be :—

Bank Account Dr.
To Bank for Collection Account.

If the bill is not honoured, the entry will be :—

The party from whom the bill was received Dr.

To Bank for Collection Account.

Bills Receivable and Bills Payable Books. So far we have considered only journal entries for transactions in bills of exchange. Journal entries are quite suitable when the transactions are few. But if a firm receives a number of bills and issues a large number of bills, it is better to make a record of these in special books. Besides reducing clerical labour involved in passing journal entries, these books will also have a systematic and permanent record of all bills received and bills accepted and their subsequent disposal. The name of the book to record receipts of bills is Bills Receivable Book and the book to record issues of bills is called Bills Payable Book. The rulings are given on the next page.

Posting. The total of the Bills Receivable Book shows the total amount of bills received. This total is debited to Bills Receivable Account. The parties from whom the bills have been received will be credited with the amount shown against their names. The total of the Bills Payable Book is credited to Bills Payable Account. The parties at whose request the bills were accepted will be debited.

If a firm maintains Bills Receivable and Bills Payable Books the use of the journal will be much curtailed in respect of bill transactions. It will then be used to record only :

(*a*) endorsement of bills receivable in favour of creditors ; and

Bills Receivable Book

Serial No.	Date	From whom received	Name and Address of Acceptor	Date of Bill	Term	Date of Maturity	Where Payable	Amount Rs.	Amount P.	How Disposed of	Remarks

Bills Payable Book

Serial No.	Date	Name of Drawer	Name of Payee	Term	Date of Maturity	Where Payable	Amount Rs.	Amount P.	Remarks

(*b*) dishonour of bills receivable and bills payable (but if a bill receivable was discounted the dishonour will be recorded in the Cash Book).

Illustration Akbar's debtors and creditors on 1st January, 1978 were :

Debtors	Rs.	*Creditors*	Rs.
John	1,500	Wahid	900
Brown	1,100	Rao	1,000
Smith	900	Ram	600

He received bills from his debtors as under :

On January	10	John's acceptance for Rs. 1,500 at 3 months payable at Bank of India, Delhi (No. 101).
,, ,,	15	Acceptance of White for Rs. 1,100 dated 20th November, 1977 for 2 months sent by Brown. (Payable at Punjab National Bank, Delhi).
,, ,,	20	Smith's own acceptance for Rs. 900 at 2 months payable at the United Commercial Bank, New Delhi.

He passed on Smith's acceptance to Wahid immediately. He issued his own acceptances to Rao and Ram, both dated 16th January, 1978 at 3 months and payable at the Bank of India, New Delhi. (No. 85 & 86.)

Bill No. 102 was returned dishonoured and noting charges had to be paid, Rs. 10. The other bills were all met (including Akbar's own) through the Bank. Write up the books of Akbar.

Solution :

(For Bill Books, Cash Book and Ledger see the following pages)

Journal

1978				Rs.	Rs.
Jan.	20	Wahid Dr. To Bills Receivable A/c Smith's acceptance (No. 103) endorsed in favour of Wahid.		900	900
Jan.	20	Brown Dr. To Bills Receivable A/c White's acceptance sent by Brown (No. 102) dishonoured (Noting Charges in Cash Book).		1,100	1,100

Bills Receivable Book

Serial No.	Date	From whom Received	Acceptor	Date of Bill	Term	Date of Maturity	Where Payable	Amount Rs.	Amount P.	How Disposed of	Remarks
	1978			1978							
101	Jan. 10	John	John	Jan.10	3 months	April 13	Bank of India	1,500	—	Collected	
				1977							
102	,, 15	Brown	White	Nov.20	2 ,,	Jan. 23	Punjab National Bank	1,100	—	Dishonoured	
				1978							
103	,, 20	Smith	Smith	Jan.20	2 ,,	March 23	United Commercial Bank	900	—	Endorsed to Wahid	
							Rs.	3,500	—		

Bills Payable Book

Serial No.	Date	Name of Drawer	Payee	Term	Date of Maturity	Where Payable	Amount Rs.	P.	Remarks
	1978								
85	Jan. 16	Rao	Rao	3 months	April 19	Bank of India	1,000	—	
86	,, ,,	Ram	Ram	3 months	April 19	,,	600	—	
							1,600	—	

Cash Book

Dr. | Cr.

Date		Particulars	L.F.	Discount Rs.	Cash Rs.	Bank Rs.		Date		Particulars	L.F.	Discount Rs.	Cash Rs.		Bank Rs.	
1978 April	13	To Bills Receivable A/c (No. 101)				1,500	—	1978 Jan.	23	By Brown (Noting charges)			10	—		
								April	19	By Bills Payable A/c (No. 85)					1,000	—
								,,	,,	By Bills Payable A/c (No. 86)					600	—

Ledger Accounts

John

Date		Particulars	Folio	Amount Rs.	P.	Date		Particulars	Folio	Amount Rs.	P.
1978 Jan.	1	To Balance b/d		1,500	—	1978 Jan.	10	By Bills Receivable A/c		1,500	—

Brown

Date		Particulars	Folio	Amount Rs.	P.	Date		Particulars	Folio	Amount Rs.	P.
1978 Jan.	1	To Balance b/d		1,100	—	1978 Jan.	15	By Bills Receivable A/c		1,100	—
,,	23	To Bills Receivable A/c (Dishonour)		1,100	—	,,	31	By Balance b/d		1,110	—
	,,	To Cash (Noting charges)		10	—						
				2,210	—					1,210	—
Feb.	1	To Balance b/d		1,110	—						

Smith

Date		Particulars	Folio	Amount Rs.	P.	Date		Particulars	Folio	Amount Rs.	P.
1978 Jan.	1	To Balance b/d		900	—	1978 Jan.	20	By Bills Receivable A/c		900	—

Wahid

Date		Particulars	Folio	Amount Rs.	P.	Date		Particulars	Folio	Amount Rs.	P.
1978 Jan.	20	To Bills Receivable A/c		900	—	1978 Jan.	1	By Balance b/d		900	—

Rao

Date		Particulars	Folio	Amount Rs.	P.	Date		Particulars	Folio	Amount Rs.	P.
1978 Jan.	16	To Bills Payable A/c		1,000	—	1978 Jan.	1	By Balance b/d		1,000	—

Ram

Date		Particulars	Folio	Amount Rs.	P.	Date		Particulars	Folio	Amount Rs.	P.
1978 Jan.	16	To Bills Payable A/c		600	—	1978 Jan.	1	By Balance b/d		600	—

Bills Receivable Account

Date		Particulars	L.F.	Amount Rs.		Date		Particulars	L.F.	Amount Rs.	
1978						1978					
Jan.	31	To Sundries as per Bills Receivable Book		3,500	—	Jan.	20	By Wahid		900	—
						Jan	23	By Brown		1,100	—
						April	13	By Bank		1,500	—
				3,500	—					3,500	—

Bills Payable Account

Date		Particulars	L.F.	Amount Rs.		Date		Particulars	L.F.	Amount Rs.	
1978						1978					
April	19	To Bank		1,000	—	Jan.	31	By Sundries as per Bills Payable Book		1,600	—
	,,	To Bank		600							
				1,600						1,600	—

Exercises

1. X purchases goods from Y for Rs. 1,000 on 1st January, 1977. Y pays Rs. 500 in cash and sends his acceptance to X for the balance. The acceptance is for three months. On the due date the bill is duly met. Pass journal entries in the books of the two parties.

2. Ram owed Rs. 5,000 to Ali on 1st July, 1978. Ram satisfied this balance by sending his promissory note payable three months after date. On the due date the bill was dishonoured. Ram paid Rs. 10 as noting charges. Pass journal entries in the books of the two parties and give Ledger Accounts.

3. Rao purchased goods worth Rs. 3,000 from Krishna on 1st October, 1978. He pays Rs. 1,000 immediately in cash and sends his acceptance for three months to Krishna for the balance payable at the Bank of India Ltd. New Delhi. Krishna gets the bill discounted at six per cent per annum. On the due date the bill was met. Give journal entries in the books of the two parties.

Suppose, further, the bill was dishonoured and the noting charges were Rs. 15. What difference would this make to the entries passed by you already ?

4. E owes Rs. 2,000 to Q. He gives him three acceptances, one for Rs. 600 at two months, second for Rs. 900 at three months and the third for Rs. 500 at four months. Q endorses the first bill in favour of his creditor R and gets the second bill discounted with his banker at 9% per annum. He retains the third bill. On the date of maturity all the three bills are dishonoured. The noting charges in each case were Rs. 5. Give journal entries in the books of E and Q.

5. Black owes Rs. 1,500 to White. He sends his acceptance to White payable after three months at the Punjab National Bank, Delhi. On the due date Black requests White to renew the bill for another two months. White agrees to his request provided interest is added at 6% per annum. To this Black is agreeable. Record these transactions in the journal and ledger of both the parties.

6. On 1 January, 1979, Sood owed Rs. 600 to Ghosh. This debt was discharged by a promissory note payable after three months. On the due date Sood requested Ghosh to accept Rs. 200 in cash and a new

bill for three months for the balance together with interest at 9 per cent per annum. Ghosh agreed to this arrangement. On July 7, Sood dishonoured the second acceptance. Journalise the transactions in the books of both Sood and Ghosh.

7. Merchant sold goods worth Rs. 6,000 to Trader on 1st October, 1977. Trader discharged this debt as follows :—

(*a*) by a cheque for Rs. 1,500,

(*b*) by a bill accepted by Bhalla for Rs. 2,000 (payable on 15th November, 1978, and

(*c*) by his own acceptance for three months for the balance.

Bhalla's bill was dishonoured and noting charges of Rs. 15 had to be paid. But Trader's own acceptance was duly met. Trader issued his own acceptance for three months in favour of Merchant for the amount due in respect of Bhalla's bill together with Rs. 35 as interest. Trader retired this bill one month before the due date and received Rs. 10 as discount. Record these transactions in the books of Merchant and Trader.

8. M/s Gopi & Co. gave you the following lists of debtors and creditors on 1st January, 1979 :—

Debtors		*Creditors*	
1. M/s Munshi & Co.	Rs. 6,000	1. M/s Lall & Co.	Rs. 1,000
2. M/s Ali & Rao.	Rs. 1,500	2. Sethi & Co.	Rs. 1,500
3. M/s Krishna & Co.	Rs. 2,500	3. Kohli Bros.	Rs. 3,000
4. M/s Gupta & Co.	Rs. 900		

During the month of January 1969 the following bill transactions took place (all acceptances of M/s Gopi & Co. are payable at the Bank of India, New Delhi) :—

4 Jan. Received acceptance from Munshi & Co. for Rs. 6,000 at two months payable at the Central Bank of India, New Delhi (Bill No. 59).

4 Jan. Bill No. 59 discounted at bank at 6% discount.

6 Jan. Kohli Bros. draw a bill on us for Rs. 2,900 in full settlement. Bill returned after acceptance (No. 84).

8 Jan. M/s Krishna & Co. send acceptance of M/s Reed and Wright for Rs. 2,500. The bill is dated 15th November, 1978 and is payable after 2 months at the Chartered Bank, Delhi.

9 Jan. M/s Ali & Rao send their acceptance for the amount due payable after three months at the United Commercial Bank, Delhi.

10 Jan. Received from Gupta & Co., promissory note of date payable after two months for Rs. 850 in full settlement.

10 Jan. We endorse Ali & Rao's acceptance to M/s Sethi & Co.

18 Jan. The acceptance of M/s Reed and Wright is returned dishonoured by bank, noting charges being Rs. 20.

20 Jan. Sent own acceptance to Lall & Co. at 2 months for Rs. 1,000. Prepare Bills Receivable Book, Bills Payable Book, Cash Book, Bills Receivable and Bills Payable Accounts in the books of M/s Gopi & Co.

9. Journalise the following transactions in K. Katrak's books :—

(*i*) Katrak's acceptance to Basu for Rs. 2,500 discharged by a cash payment of Rs. 1,000 and a new Bill for the balance plus Rs. 50 for interest.

(*ii*) G. Gupta's acceptance for Rs. 4,000 which was endorsed by Katrak to M. Mehta was dishonoured. Mehta paid Rs. 20 noting charges. Bill withdrawn against cheque.

(*iii*) D. Dalal retires a Bill for Rs. 2,000 drawn on him by Katrak for Rs. 10 discount.

(iv) Katrak's acceptance to P. Patel for Rs. 5,000 discharged by M. Mody's acceptance to Katrak for a similar amount.

(v) Katrak's acceptance to S. Sen for Rs. 4,000 was discharged by a cash payment of Rs. 2,020 and a new bill for Rs. 2,000.

10. Murli draws a bill of exchange for Rs. 500 at three months on Manohar. On the same date Manohar draws on Murli a similar bill for Rs. 500. Both parties accept the bills and get the bills discounted at Bank at 5%. On the due date the bills are met. Give ledger accounts in the books of the two parties.

11. R 1 Manohar & Co. are in need of funds and they persuade M/s Sunder & Bros. to accept a bill for Rs. 5,000 at three months. The bill is duly accepted and discounted at bank @ 6% per annum. On the due date M/s Ram Manohar & Co. remit the amount to the acceptors and the bill is duly met. Pass journal entries in the books of the two parties.

12. Gupta draws a bill for Rs. 800 on Jain at three months. Jain also draws a similar bill on Gupta on the same date. Both bills are duly accepted and discounted by the two parties at their respective banks at 6%. On the due date, Jain meets his acceptance but Gupta fails to do so. Give ledger accounts in the books of the two parties.

13. Rao drew on Raghavan a bill for Rs. 6,000 at three months on 1st July, 1978. The bill was accepted by Raghavan and returned to Rao who got it discounted at his bank @6% per annum. He then remitted 1/3rd of the proceeds to Raghavan. On the due date he sent the necessary amount to Raghavan who met the bill. Give journal entries in the books of both the parties.

14. Khan accepts a bill at three months for Rs. 5,000 drawn on him by Ali. Ali gets the bill discounted at his bank at 9%. He remits half the proceeds to Khan. On the due date Ali sends his own acceptance to Khan for Rs. 2,600 at three months (extra amount to cover interest). This bill is discounted by Khan at his bank for Rs. 2,550. Ali's acceptance is dishonoured and noting charges of Rs. 20 are paid. Give ledger accounts in the books of Khan.

15. On 31st December, 1977, Varma wrote off as a bad bebt a balance of Rs. 1,000 on an account due to him by Sethia. On 30th June, 1968 Sethia paid cash Rs. 600 to Varma in full settlement of the account.

On the 1st July, Varma sold further goods to Sethia invoiced at Rs. 1,560 which Sethia paid for by a cheque Rs. 300 and a bill for Rs. 1,260 at two months. Varma discounted the bill at his bank for Rs. 1,228. This bill was not honoured when it became due and Varma was called upon to take it up and pay the noting charges of Rs. 14. The following day Sethia met his obligation with a bill at one month for the amount and paid cash for noting charges and interest at 9%. When this bill became due Sethia met it by paying cash Rs. 600 and, accepting a fresh bill at three months for Rs. 695. On 11th January, 1979 Sethia, having become insolvent, paid a composition of 50 P. in the rupee.

Journalise the above transactions in Varma's books. Also show the Bills Receivable Account.

16. X was indebted to Y for Rs. 6,000. On 1st January, 1969 he accepted a bill for the amount drawn by Y at three months. Y discounted the bill with his banker at 8% on the same date. On maturity, X failed to meet the bill and requested Y to renew it at two months by adding 9% interest to this amount. Y agreed to the proposal on X's furnishing security; whereupon X endorsed three of his customers' bills, *viz.*, Rs. 3,000 due on 17th May, 1979, Rs. 2,000 due on 28th May, 1979, and Rs. 1,100 due on 4th June, 1979. Y discounted these three bills as well as the renewed bill of X at 6% with his bankers. The first two bills were duly met but the third one and the renewed bills were dishonoured. Show X's account in Y's ledger.

17. X draws on Y, for the mutual accommodation of both, a bill for Rs. 2,000 at three months. X discounts the bill for Rs. 1,960 and remits half the proceeds to Y. On maturity, X is unable to send the amount due and, therefore, Y draws on X a bill for Rs. 2,500 which is duly accepted by X, Y discounts the bill for Rs. 2,500 and remits Rs. 200 to X. Before the bill is due for payment, X becomes insolvent. Later 30% dividend is received from his estate.

Give X's Account in Y's books and Y's Account in X's books.

X promises to subsequently pay the amount due from him. How should Y treat the amount at the time of the preparation of the Balance Sheet ?

18. Journalise the following in the books of Don :—

(i) Bob informs Don that Ray's acceptance for Rs. 3,000 has been dishonoured and that noting charges are Rs. 40. Bob accepts Rs. 1,000 cash and the balance as a bill at 3 months at interest @ 10%.

Don accepts from Ray his aceeptance at 2 months plus interest @12%.

(ii) James owes Don Rs. 3,200; he sends Don's own aceeptance in favour of Ralph for Rs. 3,160 in full settlement.

(iii) Don meets his acceptance in favour of Singh for Rs. 4,500 by endorsing John's acceptance for Rs. 4,450 in full settlement.

(iv) Roy's acceptance in favour of Don for Rs. 3,000 retired one month before the due date, interest is taken @ 6%.

CHAPTER VIII

FINAL ACCOUNTS *

The term final accounts means statements which result finally from the preparation of accounts showing the profit earned or loss suffered by the firm and the financial state of affairs of the firm at the end of the period concerned. As already stated, the statement showing the profit or loss is known as Profit and Loss Account and the statement showing the financial state of affairs is called the Balance Sheet. In this chapter we shall study the method of preparing these two vital statements. The student must realise that in every concern, big or small, the accountant will be required to prepare these statements. Therefore, those who learn Accountancy should become proficient in this. It is the trial balance that is the basis for these two statements and unless the student has mastered the preparation of the various books and ledger accounts and also of the trial balance, he will not be able to fully grasp the significance of the Profit and Loss Account and the Balance Sheet and master the technique of preparing them. Therefore, students are well advised to master the fundamental rules according to which transactions are entered in the books of various firms.

Financial Statements and their Nature

The traditional purpose of accounting is to prepare two statements—one to show up the result of operations during the period concerned and the other to portray the financial position as at the end of the period. The first is called the Income Statement or the Profit and Loss Account in case of business houses and Income and Expenditure Account in case of non-profit organisations. The second statement is called Balance Sheet. The profit and loss account (or its equivalent) should be drawn up in such a manner as to enable those who go through it carefully to have a fair idea of the results of the day to day operations (like producing goods and selling them) together with significant details. In case of a joint stock company the profit and loss account is legally required to give a true and fair view of the profit earned or loss suffered during the year.

The balance sheet, similarly, is required in case of joint stock companies to give a true and fair view of the financial position at the end of the year. It would be proper to keep the same object in mind while drawing up the balance sheets of other concerns or institutions. In other words, those who study the balance sheet should be able to judge whether the firm or institution is financially sound or not.

The profit and loss account gives information about (1) the revenues or incomes earned and other gains made by the concern and (2) moneys spent to earn the revenues or incomes and other losses that may have been suffered. The difference between (1) and (2) is profit, if (1) is bigger, or loss in the other case. The balance sheet records on one side what the firm (or institution) possesses, called assets. Assets may be convertible into cash or they may enable the firm to carry on its work (for example patents which per-

*See also Ch, XIII, page 534 onwards.

mit goods of a certain type to be produced) or the firm may enjoy some benefit without further payment (like insurance premium relating to the next year). On the other side is recorded the sources from which the necessary funds have been derived contribution by the proprietors (capital) and loans raised and credit received from outsiders. The balance sheet may also be looked upon as indicating the total of the resources placed at the disposal of the firm and then showing how the resources have been utilised.

It should be noted that a firm's financial position is bound to be affected by the results of its operations—a firm which suffers a loss must find itself in a less fortunate position than previously and *vice versa.* The two statements therefore are interlinked—the balance sheet portrays the financial position while the profit and loss account supplies much, though not all, of the exp anation of the causes leading to the change in the financial position.[1] This connection will also be clear from a discussion of the basic principle governing the preparation of the two statements. The principle is called "Matching Principle".

Matching Principle. According to this principle, the revenues and the relevant expenses incurred should be correlated and matched so that a complete picture is available. The implications of this principle are the following :—

(i) When an item of revenue is entered in the profit and loss account, all the expenses incurred (whether paid for in cash or not) should be set down on the expenses side.

(ii) If an amount is spent but against it revenue will be earned in the next period, the amount should be carried down to the next period (and shown in the balance sheet as an asset) and then treated as an expense, next year. This applies also to a part of the amount incurred. Examples :

1. At the end of the year, some of the goods purchased remain unsold . The cost of the goods concerned should be carried forward to the next year and set against sales of the next year.
2. Machinery purchased will last for ten years. Then only one-tenth of the cost should be treated as expense and the remaining amount should be shown in the balance sheet as an asset.
3. Tax paid is partly for the next year also—the part relating to the next year should be shown as an expense only next year and not this year.

The above can be summed up by saying that of the total amount spent, that part against which benefit will be received or revenue earned in the future is shown in the balance sheet as an asset and the rest is treated as expense or loss. In this sense, assets are only unamortised expenses—amounts not yet absorbed in the profit and loss account.

(iii) If an amount of a revenue nature is received but against it service is to be rendered or goods are to be supplied in future, the amount must not be treated as revenne this year but only next year—this year it will be shown as a liability. This nature of the amounts shown in the balance sheet establishes a very significant relationship between the two statements.

Limitations. Even though the two statements are drawn up in a manner which gives an impression of exactitude, they suffer from some serious limitations. These are stated below :

(i) Though the accounting record is maintained on the basis of the concern enjoying a long life, the profit and loss account and the balance sheet have to be prepared every year. This involves many an expenditure to be apportioned over a number of years. This apportionment is done only on an estimated basis regarding which judgement may differ. Results will be different if a different basis is adopted. This is bad enough but it will be much worse if the basis is changed from year to year. This is why if there is such a change, not only should the fact of the change be disclosed but also the effect of it. If this is not done, the financial statements may become quite misleading.

(ii) With assets being only unamortised or unabsorbed costs incurred in the past, in other words assets being shown only at actual cost less whatever amounts may have been charged off in the profit and loss account, the balance sheet may not correctly show the financial position. Financial position depends upon the current economic values of assets and not upon amounts actually spent on them. In other words, to judge the financial position of a concern, it is necessary to know the present values of assets but, as position stands at present, balance sheets do not usually reflect them.

(iii) The future of a firm depends upon a number of factors, besides the assets possessed by it, which cannot be shown in the financial statements. For example, the research effort of the firm or the quality and calibre of the staff will have a deciding influence on its future prosperity but there is no accepted way as yet to put these on the balance sheet.

(*iv*) Due to the choice made by managements in respect of method of valuation of inventories, depreciation method, etc. (*i.e.*, accounting policies), the financial statements of various companies are not easily comparable. In other words, one must have knowledge of the accounting policies adopted by the management concerned.

(*v*) As a result of continuous rise in prices over a very long period, the balance sheet and the profit and loss account may not reflect present day conditions. For example, the fixed assets are stated normally at cost less depreciation but the real value of the asset is much higher; and, therefore, the depreciation charged in the profit and loss account is much less than the real amount in terms of present day prices. Inflation thus has distorted both the picture of profits and the financial position.

In view of the limitations mentioned above, one must be very careful in forming judgement on the basis of the financial statements.

One should not depend on the statements of a single or a few years—statements of a number of years should be studied systematically through proper analysis, chiefly ratio analysis.

Distinction between Capital and Revenue Items. Before we take up the task of preparing the Profit and Loss Account and the Balance Sheet, we must have a clear idea as to which items go into the former and which into the latter. Balance Sheet consists of only assets and liabilities (including sums owing to the proprietor). The financial state of affairs can only be concerned with these and the capital which the proprietor has contributed. Profit or loss can be determined only by comparing expenses and incomes. Therefore, a student should know whether an expenditure it is to be treated as an asset or as an expense ; also whether a receipt of funds is to be treated as an income or as a liability. In other words we must know which item is of capital nature and which item is of revenue nature.

An expenditure will be treated as capital in the following circumstances :—

1. If it results in the acquisition of an asset*. Clearly if, say, Rs. 50,000 is spent upon the purchases of a building, we cannot treat it as an expense or of revenue nature (unless the firm deals in, *i.e.*, purchases and sells, houses). Such an expenditure can be converted into cash, whenever the firm wishes and, therefore, it is an asset and has to be shown in the Balance Sheet. **Acquisition of a tangible thing is treated as capital expenditure.**
2. If the expenditure results in a benefit which will last for a long time. Suppose, a new firm spends a very large sum of money on advertising in order to capture a share of the market. It is no doubt an expense but, strictly speaking, this benefit will last the company for a number of years. Therefore, for that number of years the expenditure can be treated like an asset and shown in the Balance Sheet. Expenditure on trade marks or patents is of similar nature because with the use of the trade marks and patents, goods will be sold or manufactured for a fairly long time.
3. If the expenditure is incurred in putting a new asset in working condition. Suppose, a second hand machinery is purchased and a sum of money is spent upon overhauling it and then installing it. The expenditure in overhauling and installation will be capital expenditure. Similarly, if new machinery is purchased and installed the expenditure up to the point the machine is ready to work will be capital expenditure, but expenditure after it is ready to work will not be treated as capital.

Costs incurred in acquiring an asset, *e.g.*, amount paid to a lawyer while purchasing land, is capital expenditure. Even

*This does not apply to goods dealt in by the firm.

interest on loan taken to acquire an asset, *upto the date the asset is ready for use*, can be added to the cost of the asset.

4. If the expenditure results in extra capacity. Suppose, extensive alternations are made in a building so that more floor space is now available. In such a case, the amount spent can be treated as an asset and capitalised.
5. If the expenditure results in reduction of cost of production. Suppose, previously goods are produced at a cost of Rs. 20 per unit, but with various alterations made in plant and machinery, the goods can be produced at Rs. 18 per unit. In that case the expenditure involved can be properly capitalised.

All capital expenditure, to repeat, is treated as asset and shown in the Balance Sheet. It is an expenditure whose benefit will last for a long time. Usually, but not always it can be reconverted into cash.

Revenue Expenditure. Expenditure will be treated as of revenue type, that is to say it will be treated an expense, in the following cases :—

1. Expenditure to acquire raw materials or stock of finished goods. This means that the expenditure for purchase of goods or raw materials to make goods is to be treated as revenue expenditure and taken into account while determining profit.
2. Expenditure whose benefit will expire within the year. Suppose, salaries are paid to clerks. The benefit of this expenditure has already been taken and if further services are required, more salaries will have to be paid. This is clearly an expense or revenue expenditure.
3. Expenditure to maintain assets in working order. If a machine has gone out of order and if money is spent upon repairing it, the expenditure will be revenue expenditure. If alterations are made to an existing asset, only that portion of the expenditure which results in extra capacity will be capitalised and the remaining amount will have to be treated as revenue expenditure. Suppose, certain additions and renewals are made in a machine. The total cost is Rs. 10,000. The machine can produce extra 500 units now. It is estimated that if a new machine had been installed to produce 500 units, it would have cost Rs. 7,000. Therefore, out of Rs. 10,000 spent, Rs. 7,000 only can be capitalised and Rs. 3,000 will have to be treated as revenue expenditure.
4. **Expenditure incurred to defend one's right to an asset is treated as revenue.**
5. Loss of all types whether of stock-in-trade or of other current assets or of fixed assets.

All revenue expenditure has to be deducted from the income earned by the firm. That is to say, all revenue items will be taken to the Profit and Loss Account.

Deferred Revenue Expenditure. Sometimes an expenditure is of a revenue nature but the benefit of the expenditure is available for three or four years. In such a case it is fair that the total expenditure should not be debited to the Profit and Loss Account only in one year. It should be charged over the full period over which the benefit will be available. Suppose, a heavy advertisement campaign is carried out. The benefit of this campaign will be available for the next three or four years. In such a case the advertisement expenditure should be charged to the Profit and Loss Accounts of these three or four years. If this is so, the expenditure will be known as deferred revenue expenditure. Sometimes extraordinarily heavy losses are also treated as deferred revenue expenditure and charged to the Profit and Loss Accounts of three or four years. The amount which is not yet charged to the Profit and Loss Account is shown in the Balance Sheet as a sort of asset.

Capital and Revenue Receipts. Just as it is important to make a distinction between capital and revenue expenditure, it is also necessary to distinguish between capital and revenue receipts. The following rules can be observed :—

1. If stock-in-trade, that is to say, the goods in which the firm deals are sold and money is received, the receipts will be treated as revenue receipt and will be credited to the Profit and Loss Account.
2. If money is received by converting other assets into cash, then it is a capital receipt. Suppose, investments are sold and cash is received. In that case the amount received is not revenue and must not be credited to the Profit and Loss Account.
3. If an amount is borrowed or is received from the proprietor, then, clearly, it is not income and has to be shown as a liability. It is a capital receipt.
4. If, however, money is received without having to be returned again to anybody and if the benefit of that amount has already been given by the firm, it is a revenue receipt. For instance, when interest is received on investments or when rent is received for premises sublet or when commission is received for work done for others, the receipts are all revenue receipts and have to be credited to the Profit and Loss Account.
5. If an asset is sold and some profit is made on the sale of the asset, it can be treated as a revenue profit. But a better practice is to treat large profits on fixed assets as special profits or capital profits. Such special or capital profits should be put to Capital Reserve or General Reserve and should not be included in the Profit and Loss Account for calculating the year's profit.

The student is reminded that only revenue items, that is to say revenue expenditure and revenue incomes, are entered in the Profit and Loss Account. Only then can one ascertain the true profit or loss.

Illustration Which of the following expenditures are capital, revenue and deferred revenue expenditure ?

(*a*) Cost of air-conditioning the office of the general manager.
(*b*) Cost of overhauling and painting a secondhand truck newly purchased.
(*c*) Cost of the annual taxes paid and the annual insurance premium paid on the truck mentioned above.
(*d*) Wages paid to workers for installation of machinery.
(*e*) Cost of making more exits in a cinema hall under orders of the Government.
(*f*) Cost of re-decorating a cinema hall.
(*g*) Cost of putting up a gallery in a theatre hall.
(*h*) Cost of acquiring the goodwill of an old firm.
(*i*) Cost of heavy advertisements for a new product and removal of works to a new and better site.
(*j*) Temporary rooms constructed for storing raw materials for the construction of a big building.
(*k*) A machinery costing Rs. 5,000 has to be sold. It realises Rs. 3,000. A new machine is purchased for Rs. 9,000.

Solution :

(*a*) This is capital expenditure because the benefit of this expenditure will be available for a number of years. In any case, the machine which has been installed will be there and can be disposed of whenever desired.

(*b*) When a secondhand machine is purchased, all expenditure incurred in the beginning to make it fit for working is treated as capital expenditure. The value of the machine is increased by the amount spent. Therefore, the cost of overhauling and painting the truck will be capital expenditure.

(*c*) Annual taxes and annual premium paid on the truck are revenue expenditures because they do not add to the value of the truck and their benefit will be exhausted within the year.

(*d*) This is capital expenditure because it is necessary to put the machine in working condition. [See (b) above].

(*e*) Making more exits in a cinema hall does not increase the capacity of the hall and, therefore, it should be treated as revenue expenditure.

(*f*) Cost of re-decorating a cinema hall is also not capital expenditure because it does not add to the capacity of the hall. But the cost is fairly heavy and the benefit will be there for a number of years. Therefore, the cost of re-decoration should be treated as deferred revenue expenditure.

(*g*) When a new gallery is put up, it will increase the number of seats in (or capacity of) the hall. Therefore, this cost should be treated as capital expenditure.

(*h*) This is capital expenditure because the use of that firm's name will benefit the purchaser for a long time.

(*i*) This expenditure is heavy but not of capital nature because no new asset is acquired. But since the benefit of the expenditure will be available for a number of years, it should be treated as deferred revenue expenditure.

(*j*) The cost of construction of temporary rooms should be treated as capital expenditure because it is necessary for the construction of the main building. The cost of the rooms will be added to the cost of the building.

(*k*) There is a loss of Rs. 2,000 on sale of the old machinery. This is revenue loss. Rs. 9,000 has been spent on acquiring a new machinery. It is capital expenditure.

Illustration State which of the following receipts are of capital nature and of revenue nature :—

(*a*) Amount realised from sale of old furniture.

(*b*) Amount received from a debtor whose account was previously written off as bad.

(*c*) Amount of loan taken from a bank.

(*d*) Fees received from apprentices.

(*e*) Amount realised from debtors against their debts.

(*f*) Amount contributed by the proprietor to augment his capital.

(*g*) Rs. 10,000 received from sale of machinery which had cost Rs. 6,000.

Solution :

(*a*) Sale of old furniture only means conversion of one asset into another. Therefore, it is a capital receipt.

(*b*) This amount is to be treated as a revenue receipt because this amount is not refundable to the customer and the amount was previously written off as a loss.

(*c*) The loan taken from a bank is repayable and, therefore, is a liability. This is a capital receipt.

(*d*) Fees received from apprentices are not returnable and, therefore, they are an income of the firm. They are revenue receipts.

(*e*) Amount realised from debtors against their debts is not revenue ; it is merely conversion of one asset into another.

(*f*) This item is a capital receipt since it increases the firm's liability to the proprietor.

(g) Out of Rs. 10,000, Rs. 6,000 will be treated as capital receipt as conversion of one asset into another (machinery into cash); the excess amount received, Rs. 4,000, is a profit and, therefore, a revenue receipt.

Preparation of the Profit and Loss account.

The student realises that one of the aims of Accountancy is to ascertain at the end of, say, a year how much profit the firm has earned. This is done by preparing an account called Profit and Loss account. Into this account all revenue items, both incomes and expenses, are transferred. The net result is profit or loss. This account is usually divided into two portions. The first portion, known as the Trading Account, shows the broad result of trading or manufacturing. In trading concerns the sales proceeds are compared with the amount paid for purchases together with the expenses *directly* related to purchases. The difference between the amount realised by sale and the purchase price paid is gross profit ; if the purchase price is more than the sale price, there is a gross loss. In case of a manufacturing concern, the sale proceeds will be compared to the total cost incurred in making or manufacturing the goods. If the sale proceeds exceed the cost of manufacture, the difference will be gross profit, but if the sale proceeds are less than the cost of manufacture, the difference will be gross loss.*

There is one very obvious adjustment to be made before gross profit or gross loss can be ascertained, *viz.*, for stocks. Suppose, a firm has Rs. 15,000 worth of goods on hand on 1st January 1967 and it purchases goods to the extent of Rs. 80,000 during 1967. This makes a total of Rs. 95,000. Suppose, out of these goods, goods costing Rs. 20,000 are still on hand. In that case, it is quite clear that goods costing only Rs. 75,000 have been sold. If the sales amount to Rs. 91,000, the gross profit comes to Rs. 16,000, *i.e.*, Rs. 91,000 *minus* Rs. 75,000. In manufacturing concerns also this adjustment for opening and closing stocks has to be made. Here it should be noted that the figure of opening stock will be there in the books itself since the opening stock of the current year must have been the closing stock of the previous year and must have been entered in books in the current year through the opening entry. The Trial Balance usually contains an account called Opening Stock. Usually, there will be no account for closing stock in the books. This figure is to be ascertained and then entered in the books. The entry is —

Closing Stock Account Dr.

To Trading Account

The method of ascertaining the stock is discussed later in this chapter.

---

* The student should note that gross profit (or loss) is not the same thing as net profit (or loss). Far arriving at net profit (or loss) all expenses not yet taken into account, say, for running the office or advertising, must also be adjusted. See p. 164 below.

Trading Account. One can ascertain the gross profit by means of a statement which may appear as follows (figures assumed) :—

	Rs.
Opening stock of goods	35,000
Add purchases made during the year	2,00,000
Add freight inwards, etc.	10,000
Total	245,000
Less closing stock of goods	40,000
Cost of goods sold	2,05,000
Sales	2,50,000
Profit (sales *minus* cost of goods sold)	45,000

In actual practice, however, gross profit is ascertained by preparing an account which is called "Trading Account." The heading of the account is Trading Account of such and such firm for the year ended, say, 31st December 1977. The account will appear as under (using the figures already given above) :—

Trading Account of..............for the year ended...........

	Rs.			Rs.	
Opening Stock	35,000	—	Sales	2,50,000	—
Purchases	2,00,000	—	Closing Stock	40,000	—
Freight Inwards	10,000	—			
Gross Profit carried to Profit and Loss A/c	45,000	—			
	2,90,000	—		2,90,000	—

The student will have noted that except for closing stock all the figures must have been there in the ledger from which the Trial Balance is extracted.

Main Principles of preparing Trading and Profit and Loss Accounts. The Trading and Profit and Loss Accounts are prepared for a particular period, say, for six months or for a year. The following principles should be kept in mind while praparing both these accounts :—

1. Only revenue receipts, that is to say, sale proceeds and other incomes should be entered.
2. Similarly, only revenue expenses together with losses should be taken into account. Amount paid for purchase of goods or materials used in manufacture of goods will, of course, be revenue expense.
3. Expenses and incomes relating only to the period for which the accounts are being prepared should be considered. Suppose accounts are being prepared for 1977. In that case no income relating to 1976 or 1978 should be

treated as income for 1977 and entered in the Trading or Profit and Loss Account of that year. This is so even if the amount has been received. Suppose, a customer has paid an amount of Rs. 5,000 for goods to be supplied to him during 1978; it is not a sale for 1977 and must not be credited to Sales Account, even if the amount is not returnable to him. Similarly, if the firm has given a loan to an employee and if the interest for 1978 has already been received, the interest will not be treated as income for 1977. In the same way, no expense relaling to 1976 or 1978 should be debited to Trading or Profit and Loss Account even if the amount has been actually paid in 1977.

This means that while preparing the Trading and Profit and Loss Accounts for a year, suitable adjustments have to be made in order to ensure that the figure relates to that period only, not to the previous period or a future period.

4. All expenses and incomes relating to the period concerned should be considered even if the expense has not yet been paid in cash or the income has not yet been received in cash. Suppose, salaries for December 1977 are paid in January, 1978. In such a case the salaries to be debited to the Profit and Loss Account must include the amount for December also. In the same way, if a firm has yet to receive some income, it must be credited to the Profit and Loss Account. Suppose, the firm has sublet premises and the rent for the month of December 1977 has not yet been received. This amount must be credited to the Profit and Loss Account.
5. While preparing Trading and Profit and Loss Account, distinction must be made between the personal expenses of the proprietor or partners and the expenses relating to the firm. All personal expenses of the proprietor and partners must be debited to the capital or drawings accounts and must not be debited to the Trading or Profit and Loss Accounts. Similarly, if the firm has received any income but which, strictly speaking, has been earned from the private assets of the proprietor, it must be credited to the capital or drawings account.

The points discussed above will enable a firm to know its profit or loss properly. But for the proper preparation of the Balance Sheet also, the above points will be very important.

Now we shall discuss the items of the Trading Account one by one.

Opening Stock. This figure will be available from the Trial Balance. In case of trading concerns, the figure will consist of only finished goods or goods to be sold without alteration. In case of a manufacturing concern, the opening stock will consist of three parts : (*a*) stock of raw materials, (*b*) stock of partly finished goods or work-in-progress, and (*c*) stock of finished goods. Opening stock is always debited to the Trading Account. There will, of course, be no opening stock in case of a new business.

Purchases and Purchase Returns. The Purchases Account in the Trial Balance represents the total value of goods purchased. But it does not include goods received on behalf of others or on approval. Some goods may be returned to the suppliers. While returning the goods, the Purchases Account can be credited but, usually, a separate account, called Returns Outwards Account or Purchase Returns Account, is opened. This account naturally shows a credit balance. While preparing the Trading Account, the usual practice is to deduct the balance of this account from the Purchase Account and show the net figure in the Trading Account. Thus :

	Rs.	Rs
To Purchases	5,00,000	
Less Returns Outwards	20,000	4,80,000

In case of purchases, the following points should be kept in mind :—

(*a*) It is possible that some goods may have been purchased and received before the close of the year but the invoice for the goods may not have been received till after the close of the year. Care must be taken to include the amount of such items in the Purchases Book. If, however, the Purchases Book has been closed, a journal entry will be necessary, *i.e.*,

Purchases Account Dr.
To the Supplier's A/c

An alternative is to keep such goods separately and not to include them in closing stock. But this method is not desirable; it will have the effect of not stating fully the total amount due to suppliers of goods.

(*b*) Purchases Account should not include any goods received but to be sold on behalf of others, that is to say, goods received on consignment.

(*c*) Forward purchases, that is to say, goods which will be purchased in future but for which a contract has already been entered into should not be included in purchases.

Adjusted Purchases. Some firms like to show a figure of cost of goods sold for proper comparison with sales. These firms will adjust the purchases for opening and closing stocks. The entries which they pass are two :—

(*a*) Purchases Account Dr.
To Opening Stock

By this entry the opening stock account is closed and the amount of Purchase is increased.

(*b*) Closing Account Dr.
To Purchases Account

By this entry the amount of purchases is reduced and a new account, Closing Stock Account, is opened. This will appear in the Trial Balance. The student should know that this account represents an asset and should, therefore, appear only in the Balance Sheet. Adjusted Purchases Account, of course, will be transferred to the Trading Account.

Carriage, freight or cartage. All expenses that are incurred to bring the goods or materials to the firm's premises and godowns have to be debited to the Trading Account. Again, care must be taken to see that if the amount has been incurred but not yet paid, it should be brought into account. The entry is :

Carriage Inwards Account Dr.
To Expenses Payable A/c

Expenses Payable Account will be a liability and will be shown in the Balance Sheet.

Customs Duty, Octroi Duty, etc. When goods are purchased from a foreign country, import duty will be payable. When goods are received from another city, the municipal corporation may charge octroi duty. Both of these expenses increase the value of the goods or materials purchased and, therefore, should be debited to the Trading Account. If there is any amount which has yet to be paid in respect of these duties, it should be brought into books as shown in the case of carriage.

Wages. Wages paid to workers in the factory for manufacture of goods have to be debited to the Trading Account. Similarly, salaries paid to anybody working in the factory will also be debited to the Trading Account. The following points should be noted :—

(*a*) Wages for the full period have to be debited to the Trading Account. Therefore, if some of the wages have not yet been paid, the following entry will be passed :—

Wages Account Dr.
To Unpaid Wages A/c

Unpaid Wages Account is a liability.

(*b*) Wages paid for the previous period must be excluded. Suppose in 1968 wages are paid for December 1967. At the end of 1967 an Unpaid Wages Account must have been opened as shown in (*a*) above, and carried forward to the next year. While starting the books for 1968, this account will show an opening credit balance. This account will be reversed in 1968 by the following entry :—

Unpaid Wages Account Dr.
To Wages Account

By this entry the amount paid for 1967 in 1968 will be automatically deducted from the Wages Account.

(*c*) If wages are paid to workmen who are engaged on the making of some asset for the firm, the wages paid to such workers should be capitalised. Suppose, Rs. 1,000 is paid to carpenters who are making furniture for the firm for use in office. In such a case the wages to be debited to the Trading Account must be reduced by Rs. 1,000. This amount will be added to the cost of furniture. This entry is—

Furniture Account Dr.
To Wages Account

Fuel and Power. Electricity used for running machines is known as power and the amount paid for it has to be debited to the Trading Account. Similarly, if production is carried on with the help of steam, coal will be used. The cost of coal used will also be debited to the Trading Account.

Lighting. The amount spent upon electricity used for lighting the factory premises will be treated as a manufacturing expense and, therefore, debited to the Trading Account. But lighting of office should not be debited to the Trading Account.

Rent and Rates. Rent paid for the factory premises will be debited to Trading Account and so also taxes paid to municipal committees in respect of the factory buildings. Municipal taxes are often known as rates. If the office and the factory are situated in the same building, rent and rates must be apportioned between the two on the basis of the area occupied. But because the office will be using a more advantageous position, it should be charged with a correspondingly higher amount. The exact amount will, of course, differ in each case. The Trading Account will be debited only with the proportion of rent and rates relating to the factory premises. Rent is usually paid after a month is over and, therefore, it is possible that at the end of a year one month's rent may still be unpaid. This has to brought into account by the entry—

Rent Account Dr.
To Rent Outstanding Account

Municipal taxes may be paid in advance and, therefore, it is possible that the municipal taxes are paid, say, in 1967 to cover the period up to 31st March, 1968. In that case the taxes for three months, *i.e.*, from 1st January, 1968 to 31st March, 1968 will be treated as pre-paid. For preparing the Trading Account for 1967 this amount must be deducted from the amount of taxes paid. The entry is :—

Prepaid Expenses Account Dr.
To Municipal Taxes Account

Royalties. Royalty is an amount paid to a person for exploiting rights possessed by him. Suppose, a scientist has invented a new device and has taken out a patent. He may allow some industrialist to use that patent and make goods with its help. He may receive a lump sum for it. In other words he may sell the patent. In this case the industrialist will treat the patent as an asset. There is another method and that is that the scientist may receive a certain sum, say, Rs. 2 for every unit produced or for every unit sold. The payment thus made by the industrialist will be known as royalty. If the payment depends upon output, it is a manufacturing expense and should be debited to the Trading Account. But if the payment depends upon sales, it is not a manufacturing expense and will be then debited to the Profit and Loss Account.

Excise Duty. Excise duty is a tax levied by the Government. Sometimes, it is levied on production and sometimes on sales. If the tax is levied on production, it will be treated as a manufacturing expense and debited to Trading Account, but if it is levied on sales, it will be debited to the Profit and Loss Account and not to the Trading Account.

The student will note that a trader will not be concerned with all the items discussed above. In fact, he will be concerned only with purchases, carriage, import duty or octroi duty, etc. Wages, fuel and power, excise duty, royalties, etc. concern only a manufacturer and not a trader.

Sales and Sales Returns. The term sales includes only the sales of the goods in which the firm deals or the goods which are manufactured by the firm. Some customers will certainly return the goods on one pretext or another and usually a separate account called, Returns Inwards Accounts or Sales Returns Account, is opened. While preparing the Trading Account the amount of Returns Inwards is deducted from sales. The following points should be noted for arriving at a proper figure for crediting the Trading Account in respect of the sales :—

(*a*) If goods have been sold but not yet despatched, care should be exercised to see that the goods are not included in the closing stock. Such goods should be kept apart If property in the goods has not yet passed to the buyer, say, because the seller still has to carry out some operation, then it should not he treated as a sale. In such a case, the entry for sale should be reversed, debiting Sales Account and crediting the customer. The goods then will be included in stock.

(*b*) No sales out of goods received on behalf of others, that is to say, goods received on consignment, should be treated as sales. Such sales have to be credited to the account of the consignor or the principal. If such sales have been already credited to Sales Account, the following entry will be necessary :—

Sales Account Dr.

To Consignor's Account

(*c*) Sales of fixed assets or of investments or any other thing which is not usually dealt in by the firm should be excluded from sales. Thus if old furniture is sold, it must not be credited to Sales Account. If it has been the following entry will be necessary :—

Sales Account Dr.

To Furniture Account

(*d*) Sometimes goods are sold on sales or return basis, that is to say, the customer has the right to return the goods within a stipulated time without any obligation. If goods have been sold on this basis, then at the end of the trading period a list of goods which can still be returned by customers should be prepared. It will not be proper to treat the amount involved as sales. Therefore, the following entry should be made :—

Sales Account Dr,

To Customer's Account

Care must be taken to include the cost of such goods in closing stock. The goods are lying with customers but they still belong to the firm. Since they have not yet been treated as sales, they should be treated as part of closing stock.

(*e*) Forward sales, *i.e.*, sales yet to be made in future, although contracted for, should not be treated as sales.

Stock. Almost all firms ascertain the value of closing stock by means of compilation of list of materials, stores and goods actually in their possession at the close of the trading period. This work is known as taking the inventory or stock-taking. Business is suspended for two or three days and all employees are drafted in order to make a complete inventory of every thing that is lying in the godowns. These are then faired and valued. The total of the lists will be the closing stock. The lists are also known as stock sheets.

The student knows that the closing stock is credited to the Trading Account and, therefore, the figure of gross profit will depend very much upon the value placed upon this item. If the figure of closing stock is increased, say, by Rs. 50,000, the gross profit will increase accordingly and if the figure of closing stock is reduced by Rs. 40,000, then, to that extent, the gross profit will be less. Therefore, extreme care has to be taken to see that the figure of closing stock is neither inflated, *i.e.*, unnecessarily increased or deflated, *i.e.*, unnecessarily reduced. This involves two points. The first is that, while preparing stock sheets, the physical quantities must not be over-stated or under-stated. All items must be taken in stock. No fictitious items should be included and nothing should be left out. The second point is that the value placed against each item has to be the proper one.

Valuation . The principle of valuation of stock is that no profit which has not yet been earned should be taken into account but if a loss has taken place, it must be provided for. This principle is expressed by saying that stock should be valued at cost or replacement price or the expected realizable price, whichever is the lowest. Suppose, goods purchased for Rs. 10,000 are still in stock and the present replacement price is Rs. 12,000 (replacement price means the amount which will have to be paid for buying new stocks). The goods can be sold in the market for Rs. 13,000. In this case the value of the closing stock will be Rs. 10,000. Suppose, the costs were Rs. 14,000. In that case the closing stock would have been valued at Rs. 12,000.

There are two ways in which the cost or market price or replacement price can be compared. We may consider every item and each item may be taken at the lowest of the three prices mentioned above or we may value the entire stock firstly according to cost, secondly according to replacement price and thirdly according to the market price. Then the lowest of the three can be taken.

There is some difference of opinion regarding the applicability of the above principle to raw materials and stores* to be used in the factory. There is no difference of opinion as regards finished goods. Finished goods must always be valued at the lowest of the three values pointed out above. But some people maintain that since raw materials and stores are not to be sold but have to be used by the factory itself, they should always be valued at cost. There may be nothing wrong, strictly speaking, with this statement but it will be better if raw materials are valued at cost or replacement price, whichever is lower. This is because if the price of raw materials falls, the price of finished goods is also bound to fall. Therefore, there may be a loss in future. It is better to provide for such a loss now. In case of stores, it does not really matter very much whether they are valued at cost or replacement price since the amount involved is not likely to be very heavy. Therefore, it may be alright if stores are always valued at cost.

Adjusted Selling Price. In certain cases finished goods are valued at adjusted selling price, that is to say selling price minus the expenses to be incurred on making the sales. This principle is followed chiefly by plantations. A tea plantation will always value the closing stock of tea on the basis of the current auction prices of tea less the expenses to be incurred in despatching the tea from the garden to the market and also less the commission, etc., to be paid.

---

*Stores means materials which do not form part of the product but are necessary to keep machines working, such as lubricating oil, fuel oil, etc.

How to ascertain cost. In case of finished goods, cost means the cost of production. Cost of production consists of materials used, wages and expenses incurred in the factory for production*. The total cost incurred is divided by the number of units produced in order to find out the cost per unit. Suppose the following information is given :—

	Rs.
Materials	2,00,000
Wages	1,50,000
Factory Expenses	1,00,000
Total :	4,50,000

If 1,00,000 units are produced, the cost per unit comes to Rs. 4.50. If out of 1,00,000 units produced, 20,000 units are still in stock, the value of the closing stock will be Rs. 20,000 × 4.50, namely, Rs. 90,000. In case of work-in-progress, that is, partly finished goods, cost will mean the amount of materials, wages and proportionate factory expenses. Factory records will show how much has been spent by way of materials and how much by way of wages upon those units which have not yet been completed. To the total of those items a fair share of factory expenses should be added.

In case of raw materials and stores and finished goods cost may be determined in one of the following ways :—

(*a*) First in and first out (FIFO) basis. Under this method the goods are supposed to be issued out of the earliest consignments in hand. Therefore, the stock will be out of the latest consignments. The stock should accordingly be valued according to the value paid for the goods on hand. Suppose, the following purchases were made :—

on 15th October, 100 units @ Rs. 5
on 20th December, 60 units @ Rs. 6

Suppose on 20th November, 80 units were issued. The stock on hand will be 80 units. The value according to the FIFO method will be 20 units (out of the first lot) and 60 units of the second lot. Hence the value is :—

	Rs.
20 units @ Rs. 5	100
60 units @ Rs. 6	360
Total	460

(*b*) Last in first out (LIFO) basis. In case of LIFO basis, the presumption is that goods are first issued out of the latest consignment in hand. In this case, one has to find out which consignment has not yet been issued and the stock will be valued according to that. Suppose, goods were purchased as follows :—

* For this purpose, office and selling expenses should be ignored.

10th October, 50 units @ Rs. 4
15th November, 40 units @ Rs. 5
15th December, 30 units @ Rs. 5.50

Suppose, on 10th December, 30 units were issued. In this case the total stock on hand will be 90. The issue must have been made out of the lot purchased on 15th November. Therefore, the stock consists of the following :—

	Rs.
50 units purchased on 10th October @ Rs. 4	200
10 units purchased on 15th November @ Rs. 5	50
30 units purchased on 15th December @ Rs. 5.50	165
	Rs. 415

One should note that a different method leads to a different value being put on closing stock.

(*c*) Average basis. Average may be of two types, simple and weighted. In case of simple average, the prices are added and then divided by the number of items. If 100 units are purchased at Rs. 6 and 50 units are purchased at Rs. 7, the simple average will be Rs. $\frac{6 \text{ plus } 7}{2}$ or Rs. 6.50. In case of weighted average quantities are also taken into account. The price paid is multiplied by the quantity and the products are added. The total of the products is divided by the total number of units involved. In the above case, the weighted price will be :

$$\frac{100\times 6+50\times 7}{150}=\text{Rs. } 6.33.$$

Weighted average is definitely better than simple average. The weighted average arrived at will be used to evaluate the stock at hand.

(*d*) Base Stock Method. Every factory has to maintain a minimum level of stock for almost every item. It can be used sometimes, but as soon as it is used, it has to be replenished. The carrying of minimum stock, therefore, is treated like fixed assets, *i.e.*, not to be converted into cash. The base stock method of valuing stock recognises this. The minimum quantities to be carried are valued always on the price originally paid. Any excess stock is valued to current costs, *i.e.*, according to methods (*a*), (*b*) or (*c*) discussed above. Suppose, a firm has decided that it will carry a minimum stock of 50 kg. Suppose, the cost of per kg. is Rs. 3, but was Rs. 2. when the factory started working. The actual stock is 80 kg. In that case, 50 kg. will be valued at Rs. 2 and 30 kg. will be valued at Rs. 3

Stock-taking over an extended period. Since taking of stock involves good deal of work and inconvenience, some firms may extend the process over a number of days without stopping work. In such a case, the figure of stock arrived at will have to be adjusted for sales and purchases made during the period of stock-taking. From the stock (as ascertained) the purchases made during that particular period will have to be deducted. The cost of goods sold during the period will be added. The cost of sales will be arrived at by deducting gross profit from sales.

Illustration M/s Kumar & Brothers close their financial books on 31st March. Stock taking is completed over a period of two weeks. In 1978 the value of the closing stock thus arrived at was Rs. 25,000. During the two weeks (*a*) purchases made were Rs. 1,000 and (*b*) sales totalled Rs. 4,000. The firm makes a gross profit of 30% on sales. Ascertain the value of closing stock on 31st March, 1978.

Solution :

1. The closing stock includes Rs. 1,000 for goods purchased after 31st March, 1968. This should be deducted. Therefore, the closing stock is Rs. 24,000 except for the following.

2. Total sales are Rs. 4,000. Out of this 30% or Rs. 1,200 is gross profit. Rs. 2,800, therefore, is the cost of the goods sold. These goods have not been included in the closing stock and therefore should now be added. Therefore, the value of closing stock is Rs. 26,800.

Illustration. For certain reasons, stock taking in a firm was completed on 15th June, 1981 even though the books were closed on 30th June. The stock taking revealed that the stock was Rs.35,600 (cost). The following further information is available :—

(*i*) The purchases as recorded in the Purchase Book after 15-6-81 totalled Rs.8,100 but of these goods costing Rs.600 were found unsuitable and returned.

(*ii*) The Sales Book showed Sales at the total figure of Rs.12,500 for the last fortnight of June, 1981.

(*iii*) Out of certain sales made before 15-6-81, goods of the sale value of Rs.1,200 were received back from customers after the date mentioned above.

(*iv*) The stock as at 15-6-81 included goods costing Rs.5,000 received on behalf of another firm for safe keeping.

(*v*) The firm sells goods at cost plus 25% normally but the sales after 15-6-81 included one item costing Rs.500 and sold for Rs.450.

Ascertain the value of the closing stock as on June 30, 1981.

Solution :

Statement Showing Stock as on June 30, 1981.

			Rs.
Stock as on June 15, 1981			35,600
Add : Purchases since 15th June		8,100	
Less Returns		600	7,500
			43,100
Less: Goods not belonging to the firm		5,000	
Cost of goods sold : Sales	12,500		
Less Returns	1,200		
	11,300		
Less Sale below cost	450		
	10,850		
Profit Margin @ 25/125	2,170	8,680	13,680
Cost of Stock as on 30th June, 1981			29,420

Illustration, A firm has two products *A* and *B*. It analyses its costs for the two products as follows :

	A Rs.	*B* Rs.
Materials	1,20,000	1,40,000
Labour	80,000	1,00,000
Production Expenses	70,000	70,000
Administration Expenses	50,000	50,000
Advertising	30,000	30,000
	3,50,000	3,90,000

Production was 20,000 units of *A* and 30,000 units of *B*. The selling price was Rs. 20 per unit of A but the price of B was only Rs.10; agents in both cases received commission @ 5% of the selling price. The closing stock was 2,000 units and 3,000 units respectively. What is the value that should be put on the closing stock ?

Solution :

Statement Showing Valuation of Stock as on....

Cost of Production :

		A	*B*
Materials	Rs.	1,20,000	1,40,000
Labour		80,000	1,00,000
Production Expenses		70,000	70,000
Total	(*i*) Rs.	2,70,000	3,10,000
No. of units produced	(*ii*)	20,000	30,000
Cost per unit [(*i*)÷(*ii*)]	Rs.	13.50	10.33
Net Selling Price (Price less 5%)	Rs.	19.00	9.50

Lower of Cost or Selling Price	Rs.	13.50	9.50
No. of units in Stock		2,000	3,000
Value of Stock (at cost or selling price whichever is lower)	Rs.	27,000	28,500
Total Value : Rs. 55,500			

Entries to prepare the Trading Account. The student must have learnt that usually the accounts mentioned below are transferred to the Trading Account for ascertaining the gross profit :—

Stock Account, Purchases Account, Wages Account, Carriage Inwards Account, Customs Duty Account, Factory Light and Heating Account, Factory Rent Account, Sales Returns Account, Purchases Returns Account.

Of these usually the Sales Account and the Purchases Returns Account show a credit balance and the others show debit balance. As already pointed out, net purchases are shown, *i.e.*, purchases less purchase returns. Similarly, net sales are shown, *i.e.*, sales minus sales returns. Therefore, first of all, the Returns Accounts must be closed. The entries are the following :—

(1) Purchases Returns Account Dr.

To Purchase Account

This entry will close Purchases Returns Account and reduce the amount of purchase.

(2) Sales Account

To Sales Returns Account Dr.

By this entry the Sales Returns Account is closed and the amount of sales is reduced.

The other journal entries for preparing the Trading Account will be as under :—

(1) Trading Account Dr.

To Sundries—
(Opening) Stock Account, Purchases Account, Wages Account, Carriage Inwards Account, Factory Light and Heating Account, etc.

By this entry the accounts which are transferred to the debit of Trading Account are closed.

(2) Sales Account Dr.

To Trading Account

By this entry the Sales Account is closed and put on the credit side of the Trading Account.

(3) Closing Stock Account Dr.
To Trading Account

By this entry a new account, namely, Closing Stock Account is opened and is debited. This is an asset at the date of the Balance Sheet. The Trading Account is credited to show that so much of the goods purchased have not yet been sold.

(4) Trading Account Dr.
To Profit & Loss Account

With the gross profit, *i.e.*, the excess of credit side of the Trading Account over the debit side.

If, however, the debit side is bigger than the credit side, it will reveal gross loss. In that case the entry will be :—

Profit and Loss Account Dr.
To Trading Account

Illustration Desai's books show the following balances on 31st Dec., 1977.

Debits	Rs.	*Credits*	Rs.
Opening Stock	28,000	Sales	1,38,600
Purchases	73,000	Purchases Returns	2,000
Wages	25,000		
Freight Inwards	5,000		
Sales Returns	4,500		
Fuel and Power	11,000		

Stock on 31st December, 1977 was valued at Rs. 26,400. Wages for the month of December, 1977, totalling Rs. 2,300, have still to be paid. A customer returned goods worth Rs. 600 on December 30th. These have been included in stock but no entry has yet been passed. Prepare ledger accounts and the Trading Account. Also give the journal entries required.

Solution :

Journal

Date		Particulars		*Dr.* Rs.		*Cr.* Rs.	
1977 Dec.	31	Sales Returns Account To Customer's Account The entry to record return of goods by...	Dr.	600	—	600	—
	,,	Wages Account To Wages Unpaid Account The entry to bring into account the wages of Rs. 2,300, due for December, 1967.	Dr.	2,300	—	2,300	—

Date		Particulars		Rs.		Rs.	
1977 Dec.	31	Purchase Returns Account To Purchases Account Purchase Returns A/c closed by transfer to Purchases A/c	Dr.	2,000	—	2,000	—
	,,	Sales Account To Sales Returns Account Sales Returns Account closed by transfer to Sales Account.	Dr.	5,100	—	5,100	—
	,,	Trading Account To Opening Stock Account To Purchases Acccount To Wages Account To Freight Inwards Account To Fuel & Power Account Various accounts transferred to Trading Account.	Dr.	1,42,300	—	 28,000 71,000 27,300 5,000 11,000	 — — — — —
	,,	Sales Account To Trading Account Sales Account transferred to Trading Account.	Dr.	1,33,500	—	1,33,500	—
	,,	Closing Stock Account To Trading Account The entry to record Closing Stock.	Dr.	26,400	—	26,400	—
	,,	Trading Account To Profits & Loss Account Transfer of gross profit.	Dr.	17,600	—	17,600	—

Ledger Account

Opening Stock Account

Dr. *Cr.*

Date		Particulars		Rs.		Date		Particulars		Rs.	
1977 Jan.	1	To Balance b/d		28,000	—	1977 Dec.	31	By Trading A/c —transfer		28,000	—

Purchase Account

Date		Particulars		Rs.		Date		Particulars		Rs.	
1977		To Sundries		73,000	—	1977 Dec.	31	By Purchase Returns A/c		2,000	—
								By Trading A/c —transfer		71,000	—
				73,000	—					73,000	—

Wages Account

Date		Particulars		Rs.		Date		Particulars		Rs.	
1977 Dec.	31	To Sundries—		52,000	—	1977 Dec.	31	By Trading A/c —transfer		27,300	—
		To Wages Unpaid A/c		2,300							
				27,300	—					27,300	—

Freight Inwards Account

Date		Particulars		Rs.		Date		Particulars		Rs.	
1977		To Sundries		5,000	—	1977 Dec.	31	By Trading A/c —transfer		5,000	—

Sales Returns Account

Date		Particulars		Rs.		Date		Particulars		Rs.	
1977 Dec.	31	To Sundries		4,500	—	1977 Dec.		By Sales A/c —transfer		5,100	—
		To Customer		600	—						
				6,100	—					5,100	—

Fuel & Power Account

Date		Particulars		Rs.		Date		Particulars		Rs.	
1977		To Sundries		11,000	—	1977 Dec.	31	By Trading A/c —transfer		11,000	—

Sales Account

Date		Particulars		Rs.		Date		Particulars		Rs.	
1977 Dec.	31	To Sales Returns		5,100	—	1977		By Sundries		1,38,600	—
”		To Trading A/c —transfer		1,33,500	—						
				1,38,600	—					1,38,600	—

Purchase Returns Account

Date		Particulars		Rs.		Date		Particulars		Rs.	
1977 Dec.	31	To Purchase A/c —transfer		2,000	—	1977		By Sundries		2,000	—
”											

Wages Unpaid Account

Date		Particulars		Rs.		Date		Particulars		Rs.	
1977 Dec.	31	To Balance c/d		2,300	—	1977 Dec.	31	By Wages A/c		2,300	—
						1978 Jan.	1	By Balance b/d		2,300	—

Customer

			?	1977 Dec.	31	By Sales Returns Account		Rs. 600

Closing Stock Account

Dr.							Cr.
1977 Dec.	31	To Trading A/c	Rs. 26,400	1977 Dec.	31	By Balance c/d	Rs. 26,400
1978 Jan.	1	To Balance b/d	26,400				

Trading Account of Desai for the year ended December 31, 1977

	Rs.	Rs,		Rs.	Rs,
To Opening Stock		28,000	By Sales :	1,38,600	
To Purchases :	73,000		*Less* Returns	5,100	1,33,500
Less Returns	2,000	71,000	By Closing Stock		26,400
To Wages	25,000				
Add Unpaid	2,300	27,300			
To Freight Inwards		5,000			
To Fuel & Power		11,000			
To Gross Profit carried to Profit & Loss A/c		17,600			
		1,59,900			1,59,900

Profit & Loss Account

				1977 Dec.	31	By Trading A/c —transfer		Rs. 17,600

Profit and Loss Account.

The Profit and Loss Account is opened with gross profit transferred from the Trading Account (or with gross loss which will be debited to the Profit and Loss Account). After this, all expenses and losses (which have not been dealt with while preparing the Trading Account) are transferred to the debit side of the Profit and Loss

Account. If there are any incomes or gains, for instance, rent received on premises sublet, interest received on investments, discount received from suppliers, these will be credited to the Profit and Loss Account.

Illustration Prepare the Trading and Profit and Loss Accounts of Surya for 1978 from the following :—

	Dr.	Cr.
	Rs.	Rs.
Surya's Capital Account		25,000
Stock, 1st Jan., 1978	6,200	
Cash	1,700	
Sundry Debtors	9,100	
Purchases	61,300	
Sales	...	93,600
Returns Outwards	...	1,800
Returns Inwards	500	
Freight inwards	3,700	
Freight outwards	7,200	
Salaries	10,500	
Rent	6,000	
Sundry Creditors		4,000
Miscellaneous receipts (old boxes)		100
Drawings Account	6,300	
Furniture and Fittings	10,800	
Depreciation of Furniture Fittings	1,200	
	1,24,500	1,24,500

The closing stock on December 31, 1978 was valued at Rs. 7,800.

Solution :

Trading Account of Surya for the year ended December 31, 1978

		Rs.		Rs.
To Opening Stock		6,200	By Sales	93,600
To Purchases	61,300		Less Returns	500
				93,100
Less Returns	1,800	59,500	By closing Stock	7,800

	Rs.		Rs.
To Freight inwards	3,700		
To Gross Profit, carried to Profit and Loss Account	31,500		
	1,00,900		1,00,900

Profit and Loss Account of Surya for the year ended December, 31st, 1978

	Rs.		Rs.
To Freight Outwards	7,200	By Gross Profit brought down from Trading Account	31,500
To Salaries	10,500	By Miscellancous Receipts	100
To Rent	6,000		
To Depreciation of Furniture and Fittings	1,200		
To Net Profit, transferred to Capital Account	6,700		
	31,600		31,600

Note : In the trial balance, there are certain accounts which have not been dealt with while preparing the Trading and Profit and Loss Accounts. Of these, Drawings Account will be transferred to the Capital Account; it means money drawn by Surya for domestic purposes. Others are assets or liabilities and will reflect the financial position in the balance sheet.

Adjustments. The student is reminded that while preparing the Profit and Loss Account for a particular period it is absolutely essential that the expenses, losses, incomes and gains relating only to that period are considered. Similarly, *all* the expenses, losses, incomes and gains relating to that period must be considered. For example, if accounts are being prepared for 1978, then no income, gain, expense or loss relating to 1977 or 1979 should be included while preparing the Profit and Loss Account. Similarly, even if some of these items remain to be settled in case at the end of 1968, these must be included. The above means that the figure as shown by the Trial Balance should not be blindly accepted. It is one of the important duties of the accountant of any concern to adjust the figures of the Trial Balance to make them suitable for inclusion in the Profit and Loss Account. In fact, the final Trial Balance itself will be prepared only after adjusting the various ledger accounts. The student is usually asked in examination problems to make suitable adjustments for various expenses, etc. which may have been paid for in advance or which may yet remain unpaid and, similarly, for incomes

*For treatment of adjustments relating to previous year, please see Chapter XIII

which may ha. een received for the next period of which have yet to be received.

The following are some of the usual adjustments (in addition to those already dealt with) :

(a) During the year concerned a fire may have occurred and goods, say, worth Rs. 10,000 may have been destroyed. In case there was no insurance, the whole of this sum will represent a loss. In order to find out the proper gross profit, the amount should be credited to the Trading Account and debited to the Profit and Loss Account because if there were no fire, the closing stock would have been higher and, therefore, the gross profit would have been more. The entry is :—

		Rs.	Rs.
Profit and Loss Account	Dr.	10,000	
To Trading Account			10,000

In case the goods were insured and the insurance company agrees to pay the full amount, the entry is :—

Insurance Company	Dr.	10,000	
To Trading Account			10,000

In case the insurance company agrees to pay only part of the claim, say, Rs. 6,000, it is clear that the remaining Rs. 4,000 is a loss. The entry, therefore, is :—

Insurance Company	Dr.	6,000	
Profit and Loss A/c	Dr.	4,000	
To Trading A/c			10,000

(b) During 1978 rent for 1978 and 1969 amounting to Rs. 6,000 in all was paid and debited to Rent Account. It is clear that half of the rent relates to the next period and its benefit will be enjoyed then; for the current year the rent is Rs.8,000. Therefore, the entry is :—

Pre-paid Rent Account	Dr.	8,000	
To Rent Account			8,000

(c) Lease rent amounting to Rs.15,000 for two years 1978 and 1979 was debited to Buildings Account. In this case, the debit to the Buildings Account is inappropriate because lease rent is an expense. Further, the lease rent relates to two years and, therefore, half of it should be carried forward to the next year. Therefore, the entry will be :—

		Rs.	Rs.
Lease Rent Account	Dr.	7,500	
Lease Rent paid in Advance	Dr.	7,500	
To Buildings A/c			15,000

(*d*) The firm has apprentices from which fees are charged. An apprentice has paid a full two years' premium in advance amounting to Rs. 1,000. This amount has been credited to the Apprentices' Premium Account. This represents an income of the firm but only half of it relates to the current year. Hence, at the end of the current year, the following entry should be passed :—

Apprentices' Premium A/c	Dr.	500	
To Apprentices' Premium Received in Advance Account			500

By this entry the Apprentices' Premium Account will be reduced to Rs. 500 and the Apprentices Premium Received in Advance Account will be a sort of liability to be taken to the Balance Sheet.

(*e*) A delivery van standing in the books at Rs. 10,000 is exchanged for a new one. The value of the old van is taken to be Rs. 8,000 and the new van is valued at Rs. 60,000. The amount of Rs. 12,000 paid has been debited to the Delivery Van Account. It will be clear that there has been a loss of Rs. 2,000 on the exchange of the delivery van, *i.e.*, Rs. 10,000—Rs. 8,000. This loss of Rs. 2,000 should be brought into account. The entry is :—

Profit and Loss Account	Dr.	2,000	
To Delivery Van Account			2,000

(*f*) A machine for Rs. 90,000 is acquired by a firm and is installed by own workmen to whom wages totalling Rs. 500 were paid. This amount stands debited to Wages Account, whereas the purchase of machinery has not yet been recorded. The entry for this will be :—

		Rs.	Rs.
Machinery Account	Dr.	10,500	
To Supplier			10,000
To Wages Account			500

(*g*) A firm dealing in cloth incurs advertisement expenditure totalling Rs. 1,000. This amount is settled by paying Rs. 600 in cash and by giving cloth worth Rs. 400. The only entry in books is regarding the payment of cash. To record the giving of cloth worth Rs. 400, the following entry will be necessary :—

Advertisement Account	Dr.	400	
To Sales Account			400

(*h*) Books (closed on 31st December each year) show that there is a loan of Rs. 20,000 taken at 16 per cent per annum on 1st July, 1978. Books show that there is no payment of interest. The liability to pay interest for 6 months up to 31st December must be brought into account.

The interest is Rs.1600 and, therefore, the entry should be :—

Interest Account	Dr.	1600	
To Interest Outstanding Account			1600

(*i*) Wages for the month of June (books closed on 30th June), amounting to Rs.25,400 were paid on 7th July, there being no other entry in the books. It is obvious that there is the liability to pay Rs.25,400 to the workmen and the amount of wages as recorded in the books so far has to be increased by this figure. The entry is :

Wages Account	Dr.	25,400	
To Outstanding Wages Account			25,400

(*j*) Goods of the cost of Rs.2,100 have been used by the proprietor at his home. It is clear that the cost of the goods sold has to be arrived at by deducting this amount and proprietor's drawings have increased. The entry :

Drawings Account	Dr.	2,100	
To Purchases Account			2,100

(*k*) On 1st May 1980 a policy was taken out to insure the premises against fire, the premium being Rs.900. The books are closed on 31st December each year. The policy will run till 30th April 1981, i.e. protection will be available for four months in 1981 also. Hence 4 months' premium, Rs.300, relates to 1981 and the premium for 1980 is only Rs.600. The entry required is :

Prepaid Insurance A/c	Dr.	300	
To Insurance Premium A/c			300

(*l*) A publisher of a monthly magazine receives one annual subscription, Rs.60, in August 1980, the books being closed on 31st Dec. each year. Since 7 issues will have to be supplied in 1981, the subscription relating to these issues, Rs.35, should be carried forward to the next year; this year, this amount is income received in advance. The required entry is :

Subscription Account	Dr.	35	
To Subscription Received in Advance A/c			35

Some Important Items. We now consider some of the important items which usually find a place in the Profit and Loss Account.

Provision* for Bad and Doubtful Debts. Bad debt means the amount which is lost because a customer fails to pay. When a bad debt occurs, Bad Debts Account is debited and the customer's account is credited, thus closing the account of the customer. (Should the amount be later on recovered, the customer must not be credited ; it is the Bad Debts Recovered Account that will receive the credit. This account represents gain.) Properly speaking, all bad debts should be debited to the Profit and Loss Account of the year in which the sale takes place. But this is very difficult since the actual writing off of the bad debt will be in some subsequent year. This is because debts must not be written off unless all efforts have been made to recover them. To ensure that the account of the year in which the sale took place receives the debit, an estimate is made of the likely bad debts and then, for this purpose, an amount equal to the estimated bad debts is set aside. This estimate is prepared in actual practice by carefully considering the position of each individual person who owes money to the firm. Hence the entry is :

Profit and Loss Account Dr.
To Provision for Bad Debts A/c

Thus the profit will be reduced. The Provision for Bad Debts Account is carried forward to the next year. While preparing the Balance Sheet, the amount of the provision is deducted from the sundry debtors.† The student must, however, realise that the Provision for Bad Debts Account is entirely separate from the Sundry Debtors Account.

Next year, the various debts will be written off and debited to the Bad Debts Account. At the end of the year, the Bad Debts Account will be transferred to the Provision for Bad Debts Account and *not* to the Profit and Loss Account. This will reduce the provision or may even wipe it off completely. Suppose, the provision in the beginning of 1977 was Rs. 1,000 and bad debts during the year totalled Rs. 800. This means that by transferring the Bad Debts Account to the Provision of Bad Debts Account a sum of Rs. 200 will remain in the latter account. Now suppose a total provision of Rs. 900 is considered necessary. This means that we

* The term 'provision' means an estimated amount set aside to meet a loss which is likely to occur but is uncertain in amount.

† Sundry debtors means various debtors and includes the total amount owing by them.

need only Rs. 700 more to make up the provision to Rs. 900. The Profit and Loss Account, therefore, will be debited by only Rs. 700. The Provision for Bad Debts Account in this example will appear as under :—

Provision for Bad Debts Account

Dr. *Cr.*

			Rs.				Rs.
1977 Dec.	31	To Bad Debts A/c	800—	1977 Jan.	1	By Balance b/d	1,000—
		To Balance c/d (required)	900—	Dec.	31	By Profit & Loss A/c (balancing figure)	700—
			1,700—				1,700—
				1978 Jan.	1	By Balance b/d	900—

The student should note that the Profit and Loss Account will contain a debit of only Rs. 700 and not more. The Bad Debts Account is transferred to the Provision for Bad Debts Account and not to the Profit and Loss Account. In the Profit and Loss Account the entry will be made as under :—

	Rs.	Rs.
"To Provision for Bad Debts required	900	
Add Bad Debts written off	800	
	1,700	
Less Existing Provision for Bad Debts	1,000	700

Suppose, in 1978 (to continue the example), the total bad debts are only Rs. 300 and the provision required is Rs. 500. This means that out of the existing provision of Rs. 900, Rs. 600 will remain after writing off the bad debts ; and Rs. 100 will still remain after leaving the required provision. This sum of Rs. 100 represents a sort of profit and should be placed on the credit side of the Profit and Loss Account. The entry is :—

Provision of Bad Debts A/c	Dr. 100	
To Profit & Loss Account		100

In the Profit and Loss Account it will be shown as under (on the credit side) :—

	Rs.	Rs.	Rs.
"By Existing Provision for Bad Debts		900	
Less : Bad Debts written off	300		
Required Provision	500	800	100

The Provision for Bad Debts Account will appear as follows :—

Provision for Bad Debts Account

Dr. Cr.

			Rs.				Rs.
1978 Dec.	31	To Bad Debts A/c	300	1978 Jan.	1	By Balance b/d	900
	,,	To Profit & Loss A/c (balancing figure)	100				
	,,	To Balance c/d	500				
			900				900
				1979 Jan.		By Balance b/d	500

The student should remember to :—

(1) put the opening balance on the credit side ;

(2) transfer bad debts to the debit side ;

(3) put the balance required at the end of the year on the debit side (to be carried down to the next year) ; and

(4) close the Provision for Bad (or Doubtful) Debts Account by transferring the balance to the debit of P & L A/c (if the credit side is short) or to the credit of P & L A/c (if debit side is short.)

Illustration On 31st December, 1976 the debtors of M/s Nanda and Bhalla totalled Rs. 50,000. A provision of 5 per cent was made for bad and doubtful debts. In 1977 the total bad debts written off were Rs. 1,400. The debtors on 31st December, 1977, were Rs. 40,000. In 1978 the total bad debts were Rs. 600 and the debtors at the end of 1978 totalled Rs. 25.000. The provision for bad debts has been maintained at 5 per cent of the debtors.

Give the necessary journal entries. Show the Bad Debts Account and the Provision for Doubtful Debts Account for the years 1977 and 1978. Also show the entries in the Profit & Loss Account.

Solution

Journal

Date		Particulars	Dr. Rs.	Cr. Rs.
1977 Dec.	31	Provision for Doubtful Debts A/c Dr.	1,400 —	
		To Bad Debts Account		1,400 —
		Transfer of Bad Debts in 1967 to the Provision for Doubtful Debts Account.		
		Profit & Loss Account Dr.	900 —	
		To Provision for Doubtful Debts A/c		900 —
		The amount required to make up the balance in the Provision for Doubtful Debts A/c to Rs. 2,000, i.e., 5% of Rs. 40,000.		
1978 Dec.	31	Provision for Doubtful Debts A/c Dr.	600 —	
		To Bad Debts Account		600 —
		Transfer of bad debts in 1968 to the Provision for Doubtful Debts A/c.		
	”	Provision for Doubtful Debts A/c Dr.	150 —	
		To Profit and Loss Account		150 —
		Balance left in the Provision for Doubtful Debts A/c after leaving a balance of Rs. 1,250 (5% of Rs. 25,000) transferred to P & L A/c.		

(The student should see ledger accounts to understand the above entries).

Bad Debts Account

Dr. *Cr.*

Date	Particulars	Rs.	Date		Particulars	Rs.
1977	To S. Debtors	1,400—	1977 Dec.	31	By Provision for Doubtful Debts A/c —transfer	1,400—
1978	To Sundry Debtors	600—	1978 Dec.	31	By Provision for Doubtful Debts A/c —transfer	600—

Provision for Doubtful Debts Account

Dr. *Cr.*

Date		Particulars	Rs.	Date		Particulars	Rs.
1977 Dec.	31	To Bad Debts A/c—transfer	1,400	1977 Jan	1	By Balance b/d*	2,500
		To Balance c/d (5% on 40,000)	2,000	Dec.	31	By P. & L. A/c (balancing figures)	900
			3,400				3,400
				1978 Jan.	1	By Balance b/d	2,000
1978 Dec.	31	To Bad Debts A/c—transfer	600				
		To P. & L. A/c (balancing figure)	150				
		To Balance c/d (5% on Rs. 25,000)	1,250				
			2,000				2,000
				1979 Jan.	1	By Balance b/d	1,250

Profit & Loss Account (1967)

Debit side		Rs.	
To Provision for Doubtful Debts—required		2,000	
Add Bad Debts		1,400	
		3,400	
Less Existing Provision		2,500	900

Profit & Loss Account (1968)

Credit Side			
By Existing Provision for Doubtful Debts		2,000	
Less : Bad Debts	600		
Required Provision	1,250	1,850	150

* In 1976 a sum of Rs. 2,500 (5% on Rs. 50,000) must have been credited to the Provision for Doubtful Debts Account.

Illustration 31. On 31st December, 1979, a firm considered the undermentioned book debts as doubtful and decided to maintain, as a policy, a full provision to meet the possible loss :

P Rs. 450 ; Q Rs. 720 and R Rs. 340.

During 1980 Q paid the whole of the amount due from him and R was declared insolvent, his estate paying 40 P in the rupee. On 31st December, 1980, the firm found that amounts due from T and V, Rs. 610 and Rs. 520 respectively were also doubtful of recovery.

You are required to give the personal accounts and also the Provision for Doubtful Debts Account for 1980.

Solution : **Ledger Accounts**

P

Dr.				Cr.
1980		Rs.	1980	Rs.
Jan. 1	To Balance b/d	450	Dec. 31 By Balance c/d	450
1981				
Jan. 1	To Balance b/d	450		

Q

1980		Rs.		Rs.
Jan. 1	To Balance b/d	720	? By Cash	720

R

1980		Rs.		Rs.
Jan. 1	To Balance b/d	340	? By Cash (40%)	136
			By Bad Debts A/c	204
		340		340

T

		Rs.	1980	Rs.
?	To Balance b/d	610	Dec., 31 By Balance c/d	610
1981				
Jan., 1	To Balance b/d	610		

Ledger Accounts

Dr. Cr.

V

		Rs.	1980		Rs.
?	To Balance b/d	520	Dec., 31	By Balance c/d	520
1981					
Jan., 1	To Balance b/d	520			

Provision for Doubtful Debts Account

1980		Rs.	1980		Rs.
Dec., 31	To Bad Debts Account	204	Jan., 1	By Balance b/d	1,510
	To Balance c/d	1,580	Dec., 31	By Profit and Loss A/c. (Balancing figure)	274
		1,784			1,784
			1981		
			Jan., 1	By Balance b/d	1,580

Note : Provision for doubtful debts required :

	On 31.12.79	On 31.12.80
	Rs.	Rs.
In respect of amount due by ;		
P	450	450
Q	720	—
R	340	—
T		610
V		520
	1,510	1,580

Discounts allowed and provision for discounts on debtors. Discounts are usually of two types—trade discounts and cash discounts. Trade discount is allowed to those customers who place an order above a certain level. For instance, the terms may be that those who buy 10 gross at a time will receive a special discount of 5 per cent. This 5 per cent on the total sale price will be known as trade discount and will be deducted in the invoice itself. Therefore, the sales will stand reduced by the trade discount. No further treatment of trade discount is necessary.

Cash discount is allowed to those customers who pay promptly. The terms may be that those who pay their bills before the end of the month will receive a discount of 2 per cent. If a customer has purchased goods worth Rs. 1,000, he may pay only Rs. 980 *i.e.*, Rs. 1,000 less Rs. 20 (which is 2 per cent of Rs. 1,000), if he pays before the end of the month. As the student knows, in the Cash Book, Rs. 20 will be entered in the discount column on the debit side and ultimately the Discount Account will be debited with this amount. Discount allowed is a loss to the firm and will be debited to the Profit and Loss Account.

Some firms like to maintain a provision for discount just like the provision for bad debts. The treatment for provision for discounts is exactly the same as shown for the provision for bad debts. That is to say, when the provision is to be created the Profit and Loss Account will be debited and the Provision for Discounts on Debtors Account will be credited. This amount will be carried forward to the next year. In the balance sheet, the amount will be deducted from debtors. Next year the total dicounts allowed will be debited to this account. Profit and Loss Account will be debited to make the balance equal to the required balance at the end of the year.* The student must note, however, that if he is to calculate the provision for discounts he must, first of all, deduct from the debtors the provision for bad or doubtful debts. Suppose, a firm wishes to maintain a provision for discounts at 2 per cent and provision for bad debts at 5 per cent. The debtors of the firm are Rs. 40,000. In that case the provision for bad debts will be Rs. 2,000, *i.e.*, 5 per cent of Rs. 40,000 and the provision for discounts will be Rs. 760 *i.e.*, 2 per cent of Rs. 38,000 *i.e.*, Rs. 40,000—Rs. 2,000.

Illustration On 1st January, 1978, the Provision for Bad Debts Account stood at Rs. 800 and Provision for Discounts Account stood at Rs. 500. At the end of the year the debtors totalled Rs. 20,500. Of this sum Rs. 500 are bad debts and have to be written off. During the year discounts allowed to debtors totalled Rs. 730. The firm maintains a provision at 5 per cent for bad and doubtful debts and at 2 per cent as provision for discounts.

---

*The steps are absolutely the same as given on page 186 for Provision for Doubtful Debts Account.

Give the journal entries and the Provision for Bad Debts Account and Provision for Discounts Account.

Solution :

Journal

Date		Particulars		Dr. Rs.	Cr. Rs.
1978 Dec.	31	Bad Debts Account	Dr.	500 —	
		To Sundry Debtors			500 —
		Rs. 500 written off as bad.			
	,,	Provision for Bad Debts Account	Dr.	500 —	
		To Bad Debts Account			500 —
		Transfer of bad debts to the Provision for Bad Debts Account.			
	,,	Profit & Loss Account	Dr	700 —	
		To Provision for Bad Debts Account			700 —
		Amount required to make up the Provision for Bad Debts Account to Rs. 1,000, *i.e.*, 5% of Rs. 20,000.			
	,,	Provision for Discounts A/c	Dr.	730 —	
		To Discount Allowed A/c			730 —
		The discounts allowed during the year transferred to the Provision for Discounts Account.			
	,,	Profit & Loss Account	Dr.	610 —	
		To Provision for Discounts A/c			610 —
		Amount required to make up the Provision for Discounts Account to Rs. 380, *i.e.*, 2% of Rs. 19,000 *i.e.* 20,000 minus Rs. 1,000 Provision for Bad Debts.			

Provision for Bad Debts Account

Dr.			Rs.				Cr. Rs.
1978 Dec.	31	To Bad Debts A/c —transfer	500 —	1978 Jan.	1	By Balance b/d	800 —
	,,	To Balance c/d (5% on Rs. 20,000)	1,000 —	Dec.	31	By Profit & Loss A/c (balancing figure)	700 —
			1,500 —				1,500 —
				1979 Jan.	1	By Balance b/d	500 —

Provision for Discounts Account

			Rs.				Rs.
1978				1978			
Dec.	31	To Discounts Allowed A/c—transfer	730	Jan.	1	By Balance b/d	500—
		To Balance c/d (required)	380	Dec.	31	By Profit & Loss A/c (balancing figure)	610—
			1,110—				1,110—
				1979			
				Jan.	1	By Balance b/d	380—

Discounts Received and Reserve for Discount on Creditors. Discounts received may also be of two types, namely, trade discount and cash discount. Trade discount will be deducted from the invoice received from the suppliers, and the entry in the books will be made only with the net amount of the purchase. Cash discount is received for making a prompt payment. Discount received is an income and will be shown on the credit side of the Profit and Loss Account or, alternatively, it may be deducted from the discounts allowed. Some firms like to bring into record the discounts which they expect to get next year in respect of present creditors. The amount is estimated. This amont will represent a gain which is expected to arise in the following year but in respect of present creditors. Hence the entry is :

Reserve for Discount or Creditors A/c Dr.

To Profit and Loss Account

The Reserve for Discount on Creditors Account is carried forward to the next year and will show a debit balance. It will be deducted from the creditors while preparing the balance sheet. Next year, the discount received will be credited to this account. Again an estimate will be made regarding the discount likely to be earned. This much balance will be left in the Reserve for Discount on Creditors* and suitable adjustment will be made by crediting the Profit and Loss Account. Suppose, the Reserve for Discount on Creditors on 1st January, 1977 was Rs. 600. Total discounts received during the year are 900. Creditors at the end of the year are Rs. 20,000 on which a reserve of 2 per cent is required. 2 per cent on Rs. 20,000 is Rs. 400. The total credit to the Profit and Loss Account will be Rs. 700 made up as follows :—

	Rs.	Rs.
"By Reserve for Discount on Creditors	400	
Add Discounts received during the year	900	
	1,300	
Less Reserve for Discount on Creditor in the beginning of the year	600	700

* The amount will be put on the credit side of the Reserve for Discount on Creditors Account to be carried down to next year as debit balance.

The Reserve for Discount on Creditors Account will appear as under :—

Reserve for Discount on Creditors Account

Dr.			Rs.			Cr. Rs.
1977						
Jan.	1	To Balance b/d	600—	1977 Dec.	By Discounts Received A/c —transfer	900—
Dec	31	To Profit & Loss A/c (balancing figure)	700—		By Balance c/d (2% on Rs. 20,000)	400—
			1,300—			1,300—
1978						
Jan.	1	To balance b/d	400			

Two journal entries required for the above would be as follows:—

Journal

				Dr. Rs.	Cr. Rs.
1977 Dec.	31	Discounts Received A/c To Reserve for Discount on Creditors Account Transfer of discounts received to the Reserve for Discount on Creditors Account.	Dr.	900 —	900 —
	,,	Reserve for Discount on Creditors A/c To Profit & Loss Account Amount transferred to P & L A/c after leaving(a balance of Rs. 400 in the Reserve for discount on Creditors Account.	Dr.	700 —	700 —

The practice of creating a reserve for discount on creditcrs is not recommended since it means taking credit for an income yet to be earned.

Depreciation. Assets which are used by a firm lose their value due to (*a*) wear and tear, and (*b*) efflux of time. This means that if an asset is constantly used it will surely become useless after some time. But even if an asset is not used at all, after some time it may lose its value because of new inventions, changes in products and methods of production. For instance, nobody will pay much money for a car purchased in 1949 even if it has remained completely unused. Reduction of value of an asset due to these two causes is known as depreciation. This is a loss and must be debited to the Profit and Loss Account before the profit is ascertained. If it is not done, the profit will be too high and unduly inflated. An example will make it clear. Suppose, a firm earns Rs. 5,000 per year ; in ten years it will make a total profit of Rs. 50,000. But, suppose, in the meantime an asset worth Rs. 30,000 has become useless. Obviously, the firm has not earned Rs. 50,000 but only Rs. 20,000. It would have been better to write off depreciation from the very beginning by debiting the Profit and Loss Account and crediting the Asset Account. The question of depreciation will be taken up in a later chapter, but here it should be remembered that the amount of depreciation should be calculated by every firm and debited to Profit and Loss A/c. The calculation is made with reference to the time for which the asset is in use. If a firm closes the books on 31st December every year and if it purchases a machine on 1st April, then only nine months' depreciation should be charged. The entry for providing the depreciation is :

Depreciation Account .... Dr.
To Provision for Depreciation

The asset account remains unaffected; the depreciation is accummulated in a separate account.

Depreciation Account is transferred to the debit of Profit and Loss Account. In the Balance Sheet the asset will be shown at the reduced figure, showing generally the cost less accumulated depreciation.

Depreciation Account is transferred to the debit of Profit and Loss Account and the value of the asset will be reduced by the above entry. In the Balance Sheet the asset will be shown at the reduced figure.

It is no argument to say that because the asset has been properly maintained and repaired, there is no need of depreciation. The asset will depreciate in spite of repairs and maintenance. Therefore, depreciation must be provided for in any case.

Repairs and Provision for Repairs. If an asset, say, a machine goes out of order, it has to be set right. The expense involved in this surely has to be debited to the Profit and Loss Account, Repairs and Maintenance Account is, thus, transferred to the Profit and Loss Account at the figure showing the actual amount spent. There is one point to be noted here. When an asset is newly acquired, the amount spent on repairs is very small. In later years the amount will be large. Throughout its life, the asset renders the same service. Therefore, a heavy debit to the Profit and Loss Account later and a lighter charge to the Profit and Loss Account earlier is not proper. Some firms try to see that the debit in respect of repairs and maintenance is uniform throughout the life of the asset. This is done by first estimating the amount to be spent by way of repairs during the entire life of the asset and then dividing it by the number of years the asset is likely to be used. The amount thus arrived at is debited to the Profit and Loss Account every year. The credit is placed in an account named "Provision for Repairs Account". *Actual amount spent on repairs is not debited to the Profit and Loss Account ; it is debited to the provision for Repairs Account.* The balance left in this account is shown in the Balance Sheet. Suppose, a machine is acquired for Rs. 20,000. It is expected that during the ten years of its life Rs. 4,600 will be spent on it by way of repairs and maintenance. The annual average comes to Rs. 460. This amount will be debited to the Profit and Loss Account every year, crediting the Provision for Repairs Account. Actual amount of repairs will be debited to the latter account.

Illustration Y & Co., estimate that during the 15 years of the life of their plant (acquired in 1975) they will have to spend Rs. 30,000 on repairs and maintenance. The actual amounts spent on repairs during 1975, 1966, 1977, and 1978 were, respectively, Rs. 600, Rs. 900, Rs. 1,500 and 2,100. The firm desires that the debit to the Profit and Loss Account should be uniform. Give the necessary ledger accounts.

Solution :

Dr. **Repairs Account** *Cr.*

		Rs.			Rs.
1975	To Cash A/c	600	1975	By Provision for Repairs A/c—transfer	600
1976	To Cash A/c	900	1976	By do.	900
1977	To Cash A/c	1,500	1977	By do.	1,500
1978	To Cash A/c	2,100	1978	By do.	2,100

Provision for Repairs Account

		Rs.			Rs.
1975	To Repairs A/c	600	1975	By Profit & Loss Account*	2,000
	To Balance c/d	1,400			
		2,000			2,000
1976	To Repairs A/c	900	1976	By Balance b/d	1,400
	To Balance c/d	2,500		By Profit & Loss A/c	2,000
		3,400			3,400
1977	To Repairs A/c	1,500	1977	By Balance b/d	2,500
	To Balance c/d	3,000		By Profit & Loss A/c	2,000
		4,500			4,500
1978	To Repairs A/c	2,100	1978	By Balance b/d	3,000
	To Balance c/d	2,900		By Profit & Loss A/c	2,000
		5,000			5,000
				Py Balance b/d	2,900

*Rs. 30,000 divided by 15.

Profit and Loss Account

1975	To Provision for Repairs A/c		2,000	—			
1976	To do.		2,000	—			
1977	To do.		2,000	—			
1978	To do.		2,000	—			

Accidental Losses and Gains. A Profit and Loss Account should clearly show the reasons for losses and profits. A business-house may suffer a loss due to fire or due to earthquake or such other natural calamities. If an asset is destroyed and if it is insured, the amount will be recoverable from the insurance company. The difference between the book value and the amount paid by the insurance company is loss or profit and should be transferred to the Profit and Loss Account. Suppose, a building standing in the books at Rs. 50,000 is completely destroyed by fire and the insurance company agrees to pay a claim of Rs. 40,000. This means that there is a loss of Rs. 10,000. The entry to be passed is :

		Rs.	Rs.
Insurance Company	Dr.	40,000	
Loss by Fire Account	Dr.	10,000	
To Buildings Account			50,000

If the insurance company admits the claim for Rs. 65,000 there will be a profit of Rs. 15,000. The entry to be passed is :

		Rs.	Rs.
Insurance Company	Dr.	65,000	
To Building Account			50,000
To Profit & Loss A/c			15,000

The loss by the Fire Account is closed by transfer to the Profit and Loss Account

As already stated, if goods are destroyed, the cost of the goods should be ascertained and the following entry should be passed :

Loss by Fire Account Dr.
To Trading Account

By this entry the Trading Account will show proper gross profit. If any amount is recovered from the insurance company. the insurance company should be debited and Loss By Fire Account should be credited. The remaining amount in the Loss by Fire

Account should be transferred to the Profit and Loss Account. If loss by fire is very heavy, it may be better to spread the loss over three or four years. The amount not yet written off should be shown in the Balance Sheet.

Commission Payable on Profits. Students sometimes experience difficulty in calculating the commission based upon profits. If the commission is to be calculated at, say, 5 per cent on profits, then the profit should be ascertained by deducting expenses and losses from incomes and 5 per cent of that figure will be the commission payable. This should be debited to the Profit and Loss Account. Commission Payable Account will be credited and will be a liability. This will be shown in the Balance Sheet. Suppose, before calculating commission, the profit of a firm comes to Rs. 25,000 and 6 per cent commission is payable to the manager on profits. The commission will be Rs. 1,500, *i.e.*, 6 per cent of Rs. 25,000. Rs. 1,500 will be debited to the Profit and Loss Account and the profit will be reduced to Rs. 23,500.

Sometimes, the commission is payable on net profit remaining after charging the commission. In such a case, the commission should be calculated by again ascertaining the profit (deducting expenses and losses from incomes) and then multiplying this figure by

$$\frac{\text{Percentage of commission}}{\text{100 plus Percentage of commission}}$$

Suppose, the manager is entitled to 5 per cent commission on profits after charging his commission. It means that if Rs. 100 remains finally as net profit, Rs. 5 must have been paid to the manager as commission. Therefore, before charging the commission, the profit must have been Rs. 105. So the manager gets Rs. 5 out of Rs. 105 of profits before charging his commission. Out of this, Rs. 5 will be paid and Rs. 100 will remain as net profit and commission is exactly 5 per cent.

"Expenses" that do not appear in Profit and Loss Account. The word 'expense' or 'loss' relates to expenses or losses of the firm. Therefore, the following expenses should not be entered in the Profit and Loss Account:—

1. *Domestic and household expenses.* These expenses are not incurred for the purpose of earning the profits. Therefore, these must be kept out of the Profit and Loss Account. Further, if the firm has paid any expense on behalf of the proprietor, for instance, rent for the dwelling house, it must be treated as his personal drawings and should be debited to the Capital Account. Drawings Account must never be debited to the Profit and Loss Account. It is debited to the Capital Account.

2. *Income tax* paid by the proprietor on his income is also his private expense and should not be debited to the Profit and Loss Account. It should be debited to the Drawings Account or the Capital Account. (The treatment is different in case of joint stock companies).

Closing entries for preparing the Profit and Loss Account. The student has already seen the entries for preparing the Trading Account. He has noted that the gross profit was transferred from the Trading account to the Profit and Loss Account. Now the other expenses and losses will be debited to the Profit and Loss Account. The entry is :

Profit and Loss Account Dr.

To Various Expenses and Losses, such as Salaries Account, Rent Account, Repairs and Maintenance Account, Discounts Allowed Account, etc.

If there is any income or gain, it is transferred to the credit side of the Profit and Loss Account. The entry is :

The Income Account Dr.
(Such as Discounts Received Account, Interest Received Account).

To Profit and Loss Account

By these two entries the various accounts for expenses, losses, incomes and gains will be closed. Now the two sides of the Profit and Loss Account will be totalled. If the credit side is bigger, the difference will be net profit. But if the debit side is bigger, the difference will be net loss. Net profit or net loss is transferred to the Capital Account because this much money the proprietor has earned and it belongs to him. (In case of joint stock campanies this transfer is not made). The entry to transfer the net profit is :

Profit and Loss Account Dr.

To Capital Account

In case of net loss the entry is reserved.

Illustration The following trial balance of Yusuf as at 31st December, 1978 is given to you :

Debit Balances	Rs.	*Credit Balances*	Rs.
Opening Stock	15,500	Capital	60,000
Land and buildings	35,000	Loan from Mrs. Yusuf	
Machinery	50,000	@ 9%	30,000
Furniture & Fixtures	5,000	Sundry Creditors	9,600
Purchases	1,06,000	Purchase Returns	2,100
Salaries	11,000	Miscellaneous Receipts	1,200
General Expenses	2,500	Sales	2,07,300
Rent	3,000		
Postage, Telegrams, etc.	1,400		
Stationery	1,300		
Wages	26,000		
Freight on Purchases	2,800		
Carriage on Sales	4,000		
Repairs	4,500		
Sundry Debtors	30,000		
Bad Debts	600		
Cash in hand	100		
Cash at Bank	6,400		
Sales Returns	5,100		
	3,10,200		3,10,200

The follownig further information is given :

(*a*) Wages for December, 1978 amounting to Rs. 2,100 have not yet been paid.

(*b*) Included in General expenses is insurance premium, Rs. 600, paid for the year ending March 31, 1979.

(*c*) A provision for Doubtful Debts @ 5% on debtors is necessary.

(*d*) Depreciation is to be charged as follows : Land and buildings 2%, Machinery 10% and Furniture and Fixtures 15%,

(*e*) The loan from Mrs. Yusuf was taken on 1st July, 1978. Interest has not been paid yet.

(*f*) The value of stock on hand on 31st December, 1978 was Rs. 14,900.

Give the journal entries for the above noted adjustments closing entries, ledger accounts and the Trading and Profit and Loss Account.

Solution :

Adjusting Entries

Date		Particulars		Dr. Rs.	Cr. Rs.
1978 Dec.	3	Wages Account To Wages Outstanding A/c Wages due for December, 1968 (not yet paid) brought into account.	Dr.	2,100 —	2,100 —
	,,	Prepaid Insurance Account To General Expenses Account Three months' premium (1st Jan., 1979 to 31st March, 1979) creditcd to General Expenses, being prepaid.	Dr.	150 —	150 —
	,,	Profit and Loss Account To Provision for Doubtful Debts A/c Provision for doubtful debts created @ 5% of debtors, Rs. 30,000.	Dr.	1,500 —	1,500 —
	,,	Depreciation Account To Land and Buildings Account To Machinery Account To Furniture and Fixtures Account Depreciation for the year written of— Land & Buildings : 2% on Rs. 35,000 Machinery : 10% on Rs. 50,000 Furniture & Fixtures : 15% on Rs. 5,000	Dr.	6,450 —	 700 — 5,000 — 750 —
	,,	Interest Account To Mrs. Yusuf's Loan Account Six months' interest due @ 9% p.a. on Rs. 30,000.	Dr.	1,350 —	1,350 —
	,,	Closing Stock Account To Trading Account The value of closing stock brought into accounts by crediting Trading Account.	Dr.	14,900 —	14,900 —

Closing Entries

Date		Particulars		Rs.		Rs.	
1978 Dec.	31	Purchase Returns Account	Dr.	2,100	—		
		To Purchases Account				2,100	—
		Transfer of Purchase returns to Purchases Account.					
	,,	Sales Account	Dr.	5,100	—		
		To Sales Returns Account				5,100	—
		Transfer of Sales Returns to Sales Account.					
	,,	Trading Account	Dr.	1,50,300	—		
		To Opening Stock A/c				15,500	—
		To Purchases Account				1,03,900	—
		To Wages Account				28,100	—
		To Freight on Purchase A/c				2,800	—
		Transfer of the above named accounts to Trading Account (see ledger accounts below).					
	,,	Sales Account	Dr.	2,02,200	—		
		To Trading Account				2,02,200	—
		Transfer of Sales Account to Trading Account.					
	,,	Trading Account	Ds.	66,800	—		
		To Profit and Loss Account				66,800	—
		Transfer of gross profit to Profit and Loss Account					
	,,	Profit and Loss Account	Dr.	35,950	—		
		To Salaries Account				11,000	—
		To General Expenses Account				2,350	—
		To Rent Account				3,000	—
		To Postage and Telegrams Account				1,400	—
		To Stationery Account				1,300	—
		To Carriage or Sales Account				4,000	—
		To Repairs Account				4,500	—
		To Bad Debts Account				600	—
		To Depreciation Account				6,450	—
		To Interest Account				1,350	—
		Transfer of various expenses to Profit and Loss Account (see ledger accounts below).					
	,,	Miscellaneous Receipts A/c	Dr.	1,200	—		
		To Profit and Loss Account				1,200	—
		Transfer of miscellaneous receipts to the credit of P. & L. Account.					
	,,	Profit and Loss Account	Dr.	30,550	—		
		To Capital Account				30,550	—
		Transfer of net profit to the Capital Account.					

Ledger Accounts

Opening Stock Account

Date	Particulars	L.F.	Amount Rs.	Date	Particulars	L.F.	Amount Rs.
1978 Jan. 1	To Balance b/d		15,500	1978 Dec. 31	By Trading A/c —transfer		15,500

Land & Buildings Account

Date	Particulars	L.F.	Amount Rs.	Date	Particulars	L.F.	Amount Rs.
1978 Jan. 1	To Balance b/d		35,000	1978 Dec. 31	By Depreciation A/c		700
					By Balance c/d		34,300
			35,000				35,000
1979 Jan. 1	To Balance b/d		34,300				

Machinery Account

Date	Particulars	L.F.	Amount Rs.	Date	Particulars	L.F.	Amount Rs.
1978 Jan. 1	To Balance b/d		50,000	1978 Dec. 31	By Depreciation A/c		5,000
					By Balance c/d		45,000
			50,000				50,000
1979 Jan. 1	To Balance b/d		45,000				

Furniture & Fixtures Account

Date	Particulars	L.F.	Amount Rs.	Date	Particulars	L.F.	Amount Rs.
1978 Jan.	To Balance b/d		5,000	1973 Dec. 31	By Depreciation A/c		750
					By Balance c/d		4,250
			5,000				5,000
1979 Jan.	To Balance b/d		4,250				

Purchases Account

Date	Particulars	L.F.	Amount Rs.	Date	Particulars	L.F.	Amount Rs.
1978	To Sundries		1,06,000	1978 Dec. 31	By Purchase Returns A/c		2,100
					By Trading A/c—transfer		1,03,900
			1,06,000				1,06,000

Salaries Account

Date	Particulars	L.F.	Amount Rs.	Date	Particulars	L.F.	Amount Rs.
1978	To Sundries		11,000	1978 Dec. 31	By Profit & Loss A/c—transfer		11,000

General Expenses Account

Date	Particulars	L.F.	Amount Rs.	Date	Particulars	L.F.	Amount Rs.
1978	To Sundries		2,500 —	1978 Dec. 31	By Prepaid Insurance A/c		150 —
					By Profit & Loss A/c—transfer		2,350 —
			2,500 —				2,500 —

Rent Account

Date	Particulars	L.F.	Amount Rs.	Date	Particulars	L.F.	Amount Rs.
1978	To Sundries		3,000 -	1978 Dec. 31	By Profit & Loss A/c—transfer		3,000 —

Postage & Telegrams Account

Date	Particulars	L.F.	Amount Rs.	Date	Particulars	L.F.	Amount Rs.
1978	To Sundries		1,400 —	1978 Dec. 31	By Profit & Loss A/c—transfer		1,400 —

Stationery Account

Date	Particulars	L.F.	Amount Rs.	Date	Particulars	L.F.	Amount Rs.
1978	To Sundries		1,300 —	1978 Dec. 31	By Profit & Loss A/c—transfer		1,300 —

Wages Account

Date	Particulars	L.F.	Amount Rs.	Date	Particulars	L.F.	Amount Rs.
1978	To Sundries		26,000 —	1978 Dec. 31	By Trading A/c —transfer		28,100 —
Dec. 31	To Wages Outstanding Account		2,100 —				
			28,100 -				28,100 —

Freight on Purchases on Account

Date	Particulars	L.F.	Amount Rs.	Date	Particulars	L.F.	Amount Rs.
1978	To Sundries		2,800 —	1978 Dec. 31	By Trading A/c —transfer		2,800 —

Carriage on Sales Account

Date		Particulars	L.F.	Amount Rs.	Date		Particulars	L.F.	Amount Rs.
1978		To Sundries		4,000 —	1978 Dec.	31	By Profit & Loss A/c—transfer		4,000 —

Repairs Account

Date		Particulars	L.F.	Amount Rs.	Date		Particulars	L.F.	Amount Rs.
1978		To Sundries		4,500 —	1978 Dec.	31	By Profit & Loss A/c—transfer		4,500 —

Sundry Debtors Account

Date		Particulars	L.F.	Amount Rs.	Date		Particulars	L.F.	Amount Rs.
1978		To Sundries		30,000 —	1978 Dec.	31	By Balance c/d		30,000 —
1979 Jan.	1	To Balance b/d		30,000 —					

Bad Debts Account

Date		Particulars	L.F.	Amount Rs.	Date		Particulars	L.F.	Amount Rs.
1978		To Sundries		600 —	1978 Dec.	31	By Profit & Loss A/c—transfer		600 —

Cash in Hand Account

Date		Particulars	L.F.	Amount Rs.	Date		Particulars	L.F.	Amount Rs.
1978 Dec.		To Balanced b/d		100 —	1978 Dec.	31	By Balance c/d		100 —
1979 Jan.		To Balance b/d		100 —					

*Cash at Bank Account

Date		Particulars	L.F.	Amount Rs.	Date		Particulars	L.F.	Amount Rs.
1978 Dec.	31	To Balance b/d		6,400 —	1978 Dec.	31	By Balance c/d		6,400 —
1979 Jan.	1	To Balance b/d		6,400 —					

Sales Returns Account

Date		Particulars	L.F.	Amount Rs.	Date		Particulars	L.F.	Amount Rs.
1978		To Sundries		5,100 —	1978 Dec.	31	By Sales A/c—transfer		5,100 —

*These two accounts will not be in the ledger, if a Cash Book is mentioned.

Capital Account

Date		Particulars	L.F.	Amount Rs.	Date		Particulars	L.F.	Amount Rs.
1978 Dec.	31	To Balance c/d		90,550—	1978 Jan.	1	By Balance b/d		60,000—
					Dec.	31	By Profit & Loss A/c—net profit		30,550—
				90,550—					90,550—
					1979 Jan.	1	By Balance b/d		90,550

Mrs. Yusuf's Loan Account

Date		Particulars	L.F.	Amount Rs.	Date		Particulars	L.F.	Amount Rs.
1978 Dec.	31	To Balance c/d		31,350—	1978 July.	1	By Cash		30,000—
					Dec.	31	By Interest A/c		1,350—
				31,350—					31,350—
					1979 Jan.	1	By Balance b/d		31,350

Sundry Creditors Account

Date		Particulars	L.F.	Amount Rs.	Date		Particulars	L.F.	Amount Rs.
1978 Dec.	31	To Balance c/d		9,600—	1978		By Sundries		9,600—
					1969 Jan.	1	By Balance b/d		9,600—

Purchase Returns Account

Date		Particulars	L.F.	Amount Rs.	Date		Particulars	L.F.	Amount Rs.
1978 Dec.	31	To Purchases A/c—transfer		2,100—	1978		By Sundries		2,100—

Miscellaneous Receipts Account

Date		Particulars	L.F.	Amount Rs.	Date		Particulars	L.F.	Amount Rs.
1978 Dec.	31	To Profit & Loss A/c—transfer		1,200—	1978		By Sundries		1,200—

Sales Account

Date		Particulars	L.F.	Amount Rs.	Date		Particulars	L.F.	Amount Rs.
1978 Dec.	31	To Sales Return A/c		5,100—	1978		By Sundries		2,07,300—
		To Trading A/c —transfer		2,02,200—					
				2,07,300—					2,07,300—

*Wages Outstanding Account

Date		Particulars	L.F.	Amount Rs.	Date		Particulars	L.F.	Amount Rs.
1978 Dec.	31	To Balance c/d		2,100 —	1978 Dec.	31	By Wages A/c		2,100 —
					1969 Jan.	1	By Balance c/d		2,100 —

*Prepaid Insurance Account

Date		Particulars	L.F.	Amount Rs.	Date		Particulars	L.F.	Amount Rs.
1978 Dec.	31	To General Expenses Account		150 —	1978 Dec.	31	By Balance		150 —
1969 Jan.	1	To Balance c/d		150 —					

*Provision for Doubtful Debts Account

Date		Particulars	L.F.	Amount Rs.	Date		Particulars	L.F.	Amount Rs.
1978 Dec.	31	To Balance c/d		1,500 —	1978 Dec.	31	By Profit & Loss A/c		1,500 —
					1969 Jan.	1	By Balance c/d		1,500 —

*Depreciation Account

Date		Particulars	L.F.	Amount Rs.	Date		Particulars	L.F.	Amount Rs.
1978 Dec.	31	To Sundries:			1978 Dec.	31	By Profit & Loss A/c—transfer		6,450 —
		Land & Buildings		700 —					
		Machinery		5,000 —					
		Furniture & Fixtures		750 —					
				6,450 —					6,450 —

*Interest Account

Date		Particulars	L.F.	Amount Rs.	Date		Particulars	L.F.	Amount Rs.
1978 Dec.	31	To Mrs. Yusuf's Loans A/c		1,350 —	1978 Dec.	31	By Profit & Loss A/c—transfer		1,350 —

*Closing Stock Account

Date		Particulars	L.F.	Amount Rs.	Date		Particulars	L.F.	Amount Rs.
1978 Dec.	31	To Trading A/c		14,900 —	1978 Dec.	31	By Balance b/d		14,900 —
1979 Jan.		To Balance b/d		14,900 —					

*Accounts marked with an asterisk have resulted from adjustment entries, as the student will have seen.

Trading Account of Yusuf for the year ended December 31, 1978

	Rs.	Rs.		Rs.	Rs.
To Opening Stock		15,500 —	By Sales :	2,07,300	
To Purchases :	1,06,000		Less Returns	5,100	2,02,200 —
Less Returns	21,100	1,03,900 —	By Closing Stock		14,900 —
To Wages—Paid	26,000				
Add Outstanding	2,100	28,100 —			
To Freight on Purchases		2,800 —			
To Gross Profit transferred to Profit & Loss A/c		66,800 —			
		2,17,100 —			2,17,100 —

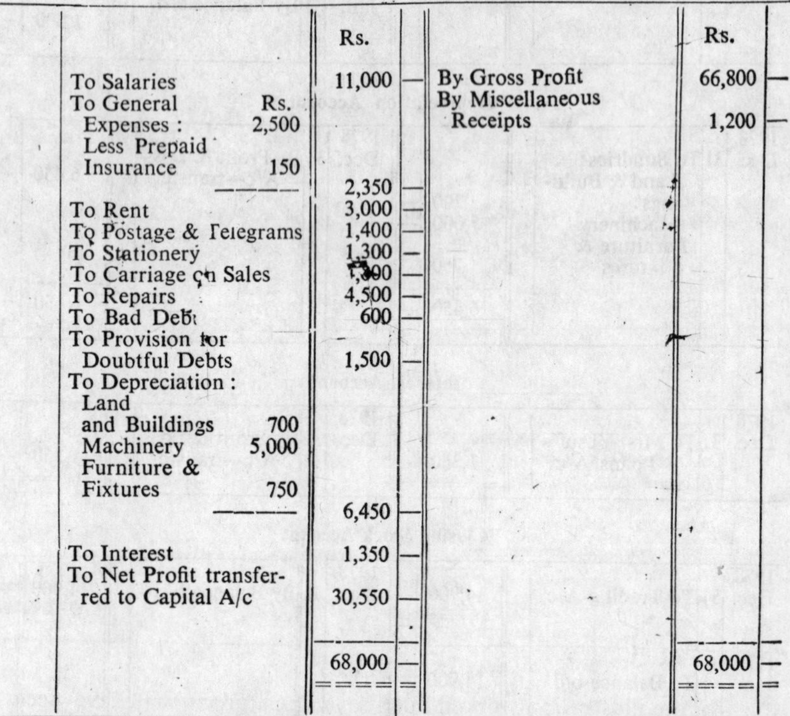

Profit & Loss Account of Yusuf for the year ended 31st December, 1978

	Rs.	Rs.		Rs.
To Salaries		11,000 —	By Gross Profit	66,800 —
To General Expenses :	2,500		By Miscellaneous Receipts	1,200 —
Less Prepaid Insurance	150	2,350 —		
To Rent		3,000 —		
To Postage & Telegrams		1,400 —		
To Stationery		1,300 —		
To Carriage on Sales		1,[illegible]00 —		
To Repairs		4,500 —		
To Bad Debt		600 —		
To Provision for Doubtful Debts		1,500 —		
To Depreciation :				
Land and Buildings	700			
Machinery	5,000			
Furniture & Fixtures	750	6,450 —		
To Interest		1,350 —		
To Net Profit transferred to Capital A/c		30,550 —		
		68,000 —		68,000 —

Usually the Trading and Profit and Loss Accounts are not given separately. They are combined as shown below :

Trading and Profit and Loss Account of Yusuf for the year ended December 31, 1978

		Rs.			Rs.	Rs.
To Opening Stock		15,500	By Sales :		2,07,300	
	Rs.		Less Returns		51,00	
To Purchases :	15,500					2,02,200
Less Returns	2,100	1,03,900	By Closing Stock			14,900
To Wages—Paid:	26,000					
Add Outstanding	2,100	28,100				
To Freight on Purchases		2,800				
To Gross Profit carried down		66,800				
		2,17,100				2,17,100
To Salaries		11,000	By Gross Profit b/d			66,800
To General Expenses :			By Miscellaneous Receipt			1,200
Paid	2,500					
Less Prepaid Insurance	150	2,350				
To Rent		3,000				
To Postage & Telegrams		1,400				
To Stationery		1,300				
To Carriage on Sales		4,000				
To Repairs		4,500				
To Bad Debts		600				
To Provision for Doubtful Debts		1,500				
To Depreciation :						
Land and Buildings	700					
Machinery	5,000					
Fixtures	750	6,450				
To Interest		1,350				
To Net Profit transferred to Capital Account		30,550				
		68,000				68,000

BALANCE SHEET

In the illustration worked out above, the student will have seen that the following accounts have still not been dealt with, that is the undermentioned accounts are still not closed :

Debit Balances	Rs.	*Credit Balances*	Rs.
Land & Buildings	34,300	Capital Account	90,550
Machinery	45,000	Mrs. Yusuf's Loan	31,350
Furniture & Fixtures	4,250	Wages Outstanding	2,100
Sundry Debtors	30,000	Sundry Creditors	9,600
Cash in Hand	100	Provision for Doubtful Debts	1,500
Cash at Bank	6,400		
Prepaid Insurance	150		
Closing Stock	14,900		
	1,35,100		1,35,100

The total of the debit balances is the same as that of the credit balances.

These accounts show what the proprietor possesses by way of assets and properties and what he owes to others on the date of the closing of the accounts. The above, of course, does not apply to the Capital Account. This is the amount which is his own but which can be treated as a sort of liability because the firm owes this sum to the proprietor. The assets and liabilities can be put down in a statement, assets on one side and liabilities on the other. When such a statement is prepared, it is known as the Balance Sheet. The Balance Sheet may be defined as a statement summarising the financial position of a firm on a given date. Traditionally, assets are shown on the right hand side and liabilites and capital are shown on the left hand side.

The Balance Sheet for the illustration given above is presented below :—

Balance Sheet of Yusuf as at December 31, 1978

Liabilities		Amount Rs.	P.	*Assets*		Amount Rs.	P.
Capital Account :				*Fixed Assets :*	Rs.		
Balance on 1st Jan.	Rs. 60,000			Land & Buildings	35,000		
*Add Profit During the year	30,550	90,550	—	*Less Depreciation	700	34,300	—
Mrs. Yusuf's Loan		31,350	—	Machinery ;	50,000		
Wages Outstanding		2,100	—	*Less Depreciation	5,000	45,000	—
Sundry Creditors		9,600	—	Furniture & Fixtures :	5,000		
				*Less Depreciation	750	4,250	—
				Current Assets :			
				Cash in Hand		100	—
				Cash at Bank		6,400	—
				Sundry Debtors :	30,000		
				**Less Provision for Doubtful Debts	1,500	28,500	—
				Closing Stock		14,900	—
				Prepaid Insurance		150	—
		1,33,600				1,33,600	—

*These details are usually given in a balance sheet.

**Provision for Doubtful Debts is deducted from Sundry Debtors in the Balance Sheet.

The assets and liabilities are shown by the Trial Balance; but during the course of preparation of the Profit and Loss Account some adjustments may have been made. These adjustments will change the amount of some assets and liabilities and may even bring into existence new accounts relating to assets and liabilities. Therefore, one can say that the Balance Sheet is intimately connected with the Trading Account and the Profit and Loss Account. Really the term final accounts includes the Balance Sheet as well as the Trading and Profit and Loss Account. The following points should be noted for preparing the Balance Sheet :—

1. The Balance Sheet is always prepared at a certain date, that is to say, at a certain point of time. It is not prepared for a period like the Profit and Loss Account which is prepared for say, a quarter, six months or a year. The Balance Sheet is true only on its date. It will not be true the next day and it would not have been true on the previous day. This is because even one single transaction will change assets and liabilities. The student can see for himself how various accounts and liabilities will change if, say, goods are sold on credit.

2. The total of assets must be equal to total of liabilities and capital. Really speaking, capital is nothing but the difference between assets and liabilities because what remains after paying off the third parties belongs to the proprietor. However, we prepare the Capital Account from books. We take the Capital Account in the ledger and add the profit (deduct the loss) and deduct drawings; and it is this figure which is put down in the Balance Sheet. Since the Trial Balance agrees, the two sides of the Balance Sheet must also agree. In an examination, the student must be very careful about this. If the total of assets does not agree with the total of liabilities and capital, there is definitely something wrong.

Arrangement of assets and liabilities. The form of Balance Sheet for a joint stock company is laid down by the Companies Act and various assets and liabilities must be shown in the order prescribed. But in case of partnerships and sole-proprietorships there is no prescribed form and, therefore, the assets can be shown as the proprietors like. However, it is better to arrange the assets in some logical order. There are two possibilities ; one is to arrange assets in the order of liquidity and the other is to arrange them in the order of permanence. If the first basis is adopted, cash in hand will come at the top and the asset which is most difficult to realize, namely, goodwill will come at the end. If the second basis is adopted, this asset will be shown right at the top.

In the order of liquidity :	In the order of permanence :
Cash in hand	Goodwill
Cash at Bank	Patents
Sundry Debtors	Furniture
Stock of Finished Goods	Machinery
Stock of Raw Materials	Pre-paid Expenses
Stock of Partly Finished Goods	Stock of Partly Finished Goods
Pre-paid Expenses	Stock of Raw Materials
Machinery	Stock of Finished Goods
Furniture	Sundry Debtors
Patents	Cash at Bank
Goodwill	Cash in hand

Whatever the order adopted, it will be better to show fixed assets together and to group current or floating assets together. Also, in case of fixed assets, the proper way is to show the cost and then deduct the total depreciation written off to date. The provision for doubtful (or bad) debts should be deducted from the debtors in the balance sheet and not shown on the liability side.

Liabilities must also be grouped in two ways, either according to the urgency of the payment or in the reverse order. Many firms show the Capital Account first and then liabilities ; other show the liabilities first and then the Capital Account. It does not matter very much which way the liabilities or capital are put down.

We now give a few illustrations of final accounts.

Illustration The following are the balances abstracted from the books of Mr. Naranlal :—

Balances—31st December, 1978.

	Rs.
Naranlal's Capital	30,000
Naranlal's Drawings	5,000
Furniture and Fittings	2,600
Bank Overdraft	4,200
Creditors	13,300
Business Premises	20,000
Stock on 1st January, 1978	22,000
Debtors	18,600
Rent from Tenants	1,000
Purchases	1,10,000
Sales	1, 50,000
Sales Returns	2,000
Discounts—Debit	1,600
Discounts—Credit	2,000

	Rs.
Taxes and Insurance	2,000
General Expenses	4,000
Salaries	9,000
Commision—Debit	2,200
Carriage on Purchases	1,800
Provision for Bad & Doubtful Debts	600
Bad Debts written off	800

Stock on hand on 31st December, 1978 was estimated at Rs. 20,000. Rent, Rs. 300, is still due from the tenant. Salaries, Rs. 750, are as yet unpaid. Write off Bad Debts Rs. 600 and depreciate Business Premises by Rs. 300 and Furniture and Fittings by Rs. 266. Make a provision of 5 per cent on Debtors for Bad and Doubtful Debts and a provision of 2% for Discounts. Allow interest on Capital at 5 per cent and carry forward Rs. 700 for unexpired insurance. The manager is entitled to a commission of 10% on profits remaining after charging his commission. Prepare Trading Account, Profit and Loss Account and Balance Sheet as on 31st December, 1978.

Solution :

In questions where a regular trial balance is not given, it is better to first prepare it in order to locate any difference that there may be. Hence :—

Trial Balance of Naranlal as at December 31, 1978

Debit Balances	Rs.	*Credit Balances*	Rs.
Naranlal's Drawings	5,000	Naranlal's Capital	30,000
Furniture & Fittings	2,600	Bank Overdraft	4,200
Business Premises	20,000	Creditors	13,300
Stock, 1st January, 1978	22,000	Rent from Tenants	1,000
Debtors	18,600	Sales	1,50,000
Purchases	1,10,000	Discounts	2,000
Sales Returns	2,000	Provision for Doubtful	
Discounts	1,600	Debts	600
Taxes and Insurance	2,000		
General Expenses	4,000		2,01,100
Salaries	9,000	Suspense	500
Commission	2,200	(Difference in Trial Balance)	
Carriage	1,800		
Bad Debts	800		
	2,01,600		2,01,600

The total of the credit side is Rs. 2,01,100, whereas it is Rs. 2,01,600 for the debit side. Hence Rs. 500 has been credited to the Suspense Account.

Trading and Profit and Loss Account of Naranlal for the year ended 31st December, 1978

		Rs.			Rs.	Rs.
To Opening Stock		22,000	By Sales :		1,50,000	
To Purchases		1,10,000	Less Returns		2,000	1,48,000
To Carriage		1,800				
To Gross Profit c/d		34,200	By Closing Stock			20,000
		1,68,000				1,68,000
	Rs.					
To Salaries, Paid	9,000		By Gross Profit b/d			34,200
Add Due	750		By Rent.		Rs.	
		9,750	Received		1,000	
			Add Due		300	1,300
To General Expenses		4 000				
To Commission		2,200	By Discounts Received			2,000
To Taxes & Insurance :						
Paid	2,000					
Less Prepaid	700					
		1,300				
To Discounts		1,600				
To Depreciation :						
Business Premises,	300					
Furniture & Fittings	266					
		566				
To Provision for Bad & Doubtful Debts Required	900					
Add Bad Debts	1,400					
	2,300					
Less Existing Provision	600*					
		1,700				
To Provision for Discounts*		342				
To Interest on Capital		1,500				
To Commission Payable to Manager**		1,322				
To Net Profit to Capital A/c		13,220				
		37,500				37,500

*Rs. 600 has to be written off as bad debts. This increases total bad debts to Rs. 1,400. It reduces sundry debtors to Rs. 18,000. 5% of this is Rs. 900. Deducting this amount from sundry debtors, Rs. 17,100 is left. The Provision for Discount will be 2% of this figure.

**Before providing for the commission, the profit is Rs. 14,542 (deduct all expenses from the incomes). The manager's commission will be $\frac{10}{110}$ of this, because if net profit of the commission is 100, commission will be 10, making a total of 110.

Balance Sheet of Naranlal as at December 31, 1978

Liabilities		Amount Rs.	*Assets*		Amount Rs.
Capital Account :	Rs.		*Fixed Assets* :	Rs.	
Balance on 1st Jan., 1978	30,000		Business Premises:		
Add Interest	1,500		Cost	20,000	
Add Net Profit	13,220		Less Depreciation	300	19,700
	44,720		Furniture and Fittings :	2,600	
Less Drawings	5,000	39,720	Less Depreciation	266	2,334
Bank Overdraft		4,200	*Current Assets* :		
Creditors		13,300	Sundry Debtors	18,000	
Liability for :			Less Provision for Bad and Doubtful Debts	900	
Salaries	750			17,100	
Commission	1,322	2,072	Less Provision for Discounts	342	16,758
Suspense		500	Stock		20,000
			Amount Due from Tenant		300
			Prepaid Insurance		700
		59,792			59,792

Illustration Below is the trial balance of Shah as at December 31, 1978 :

Debit Balances	Rs.	*Credit Balances*	Rs.
Shah's Current Account	1,500	Capital Account	50,000
Adjusted Purchases	6,99,200	Loan from Desai @ 9% (taken on 1st July, 1977)	20,000
Salaries	4,200	Sales	7,20,000
Carriage on Purchases	400	Discount	500
on Sale	500	Sundry Creditors	20,000
Lighting	300		
Rates and Insurance	400		
Buildings	27,000		
Furniture	6,000		
Sundry Debtors	8,000		
Cash on hand	250		
Cash at Bank	1,500		
Stock (31st December, 1978)	61,250		
	8,10,500		8,10,500

Rates have been prepaid to the extent of Rs. 175. Bad debts totalling Rs. 500 have to be written off. A provision for doubtful debts @ 5% on debtors is necessary. Buildings have to be depreciated at 2% and Furniture @ 10%. The manager is entitled to a commission of 5% of net profits before charging such commission.

Solution :

[*Notes* : (1) The trial balance gives "Adjusted Purchases". It means that the opening stock has already been transferred to the Purchases Account and has thus been closed. Further, entry for closing stock has already been passed by debiting the Closing Stock Account and crediting Purchases Account. That is why closing stock appears *inside* the trial balance. It will now be shown in the Balance Sheet and *not* in the Trading Account since purchases already stand reduced.

(2) There is a loan of Desai @ 9% taken in 1977. The trial balance makes no mention of any interest being paid to him. Hence, interest @ 9% must be provided for the whole year.

Trading and Profit and Loss Account of Shah for the year ended December 31, 1978

		Rs.		Rs.
To Adjusted Purchases		6,99,200	By Sales	7,20,000
To Carriage on purchases		400		
To Gross Profit c/d		20,400		
		7,20,000		7,20,000
			By Gross Profit b/d	20,400
To Salaries		4,200	By Discount	500
To Carriage on Sales		500		
To Lighting		300		
To Rates & Insurance:				
Paid	400			
Less Prepaid	175			
		225		
To Bad Debts		500		
To Provision for Doubtful Debts (5% of Rs. 7,500)		375		
To Depreciation :				
Buildings (2%)	540			
Furniture (10%)	600			
		1,140		
To Interest on Desai's Loan		1,800		
To Commission Payable to Manager (5% of Rs. 11,860*)		593		
To Net Profit—to Shah's Current A/c		11,267		
		20,900		20,900

*Rs. 20,900, less Rs. 9,040 (the total of all expenses so far). Manager is entitled to 5% of this figure.

Balance Sheet of Shah as at December 31, 1978

Liabilities	Rs.	Amount Rs.	*Assets*	Rs.	Amount Rs.
			Fixed Assets		
Loan from Desai :	20,000		Buildings :	27,000	
Add Interest Due	1,800		Less Depreciation	540	26,460
		21,800	Furniture :	6,000	
Sundry Creditors		20,000	Less Depreciation	600	5,400
Commission Payable		593	*Current Assets* :		
Capital Account		50,000	Cash on hand		250
Current Account			Cash at Bank		1,500
Net Profit :	11,267		Sundry Debtors	7,500	
Less Debit balance	1,500	9,767	Less Provision for Doubtful Debts	375	7,125
			Stock		61,250
			Prepaid Rates		175
		1,02,160			1,02,160

Illustration Narain's trial balance as on 30th June, 1969 was as under :

Debit Balances	Rs.	*Credit Balances*	Rs.
Land and Buildings	20,000	Capital	80,000
Machinery	50,000	Sundry Creditors	8,000
Furniture and Fixtures	4,000	Discounts Received	400
Opening Stock	16,300	Outstanding Expenses	1,550
Purchases	80,000	Sales	1,50,500
Salaries	6,000	Repairs and Renewals Provision	6,000
Carriage on Sales	1,500		
Freight on Purchases	2,000		
Customs duty on Purchases	8,000		
Advertising	5,400		
Wages	15,000		
Rent	3,000		
Postage and Stationery	1,500		
General Expenses	3,200		
Repairs to Machinery	2,000		
Loan to Kumar @ 9% (given on 1st January, 1979)	5,000		
Prepaid Insurance	200		
Sundry Debtors	20,000		
Cash in hand	250		
Cash at Bank	3,100		
	2,46,450		2,46,450

The following further information is given :

(*a*) Stock on 30th June, 1979 was Rs. 14,900.

(*b*) Machinery was purchased on 1st January, 1979 for Rs. 10,000 and was installed by own workmen. The wages for this purpose amounted to Rs. 500. This amount is included in Wages Account.

(*c*) Depreciation is to be written off @
3% on Land and Buildings ;
10% on Machinery ; and
5% on Furniture and Fixtures.

(*d*) Provision for Repairs and Renewals is credited with Rs. 1,500 every year.

(*e*) A reserve of 2% is to be made on creditors for discount.

From the information given above, prepare Trading Account and Profit and Loss Account for the year ended June 30, 1979 and Balance Sheet as at that date.

Solution :

[*Note* : The attention of the student is drawn to Prepaid Insurance and Outstanding Expenses which appear in the trial balance. This means that double entry in respect of these items has been completed. Hence, these items will now be shown only in the Balance Sheet.]

Trading and Profit and Loss Account of Narain for the year ended June 30, 1979.

	Rs.		Rs.
To Opening Stock	16,300	By Sales	1,50,500
To Purchases	80,000	By Closing Stock	14,900
To Freight on Purchases	2,000		
To Customs Duty	8,000		
To Wages : 15,000			
Less Charged to Machinery 500	14,500		
To Gross Profit c/d	44,600		
	1,65,400		1,65,400
To Salaries	6,000	By Gross Profit b/d	44,600
To Carriage on Sales	1,500	By Discount Received	400
To Advertising	5,400	By Reserve for Discount on Creditors (2% on Rs. 8,000)	160
To Rent	3,000	By Interest due on Loan to Kumar for 6 months	225
To Postage & Telegrams	1,500		
To General Expenses	3,200		
To Depreciation : Rs. Land & Buildings : 600; Machinery 4,525; Furniture & Fixtures 200	5,325		
To Provision for Repairs	1,500		
To Net Profit, transferred to Capital Account	17,960		
	45,385		45,385

Balance Sheet of Narain as at June 30, 1979

Liabilities		Amount Rs.	*Assets*		Amount Rs.
	Rs.		*Fixed Assets* :		
Sundry Creditors :			Land & Buildings	20,000	
	8,000		Less Depreciation	600	
Less Reserve for Discounts	160				19,400
		7,840	Machinery :	50,500*	
Outstanding Expenses		1,550	Less Depreciation	4,525	
Provision for Repairs & Renewals :**	6,000				45,975
Add Addition	1,500		Furniture & Fixtures	4,000	
	7,500		Less Depreciation	200	
Less Actual Repairs	2,000				3,800
		5,500	*Current Assets* :		
Capital Account :			Cash in hand		250
	80,000		Cash at Bank		3,100
Add Profit	17,960		Sundry Debtors		20,000
		97,960	Stock		14,900
			Loan to Kumar	5,000	
			Add Interest Due	225	
					5,225
			Prepaid Insurance		200
		1,12,850			1,12,850

*Machinery stands @ Rs. 50,000. Out of this Rs. 10,000 was added on 1st January, 1979. Hence on 1st July, 1978 the machinery account must have stood at Rs. 40,000. On 1st Jan. 1979 another Rs. 500 have to be transferred to the debit of Machinery A/c by crediting Wages A/c. Total Machinery Account will stand at a debit of Rs. 50,500. Depreciation has to be charged—

	Rs.
on Rs. 40,000 @ 10% for full year	4,000
on Rs. 10,500 @ 10% for six months	525
Total	4,525

**There is a Provision for Repairs and Renewals. Actual repairs will therefore, be debited to this account and not to the Profit and Loss Account. The Provision for Repairs and Renewals Account will be credited by Rs. 1,500 by debiting Profit and Loss Account.

Illustration The following figures were taken from the books of Dutt on 31st December, 1978.

	Rs.		Rs.
Cash at Bank	26,400	Royalties Received	400
Cash in hand	30	Trade & General Expenses	5,020
Sales	2,61,230	Reserve on Patents	5,000
Stock (1st Jan. 1978)	27,410	Interest on Loan	1,240
Sales Returns	3,300	Repairs	840
Discount (Dr.)	6,380	Sundry Creditors	20,780
Bills Receivable	1,820	Buildings	95,820
Sundry Debtors	52,720	Patent Rights	50,000
Depreciation	4,780	Loan (raised on Mortgage of Buildings)	45,000
Purchases	1,84,030	Agents' Commission	6,500
Discount on Purchases	3,900	Bad Debts	1,900
Wages	14,040	Plant and Machinery	30,000
Provision for Bad Debts	5,400	Capital	2,00,000
Provision for Discount on Drs.	1,970	Drawings	30,000
		Advertising	1,000
		Carriage	450

In addition, the following information is given :

(*a*) Stock on 31st December, 1978 was Rs. 32,250.

(*b*) The stock includes materials worth Rs. 2,250 for which bills had not been received and, therefore, not accounted for yet.

(*c*) During the year a sum of Rs. 3,000 was paid as ground rent for 1978 and 1979. This sum stands debited to Buildings Account.

(*d*) Included in sales is an amount of Rs. 7,500 representing goods on sale or return, the customers still having the right to return the goods. The goods were invoiced showing a profit of 20% on sales.

(*e*) A customer's bill for Rs. 2,780 had been discounted with bank. The bank has sent an intimation that the bill has been dishonoured. No entry has yet been passed in respect of this.

(*f*) A provision for bad debts is to be maintained at 5% of the debtors and a provision for discounts on debtors is also to be maintained @ 2% of the debtors.

Prepare Trading and Profit and Loss Account of Dutt for the year ended December 31, 1978 and his Balance Sheet as on that date.

Solution :

Notes : (1) The student is advised to prepare a regular trial balance first.

(2) He will note that Depreciation appears in the trial balance. This means that the assets concerned have already been credited in respect of depreciation.

(3) Goods purchased, Rs. 2,250 have not yet been brought into account. Hence an entry is necessary

debiting Purchases Account and crediting Sundry Creditors.

(4) There is a "sale" of Rs. 7,500. The goods can still be returned by the customer. It is not proper to treat it as a sale. Hence an entry will be necessary :

		Rs.	Rs.
Sales Account		Dr. 7,500	
	To Sundry Debtors		7,500

The entry reduces both sales and debtors. Debtors now stand at Rs. 45,220.

Further, the goods lying with the customer should be included in stock *at cost.* The cost is Rs. 7,500 less 20%, *i.e.*, Rs. 6,000.

(5) Entry for Bills Discounted dishonoured will be necessary :

Sundry Debtors		Dr. 2,780	
	To Bank Account		2,780

By this entry the cash at bank will be reduced to Rs. 23,620 and debtors will increase to Rs 48,000 *i.e.*, Rs. 45,220 (*see* (4) above) plus Rs. 2,780. The Provision for Bad Debts will be 5% of this figure *viz.*, Rs, 2,400. The provision for Discount should be 2% of Rs. 45,600 (*i.e.*, Rs. 48,000—Rs. 24,00) or Rs. 912].

Trading and Profit and Loss Account of Dutt for the year ended December 31, 1978

	Rs.	Rs.			Rs.
To Opening Stock		27,410	By Sales :	2,61,230	
To Purchases	,84,030		Less Returns	3,300	
Add still un accounted for	2,250			2,57,930	
		1,86,280	Less Returnable	7,500	2,50,430
To Wages		14,040	By Stock :	32,250	
			Add in hands of Customer	6,000	
To Carriage		450			38,250
To Gross Profit c/d		60,500			
		2,88,680			2,88,680
To Provision for Discounts on Debtors :			By Gross Profit b/d		60,500
Required	912		By Discount Received		3,900
Add Discounts	6,380		By Royalties Received		400
	7,292		By Provision for Bad Debts.		
Less Existing Provision	1,970		Existing	5,400	
		5,322	Less : Bad Debts 1,900		
To Depreciation		4,780	Provisions required 2,400	4,300	
To Trade & General Expenses		5,020			1,100
To Interest on Loan		1,240			
To Ground Rent		1,500			
To Repairs		840			
To Agents' Commission		6,500			
To Advertising		1,000			
To Net Profit transferred to Capital Account		39,698			
		65,900			65,900

Balance Sheet of Dutt as at December 31, 1978

Liabilities		Amount Rs.	*Assets*		Amount Rs.
			Fixed Assets :		
Sundry Creditors (20,780 + 2,250)		23,030	Buildings	95,820	
Loan on Mortgage of Buildings		45,000	Less Transferred to Ground Rent	3,000	92,820
	Rs.		Plant & Machinery		30,000
Capital :	2,00,000		Patent Rights	50,000	
Add Profit	39,698		Less Reserve	5,000	45,000
	2,39,698		*Current Assets :*		
Less Drawings	30,000	2,09,698	Cash on hand		30
			Cash at Bank		23,620
			Bills Receivable		1,820
			Sundry Debtors :	48,000	
			Less Provision for Bad Debts	2,400	
				45,600	
			Less Provision for Discounts	912	44,688
			Stock		38,250
			Ground Rent paid in Advance		1,500
		2,77,728			2,77,728

Illustration Mahant gives you the following figures from his books as on 30th June, 1967 :—

	Rs.		Rs.
Capital	50,000	Purchases	48,000
Trade Creditors	10,000	Discounts Received	400
Bills Payable	1,000	Buildings	10,000
General Reserve	5,000	Plant & Machinery	15,000
Provision for Bad Debts	1,000	Book Debts	16,400
Mahant's Current A/c (Cr.)	450	Bank Balance (Dr.)	3,400
Sales	75,000	Investments (4%)	10,000
Discounts allowed	750	Bills Receivable	2,500
Stock (1st July, 1978)	15,000	Wages & Salaries	13,000
Audit Fees	2,000	Repairs & Renewals	1,800
Office Expenses	4,500	Interest Paid	700
		Bad Debts Recovered	200

The trial balance *had* shown a difference of Rs.2,500, the debit side being short. It was transferred to Office Expenses A/c.

The value of stock on hand on 30th June, 1979 was Rs. 18,000. During June 1979 there was a fire which destroyed goods worth Rs. 3,500. The insurers admitted claim for Rs. 2,500. This amount had not yet been received and no entries have been passed yet. Buildings are to be depreciated at 2% p.a. and Plant and Machinery at 10% p.a. Rs. 2,000 is to be transferred to General Reserve out of profits, if any. The manager is entitled to a commission of 10% of net profits after charging his commission

The following errors were located :—

(1) The total of the Purchases Book in May was found to be Rs.1,000 short.

(2) A sale of Rs.500 to a credit customer in April was posted twice to his account.

(3) Rs.1,000 paid to a creditor was credited to his account.

Prepare Mahant's Trading Account, Profit and Loss Account and Balance Sheet.

Solution .

Trading and Profit and Loss Account of Mahant for the year ending June 30, 1979

		Rs.			Rs.
To Opening Stock		15,000	By Sales		75,000
To Purchases		49,000	But Goods Lost by Fire :		
To Wages and Salaries		13,000	Claim Admitted	2,500	
To Gross Profit c/d		19,500	Not Admitted	1,000	
					3,500
			By Closing Stock		18,000
		96,500			96,500
To Discount Allowed		750	By Gross Profit b/d		19,500
To Audit Fees		2,000	By Discounts Received		400
To Office Expenses		2,000	By Bad Debts Recovered		200
To Repairs & Renewals		1,800	By Interest Due on Investments (4% on Rs. 10,000)		400
To Interest Paid		700			
To Loss by Fire (not admitted)		1,000			
The Depreciation :	Rs.				
Buildings (2%)	200				
Plant & Machinery (10%)	1,500	1,700			
Total		9 950			
To Manager's Commission*		959			
To Profit transferred to :					
General Reserve		2,000			
Current Account		7,591			
		20,500			20,500

* $\frac{10}{110} \times 10,550$ (*i.e.*, Rs. 20,500 − 9950).

Balance Sheet of Mahant as at June 30, 1979

Liabilities		Amount Rs.	*Assets*		Amount Rs.
Trade Creditors		8,000	*Fixed Assets* :	Rs.	
Bills Payable		1,000	Buildings :	10,000	
Amount due to Manager as Commission		959	Less Depreciation	200	9,800
General Reserve :			Plant & Machinery :	15,000	
Previous Balance	5,000		Less Depreciation	1,500	13,500
Addition this year	2,000	7,000	*Current Assets* :		
Mahant's Current Account :			Cash at Bank		3,400
Previous Balance	450		Investments		10,000
Profit this year	7,591	8,041	Interest Due on above		400
Mahant's Capital A/c		50,000	Bills Receivable		2,500
			Sundry Debtors	15,900	
			Less Provision for Bad Debts	1,000	14,900
			Insurance Company		2,500
			Stock		18,000
		75,000			75,000

Notes : (1) The following corrections have to be made before the final accounts are prepared :

(*i*) Purchases Account	Dr.	1,000	
To Office Expenses Account*			1,000
(*ii*) Office Expenses Account*	Dr.	500	
To Sundry Debtors			500
(*iii*) Sundry Creditors	Dr.	2,000	
To Office Expenses Account*			2,000

* Since the difference was transferred to the Office Expenses A/c.

(2) There has been a fire. The students should note that the figure of stock (Rs. 18,000) is after the fire and hence cannot include the goods destroyed. The total loss is credited to Trading Account, debiting the Insurance Company with the amount admitted as claim and debiting the Profit and Loss Account with the balance.

(3) There are 4% investments. The trial balance makes no mention of any interest received. Hence, the student must himself calculate the amount and pass entry for the interest due.

(4) In absence of instructions it is better to maintain the Provision for Bad Debts at the figure already given.

Manufacturing Accounts. Industrial concerns may like to find out the cost of goods manufactured by them during the year. The Trading Account as usually prepared cannot give this figure because

(1) it includes figures of stocks of finished goods also, both opening and closing; and (2) it ignores some of the manufacturing expenses, for example, repairs to machinery, depreciation of machinery, etc. If the cost of manufacturing goods is to be ascertained, an account called Manufacturing Account will have to be prepared. The chief features of a Manufacturing Account are the following :

(1) It is debited with all expenses that are incurred in manufacturing goods. This means that besides such expenses as freight on purchases of raw materials, customs duty, wages, rent and lighting of factory premises, we must also debit the Manufacturing Account with repairs to plant and machinery, depreciation of machinery, loose tools, etc. [The student will have noted that, otherwise, repairs and depreciation are debited to the Profit and Loss Account. This is not so if a Manufacturing Account is prepared.]

(2) Instead of showing figures of opening stock, purchases and closing stock separately, we have to show one figure for *materials consumed*. This figure is obtained by adding opening stock of raw materials and purchases of raw materials and then deducting the closing stock of raw materials. Thus—

	Rs.
"To Raw Materials consumed :	
Opening Stock (of Raw Materials), say,	16,400
Add Purchases (,,)	83,700
	1,00,100
Less Closing Stock (,,)	24,300
	75,800"

Opening and closing stocks of finished goods are not entered in the Manufacturing Account.

(3) Usually, at the end of every period certain goods are in a semi-finished state. It means that still some work remains to be done on some units. This is called "Work in Progress" or "Work in Process". It is an asset of the firm and has to be valued carefully. The usual basis of valuation is the actual materials used and labour spent on these unfinished units plus a proper proportion of manufacturing expenses, generally on the basis of labour. Suppose, in a factory total wages in a year are Rs. 2,00,000 and total manufacturing expenses are Rs. 1,20,000. This means that manufacturing expenses are 60% of wages. This can be used to determine

how much should be added to materials and labour in order to find out the value of work in progress. Suppose, materials worth Rs. 5,000 and labour worth Rs. 4,000 has been spent on units that are still in progress. Then the value of work in progress will be Rs. 11,400 taking the figures given above. Thus—

	Rs.
Materials	5,000
Labour	4,000
Manufacturing Expenses (60% wages)	2,400
	11,400

In the Manufacturing Account, the opening stock of work in progress is debited and the closing stock of work in progress is credited. The entry is :—

Work in Progress Account Dr.
To Manufacturing Account.

Alternatively, the amount of the closing work in progress may be deducted from the total of the debit side of the Manufacturing Account.

The closing stock of work in progress is an asset and has to be the shown in Balance Sheet.

(4) In the course of manufacturing, some waste material always emerges. This is sold. The amount realised is credited to "Scrap Account". This account is transferred to the credit side of the Manufacturing Account.

(5) The balance in the Manufacturing Account, the difference between the debit and credit sides, is the cost of the goods produced during the period. This is transferred to the debit side of the Trading Account; of course, the Manufacturing Account is credited and is, thus, closed.

To find out the cost per unit of the goods produced, what is needed is to divide the total cost, as revealed by the Manufacturing Account, by the total number of units produced. For example, if the total cost is Rs. 20,00,000 and the total number of units is 1,25,000, the cost per unit is Rs. 16, *i.e.*, $\frac{20,00,000}{1,25,000}$. If possible, a column should be added on both sides of the Manufacturing Account for cost per unit. In such a case, cost per unit should be calculated for each element—materials, labour, etc.

In addition to the Manufacturing Account, Trading Account will also be prepared. But this account will show only opening stock of finished goods and cost of goods produced on the debit side, and sales and closing stock of finished goods on the credit side. The resultant gross profit (or loss) will, of course, be transferred to

Profit and Loss Account. Expenses and losses (except those already debited to the Manufacturing Account) will be debited to the Profit and Loss Account. Incomes, if any (except that by sale of waste and scrap), will be credited. The Profit and Loss Account will reveal net profit or loss which is transferred to the Capital Account. After this the Balance Sheet is prepared, as already explained.

Illustration On 31st December, 1978 the Trial Balance of Topa was as follows :—

Debit Balances	Rs.	*Credit Balances*	Rs.
Stock on 1st Jan. 1968 :			
Raw Materials	21,000	Sundry Creditors	15,000
Work in Progress	9,500	Bills Payable	7,500
Finished goods	15,500	Sale of Scrap	2,500
Sundry Debtors	24,000	Commission	450
Carriage on Purchases	1,500	Provision for Doubtful	
Bills Receivable	15,000	Debts	1,650
Wages	13,000	Capital Account	1,00,000
Salaries	10,000	Sales	1,67,200
Telephone, Postage, etc.	1,000	Current Account of Topa	8,500
Repairs to Plant	1,100		
Repairs to Office Furniture	350		
Purchases	85,000		
Cash at Bank	17,000		
Plant and Machinery	70,000		
Office Furniture	10,000		
Rent	6,000		
Lighting	1,350		
General Expenses	1,500		
	3,02,800		3,02,800

The following additional information is available :—

(*a*) Stocks on 31st December, 1978 were :

Raw Materials	16,200
Finished goods	18,100
Semi-finished goods	7,800

(*b*) Salaries and wages unpaid for December 1978 were respectively, Rs. 900 and Rs. 2,000.

(*c*) Machinery is to be depreciated by 10% and office furniture by 7½%.

(*d*) Provision for Doubtful Debts is to be maintained @ 1% sales.

(*e*) Office Premises occupy ¼ of total area. Lighting is to be charged as to ⅔ to factory and ⅓ to office.

Solution :

Manufacturing Account of Topa for the year ended December 31, 1978.

		Rs.		Rs.
To Work in Progress, opening		9,500	By Work in Progress (on 31st Dec.)	7,800
To Materials Consumed :			By Sale of Scrap	2,500
Opening Stock	21,000		By Cost of Goods manufactured—transferred to Trading Account	1,19,000
Add Purchases	85,000			
	1,06,000			
Less Closing Stock	16,200			
		89,800		
To Wages	13,000			
Add Outstanding	2,000			
		15,000		
To Carriage on Purchases		1,500		
To Repairs to Plant		1,100		
To Rent (3/4)		4,500		
To Lighting (2/3)		900		
To Depreciation of Plant		7,000		
		1,29,300		1,29,300

Trading and Profit and Loss Account of Topa for the year ended December 31, 1978.

	Rs.			Rs.
To Opening Stock of Finished Goods		15,500	By Sales	1,67,200
To Cost of Goods Manufactured		1,19,000	By Closing Stock (Finished goods)	18,100
To Gross Profit c/d		50,800		
		1,85,300		1,85,300
To Salaries :	10,000		By Gross Profit c/d	50,800
Add Outstanding	900		By Commission	450
		10,900		
To Telephone & Postage		1,000		
To Repairs to Furniture		350		
To Depreciation of Furniture		750		
To Rent (1/4)		1,500		
To Lighting (1/3)		450		
To General Expenses		1,500		
To Provision for Doubtful Debts : Required (1% of Rs. 1,67,200)	1,672			
Less Existing Provision	1,650			
		22		
To Net Profit, transferred to Topa's Current Account		34,778		
		51,250		51,250

Prepare the Manufacturing Account, Trading Account, Profit and Loss Account and the Balance Sheet relating to 1978.

Balance Sheet of Topa as at December 31, 1978

Liabilities		Rs.	*Assets*		Rs.
Sundry Creditors		15,000	*Fixed Assets :*		
Bills Payable		7,500	Plant & Machinery :		
Expenses Payable :	Rs.		Balance	70,000	
Salaries	900		Less Depreciation	7,000	
Wages	2,000				63,000
		2,900	Office Furniture :		
Current Account of Topa :			Balance	10,000	
			Less Depreciation	750	
Previous Balance	8,500				9,250
Add Net Profit	34,778		*Current Assets :*		
		43,278	Cash at Bank		17,000
Capital Account		1,00,000	Sundry Debtors :	24,000	
			Less Provision for Doubtful Debts	1,672	
					22,328
			Bills Receivable		15,000
			Stocks :		
			Raw Materials	16,200	
			Finished Goods	18,100	
			Work in Progress	7,800	
					42,100
		1,68,678			1,68,678

Illustration : On 31st December 1973, the following balances appeared in the books of Mr. Sadhu Ram of Ludhiana:—

	Rs.
Capital Account ..	1,00,000
Mr. Sadhu Ram's Current Account ..	15,000
Drawings during the year ..	12,000
Loan from Mrs. Sadhu Ram taken on 1st April, 1973 bearing interest at 12 per cent per annum ..	6,000
Investments (market value Rs.15,000) ..	16,250
Cash in Hand ..	2,500
Cash at Bank ..	15,700
Sundry Creditors ..	66,156
Sundry Debtors ..	35,000
Bad Debts Reserve ..	1,000
Sales ..	3,25,700
Purchases of Raw Materials ..	1,15,000
Discount Received ..	1,100
Purchases Returns ..	3,750
Bills Payable ..	15,300
Outstanding Sundry Expenses as on 1st January, 1973 ..	9,300
Outstanding Sundry Expenses paid during the year ..	9,000
Sundry Receipts ..	74
Plant and Machinery ..	55,800
Land and Building (3/4 in use of the Factory) ..	60,000
Sales Returns ..	2,300
Opening Balances as on 1st January, 1973—	
Raw Materials ..	25,000
Work-in-Progress ..	9,800
Finished Goods ..	57,000
Carriage Inward ..	2,000
Wages ..	60,000
Interest paid on Loan from Mrs. Sadhu Ram ..	480
Salary of Works Manager ..	9,600
Salaries ..	10,000
Rates and Taxes on Buildings ..	3,200
Royalties paid (payable at 1 per cent on net sales) ..	3,000
Advertisement ..	7,000
Insurance of Building ..	2,000

	Rs.
Insurance of Plant and Machinery (includes one annual premium of Rs.1,200 paid on 30th June, 1973) ..	3,000
Printing and Stationery ..	2,000
Audit Fee ..	2,000
Carriage Outward ..	3,750
Bad Debts ..	3,000
Loose Tools ..	5,000
Repairs of Plant and Machinery ..	3,000
Furniture and Fittings ..	7,000
General Expenses ..	2,000

From the balances and the undermentioned information, prepare the Manufacturing, Trading and Profit and Loss Account of Mr. Sadhu Ram for the year ending 31st December, 1973 and the Balance Sheet as on that date:—

(1) Provide depreciation on Land and Buildings at 5 per cent, Plant and Machinery at 20 per cent, Loose Tools at 25 per cent and Furniture and Fittings at 10 per cent.

(2) Sundry Expenses outstanding as at 31st December, 1973 amounted to Rs.5,600.

(3) Closing Balances as at 31st December, 1973 were:—

	Rs.
Raw Materials	22,000
Work-in-Progress	11,000
Finished Goods	38,000

(4) Provision for Bad Debts should be maintained at 5 per cent.

(5) Salaries include advance for the next period amounting to Rs.600.

(6) Advertisement includes Rs.3,000 spent on Neon-signs.

(7) It was discovered that stock sheet of Finished Goods as on 31st December 1972 were overcast to the extent of Rs.1,000.

(*C.A. Inter*)

Solution:

Manufacturing Account of Sadhu Ram for the year ending 31st December, 1973

	Rs.	Rs.		Rs.
To Opening Work-in Progress		9,800	By Work-in-Progress (closing)	11,000
To Raw Material consumed:	Rs.		By Trading A/c, transfer (cost of goods manufactured)	2,08,610
Opening Stock	25,000			
Add: Purchases (Net)	1,11,250			
	1,36,250			
Less: Closing Stock	22,000	1,14,250		
To Carriage Inward		2,000		
To Wages		60,000		
To Salary of Works Manager		9,600		
To Repairs, Plant & Machinery		3,000		
To Depreciation:				
Land & Building		2,250		
Plant & Machinery		11,160		
Loose-tools		1,250		
To Insurance:				
Factory Building	1,500			
Plant & Machinery	2,400	3,900		
To Rates & Taxes, Buileding		2,400		
		2,19,610		2,19,610

Trading and Profit and Loss Account of Sadhu Ram for the year ending 31st December, 1973

		Rs.		Rs.
To Opening Stock (adjusted)		56,000	By Sales *less* Returns	3,23,400
To Manufacturing A/c, cost of goods produced		2,08,610	By Closing Stock, Finished goods	38,000
To Gross Profit c/d		96,790		
		3,61,400		3,61,400
To Salaries		9,400	By Gross Profit b/d	96,790
To Rates & Taxes on Building		800	By Discount	1,100
To Printing & Stationery		2,000	By Sundry Receipts	74
To Depreciation:	Rs.			
Land & Building	750			
Furniture & fittings	1,000	1,750		
To Insurance on Building		500		
To General Expenses		2,000		
To Audit Fee		2,000		
To Carriage Outward		3,750		
To Royalties		3,234		
To Advertisement		4,000		
To Provision for Bad & Doubtful Debts:				
Provision required	1,750			
Add Bad Debts	3,000			
	4,750			
Less Existing Provision	1,000	3,750		
To Interest on Loan		540		
To Expenses Outstanding*		5,300		
To Net Profit		58,940		
		97,964		97,964

*Rs. 5,600 less Rs.300 credit balance of previous year less the amount paid.

Balance Sheet of Sadhu Ram as on 31st December, 1973

Liabilities and Capital		Rs.	*Assets*		Rs.
	Rs.		*Fixed Assets*:	Rs.	
Capital:		1,00,000	Land & Building	60,000	
Proprietor's Current Account:			*Less*: Depreciation	3,000	57,000
Balance as shown	15,000		Plant & Machinery	55,800	
Add: Net Profit	58,940		*Less*: Depreciation	11,160	44,640
	73,940				
Less: Drawings	12,000		Loose-tools	5,000	
	61,940		*Less*: Depreciation	1,250	3,750
Less: Adjustment of Opening Stock	1,000	60,940	Furniture & Fittings	10,000	
Liabilities:					
Mrs. Sadhu Ram's Loan	6,000		*Less*: Depreciation	1,000	9,000
Add: Interest due	60	6,060	*Investments* (Market Value Rs.15,000)		16,250
Sundry Creditors		66,156			
Bills Payable		15,300			
Outstanding Expenses		5,600	*Current Assets*:		
Royalties Payable		234	Stock-in-trade:		
			Finished goods	22,000	
			Work-in-Progress	11,000	
			Raw Materials	38,000	71,000
			Sundry Debtors	35,000	
			Less: Provision for Doubtful Debts	1,750	33,250
			Cash in hand		2,500
			Cash at Bank		15,700
			Prepaid Expenses		1,200
		2,54,290			2,54,290

Exercises

1. Ascertain the gross profit from the following figures :

	Rs.
Opening Stock	20,800
Closing Stock	18,700
Purchases	85,000
Carriage on Purchases	2,300
Carriage on Sales	3,000
Rent of Office	4,800
Sales	1,40,000

(Gross Profit, Rs. 50,600)

2. Find out the gross profit and net profit from the following :

	Rs.		Rs.
Sales	1,60,000	Closing Stock	22,100
Purchases	91,300	Purchases Returns	4,000
Wages	18,100	Sales Returns	5,000
Rent—Factory	3,000	Salaries (Office)	6,000
Office	2,000	General Expenses	4,500
Freight—Purchases	3,000	Discount from Creditors	1,100
Sales	1,500	Discount to Customers	1,800
Opening Stock	24,000		

(Gross Profit Rs. 41,700 ; Net Profit Rs. 27,000)

3. The trial balance of Chatterji on 31st December, 1978 reevealed the following balances :

Debit Balances	Rs.	*Credit Balances*	Rs.
Plant & Machinery	80,000	Capital Account	1,00,000
Purchases	68,000	Sales	1,27,000
Sales Returns	1,000	Purchases Returns	1,275
Opening Stock	30,000	Discounts Received	800
Discount Allowed	350	Sundry Creditors	25,000
Bank Charges	75		
Sundry Debtors	45,000		
Salaries	6,800		
Wages	10,000		
Freight : In	750		
Out	1,200		
Rent, Rates, Taxes	2,000		
Advertisements	2,000		
Cash in Bank	6,900		
	2 54,075		2,54,075

The stock on 31st December, 1978 was valued at Rs. 35,000. Prepare Trading and Profit and Loss Account for the year ended 31st December, 1978 and Balance Sheet as on that date.

(Gross Profit, Rs. 53,525 ; Net Profit, Rs. 41,900; Total of Balance Sheet, Rs. 1,66,900)

4. On 1st January, 1978 the Provision for Bad Debts stood at Rs. 1,100. During the year Bad Debts totalled to Rs. 800. At the end of the year the Sundry Debtors were Rs. 20,000. The firm wishes to maintain the Provision for Bad Debts @ 5% of the Sundry Debtors. Give the necessary journal entries and the Provision for Bad Debts Account. *(P. & L. A/c debited with Rs. 700)*

5. On 1st January, 1966 the Provision for Bad Debts stood at Rs. 1,500. The total debtors on 31st December, 1977 were Rs. 12,500 but out of these, Rs. 500 were bad and had to be written off. The Provision is to be maintained

at 5% of the debtors. Give the journal entries and the Provision for Bad Debts Account.
(P. & L. A/c credited with Rs. 400)

6. The following information is supplied to you :

	Rs.
Provision for Doubtful Debts on 1st Jan. 1978	**1,200**
Provision for Discount on Debtors („)	**500**
Bad Debts written off during 1978	**900**
Discounts allowed during 1978	**1,400**
Sundry Debtors on 31st December, 1978	**20,000**

The Provision for Doubtful Debts is maintained at 4% of debtors and the Provision for Discounts is maintained @ 2% of the debtors. Give the accounts relating to the two provisions.
(Profit & Loss A/c debited with : Rs. 500 for Provision for Doubtful Debts : and Rs. 1,284 for Provision for Discounts)

7. (*a*) The Reserve for Discounts on Creditors as on 31st December, 1977 was Rs. 600. During 1978, discounts received from creditors were Rs. 950. On 31st December, 1978 the creditors totalled Rs. 18,000. The Reserve for Discounts on creditors is to be kept @ 2% of the creditors. Give the required journal entries and the Reserve for Discount on Creditors Account.
(Profit and Loss A/c credited with Rs. 710)

(*b*) For the first time in 1979, a firm decided to make appropriate provision for doubtful debts. On 31st December, 1979 it considered the following debts to be doubtful of recovery :—

Pee	Rs.	1,100
Que	Rs.	650
Aar	Rs.	1,340
Ess	Rs.	810

Que paid the amount due but Pee became insolvent and only 30 P in the rupee was recovered from the Receiver. At the end of 1980, it was clear that Ess would pay the amount (in fact it was recovered in January 1981) but it was thought that Wye and Zed respectively owing Rs.1,500 and Rs.900 would not be able to pay.

Prepare the Provision for Doubtful Debts Account for 1980.

8. A firm wishes to equalise the charge to Profit and Loss Account in respect of repairs and renewals to plant. It ascertains that the total expenditure on repairs and renewals on plant (life 15 years) will be Rs. 28,500. The actual expenditure on repairs and renewals in the first three years was Rs. 600, Rs. 1,200, and Rs. 2,100. Give journal entries to record the above and show the accounts relating to repairs and renewals.
(Annual debit to Profit and Loss A/c, Rs. 1,900 ; Balance in Repairs and Renewals Provision A/c (3rd year), Rs. 1,500)

9. The Sundry Debtors and Sundry Creditors of a firm on 31st December 1970 were Rs.20,000 and Rs.15,000 respectively. During 1970, the Discounts received were Rs. 750 and Discounts allowed Rs.860.

On 31st December 1970, it was decided to create Reserve for Discounts at $2\frac{1}{2}$ per cent on Sundry Debtors and 3 per cent on Sundry Creditors.

Show the Journal, Ledger, Profit and Loss and Balance Sheet entries.
(B. Com. Madars)

10. The Swan Industries Ltd. removed their works to more suitable premises and given below are some of their transactions :

(*a*) A sum of Rs.4,750 was expended on dismantling, removing and reinstalling Plant, Machinery and Fixtures.
(*b*) The removal of Stock from the old works to the new cost Rs.500.
(*c*) Plant and Machinery which stood in the books at Rs.75,000 included a machine at a book value of Rs.1,500. This being obsolete was sold off at Rs.500 and was replaced by a new machine costing Rs.2,400.
(*d*) The freight and carriage on the new machine amounted to Rs.150, and erection charges cost Rs.275.
(*e*) A sum of Rs.1,200 was spent on painting the new factory.

State which items of expenditure would be charged to Capital and which to Revenue. *(B. Com. Madras)*

11. After the preparation of the Trial Balance on 31st Dec., 1978, the accountant of a firm found that entries in respect of the following had not yet been passed or passed wrongly :—

(*a*) Wages due but not yet paid, Rs. 1,500.

(*b*) Wages incurred on installation of machinery, Rs. 2,000. The amount stands debited to the Wages Account.

(*c*) Goods destroyed by fire, Rs. 4,000. The goods were not insured.

(*d*) Goods returned by customers, Rs. 1,100 ; goods included in stock.

(*e*) Purchases made, Rs. 1,500. The goods have not been included in the closing stock.

(*f*) On 31st July a policy had been taken out against fire on which the premium paid was Rs. 3,000; the amount stands debited to Insurance A/c.

(*g*) An apprentice had been taken on 1st April, 1978 on payment of Rs. 2,000. This was the fee for two years. The amount was credited to General Expenses Account.

(*h*) Goods worth Rs. 600 were used by the proprietor at his house.

(*i*) Stamp Duty on purchase of buildings, Rs. 4,500 stands debited to Legal Expenses Account.

(*j*) Lease Rent for 1978 and 1979 was paid totalling Rs. 3,000. This stands debited to Rent Account.

Pass the necessary adjustment entries. What will the net effect on the profit of the firm ?

(As a result of adjustment entries, profit will be increased by Rs. 6,500)

12. Below is given the Trial Balance of Sarkar as at 31st March, 1978.

You are required to prepare the Trading and Profit and Loss Account for the year ended 31st March, 1978 and a Balance Sheet as at this date :

TRIAL BALANCE

	Rs.	Rs.
Capital Account		75,000
Stock	45,000	
Purchases	2,25,000	
Plant and Machinery	75,000	
Trade Charges	10,000	
Sales		4,20,750
Carriage In	2,500	
Carriage Out	1,500	
Factory Rent	1,500	
Discount	350	
Insurance	700	
Sundry Debtors	60,000	
Sundry Creditors		15,000
Office Rent	3,000	
Bad Debts Provision		200
Printing and Stationery	600	
General Expenses	2,800	
Advertising	15,000	
Bills Receivable	3,000	
Drawings	6,000	
Bills Payable		2,000
Salaries	18,000	
Manufacturing Wages	20,000	
Furniture & Fixtures	7,500	
Coal, Gas & Water	1,000	
Cash in Hand	2,000	
Cash at Bank	12,500	
Rs.	5,12,950	5,12,950

The following adjustments are required :—

(*a*) The closing stock amounted to Rs. 35,000.

(*b*) Plant & Machinery and Furniture & Fixture are to be depreciated at 10% and 5% respectively.

(*c*) Bad Debts Reserve to be raised to 2½% on Debtors

(*d*) Provide for Outstanding Liabilities :—

	Rs.
Factory Rent	300
Office Rent	600

(*e*) Insurance includes Rs. 100 respect of 1978-79

(*Gross Profit, Rs. 1,60,450 ; Net Profit. Rs. 98,825, Balance Sheet Totals, Rs. 1,85,725*)

13. Prepare Trading and Profit and Loss Account and Balance Sheet as on 31st March, 1976 from the following balances :

	Rs.
M. Mirza's Capital Account	1,19,400
M. Mirza's Drawings Account	10,550
Sundry Creditors	59,630
6% Loan Account (Credit)	20,000
Cash in hand	3,030
Cash at bank	18,970
Sundry Debtors	62,000
Bills Receivable	9,500
Provision for Doubtful Debts	2,500
Fixtures and Fittings	8,970
Plant & Machinery	28,800
Stock, 1st April, 1975	89,780
Purchases	2,56,590
Manufacturing Wages	40,970
Sales	3,56,530
Returns Inwards	2,780
Salaries	11,000
Rent and Taxes	5,620
Interest and Discount (Debit)	5,870
Travelling Expenses	1,880
Repairs and Renewals	3,370
Insurance (including Premium @ Rs. 300 per annum paid up to 30th Sept., 1976)	400
Bad Debts	3,620
Commission Received	5,640

Stock on hand on 31st March, 1976 was Rs. 1,28,960. Create a Provision of 5% on Sundry Debtors. Charge 5% Interest on Capital. Manufacturing Wages include Rs. 1,200 for erection of new machinery purchased last year. Depreciate Plant and Machinery by 5% and Fixtures and Fittings by 10% per annum. Commission earned but not received amounts to Rs. 600. Interest on Loan for the last 2 months is not paid.

(*Gross Profit, Rs. 96,570 ; Net Profit Rs. 62,033 ; Total of Balance Sheet, Rs. 2,56,683*)

14. From the undermentioned Trial Balance of Govinda prepare a Trading and Profit and Loss Account for the year ended 31st December, 1978 and Balance Sheet as at that date :

	Rs.	Rs.
Capital Account		1,00,000
Stock	30,000	
Purchases	1,00,000	
Sales		2,00,000
Returns In and Out	2,500	1,500
Bad Debts Provision		750
Bills Receivable and Payable	45,000	10,000
Carriage	7,500	
Plant and Machinery	65,000	
Office Furniture	3,500	
Sundry Debtors	60,000	
Sundry Creditors		28,000
Coal, Gas and Water	1,200	
Wages	10,000	
Duty and Clearing Charges	1,500	
Office Rent	2,500	
Printing and Stationery	500	
Insurance	350	
Carriage Out	4,200	
Salaries	18,000	
Factory Rent	1,900	
Electricity and Telephone	800	
Loan @ 9% (taken on May 1, 1978)		25,000
Bank Charges	25	
Drawings	5,000	
Cash in hand	1,250	
Cash at Bank	4,525	
Rs.	3,65,250	3,65,250

The following adjustments are to be taken into consideration : Closing Stock, Rs. 40,000. Outstanding Liabilities to be provided for : Salary—Rs. 2,400, Factory Rent 1,500 and Office Rent 550. Bad Debts Provision to be adjusted to 2½% of Sundry Debtors after elimination of Bad Debts amounting to Rs. 2,000. Goods withdrawn Rs. 2,525 for private use. Depreciation on Plant 10%. Interest on Capital at 5% per annum.

The manager is allowed a commission of 5% of net profit before charging the commission.

(Gross Profit Rs. 87,925 ; Net Profit, Rs. 40,755 ; Total of Balance Sheet, Rs. 2,09,325)

15. The following Trial Balance has been taken from the books of Chandra as on 31st December, 1967—

You are required to prepare the Trading and the Profit and Loss Account for the year ended 31st December, 1977 and the Balance Sheet as at that date—

	Rs.	Rs.
Capital A/c		80,000
Drawings	4,800	
Stock 31st Dec., 1977	40,000	
Office Furniture	13,000	
Printing and Stationery	1,200	
Coal Gas and Water	600	
Freight and Clearing Charges	3,500	
Purchases adjusted	65,000	
Sundry Creditors		15,000
Bank Loan (at 16%, taken on 1st Jan., 1977)		20,000
Discount	950	400
Repairs to Plant	1,000	
Sales		2,05,350
Factory Rent	2,500	
Salaries	2,800	
Manufacturing Wages	24,000	
Advertising	19,000	
Plant and Machinery	70,000	
Office Rent	3,600	
Miscellaneous Expenses	1,000	
Bad Debts Provision		600
Bills Receivable	22,000	
Bills Payable		1,500
Carriage Out	1,500	
Insurance	600	
Interest on Bank Loan	1,000	
Cash at Bank	7,500	
Cash in h	3,500	
Sundry Debtors	33,800	
	3,22,850	3,22,850

The following adjustments are required :—

(*a*) Depreciate :
Plant and Machinery @ 10%.
Office Furniture @ 7½%.

(*b*) Provision for Bad Debts to be raised to 5% and Reserve for Discount on Creditors to 1%.

(*c*) Insurance Premium was paid for six months up to 31st March, 1978.

(*d*) Sales include Rs. 350 worth of goods which were taken by the proprietor.

(*e*) Half of the Advertising A/c is to be carried to a Suspense A/c and to be written off in the subsequent 2 years.

(*f*) Rs. 100 were paid in advance for Factory Rent ; and

(g) An outstanding bill for Repairs amounting to Rs. 250 remains to be paid.

(Gross Profit, Rs. 1,09,850, Net Profit, Rs. 76,035 ; Total of Balance Sheet, Rs. 1,90,035)

16. (a) What do you understand by the term "Work-in-progress" in connection with a manufacturing concern and how would you value the same ?

(b) Draw up the Manufacturing Account showing cost of production and the Trading account showing gross profit from the following :—

	Rs.
Purchase of Raw Materials	3,000
Electric Power consumed	750
Opening stock—finished goods	5,000
Carriage on raw materials	100
Opening stock—partly finished goods	1,000
Returns—raw materials	200
Opening stock—raw materials	2,500
Sales	10,000
Repairs—Plant and Machinery	200
Wages Manufacturing	2,500
Factory rent and taxes	400
Sales returns	500
Depreciation—Factory Buildings	100
Depreciation—Plant and Machinery	300
Factory Insurance	150

The closing stock was : raw materials, Rs. 2,000, partly finished goods. Rs. 1,600 and finished goods, Rs. 8,000.

(Cost of goods manufactured, Rs. 7,200 ; Gross Profit, Rs. 5,300)

17. The following are the balances taken on 31st December, 1978, from the books of Mr. R. Gupta :—

Capital	8,794
Opening stock (1st January, 1978)	8,560
Discount (Cr.)	35
Wages	3,000
Advertising	470
Plant and Machinery	2,000
Sales	36,000
Electric energy and water	70
Returns outwards	190
Office rent	150
Purchases	26,270
Bills receivable	200
Cash at Bank	666
Furniture and Fittings	250
Cash in hand	5
Sundry creditors	845
Rates and taxes	30
Printing and Stationery	50
Sundry Debtors	1,800
Drawings	1,250
General Expenses	123
Insurance	42

Stock as on 31st December, 1978 was Rs. 3,980.

You are asked to prepare manufacturing and profit and Loss account for the year ending 31st December. 1978, and the balance-sheet as on that date after taking into consideration the following :—

(a) Rs. 15 owing for premises sublet, were not taken into account.

(b) Bad debts provision required is Rs. 250.

(c) Depreciation is to be written off at 10 per cent on Plant and Machinery and Furniture and Fittings.

(d) Insurance was prepaid to the extent of Rs. 13.

(*e*) Bills receivable Rs. 100, not yet due, were discounted on 31st December, 1978.

(*f*) The manager is entitled to a commission of 25 per cent on the net profits after charging such commission.

Prepare the Final Accounts and Balance Sheet relating to 1978.

(*Gross Profit. Rs. 2,270 ; Net Profit, Rs. 794 ; Total of Balance Sheet, Rs. 9,382*)

(*Hint* : Prepare Trial Balance first).

18. From the following Trial Balance, prepare the Trading and Profit and Loss Account for the year ended 31st December, 1977, and the Balance Sheet as at that date, of Mr. E.P. Taxwallah :—

	Dr. Rs.	*Cr.* Rs.
Capital Account		50,000
Provision for Bad Debts		3,000
10 per cent Mortgage Loan (as on 1st Jan. 1977)		45,000
Sundry Creditors		10,960
Bills Payable		8,150
Commission		2,870
Sales		1,22,040
Sundry Debtors	48,000	
Bills Receivable	13,795	
Goodwill	40,000	
Machinery and Plant	55,500	
Stock (1-1-1977) —Finished Goods	17,180	
Cash in Hand	860	
Manufacturing Charges	7,840	
Wages	8,000	
Wages Unpaid		1,500
Salary	4,340	
Postage & Telephone	540	
Rent	950	
Stationery & Printing	860	
Charges General	170	
Purchases (adjusted)	34,860	
Interest on Mortgage Loan	1,125	
Returns	3,500	5,000
Bad Debts	1,500	
Depreciation on Machinery	4,500	
Stock of Materials (31-12-77)	5,000	
	2,48,520	2,48,520

The following points, amongst others, are to be taken into consideration before preparing the final accounts :—

Closing Stock of Finished Goods is valued at Rs.10,000; Provision for Bad Debts is to be made up to 5 per cent and Provision for Discount on Debtors is required @ 2% of the Sundry Debtors. Unpaid bills for Purchases amounted to Rs.3,500; Intangible asset, if any, is to be written off to the extent of 25 per cent.

(*Gross Profit Rs.* 62,160; *Net Profit Rs.*37,358; *Total of Balance Sheet, Rs. 1,59,843*)

19. The balance sheet of Thapar on 1st January, 1978 was as follows :

	Rs.		Rs.
Sundry Creditors	15,000	Plant & Machinery	30,000
Expenses Payable	1,500	Furniture & Fixture	3,000
Capital	50,000	Stock	13,000
		Sundry Debtors	14,000
		Cash at Bank	6,500
	66,500		66,500

During 1978, his Profit and Loss Account revealed a net profit of Rs. 15,300. This was after allowing for the following :

(*a*) Interest on capital @ 6% p.a.

(*b*) Depreciation on Plant and Machinery @ 10% and on Furniture and Fixtures @ 5%.

(*c*) A Provision for Doubtful Debts @ 5% of the debtors as at 31st December, 1978.

But while preparing the Profit and Loss A/c he had forgotten to provide for (1) outstanding expenses totalling Rs. 1,800 and (2) prepaid insurance to the extent of Rs. 200.

His current assets and liabilities on 31st Dec. 1978 were : Stock Rs. 14,500 ; Debtors, Rs. 20,000 ; Cash at Bank, Rs. 10,350 and Sundry creditors, Rs. 11,400.

During the year he withdraw Rs. 6,000 for domestic use. Draw up his Balance Sheet at the end of the year. *(Total of Balance Sheet, Rs. 73,900)*

20. From the following Trial Balance of Alam, prepare Trading and Profit and Loss Account for the year ended 31st March, 1976 and a Balance Sheet as on that date :—

	Debits Rs.	*Credits* Rs.
Plant and Machinery	19,720	
Fixtures and Fittings	9,480	
Freehold Works	25,000	
Goodwill	30,000	
Sundry Debtors	78,140	
Horses and Carts	5,165	
Cash at Bank	7,540	
Cash in hand	145	
Alam's Capital Account		1,20,000
Sundry Creditors		54,160
Bank Loan		10,000
Provision for Bad and Doubtful Debts		2 000
Purchase Returns		1,140
Sales		2,06,850
Stock, 1st April, 1965	34,170	
Purchases	97,165	
Manufacturing Wages	34,965	
Carriage Inwards	1,980	
Manufacturing Expenses	9,455	
Factory Fuel & Power	1,276	
Factory Lighting	986	
Salaries	15,965	
Carriage Outwards	2,150	
Insurance & Taxes	3,685	
General Expenses	8,142	
Stable Expenses for Distribution	2,473	
Sales Returns	3,170	
Import Duty	928	
Bad Debts	1,485	
Interest and Bank Charges	475	
Prepaid Expenses	490	
Rs.	3,94,150	3,94,150

Adjustments :

(*a*) Stock on 31st March, 1976 Rs. 39,630.

(*b*) Depreciation—Plant & Machinery, 10 per cent, Fixtures & Fittings, 5 per cent and Horses & Carts, Rs. 1,000.

(*c*) Bring up Provisions for Bad and Doubtful Debts to 5 per cent.

(d) A Commission of one per cent on the Gross profit to be provided for Works Manager.

(e) A Commission of 5 per cent of net profits (after charging such commission) to be credited to the General Manager.

Make your calculations to the nearest rupee.

(Gross Profit, Rs. 63,525 ; Net Profit, Rs. 22,059 ; Total of Balance Sheet, Rs. 2,07,957)

21. From the following Trial Balance of Asif and Bimal, as at 31st December, 1977, you are requested to prepare Profit and Loss Account for the year ended on that date, and Balance Sheet as at that date.

	Debit Rs.	*Credit* Rs.
Salaries	24,000	
Rent, Rates, etc.	6,000	
Fire Insurance Premium (paid upto 30th June, 1978)	4,000	
General Expenses	6,000	
Asif's Capital		35,000
Bimal's Capital		25,000
Gross Profit		69,000
Loan from John taken on 1st July, 1977 @ 10% p.a.		20,000
Sundry Creditors		45,000
Plant and Machinery	75,000	
Sundry Debtors	45,000	
Dividend on Shares		1,000
Provision for Depreciation		15,000
Cash and Bank Balances	21,000	
Closing Stock	20,000	
Goods lost by fire	4,000	
Outstanding Salaries		1,000
Free distribution of samples	1,000	
Investment in shares	5,000	
	2,11,000	2,11,000

The following information is relevant :

(1) Sundry Debtors include an account of Shri Chenoy for Rs.3,000 for a dishonoured bill. Nothing is likely to be received from him.

(2) Rs.2,000 paid as donation to Bombay Education Society stands debited to the society's account, included in Sundry Debtors.

(3) Sundry Creditors include an amount of Rs.5,000 received from Mr. Shah and credited to his account. The amount was written off as a bad debt in a previous year.

(4) Sundry Debtors and Sundry Creditors both include the account of Mr. Tanna, showing debit and credit respectively of Rs.2,000 and Rs.1,500.

(5) Each partner has withdrawn Rs.500 p.m.; it has been included in the Salaries A/c.

(6) Rs.20,000 was added to Plant & Machinery on 1st July, 1977.

(7) Depreciation @ 10% p.a. has to be provided on Plant & Machinery.

(8) Profit is to be distributed equally among the partners.

(Adapted from F.Y. B. Com., Bombay)

*(Profit Rs.*33,000; *Total of Balance Sheet Rs.*1,41,500)

22. The manager of a manufacturing concern is paid partly by salary and partly by commission. You are required to ascertain the profit and the percentage of net profit to the manufacturing cost from the following figures :

	Rs.
Stock, 1st January	**10,600**
Purchases	**30,000**
Wages	**25,000**
Office salaries	**6,000**

Discount on sales	2,000
Carriage inwards	3,200
Carriage outwards	6,000
Printing and stationery	300
Rent (3/4 to Factory)	4,800
Postage and telegrams	350
Travelling	2,500
General Charges	350
Commission	2,600
Workshop power	5,500
Rebate on purchases	1,000
Sales	1,00,000
Stock, 31st December	20,000

Note : Assume the opening and closing stocks are of raw materials,

(Cost of goods produced, Rs. 56,900 ; Net Profit, Rs. 21,800)

23. The undernoted figures were extracted from the Books of Mr. A. Prepare a comparative Manufacturing Account from these figures, showing the profit earned.

	1977 Rs.	1978 Rs.
Purchases	3,87,200	4,56,100
Manufacturing wages	1,57,200	1,64,300
Factory power	94,100	95,000
Carriage Inwards	43,000	48,100
Initial stock (Raw Materials)	2,75,100	2,64,000
Final stock (,,)	2,64,000	2,98,000
Office Expenses	1,00,000	1,15,000
Sales	9,45,000	10,17,000

(Cost of Production : 1977, Rs. 6,92,600 ; 1978, Rs. 7,29,500)

24. The following are the balances of X, as on 31st December, 1978 :—

	Rs.	Rs.
Sundry Debtors		60,000
Sales		2,50,000
Sundry Creditors		10,000
General Trade Expenses		12,000
Factory Rent		2,000
Interest received		1,200
Purchase returns		2,000
Manufacturing Wages		20,000
Purchases		1,00,000
Discounts received		1,800
Provision for Bad Debts		2,000
Fixtures and Fittings		5,000
Carriage and Freight on Raw Materials		5,500
Capital		2,00,000
Drawings		35,000
Stock. 1st Jan. 1978		
Raw Materials	20,000	
Work in Progress	9,000	
Finished goods	21,000	50,000
Sales Returns		3,000
Plant and Machinery		60,000
Motor Vehicles		20,000
Freehold Offices		20,000
Balance at Bank		23,000
Advance on Mortgage (Dr.)		20,000
Cash Balance		100
Travelling Expenses		6,000
Discounts allowed		2,200
Office Salaries		22,000
Rates, Taxes and Insurance		1,200

Taking into account the undermentioned information, prepare—

(1) Manufacturing and Trading Accounts, showing gross profit for the year;

(2) Profit and Loss Account, showing net profit available for division among partners; and

(3) Balance Sheet as on 31st December, 1978.

Stock on hand, on 31st December, 1978 amounted to Rs. 75,000 made up as : Raw materials, Rs. 30,000; Work-in-Progress, Rs. 11,000; Finished goods, Rs. 34,000.

In December, 1978, finished goods were destroyed by fire. The total claim lodged was Rs. 6,000 out of which insurers admitted claim for Rs. 5,000. The amount had not been received yet.

Write off 5 per cent from Plant and Machinery.

Write off 10 per cent of Motor Vehicles and Fixtures and Fittings. Increase the Provision for Bad Debts to Rs. ¼,000.

(*Cost of Production, Rs.* 1,16,500 ; *Gross Profit, Rs.* 1,49,500. ; *Net Profit, Rs.* 1,03,600 ; *Total of Balance Sheet, Rs.* 2,78,600)

25. From the following Trial Balance prepare the Manufacturing and Profit and Loss Accounts for the year ended December, 1978 as well as the Balance Sheet as on that date :—

	Dr. Rs.	*Cr.* Rs.
Land and Buildings (Factory)	26,000	
Sundry Debtors	40,500	
Sundry Creditors		45,000
Plant and Machinery	20,000	
Purchases—Raw Materials (less Returns)	35,000	
Sales (Less Returns)		1,23,400
Finished Stock— 1st January, 1978	18,000	
Raw Materials— 1st January, 1978	3,500	
Work in process— 1st January, 1978	2,000	
Wages	27,000	
Factory Rent and Taxes	2,500	
Salaries of Works staff	6,800	
Advertising	3,000	
Office Rent and Insurance	4,800	
General Expenses (including salaries)	6,800	
Carriage Inwards	1,700	
Discounts allowed	1,400	
Discounts received		1,100
Bad Debts	750	
Provision for Doubtful Debts		1,000
Factory Expenses	3,400	
Patent Rights	2,000	
X's Capital Account		20,000
Y's Capital Account		25,000
X's Drawings	3,600	
Y's Drawings	2,500	
Cash at Bank	4,000	
Cash in hand	250	
	2,15,500	2,15,500

Stocks on 31st December. 1978, were as follows :—

	Rs.
Raw Materials	4,000
Work-in-process	4,500
Finished Goods	28,000

The outstanding expenses were :—Factory Rent, Rs. 250, Wages Rs. 600 and Office Salaries, Rs. 3,000. Write off Rs. 500 as Bad Debts and provide 5 per cent Provision for Doubtful Debts and 2 per cent. Provision for Discounts. Depreciate Buildings by 2 per cent, Plant by 7½ per cent and Patents by 10%.

The General Manager is entitled to a commission of 25 per cent of the net profits after charging such commission.

The profits were shared between X and Y in the proportion of 3 : 2.

(Figures to be worked to the nearest rupee.)

(Cost of goods manufactured, Rs. 76,470, ; Gross Profit, Rs. 56,930 ; Net Profit, Rs. 28,816 ; Total Balance Sheet, Rs. 1,23,770)

26. Show by means of journal entries how the following matters should be adjusted when preparing the annual accounts of a firm for the year ended 30th September 1984 :

(*a*) Goods sold and recorded as sales for Rs. 4 000 were packed and the invoice for them sent to the customer. Stocktaking intervened, and the parcel of goods was not dispatched but was included in Stock-in-hand.

(*b*) Serveral employees took their salary in advance in the month of September 1984, which was payable to them in October, 1984 amounting to Rs. 2,500.

(*c*) A purchase was made for a staff member of Rs. 1 000 and the cost was included in purchases. A deduction of similar amount was made from his salary and the net payment to him posted to salaries account.

(*d*) Wages paid to the firm's own workmen for making certain additions to machinery amounting to Rs. 750, were posted to wages account.

(*e*) A dishonoured bill receivable for Rs. 500 returned by she Bank with whom it had been discounted, had been credited to Bank Account and debited to Bills Receivable Account.

(*f*) A cheque amounting to Rs. 270 received from a customer Mr. X was dishonoured. The returned cheque was correctly entered in the Cash Book but was posted there-from to Allowances Account.

(*g*) A duplicate invoice for a purchase of machinery costing Rs. 10,000 was erroneously passed again and entered into the books.

(*h*) A sum of Rs. 1,000 drawn by the proprietor was debited to Travelling Expenses. *(C.A., Entrance Ahapsed)*

What wjll be that the effect on the profit of the year as a result of the evrors given above ? *[Profit reduced by Rs. 520]*

CHAPTER IX

CONSIGNMENT ACCOUNTS

The word 'consignment' technically means sending of goods to another person without transferring the ownership to that person, but requiring that person to effect sales thereof. The ownership remains with the sender or the consignee. If the goods are destroyed, the receiver (or the consignee) is not at all responsible; the loss will fall on the consignor. The consignee will try to sell the goods according to the instructions of the consignor and will deduct the expenses incurred by him and also his remuneration for making the sales. The amount of the sale proceeds, after deducting expenses and remuneration, is remitted to the consignor.

The relationship between the consignor and the consignee is that of principal and agent. The consignee is the agent. The law of agency applies. The consignee acts entirely on behalf of the consignor and, therefore, the loss or profit is that of the consignor and not the consignee. The consignee is entitled to his remuneration which is generally fixed on the basis of a commission on sales. Usually theexpenses incurred by him must also be reimbursed by the principal but this depends upon the agreement. It is possible to make the agent responsible for expenses and to compensate him only by way of a flat commission. The student must remember that the consignee does not buy the goods ; he merely receives possession of the goods. Therefore, the consignor does not send him an invoice which is made out when goods are sold. But a statement similar to invoice will be made out and sent to the consignee. Such a statement is called "Proforma invoice", *i.e.*, invoice for form s sake.

The consignee informs the agent about the sale effected and expenses incurred through a statement known as Account Sales. Account Sales is periodically prepared. The following is a specimen.

Account Sales of Telly Radio Sets received from and sold on behalf and at the risk of Airwaves Ltd.

Particulars	Details Rs.	P.	Amount Rs.	P.
100 Sets sold @ Rs. 250 per set	25,000	—		
60 Sets sold @ Rs. 240 per set	14,400	—	39,400	—
Less : Expenses incurred :				
Freight & Cartage	500	—		
Godown Rent	100	—		
Insurance	150	—		
Commission @ 10% of Sales	3,940	—	4,690	—
			34,710	—
Less Bill already accepted			20,000	—
Bank Draft now enclosed.			14,710	—

E. & O. E. For Pleasant Sounds & Co.

Delhi, the 26th October, 1978 G. Ram

Partner

The above statement shows that M/s. Pleasant Sounds & Co. have sold 160 radio sets for a total amount of Rs. 39,400 on behalf of Airwaves Ltd. This amount belongs to them. But out of this amount, the agent or the consignee is deducting expenses totalling Rs. 750, and commission @ 10%, *i.e.*, Rs. 3,940 and also Rs. 20,000 the amount of the bill of exchange already issued in favour of the principal. The balance Rs. 14,710 is now remitted by bank draft. E. &. O. E. stands for "errors and omissions excepted". It means that clerical errors can be rectified later.

Usually the agent or the consignee is asked to accept a bill of exchange to cover part of the value of the goods. This is a guarantee by the agent that when sales are effected, he will make the necessary payment. Of course, instead of a bill of exchange, the agent may remit a sum of money to the principal as an advance. This advance or the amount of the bill of exchange will be adjusted when the goods are sold.

Del Credere Commission. Ordinarily agents do not guarantee the performance of the contract on behalf of third parties. This means that if the agent sells the goods on behalf of the principal to, say A, the agent does not guarantee that A will make the payment. If A fails to pay, the loss will fall on the principal. If the agent is to be made responsible for the payment of the sale proceeds by purchasers of the goods, he will require an extra commission which is known as del credere commission. This commission is payable on the total sale proceeds. Such agents are known as del credere agents.

Entries in the Books of the Consignor. Before we give the entries, we should again make it clear that the property or ownership in the goods does not pass to the agent and, therefore, when goods are sent on consignment to someone, it cannot be treated as a sale. In fact, the profit or loss on the consignment of the goods cannot be known immediately, *i.e.*, not till the agent has effected sales. It is possible that the principal makes no record of the transactions in his books when goods are sent. He may pass entries only when he receives an Account Sales from the agent. He may debit the agent and credit Sales Account with the sale proceeds and, then, he may debit expenses and credit the agent for the commission earned by him and expenses incurred by him. In this manner the profit or loss on the particular consignment will not be known separately and will be merged with the total profit or loss of the firm.

It is advisable, however, that we should know the profit made or loss suffered on such ventures. Therefore, the usual method of dealing with consignment is to have such accounts as will show the profit or loss on every consignment separately. This system merely consists of opening an account for every consignment. Now we give detailed entries for recording consignments with the purpose mentioned above.

(1) On despatch of goods :—

Consignment Account To Goods Sent on Consignment Account	Dr.	with the cost of goods.

(2) On payment of expenses on despatch :—

Consignment Account To Bank Account	Dr.	with the amount spent as expenses

(3) On the consignee accepting a bill of exchange :—

Bills Receivable Account To Consignee's Personal Account	Dr.	with the amount of the bill.

(4) On the consignee reporting sale (as per Account Sales) :—

Consignee's Personal A/c. To Consignment Account	Dr.	with gross proceeds of sales.

(5) For expenses incurred by the consignee (according to the Account Sales) :—

Consignment Account To Consignee's Personal Account	Dr.	with the amount of the expenses.

(6) For commission payable to the consignee :—

Consignment Account To Consignee's Personal Account	Dr.	with the amount of the commission due to the consignee.

Assuming that all the goods sent have been sold, the Consignment Account, at this stage, will reflect profit or loss. This should be transferred to the Profit and Loss Account. The entry in case of profit is :

Consignment Account Dr.

To Profit and Loss A/c.

In case of loss, the entry is the reverse.

Note : The "Goods Sent on Consignment Account" is transferred to the credit of Purchases Account in case of trading concerns and Trading Account in case of industrial concerns.

Stock. If at the end of the year some goods remain unsold with the consignee the value of such goods must be ascertained and the profit or loss should be found out by taking this stock into account; an additional entry should be passed :

Stock on Consignment Account Dr.

To Consignment Account

"Stock on Consignment Account" is an asset and will be shown in the Balance Sheet of the consignor. Valuation of stock is discussed a little later.

Illustration White of Bombay sends woollen goods costing Rs. 10,000 to Black of Calcutta to be sold on consignment basis. White pays Rs. 200 as expenses. The goods are received by Black and he accepts a bill of exchange immediately, payable after three months, for Rs. 6,000. The bill was immediately discounted @ 6%. Later, Black sends an Account Sales to White showing that sales have been effected totalling Rs. 11,000. His expenses are: freight Rs. 500, godown rent Rs. 100 and insurance Rs. 100. Black is entitled to a commission of 8 per cent. The cost of the goods still lying unsold with Black is ascertained to be Rs. 4,500.

Prepare the Account Sales to be submitted by Black to White. Give journal entries and ledger account in the books of White, assuming that Black has remitted all the amount due from him.

Solutions :

Account sales of woollen goods received from and sold

on behalf of and at the risk of White

Particulars		*Details* Rs.	P.	*Amount* Rs.	P.
Woollen goods sold				11,000	—
Less : Expenses	Rs.				
Freight	500				
Godown Rent	100				
Insurance	100	700	—		
Commission @ 8%		880	—	1,580	—
				9,420	—
Less Bill accepted already				6,000	—
Remittance enclosed				3,420	—

E. & O.E. Black

Calcutta, the....................

Solution :

White's Journal

				Dr. Rs.		Cr. Rs.	
?	?	Consignment to Calcutta A/c Dr. To Goods Sent on Consignment Account Cost of goods sent to Black of Calcutta to be sold on consignment basis.		10,000	—	10,000	—
		Consignment to Calcutta A/c Dr. To Bank Account Expenses incurred on the consignment to Calcutta.		200	—	200	—
		Bills Receivable Account Dr. To Black Acceptance received from Black as advance.		6,000	—	6,000	—
		Bank Account Dr. Discount Account Dr. To Bills Receivable Account Black's acceptance discounted @ 6% ; discount being Rs. *i.e.*, $\frac{6,000\times6}{100}\times\frac{3}{12}$		5,910 90	— —	6,000	—
		Black Dr. To Consignment to Calcutta Account Sales effected by Black as per Account Sales.		11,000	—	11,000	—
		Consignment to Calcutta A/c Dr. To Black Expenses incurred by Black on the consignment as per Account Sales.		700	—	700	—
		Consignment to Calcutta A/c Dr. To Black Commission @ 8% on sales due to Black.		880	—	880	—
		Bank Account Dr. To Black Amount received from Black in settlement.		3,420	—	3,420	—
		Stock on Consignment A/c Dr. To Consignment to Calcutta A/c Value of stock still unsold with Black.		4,500	—	4,500	—
		Consignment to Calcutta A/c Dr. To Profit and Loss Account Profit on the consignment to Calcutta transferred to Profit and Loss Account (*See* consignment A/c)		3,720	—	3,720	—
		Goods sent on Consignment A/c Dr. To Purchases Account Transfer of Goods sent on Consignment Account to Purchases Account		10,000	—	10,000	—

LEDGER ACCOUNTS

Consignment to Calcutta Account

Dr. | | | | | | | *Cr.*

		Rs.				Rs.	
?	To Goods sent on Consignments A/c	10,000	—		By Black— Sale Proceeds	11,000	—
	To Bank— Expenses	200	—		By Stock on Consignment Account	4,500	—
	To Black— Freight 500, Godown Rent 100, Insurance 100	700	—				
	To Black— Commission	880	—				
	To Profit and Loss A/c— Profit transferred	3,720	—				
		15,500	—			15,500	

Goods sent on Consignment A/c

		Rs.				Rs.	
?	To Purchases A/c— transfer	10,000	—	?	By Consignment to Calcutta A/c	10,000	—

Bank Account

		Rs.				Rs.	
	To Bills Receivable Account	5,910	—		By Consignment to Calcutta A/c	200	—
	To Black	3,420	—				

Black

		Rs.				Rs.	
?	To Consignment to Calcutta A/c—Sale Proceeds	11,000	—	?	By Bills Receivable A/c	6,000	—
					By Consignment to Calcutta A/c—		
					Expenses	700	—
					Commission	880	—
					By Bank A/c	3,420	—
		11,000				11,000	

Bills Receivable Account

		Rs.				Rs.	
	To Black	6,000			By Bank A/c	5,910	—
					By Discount A/c	90	—
		6,000	—			6,000	—

Discount Account

		Rs.				Rs.	
	To Bills Receivable Account	90	—		By Profit & Loss A/c—transfer	90	—

Purchases Account

						Rs.	
		?			By Goods sent on Consignment A/c	10,000	—

Profit & Loss Account

		Rs.				Rs.	
	To Discount	90	—		By Consignment to Calcutta Account	3,720	—

Stock on Consignment Account

		Rs.			Rs.
	To Consignment to Calcutta A/c	4,500 —		By Balance c/d	4,500 —
Next Year	To Balance b/d	4,500 —			

Books of Consignee. As we already know, the consignee is not the owner of the goods and, therefore, he makes no entry when he receives the goods. One should also note that the consignee is not at all concerned with the profit or loss on the goods. Usually, therefore, the following entries will be found in the books of the agent or consignee :—

(1) On despatch of goods by the consignor ... no entry

(2) On payment of expenses by the consignor ... no entry

(3) On the consignee accepting a bill of exchange :

Consignor's Personal A/c Dr. } with the amount of the bill.
To Bills Payable Account

(4) On expenses incurred by the consignee on the consignment :

Consignor's Personal A/c Dr.
To Cash Account

(5) On sales being effected :

Cash (or Bank) Account Dr.
To Consignor's Personal A/c

(6) On commission being earned :

Consignor's Personal A/c Dr.
To Commission Account

Taking illustration No. 40, the journal entries and ledger accounts in the books of Black will be as follows :—

Black's Journal

			Dr. Rs.	Cr. Rs.
?	White ... ... Dr. To Bills Payable Account Acceptance sent to White as advance against consignment.		6,000 —	6,000 —
	White ... ... Dr. To Bank Account Expenses incurred on the consignment on behalf of White.		700 —	700 —
	Bank Account ... ... Dr. To White Sales effected out of goods received on consignment on behalf of White.		11,000 —	11,000 —
	White ... ... Dr. To Commission Account Commission @ 8% due from White for effecting sales.		880 —	880 —
	White ... ... Dr. To Bank Account Remittance of the amount due to White to settle his account.		3,420 —	3,420 —
	Bills Payable Account ... ... Dr. To Bank Account Amount paid against acceptance given to White.		6,000 —	6,000 —

LEDGER ACCOUNTS

White

Dr. Cr.

	Rs.			Rs.
To Bills Payable A/c	6,000 —	?	By Bank Account Sale Proceeds	11,000 —
To Bank A/c-expenses	700 —			
To Commission A/c	880 —			
To Bank A/c	3,420 —			
	11,000 —			11,000 —

Bank Account

		Rs.				Rs.	
	To White—Sale Proceeds	11,000	—	?	By White	700	—
					By Bills Payable A/c	6,000	—

Bills Payable Account

		Rs.				Rs.	
?	To Bank A/c	6,000	—		By White	6,000	—

Commission Account

					By White	880	—

Valuation of Stock. The valuation of stock lying with the consignee is done on the same basis as ordinary stock, that is, cost or market price whichever is lower. Thus if 100 units are consigned at a cost of Rs. 50 each and if, out of these, 20 units remain unsold, then the cost is Rs. 1,000. If the selling price of these units is, say Rs. 60 each, the value of the stock will be still Rs. 1,000. But if the selling price is, say, Rs. 45 each, then, on the basis of market price which is lower, the value of the stock will be Rs. 900.

The meaning of cost, however, should be properly understood. Cost is not merely the amount paid by the consignor to purchase the goods. It should also include the expenses which are incurred to move the goods from the consignor's premises to the premises of the consignee. All expenses which are incurred up to the moment the goods are received into the godown of the consignee are treated properly as part of cost. Therefore, such expenses should be included while valuing the stock. But expenses incurred after the goods have been put into the godown should not be included in the cost because such expenses do not increase the value of the goods usually. It does not matter who pays the expenses. It is the nature of expenses which will determine whether they should be included in the cost or not. Suppose, 1,000 units are despatched at a cost of Rs. 20 each. The consignor pays Rs. 100 for insurance in transit and Rs. 200 for packing. The consignee pays Rs. 700 for freight, Rs. 100 as octroi duty and another Rs. 100 as cartage. He also pays Rs. 200 as godown rent and Rs. 150 as insurance premium. The last two items will be excluded while calculating the cost. Therefore, the total cost will be Rs. 21,200. The cost of one unit therefore, comes to Rs. 21.20. If 150 units remain unsold, the value of the stock will be : 150×21.20, *i.e.*, Rs. 3,180. Of course, if the market price is less than this figure, the value of the stock will be on the basis of market price.

Normal Loss. Normal loss of goods should also be considered while valuing the stock. Normal loss means inherent and unavoidable loss, that is to say, a loss which will occur in spite of all care. Suppose 100 tonnes of coal are despatched. The cost of 1 tonne of coal is Rs. 80 and the freight incurred is Rs. 360. To the consignor the total cost comes to Rs. 8,360. In the nature of coal some shortage is unavoidable. Suppose, the consignee receives only 95 tonnes. It is legitimate to say that the cost is Rs. 8,360 for 95 tonnes. In that case the consignor can properly say that the cost of 1 tonne of coal is Rs. $\frac{8,360}{95}$ or Rs. 88. If 20 tonnes of coal are left unsold with the consignee, the value of stock will be 20×88, *i.e.* Rs. 1,760

Abnormal Loss. Abnormal loss is a loss which arises due to mischief, bad luck or inefficiency. Suppose part of the goods is stolen. This will surely reduce the value of the stock and, therefore, the profit on consignment. But if we do not remember that the loss has occurred because of the theft, we might be misled by the result. In order to see the effect of theft clearly, it is better to find out the cost of the goods thus lost. The method to find out the value is exactly the same as for valuing the stock. After finding out the value, the Consignment Account is credited and Profit and Loss Account is debited. The effect of this will be that the Consignment Account will show its proper profit and in the Profit and Loss Account this profit will be reduced to show actual profit. Of course, if part of the loss is recoverable, because an insurance company is liable or because the goods are there in some defective shape, the amount which can be recovered like this should be deducted from the loss for the purpose of debiting the Profit and Loss Account.

Illustration Wali sent 1,000 kg. wool to Gope to be sold on consignment basis. The terms were that Gope would get 5% commission plus 2% del credere commission and would be reimbursed for expenses incurred.

The cost to Wali was Rs. 30 per kg. He incurred Rs. 300 as packing and forwarding charges. On receipt of the wool, Gope accepted a bill for Rs. 20,000. Gope also paid Rs. 800 as freight and cartage and Rs. 400 as rent and insurance.

Gope sold 800 kg. at Rs. 40 per kg. One-quarter of the sales were on credit. One customer failed to pay the amount of Rs. 1,500 due from him. Gope remitted the necessary amount to Wali. Give the Consignment Account and Gope's account in the books of Wali and important ledger accounts in the books of Gope.

Solution :

Books of Wali

Consignment Account

Dr. *Cr.*

	Rs.			Rs.	
To Goods Sent on Consignment Account	30,000	—	By Gope—Sale proceeds	32,000	—
To Bank A/c—expenses	300	—	By Stock on Consignment Account*	6,220	—
To Gope-Expenses	1,200	—			
To Gope-Commission	2,240	—			
To Profit and Loss A/c—profit transferred	4,480	—			
	38,220	—		38,220	—

Gope

	Rs.			Rs.	
To Consignment Account—sale proceeds	32,000	—	By Bills Receivable A/c	20,000	—
			By Consignment A/c—Expenses	1,200	—
			Commission	2,240	—
			By Bank A/c	8,560	—
	32,000	—		32,000	—

* Stock has been valued as under:

	Rs.
200 kg. @ Rs. 30	6,000
Add : $\frac{200}{1,000}$ of consignor's expenses	60
$\frac{200}{1,000}$ of freight	160
	6,220

Books of Gope

Wali

Dr. | | | | | Cr.

	Rs.			Rs.	
To Bills Payable A/c	20,000	—	By Bank A/c (3/4 of sale proceeds)	24,000	—
To Bank—Expenses	1,200	—	By Sundry Debtors (1/4 of sale proceeds)	8,000	—
To Commission A/c	2,240	—			
To Bank A/c	8,560	—			
	32,000	—		32,000	—

Bank

	Rs.			Rs.	
To Wali—3/4 of sale proceeds	24,000		By Wali	1,200	—
To Sundry Debtors	6,500	—	By Wali	8,560	—
			By Bills Payable A/c	20,000	—

Sundry Debtors

	Rs.			Rs.	
To Wali—1/4 of sale proceeds	8,000	—	By Bank A/c	6,500	—
			By Bad Debts A/c	1,500	—
	8,000	–		8,000	–

Bad Debts Account

	Rs.			Rs.	
To Sundry Debtors	1,500	—	By Commission A/c—transfer	1,500	—
	1,500	—		1,500	–

Commission Account

	Rs.			Rs.	
To Bad Debts A/c	1,500	—	By Wali	2,240	—
To Profit and Loss A/c	740	–			
	2,240	–		2,240	–

Note. Since the bad debts have arisen out of sales ex-consignment and have to be borne by the consignee (because of del credere commission), these have been debited against Commission Account and not against Profit and Loss Account, as is usual.

Consigning goods at a value higher than cost. So far we have considered the consignments as invoiced at cost. That is to say, entries are passed in the books of the consignor on the basis of cost. But when the pro forma invoice is sent to the consignee, it may be desirable not to tell him the cost. Therefore, the invoice price may be something higher than cost, say, cost plus 25 per cent. If the cost of goods consigned is Rs. 10.000, the pro forma invoice will be made out at Rs. 12,500. The following differences will then arise in the matter of treatment of goods sent on consignment and invoiced in such a manner :—

1. The entry to record the consigning of goods will be on the basis of invoice price, *i.e.*, higher than the cost. The entry, of course, is :

   Consignment Account Dr.

   To Goods Sent on Consignment Account.

2. At the end of the year the difference between the invoice price and the cost will be credited to the Consignment Account by debiting Goods Sent on Consignment Account Thus, if goods costing Rs. 10,000 are invoiced at Rs. 12,500, an entry will have to be made at the end of the year for Rs. 2,500. The entry is :

   Goods Sent on Consignment Account Dr.

   To Consignment Account

   The purpose of this entry is first of all, to show the cost of goods sent out and secondly to calculate the profit on consignment. Profit can be calculated only by comparing the cost with the sale proceeds. Goods Sent on Consignment Account, of course, is transferred to the Trading Account or Purchases Account, as already stated.

3. The stock in the hands of the consignee will also be val according to the invoice price plus the share of expen

which normally add to the value of goods. The usual entry will be made, namely :

Stock on Consignment Account Dr.

To Consignment Account.

4. It is a fixed principle that stock must not be shown at more than the cost, but entry No. 3, shown above, is at an amount which is higher than the cost. The difference will be calculated and the following entry will be passed to show the stock at cost in the balance sheet :—

Consignment Account Dr.

To Consignment Stock Reserve Account

Consignment Stock Reserve Account will be a credit balance and if deducted from the Stock on Consignment Account will give the cost of stock in the hands of the consignee.

The other entries given already on pages 222 and 223 hold good. There is also no difference in the entries to be passed in the books of the consignee.

Illustration Roy of Calcutta sends 100 sewing machines on consignment to Malik at Patna. The cost of each machine is Rs. 130 but the invoice price is at the rate of Rs. 160 each. Roy spends Rs. 400 on packing and despatch. Malik receives the consignment and immediately accepts Roy's draft for Rs. 8,000. Subsequently, Malik informs Roy that 80 machines have been sold at Rs. 175 each. Expenses paid by Malik are : Freight Rs. 600 (Calcutta to Patna), Godown Rent Rs. 50, and Insurance Rs. 100. Malik is entitled to a commission of 6 per cent on sales and $1\frac{1}{2}$ per cent as del credere commission. One customer who purchased 4 machines on credit failed to pay because of insolvency ; another customer deducted Rs.50 because of defective parts in machines bought by him.

Give journal entries in the books of Roy. Also prepare important ledger Accounts in Roy's books,

Solution :

Roy's Journal

Particulars		Dr. Rs.	Cr. Rs.
Consignment to Patna Account To Goods Sent on Consignment Account 100 machines sent on consignment to Malik at Rs. 160 each (cost price Rs. 130 each).	Dr.	16,000 —	16,000 —
Consignment to Patna Account To Cash Account Amount spent on packing and despatch of the consignment to Patna.	Dr.	400 —	400 —
Bills Receivable Account To Malik Malik's acceptance received for Rs. 8,000 as advance.	Dr.	8.000 —	8,000 —
Malik To Consignment to Patna Account 80 machines sold by Malik at Rs. 175 each as per Account Sales.	Dr.	14,000 —	14,000 —
Consignment to Patna Account To Malik Expenses incurred by Malik on consignment as under : Freight Rs. 600, Godown Rent Rs. 50 and Insurance Rs. 100.	Dr.	750 —	750 —
Consignment to Patna Account To Malik Commission at 6% plus $1\frac{1}{2}$% on sales made by Malik.	Dr.	1,050 —	1,050 —
Stock on Consignment Account To Consignment to Patna Account Value of 20 machines in the hands of Malik, valued as 20×160 plus $\frac{20}{100}$ of Rs. 1,000, freight and expenses incurred by Roy.	Dr.	3,400 —	3,400 —
Goods Sent on Consignment Account To Consignment to Patna Account The loading in the invoice value, namely, Rs. 30 per machine written back.	Dr.	3,000 —	3,000 —

	Particulars		Rs.		Rs.	
	Consignment to Patna Account Dr. To Consignment Stock Reserve Account The loading in the value of stock, *viz.*, Rs. 30 each on 20 machines, provided for.		600		600	—
	Goods Sent on Consignment A/c Dr. To Trading Account Transfer of Goods Sent on Consignment A/c to Trading Account.		13,000	—	13,000	—
	Consignment to Patna Account Dr. To Malik Amount deducted from sale proceeds because of defects.		50		50	
	Consignment to Patna Account Dr. To Profit and Loss Account Transfer of Profit on consignment.		1,550	—	1,550	—

LEDGER ACCOUNTS

Consignment to Patna Account

Dr. **Cr.**

	Rs.			Rs.	
To Goods Sent on Consignment A/c	16,000	—	By Malik—Sale Proceeds	14,000	—
To Bank—Expenses	400	—	By Stock on Consignment A/c	3,400	—
To Malik—Expenses: Freight 600 Rent 50 Insurance 100 Amount deducted by customer 50	800	—	By Goods Sent on Consignment A/c—loading	3,000	—
To Malik—Commission	1,050	—			
To Consignment Stock Reserve Account	600	—			
To Profit and Loss A/c—profit transferred	1,550	—			
	20,400	—		20,400	—

Goods Sent on Consignment Account

		Rs.				Rs.	
	To Consignment to Patna A/c — loading	3,000	—		By Consignment to Patna A/c	16,000	—
	To Trading A/c—transfer	13,000	—				
		16,000	—			16,000	—

Stock on Consignment Account

		Rs.				Rs.	
	To Consignment to Patna A/c	3,400	—		By Balance c/d	3,400	—
Next Year	To Balance *b/d*	3,400	—				

Consignment Stock Reserve Account

		Rs				Rs.	
	To Balance *c/d*	600	—		By Consignment to Patna A/c	600	—
				Next Year	By Balance *b/d*	600	—

Malik

		Rs.				Rs.	
	To Consignment to Patna A/c—Sale Proceeds	14,000	—		By Bills Receivable A/c	8,000	-
					By Consignment to Patna A/c—		
					Expenses	750	—
					Commission	1,050	—
					Amount deducted by customer	50	
					By Balance *c/d*	4,150	—
		14,000	—			14,000	—
Next Year	To Balance *b/d*	4,150	—				

Note : The bad debt will have to be borne by Malik.

Memorandum Columns. Sometimes the consignment Account and the Goods sent on Consignment Account and Consignment Stock Account are prepared on cost basis but columns are provided to record the invoice value also. One column is provided on each side to record the invoice value. Such columns will be known as

Memorandum Columns. They will not be really taken into account while determining the profit and loss but are useful to show the profit which would have been there on the basis of invoice value. The Accounts in the above illustration will be worked out as follows under this method.

Dr. **Consignment to Patna Account** *Cr.*

Particulars	*Memorandum* Rs.	P.	*Actual* Rs.	P.	*Particulars*	*Memo randum* Rs.	P.	*Actual* Rs.	P.
To Goods Sent on Consignment A/c	16,000	—	13,000	—	By Malik—Sale Proceeds	14,000	—	14,000	—
To Bank—Expenses	400	—	400	—	By Stock on Consignment A/c	3,400	—	2,800	—
To Malik—Expenses	750	—	750	—	By Loss	800	—		
To Malik—Commission	1,050	—	1,050	—					
To Profit & Loss A/c—Profit transferred			1,600	—					
	18,200	—	16,800	—		18,200	—	16,800	—

Goods Sent on Consignment Account

Particulars	Memorandum Rs.	P.	Actual Rs.	P.	Particulars	Memorandum Rs.	P.	Actual Rs.	P.
To Trading A/c—transfer	16,000	—	13,000	—	By Consignment to Patna A/c	16,000	—	13,000	—

Stock on Consignment Account

Particulars	Memorandum Rs.	P.	Actual Rs.	P.	Particulars	Memorandum Rs.	P.	Actual Rs.	P.
To Consignment to Patna A/c	3,400	—	2,800	—	By Balance *c/d*	3,400	—	2,800	—
To Balance *b/d*	3,400	—	2,800	—					

Illustration Shah sends goods on consignment to Rao. The terms are that Rao will receive 10% commission on the invoice price (which is cost plus 25%) and 20% of any price realised above the invoice price. Rao will meet his expenses himself, goods to be sent freight paid.

Shah sent goods whose cost was Rs. 16,000 and spent Rs. 1,500 on freight, forwarding, etc. Rao accepted a bill for Rs. 16,000 immediately on receiving the consignment. His expenses were Rs. 200 as rent and Rs. 100 as insurance. Rao sold 3/4 of the goods for Rs. 19,500. Part of the sales were on credit and one customer failed to pay Rs. 400. Give Consignment Account and Rao's account in the books of Shah and important ledger accounts in the books of Rao.

Solution :

SHAH'S LEDGER

Consignment to Rao Account

Dr.		Rs.			Cr.	Rs.	
	To Goods Sent on Consignment A/c (Rs. 16,000 +25%)	20,000	—		By Rao—Sale Proceeds	19,500	—
	To Bank—Expenses	1,500	—		By Stock on Consigment A/c.**	5,375	—
	To Rao—Commission*	2,400	—		By Goods Sent on Consignment A/c—loading	4,000	—
	Bad Debt	400	—				
	To Consignment Stock Reserve A/c	1,000	—				
	To Profit & Loss A/c—profit	3,575	—				
		28,875	—			28,875	—

Rao

		Rs.				Rs.	
	To Consignment to Rao A/c—Sale proceeds	19,500	—		By Bills Receivable A/c	16,000	—
					By Consignment to Rao A/c—Commission	2,400	—
					Bad Debt	400	—
					By Balance c/d	700	—
		19,500	—			19,500	—
Next Year	To Balance b/d	700	—				

* Commission has been calculated as under :

$\frac{3}{4}$ of invoice of goods sent (invoice value)	Rs. 15,000
10% commission on this figure	Rs. 1,500
Excess value realised : Rs. 19,500 – Rs. 15,000 = Rs. 4,500	
20% of excess value realised	Rs. 900
	Rs. 2,400

** Stock has been valued as :

$\frac{1}{4}$ of goods left unsold	Rs. 5,000
Add $\frac{1}{4}$ of expenses	Rs. 375
	Rs. 5,375

RAO'S LEDGER

Shah

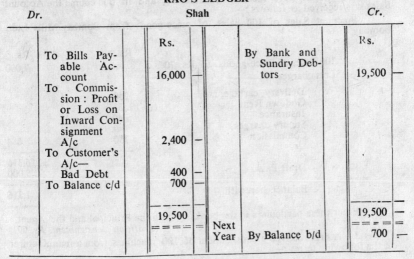

Dr.					Cr.
		Rs.			Rs.
	To Bills Payable Account	16,000		By Bank and Sundry Debtors	19,500
	To Commission : Profit or Loss on Inward Consignment A/c	2,400			
	To Customer's A/c—Bad Debt	400			
	To Balance c/d	700			
		19,500			19,500
			Next Year	By Balance b/d	700

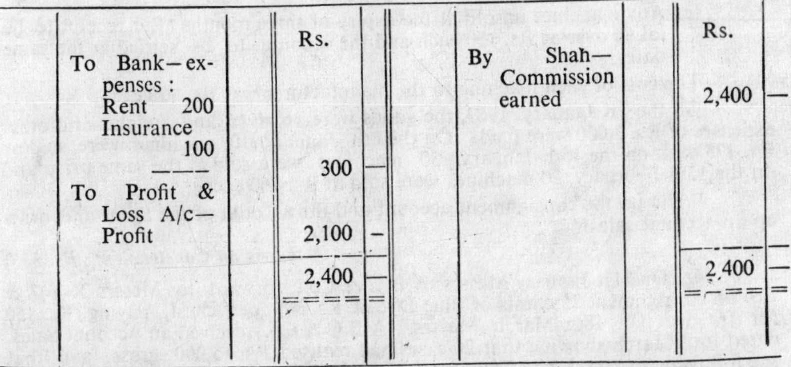

Profit or Loss on Inward Consignment A/c

		Rs.			Rs.
	To Bank—expenses : Rent 200, Insurance 100	300		By Shah—Commission earned	2,400
	To Profit & Loss A/c—Profit	2,100			
		2,400			2,400

Note. The student should note that Rao is to bear the expenses as per the terms of agreement with Shah. Hence the expenses have been set against the commission earned and not debited to Shah. But Rao is not a del credere agent, hence the bad debt of Rs. 400 has to be borne by Shah.

Exercises

1. Dutt sends 100 radio sets to Ray to be sold on Consignment basis. Dutt spends Rs. 300 on packing, etc. The cost of each set is Rs. 150.

Ray sends a bank draft as advance to Dutt for Rs. 10,000 as advance. He spends Rs. 800 on freights, Rs. 200 on salesmen's salary and Rs. 150 as rent and insurance.

Ray sells all the sets @ Rs. 200 each. He is entitled to a commission of 10% on sales. He settles his account. Prepare the Account Sales and various ledger accounts in the books of both Dutt and Ray.

(*Profit on Consignment*, *Rs. 1,550*)

2. The Bombay Mills Ltd. of Bombay consign to their Calcutta Agent Rs. 5,000 worth of piece-goods, drawing on Calcutta for the amount.

They pay charges, freight and insurance on the consignment amounting to Rs. 325 and discount the bill at a discount of Rs. 100.

The goods were received in Calcutta, and in due course the Account Sales was received as follows :—

Account Sales of 100 bales of piece-goods from Bombay Mills Ltd., Bombay.

	Rs.	Rs.
100 Bales of Piece-goods @ Rs. 70		7,000
Less charges—		
Delivery, cartage, etc.	250	
Godown Rent	35	
Insurance	40	
Sundry charges	9	
Commission	350	684
		6,316
Draft Paid		5,000
Balance herewith		1,316

Enter these particulars in the books of both the Principal and the Agent.

(*Profit on Consignment, Rs. 991*)

3. A firm received a consignment of 100 machines from a manufacturer on the following terms :—

(*a*) The machines to be sold at the best price obtainable above Rs. 150.

(*b*) Selling commission to be 15 per cent.

(*c*) Any machines unsold at the expiry of three months after receipt to be taken over at Rs. 150 each and the account to be settled at the same date.

The cost of each machine to the manufacturer was Rs. 120 each.

On the 1st January, 1967, the goods were received and freight and other expenses of Rs. 3,000 were paid. On the 8th January 10 machines were sold at Rs. 175 each on the 15th January,. 30 machines were sold at the same price and on the 15th February, 20 machines were sold at Rs. 160 each.

Write up the consignment account and the account of the agent and draw up an account sales.

(*Loss on Consignment, Rs. 330*)

4. On 21st January Messrs. A B C & Co., forward to Messrs X Y Z & Co. on consignment 25 chests of Blue Dye at Rs. 500 per chest, paying Rs. 150 for freight. On 18th March Messrs. A B C & Co. received an Account Sales, dated 16th March showing that 20 cases had realised Rs. 15,000 gross, and that the following expenses had been incurred :—

	Rs,
Octroi Duty	100
Storage and Insurance	30
Delivery charges, etc.	150
Commission 3 per cent	
Del Credere Commission 2 per cent	

Messrs. XYZ & Co. enclosed a bill at three months for the amount due. You are requested to record the above transactions (*i*) in Messrs. ABC & Co's. books, and (*ii*) in Messrs. XYZ & Co's books. Show also the Account Sales.

(*Profit on Consignment, Rs 3,870*)

5. Ali Hussain of Calcutta sent a consignment of cotton goods to Osman Khan of Singapore costing Rs. 1,000. The invoice price was made by adding 25 per cent to the cost. The expenses incurred by Ali Hussain were: Packing Rs. 24, Carriage etc. Rs. 16, Insurance Rs. 12 and other expenses Rs. 26.

After three months he received an Account Sales intimating that half the consignment was sold at Rs. 900. The expenses incurred by the consignee were : Freight Rs. 30, Fire Insurance Rs. 18 and other expenses

Rs. 10. His commission was 6 per cent on sales and del credere commission 2 per cent.

(*Profit on Consignment, Rs. 246*)

6. Shri Gopalan from Madras consigned 10,000 cases of tinned fruit (cost Rs.75,000) to Sengupta of Calcutta on 1st January 1973 charging him a proforma invoice to show a profit of 25 per cent on sales. Gopalan paid on the same date Rs.7,000 in respect of freight, etc. During the half year ending 30th June 1973, Sengupta, incurred expenses of Rs.3,000 on godown rent and sold 8,000 cases on consignment for Rs.80,000. Sengupta is entitled to 5 per cent commission on sales which is duly charged up. Record the entries in the books of Shri Gopalan.

(*C.A. Inter*)

(*Profit, Rs.*7,400)

7. Somesh of Calcutta consigned 100 cases of candles to Sailesh of Bankura, which costs him Rs. 30 per case. The invoice price was Rs. 45 per case. He incurred the following costs :—Packing Rs. 40 ; Carriage Rs. 20 and Railway Freight Rs. 40. Some of the cases were damaged in transit and Sailesh took delivery of 90 cases only. He (Sailesh) spent Rs. 9 for cartage (to the godown) and Rs. 40 for godown rent and sold 80 cases at Rs. 50 per case. He sent the net amount to Somesh after deducting his expenses and commission at the rate of 8 per cent on the sale proceeds together with his Account Sales. Somesh also received Rs. 180 from the Railway as damages. Show how the transactions would appear in the books of Somesh.

(*Profit on Consignment, Rs. 1,152 subject to abnormal loss of Rs. 130*)

8. Nissar sent goods to Mumtaz to be sold on consignment basis. The invoice price was Rs. 24,000 which was 20% above cost. Mumtaz was entitled to a commission of 5% on the invoice price of the goods sold and 15% of any excess price realised. He was to be reimbursed for expenses.

On receiving the goods, Mumtaz paid Rs. 920 as freight and Rs. 500 as godown rent, insurance, etc. He sold 5/8 of the goods for Rs. 19,000. Part of the sale was on credit and there was a bad debt of Rs. 600. Mumtaz settled his account.

Show ledger account in the books of both the parties.

(*Profit on Consignment, Rs. 3,475*)

9. Panther sent 100 bicycles, each costing Rs. 150 each, to Tiger to be sold at his risk. Tiger was to get, for his services, a commission at the rate of Rs. 8 per bicycle and was to be reimbursed for expenses. Tiger spent Rs. 500 on freight and Rs. 600 for salesmen's salaries, godown rent, etc.

Tiger sold 80 bicycles @ Rs. 145 each and settled his account with Panther. Prepare the Consignment Account in Panther's books.

(*Loss on Consignment, Rs. 2,040*)

10. Active of Bombay sent a consignment of goods to Strong of Delhi on the basis that Strong was to affect sales on behalf of Active and receive a commission of 20% on the selling price. Strong was to be responsible for all expenses at his end, but the goods were to be forwarded f.o.r. Delhi. The commission was considered to include del credere commission also.

Active sent the goods costing Rs. 20,000 at an invoice price of Rs. 25,000. He spent Rs. 400 on packing and forwarding. On receiving the goods, Strong accepted Active's draft for Rs. 16,000 and paid the following expenses :

	Rs.
Freight (Bombay to Delhi)	1,500
Godown Rent	500
Insurance (godown)	200
Miscellaneous	

He sold 4/5 of the goods for Rs. 30,000. There was a bad debt of Rs. 600. Give journal entries in the books of both the parties and prepare important ledger accounts.

(*Profit to Active, Rs. 6,480 ; to Strong Rs. 4,700*)

11. Bose of Patna sent a consignment to his agent, Roy of Delhi. The invoice price of the goods was Rs. 20,000 which was 25% above cost. On receiving the goods. Roy accepted a 3 months' draft for Rs. 10,000 (which was discounted by Bose @ 6%). He also spent the following sums :

On freight and cartage	Rs. 500
On godown insurance and rent	Rs. 300

Four-fifths of the goods were sold for Rs. 17,400. Bose is entitled to a commission of 10% on the invoice price plus 1/4 of any profit (finally remaining) that Bose might make.

Prepare accounts in the books of Bose with memorandum columns.

(*Profit on Consignment, Rs. 1,840*)

12. Tai of Singapore is the agent for sewing machines manufactured by Mehta in Delhi. A machine costs Rs. 150, the invoice price to Tai is Rs. 200; Tai is entitled to a commission of 15% of this plus 40% of the excess realised over Rs. 200 ; he is also responsible for all expenses incurred by him but not for freight to Singapore or customs duty.

Mehta despatched 200 machines in January 1969, drawing on Tai for Rs. 20,000 at 3 months. Tai accepted the draft. Expenses paid by Tai were :—

	Rs.
Freight	2,000
Customs Duty	1,000
Storage	500
Insurance	400
Commission on Sales @ 8%	

At the end of March, 1969 Tai reported that he had sold 150 machines at an average price of Rs. 220. It was agreed then that Tai would take over the remaining machines on his own account at landed cost plus 20%. Prepare the Consignment Account in the books of Mehta.

(*Profit on Consignment, Rs. 4,200*)

13. Murty of Madras sent some piece-goods to Bose of Calcutta to be sold on behalf of Murty, Bose getting a commission (including del credere commission) of 10% on sales affected by him. All expenses were to be borne by Murty. The invoice value of the goods was Rs. 30,000 made up as cost plus 20%. Murty spent Rs. 500 on forwarding and packing.

Bose paid the following:—

	Rs.
Freight and Cartage to godown	1,600
Storage	300
Insurance	200
Miscellaneous	100

At the end of 3 months Bose reported that he had sold 3/5 of the goods for Rs. 20,000. He returned 1/5 of the goods to Murty as unsaleable in Calcutta but he was confident of selling the remaining goods. Murty paid Rs. 350 as freight on the returned goods. One customer, who had bought on credit, failed to pay Rs. 800 due from him.

Ascertain, by preparing relevant accounts, the profit or loss suffered by the two parties.

(*Murty earns Rs. 370 and Bose earns Rs. 1,200*)

[**Hint :** The returned goods should be valued by Murty at the original cost —no expenses should be included.]

14. Garments costing **Rs. 36,000** were sent by Teng of Delhi to Smith of London on consignment basis. Teng spent Rs. 6,000 on freight, insurance, etc. On receipt of the goods. Smith had to pay £ *1*,000 as customs duty, clearing charges. All the goods, except 5% of the stock which were stolen by someone, were sold for £ 4,500. Smith is entitled to a commission of 10% and expenses incurred by him. He remitted the amount due to Teng immediately after the sale was effected. When the goods were sent, the £ was worth Rs. 18 but when Smith remitted the amount it was worth Rs. 17.

Ascertain by preparing proper accounts the profit or loss of Teng on the transaction. (*Profit, Rs.* 8,850)

15. J & Co of Calcutta sent on consignment account goods to H & Co of Bombay at an invoice price of Rs.29,675 and paid for freight Rs.762, cartage Rs.231 and insurance Rs.700. Half the goods were sold by the agents for Rs.17,500 subject to agent's commission of Rs.875, storage expenses of Rs.200 and other selling expenses of Rs.350. One-fourth of the consignment was lost by fire and a claim of Rs.5,000 was recovered. The agent reported that the rest of the goods, due to a fall in prices, would fetch 20% less than realised earlier subject to selling commission of 5%.

Write up accounts in the books of J & Co. to show the profit or loss on the consignments. (*Adapted from B. Com. Madras*)
(*Loss Rs.*801, *besides abnormal loss of Rs,*2,842)

CHAPTER X

JOINT VENTURES

The term joint venture means an association of two or more persons for a short while to exploit a particular business opportunity. Suppose A and B jointly undertake the construction of a building. They share the cost in agreed proportions, say, equally and also agree that any profit that may arise or any loss that may occur will also be borne equally. As soon as the construction of the building is over, the business association of A and B will come to an end. This is a case of joint venture. Legally, joint venture is not distinct from partnership. We shall, of course, consider partnership accounts in a later chapter ; but it is better from the accountancy point of view to deal with joint ventures separately from partnerships, simply because joint ventures are of short duration. One should note that profits and losses are shared according to the agreement between the parties but, in the absence of any such agreement, all parties will share profits and losses from joint ventures equally.

Joint ventures must be distinguished from joint ownership. If two brothers purchase a building jointly, without any idea of earning an income from it, it will be a case of joint ownership. In the case of joint ventures, the earning of profit is an essential point ; the profit or loss will be shared by the co-venturers.

Distinction from Consignments. Joint ventures differ from Consignments in the following respects :

(*i*) In the case of consignments, the relationship is that of principal and agent, the consignee is the agent and he has to work according to the instructions of the consignor (the principal). The parties to a joint venture (may be even more than two) are of equal status ; decisions are made jointly. (Strictly speaking, each co-venturer is principal as well as agent.)

(*ii*) All the risks and the profit or loss, in the case of a consignment, are those of the consignor. The consignee gets a commission for his work ; he is not concerned with the profit or loss made by the consignor. The profit or loss, in the case of a joint venture, belongs to all the co-venturers and will be shared equally, unless otherwise agreed upon.

(*iii*) A joint venture is usually of a small duration ; in any case it is over when the particular venture is over. The relationship between the consignor and the consignee may subsist for many years—consignment after consignment may be sent to the consignee.

(*iv*) The consignee supplies information to the consignor in the form of Account Sales. But co-venturers may merely exchange copies of the relevant account in their respective books or one party may prepare a Memorandum Joint Venture Account and circulate it among the co-venturers.

(v) Consignments concern only movable goods but joint ventures may concern other things also such as procuring subscriptions for shares or debentures of a company, construction of a building, making a film etc.

Accounts. There are two ways in which joint ventures accounts can be kept, *i.e.*, (1) a record of the transactions in the books of the various parties; (2) a separate set of books to record joint venture transactions. We shall first consider the record to be made in the books of the various parties. Each party opens a joint venture account and the accounts of other parties. Suppose P and Q enter into a joint venture. Then P will open a joint venture account and also an account of Q. Similarly, Q will open, in his books, a joint venture account and the account of P. The following entries are made :

1. When an expenditure is incurred on account of joint venture :

   Joint Venture Account Dr.
   To Cash Account
   or
   To Goods Account (if goods are used from stock)

2. When an expenditure is incurred by the other party :

   Joint Venture Account Dr.
   To the other party's account

3. If any advance is received from the other party, say, in the form of bill of exchange :

   Bills Receivable Account Dr.
   To the other party's account

4. If any advance is given to the other party, say, in the form of a promissory note :

   The other party's account Dr.
   To Bills Payable Account

5. (*a*) If the bill receivable is discounted, the usual entry will be passed, *viz*.,

   Cash Account Dr.
   Discount Account Dr.
   To Bills Receivable Account

   (*b*) The discount account should be transferred to the Joint Venture Account. The entry is :

   Joint Venture Account Dr.
   To Discount Account

   (*c*) If a bill payable was issued in favour of the other party and that party has got it discounted, the discount will have to be debited to the Joint Venture Account, the credit will be in the other party's account.

6. (*a*) When money is received on account of joint venture :

   Bank Account Dr.

To Joint Venture Account

(*b*) If money is received by the other party on account of joint venture :

The other party's account Dr.

To Joint Venture Account

7. (*a*) **If any special commission is receivable on account of joint venture :**

Joint Venture Account Dr.

To Commission Account

(*b*) **If any commission is payable to the other party :**

Joint Venture Account Dr.

To the other party's account

(commission may have to be paid for making sales or even for making purchases).

8. (*a*) **Sometimes some goods are left unsold and one of the parties takes them. The entry is :**

Purchases Account Dr.

To Joint Venture Account

(*b*) **If the other party has taken the goods, the entry will be :**

The other party's account Dr.

To Joint Venture Account

9. Now the Joint Venture Account will show a profit or loss. The profit will be divided in the agreed proportions. The entry is :

Joint Venture Account Dr.

To the other party's account

To Profit and Loss Account

In case of loss this entry will be reversed.

Illustration Ali and Akbar enter into a joint venture sharing profits 3/5ths and 2/5ths. Ali is to purchase timber in Madhya Pradesh and forward it to Akbar in Delhi. Ali purchased timber worth Rs. 10,000 and paid Rs. 1,000 as expenses. Akbar received the consignment and immediately accepted Ali's draft for Rs. 8,000, Ali got it discounted for Rs. 7,850. Akbar disposed of the timber for Rs. 16,000. He had to spend Rs. 350 for fire insurance and Rs. 300 for rent. Under the agreement he is entitled to a commission of 5 per cent on sales.

Give journal entries and ledger accounts in the books of both the parties.

Solution :

Ali's Journal

Date	Particulars		L.F.	Dr. Rs.	Cr. Rs.
	Joint Venture Account To Bank Account Amount spent on timber forwarded to Akbar	Dr.		10,000 —	10,000 —
	Joint Venture Account To Bank Account Expenses incurred on timber sent to Akbar.	Dr.		1,000 —	1,000 —
	Bills Receivable Account To Akbar Acceptance received from Akbar as an advance.	Dr.		8,000 —	8,000 —
	Bank Account Discount Account To Bills Receivable A/c. Akbar's acceptance discounted for Rs. 7,850.	Dr. Dr.		7,850 — 150 —	8,000 —
	Joint Venture Account To Discount Account Discount on Akbar's acceptance transferred to Joint Venture Account.	Dr.		150 —	150 —
	Akbar To Joint Venture Account Sales effected by Akbar.	Dr.		16,000 —	16,000 —
	Joint Venture Account To Akbar Expenses incurred by Akbar on Joint Venture.	Dr.		650 —	650 —
	Joint Venture Account To Akbar Commission due to Akbar on sales.	Dr.		800 —	800 —
	Joint Venture Account To Profit & Loss Account To Akbar Profit on Joint Venture, Rs. 3,400 ; 3/5ths to self and 2/5th to Akbar.	Dr.		3,400 —	2,040 — 1,360 —

Ali's LEDGER

Joint Venture Account

Dr.	Rs.		Cr.	Rs.	
To Bank A/c—Timber purchased	10,000	—	By Akbar—Sale Proceeds	16,000	—
To Bank A/c—Expenses	1,000	—			
To Discount Account	150	—			
To Akbar—Expenses	650	—			
To Akbar—Commission	800	—			
To Profit to : Akbar (2/5) 1,360; P & L A/c (3/5) 2,040	3,400	—			
	16,000	—		16,000	—

Bills Receivable Account

	Rs.			Rs.	
To Akbar	8,000	—	By Bank A/c	7,850	—
			By Discount A/c	150	
	8,000	—		8,000	—

Discount Account

	Rs.			Rs.	
To Bills Receivable A/c	150	—	By Joint Venture A/c—transfer	150	—

Bank Account

	Rs.			Rr.	
To Bills Receivable Account	7,850	—	By Joint Venture A/c—Timber	10,000	—
			By Joint Venture A/c—Expenses	1,000	—

Akbar

	Rs.			Rs.	
To Joint Venture A/c—Sale Proceeds	16,000	—	By Bills Receivable Account—	8,000	=
			By Joint Venture Account :		
			Expenses	650	—
			Commission	800	—
			Profit (2/5)	1,360	—
			By Balance c/d	5,190	—
	16,000	—		16,000	—
To Balance b/d	5,190	—			

Profit & Loss Account

				Rs.	
			By Joint Venture A/c	2,040	—

Books of Akbar

Journal

		Dr. Rs	Cr. Rs.
Joint Venture Account To Ali Amount spent by Ali on joint venture, *viz.*, Rs. 10,000 on timber and Rs. 1,000 as expenses.	Dr.	11,000 —	11,000 —
Ali To Bills Payable Account Acceptance sent to Ali as advance.	Dr.	8,000 —	8,000 —
Joint Venture Account To Ali Discount Rs. 150, paid by Ali.	Dr.	150 —	150 —
Joint Venture Account To Bank Account Rent Rs. 300 and insurance Rs. 350 paid on account of joint venture.	Dr.	650 —	650 —
Bank Account To Joint Venture Account Sales effected on account of joint venture.	Dr.	16,000 —	16,000 —
Joint Venture Account To Commission Account 5% commission on Rs. 16,000.	Dr.	800 —	800 —
Joint Venture Account To Profit & Loss Account To Ali Profit on joint venture, Rs. 3,400, divided as 2/5ths to self and 3/5ths to Ali.	Dr.	3,400 —	1,360 — 2,040 —
Bills Payable Account To Bank Account Acceptance to Ali met.	Dr.	8,000 —	8,000 —

LEDGER

Joint Venture Account

Dr.	Rs.		Cr.	Rs.	
To Ali—Timber and Expenses	11,000	—	By Bank Account—Sale Proceeds	16,000	—
To Bank Account—Expenses	650	—			
To Commission A/c	800	—			
To Ali—Discount	150	—			
To Profit to : Ali (3/5)	2,040	—			
P & L A/c. (2/5)	1,360	—			
	16,000	—		16,000	—

Ali

	Rs.			Rs.	
To Bills Payable A/c	8,000	—	By Joint Venture A/c	11,000	—
To Balance c/d	5,190	—	By Joint Venture A/c—Discount	150	—
			Profit	2,040	—
	13,190	—		13,190	—
			By Balance b/d	5,190	—

Will the student please prepare the remaining accounts ?

An alternative method to record the transactions. There is another method to record the transactions in the books of the various parties. In such a case the profit or loss on joint venture is ascertained on memorandum basis. A joint venture account will be prepared but not as part of financial books. The name of such an account is Memorandum Joint Venture Account. It is not really a part of the books. In books only one account is opened named as "Joint Venture with...... Account". Suppose Ram and Mohan have entered into a joint venture. Then Ram will open an account named, Joint Venture with Mohan Account or Mohan in Joint Venture Account.

Similarly, Mohan will open, in his books, Joint Venture with Ram Account or Ram in Joint venture Account. This account is prepared in the following manner.

1. Goods sent or cash spent on joint venture is debited to this account.
2. No account is taken of goods used or cash spent on joint venture by the other party.
3. If any cash or acceptance is received on account of joint venture, or from the other party, this account is credited.
4. This account is then debited with own share of profit, the credit being given to Profit and Loss Account. If the Memorandum Joint Venture Account shows a loss, the Profit and Loss Account is debited and this account will be credited with own share of loss. The balance in this account will now show the amount owing to the other party, *i.e.*, if the credit side is bigger or amount owed by the other party, *i.e.*, if the debit side is bigger.

The above illustration is now worked out under this method. (Narrations have been omitted; the student should supply them). The Joint Venture Account already given, should serve as the Memorandum Joint Veuture Account.

Ali's Journal

			Dr. Rs.		Cr. Rs.	
	Joint Venture with Akbar Account Dr. To Bank Account.		11,000	—	11,000	—
	Bills Receivable Account Dr. To Joint Venture with Akbar Account		8,000	—	8,000	—
	Bank Account Dr. Discount Account Dr. To Bills Receivable A/c		7,850 150	— —	8,000	—
	Joint Venture with Akbar A/c Dr. To Discount Account		150		150	—
	Joint Venture with Akbar Account Dr. To Profit & Loss Account.		2,040	—	2,040	—

The accounts will appear as follows :

Joint Venture with Akbar Account

Dr. *Cr.*

	Rs.			Rs.	
To Bank Account—			By Bills Receivable A/c	8,000	—
Timber	10,000	—	By Balance *c/d*	5,190	—
Expenses	1,000	—			
To Discount A/c	150	—			
To Profit and Loss Account—3/5 Share of profit	2,040	—			
	13,190	—		13,190	—
To Balance *b/d*	5,190				

Profit and Loss Account

				Rs.	
			By Joint Venture with Akbar A/c	2,040	—

Bank Account and Bills Receivable Account have not been shown. The student is advised to prepare the necessary account in Akbar's books using this method.

Illustration Ram and Rahim entered into a joint venture for sale of gur. Ram was to purchase gur in Meerut and Rahim was to sell it in Bombay. Each party was to receive 6% p.a. interest on its investment and to pay similar interest on moneys received on account of joint venture. Rahim was to get 5% commission on sales and the profits were to be shared as to 5/8 to Ram and 3/8 to Rahim.

On 1st January, 1978 Ram purchased gur for Rs. 10,000 and forwarded it to Rahim. Ram had to pay Rs. 1,001 as expenses and freight. On the same date Rahim sent Rs. 6,000 to Ram as advance. 9/10 of the consignment was sold for Rs. 16,000 on 1st March, 1968. The remaining 1/10 was taken by Rahim at cost plus 10% on 31st March. On the same date Rahim remitted the necessary amount to Ram. Prepare Joint Venture Account and Rahim's account in the books of Ram. Also show how the transactions can be recorded alternatively. Ignore paise.

Solution :

Joint Venture Account

Dr.		Rs.		Cr.		Rs.
1978 Jan. 1	To Bank Account—Gur	10,000	1978 Mar. 1	By Rahim—Sale		16,000
,,	To Bank Account—Expenses	1,001	,, 31	By Rahim—Stock taken over : cost (1/10)	1,100	
March	To Rahim—Commission	800		Add 10%	110	1,210
,, 31	To Interest Account*	75				
,, 31	To Rahim—Interest**	14				
,, ,,	To Profit to : Rahim, 3/8	1,995				
	Ram, 5/8	3,325				
		17,210				17,210

Rahim

		Rs.			Rs
1978 March 1	To Joint Venture Account—Sale	16,000	1978 Jan. 1	By Bank Account	6,000
	To Joint Venture Account—Stock taken over	1,210		By Joint Venture A/c—Commission	800
				Interest	14
				Profit, 3/8	1,995
				By Bank Account	8,401
		17,210			17,210

* Interest due to Ram has been calculated as under :

	Rs.
Interest on Rs. 11,001 for 3 months (from 1/1/78 to 31/3/78 @ 6% *p.a.*)	165
Less interest on Rs. 6,000 received from Rahim @ 6% *p.a.* from 1/1/78 to 31/3/78	90
	75

** Interest due to Rahim has been calculated as under :

Interest on Rs. 6,000 for 3 months @ 6% *p.a.*	90
Less interest on Rs. 15,200 (Rs. 16,000, sale, less Rs. 800, commission) for one month—1/3/78 to 31/3/78	76
	14

Alternatively :—

Rahim in Joint Venture Account

Dr.		Rs.	1968		Cr. Rs.
1968					
Jan. 1	To Bank Account—Gur	10,000	Mar. 1	By Bank Account	6,000
Mar. 31	Expenses	1,001	,, 31	By Bank A/c	8,401
,,	To Interest Account	75			
	To Profit & Loss A/c (5/8 of Profit)	3,325			
		14,401			14,401

The Joint Venture Account given already may be taken to be the Memorandum Joint Venture Account.

In the books of Rahim, the account will be as follows :

Rahim in Joint Venture Account

Dr.		Rs.	1968		Cr. Rs.
1968					
Jan. 1	To Bank A/c—Cash remitted to Ram	6,000	Mar. 1	By Bank A/c—Sale	16,000
Mar. 1	To Commission A/c	800	,, 31	By Stock A/c—value of gur taken over	1,210
,, 31	To Interest A/c	14			
,, 31	To Profit & Loss A/c (3/8 profit)	1,995			
,, 31	To Bank A/c—Cash sent	8,401			
		17,210			17,210

Illustration. Bittoo and Guttoo joined together to take a contract for earthwork for one of the Asiad 1982 Projects—the contract was for Rs.1,00,000, the work to be completed by 30th June 1981, delay to be penalised at Rs.2,000 per day after that date. Bittoo had a truck which he agreed to use for the contract, Guttoo paying the wages for the workers as well as other expenses. For the use of the truck, Bittoo was to be allowed Rs.4,000 per month; otherwise the profit/loss was to be shared equally.

The work commenced on 1st May and was completed on 5th July on which date the payment was received by Guttoo from the contractee. Wages came to Rs.500 per day and diesel cost Rs.160 per day. Other expenses were Rs. 14,000. Bittoo waived the payment due to him for use of the truck after the 30th June.

Prepare the Memorandum Joint Venture Account and the account(s) relating to the joint venture in the books of the two parties.

Solution :

Memorandum Joint Venture Account

	Rs.		Rs.
To Truck-hire—Bittoo	8,000	By Cash—contract price	
To Wages (500 × 66)	33,000	*Less* penalty for 5 days	90,00
To Diesel (160 × 66)	10,560		
To Other Expenses	14,000		
To Profit : Bittoo	12,220		
Guttoo	12,220		
	90,000		90,00

Books of Guttoo

Bittoo in Joint Venture Account

	Rs.		Rs.
To Cash —Wages	33,000	By Cash—paid by the contractee	90,00
—Diesel	10,560		
—Other Expenses	14,000		
To Profit & Loss A/c —Share of profit	12,220		
To Cash—paid to Bittoo	20,220		
	90,000		90,0

Books of Bittoo

Guttoo in Joint Venture Account

	Rs.		Rs.
To Truck-hire	8,000	By Cash—received from Guttoo	20,2
To Profit & Loss A/c—Share of profit	12,220		
	20,220		20,2

Truck Hire Account

o Profit & Loss A/c —Transfer	8,000	By Guttoo in J.V. A/c	8,000

Illustration. Varma and Sanon entered into a joint venture to ırry out the interior decoration of a pavilion at the 1981 Trade Fair New Delhi. Varma provided the necessary capital of Rs.30,000 hich he handed over to Sanon and for which he was to be allowed terest at 20% p.a. Sanon was to personally supervise the work and ake the necessary arrangements for which he was allowed remunera-on at Rs. 3,000 per month; he would be liable for any penalty for lay to the extent of 50%. The contract provided for a payment f Rs. 1,00,000 with a clause stating that for every week's or part of eek's delay Rs. 10,000 would be deducted. According to the rms agreed upon, the work was to be completed by 31st October 981. The work commenced on 1st Sept. and was completed on the h November actually. The following payments were made :

	Rs.
Expenses in connection with obtaining the contract	5,000
Workmen	6,000
Art-work	20,000
Entertainment	2,000

The contractee paid the amount due to Sanon and the two -venturers settled the accounts between themselves on the 7th ovember, 1981.

Prepare the Memorandum Joint Venture Account and the count that each party would have in respect of the joint venture.

lution :

Memorandum Joint Venture Account

		Rs.		Rs.
Expenses—Obtaining the contract		5,000	By Amount paid by the contractee	90,000
—Workmen's wages		6,000		
—Art-work		20,000		
—Entertainment		2,000		
Remuneration for Sanon for 2 months and 7 days	6,700			
ess Penalty (½)	5,000	1,700		
Interest to Varma for 68 days on Rs.30,000 at 20%		1,118		
Profit—Varma		27,091		
Sanon		27,091		
		90,000		90,000

Books of Varma

Sanon in Joint Venture Account

	Rs.		Rs.
To Cash—amount remitted	30,000	By Cash—received from Sanon	58,2[illegible]
To Interest Due	1,118		
To Profit & Loss—Share of profit	27,091		
	58,209		58,2[illegible]

Books of Sanon

Varma in Joint Venture Account

	Rs.		Rs.
To Cash—expenses on obtaining the contract	5,000	By Cash—received from Varma	30,0[illegible]
—Wages	6,000	By Cash—received from the contractee	90,0[illegible]
—Art-work	20,000		
—Entertainment	2,000		
To P. & L. A/c—net remuneration	1,700		
To P. & L. A/c—Share of profit	27,091		
To Cash—remitted to Varma	58,209		
	1,20,000		1,20,[illegible]

Illustration. Fast and Quick, two share brokers, jointly und[illegible] wrote a public issue of 10,000 shares of Rs.100 each; the underwriti[illegible] commission was 5% of which 2/5 was to be in the form of fully pa[illegible] shares. Fast circularised the issue at a cost of Rs.10,000. T[illegible] public subscribed for 9,000 shares and for the balance Quick provid[illegible] the funds. Of the shares held on joint venture 700 were sold by F[illegible] at Rs.90 and the balance by Quick at Rs.95, the amounts being receiv[illegible] by the two respectively. Quick also received the commission fr[illegible] the company. The accounts were then settled.

Prepare Joint Venture Accounts in the books of the two partie[illegible]

Solution :

(*Note* : The profit sharing ratio between Fast and Quick not been stated; therefore, it will be equal.)

Books of Fast

Joint Venture Account

	Rs.		Rs.
To Cash—expenses on circularisation	10,000	By Quick—underwriting commission in cash (3/5 of total)	30,000
To Quick—1,000 shares acquired in accordance with the underwriting obligation	1,00,000	By Cash—sale of 700 shares at 90/-	63,000
To Profit : Quick	15,250	By Quick—Sale of 500 shares* at 95/-	47,500
P. & L. A/c	15,250		
	1,40,500		1,40,500

Books of Quick

Joint Venture Account

	Rs.		Rs.
To Cash—shares acquired	1,00,000	By Cash—commission received	30,000
To Fast—expenses	10,000	By Cash—sale proceeds of 500 shares	47,500
To Profit : Fast	15,250	By Fast—sale proceeds of 700 shares	63,000
P. & L. A/c	15,250		
	1,40,500		1,40,500

Separate books. In case it is decided to maintain separate books for the record of joint venture transactions, the various parties will open in their own books one account, named Joint Venture Investment Account and debit to this account the amount invested by them. Later, whatever they receive back from the joint venture will be credited to this account. The two sides will then show profit or loss, which will be transferred to the Profit and Loss Account. In the books of the joint venture itself an account will be opened for every party which will be credited with the respective amount contributed by them. A Joint Bank Account will be opened to which the contributions made by parties will be debited. Another account necessary is Joint Venture Account to which all expenditure must be debited, credit being given either to the Joint Bank Account (if money is drawn from bank) or to the various parties (if they have made the payment). The amount received on

---

*Total Shares :		
	Acquired for cash	1,000
	Received as underwriting commission (20,000 ÷ 100)	200
		1,200
	Sold by Fast	700
	Sold by Quick	500

account of joint venture is debited to Joint Bank Account and credited to Joint Venture Account. If the parties have taken over plant or materials, the value will be debited to the account of the party concerned and credited to Joint Venture Account. The Joint Venture Account will now show profit or loss which will be transferred to the various parties in the agreed ratio. Now the accounts of the parties will show how much money is due to them. This money will be paid by debiting their accounts and crediting the Joint Bank Account.

Illustration *ilars* Shah and Desai undertake the making of a film for the Government for a payment of Rs. 1,50,000. For this purpose Shah contributes Rs. 30,000 and Desai contributes Rs. 25,000 These moneys were deposited in a Joint Bank Account. The following expenditure was made :—

	Rs.
On wages	40,000
On materials	25,000
On camera	5,000

These payments were made out of the Bank Account but, in addition, Shah supplied certain sets which were valued at Rs. 5,000. The film was made but, due to certain defects, the Government deducted Rs. 30,000 from the payment which was made gradually The camera was taken over by Desai at Rs. 2,000 and the sets were taken back by Shah at a value of Rs. 1,000.

Prepare the necessary accounts in the books of both Shah and Desai and also give the accounts in the separate books of the joint venture.

Solution :

Separate Books of Joint Venture

Dr. **Joint Bank Account** *Cr.*

		Rs.				Rs.	
	To Shah	30,000	—		By Joint Venture A/c—		
	To Desai	25,000	—		Wages	40,000	—
	To Joint Venture A/c— Amount received from Government	1,20,000	—		Materials	25,000	—
					Camera	5,000	—
					By Shah	58,000	—
					By Desai	47,000	—
		1,75,000	—			1,75,000	—

Joint Venture Account

Dr.	Rs.		Cr.	Rs.	
To Joint Bank A/c—			By Joint Bank A/c	1,20,000	—
Wages	40,000	—	By Desai—camera	2,000	—
Materials	25,000	—	By Shah—sets	1,000	—
Camera	5,000	—			
To Shah—sets	5,000	—			
To Profit transferred to : Shah (½) 24,000; Desai (½) 24,000	48,000	—			
	1,23,000	—		1,23,000	—

Shah

	Rs.			Rs.	
To Joint Venture A/c—sets	1,000	—	By Joint Bank A/c	30,000	—
To Joint Bank A/c—amount paid	58,000	—	By Joint Venture A/c—sets	5,000	—
			By Joint Venture A/c—profit	24,000	—
	59,000	—		59,000	—

Desai

	Rs.			Rs.	
To Joint Venture A/c—camera	2,000	—	By Joint Bank A/c	25,000	—
To Joint Bank A/c	47,000	—	By Joint Venture A/c—profit	24,000	—
	49,000	—		49,000	—

Books of Shah

Dr. **Joint Venture Investment Account** Cr.

	Rs.			Rs.	
To Bank A/c—Amount deposited in Joint Bank Account	30,000	—	By Bank A/c—Amount received	58,000	—
To Sets Account	5,000	—	By Sets Account	1,000	—
To Profit & Loss A/c	24,000	—			
	59,000	—		59,000	—

Books of Desai

Dr. **Joint Venture Investment Account** Cr.

	Rs.			Rs.	
To Bank Account	25,000	—	By Camera A/c	2,000	—
To Profit & Loss A/c	24,000	—	By Bank A/c	47,000	—
	49,000	—		49,000	—

Interest calculations. In case of joint venture where different sums of money are invested by different parties, it is often agreed upon that interest will be allowed at a certain rate. It may also be agreed that if a party receives a sum of money on account of joint venture, it should pay interest. As everyone knows, interest is always calculated with reference to the period. Of course, interest can be calculated for every transaction separately. For this purpose tables are available. Such tables give interest at various rates for periods ranging from 1 to 100 days or even more. For example, if interest is to be calculated on Rs. 350 for 85 days @ 5%, the tables will readily give the figure.

In absence of tables, the product method of calculating interest is more economical. The product method simply consists of firstly multiplying the amount concerned by the relevant number of days, secondly adding up the products and then calculating interest on the total of the products for one day. (Instead of days sometimes months are taken.) The method is really simple ; it is based on the fact that, say, interest on Rs. 500 for 10 months must be the same as interest on Rs. 5,000 for one month. For calculating the number of days, the date of the transaction is left out.*

* A modification of the product method is the method of "Interest Numbers". In this case the product is immediately divided by 100. The numbers thus arrived at are added. Interest is arrived at by the formula—
Total of the numbers × Rate × Period.

Illustration On 1st January, 1977 P owed Q Rs. 600. Further transactions between P and Q were as under :—

		Rs.
20th January	P purchases goods	700
20th February	P pays cash	800
10th March	P purchases goods	300

P makes the total payment due from him on 30th April together with interest at 6 per cent per annum.

Calculate the interest payable by P.

Solution :

Amount Rs.	Due Date	No. of Days to 30th April	Products Dr.	Products Cr.
600 (Dr.)	1-1-77	120	72,000	
700 (Dr.)	20-1-77	100	70,000	
800 (Cr.)	20-2-77	69		55,200
300 (Dr.)	10-3-77	51	15,300	
		Total	1,57,300	55,200

The difference in the two "products" is 1,02,100. Interest on Rs. 1,02,100 @ 6% for one day comes to Rs. 16.78, *i.e.*,

$$\frac{1,02,100 \times 6 \times 1}{100 \times 365}$$

Average Due Date. Average Due Date is that date on which a person can pay all the amounts due from him without loss or gain of interest. If the sum is paid early, the person making the payment loses interest but the other party gains. But a date can be arrived at on which all payments can be made so that no party loses or gains by way of interest. Such a date will be known as "average due date". The steps required to calculate average due date are :

1. Fix one of the due dates as the base date. It is better to take the first due date as the base date.

2. Calculate the number of days between the base date and the due date of every transaction. The base date is not to be taken into account.

3. Multiply each amount by the number of days arrived at in step No. 2.

4. Add up the products and the amounts.

5. Divide the total of products by the total of amounts. This will give the number of days between the base date and the average due date. The number of days added to the base date will give the average due date.

Illustration Slow owed to Sure the following sums :

	Rs.
On 20th January, 1979	400
On 10th February, 1979	300
On 25th March, 1979	600
On 18th April, 1979	700

Slow wishes to make one payment without loss or gain of interest. Ascertain the date on which the payment should be made.

Solution :

The base date is assumed to be 20th January, 1979.

Amount Rs.	Due Date	No. of days from the base date	Product (2×3)
(1)	(2)	(3)	(4)
400	20th Jan.	0	0
300	10th Feb.	21	6,300
600	25th March	64	38,400
700	18th April	88	61,600
2,000			1,06,300

Dividing 1,06,300 by 2,000 we get 53 days. The average due date is 53 days after 20th January, 1979. It is 14th March, 1979.

It is not necessary to take the first due date as the base date. Any date can be chosen as the base date. If the last due date is so chosen, the number of days arrived at by dividing the total of products by the total of amounts will have to be deducted. The last but one Illustration is worked out below taking 18th April as the base date.

Amount Rs.	Due Date	No. of days from the base date	Product
400	20th Jan.	88	35,200
300	10th Feb.	67	20,100
600	25th March	24	14,400
700	18th April	0	0
2,000			69,700

Dividing 69,700 by 2,000 we get 35 days. The average due date is 35 days prior to 18th April. It comes to 14th March, 1979.

If any of the middle dates is chosen to be the base date, the products prior to the date should be totalled separately (minus) and similarly, products after that date should be totalled separately (plus). The difference of the two products should be ascertained and then divided by the total of the amounts. If the minus products are higher the days thus arrived at should be deducted from the base date. If the plus total is higher, the days should be added to the base date. Illustration 48 is worked out below taking 25th March, 1979 as the base date.

Amount Rs.	Due Date	No. of Days from the base date	Products +	Products —
400	20th Jan.	64		25,600
300	10th Feb.	43		12,900
600	25th March	0		
700	18th April	24	16,800	
2,000			16,800	38,500

The difference of the two products 21,700 (minus). Dividing 21,700 by 2,000 we get 11 days. The average due date is 11 days prior to 25th March, 1978 or 14th March, 1978.

Calculation of interest with the help of Average Due Date. We have discussed above how interest calculations are made. We can also calculate interest with the help of the average due date. If full payment is made on the average due date, no interest is due. If payment is made after the average due date, interest is due for the number of days from the average due date to the actual date of payment. Suppose, the sum of Rs. 2,000 due by Slow (Illustration 48) is paid on 30th April, 1979. The rate of interest is 6%. Slow will have to pay interest for 47 days (*i.e.*, from 14th March to 30th April) on Rs. 2,000 @ 6%. The interest comes to Rs. 15.46, *i.e.*, $\frac{2{,}000 \times 6 \times 47}{100 \times 365}$.

Account Current. If two parties have a number of transactions between themselves, they will exchange statements confirming the amounts involved. Usually, such statements are merely a copy of the ledger account for the period concerned. But one party may calculate interest due to or due by the other party. The statement, then will include not only the amount of the transactions but also the interest involved. Such a statement is known as "Account Current". Account Current is common between a principal and his agent and between parties to a joint venture. The statement is headed, as, say, Ram in Account Current with Sita. It means that

Sita is sending the statement to Ram, showing the transactions between Ram and Sita.

Interest may be calculated for each transaction by means of tables. A better method is to calculate the interest by products. The amount of each transaction is multiplied by the number of days between the date of the transaction to the date of closing. Products of the debit side and products of the credit side are totalled separately (the Account Current will have a column for products on each side). Interest is calculated for one day on the difference of the two totals and is entered on the bigger side.

Care will have to be exercised on one point. The amount in respect of some transactions may be due after the closing. For instance, if an acceptance is received from X for 3 months on 15th April and the date of closing is 30th June, X will pay the amount on 18th July. This is 18 days after the date of closing. X will be naturally credited on 15th April with the amount of the acceptance but no interest is due to him since he has not made an actual payment. On the contrary, he will make the payment 18 days after the closing. He should, therefore, be charged interest for 18 days in this period. If this is done the task of calculating interest in the next period will be simplified because, then, interest can be calculated straightaway on the opening balance without having to remember that a certain sum was due only 18 days after the previous closing. The rule, therefore, is that in respect of amounts due after the closing date, interest should be charged or paid for the days between the date of closing and the actual due date. In actual practice, the amount is multiplied by the respective number of days and is entered in red ink on the same side as that of the transaction. In the example given above, the amount of the acceptance will be multiplied by 18 and entered on the credit side (because the acceptance was received from X) in red ink. Products entered in red are deducted from the other products. This interest is known as "red ink interest".

Illustration Yusuf owed Rs. 1,100 to Punnu on 1st January, 1979. The following transactions took place between the two parties :—

1979 Jan.	15	Yusuf sells goods to Punnu, Rs. 500
Feb.	10	Yusuf purchases goods from Punnu, Rs. 400 (due* date March 15).
Feb.	20	Punnu sends cash to Yusuf, Rs. 200.
March	5	Yusuf sells goods to Punnu, Rs. 300 (due date March 31).
April	25	Yusuf receives 3 months' acceptance from Punnu, for Rs. 600.
May	10	Yusuf pays cash, Rs. 700.
June	15	Yusuf sells goods to Punnu, Rs. 500 (due date July 15).

Interest is @ 6% p.a. Prepare the Account Current to be sent by Punnu to Yusuf on 30th June, 1979.

*Due date here means that the amount is payable on 15th March, even though the transaction took place on 10th Feb.

Yusuf in Account Current with Punnu

Dr. | Cr.

Date	Due Date	Particulars	Amount Rs.	P.	No. of Days to 30/6	Products	Date	Due Date	Particulars	Amount Rs.	P.	No. of Days to 30/6	
1979	1979						1979	1979					
Jan. 1	Jan. 1	To Balance b/d	1,100	—	181	1,99,100	Jan. 15	Jan. 15	By Purchases A/c	500	—	166	83,000
Feb. 10	March 15	To Sales A/c	400	—	107	42,800	Mar. 5	March 31	By Purchases A/c	300	—	61	18,300
Feb. 20	Feb. 20	To Cash A/c	200	—	130	26,000							
Apl. 25	July 28	To Bills Payable A/c	600	—	– 28	—16,800	May 10	May 10	By Cash A/c	700	—	51	35,700
June 30	June 30	To Interest A/c $\frac{1,21,600 \times 6}{100 \times 365}$	19	99			June 15	July 15	By Purchases A/c	500	—	–15	—7,500
							June 30		By Difference in Products				1,21,600
							”		By Balance c/d	319	99		
			2,319	99		2,51,100				2,319	99		2,51,100
July 1		To Balance b/d	319	99									

Alternatively, if interest is to be calculated for each transaction separately :

Yusuf in Account Current with Punnu

Dr.															Cr.
Date	Due Date	Particulars	Amount		No. of Days to 30/6	Interest		Date	Due Date	Particulars	Amount		No of Days to 30/6	Interest	
			Rs.	P.		Rs.	P.				Rs.	P.		Rs.	P.
1979	1979							1979	1979						
Jan. 1	Jan. 1	To Balance *b/d*	1,100	—	181	32	70	Jan. 15	Jan. 15	By Purchases A/c	500	—	166	13	64
Feb. 10	March 15	To Sales A/c	400	—	107	7	04	March 5	March 31	By Purchase A/c	300	—	61	3	01
Feb. 20	Feb. 20	To Cash	200	—	130	4	28	May 10	May 10	By Cash A/c	700	—	51	5	86
Ap. 25	July 28	To Bills Payable A/c	600	—	—28	—2	76	June 15	July 15	By Purchases A/c	500	—	—15	—1	23
June 30		To Interest A/c	19	98				June 30		By Differences in Interest				19	98
								June 30		By Balance c/d	319	98			
			2,319	98		41	26				2,319	98		41	26
July 1		To Balance b/d	319	98											

Exercises

1. A and B were partners in a joint venture sharing profits and losses in the proportion of four-fifths and one-fifth respectively. A supplies goods to the value of Rs. 5,000 and incurs expenses amounting to Rs. 400. B supplies goods to the value of Rs. 4,000 and his expenses amount to Rs. 300. B sells goods on behalf of the Joint Venture and realises Rs. 12,000. B is entitled to a commission of 5 per cent on sales. B settles his account by Bank Draft. Give the journal entries and the necessary accounts in the books of both the partners. *(Profit Rs. 1,700)*

2. Active and Sharp entered into a joint venture to buy old motor vehicles, recondition them and sell them. Active was to receive 6% p.a. interest on capital invested by him and Sharp was to get a remuneration of Rs. 500 per month and share profits or losses equally. Active invested Rs. 25,000 in purchase of motor vehicles. Costs of reconditioning and overhauling came to Rs. 15,000. These were paid for after sale. The vehicles were sold for Rs. 50,000, the proceeds being received by Active. The whole operation took six months. The accounts were settled.

Prepare accounts in the books of both the parties. *(Profits, Rs. 6,250)*

3. Heer and Sassi agreed to take up a venture to carry out repairs to Government quarters. Heer supplied materials worth Rs. 6,000. Sassi supplied tools worth Rs. 1,000. Sassi also paid the workers totalling Rs. 7,500. The whole work was completed in three months for which a total payment of Rs. 20,000 was received. The payment was received by Heer. The tools were considered worth Rs. 500 and were taken back by Sassi. Profits were to be shared equally. Prepare the necessary accounts in the books of both the parties, assuming that the accounts were settled in cash. *(Profit Rs. 6,000)*

4. A of Ahmedabad and B of Bombay enter into a joint venture to consign 100 bales of cotton piece-goods to C of Ceylon to be sold by the latter on the joint risk of A and B, sharing in proportion of 3/5 and 2/5 respectively. A sends 60 bales at Rs. 1,300 each, paying freight and other charges amounting to Rs. 900. B sends 40 bales at Rs. 1,250 each, and pays for freight and other charges Rs. 800. All the bales are sold by the consignee for Rs 1,50,000, out of which he deducts Rs. 1,500 for his expenses and his commission at 3 per cent. He remits a bank draft for Rs. 70,000 to A and the balance to B.

Give journal entries and ledger accounts to record these transactions in the books of both A and B. *(Profit Rs. 14,300)*

5. Ram and Hanuman decided to take up a venture in blankets. Ram was to purchase them and send them to Hanuman who was to sell them. Ram was entitled to interest @ 6% on the money invested by him (taking into account any money received) and Hanuman was to get a commission @ 3% on sales. Profits and losses were to be shared equally. On 1st September, 1968 Ram purchased 1,000 blankets @ Rs. 20 each. He spent Rs. 500 on packing, etc. Hanuman spent Rs. 1,000 on freight.

He sold : 200 blankets on 1st October @ Rs. 30

500 „ „ 31st October @ Rs. 35

200 „ „ 15th November @ Rs. 40

He remitted to Ram :

Rs. 5,000 on 1st October.

Rs. 15,500 on 1st November.

He took the remaining 100 blankets into his own stock at cost plus 20%. On 30th November the accounts were settled.

Prepare accounts in the books of both the parties.

(Profit, Rs. 11,455)

6. Amarchand and Balkrishna were partners in a joint venture sharing profits and losses in the ratio of 3 : 2.

Amarchand purchased goods worth Rs. 62,000 and sent them to Balkrishn and in so doing he had to pay Rs. 1,300 for insurance and Rs. 3,700 for carriag freight and other expenses.

Balkrishna reported after some time that he had sold some goods for R 60,000 and that the remaining goods could not be sold on account of bad marke conditions. Amarchand and Balkrishna then handed over the unsold goods t a local merchant Cowasji, at Bombay, who agreed to sell the goods on their be half. Cowasji was to be paid all the expenses in that connection and was to b allowed a commission at the rate of 2½ per cent on the sale price of the goo sold.

After some time Cowasji sent to Balkrishna a cheque for Rs. 4,500 afte deducting his expenses Rs. 375 and commission. The sale price of goods sold b Cowasji was Rs. 5,000. Cowasji returned the unsold goods to Balkrishna.

Amarchand and Balkrishna then decided to close the joint ventur Balkrishna taking the balance of the goods unsold which cost Rs. 25,000 at discount of 8 per cent.

Balkrishna sent a statement of account to Amarchand showing the follow ing payments made by him :—

Carriage, Rs. 1,600 ; Office expenses, Rs. 2,800 ; Insuranc Rs. 2,500 ; Office and Godown Rent, Rs. 1,500 ; Brokerage Rs. 3,60

He also sent a cheque for Rs. 70,000 to Amarchand.

You are required to prepare the necessary account or accounts in Amar chand's Ledger showing his share of profit or loss on the joint venture and th amount due to or by Balkrishna. *(Profit; Rs. 8,50*

7. X and Y undertake jointly to build a building for a newly started join stock company for a contract price of Rs. 1,00,000, payable as to Rs. 80,000 b instalments in cash and Rs. 20,000 in fully paid shares of the new company. banking account is opened in the joint name, X contributing Rs. 25,000 and Rs. 15,000. They are to share profits and losses in the proportion of 2/3 and 1/ respectively. Their transactions were as follows :—

	Rs.
Paid wages	30,00
Bought materials	78,50
Paid Architect's fees, on credit from Z.	2,00

The contract was completed and the price duly received ; Z's dues wer duly paid off. The joint venture was closed by X taking up all the shares of th company at an agreed valuation of Rs, 24,000 and Y taking up unused stock c materials for Rs. 2,000 as mutually valued.

Prepare accounts to record the above transactions in separate books c joint venture and also in the books of X and Y. *(Loss, Rs. 4,50*

8. Contractor and Architect undertook the construction of a cinem hall for Rs. 5,00,000. Contractor put Rs. 50,000 and Architect put Rs. 10,00 in the joint bank account opened for the purpose. Both were to be equa partners subject to interest on money invested @ 6% p.a. Amounts sper were :

	Rs.
On Wages	1,90,00
On Materials	2,30,00
On Plant and Stores	40,00

The whole work took one year. Payment was received in instalment except that due to certain defects Rs. 15,000 were deducted. The plant wa considered as having depreciated at 20%. Half of the plant was taken over b contractor. The other half was sold for Rs. 15,000. Prepare the separat books of the joint venture. *(Profit, Rs. 52,40*

9. R and B entered into a joint venture to carry out extensive repairs to certain buildings. The amount of the contract was Rs. 50,000 subject to completion by a certain date. The amounts spent by R and B were as follows

	Rs.	Rs.
Materials	10,000	2,000
Wages	5,000	15,000
Rent of equipment	—	2,000

The contract was delayed for which a fine of Rs. 2,000 was imposed. This was ascribed wholly to R.

Prepare relevant accounts to show the profit or loss of each party.

(R earns Rs. 6,000 and B Rs. 8,000)

10. A, B and C entered into a joint venture and agreed to divide profits in the ratio of 6:3:1 respectively. They agreed to contribute the following amounts which they put in a joint banking account: A, Rs.6,000; B, Rs.4,000 and C, Rs.2,000. They purchased goods for Rs.25,000. Some goods were spoilt and they were taken away by C at an agreed value of Rs.150. The remaining goods were sold for Rs.31,000. C was entitled to a commission @ 4% of the sale proceeds. Following expenses were paid by the co-ventures: A, Rs.490; B, Rs.250; and C, Rs.250. Open ledger accounts and record the transactions when separate set of books are maintained for the joint venture. *(Adapted from B. Com. Madras)*

(Profit Rs.3,920)

11. Raman and Laxman are participants in a joint, sharing profits and losses in the proportion of 2/3 and 1/3 respectively. Each party maintains a complete record in its books. Raman supplied goods to the value of Rs.15,000 and incurs an expenditure of Rs.600 on them; Laxman supplies goods to the extent of Rs.12,000 and his expenses thereon amount to Rs.900. Raman sells all the goods for Rs.36,000 for which he is entitled to receive a commission at 5 per cent. Accounts are settled by bank draft. Give journal entries in the books of Raman to record the above transactions. *(C. A. Inter)*

(Profit Rs.5,700)

12. The following transactions took place between Ramesh and Prakash between 1st January and 30th June, 1977 :—

			Rs.
1977	Jan. 1	Sold goods to Prakash	1,120
	,, 10	Received his acceptance at 6 mos.	500
	Feb. 15	Cash received from Prakash	600
	March 2	Bought goods from Prakash	2,750
	,, 3	Accepted Prakash's draft at 1 month	1,000
	April 11	Cash paid to Prakash	1,000
	,, 30	Goods sold to Prakash due end of May	1,200
	May 11	Bought goods from Prakash	750
	,, 31	Sold goods to Prakash due 10th June	1,100
	June 15	Bought goods from Parkash	1,500

Make out an account current to be rendered by Ramesh to Prakash as on 30th June, 1967, taking interest into account at 5% per annum.

[Interest, Rs 5.47 (Cr.)]

13. Dutt owed Rs. 600 to Bose on 1st January, 1979. There were some other transactions also between Dutt and Bose, as follows :

1979		Rs.
Jan. 15	Dutt purchases goods (due date 15th February)	300
Feb. 10	Dutt sends cash	400
" 28	Dutt sells goods (due date March 15)	600
March 1	Dutt accepts promissory note at 2 months	500
March 15	Dutt purchases goods (due date April 15)	700

Prepare the Account Current to be rendered by Bose to Dutt on March 31, 1969. Interest is to be charged @ 6% p.a. [*Interest, Rs. 7.31 (Dr.)*]

14. A merchant has purchased goods, the due dates for the payment of which are as follows :—

On March 5 Rs. 300, due date of payment April 8.
On April 15 Rs. 200, " " " May 18.
On May 10 Rs. 275, " " " June 4.
On June 10 Rs. 470, " " " July 8.

He wishes to give a bill for the total amount due, the bill to be payable on the average due date. Ascertain this date. (*31st May*)

15. Mohan had accepted the following bills payable to Sham :—

Amount Rs.	Date	Term
400	15th Jan., 1979	3 months
500	10th February, 1979	2 months
300	9th March, 1979	2 months
600	15th March, 1979	3 months

Mohan wishes to pay all the bills on one day. When should he pay ? Suppose, actually, Mohan makes the payment on 30th June, 1969. Assuming interest @ 6% p.a., what will be the amount of the interest ? Check your answer by calculating the interest on each item and by calculating it using the average due date.

16. Chen had accepted the undermentioned bills in favour of Sho :—

Date of acceptance 1979	Term (months)	Amount Rs.
January, 25	2	1,000
February, 10	3	4,000
March, 6	2	3,000

Chen now wishes to consolidate the bills into one bill payable at 2 months on such a date as will enable him to earn a rebate of Rs. 6 @ 9% p.a. Ascertain the date.

(*February 18*)

CHAPTER XI

DEPRECIATION

Meaning and need. Depreciation means a fall in the value of an asset. The net result of an asset's depreciation is that sooner or later the asset will become useless. (However, land is not considered to depreciate at all.) The main causes of depreciation are :—

1. Wear and tear due to actual use ;

2. Efflux of time—mere passage of time will cause a fall in the value of an asset, even if it is not used *;

3. Obsolescence—a new invention or a permanent change in demand may render the asset useless;

4. Accidents ; and

5. Fall in market price.

Only in a few cases do assets appreciate. Land and old paintings may go up in value. But usually the value of assets diminishes continuously. This is even if an asset is not used. Mere passage of time is sufficient.

One unfortunate thing about depreciation is that it is not visible like other expenses till the very end. In case of other expenses, the expenditure is obvious and, hence, everybody provides for such expenses while calculating loss or profit. It is not so with depreciation. Many people do not deduct depreciation from the gross earning to ascertain their net profit simply because there is no payment for it. This is fallacious. It will be clear by an example. Suppose : (1) A starts a small manufacturing business and buys machinery worth Rs. 20,000; (2) he does not realise that this machinery is depreciating and, therefore, uses up all the 'profits' which his business gives ; (3) by the end of ten years he has earned a net income of Rs. 30,000, without considering depreciation ; and (4) the machinery bought by A is useless at the end of 10 years. It is elear that A's net income is not Rs. 30,000 but only Rs. 10,000, because out of the Rs. 30,000 he must deduct the loss of machinery worth Rs. 20,000. Would it not have been better if A had deducted every year a due proportion of his expenditure on the machinery before ascertaining his profit ?

*This is because new machines come constantly on the market and old machines have to give way to new ones.

Further, if A has already used up the Rs. 30,000, which according to his mistaken idea are his profits for the 10 years, he cannot continue to run his business for his machinery is no longer serviceable unless he raises funds, say, as a loan. If he had provided proper depreciation he would have retained sufficient funds to buy new machinery when the old one became useless. Provision of depreciation, therefore, is necessary firstly for ascertaining the true profit and secondly for retaining funds in the business so that the asset can be replaced (when its life is over) by a new one.

Depreciation of current assets is taken care of by valuing them, for balance sheet purposes, at cost or market price whichever is lower. This chapter, therefore, is concerned only with depreciation of fixed assets.

Functions of Depreciation. Providing depreciation, before the profit or loss of the period concerned is ascertained, has three main objectives. These are the following :—

(*i*) Stating the assets in the balance sheet at their proper values. If, say, machinery purchased some years ago continues to be shown at its cost, the asset values will be inflated. All fixed assets should be shown at cost less the amount of depreciation suffered by them till the date of the balance sheet.

(*ii*) Reporting correct profits or losses. This point has been covered above already.

(*iii*) Seeing to it that the firm retains enough funds for the replacement of the asset at the end of its commercial life. If no depreciation is provided, the reported profit may all be withdrawn by the properietors but if depreciation is charged to the Profit and Loss Account, funds equal to the amount of the depreciation will remain in the firm and will be available at the time the replacement is due.

The Basic factors. For calculating depreciation the basic factors are :

1. The cost of the asset ;

2. The estimated residual or scrap value at the end of its life ; and

3. The estimated number of years of its commercial life. One should not consider the actual number of years that it can physically run but the number of years it is likely to be used by the firm. A machinery may be capable of running for 20 years but, say, due to new inventions, it is expected to be used only for 10 years; then the estimated life is 10 years and not 20 years.

So much depreciation has to be provided as will reduce the value of the asset to its scrap value at the end of its estimated life.

Suppose a machine is purchased at a cost of Rs. 50,000. It is expected that it will be used for 15 years at the end of which period it will have a scrap value of Rs. 5,000. We must provide a total "depreciation" of Rs. 45,000 in 15 years.

Entries required. The entry to be made on writing off depreciation is :

Depreciation Account Dr.

To Asset Account

The Depreciation Account goes to the debit of Profit and Loss Account. The asset appears at its reduced value in the Balance Sheet. An alternative entry is :

Depreciation Account Dr.
To Provision for Depreciation Account

In this case Depreciation Account, of course, goes to the debit of Profit and Loss Account. The value of the asset continues to be the same every year in the Balance Sheet. The depreciation written off is accumulated in a separate account—Provision for Depreciation Account—which may appear on the liability side of the Balance Sheet but is better deducted from the asset concerned.

Methods for providing depreciation. The following are the various methods for providing depreciation :—

(*a*) Fixed Percentage on Original Cost or Fixed Instalments or Straight Line Method ;

(*b*) Fixed Percentage on Diminishing Balance or Reducing Instalments Method ;

(*c*) Sum of the years (or digits) Method ;

(*d*) Annuity Method ;

(*e*) Depreciation Fund Method ;

(*f*) Insurance Policy Method ;

(*g*) Revaluation Method ;

(*h*) Depletion Method ; and

(*i*) Machine Hour Rate Method.

We will now consider these methods.

(*a*) *Fixed Percentage on Original Cost.* In this method a suitable percentage of original cost is written off the asset every year. Thus if an asset costs Rs. 20,000 and 10 per cent depreciation is thought proper, Rs. 2,000 would be written off every year. The assumption in this case is that the life is 10 years and that at the end of 10 years there will be no scrap or residual value. In this method, the amount to be written off every year is arrived at as under :—

$$\frac{\textit{Cost}-\textit{estimated scrap value}}{\textit{Estimated life in years}}$$

While calculating depreciation for a particular year, the period for which the asset is used in the year concerned should also be taken into account. Thus if the asset is purchased on 1st April and the books are closed on 30th June, only three months' depreciation should be written off in that year. However, income tax authorities permit depreciation for the full year even if the asset concerned was used only for one day during the year.

Illustration Jain Bros. acquired a machine on 1st July, 1963 at a cost of Rs. 14,000 and spent Rs. 1,000 on its installation. The firm writes off depreciation at 10% of the original cost every year. The books are closed on 31st December every year. Show the Machinery Account and Depreciation Account for three years.

Solution :

Machinery Account

Dr. *Cr.*

Date	Particulars	Rs.	Date	Particulars	Rs.
1973		Rs.	1973		Rs.
July 1	To Bank	14,000 —	Dec. 31	By Depreciation A/c— 10% on Rs. 15,000 for 6 months	750 —
,,	To Bank—Installation Expenses	1,000 —	,,	By Balance c/d	14,250 —
		15,000 —			15,000 —
1974			1974		
Jan. 1	To Balance b/d	14,250 —	Dec. 31	By Depreciation A/c—10% on Rs. 15,000	1,500 —
				By Balance e/d	12,750 —
		14,250 —			14,250 —
1975			1975		
Jan. 1	To Balance c/d	12,750 —	Dec. 31	By Depreciation A/c	1,500 —
			,,	By Balance c/d	11,250 —
		12,750 —			12,750 —
1976					
Jan. 1	To Balance b/d	11,250 —			

Depreciation Account

Date	Particulars	Rs.	Date	Particulars	Rs.
1973		Rs.	1973		Rs.
Dec. 31	To Machinery A/c	750 —	Dec. 31	By Profit & Loss A/c	750 —
1974			1974		
Dec. 31	To Machinery A/c	1,500 —	Dec. 31	By Profit & Loss A/c	1,500 —
1975			1975		
Dec. 31	To Machinery A/c	1,500 —	Dec. 31	By Profit & Loss A/c	1,500 —

Sale of Asset. If the asset is disposed of in the middle of the year, the amount realised should be credited to the asset account. Depreciation should be credited to the asset for the time it has been in use. Any balance left in the account of the asset will then be profit or loss and should be transferred to Profit and Loss Account. Continuing the Illustration, suppose the machine is sold on March 31, 1976 for Rs. 9,500. The depreciation for 3 months is Rs. 375, *i.e.*, $\frac{3}{12}$ of Rs. 1,500. This amount will be credited to the Machinery Account. Rs. 9,500 will also be credited. A balance of Rs. 1,375 remains. This is loss and should be transferred to the Profit and Loss Account. The Machinery Account for 1976 wiil appear as under :

Machinery Account

Dr.		Rs.				Cr. Rs.	
1976 Jan. 1	To Balance b/d	11,250	—	1976 Mar. 31	By Bank Account—sale proceeds	9,500	—
				,,	By Depreciation Account—3 months' depreciation	375	—
				,,	By Profit and Loss A/c—loss transferred	1,375	—
		11,250	—			11,250	—

(*b*) *Fixed Percentage on Diminishing Balance.* In this method the rate or percentage of depreciation is fixed, but it applies to the value at which the asset stands in the books in the beginning of the year. (In the first year depreciation is written off proportionate to the actual period in use). The depreciation on Rs. 20,000, the cost of the asset, at the rate of 10% will be Rs. 2,000 in the first year. When this amount is written off, the value of the asset is reduced to Rs. 18,000 (*i.e.*, Rs. 20,000 minus Rs. 2,000). Depreciation in the second year will be Rs. 1,800, *i.e.*, 10% of Rs. 18,000. In the third year it will be Rs. 1,620.

The above Illustration is worked out below under this method.

Machinery Account

Dr.		Rs.				Cr. Rs.	
1973 July 1	To Bank	14,000	—	1973 Dec. 31	By Depreciation A/c	750	—
,,	To Bank	1,000	—	,,	By Balance c/d	14,250	—
		15,000	—			15,000	—
1974 Jan. 1	To Balance b/d	14,250	—	1974 Dec. 31	By Depreciation A/c	1,425	—
				,,	By Balance c/d	12,825	—
		14,250	—			14,250	—
1975 Jan. 1	To Balance b/d	12,825	—	1973 Dec. 31	By Depreciation A/c	1,282	50
				,,	By Balance c/d	11,542	50
		12,825	—			12,825	—
1976 Jan. 1	To Balance b/d	11,542	50				

Continuing the example and assuming the machinery was sold on March 31 at Rs. 9,500—

Machinery Account

Dr.							Cr.
1976 Jan. 1	To Balance b/d	Rs. 11,542	50	1976 Mar. 31	By Bank A/c	Rs. 9,500	—
				,,	By Depreciation A/c (10% on Rs. 11,542.50 for 3 months)	288	56
					By Profit & Loss A/c	1,753	94
		11,542	50			11,542	50

Note : It should be noted that for a given life of an asset, the rate of depreciation under the Diminishing Value Method will be roughly 2·8 times the rate under the straight line basis. If, for example, the life is 10 years, the rate of depreciation under the Straight Line Basis will be 10% whereas under the other method it will be about 28 %.

Advantages. The expense involved in using an asset is the depreciation to be written off plus the amount spent on repairs of the asset. In the first year of the life of an asset repairs are light. They rise as the asset gets older. If one follows the first method of depreciation, the total cost of using the asset *viz.*, depreciation (which is constant every year) plus repairs will rise. Later years will show heavier expense. This is not proper because the asset gives the same service in the later years as in the earlier years. The charge to Profit and Loss Account should be uniform. If one follows the second method, depreciation in the earlier years will be heavy but will be lighter as the asset gets old. Repairs, on the other hand, are light in the earlier years and heavier later. The total of the two—depreciation and repairs—will be roughly constant. Thus this method is better than the Fixed Instalments Method. It also recognises one more fact. As soon as an asset is put to use, its value, for sale purposes, falls heavily. Under this method the depreciation is heaviest in the first year. Thus it reduces the book figure to its proper value or quite near it.

Illustration. M/s. Pee and Que had machinery in their works as per the following details :—

Date Installed	Cost Rs.
15-4-55	1,30,000
20-6-70	80,000
17-10-74	1,00,000
18-1-79	40,000

The firm had the practice of writing off 90% of the cost over 10 years, a whole year's depreciation being charged irrespective of the date of installation. No depreciation was charged if an item was sold. The accounting year adopted by the firm was the calender year

During 1979 a machine installed in 1955 at a cost of Rs.30,000 was sold for Rs.10,000; another machine installed in 1974 at a cost of Rs.60,000 was discarded, its scrap value being estimated at Rs.9,000. Draw up the Machinery Account for 1979 as also the Discarded Machines A/c.

Solution :

Note : The book value of the machinery in use on 1-1-79 was Rs. 83,200 as shown below :

		Rs.
10% of machinery installed in 1955		13,000
Machinery installed in 1970 : Cost	80,000	
9 years' depreciation @ Rs. 7,200 p.a.	64,800	15,200
Machinery installed in 1974 : Cost	1,00,000	
5 years' depreciation @ Rs. 9,000 p.a.	45,000	55,000
		83,200

Machinery Account

		Rs.		Rs.
1979				
Jan. 1	To Balance b/d	83,200	By Cash	10,000
18	To Bank	40,000	By Discarded Machines A/c	33,000
	To P.&L. A/c — Profit on Sale	7,000	By Depreciation	14,400
			By Balance c/d	72,800
		1,30,200		1,30,200
1980				
Jun. 1	To Balance b/d	72,800		

Discarded Machines Account

1979		Rs.	1979		Rs.
	To Machinery A/c	33,000		By P.&L. A/c—loss (balancing figure)	24,000
			Dec. 31	By Balance c/d	9,000
		33,000			33,000
1980					
Jan. 1	To Balance b/d	9,000			

Working Notes :

(1) The machine sold has a book value of Rs. 3,000, i.e., 10% of Rs. 30,000; since it has been sold for Rs.10,000, there is profit of Rs.7,000, transferred to P. & L. A/c

(2) The discarded machine has a book value of Rs. 33,000, as shown below :

	Rs.
Cost in 1974	60,000
Less 5 years' depreciation @ Rs.5,400 p.a.	27,000
	33,000

(3) Depreciation to be written off during 1979 :

On machines installed in 1970	7,200
On balance of machines installed in 1974	3,600
On machines installed in 1979	3,600
	14,400

(*c*) *Sum of the Digits Method.* This is a variant of the Reducing Instalments or Diminishing Balance Method. Under this method, depreciation is written off each year by the formula.

$$\text{Amount to be written off} \times \frac{\text{The number of years of the remaining life of the asset (including the current year)}}{\text{The total of all the digits representing the life of the asset (in years)}}$$

Suppose, a machine is bought for Rs. 20,000 with an estimated scrap value of Rs. 1,000 and an estimated life of 10 years. The amount to be written off in the first year will be Rs. 3,455, *i.e.*, $19{,}000 \times \frac{10}{10+9+8+7+6+5+4+3+2+1}$ or $19{,}000 \times \frac{10}{55}$. In the second year the amount of depreciation will be Rs. 3,109, *i.e.*, $19{,}000 \times \frac{9}{55}$, and in the last year of its life the depreciation will be $19{,}000 \times \frac{1}{55}$ or Rs. 345.

The three methods stated above ignore interest, By using an asset, one "loses" not only the money spent on acquiring it but also the interest which would have been earned on the money. Therefore, depreciation should cover not only the cost of the asset but also an appropriate amount for interest. This is done in the Annuity method. However, one must note that in actual practice the Fixed Instalments Method or the Fixed Percentage on Original Cost Method is the most popular these days. But Income Tax authorities, calculate depreciation according to the Reducing Instalments Method.

(*d*) *Annuity Method.* As has been pointed out, the first three methods ignore interest. The annuity method takes into account the interest lost on the acquisition of an asset. Interest is calculated on the book value of the asset at the proper rate (say, 8%) and debited to the asset. The amount is credited to Interest Account, which then goes to the credit side of the Profit and Loss Account. The amount to be written off as depreciation is calculated from the Annuity Tables. The depreciation will be different according to the rate of interest and according to the period over which the asset is to be written off. Below is an extract from the Annuity Tables.

Annuity Table

Years	3%	3½%	4%	4½%	5%
3	0·353530	0·356934	0·360349	0·363773	0·367209
4	0·269027	0·272251	0·275490	0·278744	0·282012
5	0·218355	0·221481	0·224627	0·227792	0·230975
6	0·184598	0·187668	0·190762	0·193878	0·197017
7	0·160506	0·163544	0·166610	0·169701	0·172820
8	0·142456	0·145477	0·148528	0·151610	0·154722
9	0·128434	0·131446	0·134493	0·137574	0·140690
10	0·117231	0·120241	0·123291	0·126379	0·129505
15	0·083767	0·086825	0·089941	0·093114	0·096342
20	0·067216	0·070361	0·073582	0·076876	0·080243

The above table indicates the annual sum which can be paid annually if there is Re. 1 in the beginning and if it earns a given rate of interest. Thus if the prevailing rate of interest is 5%, then, given one rupee in the beginning, a sum of Rs. 0·096342 can be paid at the end of each year for 15 years or Re. 0·080243 at the end of each year for 20 years. These figures also give the amount to be written off each year to reduce to zero an asset valued at Re. 1 in the beginning by the time its life is over, assuming it to earn a given rate of interest.

Illustration A lease is purchased on 31st January, 1970 for 4 years at a cost of Rs. 20,000. It is proposed to depreciate the lease by the annuity method charging 5 per cent interest.

Show the Lease Account for four years and also the relevant entries in the Profit and Loss Account.

Solution :

A reference to the above table shows that to depreciate Re. 1 by annuity method over 4 years, charging 5% interest, one must write off a sum of Re. 0·282012. To write off Rs. 20,000 one requires to write off every year Rs. 5,640·24 *i.e.*, ·282012×20,000.

Dr. **Lease Account** **Cr.**

Date	Particulars	Rs.		Date	Particulars	Rs.	
1970 Jan. 1	To Bank Account	20,000	—	1970 Dec. 31	To Depreciation A/c	5,640	24
Dec. 31	To Interest A/c (5% on Rs. 20,000)	1,000	—	,,	By Balance c/d	15,359	76
		21,000	—			21,000	—
1971 Jan. 1	To Balance b/d	15,359	76	1971 Dec. 31	By Depreciation A/c	5,640	24
Dec. 31	To Interest A/c (5% on Rs. 15,359·76)	767	99	,,	By Balance c/d	10,487	51
		16,127	75			16,127	75
1972 Jan. 1	To Balance b/d	10,487	51	1972 Dec. 31	By Depreciation A/c	5,640	24
Dec. 31	To Interest A/c	524	38	.,	By Balance c/d	5,371	65
		11,011	89			11,011	89
1973 Jan. 1	To Balance b/d	5,371	65	1973 Dec. 31	By Depreciation A/c	5,640	24
Dec. 31	To Interest A/c	268	59				
		5,640	24			5,640	24

Profit and Loss Account

Date	Particulars	Rs.		Date	Particulars	Rs.	
1970 Dec. 31	To Depreciation A/c	5,640	24	1970 Dec. 31	By Interest A/c	1,000	—
1971 Dec. 31	To Depreciation A/c	5,640	24	1971 Dec. 31	By Interest A/c	769	99
1972 Dec. 31	To Depreciation A/c	5,640	24	1972 Dec. 31	By Interest A/c	524	38
1973 Dec. 31	To Depreciation A/c	5,640	24	1973 Dec. 31	By Interest A/c	268	59

It will be seen from the above example that the amount to be written off as depreciat. n is larger than what would have been under the straight line or the reducing instalments method. But there is no effect on the Profit and Loss Account, because the interest debited to the asset is credited to the Profit and Loss Account. The Annuity Method, therefore, merely draws attention to the amount which is being "lost" by the use of the asset, *viz.*, the cost and the interest that has been lost.

(*e*) *Depreciation Fund Method.* When one writes off depreciation one makes sure that sufficient assets are retained in the business to replace the asset (unless the proprietor draws out more than is warranted by the figure of his net profits). Under the first three methods, however, ready cash may not be available when the time for replacement comes. The amount collected by writing off depreciation may be dispersed in all sorts of assets, making it difficult to buy new asset in place of the old one. The Depreciation Fund ensures that when replacement is due, ready cash will be available.

In a nutshell, the system is that the amount written off as depreciation should be kept aside and invested in readily saleable securities, preferably government securities. The interest received is reinvested. The securities accumulate and when the life of the asset expires, the securities are sold and a new asset is purchased with the sale proceeds. Since the securities always earn some interest it is not necessary to use the full amount of the depreciation; something less will do. Rs. 10,000 accumulated annually for ten years will be much more than Rs. 1,00,000 because of interest. Hence if Rs. 1,00,000 is required exactly, the annual instalment will be less than Rs. 10,000. How much amount is to be invested every year so that a given sum is available at the end of a given period depends on the rate of interest. The following table—known as the Sinking Fund Table—shows how much is to be invested every year together with the interest earned so that at the end of the period one gets Re. 1.

Sinking Fund Table

Years	3%	3½%	4%	4½%	5%
3	0·323530	0·321934	0·320349	0·318773	0·317209
4	0·239027	0·237251	0·235490	0·233744	0·232071
5	0·188355	0·186181	0·184627	0·182792	0·180975
6	0·154598	0·152668	0·150762	0·148878	0·147017
7	0·130506	0·128544	0·126610	0·124701	0·122820
8	0·112456	0·110477	0·108528	0·106610	0·104722
9	0·098434	0·096446	0·094493	0·092575	0·090690
10	0·087231	0·085241	0·083291	0·081379	0·079505
15	0·055767	0·051825	0·049941	0·048114	0·046342
20	0·037216	0·035361	0·033582	0.031876	0·030243

The above table shows that if investments earn 5% to get Re. 1 at the end of 5 years, one has to invest Re. ·180975 every year together with any interest that will be earned. To get at the instalment to be invested, one has to multiply this figure with the sum required. One must note that this instalment is really the depreciation to be written off. However, instead of crediting the asset, another account known as 'Depreciation Fund Account' is credited. The amount together with any interest earned will be invested. The journal entries are as follows :

First Year (at the end) :

(1) Depreciation Account ... Dr.
 To Depreciation Fund Account

(2) Depreciation Fund Investments Account ... Dr.
 To Bank

} with the instalment calculated from the S.F Tables.

The first entry not only provides depreciation but also signifies the intention to buy investments. The second entry records the actual carrying out of the intention. The Depreciation Account, of course, is transferred to the debit of the Profit and Loss Account. The Depreciation Fund Account and the Depreciation Fund Investments Account are balanced and are shown in the Balance Sheet, the former on the liability side (or as a deduction from the asset) and the latter on the asset side. The asset generally continues to be shown at its original cost in the Balance Sheet.

In subsequent years the following entries are necessary :—

(1)	Bank To Interest on Depreciation Fund Investments Account	Dr.	with the amount of interest actually received on investments.
(2)	Interest on Depreciation Fund Investments Account To Depreciation Fund A/c	Dr.	the interest received, transferred to the credit of Dep. Fund A/c.
(3)	Depreciation Account To Depreciation Fund A/c	Dr.	with the annual instalment
(4)	Depreciation Fund investments Account To Bank	Dr.	the annual instalment plus interest earned.

In the last year also, interest will be received on Depreciation Fund Investments and the sum will be transferred to the Depreciation Fund Account. The annual instalment will be, as usual, debited to the Depreciation Account and credited to the Depreciation Fund Account. But no investments will be purchased because at the end of the last year—when the asset has become useless—a new asset must be purchased which will necessitate the selling of all the investments. Hence there is no point in making an investment and realising it on the same day. In the last year, therefore, entries Nos. (1) and (2) and (3) will be repeated. Entry No. 4 will, naturally, not be made.

The position now will be that the asset will show a debit balance equal to the original cost, the Depreciation Fund Account will show a credit equal (almost) to the value of the asset and the Depreciation Fund Investments Account will show a debit balance somewhat less (because no investment has been made at the end of the last year) than the balance of the Depreciation Fund Account. The investments will be sold, the proceeds being utilised to buy a new asset. If there is any profit or loss on the sale of investments, it will be transferred to the Depreciation Fund Account. The old asset is written off by transfer to the debit of Depreciation Fund Account. If the Depreciation Fund Account shows some balance, it is closed by transfer to the Profit or Loss Account.

In the last year, therefore, the following entries are made :—

(1)	Bank To Interest on Depreciation Fund Investments Account	Dr.	with the amount of interest received on investments.
(2)	Interest on Depreciation Fund Investments Account To Depreciation Fund Account	Dr.	with the amount of the interest.
(3)	Depreciation Account To Depreciation Fund Account	Dr.	with the annual instalment.
(4)	Bank To Depreciation Fund Investments Account	Dr.	with the net sale proceeds of Depreciation Fund Investments.
(5)	Depreciation Fund Investments Account To Depreciation Fund Account or Depreciation Fund Account To Depreciation Fund Investments Account	Dr. Dr.	profit (or loss) on sale of investments transferred to the Depreciation Fund Account
(6)	Depreciation Fund Account To Asset Account	Dr.	with the book value of the asset.
(7)	Depreciation Fund Accont To Profit & Loss Account or Profit & Loss Account To Depreciation Fund Account	Dr. Dr.	any balance remaining in the Depreciation Fund Account transferred to the Profit and Loss Account.

The student should note that the above arrangement for writing off depreciation and providing for replacement of the old asset by a new one is also known as "Sinking Fund to Replace a Wasting Asset".

A point to remember is that, in the market, the price of investments is generally higher than or lower than the face value. A government security of Rs. 100 may sell at Rs. 95. If one purchases such a security, the investments account will be debited with the actual amount spent (Rs. 95 in the above example), but the interest will be calculated on the face value of the security.

Illustration On 1st January, 1970 a lease was purchased for Rs. 20,000. It is to be replaced at the end of 4 years. It is expected that investments will yield a net interest of 4% per annum. A Depreciation Fund is established to collect the necessary amount.

On 31st December, 1973 the firm had a balance of Rs. 9,100. The Depreciation Fund Investments realised Rs. 14,700. The new lease cost Rs. 21,500.

Give journal entries and the necessary ledger accounts.

Solution :

Sinking Fund Tables show that to get Re. 1 at the end of 4 years @ 4% p.a. an annual investment of Re. ·235490 is necessary. Therefore, for Rs. 20,000, an annual investment of 4,709·80, *i.e.*, ·235490 × 20,000 will be necessary.

[*Note*—The student is advised to see the progress of ledger accounts constantly while he studies the journal entries.]

Journal

Date		Particulars		Dr. Rs.		Cr. Rs.	
1970 Jan.	1	Lease Account To Bank Account Purchase of lease for 5 years.	Dr.	20,000	—	20,000	—
Dec.	31	Depreciation Account To Depreciation Fund Account Annual depreciation to be provided as per S.F. Tables.	Dr.	4,709	80	4,709	80
	,,	Depreciation Fund Investment A/c To Bank Account The amount of annual instalment invested.	Dr.	4,709	80	4,709	80
1971 Dec.	31	Bank Account To interest on Dep. Fund Investments A/c Interest received on Investments (Rs. 4,709·80) @ 4% p.a.	Dr.	188	39	188	39
	,,	Interest on Dep. Fund Investments A/c To Depreciation Fund Account Interest on Dep. Fund Investments transferred to Depreciation Fund Account	Dr.	188	39	188	39
	,,	Depreciation Account To Depreciation Fund Account Annual Depreciation credited to Depreciation Fund Account	Dr.	4,709	80	4,709	80
	,,	Depreciation Fund Investment A/c To Bank Account Investments made to cover annual depreciation (Rs. 4,709·80) and interest Rs. 188·39.	Dr.	4,898	19	4,898	19
1972 Dec.	31	Bank Account To interest on Dep. Fund Investments A/c Interest received on Investments (4% on Rs. 9,607·99).	Dr.	384	32	384	32

				Dr.		Cr.	
1972				Rs.		Rs.	
Dec.	3	Interest on Dep. Fund Investments A/c To Depreciation Fund A/c Transfer of interest on Depreciation Fund Investments to Dep. Fund A/c	Dr.	384	32	384	32
	"	Depreciation Account To Depreciation Fund Account Annual depreciation credited to Depreciation Fund A/c	Dr.	4,709	80	4,709	80
	"	Depreciation Fund Investments A/c To Bank Account Annual depreciation and interest received invested.	Dr.	5,094	12	5,094	12
1973 Dec.	31	Bank Account To Interest on Dep. Fund Investments A/c Interest received on Depreciation Fund Investments	Dr.	588	09	588	09
	"	Interest on Dep. Fund Investment A/c To Depreciation Fund A/c Interest on Dep. Fund Investments transferred to Depreciation Fund A/c.	Dr.	588	09	588	09
	"	Depreciation Account To Depreciation Fund Account Annual depreciation credited to Depreciation Fund A/c.	Dr.	4,709	80	4,709	80
Dec.	31	Bank Account To Depreciation Fund Investment Account Sale of Dep. Fund Investments for Rs. 14,700.	Dr.	14,700	—	14,700	—
	"	Depreciation Fund Account To Lease Account Transfer of Lease Account to Depreciation Fund A/c upon its expiry.	Dr.	20,000	—	20,000	—

				Dr. Rs.		Cr. Rs.	
1972 Dec.	31	Depreciation Fund Account To Dep. Fund Investments Account Transfer of loss on sale of Dep. Fund Investments.	Dr.	2	11	2	11
	"	Profit & Loss Account To Depreciation Fund A/c The latter account closed by transfer to P. & L. A/c	Dr.	2	11	2	11
	"	New Lease Account To Bank Account New Lease acquired for Rs. 21,500.	Dr.	21,500	—	21,500	—

Ledger Account

Lease Account

Dr.		Rs.				Rs. Cr.	
1970 Jan. 1	To Bank Account	20,000	—	1970 Dec. 31	By Balance c/d	20,000	—
1971 Jan. 1	To Balance b/d	20,000	—	1971 Dec. 31	By Balance c/d	20,000	—
1972 Jan. 1	To Balance b/d	20,000	—	1972 Dec. 31	By Balance c/d	20,000	—
1973 Jan. 1	To Balance b/d	20,000	—	1973 Dec. 31	By Depreciation Fund A/c—transfer	20,000	—

New Lease Account

		Rs.					
1973 Jan. 1	To Bank A/c	21,500	—				

Depreciation Fund Account

Dr.		Rs.				Cr. Rs.	
1970 Dec. 31	To Balance c/d	4,709	80	1970 Dec. 31	By Depreciation A/c	4,709	80
1971 Dec. 31	To Balance c/d	9,607	99	1971 Jan. 1	By Balance b/d	4,709	80
				Dec. 31	By Interest on Dep. Fund Investment A/c	188	39
				,,	By Depreciation A/c	4,709	80
		9,607	99			9,607	99
1972 Dec. 31	To Balance b/d	14,702	11	1972 Jan. 1			
				Dec. 31	By Balance b/d	9,607	99
					By Interest on Dep. Fund Investments A/c	384	32
				,,	By Depreciation Account	4,709	80
		14,702	11			14,702	11
1973 Dec. 31	To Lease Account—transfer	20,000	—	1973 Jan. 1	By Balance b/d	14,702	11
	To Depreciation Fund Investments A/c—Loss	2	11	Dec. 31	By Interest on Dep. Fund Investments A/c	588	09
				,,	By Depreciation A/c	4,709	80
				,,	By Profit & Loss A/c—transfer	2	11
		20,002	11			20,002	11

Depreciation Fund Investments Account

Dr. *Cr.*

Date	Particulars	Rs.		Date	Particulars	Rs.	
1970 Dec. 31	To Bank Account	4,709	80	1970 Dec. 31	By Balance c/d	4,709	80
1971 Jan. 1	To Balance b/d	4,709	80	1971 Dec. 31	By Balance c/d	9,607	99
Dec. 31	To Bank Account (Rs. 4,709·80 +188·39)	4,898	19				
		9,607	99			9,607	99
1972 Jan. 1	To Balance b/d	9,607	99	1972 Dec. 31	By Balance c/d	14,702	11
Dec. 31	To Bank Account	5,094	12				
		14,702	11			14,702	11
1973 Jan. 1	To Balance b/d	14,702	11	1973 Dec. 31	By Bank Account	14,700	—
					By Depreciation Fund A/c—loss transferred	2	11
		14,702	11			14,702	11

Depreciation Account

Date	Particulars	Rs.		Date	Particulars	Rs.	
1970 Dec. 31	To Depreciation Fund A/c	4,709	80	1970 Dec. 31	By Profit & Loss A/c	4,709	80
1971 Dec. 31	To Dep. Fund A/c	4,709	80	1971 Dec. 31	By P. & L. A/c	4,709	80
1972 Dec. 31	To Dep. Fund A/c	4,709	80	1972 Dec. 31	By P. & L. A/c	4,709	80
1973 Dec. 31	To Dep. Fund A/c	4,709	80	1972 Dec. 31	By P. & L. A/c	4,709	80

Interest on Depreciation Fund

Investments Account

		Rs.				Rs.	
1971 Dec. 31	To Depreciation Fund A/c—transfer	188	39	1971 Dec. 31	By Bank A/c	188	39
1972 Dec. 31	To Depreciation Fund A/c	384	32	1972 Dec. 31	By Bank A/c	384	32
1974 Dec. 31	To Dep. Fund A/c	588	09	1973 Dec. 31	By Bank A/c	588	09

Bank Account

		Rs.				Rs.	
1973 Dec. 31	To Balance b/d	9,100	—	1973 Dec. 31	By New Lease Account	21,500	—
,,	To Dep. Fund Investments A/c	14,700	—		By Balance c/d	2,300	—
		23,800	—			23,800	—
1974 Jan. 1	To Balance b/d	2,300	—				

Illustration. A company established a depreciation fund for replacement of plant and equipment whose cost was Rs.10,00,000. On 1st Jan., 1979 the Depreciation Fund stood at Rs.3,20,000 represented by 7% Port Trust Bonds with a face value of Rs.3,50,000. The annual depreciation was Rs.60,000.

On 1st July 1980 the plant was replaced at a cost of Rs.15,00,000 exclusive of old plant of the value of Rs.80,000 which was continued in use; the rest of the old plant was sold for Rs.5,40,000.

Prepare the various ledger accounts for 1979 and 1980, assuming that at the end of 1979 the required investment was made in Port Trust Bonds at par and towards the end of June 1980 the bonds were sold for Rs.4,36,000 of which Rs.14,000 represented interest after 1st Jan., 1980.

Solution :

Plant & Equipment Account

		Rs.			Rs.
1979 Jan., 1	To Balance b/d	10,00,000	1979 Dec., 31	By Balance b/d	10,00,000
1980 Jan., 1	To Balance b/d	10,00,000	1980 July 1	By (New) Plant and Equipment A/c	80,000
				By Bank	5,40,000
				By Depreciation Fund A/c—transfer	4,80,000
		10,00,000			10,00,000

(New) Plant & Equipment A/c

		Rs.			Rs.
1980 July 1	To Bank	15,00,000	1980 Dec., 31	By Balance c/d	15,80,000
	To (Old) Plant & Equipment A/c	80,000			
		15,80,000			15,80,000
1981 Jan., 1	To Balance b/d	15,80,000			

Depreciation Fund Account

		Rs.			Rs.
1979 Dec. 31	To Balance c/d	4,04,500	1979 Jan., 1	By Balance b/d	3,20,000
			Dec., 31	By Interest on D.F. Inv. A/c	24,500
			"	By Profit & Loss A/c—Depreciation	60,000
		4,04,500			4,04,500
1980 July 1	To Plant & Equipment A/c—transfer	4,80,000	1980 Jan. 1	By Balance b/d	4,04,500
				By Dep. Fund Inv. A/c—Profit	17,500
			July 1	By Interest on D.F. Investment A/c	14,000
				By P.&L. A/c	44,000
		4,80,000			4,80,000

Depreciation Fund Investments Account

		Rs.			Rs.
1979			1980		
Jan. 1	To Balance b/d (Face Value Rs.3,50,000)	3,20,000	Dec. 31	By Balance c/d	4,04,500
Dec. 31	To Bank (Face Value Rs.84,500)	84,500			
		4,04,500			4,04,500
1980			1980		
Jan., 1	To Balance b/d	4,04,500	July 1	By Bank (Rs. 4,36,000 *Less* Rs. 14,000 Interest)	4,22,000
July 1	To Dep. Fund A/c —profit on sale	17,500			
		4,22,000			4,22,000

Interest on Dep. Fund Investments A/c

		Rs.			Rs.
1979			1979		
Dec. 31	To Dep. Fund A/c —transfer	24,500	Dec. 31	By Bank (7% on Rs. 3,50,000)	24,500
1980			1980		
July 1	To Dep. Fund A/c—transfer	14,000	July 1	By Bank	14,000

Profit & Loss Account

		Rs.
1979	To Dep. Fund A/c—Depreciation	60,000
1980	To Dep Fund A/c —amount written off	44,000

Bank Account

		Rs.			Rs.
1979			1979		
Dec. 31	To Balance b/d	?	Dec. 31	By Dep. Fund Investments A/c	84,500
	To Interest on Dep. Fund Investments A/c	24,500	"	By Balance c/d	?
1980			1980		
Jan. 1	To Balance b/d	?	July 1	By Plant & Equipment A/c	15,00,000
July 1	To Dep. Fund Inv. A/c	4,22,000			
"	To Interest on D.F. Inv. A/c	14,000		By Balance b/d	?

(*f*) *Insurance Policy Method.* Insurance policy method is similar to the Depreciation Fund Method. Instead of making investments, arrangements are made with an insurance company which will receive premiums annually and pay at the end of the fixed period, say 15 years, the required amount. Premiums have to be paid in the beginning of each year. The annual premium is treated as the annual depreciation. The amount is credited every year to the Depreciation Fund Account (by debiting Depreciation Account). On payment of the premium, Depreciation Fund Policy Account is debited. The two accounts are balanced year by year. There is no need to pass any entry for interest ; in any case, no interest will be received from the insurance company.

At the end of the period the fixed amount will be received and credited to Depreciation Fund Policy Account. This account will then show a credit balance which will be transferred to the Depreciation Fund Account. The asset account is closed by transfer to the Depreciation Fund Account.

Illustration A machine is purchased for Rs. 20,000. At the end of 4 years it has to be replaced. For this purpose an insurance policy is taken out, the annual premium being Rs. 4,600. At the end of 4 years, a new machine costing Rs. 23,000 is installed and the old machine is written off. Give the necessary ledger accounts.

Solution :

Machinery Account

Dr. Cr.

		Rs.			Rs.
Year 1	To Bank A/c	20,000	Year 1	By Balance c/d	20,000
Year 2	To Balance b/d	20,000	Year 2	By Balance c/d	20,000
Year 3	To Balance b/d	20,000	Year 3	By Balance c/d	20,000
Year 4	To Balance b/d	20,000	Year 4 (end)	By Depreciation Fund A/c	20,000

(New) Machinery Account

		Rs.			
Year 4 (end)	To Bank A/c	23,000			

Depreciation Fund Account

		Rs.			Rs.
Year 1 (end)	To Balance c/d	4,600	Year 1 (end)	By Depreciation A/c	4,600
Year 2	To Balance c/d	9,200	Year 2	By Balance b/d	4,600
				By Depreciation A/c	4,600
		9,200			9,200
Year 3	To Balance c/d	13,800	Year 3	By Balance b/d	9,200
				By Depreciation A/c	4,600
		13,800			13,800
Year 4	To Machinery Account—transfer	20,000	Year 4	By Balance b/d	13,800
				By Depreciation A/c	4,600
				By Dep. Fund Policy A/c—profit transferred	1,600
		20,000			20,000

Depreciation Fund Policy Account

Dr. *Cr.*

		Rs.			Rs.
Year 1 (beginning)	To Bank Account	4,600	Year 1 (end)	By Balance c/d	4,600
Year 2	To Balanee b/d	4,600	Year 2	By Balance c/d	9,200
	To Bank A/c	4,600			
		9,200			9,200
Year 3	To Balance b/d	9,200	Year 3	By Balance c/d	13,800
	To Bank A/c	4,600			
		13,800			13,800
Year 4	To Balance	13,800	Year 4 (end)	By Bank A/c	20,000
	To Bank	4,600			
	To Dep. Fund—profit transferred	1,600			
		20,000			20,000

(g) *Revaluation Method.* This method is used in case of loose tools, live stock, etc. At the end of every year, the loose tools in hand are valued properly and enough depreciation is written off to bring the value of the assets to its proper figure. Suppose, a firm had, in the beginning of a year, loose tools of the value of Rs. 1,100. During the year it purchased new tools costing Rs. 400, thus making a total of Rs. 1,500. At the end of the year the loose tools are found to be worth Rs. 1,150. The depreciation to be written off is Rs. 350, *i.e.*, Rs. 1,500 less Rs. 1,150.

(h) *Depletion Method.* This method is most suitable for mines, quarries, etc. from which a certain quantity of output is expected to be obtained. The value of mine depends only upon the quantity of minerals that can be obtained. When the whole quantity is taken out, the mine loses its value. Hence, one can say that the mine depreciates according to the quantity mined. The rate of depreciation is worked out as so much per tonne. It is obtained by simply dividing the cost of the mine by the total quantity of the mineral expected to be available. Thus if a mine is acquired at a cost of Rs. 6,00,000 and if it is thought that a total of 4,00,000 tonnes of minerals will be available, the depreciation rate is Rs. 1·50, *i.e.*, Rs. 6,00,000 divided by 4,00,000. The total depreciation to be written off will depened upon the quantity mined. If in the above example, in the first year 30,000 tonnes are taken out, the depreciation will be 30,000 × 1·50 or Rs. 45,000. If in the next year the output is 40,000 tonnes, the depreciation will be 40,000 × 1·50 or Rs. 60,000.

(i) *Machine Hour Rate Method.* This method is useful in case of machines. The life of the machine is fixed in terms of hours. Hourly rate of depreciation is worked out by dividing the cost of the machine by the total number of hours for which the machine is expected to be used. Suppose, a machine costing Rs. 42,000 and having an estimated scrap value of Rs. 2,000 is expected to be used for 25,000 hours in all. The hourly rate of depreciation is then Rs. $\frac{40,000}{25,000}$, or Rs. 1·60. Depreciation to be written off in a year will be ascertained by multiplying the hourly rate of depreciation by the number of hours that the machine actually runs in the year. Suppose to continue the example, the machine runs for 1,000 hours in the first year and 1,500 hours in the next. The depreciation for the first year will be Rs. 1,600 (*i.e.*, Rs. 1·60 × 1,000) and Rs. 2,400 in the next. The student will have seen that this method is similar to the first method—fixed instalment method.

Consistency. It is extremely desirable that the same method of depreciation should be followed from year to year as otherwise the reported profit or loss will not be comparable. However, sometimes a change in the method, say from the Diminishing Value Method to the Staight Line Method, becomes necessary for various reasons. In such a case, the Profit and Loss Account should bear a note stating (*i*) the fact of the change and (*ii*) the difference in the amount of depreciation charged to the P & L A/c because of the change. If adjustment is made for previous years also, the amount should be shown as a separate item in the Profit and Loss Account.

If no depreciation in charged, this should be made clear by way of a note which should also state the amount of the depreciation that should have been charged. This is necessary to enable people to judge the true profit or loss of the firm.

Illustration. On 1st April 1972, a firm commenced operations with machinery installed at a cost of Rs.2,00,000; its scrap value was estimated at 5% and life at 10 years. The firm decided to provide depreciation at 25% p.a. on the diminishing value, its books being closed on 30th September each year. In 1975-76 it decided to change the method of depreciation to straight line basis from the very beginning.

Prepare Machinery Account for 1975-76 and show the relevant entries in the Profit and Loss Account. Work to the nearst rupee.

Solution :

Machinery Account

1975		Rs.	1976		Rs.
Oct. 1	To Balance b/d	73,828	Sept. 30	By Depreciation	19,000
"	To Profit & Loss A/c—adjustment of depreciation on change of method	59,672	"	By Balance c/d	1,14,500
		1,33,500			1,33,500
1976					
Oct. 1	To Balance b/d	1,14,500			

Profit and Loss Account for 1975-76

To Depreciation	19,000	By Adjustment of Depreciation for previous years	59,672

During the year the method of depreciation was changed; according to the previous method the depreciation would have been Rs.18,457.

Notes : (1) The balance on 1-9-75 in the Machinery Account was Rs.73,828 as shown below :

	Rs.
Cost on 1-4-72	2,00,000
Depreciation for half year upto 30-9-72 @ 25% p.a.	25,000
	1,75,000
Depreciation for 1972-73	43,750
	1,31,250
Depreciation for 1973-74	32,813
	98,437
Depreciation for 1974-75	24,609
	73,828

(2) The balance on straight line basis would have been Rs.1,33,500 i.e. Rs.2,00,000 *less* depreciation for 3½ years @ Rs.19,000 p.a. Hence Rs.59,672 i.e. Rs. 1,33,500 *less* Rs.73,828 has to be added to the Machinery Account by credit to the Profit & Loss Account.

Illustration. In 1975, a company leased a mine at a cost of Rs.20,00,000 for 20 years and decided to amortise the lease over the life equally. The output was estimated at 4,00,000 tonnes in total and the actual output was as follows :—

1975	10,000 tonnes
1976	15,000 "
1977	25,000 "
1978	32,000 "

In 1978 the company decided to adopt the Depletion Method with retrospective effect.

Show the Mine Account and entries in the Profit & Loss Account for 1978.

Solution :

Mine Account

1978		Rs.	1978		Rs.
Jan. 1	To Balance b/d	17,00,000	Dec. 31	By Depreciation—Rs. 5 per tonne on 32,000 tonnes	1,60,000
	To Profit & Loss A/c—adjustment of depreciation on change of method	50,000	"	By Balance c/d	15,90,000
		17,50,000			17,50,000
1979					
Jan. 1	To Balance b/d	15,90,000			

Profit and Loss Account for 1978

To Depreciation	1,60,000	By Adjustment of Depreciation for previous years	50,000

During the year, the method of depreciation was changed; according to the previous method, the amount of depreciation would have been Rs.1,00,000.

Note : According to the Depletion Method, the amount to be written off is Rs.5 per tonne i.e. Rs.20,00,000 ÷ 4,00,000. The output in the previous 3 years is 50,000 tonnes and hence Rs.2,50,000 should have been written off, leaving a balance of Rs.17,50,000.

Exercise

1. M/s. X and Y purchased (second hand) a machine for Rs. 8,000 on 1st April, 1976. They spent Rs. 3,500 on its overhaul and installation. Depreciation is written off @ 10% p.a. on the original cost. On 30th June, 1979 the machine was found to be unsuitable and sold for Rs. 6,500. Prepare the Machine Account from 1976 to 1979, assuming that the accounts are closed on 31st December every year. *(Loss to be written off, Rs. 1,262·50)*

2. M/s. P & Q purchased mashinery for Rs. 40,000 on 1st July, 1976. Depreciation is provided @ 10% p.a. on the diminishing balance. On 31st October, 1978, one-fourth of the machinery was found unsuitable and disposed of for Rs. 5,600. On the same date new machinery at a cost of Rs. 15,000 was purchased. Write up the Machinery Account from 1976 to 1979. The accounts are closed on 31st December. *(Loss to be written off Rs. 2,308·75 ; Balance in Machinery A/c. Rs. 33,939)*

3. A firm purchased a lorry for Rs. 50,000 on 1st Jan. 1975 and wrote off depreciation @ 15% on the diminishing value balance. At the end of 1968 it decided that the depreciation should be on the basis of 15% of the original cost from the very beginning and write off the necessary amount in 1968. Assuming the firm closes the books on 31st December, write up the Lorry Account up to the end of 1978. *(Balance Rs. 20,000, excess depreciation to be written off for 1965-67, Rs. 3,206·25)*

4. The balance on 1st July, 1976 on machinery acquired on 1st July, 1974 was Rs. 40,500. The firm had been writing off depreciation @ 10% p.a. on the diminishing value basis. Accounts are made up to 30th June each year. It was decided that during 1976-77 enough depreciation should be written off to make up depreciation to @ 10% on the basis of original cost. On 1st January, 1977 a machine whose book value was Rs. 12,150 on 1st July, 1974 was disposed of for Rs. 8,400. Prepare the Machinery Account for 1976-77. *(Balance in Machinery Account Rs. 26,495)*

5. A machine was acquired on 1st April, 1977 at a cost of Rs. 15,000 ; the cost of installation being Rs. 1,000. It is expected that its total working life will be 25,000 hours. During 1977 it worked for 1,200 hours and during 1978 for 2,000 hours. Write up the Machinery Account for 1977 and 1978.

6. A mine was acquired at a cost of Rs. 4,00,000 on 1st June, 1976 ; it was expected it would yield 2,50,000 tonnes of minerals in all. The actual output was as under :

1976	20,000	tonnes
1977	35,000	tonnes
1978	40,000	tonnes.

Write up the Mine Account for 1966, 1977 and 1968.

7. A lease of land was acquired for a period of 25 years on 1st January, 1970 at a cost of Rs. 24,000. Buildings were commenced on the same day and completed at a cost of Rs. 96,000 on 31st December, 1970. During 1962 repairs were carried out and cost Rs. 3,000 and on 1st January, 1972 additional rooms were completed at a cost of Rs. 18,400. Prepare the Land & Buildings Accounts for the 4 years ended 31st December, 1973. *(Balance, Rs. 1,21,800)*

8. A Lease of land was acquired on 1st January, 1972 at a cost of Rs. 30,000. It was decided to depreciate it under the Annuity Method, using 5% interest. Annuity Tables show that @ 5% Re. 1 over 5 years is equivalent to Re. ·230975 annually. Write up the Lease Account for 5 years.

9. Machinery was acquired on 1st January, 1972 at a cost of Rs. 40,000. The life of the machinery was 5 years. It was decided to establish a Deprecia-tion Fund to provide funds for replacement. Investments are expected to yield net 5% p.a. Sinking Fund Tables show that Re. ·180975 invested annually at 5% produces Re. 1 in five years. Prepare the necessary ledger accounts for all the five years, assuming that new machinery costs Rs. 43,000 on 1st January, 1977.

10. A firm had purchased machinery for Rs. 60,000 on 1st January, 1960. Its expected life was 15 years. Depreciation Fund was established to provide for replacement. Investments produced 5% interest annually. On 1st January, 1972 the Depreciation Fund stood at Rs. 52,000. The annual amount credited to the Depreciation Fund was Rs. 2,800.

In December, 1972 it was decided to replace the entire machinery. Certain parts of the old machinery, valued at Rs. 2,000, were retained and the remaining machinery was auctioned for Rs. 11,000. For the purposes of replacement, the Depreciation Fund investments were realised at Rs. 51,000 on 31st December. New machinery cost Rs. 90,000.

Write up for 1972 the Machinery Account and Depreciation Fund Account. *(Amount transferred to General Reserve, Rs. 9,400)*

11. A company purchased a machine for Rs. 18,000 on 1st July, 1972. The machine had a life of 4 years only. In order to provide for replacement of the machine, an insurance policy was taken out with an annual premium of Rs. 4,100. At the end of 4 years, a new machine was acquired for Rs. 21,000.

Write up the various ledger accounts for 4 years.

CHAPTER XII

PARTNERSHIP ACCOUNTS

General. The Indian Partnership Act defines partnership as "the relation between persons who have agreed to share the profits of a business carried on by all or any of them acting for all." The essential features of partnership, therefore, are:

1. An association of two or more persons;
2. An agreement entered into by all persons concerned;
3. Existence of a business;
4. The carrying on of business by all or any of them acting for all; and
5. Sharing of profits of the business (including losses).

From the accounts point of view, the main thing to remember is that the relations among the partners will be governed by mutual agreement. The agreement is known as Partnership Deed. It should be comprehensive to avoid disputes later on. It is usual, therefore, to find the following clauses in a Partnership Deed :

1. The name of the firm and the nature of the partnership business.
2. The commencement and duration of the business.
3. The amount of capital to be contributed by each partner.
4. The rate of interest to be allowed to each partner on his capital and on his loan to the firm, and to be charged on his drawings.
5. The disposal of profits, particularly the ratio in which profits are to be shared.
6. The amount to be allowed to each partner as drawings and the timing of such drawings.
7. Whether a partner will be allowed a salary.
8. Any variations in the usual rights and duties of partners.
9. The method by which goodwill is to be calculated on the retirement or death of a partner.
10. The procedure by which a partner may retire and the method of payment of his dues to him.
11. The basis of determination of the sums due to the executors of a deceased partner and the method of payment.
12. The treatment of losses arising out of the insolvency of a partner.
13. The procedure to be followed for settlement of disputes among partners.
14. Preparation of accounts and their audit.

The Deed has to be properly stamped.

Often there is no Partnership Deed or, if there is one, it may be silent on a particular point. In that case relevant sections of the Act will apply. If on any point the Partnership Deed contains a clause, it will be held good; otherwise the provisions of the Act relating to the question will apply. Broadly, the provisions of the Act are as under:

Rights of partners :

(*a*) Every partner has a right to take part in the conduct and management of business.

(*b*) Every partner has a right to be consulted and heard in all matters affecting the business of the partnership.

(*c*) Every partner has a right of free access to all records, books and accounts of the business, and also to examine and copy them.

(*d*) Every partner is entitled to share in the profits equally (unless the partnership deed says otherwise).

(*e*) A partner who has contributed more than the agreed share of capital is entitled to interest at the rate of 6 per cent per annum on the excess amount. But no interest can be claimed on capital unless agreed upon.

(*f*) A partner is entitled to be indemnified by the firm for all acts done by him in the course of the partnership business, for all payments made by him in respect of partnership debts or liabilities and for expenses and disbursements made in an emergency for protecting the firm from loss, provided he acted as a person of ordinary prudence would have acted in similar circumstances for his own personal business.

(*g*) Every partner is, as a rule, a joint owner of the partnership property. He is entitled to have the partnership property used exclusively for the purpose of the partnership.

(*h*) A partner has power to act in an emergency for protecting the firm from loss, but he must act reasonably.

(*i*) Every partner is entitled to prevent the introduction of a new partner into the firm without his consent.

(*j*) Every partner has a right to retire according to the deed or with the consent of the other partners. If the partnership is at will, he can retire by giving notice to other partners.

(*k*) Every partner has a right to continue in the partnership.

(*l*) A retiring partner or the heirs of a deceased partner are entitled to share in the profits earned with the aid of the assets belonging to such outgoing partner or interest at six per cent per annum at the option of the outgoing partner (or his representative) until the accounts are finally settled.

Duties of partners :

(*a*) Every partner is bound to diligently carry on the business of the firm to the greatest common advantage. Unless the agreement provides, there is no salary.

(*b*) Every partner must be just and faithful to the other partners.

(*c*) A partner is bound to keep and render true, proper, and correct accounts of the partnership and must permit other partners to inspect and copy such accounts.

(*d*) Every partner is bound to indemnify the firm for any loss caused by his wilful neglect or fraud in the conduct of the business.

(*e*) A partner must not carry on a competing business, nor use the property of the firm for his private purposes. In both cases he must hand over to the firm any profit or gains made by him but he must himself suffer any loss that might have occurred.

(*f*) Every partner is bound to share the losses equally with the others.

(*g*) A partner is bound to act within the scope of his authority.

(*h*) No partner can assign or transfer his partnership interest to any other person so as to make him a partner in the business.

Powers of partners. The above relates to relations among the partners themselves. When it comes to dealing with outsiders or third parties, the partners are supposed to have the power to act in certain matters and not to have such power in others. In other words, unless a public notice has been given to the contrary, certain contracts entered into by a partner on behalf of the partnership, even without consulting other partners, will be binding on the firm. In case of a trading firm, the implied powers of partners are the following :

(*a*) Buying and selling goods.

(*b*) Receiving payments on behalf of the firm and giving valid receipts.

(*c*) Drawing cheques and drawing, accepting and endorsing bills of exchange and promissory notes in the name of the firm.

(*d*) Borrowing moneys on behalf of the firm with or without pledging the stock in trade.

(*e*) Engaging servants for the business of the firm.

In certain cases a partner has no powers. This is to say that third parties cannot bind the firm unless the partners have agreed. These cases are :—

(*a*) Submitting a dispute relating to the firm to arbitration.

(*b*) Opening a bank account on behalf of the firm in the name of a partner.

(c) Compromise or relinquishment of any claim or portion of claim by the firm.

(d) Withdrawal of a suit or proceedings filed on behalf of the firm.

(e) Admission of any liability in a suit of proceedings against the firm.

(f) Acquisition of immovable property belonging to the firm.

(g) Entering into partnership on behalf of the firm.

The rights, duties and powers of partners can be changed by mutual consent.

Kinds of partners. Besides the usual partners who contribute to the capital of the firm and take part in its business, the following special types of partners may be noted.

Sleeping or Dormant Partner is one who is in reality a partner but whose name does not appear in any way as partner and who is not known to outsiders as partner. He is liable to those third parties who subsequently discover that he was or is a partner. He has no duties to perform but he has the right of access to books of account and of examining and copying them.

Nominal Partner is a person whose name is used as if he were a member of the firm, but who, really, is not a partner. He is liable to third parties for all acts of the firm as if he were a real partner.

Partner in Profit Only is one who gets a share of the profits and does not share losses. He is liable to outsiders. He does not take part in the management of the business.

Partner by Estoppel or Holding Out is one who without really being a partner, so behaves as to lead others to believe him to be a partner. Similarly, if one is declared to be a partner and does not disclaim the partnership, one will be treated as partner by holding out Such persons are liable to those third parties who extend credit to the firm on the belief that such persons are partners.

Sub-Partner is one who gets a share of profits of the firm from one of the partners. A sub-partner has no rights against the firm and he is not liable for its debts.

An Incoming Partner is one who is newly admitted to the firm. He is not liable for the debts and obligations of the firm incurred before his joining the firm unless he so agrees.

A Retiring or Outgoing Partner continues to be liable for obligations incurred before his retirement, and will continue to be liable even for future obligations if he does not give public notice of his retirement.

Minor Partner . A minor can be admitted to the benfits of an existing partnership with the consent of all the partners. The minor is not personally liable for the debts of the firm but his share in the partnership property and profits of the firm will be liable for the firm's debts and obligations. He can bring a suit for accounts and for his distributive share when he wants to sever his connections with the firm, but not otherwise. But he has the right of access to the account of the firm including the right to examine and copy. Within six months of his attaining majority or on his coming to know that he enjoys the benefits of partnership (whichever date is later), he has to elect whether or not he wants to continue as partner. He must give public notice of his decision not to continue as partner, otherwise he will be deemed to have elected to be a full-fledged partner. On his election as a partner, he will become liable for the debts of the firm since he was admitted to the benefits of the firm. If he repudiates his partnership, all his liabilities will cease from the date of the public notice to this effect.

The student should remember that in the absence of any agreement to the contrary :

(1) no partner has the right to a salary,

(2) no interest is to be allowed on capital,

(3) no interest is to be charged on drawings,

(4) interest at the rate of 6 per cent is to be allowed on a partner's loan to the firm, and

(5) profits and losses are to be shared equally.

Note : **In absence of agreement. the interest and salary payable to a partner will be paid only if there is a profit.**

Accounts

There is not much difference between the accounts of a partnership firm and that of sole proprietorship (provided there is no change in the firm itself). The only difference to be noted is that instead of one capital account there will be as many as capital accounts as there are partners. If for instance, there are three partners, A, B & C, there will be a capital account for each one of these partners. A's Capital Account will be credited by the amount contributed by him as capital and similarly B's and C's Capital Accounts will be credited with the amounts brought in by them respectively as capital.

When a partner takes money for his domestic purpose, either his Capital Account can be debited or a separate account, named as Drawings Account, can be opened in his name and that account may be debited. In a Trial Balance of a partnership firm, therefore, one may find Capital Accounts of partners as well as Drawings Accounts of partners. Finally, the Drawing Account of a partner may be transferred to his Capital Account so that a net figure is available. But often, the Drawings Account or Current Account (as it is sometimes called) remains separate.

During the course of business, a partnership firm will prepare Trading Account and a Profit and Loss Account at the end of every year. This is done exactly on the lines already given in the chapter on Final Accounts. This is to say that the final accounts of a sole proprietor concern will not differ from the final accounts of a partnership firm. The Profit and Loss Account will show the profit earned by the firm or loss suffered by it. This profit or loss has to be transferred to the Capital Accounts of partners according to the terms of the Partnership Deed or according to the provisions of the Indian

Partnership Act (if there is no Partnership Deed or if the Deed is silent on a particular point). Suppose, the Profit and Loss Account reveals a profit of Rs. 30,000. There are two partners, A and B. A devotes all his time to the firm; B does not. A's capital is Rs. 50,000 and B's capital is Rs. 20,000. There is no Partnership Deed. In such a case the profit will he distributed among A and B equally. This is irrespective of the fact that B does not work as much as A does and B's capital is much less than that of A. But if the Partnership Deed lays down that A is to get a salary and interest is to be allowed on capital, then, first of all, from the profit earned, A's salary must be deducted and interest on the capital accounts of both partners will be deducted. The remaining profit will be divided equally between A and B. Further, if the Partnership Deed says that profits are to be divided in the ratio of, say, three-fourths to A and one-fourth to B, then this will be the ratio to be adopted.

The student can see for himself that if a salary is to be allowed to a partner, the Profit and Loss Account will be debited and that partner's Capital Account will be credited. Similarly, if interest is to be allowed on capitals, the Profit and Loss Account will be debited and the respective Capital Accounts will be credited. But these entries should be passed only if the P. & L. Account otherwise reveals a profit. Usually, the profit as per the P & L A/c is transferred to the Profit and Loss Appropriation Account and entries for interest salary and profit to partners will be passed only in that account.

Illustration 55. A and B start business on 1st January, 1966 capitals of Rs. 30,000 and 20,000. According to the Partnership d, B is entitled to a salary of Rs. 500 per month and interest o be allowed on capitals at 6% per annum. The remaining ofits are to be distributed amongst the two partners in the ratio of 3. During 1966 the firm earned a profit, before charging salary to B and interest on capitals, amounting to Rs. 25,000. During the year A withdrew Rs. 8,000 and B withdrew Rs. 10,000 for domestic purposes.

Give journal entries relating to division of profit, the Profit and Loss Account and the Capital Accounts of partners.

Solution :

Journal Entries

Date		Particulars		Dr. Rs.	Cr. Rs.
1976 Dec.	31	Profit and Loss Account	Dr.	6,000 —	
		To B's Capital Account			6,000 —
		Salary due to B @ Rs. 500 per month			
		Profit and Loss Account	Dr.	3,000 —	
		To A's Capital Account			1,800 —
		To B's Capital Account			1,200 —
		Interest due on capital @ 6% p.a.— A Rs. 1,800 B Rs. 1,200			
		Profit and Loss Account	Dr.	16,000 —	
		To A's Capital Account			10,000 —
		To B's Capital Account			6,000 —
		Remaining Profit of Rs. 16,000 divided between A and B in the ratio of 5 : 3.			

Profit and Loss Account*

Dr.	Rs.		Cr.	Rs.
To B's Capital A/c— Salary	6,000 —		By Net Profit	25,000 —
To A's Capital A/c— Interest	1,800 —			
To B's Capital A/c— Interest	1,200 —			
To Profit Transferred to :				
A's Capital A/c (5/8)	10,000 —			
B's Capital A/c (3/8)	6,000 —			
	25,000 —			25,000 —

* The account showing division of profit among partners is better called Profit and Loss Appropriation Account.

A's Capital Account

		Rs.				Rs.	
1976 Dec. 31	To Cash (Drawings)	8,000	—	1976 Jan. 1	By Cash	30,000	—
	To Balance c/d	33,800	—	Dec. 31	By Profit and Loss A/c—Interest	1,800	—
				,,	By Profit and Loss A/c—5/8 profit	10,000	—
		41,800	—			41,800	—
				1977 Jan. 1	By Balance b/d	33,800	—

B's Capital Account

Dr. *Cr.*

		Rs.				Rs.	
1976 ?	To Cash (Drawing)	10,000	—	1976 Jan. 1	By Cash	20,000	—
	To Balance c/d	23,200	—	Dec. 31	By Profit and Loss A/c—Salary	6,000	—
					Interest	1,200	—
					By Profit and Loss A/c—3/8 profit	6,000	—
		33,200	—			33,200	—
				1977 Jan. 1	By Balance b/d	23,200	—

Fixed and fluctuating capitals. The student will have seen in the working of the above example that the Capital Account of A has changed from Rs. 30,000 in the beginning to Rs. 33,800 at the end and, similarly, B's Capital Account has changed from Rs. 20,000 to Rs. 23,200. This is because we have made entries in respect of interest, salary, profit earned during the year and money taken out by partners in the Capital Account itself. If the Capital Accounts are prepared on this basis, capitals are said to be fluctuating. Some firms, however, prefer to continue to show the Capital Accounts of partners at the s me old figure. This means that no entry is to be made in the Capital Account in respect of interest, salary, profit, drawings, etc. A separate account is opened for this purpnse. The account is known as Current Account or even as Drawings Account*.

* Under this system interest on capital, if allowed, should be calculated only on the amount of the fixed capital.

If this system is followed the capitals will be said to be fixed. The above example can be worked out as follows with capitals treated as fixed.

A's Capital Account

Dr. *Cr.*

Date	Particulars	Rs.		Date	Particulars	Rs.	
1976 Dec. 31	To Balance c/d	30,000	—	1976 Jan. 1	By Cash	30,000	—
				1977 Jan. 1	By Balance b/d	30,000	—

B's Capital Accovnt

Date	Particulars	Rs.		Date	Particulars	Rs.	
1976 Dec. 30	By Balance c/d	20,000	—	1976 Jan. 1	By Cash	20,000	—
				1977 Jan. 1	By Balance b/d	20,000	—

A's Current Account

Date	Particulars	Rs.		Date	Particulars	Rs.	
1976 ?	To Cash (Drawings)	8,000	—	1976 Dec. 31	By Profit and Loss A/c—Interest	1,800	—
Dec. 31	To Balance c/d	3,800	—		By Profit and Loss A/c 5/8 Profit	10,000	—
		11,800	—			11,800	—
				1977 Jan. 1	By Balance b/d	3,800	—

B's Current Account

1976		Rs.	1976		Rs.
?	To Cash (Drawings)	10,000	Dec. 31	By Profit and Loss A/c— Salary	6,000
				Interest	1,200
Dec. 31	To Balance c/d	3,200		By Profit and Loss A/c— 3/8 profit	6,000
		13,200			13,200
			1977 Jan. 1	By Balance b/d	3,200

Interest on drawings. Sometimes interest is not only allowed on capitals but is also charged on drawings. In such a case, the interest will be charged according to the time that elapses between the taking out of the money and the end of the year. Suppose X, a partner, has drawn the following sums of the money :—

	Rs.
On 28th February, 1976	500
On 31st March, 1976	400
On 30th June, 1976	600
On 31st October, 1976	800

Accounts are closed on 31st December every year. Interest is chargeable on drawings at 6% per annum. The interest on X's drawings will be calculated as under :

1. On Rs. 500 for 10 months, *i.e.*, Rs. 25
2. On Rs. 400 for 9 months. *i.e.*, Rs. 18
3. On Rs. 600 for 6 months, *i.e.*, Rs. 18
4. On Rs. 800 for 2 months, *i.e.*, Rs. 8

Total Rs. 69

Alternatively, it can be calculated as follows :—

Amount Rs.	Number of months	Product
500	10	5,000
400	9	3,600
600	6	3,600
800	2	1,600
23,00		13,800

Interest on Rs. 13,800 for one month at 6% per annum is Rs. 69.

If the dates on which amounts are drawn are not given, the student will do well to charge interest for six months on the whole of the amount on the assumption that the money was drawn evenly throughout the year. In the above example, the total drawings come to Rs. 2,300 ; at 6% for six months, the interest comes to

Rs. The entry to record interest on drawings is to debit the Capital Account of the partner concerned (or his Current Account if capitals are fixed) and credit the Profit and Loss Account.

If withdrawals are made evenly in the beginning of each month, interest can be calculated easily for the whole of the amount (annual) for 6½ months; if withdrawals are made at the end of each month, interest should be calculated for 5½ months.

Illustration Ram and Rahim start business with capitals of Rs. 50,000 and Rs. 30,000 on 1st January, 1976. Rahim is entitled to a salary of Rs. 400 per month. Interest is allowed on capitals and is charged on drawings at 6% per annum. Profits are to be distributed equally after the above noted adjustments. During the year, Ram withdraw Rs. 8,000 and Rahim withdrew Rs. 10,000. The profit for the year, before allowing for the terms of the Partnership Deed, came to Rs. 30,000. Assuming the capitals to be fixed, prepare the Profit and Loss Appropriation Account and the accounts relating to the partners.

Solution :

Profit & Loss (Appropriation) Account

Dr. *Cr.*

		Rs.				Rs.	
1976 Dec. 31	To Rahim's Current A/c—Salary	4,800	—	1976 Dec. 31	By Net Profit	30,000	—
	To Sundries—Interest on Capitals :				By Sundries—Interest on drawings :		
	Ram's Current A/c	3,000	—		Ram's Current A/c (6% on Rs. 8,000 for 6 months)	240	—
	Rahim's Current A/c	1,800	—		Rahim's Current A/c (6% on Rs. 10,000 for 6 months)	300	—
"	To Profit transferred to :						
	Ram's Current A/c (1/2)	10,470	—				
	Rahim's Current A/c (1/2)	10,470	—				
		30,540	—			30,540	—

Ram's Capital Account

		Rs.				Rs.	
1976 Dec. 31	To Balance c/d	50,000	—	1976 Jan. 1	By Cash	50,000	—
				1967 Jan. 1	By Balance b/d	50,000	—

Rahim's Capital Account

Date	Particulars	Rs.		Date	Particulars	Rs.	
1976 Dec. 31	To Balance c/d	30,000	—	1976 Jan. 1	By Cash	30,000	—
				1967 Jan. 1	By Balance b/d	30,000	—

Ram's Current Account

Dr. *Cr.*

Date	Particulars	Rs.		Date	Particulars	Rs.	
1976 ?	To Cash (Drawings)	8,000	—	1976 Dec. 31	By Profit & Loss A/c—Interest	3,000	—
Dec. 31	To Profit & Loss A/c—Interest on Drawings	240	—	"	By Profit & Loss A/c—1/2 Profit	10,470	—
"	To Balance c/d	5,230	—				
		13,470	—			13,470	—
				1977 Jan. 1	By Balance b/d	5,230	—

Rahim's Current Account

Date	Particulars	Rs.		Date	Particulars	Rs.	
1976 ?	To Cash (Drawings)	10,000	—	1976 Dec. 31	By Profit & Loss A/c—Salary	4,800	—
					Interest	1,800	—
Dec. 31	To Profit & Loss A/c—Interest on Drawings	300	—		By Profit & Loss A/c—1/2 profit	10,470	—
"	To Balance c/d	6,770	—				
		17,070	—			17,070	—
				1977 Jan. 1	By Balance b/d	6,770	—

Illustration A presents the following Profit and Loss Appropriation Account to his partner, B :—

Profit & Loss Appropriation Account

	Rs.		Rs.
To Salary to A	10,000	By Profit earned	29,400
To Salary to B	7,000		
To Interest on capitals at 6% :			
A on Rs. 50,000	3,000		
B on Rs. 20,000	1,200		
To Interest on A's loan at 6%	1,200		
To Profit			
5/7th to A	5,000		
2/7th to B	2,000		
	29,400		29,400

There is no Partnership Deed. B feels that he has not been treated fairly. Point out whether A has contravened the provisions of law and draw out new Profit and loss Appropriation Account on proper lines.

Solution :

The account presented by A is wrong because in the absence of agreement :

(*a*) no salary is due to any of the partners;
(*b*) interest on capitals is not to be allowed; and
(*c*) both partners must share equally.

The interest charged on A's loan @ 6% is correct. The correct account will be :

Profit and Loss Appropriation Account

Dr. Cr.

	Rs.			Rs.	
To Interest to A on his loan @ 6%	1,200	--	By Profit earned	29,400	
To Profit transferred to Capital A/cs : A(1/2) 14,100 B(1/2) 14,100	28,200	—			
	29,400	—		29,400	—

Illustration Marsh and Mallow were in partnership as confectioners, sharing profits and losses in the proportion—Marsh three-fifths and Mallow two-fifths. Interest is allowed on capitals and charged on drawings @ 6% per annum. The following balances were given as at December 31, 1976 :—

	Rs.		Rs.
Marsh's Capital A/c	32,500	Sales	6,53,000
Mallow's Capital A/c	27,000	Creditors	44,510
Marsh's Drawings	26,000	Purchases	4,98,800
Mallow's Drawings	17,000	Motor Lorry at cost	29,400
Stock, 1st Jan. 1976	39,000	Petty Cash Account	1,920
Provision for Depreciation on motor lorry to 31st December, 1975	10,800	Lighting	1,300
		Motor expenses	15,380
Provision for Depreciation of Shop Fittings to December 31, 1975	3,240	Shop Fittings at cost	32,400
		Balance at Bank	18,270
		General Expenses	4,340
Rates & Insurance	2,200		
Debtors	17,830		
Salaries and Wages	67,210		

You are given the following additional information :—

1. On December 31, 1976 the stock was valued at Rs. 41,000.

2. Provision is to be made for depreciation on the motor lorry at 20% per annum on cost and on shop fittings at 5% per annum on cost.

3. The cost of goods taken during the year by partners for their own use was : Marsh 1,600 ; Mallow Rs. 900.

4. The business premises belongs to Marsh who lets them to the firm at a rent of Rs. 6,000 a year. Nothing has been paid or credited to Marsh in respect of rent for 1976.

5. Petty cash balance on hand was Rs. 40.

Prepare Trading and Profit and Loss Account for 1976 and Balance Sheet as at December 31, 1976.

Solution :

Trading and Profit and Loss Account of Marsh and Mallow for the year ending December 31, 1976

Dr.	Rs.	Cr.	Rs.
To Opening Stock	39,000	By Sales	6,53,000
To Purchases : 4,98,800 Less taken by Partners 2,500	4,96,300	By Closing Stock	41,000
To Gross Profit c/d	1,58,700		
	6,94,000		6,94,000
To Salaries and Wages	67,210	By Gross Profit b/d	1,58,700
To Motor Expenses	15,380		
To General Expenses	4,340		
To Rates and Insurance	2,200		
To Lighting	1,300		
To Petty Expenses (Rs. 1,920—Rs. 40)	1,880		
To Depreciation Motor Lorries : 20% on Rs. 29,400 5,880 Shop Fittings : 5% on Rs. 32,400 1,620	7,500		
To Marsh's Capital A/c: rent of premises	6,000		
To Net Profit, c/d	52,890		
	1,58,700		1,58,700
To Interest on Capitals: Marsh Rs. 1,950 Mallow Rs. 1,620	3,570	By Net Profit b/d	52,890
		By Interest on Drawings Marsh Rs. 828 Mallow Rs. 537	1,365
To Profit transferred to Capital Accounts: Marsh (3/5) Rs. 30,411 Mallow (2/5) Rs. 20,274	50,685		
	54,255		54,255

Balance Sheet of Marsh and Mallow as at December 31, 1976

Liabilities		Amount Rs.		*Assets*	Rs.	Amount Rs.	
Creditors		44,510	—	*Fixed Assets* :			
Capitals—							
Marsh Rs.	42,433			Mottor Lorry Cost	29,400		
Mallow Rs,	30,457	72,890	—	Less Total Provision for Depreciation to date	16,680	12,720	—
(see Capital Accounts below)				Shop Fittings cost	32,400		
				Less Provision for Depreciation to date	4,860	27,540	—
				Current Assets :			
				Petty Cash		40	—
				Cash at Bank		18,270	—
				Debtors		17,830	—
				Stock		41,000	—
		1,17,400	—			1,17,400	—

Capital Accounts

Dr. *Cr.*

	Marsh Rs.	*Mallow* Rs.		*Marsh* Rs.	*Mallow* Rs.
To Drawing—Cash	26,000	17,000	By Balance b/d	32,500	27,000
To Purchase A/c—Goods used	1,600	900	By P.&L. A/c—Rent	6,000	—
To P.&L. App. A/c—Interest on Drawings	828	537	By P.& L. App. A/c—Interest	1,950	1,620
To Balance c/d	42,433	30,457	By P. & L. App. A/c—Profit	30,411	20,274
	70,861	48,894		70,861	48,894
			By Balance b/d	42,433	30,457

Notes : (1) Goods taken by partners could be credited to the Trading Account, but, preferably, these should be deducted from purchase.

(2) Depreciation is to be credited to the Provision for Depreciation Account. The firm obviously maintains the Motor Lorry and Shop Fittings at cost. In the balance sheet, however, the Provision for Depreciation is to be deducted from the asset.

(3) Interest on drawings is charged at 6% for 6 months. The value of goods taken by the partners for domestic use must be added to drawings for calculation of interest.

Admission of a new partner. When a new partner is admitted into a partnership, certain adjustments in accounts become necessary. Chiefly, this is because the new partner will acquire a share in the profits of the firm and, because of this, the old partner will stand to lose. Suppose, A and B are partners sharing profits in the ratio 3 : 2. If their profits are Rs. 20,000, A will get Rs. 12,000 and B will get Rs. 8,000. If C is admitted and is given one-fourth share in profits, then out of the Rs. 20,000 he will get Rs. 5,000. The remaining Rs. 15,000 will be divided between A and B; A will get Rs. 9,000 and B will get Rs. 6,000. Thus on C's admission A loses Rs. 3,000 per year and B loses Rs. 2,000 per year. C will have to compensate A and B for this loss. It is no argument to say that on C's admission the profits will not remain at Rs. 20,000; extra profits will arise and, therefore, A and B will both get more than what they previously got. But it should be noted that the additional profits will be earned by the combined efforts of all the partners, A, B and C. Therefore, if A & B get a share of the extra profits they are not particularly obliged to C. Out of the present profits of Rs. 20,000 they have to give up a share in favour of C and, therefore, they are entitled to a compensation. The problem of the compensation is the chief problem while dealing with admission of a partner. This is tackled through goodwill.

Goodwill. Goodwill is the value of the reputation of a firm in respect of profits expected in future over and above the normal rate of profits. The implication of the above is that there is always a certain normal rate of profit earned by various firms. A firm will be said to possess goodwill only if the future profits of the firm are expected to be more than this normal rate of profit. Suppose, a firm employs a capital of Rs. 1 lakh. The rate of profit earned by firms in general is 10%. If this firm earns Rs. 10,000 or less per year, there will be no goodwill for this firm. But if the profit earned is more than Rs. 10,000 say, Rs. 18,000, then the goodwill will attach to the extra Rs. 8,000. Usually this figure of extra profits (or super profits as it is known) will be multiplied by 3 or 4 or 5 representing the number of years' purchase of super profits.

In examination problems, very often goodwill is not valued in this manner but may be valued as so many years' purchase of the average profits of a number of years. If, for instance, it is said that goodwill is to be valued at three years' purchase of five years' average profits, it means that, first of all, average for 5 years profits will be ascertained and then that average will be multiplied by three. The product will be the amount of goodwill. If the profits for 5 years total Rs. 50,000, the average comes to Rs. 10,000; three years' purchase of goodwill will be Rs. 30,000.

One can see that there can be no goodwill if the firm has not been working properly and that goodwill will exist only if the firm has worked hard and well. If a new partner joins the firm he will enjoy the fruits of the past labours on the part of the previous partners. This is another reason why a new partner has to compensate the existing partners. Usually, therefore, when a new partner joins the firm, he has to bring in the required sum of capital as well as another sum of money representing the compensation for old partners. This sum will be based upon goodwill. If, in the above example, where goodwill has been valued at Rs. 30.000, the incoming partner is to have one-fifth share in future profits, he will be required to pay Rs. 6,000 in addition to whatever he has to bring in as his capital. This Rs. 6,000 belongs to old partners and will be credit to their Capital Accounts. However, it is not always necessary that the new partner should pay his share of goodwill in cash. There are various ways in which goodwill can be dealt with on the admission of a partner.

Following are the ways :—

1. **Goodwill raised** *or when the new partner cannot pay his share of goodwill in cash.* This means that goodwill is simply brought into books at its proper value. *This is what is meant by raising goodwill.* This is done by debiting goodwill and crediting the old partners in the old profit sharing ratio. Suppose, A and B carry on business sharing profits and loss in the ratio of 5 : 3. C is admitted and is given $\frac{1}{5}$ of profits. He pays Rs. 25,000 as his capital. But is unable to pay anything for goodwill which is valued at Rs. 40,000. In this case the entries will be :—

1.	Cash Account	Dr.	25,000	
	To C's Capital Account			25,000
	Amount brought in by C as his capital on his admission.			
2.	Goodwill Account	Dr.	40,000	
	To A's Capital Account			25,000
	To B's Capital Account			15,000
	Goodwill raised at its proper value in books and credited to A and B in their profit sharing ratio.			

The effect will be that the capitals of A and B will increase and there will be a new account, namely, Goodwill Account. This will appear in the Balance Sheet on the asset side.

A point to note is that if goodwill is already appearing in books, the *entry is to be made for the difference only*. Suppose, in the above case when goodwill has been valued at Rs. 40,000, goodwill already appears in books at Rs. 16,000. This means that Goodwill Account stands debited with this figure and that on C's admission this figure is to be raised to Rs. 40,000. This can be done by debiting goodwill by another Rs. 24,000. The entry, therefore, will be :—

Goodwill Account	Dr.	24,000	
To A's Capital Account			15.000
To B's Capital Account			9,000

If the amount of goodwill already appearing in books is more than the present value, then it means that there is a loss to be suffered by the old partners. Suppose, goodwill is now valued at Rs. 40,000, but appears in books already at Rs. 48,000. This means that the Goodwill Account has to be credited by Rs. 8,000 in order to reduce it to Rs. 40,000. Both A and B will be debited in their profit sharing ratio. The entry is :

A's Capital Account	Dr. 5,000	
B's Capital Account	Dr. 3,000	
To Goodwill Account		8,000

In all the cases discussed above, Goodwill will appear at Rs. 40,000 after C's admission and will be shown in the Balance Sheet at this figure.

2. Goodwill raised and written off immediately. It may not be considered proper by a firm to continue to show goodwill in the Balance Sheet. This is because goodwill is an asset which can be realised or converted into cash only if the firm is dissolved. Therefore, if goodwill is raised on the admission of a partner, it is often written off immediately. This is done by debiting *all* partners, including the new partner, in the new profit sharing ratio and by crediting goodwill. Suppose, in the above case when goodwill is raised at Rs. 40,000, it has to be written off. The entry for writing off will be :

A's Capital Account	Dr.	20,000	
B's Capital Account	Dr.	12,000	
C's Capital Account	Dr.	8,000	
The Goodwill Account			40,000

With this entry the Goodwill Account will cease to exist. Capital Accounts of all partners are reduced. Goodwill, naturally, will not appear in the Balance Sheet.

3. Goodwill brought in cash. In this case, Cash Account is debited and Goodwill Account is credited. Then, immediately, the Goodwill Account is transferred to the Capital Accounts of the old partners in the old profit sharing ratio. Suppose, A and B carry on business sharing profits and losses in the ratio of 3 : 1. C is admitted and is given one-fifth share of profits. He is required to bring in Rs. 20,000 as capital and his share of goodwill which is valued at Rs. 25,000. In this case C will have to pay Rs. 5,000 for goodwill, *i.e.*, one-fifth of Rs. 25,000. The entries will be as follows :

1.	Cash Account	Dr.	25,000	
	To C's Capital Account			20,000
	To Goodwill Account			5,000
	Amount brought in by C as his capital and goodwill.			

2. Goodwill Account	Dr.	5,000	
To A's Capital Account			3,750
To B's Capital Account			1,250
Goodwill brought in by C credited to A and B in their profit sharing ratio.			

The net effect of these two entries is that there is an increase of Rs. 25,000 in cash and an increase of Rs. 3,750 in the Capital Account of A, Rs. 1,250 in the Capital Account of B and a credit to the Capital Account of C of Rs. 20,000. Goodwill Account has been closed and, therefore, will not appear in the Balance Sheet.

One point, however, is to be noted. It has been made clear above that goodwill is a compensation to old partners. *Therefore, the amount brought in as goodwill by the incoming partner should be credited to the old partners in the ratio of their sacrifice* and not in the old profit sharing ratio. Suppose, in the above case, on C's admission the new profit sharing ratio is one-half, one-fourth and one-fourth. This means that on C's admission B does not stand to lose at all. He previously received one-fourth of profit and now also he receives one-fourth of profit. It is A who is suffering the entire loss on C's admission because his share of profit has come down from three-fourths to one-half. Therefore, the entire amount of goodwill brought in by C should be given to A. This is why the cash brought in as goodwill by the incoming partner should be credited to old partners in the ratio of sacrifice made by them. This ratio of sacrifice can be calculated by finding out how much the previous partners lose. Suppose, A and B were sharing profits in the ratio of 5 : 3. C is admitted and the new profit sharing ratio is 2 : 1 : 1. This means that A will now get one half, B will get one-fourth and C one-fourth. A loses 5/8—1/2, *i.e*, 1/8. B also loses 1/8, *i.e.*, 3/8—1/4. Therefore, on C's admission, both A and B lose equally. The amount brought in by C should he credited to the Capital Accounts of A and B equally.

There is a way in which goodwill can be credited to partners in the ratio of their sacrifices automatically. This requires the three following steps :—

(*i*) Credit the whole of the cash brought in by the new partner (for goodwill as well as for his capital) to his Capital Account. Suppose C is required to pay Rs. 40,000 as capital and Rs. 10,000 as goodwill for one-fifth share of profits. The entry under this step will be :

Cash Account	Dr.	50,000	
To C's Capital Account			50,000

(*ii*) Raise goodwill at full value and credit old partners and the old profit sharing ratio. Suppose, A and B were sharing profits and losses in the ratio of 3 : 2. Then taking the above example of C's admission, and therefore, valuing goodwill at Rs. 50,000, *i.e.*, $10,000 \times \frac{5}{1}$, the following entry will be made :—

Goodwill Account	Dr.	50,000	
To A's Capital Account			30,000
To B's Capital Account			20,000

(*iii*) Write off goodwill to all partners, including the new one, in the new profit sharing ratio. Suppose the new profit sharing ratio is 5 : 3 : 2. In that case the entry will be :—

A's Capital Account	Dr.	25,000	
B's Capital Account	Dr.	15,000	
C's Capital Account	Dr.	10,000	
To Goodwill Account			50,000

The effect of these three entries is that A has been credited with Rs. 5,000, *i.e.*, Rs. 30,000 minus Rs. 25,000. B has been credited with Rs. 5,000 *i.e.*, Rs. 20,000 minus Rs. 15,000. C's Capital Account which was previously credited at Rs. 50,000 has been debited with Rs. 10,000 and, therefore, has been reduced to Rs. 40,000. We can pass the entries in the straightforward manner also but we will have to calculate the ratio of sacrifice made by A and B on C's admission. The sacrifice is :—

A 3/5—5/10=1/10

B 2/5—3/10=1/10

The sacrifice made by both partners is equal. Therefore, we can, alternatively, pass the following entries :—

(*i*) Cash Account	Dr.	50,000	
To C's Capital Account			40,000
To Goodwill Account			10,000
(*ii*) Goodwill Account	Dr.	10,000	
To A's Capital Account			5,000
To B's Capital Account			5,000

The student must note that *this treatment of goodwill is necessary only when goodwill is brought in cash.*

If goodwill is to be withdrawn by partners, then the only additional entry required is to debit the Capital Accounts of the partners concerned and to credit cash.

4. **Goodwill paid privately.** When the amount of goodwill is paid to the old partners outside the books privately, no entry is required. In this case the amount to be paid to each partner will be calculated as shown in number 3 above but, there will be no entry in the books.

Illustration . The following is the balance sheet of Yellow and Green as at 31st December, 1977.

Liabilities	Rs.	Assets	Rs.
Creditors	20,000	Cash at Bank	10,000
Capitals—Yellow	25,000	Sundry Assets	55,000
Green	20,000	(No Goodwill A/c)	
	65,000		65,000

The partners shared profits and losses in the ratio 3 : 2. On the above date, Black was admitted as partner on the condition that he would pay Rs. 20,000 as capital. Goodwill was to be valued at 3 years' purchase of the average of four years' profits which were :—

1974 Rs. 9,000 1976 Rs. 12,000
1975 Rs. 14,000 1977 Rs. 13,000

The new profit sharing ratio is 7 : 5 : 4.

Give journal entries and balance sheets under various methods of treatment of goodwill.

Solution :

[Note- The total profit of the four years is Rs. 48,000, the average is Rs. 12,000. Hence the total value of goodwill is Rs. 36,000, i.e., 3 times Rs. 12,000].

Case (*a*)—Goodwill raised :

		Rs.	Rs.
Bank Account	...Dr.	20,000	
To Black's Capital Account			20,000
Amount brought in by Black as his capital.			
Goodwill Account	...Dr.	36,000	
To Yellow's Capital Account			21,600
To Green's Capital Account			14,400
Goodwill raised at Rs. 36,000 and credited to partners in the ratio of 3 : 2.			

Balance Sheet of Yellow, Green and Black

Liabilities		Rs.	Assets	Rs.
Creditors		20,000	Cash at Bank	30,000
Capitals—			Goodwill	36,000
Yellow	46,600		Sundry Assets	55,000
Green	34,400			
Black	20,000			
		1,01,000		
		1,21,000		1,21,000

Case (*b*) Goodwill raised and written off :

In addition to the two journal entries given under case (*a*), the following additional entry will be made :—

		Rs.	Rs.
Yellow's Capital Account	...Dr.	15,750	
Green's Capital Account	...Dr.	11,250	
Black's Capital Account	...Dr.	9,000	
To Goodwill Account			36,000
Goodwill written off to all partners in the new profit sharing ratio.			

Balance Sheet

Liabilities		Rs.	*Assets*	Rs.
Creditors		20,000	Cash at Bank	30,000
Capitals :			Sundry Assets	55,000
Yellow	30,850			
Green	23,150			
Black	11,000			
		65,000		
		85,000		85,000

Case (*c*)—Goodwill brought in cash :

Either :

		Rs.	Rs.
Bank Account	...Dr.	29,000	
To Black's Capital Account			29,000
Amount brought in by Black credited to his Capital Account (Rs. 20,000 for capital plus Rs. 9,000 for goodwill, 4/16 of Rs. 36,000).			
Goodwill Account	...Dr.	36,000	
To Yellow's Capital Account			21,600
To Green's Capital Account			14,400
Goodwill, Rs. 36,000, credited to Yellow and Green in their old profit sharing ratio.			
Yellow's Capital Account	...Dr.	15,750	
Green's Capital Account	...Dr.	11,250	
Black's Capital Account	...Dr.	9,000	
To Goodwill Account			36,000
Goodwill written off to all partners in the new profit sharing ratio.			

Or :

Bank Account	...Dr.	29,000	
To Black's Capital Account			20,000
To Goodwill Account			9,000
Amounts brought in by Black as capital and as goodwill.			

		Rs.	Rs.
Goodwill Account	...Dr.	9,000	
To Yellow's Capital Account			5,850
To Green's Capital Account			3,150
Goodwill credited to Yellow and Green in the ratio of sacrifice made by them in favour of Block*.			

Balance Sheet

Liabilities		Rs.	*Assets*	Rs.
Creditors		20,000	Cash at Bank	39,000
Capitals :			Sundry Assets	55,000
Yellow	30,850			
Green	23,150			
Black	20,000			
		74,000		
		94,000		94,000

Case (*d*)—Goodwill brought in cash, but withdrawn :

In addition to the treatment under case (*c*) above, the following additional entry will be made :

		Rs.	Rs.
Yellow's Capital Account	...Dr.	5,850	
Green's Capital Account	...Dr.	3,150	
To Bank Account			9,000
Amount withdrawn by Yellow and Green in respect of goodwill credited to them.			

Balance Sheet

Liabilities		Rs.	*Assets*	Rs.
Creditors		20,000	Cash at Bank	30,000
Capitals :			Sundry Assets	55,000
Yellow	25,000			
Green	20,000			
Black	20,000			
		65,000		
		85,000		85,000

Case (*c*)—Goodwill paid privately :

There will be no entry for goodwill but Black will pay Rs. 5,850 to Yellow and Rs. 3,150 to Green. For capital brought in by Black, the entry is :

*Sacrifice made : Yellow : $\frac{3}{5}-\frac{7}{16}=\frac{48-35}{80}=\frac{13}{80}$

Green : $\frac{2}{5}-\frac{5}{16}=\frac{32-25}{80}=\frac{7}{80}$

The ratio, therefore, is 13 : 7.

		Rs.	Rs.
Bank Account	...Dr.	20,000	
To Black's Capital Account			20,000
Amount brought in by Black as capital.			

Balance Sheet

Liabilities		Rs.	*Assets*	Rs.
Creditors		20,000	Cash at Bank	30,000
Capitals :			Sundry Assets	55,000
Yellow	25,000			
Green	20,000			
Black	20,000			
		65,000		
		85,000		85,000

Revaluation of assets and liabilities. When a new partner joins a firm, it is desirable to bring all appreciation or reduction in the value of assets into account as on the date of admission. Similarly, if the books contain any liability which has not to be paid or if the books do not contain a liability which has to be paid, suitable entries should be passed. The purpose of such entries is to make a proper Balance Sheet on the date of admission. Also, all profits which have accrued but not yet brought into books and, similarly, all losses which have occurred, but not yet recorded, should now be brought into books so that the capital accounts of the old partners reflect the proper figure. One result of passing of such entries will be that any subsequent profits or losses will be automatically shared by the incoming partner along with others. To record such profits or losses, an account, named Profit and Loss Adjustment Account or Revaluation Account, is opened. This account is debited with all reductions in the value of assets and increase in liabilities. The account is credited with increase in that value of assets and decrease in liabilities. The difference in the two sides of the account will show profit or loss. This is transferred to the capital accounts of old partners in the old profit sharing ratio. The entries to be passed are :

1. Revaluation Account	Dr.	
To the Assets (individually) which show a decrease		with the reduction in the value of the assets.
To Liabilities (individually) which have to be increased		with the increase in the liabilities.

2. Assets Account (individually)	Dr.	with the increase in the value of assets.
Liabilities Account (individually)	Dr.	with the reduction in the amount of liabilities.
To Revaluation Account		
3. Revaluation Account To Capital Accounts of old partners	Dr.	with the profit in the profit sharing ratio.
Or, Capital Account of old partners. To Revaluation Account	Dr.	with the loss in old profit sharing ratio.

As a result of the above entries the capital accounts of the old partners will change and the assets and liabilities will have to be adjusted to their proper values. It is at these figures that they will appear in the Balance Sheet.

Illustration The following is the Balance Sheet of Ram and Mohan (who share profits in the ratio of 3 : 2) as on 1st January, 1976 :—

Liabilities	Rs.	*Assets*	Rs.
Sundry Creditors	15,000	Buildings	18,000
Ram's Capital	20,000	Plant & Machinery	15,000
Mohan's Capital	25,000	Stock	12,000
		Debtors	10,000
		Bank	5,000
	60,000		60,000

On this date Sham was admitted on the following terms :—

1. He is to pay Rs. 25,000 as his capital and Rs. 10,000 as his share of goodwill for one-fifth share of profits.
2. The new profit sharing ratio will be 5 : 3 : 2.
3. The assets are to be revalued as under :—

	Rs.
Buildings	25,000
Plant & Machinery	12,000
Stock	12,000
Debtors (because of doubtful debts)	9,500

4. It was found that there was a liability for Rs. 1,500 for goods received but not recorded in books.

Give journal entries to record the above. Also give Ledger Accounts and the Balance Sheet after Sham's admission.

Solution :

Journal Entries

Date		Particulars		Dr. Rs.	Cr. Rs.
1976 Jan.	1	*Bank Account	Dr.	35,000 —	
		To Sham's Capital Account			35,000 —
		Amount brought in by Sham for capital and for goodwill.			
	,,	*Goodwill Account	Dr.	50,000 —	
		To Ram's Capital Account			30,000 —
		To Mohan's Capital A/c			20,000 —
		Goodwill raised at full value, i.e., 10,000×5/1 and credited to the old partners in the old ratio.			
	,,	*Ram's Capital Account	Dr.	25,000 —	
		Mohan's Capital Account	Dr.	15,000 —	
		Sham's Capital Account	Dr.	10,000 —	
		To Goodwill Account			50,000 —
		Goodwill written off to all partners in the new ratio.			
	,,	Revaluation Account	Dr.	5,000 —	
		To Plant & Machinery			3,000 —
		To Provision for Doubtful Debts			500 —
		To Sundry Creditors			1,500 —
		Recording of the reduction in the value of assets and the liability which has been previously omitted			
	,,	Buildings Account	Dr.	7,000 —	
		To Revaluation Account			7,000 —
		Increase in the value of buildings brought into account			
	,,	Revaluation Account	Dr.	2,000 —	
		Ram's Capital Account			1,200 —
		To Mohan's Capital A/c			800 —
		Profit on revaluation credited to Ram and Mohan in the old profit sharing ratio			

*Instead of these three entries given ab[illegible] [illegible]wing two entries can be passed :—

Journal Entries

			Dr.		Cr.	
			Rs.		Rs.	
1	Bank Account Dr. To Sham's Capital A/c To Goodwill Account		35,000	—	25,000 10,000	— —
2	Goodwill Account Dr. To Ram's Capital A/c To Mohan's Capital A/c		10,000	—	5,000 5,000	— —

Ledger Accounts

Bank Account

Dr. Cr.

		Rs.				Rs.	
1976 Jan. 1	To Balance b/d	5,000	—	1972 Jan. 1	By Balance c/d	40,000	—
„	To Sham's Capital A/c	35,000	—				
		40,000	—			40,000	—
1976 Jan. 1	To Balance b/d	40,000	—				

Goodwill Account

		Rs.				Rs.	
1976 Jan. 1	To Sundries Ram's Capital A/c (3/5) Mohan's Capital A/c (2/5)	30,000 20,000	— —	1976 Jan. 1	By Sundries— Ram's Capital A/c (5/10) Mohan's Capital A/c (3/10) Sham's Capital A/c (2/10)	25,000 15,000 10,000	— — —
		50,000	—			50,000	—

Revaluation Account

Date	Particulars	Rs.		Date	Particulars	Rs.	
1976 Jan. 1	To Sundries :			1976 Jan. 1	By Buildings A/c	7,000	—
	Plant & Machinery A/c	3,000	—				
	Provision for Doubtful Debts A/c	500	—				
	Sundry Creditors	1,500	—				
,,	To Capital A/cs–(Transfer of profit)						
	Ram (3/5)	1,200	—				
	Mohan (2/5)	800	—				
		7,000	—			7,000	—

Buildings Account

Date	Particulars	Rs.		Date	Particulars	Rs.	
1976 Jan. 1	To Balance b/d	18,000	—	1976 Jan. 1	By Balance c/d	25,000	—
,,	To Revaluation A/c	7,000	—				
		25,000	—			25,000	—
1976 Jan. 1	To Balance b/d	25,000	—				

Plant and Machinery Account

Date	Particulars	Rs.		Date	Particulars	Rs.	
1976 Jan. 1	To Balance b/d	15,000	—	1976 Jan. 1	By Revaluation A/c	3,000	—
					By Balance c/d	12,000	—
		15,000	—			15,000	—
1976 Jan. 1	To Balance b/d	12,000	—				

Stock Account

		Rs.					
1976 Jan. 1	To Balance b/d	12,000	—				

Sundry Debtors Account

		Rs.					
1976 Jan. 1	To Balance b/d	10,000	—				

Provision for Doubtful Debts Account

						Rs.	
				1976 Jan. 1	By Revaluation A/c	500	

Sundry Creditors Account

		Rs.				Rs.	
1976 Jan. 1	To Balance c/d	16,500	—	1976 Jan. 1	By Balance b/d	15,000	—
				,,	By Revaluation A/c	1,500	—
		16,500	—			16,500	—
				1976 Jan. 1	By Balance b/d	16,500	—

Ram's Capital Account

		Rs.				Rs.	
6 1	To Goodwill A/c	25,000	—	1976 Jan. 1	By Balance b/d	20,000	—
,,	To Balance c/d	26,200	—	,,	By Goodwill A/c	30,000	—
				,,	By Revaluation A/c	1,200	—
		51,200	—			51,200	—
				1976 Jan. 1	By Balance b/d	26,200	—

Mohan's Capital Account

		Rs.				Rs.	
1976 Jan. 1	To Goodwill A/c	15,000	—	1976 Jan. 1	By Balance b/d	25,000	—
,,	To Balance b/d	30,800	—	,,	By Goodwill A/c	20,000	—
				,,	By Revaluation A/c	800	—
		45,800	—			45,800	—
				1972 Jan. 1	By Balance b/d	30,800	—

Sham's Capital Account

		Rs.				Rs.	
1976 Jan. 1	To Goodwill A/c	10,000	—	1976 Jan. 1	By Bank A/c	35,000	—
,,	To Balance c/d	25,000	—				
		35,000	—			35,000	—
				1976 Jan. 1	By Balance b/d	25,000	—

Balance Sheet of Ram, Mohan and Sham as at January 1, 1966

Liab ities	Rs.		*Assets*	Rs.	
Sundry Creditors	16,500	—	Buildings	25,000	—
Capital Accounts :			Plant and Machinery	12,000	—
Ram 26,200			Stock	12,000	—
Mohan 30,800			Sundry Debtors Rs. 10,000		
Sham 25,000			Less Provision for Doubtful Debts Rs. 500		
	82,000	—		9,500	—
			Bank	40,000	—
	98,500	—		98,500	—

Reserves etc. in the Balance Sheet. Whenever a new partner is admitted, any reserves, etc. which may be lying in the Balance Sheet should be transferred to the Capital Accounts of the old partners in the old profit sharing ratio. In examination problems it should be done even if there are no instructions on this point.

Finding out the new profit sharing ratio. When a new partner is admitted, in absence of any other agreement, it is assumed that the old partners, as between themselves, will continue to share profits in the old profit sharing ratio. This means that after giving the share to the new partner as per agreement with him, the remaining share of profits should be divided among the old partners in the old ratio. For doing this the new partner's share should be deducted from 1 and then the remainder should be divided up in the old ratio. Suppose A and B share profits in the ratio of three-fourths and one-fourth. C is admitted and is given one-fifth share of profits. Deducting one-fifth from 1, we have four-fifths. If four-fifths are divided between A and B in the ratio of 3 : 1 the share of A comes to three-fifths, *i.e.*, $\frac{4}{5} \times \frac{3}{4}$. Similarly, the share of B comes to one-fifth, *i.e.*, $\frac{4}{5} \times \frac{1}{4}$. Thus the new profit sharing ratio of the three partners comes to three-fifth, one-fifth and one-fifth or 3 : 1 : 1.

Sometimes, a partner purchases a certain share of profits from one partner and another share of profit from another partner. Suppose A and B share profits in the ratio of 3 : 1. C is admitted and he purchases one-fourth share of profit from A. In that case, the share of profit of A will be three-fourths minus one-fourth, *i.e.*, one-half. There is no change in B s share of profits and, therefore, the new ratio will be one-half, one-fourth and one-fourth. Suppose A and B share in the ratio of 3 : 2 and C is admitted taking one-tenth of profits from each of the partners. In that case A's profit will be 3/5—1/10, *viz.*, 5/10 and B's share of profit will be 2/5—1/10 *viz.*, 3/10, and C's profit will be 1/10 + 1/10, *i.e.*, 2/10. The new ratio, therefore, is 5 : 3 : 2.

Capitals in the profit sharing ratio. It is sometimes agreed that on the admission of a partner the capitals of the partners should also be made in the profit sharing ratio. This question should be taken up after making all adjustments in respect of goodwill transfer of profit or loss on revaluation of assets and reserves, etc. Suppose as a result of these adjustments A's capital stands at Rs. 45,000 and B's capital stands at Rs. 34,000. C is admitted who pays Rs. 20,000 as his share of capital. The new profit sharing ratio is 5 : 3 : 2. The capitals of A and B are also to be in the same ratio as that of profits. This means that C's capital is Rs. 20,000 for one-fifth share of profits. Accordingly, the total capital of the firm should be Rs. 1 lakh. Therefore, according to the profit sharing ratio A's capital should be Rs. 50,000 and B's capital should be Rs. 30,000. A, therefore, should bring in Rs. 5,000 and B should be paid Rs. 4,000. We can get at these figures in another way also. If for one-fifth share of profits, the capital is Rs. 20,000, for three-tenths share of profits the capital should be 20,000 × 5 × 3/10 or

Rs. 30,000. This is what B's capital should be. Similarly, for five-tenth share of profits the capital should be 20,000×5/1×5/10 or Rs. 50,000.

Sometimes, the new partner is asked to bring in capital according to his profit sharing ratio. Suppose A's capital is Rs. 45,000 and B's capital is Rs. 35,000, making a total of Rs. 80,000. C is admitted for one-fifth share of profits and is to pay a proportionate amount as capital. It is clear that A and B together get four-fifths share of profits for which the capital is Rs. 80,000. For a full share the capital comes to Rs. 1 lakh, *i.e.*, 80,000×5/4. If C is to get one-fifth share of profits and has to pay a proportionate amount as capital, he must pay Rs. 20,000 *i.e.*, one-fifth of Rs. 1 lakh. This figure can also be obtained in another way. A and B's share of profit is 4/5. C's share of profit is 1/5. C's share, therefore, is 1/4 of the combined share of A and B, *i.e.*, 1/5÷4/5. Therefore, C's capital should be 1/4 of the total of A's and B's capitals. Therefore, he must pay 1/4 of Rs. 80,000 or Rs. 20,000 as his capital.

Illustration Sethi and Kohli are partners in a firm sharing profits and losses in the ratio of 3 : 2. Their Balance Sheet was as follows on 1st January, 1977 :—

	Rs.		Rs.
Sundry Creditors	15,000	Plant & Machinery	30,000
Capital Accounts		Patents	10,000
Sethi	30,000	Stock	20,000
Kohli	25,000	Debtors	18,000
General Reserve	10,000	Cash	2,000
	80,000		80,000

Bali is admitted as a partner on the above date on the following terms :—

(*a*) He will pay Rs. 10,000 as goodwill for ¼th share in the profit of the firm:

(*b*) The assets are to be valued as under :

Plant Machinery at Rs. 32,000

Stock at Rs. 18,000

Debtors at book figure less a provision of 5%.

(*c*) It was found that the creditors included a sum of Rs. 1,400 which was not to be paid. But it was also found that there was a liability for compensation to workers amounting to Rs. 2,000.

(*d*) Bali was to introduce Rs. 20,000 as capital and the capitals of the other partners were to be adjusted in the profit sharing ratio. For this purpose current accounts were to be opened.

Give journal entries to record the above and Balance Sheet after Bali's admission.

Solution :

Journal

Date		Particulars		Dr. Rs.	Cr. Rs.
1977 Jan.	1	Cash Account To Bali's Capital A/c To Goodwill Account Amount brought in by Bali as his capital and as goodwill	Dr.	30,000	 20,000 10,000
	,,	Goodwill Account To Sethi's Capital A/c To Kohli's Capital A/c Goodwill transferred to the Capital Accounts of old partners in the old profit sharing ratio	Dr.	10,000	 6,000 4,000
	,,	General Reserve Account To Sethi's Capital A/c To Kohli's Capital A/c General Reserve appearing in the books of Sethi & Kohli transferred to their Capital Accounts on the admission of Bali.	Dr.	10,000	 6,000 4,000
	,,	valuation Account To Stock To Provision for Doubtful Debts Ty Liability for Compensation to Workers Recording of— Rs. Reduction in the value of stock 2,000 Provision required for doubtful debts 900 Liability to Workmen brought into account 2,000	Dr.	4,900	 2,000 900 2,000
	,,	Plant and Machinery Sundry Creditors To Revaluation Account Increase in the value of plant and machinery and reduction in liabilities recorded	Dr. Dr.	2,000 1,400	 3,400

		Rs.	Rs.
Sethi's Capital Account	Dr.	900	
Kohli's Capital Account	Dr.	600	
To Revaluation Account			1,500
Loss on revaluation transferred to the Capital Accounts of old partners			
Sethi's Capital Account	Dr.	5,100	
To Sethi's Current A/c			5,100
Excess amount in Sethi's Capital Account transferred to his Current Account in order to bring down capital Account to Rs. 36,000			
Kohli's Capital Account	Dr.	8,400	
To Kohli's Current A/c			8,400
Excess amount in Kohli's Capital Account transferred to his Current Account in order to bring down Capital Account to Rs. 24,000*			

*The profit sharing ratio of the partners is now as under :—

Bali gets 1/4 share leaving 3/4 for others. Therefore, Sethi's share of profits will be 3/4×3/5 or 9/20. Kohli's share of profits will be 3/4×2/5 or 6/20. The capitals of Sethi and Kohli should be Rs. 36,000 and Rs. 24,000 respectively, as under :

	Rs.
For 1/4th share of profits, capital is	20,000
For full share, capital will be	80,000

For 9/20th share capital should be Rs. 80,000×9/20 or Rs. 36,000

For 6/20th share the capital should be Rs. 80,000×6/20 or Rs. 24,000

Balance Sheet of Sethi, Kohli and Bali as on 1st January, 1977

Liabilities		Rs.	Assets		Rs.
Sundry Creditors		13,600	Plant & Machinery		32,000
Liability for Compensation to Workers		2,000	Patents		10,000
			Stock		18,000
Capital Accounts :			Sundry Debtors	18,000	
Sethi	36,000		Less Provision for Doubtful Debts	900	
Kohli	24,000				17,100
Bali	20,000		Cash		32,000
		80,000			
Current Accounts :					
Sethi	5,100				
Kohli	8,400				
		13,500			
		1,09,100			1,09,100

Amounts of assets and liabilities not to be changed. Sometimes on the admission of a partner, it is desired that the effect of changes in the amounts of assets and liabilities should be brought into books *without* having to show the assets and liabilities at their new figures. This means that the partners concerned will pass entries in their capital accounts to record the changes but will leave the assets and liabilities to be shown in the balance sheet at their old figures. The method to do this is to find out the loss or profit or revaluation by a Memorandum Revaluation Account. This will be debited with losses and credited with gains, but double entry will not be completed in the accounts of the assets and liabilities concerned. The net result of this account, Memorandum Revaluation Account, is transferred to the capital accounts of old partners in the old ratio. Then, immediately this entry is reversed by transferring the amount to the capital account of all partners in the new ratio. If revaluation shows a profit, first the profit will be transferred to the credit side of old partners in

old ratio, and then the amount will be debited to the capital accounts of all partners, including the new partners, in the new ratio. If it is a loss, first the capital accounts of old partners will be debited in the old profit sharing ratio and then the capital accounts of all partners will be credited in the new profit sharing ratio. In this manner the double entry is completed by crediting and debiting the capital accounts only. The assets and liabilities will continue to appear at their old figures. It should be noted that, in a question like this, it is understood that Goodwill Account will have to be written off if it is to be raised first.

Illustration 62. The balance sheet of Arun and Chandra was as under on 1st July, 1978 :—

Liabilities		Rs.	*Assets*	Rs.
Sundry Creditors		9,000	Cash	1,000
Reserve		5,000	Debtors	10,000
Capital Accounts .			Stock	12,000
Arun	15,000		Furniture	2,000
Chandra	12,000	27,000	Buildings	16,000
		41,000		41,000

Dass was admitted as a partner and was given 1-4 share on the following terms :—

(*a*) He should bring Rs. 15,000 as his capital.

(*b*) His share of goodwill was valued at Rs. 5,000 but he was unable to bring it in cash.

(*c*) Stock and furniture be depreciated by 10%.

(*d*) A provision of 5% on debtors be created.

(*e*) An amount of Rs. 1,000 included in creditors not to be treated as a liability.

(*f*) A provision of Rs. 500 be created against bills discounted.

(*g*) The buildings be treated as worth Rs. 20,000.

It was agreed that except cash the other assets and liabilities were to be shown at the same old figure in the balance sheet.

Give journal entries to record the transactions on the admission of Dass and show the balance sheet after his admission.

Solution :

Journal

Date		Particulars		Dr Rs.		Cr. Rs.	
1978 July	1	Cash Account	Dr.	15,000	—		
		To Dass's Capital Account				15,000	—
		Amount brought in by Dass as his share of capital					
		Goodwill Account	Dr.	20,000	—		
		To Arun's Capital Account				10,000	—
		To Chandra's Capital Account				10,000	—
		Full value of goodwill (5,000×4) raised on the admission of Dass and credited to the capital accounts of the old partners in the old ratio (which is equal)					
		Arun's Capital Account	Dr.	7,500	—		
		Chandra's Capital Account	Dr.	7,500	—		
		Dass's Capital Account	Dr.	5,000	—		
		To Goodwill Account				20,000	—
		Goodwill Account written off to capital accounts of old partners in the new profit sharing ratio which is 3/8, 3/8 and 1/4					
		Reserve Account	Dr.	5,000	—		
		To Arun's Capital Account				2,500	—
		To Chandra's Capital Account				2,500	—
		Transfer of reserve to capital accounts of old partners in the old ratio					
		Memorandum Revaluation A/c	Dr.	2,600	—		
		To Arun's Capital A/c				1,300	—
		To Chandra's Capital A/c				1,300	—
		Profit on revaluation credited to the old partners in the old ratio (For Revaluation A/c see below)					
		Arun's Capital Account	Dr.	975	—		
		Chandra's Capital Account	Dr.	975	—		
		Dass's Capital Account	Dr.	650	—		
		To Memorandum Revaluation A/c				2,600	—
		Memorandum Revaluation Account closed by debiting all the partners in the new profit sharing ratio.					

The Memorandum Revaluation Account will appear as under ;

Memorandum Revaluation Account

		Rs.				Rs.
To Provision for Doubtful Debts		500	By Buildings			4,000
			By Sundry Creditors			1,000
To Stock		1,200				
To Furniture		200				
To Provision for Bills Discounted		500				
To Profit transferred to						
Arun ½	1,300					
Chandra ½	1,300	2,600				
		5,000				5,000
To Buildings		4,000	By Provision for Doubtful Debts			500
To Sundry Creditors		1,000				
			By Stock			1,200
			By Furniture			200
			By Provision for Bill Discounted			500
			By Loss transferred to			
			Arun	3/8	975	
			Chandra	3/8	975	
			Dass	¼	650	2,600
		5,000				5,000

Balance Sheet of Arun, Chandra and Dass as on 1st July, 1978

Liabilities		Rs.	*Assets*	Rs.
Sundry Creditors		9,000	Cash	16,000
Capital Accounts :			Debtors	10,000
Arun	20,325		Stock	12,000
Chandra	17,325		Furniture	2,000
Dass	9,350		Buildings	16,000
		47,000		
		56,000		56,000

Retirement of a Partner.

The problems relating to retirement are similar to those of admission. Chiefly, the problems relate to goodwill and to revaluation of assets and liabilities. In addition, there will be the problem of repayment of the amount due to the retiring partner.

Before we discuss these points we should note how the profit sharing ratio will be arrived at after the retirement of a partner. The remaining partners will have to agree amongst themselves on this point. For instance, if A, B & C were sharing profits and losses in the ratio of 5 : 3 : 2 and B retires, it is up to A and C to agree that in future the profits and losses will be shared in the ratio of say, 3/5 to A and 2/5 to C; or A and C may agree that B's share of profits will be taken equally by the other two partners. B was getting 3/10; half of this is 3/20. Therefore, 3/20 will be added to A's share and 3/20 will be added to C's share. A's share will be 5/10+3/20 or 13/20 and C's share will be 2/10+3/20 or 7/20. The new ratio, therefore, is 13 : 7.

If there is no fresh agreement among the remaining partners, it is presumed that they will take the share of the retiring partner in the same ratio as they were having previously. To continue the above example, A and C will take B's share in the ratio of 5 : 2 in absence of agreement. That means 5/7 of 3/10 or $\frac{15}{70}$ will be taken by A and 2/7 of 3/10 will be taken by C. The new share for A will be $5/10+\frac{15}{70}$ or 50/70 or 5/7. Similarly, C's share will be 2/10+6/70 or 20/70 or 2/7. We can arrive at these ratios in a more convenient manner. The previous ratio 5 : 3 : 2. The partner with '3' goes, so let us remove this figure. The ratio remains as 5 : 2. Therefore, A will get 5/7 and C will get 2/7.

Goodwill. In case of retirement of a partner there is no question of goodwill being dealt with in the form of cash. Goodwill is only raised in the books or, rather, goodwill is recorded in the books at its proper figure. If, for instance, there is no goodwill account already appearing in books. goodwill account will be raised at its full figure. But if in books there is already a goodwill account, then goodwill account should be raised only for the difference. On the other hand, if the present value of goodwill is less than the book figure, the goodwill account will have to be credited to bring it down to its proper value. Of course, goodwill is valued according to the method given in the Partnership Deed. If the Deed is silent, the retiring partner and the other partners will have to come to an agreement on question of the value of goodwill.

Assuming that there is no goodwill account already appearing in the books, goodwill may be recorded in one of the three ways :—

1. Goodwill is raised in the books of the firm.

The entry is :

Debit Goodwill Account.

Credit all partners (including the retiring one) in the old profit sharing ratio.

This entry should be passed only for the difference if already a goodwill account appears in the books. If the present value of goodwill is less than the book figure, the above noted entry will be reserved. In this case goodwill account will appear in balance sheet of the company at its present figure.

2. Goodwill Account is raised in the books but is then written off. In this case two entries will be made :

(a) Debit Goodwill.
Credit all partners (including the retiring one) in the old profit sharing ratio.

(b) Debit the remaining partners in the new profit sharing ratio and credit goodwill. Suppose A, B and C were partners sharing in the ratio of 3 : 1 : 1. B retires and goodwill on that occasion is valued at Rs. 20,000. The two entries will be :

			Rs.
(a) Goodwill Account	...Dr.	20,000	
To A's Capital A/c			12,000
To B's Capital A/c			4,000
To C's Capital A/c			4,000
Goodwill raised at Rs. 20,000 and credited to all partners.			
(b) A's Capital Account	...Dr.	15,000	
C's Capital Account	...Dr.	5,000	
To Goodwill Account			20,000
Goodwill Account written off to the capital accounts of A and C in the new profit sharing ratio which is ¾th and ¼th.			

The student will see that the net effect of the above two entries is that B has been credited with Rs. 4,000 and A has been debited with Rs. 3,000 and C with Rs. 1,000. A has been debited with ¾th of Rs. 4,000 and C with ¼th of Rs. 4,000. Therefore, the following method may be adopted :

3. Entry is passed only for the share of the retiring partner. The method is : debit the remaining partners and credit the retiring partner with his share of goodwill. Instead of one entry, two entries can be passed, *viz.*

(a) Debit Goodwill) with his share
)
Credit retiring partners,) of goodwill only.
capital account)

(*b*) Debit remaining Partners' Capital Accounts
Credit Goodwill Account } in the ratio of the gain of the remaining partners

In this case the student should note that the *debit to the remaining partners should be* not in the ratio of their profits now but, *in the ratio of the gain made by them on the retirement of the partner*. If, say, the two remaining partners gain equally on the retirement of a partner, then goodwill also should be debited to their capital accounts equally. This applies only when goodwill raised only at the amount due to the retiring partner. It does not apply when goodwill is raised at full value and written off. An example will make it clear. Suppose A, B and C are partners sharing profits and losses in the ratio of 1/2, 1/3 and 1/6. B retires and goodwill for that purpose is valued at Rs. 30,000. The new profit sharing ratio is 3/5 and 2/5. This means that A's gain is 1/10 (or 3/30), *i.e.*, 3/5—1/2. C's gain is 7/30, *i.e.*, 2/5—1/6. The ratio of gain, therefore, is 3 : 7 as between A and C. Therefore, the amount of Rs. 10,000 which will have to be credited to B as goodwill should be debited to A and C in the ratio of 3 : 7. The entry will be :

A's Capital Account	Dr.	3,000	
C's Capital Account	Dr.	7,000	
To B's Capital Account			10,000

Of course, the following two entries can be passed :

Goodwill Account	Dr.	10,000	
To B's Capital Account			10,000
Goodwill Account raised at B's share which is 1/3			
A's Capital Account	Dr.	3,000	
C's Capital Account	Dr.	7,000	
To Goodwill Account			10,000
Goodwill Account written off			

The truth of the above can be tested by raising goodwill at full value and then writing it off in the new ratio. The two entries are given below (without narration) :

Goodwill Account	Dr.	30,000	
To A's Capital Account			15,000
To B's Capital Account			10,000
To C's Capital Account			5,000
A's Capital Account	Dr.	18,000	
C's Capital Account	Dr.	12,000	
To Goodwill Account			30,000

The net effect of these two entries is that A has been debited with Rs. 3,000 and C has been debited with Rs. 7,000. These figures are the same as worked out previously.

Revaluation of assets and liabilities. Revaluation of assets and liabilities is a must on the retirement of a partner unless the Deed specifically says that they are not to be revalued. Even those assets which do not appear in the books but which belong to the firm have to be revalued. The method of recording the revaluation is the same as given in the case of admission of partners. Revaluation Account will be debited with reduction in the values of assets and increase in the amount of liabilities. This account will be credited with increase in the value of assets and reduction in the amount of liabilities. The profit or loss on revaluation must be transferred to the capital accounts of all partners (including the retiring partner) in the old profit ratio.

Reserve, etc. On the retirement of a partner any reserve built out of profits, etc. should be transferred to the capital accounts of all partners in the old profit sharing ratio. If desired, only the retiring partner's share may be credited to his capital account and debited to the reserve account.

Capital Account to be transferred to Loan Account. After ascertaining the amount due to the retiring partner and making all entries, the amount standing to the credit of the retiring partner's capital account will be transferred to his loan account and will be paid according to the agreement with the remaining partners. This means that the Loan Account will carry an interest at agreed terms. If there is no agreement, the retiring partner is entitled to receive *either* interest at the rate of 6% per annum on the amount due to him but remaining in the business, that is to say on his loan *or* the share of profits earned with his investment remaining with the firm. The retiring partner is entitled to make the choice.

Illustration A and B are partners in a business sharing profits and losses as A, 3/5ths and B, 2/5ths. Their Balance Sheet as on 1st January, 1978 is given below :—

Liabilities		Rs.	*Assets*	Rs.
Capital Accounts :			Plant & Machinery	20,000
A	20,000		Stock	16,000
B	15,000	35,000	Debtors	15,000
Reserve Account		15,000	Balance at Bank	6,000
Sundry Creditors		7,500	Cash in hand	500
		57,500		57,500

B retires from the business owing to illness and A takes it over. The following revaluations were made :

(1) The goodwill of the firm is valued at Rs. 25,000.

(2) Depreciate :

Plant & Machinery by 7½% and Stock by 15%.

(3) A bad debts provision is raised against debtors at 5% and a discount reserve against creditors at 2%

You are asked to journalise the above transactions in the books of the firm and close the partners accounts as on 1st Jan. 1978. Give also the opening balance sheet of A.

Solution :

Journal

Date		Particulars		Dr Rs.	Cr. Rs.
1978 Jan.	1	Goodwill Account	Dr.	25,000 —	
		To A's Capital Account			15,000 —
		To B's Capital Account			10,000 —
		The amount of goodwill raised on B's retirement.			
		Reserve Account	Dr.	15,000 —	
		To A's Capital Accouut			9,000 —
		To B's Capital Account			6,000 —
		Transfer of reserve to A's capital account and B's capital account in the profit sharing ratio			
		Profit and Loss Adjustment Account	Dr.	4,650 —	
		To Plant & Machinery Account			1,500 —
		To Stock Account			2,400 —
		To Provision for Bad Debts Account			750 —
		Reduction in the value of assets and creation of provision for doubtful debts as per agreement with B			
		Reserve for Discount on Creditors Account	Dr.	150 —	
		To Profit & Loss Adjustment Account			150 —
		Creation of reserve for discount on creditors at 2%			

		Rs.	Rs.
A's Capital Account	Dr.	2,700 —	
B's Capital Account	Dr.	1,800 —	
To Profit & Loss Adjustment Account			4,500 —
Transfer of loss on revaluation of assets and liabilities to capital accounts of A and B in the profit sharing ratio.			
B's Capital Account	Dr.	29,200 —	
To B's Loan Account			29,200 —
Transfer of B's Capital Account to his Loan Account on retirement			

Balance Sheet of A as on 1st January, 1978

Liabilities		Rs.	*Assets*		Rs.
Sundry Creditors	7,500		Goodwill		25,000
Less Reserve for Discount	150	7,350	Plant & Machinery		18,500
			Stock		13,600
B's Loan Account		29,200	Debtors	15,000	
A's Capital Account		41,300	Less Provision for Bad Debts	750	14,250
			Balance at Bank		6,000
			Cash in hand		500
		77,850			77,850

Illustration Sen, Sil and Som are partners in a business sharing profits $\frac{3}{4}$, $\frac{1}{8}$ and $\frac{1}{8}$ respectively and their Balance Sheet as on 31st December, 1967 was as follows :

Capital and Liabilities		Rs.	*Property & Assets*	Rs.
Sundry Creditors		25,000	Plant & Machinery	50,000
General Reserve		5,000	Sundry Debtors	35,000
Capital Account :			Stock	20,000
Sen	50,000		Cash	25,000
Sil	30,000		Patents	5,000
Som	25,000	1,05,000		
		1,35,000		1,35,000

Som retired on 31st December, 1977. **From** the following particulars ascertain the amount due to Som by **preparing** important ledger accounts. Also prepare balance sheet after **Som's** retirement.

1. Goodwill is to be valued at three years' purchase of the average profits of the last four years. The profits were as follows :

	Rs.
1974	50,000
1975	60,000
1976	40,000
1977	50,000

   Goodwill Account is not to remain in books.

2. Plant and Machinery was valued at Rs. 40,000, patents at Rs. 10,300 and stock at Rs. 18,000.
3. A provision of 5% on sundry debtors was necessary.
4. On 30th June, 1976 a shed was constructed at a cost of Rs. 10,000. This sum was charged to the Profit and Loss Account. This asset is now to be brought into books allowing 5% p.a. depreciation on the original cost.
5. Sil was to acquire the whole of the share of profits of Som.
6. The total capital of the firm was to be Rs. 80,000 and capitals of Sen and Sil were to be in their profit sharing ratio, adjustments to be made in cash.
7. Som is to leave Rs. 30,000 in the business as loan @ 9%. The remaining amount is to be paid to him immediately.

Solution :

Notes : Goodwill will be valued at Rs. 1,50,000. The total profits of four years are Rs. 2,00,000. The average comes to Rs. 50,000. At three years' purchase, the figure is Rs. 1,50,000.

The new profit sharing ratio is Sen, 3/4 and Sil 1/4 since Sil acquires the whole of Som's share.

LEDGER

Goodwill Account

1977 Dec.31	To Sundries			1977 Dec.31	By Sundries	
	Sen's Capital A/c (3/4)	1,12,500	—		Sen's Capital A/c (3/4)	1,12,500
	Sil's Capital A/c (1/8)	18,750	—		Sil's Capital A/c (1/4)	37,500
	Som's Capital A/c (1/8)	18,750	—			
		1,12,500	—			1,12,500

Revaluation Account

1977		Rs.		1977		Rs.	
Dec. 31	To Plant & Machinery A/c—Loss	10,000	—	Dec. 31	By Patents—Profit	5,300	—
"	To Stock A/c —Loss	2,000	—	"	By Shed: Cost 10,000; Less 5% Dep. for 1½ years 750	9,250	—
"	To Provision for Bad Debts A/c	1,750	—				
"	To Profit transferred to Capital A/cs— Sen (3/4) 600; Sil (1/8) 100; Som (1/8) 100	800	—				
		14,550	—			14,550	—

Sen's Capital Account

1977		Rs.		1977		Rs	
Dec. 31	To Goodwill A/c	1,12,500	—	Dec. 31	By Balance b/d	50,000	—
	To Balance b/d (3/4 of Rs. 80,000)	60,000	—	"	By Goodwill A/c	1,12,500	—
				"	By Revaluation A/c	600	—
				"	By General Reserve	3,750	—
				"	By Cash (to make capital up to Rs. 60,000)	5,650	—
		1,72,500				1,72,500	—
				1978 Jan. 1	By Balance b/d	60,000	—

Sil's Capital Account

		Rs.				Rs.	
1977 Dec.31	To Goodwill A/c	37,500	—	1977 Dec.31	By Balance b/d	30,000	—
,,	To Balance c/d (1/4 of Rs. 80,000)	20,000	—	,,	By Goodwill A/c	18,750	—
				,,	By Revaluation A/c	100	—
				,,	By General Reserve	625	—
				,,	By Cash (to make balance equal to Rs. 20,000)	8,025	—
		57,500	—			57,500	—
				1968 Jan. 1	By Balance b/d	20,000	—

Som's Capital Account

		Rs.				Rs.	
1977 Dec.31	To Cash	14,475	—	1977 Dec.31	By Balance b/d	25,000	—
	To Transfer to Som's Loan Account	30,000	—	,,	By Goodwill A/c	18,750	—
					By Revaluation A/c	100	—
					By General Reserve	625	—
		44,475	—			44,475	—

Som's Loan Accoant

						Rs.	
				1967 Dec.31	By Som's Capital A/c —Transfer	30,000	—

Balance Sheet of Sen and Sil as at Dec. 31, 1977

Liabilities		Rs.		*Assets*		Rs.	
Sundry Creditors		25,000	—	Plant & Machinery		40,000	—
Som's Loan Accounts		30,000	—				
Capital Accounts :	Rs.			Cycle Shed		9,250	—
				Patents		10,300	—
Sen	60,000			Sundry Debtors	35,000		
Sil	20,000			Less Provision for Bad Debts	1,750		
		80,000	—			33,250	—
				Stock		18,000	—
				*Cash		24,200	—
		1,35,000	—			1,35,000	—

*The student should prepare Cash Account.

Paying a partner's loan in instalments. Strictly speaking, paying a partner's loan is only a matter of arranging finance. However, sometimes it is stated that the loan is to be paid off in so many equal instalments and that the balance is to carry interest. In such a case what should be done is that the loan should be divided into equal parts. The interest for the period should be calculated and the payment should consist of the instalment on account of the loan plus interest for the period. Suppose a partner's loan stands at Rs. 30,000 and that it has to be paid in four annual equal instalments and that the loan is to carry interest at 6% per annum. The annual instalment on account of loan comes to Rs. 7,500. For the first year the interest is Rs. 1,800, *i.e.*, 6% on Rs. 30,000. In the first year the amount to be paid will be Rs. 9,300. Balance of Rs. 22,500 will now be left. Next year the interest will be Rs. 1,350. The amount to be paid therefore will be Rs. 7,500 plus interest, *viz.*, Rs. 8,850. The Loan Account will appear in the books as under :

Retiring Partner's Loan Account

		Rs.				Rs.	
I Yr.	To Cash (7,500+1,800)	9,300	—	I Yr.	By Capital A/c	30,000	—
	To Balance c/d	22,500	—		By Interest A/c	1,800	—
		31,800	—			31,800	—
II Yr.	To Cash (7,500+1,350)	8,850	—	II Yr.	By Balance b/d	22,500	—
	To Balance c/d	15,000	—		By Interest A/c (6% on Rs. 22,500)	1,350	—
		23,850	—			23,850	—
III Yr.	To Cash	8,400	—	III Yr.	By Balance c/d	15,000	—
	To Balance c/d	7,500	—		By Interest A/c	900	—
		15,900	—			15,900	—
IV Yr.	To Cash	7,950	—	V Yr.	By Balance b/d	7,500	—
					By Interest A/c	450	—
		7,950	—			7,950	—

However, it may be desired that the loan is to be paid off in absolutely equal instalments, that is to say, the instalment plus the interest to be paid every year should be equal. In such a case the Annuity Table should be consulted. A specimen of Annuity Table has been given on page 277. Suppose a loan of Rs. 30,000 is to be paid off in four years in absolutely equal instalments. Interest is to be calculated at 5% per annum. A reference to the Annuity Table shows that one rupee over four years at 5% is ·282012. The meaning of this is that if one has one rupee just now and if it is invested at 5% per annum, the sum of Rs. ·282012 can be paid annually for 4 years. Multiplying this figure by Rs. 30,000 we get Rs. 8,460·36. If every year the Loan Account is credited with 5% interest on the balance in the beginning and if every year, at the end, a sum of

Rs.8,460·36 is paid, the loan will be exhausted in four years. The Loan Account in this case is shown below :

Retiring Partner's Loan Account

		Rs.				Rs.	
I Yr.	To Cash Account	8,460	36	I Yr.	By Capital A/c	30,000	—
	To Balance c/d	23,039	64		By Interest A/c (5% on Rs. 30,000)	1,500	—
		31,500	—			31,500	—
II Yr.	To Cash Account	8,460	36	II Yr.	By Balance b/d	23,039	64
	To Balance c/d	15,731	26		By Interest A/c (5% on Rs. 23,039.64)	1,151	98
		24,191	62			24,191	62
III Yr.	To Cash Account	8,460	36	III Yr.	By Balance b/d	15,731	26
	To Balance c/d	8,057	46		By Interest A/c	786	56
		16,517	82			16,517	82
IV Yr.	To Cash	8,460	36	IV Yr.	By Balance b/d	8,057	46
					By Interest A/c	402	90
		8,460	36			8,460	36

Joint Life Policy. Partners often take out a life insurance policy on their lives jointly. Annually a sum of money, known as the premium, is paid to the life insurance company (Life Insurance Corporation of India). The company will pay the amount of the policy on the death of any one of the partners. The payment of premium also stops on death. This arrangement is usually made to provide funds for settling the claims of the heirs of the deceased partner. Of course, a joint life policy strengthens the financial position of the firm also.

It is possible to treat a joint life policy in two ways in the books of account. The annual premium can be treated as an expense and debited to the Profit and Loss Account. In such a case, there will be no joint life policy account in the books of the firm and, naturally, nothing will appear in the balance sheet. On the death of a partner, the firm will receive the full amount. This must be credited to the capital accounts of all the partners in the profit sharing ratio.

The second method is to debit the premium paid to an account called Joint Life Policy Account. It is, however, not proper to treat the whole of the amount paid as premium as an asset. This is because if the firm stops paying premiums, the life insurance company will not refund the premiums but will pay only a proportion of the premium received by it. The amount which the insurance company is prepared to pay immediately in cash in case of stoppage of further payment of premiums is called "surrender value". In the books of the firm, the Joint Life Policy Account should not be shown at more than the surrender value. Hence if premiums are debited to the Joint Life Policy Account, a sum sufficient to reduce the balance in this account equal to the surrender value should be debited to the Profit and Loss Account and credited to the Joint Life Policy Account. Thus this account will show a debit balance equal to the surrender value. This will be shown in the balance sheet. If it is so desired, the amounts necessary to reduce the Joint Life Policy Account to its surrender value may be credited to a separate account called Joint Life Policy Reserve Account. Credits will accumulate in this account and debits in the Joint Life Policy Account The difference between the balances of the two accounts will be equal to the surrender value.

If a partner dies, the firm will receive the full amount of the policy. This amount is credited in the Joint Life Policy Account If a Joint Life Policy Reserve Account is maintained it will also be transferred to the Joint Life Policy Account and thus closed The balance in the Joint Life Policy Account will represent a profit to the firm and will be transferred to the capital accounts of *all* the partners (including the deceased partner) in the profit sharing ratio.

Illustration Red, White and Black shared profits and losses in the ratio of 5 : 3 : 2. They took out a joint life policy in 1958 for Rs. 50,000, a premium of Rs. 3,000 being paid annually on 10th June The surrender value of the policy on 31st December of various years was as follows :— 1958 nil ; 1959 Rs. 900 ; 1960 Rs. 2,000 ; 196[illegible] Rs. 3,600.

Black died on 15th April, 1962. Prepare ledger accounts assuming (1) no joint life policy account is maintained, and (2) a joint life policy account is maintained on surrender value basis.

Solution :

Case (1) :

Joint Life Policy Premium Account

Dr.		Rs.				Rs.	Cr.
1958 June 10	To Bank Account	3,000	—	1958 Dec. 31	By Profit & Loss A/c	3,000	—
1959 June 10	To Bank Account	3,000	—	1959 Dec. 31	By Profit & Loss A/c	3,000	—
1960 June 10	To Bank Account	3,000	—	1960 Dec. 31	By Profit & Loss A/c	3,000	—
1961 June 10	To Bank Account	3,000	—	1961 Dec. 31	By Profit & Loss A/c	3,000	—

Profit and Loss Account

1958 Dec.31	To Joint Life Policy Premium Account	3,000	—				
1959	To Joint Life Policy Premium Account	3,000	—				
1960	To Joint Life Policy Premium Account	3,000	—				
1961	To Joint Life Policy Premium Account	3,000	—				

Joint Life Policy Account

1962 Apl. 15	To Capital Accounts (transfer) :				1962 Ap. 15	By Bank Account	50,000	—
	Red 5/10	25,000						
	White 3/10	15,000						
	Black 2/10	10,000						
			50,000	—				
			50,000	—			50,000	—

Case (*ii*) :

Joint Life Policy Account

Date	Particulars	Rs.		Date	Particulars	Rs.	
1958				1958			
June 10	To Bank A/c	3,000	—	Dec. 31	By Profit & Loss A/c	3,000	—
1959				1959			
June 10	To Bank A/c	3,000	—	Dec. 31	By Profit & Loss A/c	2,100	—
					By Balance c/d	900	—
		3,000	—			3,000	—
1960				1960			
Jan 1	To Balance b/d	900	—	Dec. 31	By Profit & Loss A/c	1,900	—
June 10	To Bank A/c	3,000	—	"	By Balance c/d	2,000	—
		3,900	—			3,900	—
1961				1961			
Jan. 1	To Balance b/d	2,000	—	Dec. 31	To Profit & Loss A/c	1,400	—
June 10	To Bank A/c	3,000	—	"	By Balance c/d	3,600	—
		5,000	—			5,000	—
1962				1962			
Jan. 1	To Balance b/d	3,600	—	Apl. 15	By Bank A/c	50,000	—
Apl. 15	To Profit transferred to Capital A/cs.						
	Red 5/10	23,200	—				
	White 3/10	13,920	—				
	Black 2/10	9,280	—				
		50,000	—			50,000	—

Profit and Loss Account

		Rs.				
1958 Dec. 31	To Joint Life Policy A/c	3,000	—			
1959 Dec. 31	To Joint Life Policy A/c	2,100	—			
1960 Dec. 31	To Joint Life Policy A/c	1,900	—			
1961 Dec. 31	To Joint Life Policy A/c	1,400	—			

Individual Policies instead of one joint life policy may also be taken out. If the premium is debited to the Drawing or Capital Accounts of partners, the policies will then be private properties of the partners and on the death of a partner, his heirs will get the full amount. The firm will get nothing and hence no entries will be required in this case. But if the firm debits the premiums to the Profit and Loss Account, the policies will be the property of the firm. On the death of a partner, the firm will receive the amount of his policy. But, on such an occasion, the surrender value of the policies on the life of the surviving partners must also be taken into account. The amount actually received and the surrender value of the continuing policies will be transferred to the capital accounts of all the partners in the profit sharing ratio.

Illustration Active, Blunt and Sharp were partners sharing profits and losses in the ratio of 3 : 2 : 1. The firm had taken out policies on the lives of the partners as under :

Active Rs. 20,000; Blunt Rs. 15,000 and Sharp Rs. 10,000. The premiums in all cases were treated as expense of the firm and debited to the Profit and Loss Account. On July 1, 1968 Blunt died. The surrender value in all cases was 30% of the amount of the policies. Give journal entries to record the happening on Blunt's death.

Solution :

Journal

Date		Particulars		Dr. Rs.	Cr. Rs.
1978 July	1	Bank Account To Insuranc cies A/c Amount receiv ınst Blunt's Policy on ıh	Dr.	15,000 —	15,000 —
	1	Surrender Value of Policies A/c To Insurance Policies A/c Surrender value of Active's Policy and of Sharp's Policy brought into account on Blunt's death	Dr.	9,000 —	9,000 —
	1	Insurance Policies A/c To Active's Capital Account To Blunt's Capital Account To Sharp's Capital Account Insurance Policies A/c closed by transfer to capital accounts of partners in the profit sharing ratio	Dr.	24,000 —	 12,000 — 8,000 — 4,000 —

"Surrender Value of Policies", in the above illustration, will appear in the balance sheet. If it is desired that it should not, it should be transferred to the debit of the remaining partners in the new profit sharing ratio. This entry, if desired in the above illustration, will be :

		Rs.	Rs.
Active's Capital Account	Dr.	6,750	
Sharp's Capital Account	Dr.	2,250	
To Surrender Value of Policies A/c			9,000
Surrender Value of Policies A/c raised on Blunt's death, closed by transfer to capital accounts of the remaining partners.			

The question of treatment of the joint policy or individual policies can also arise in case of retirement of a partner. The treatment will, of course, depend on how the accounts are kept. If an account (or accounts) are kept in respect of the policy (or policies) on surrender value basis, no further treatment is necessary if a partner retires. Also no treatment is necessary if, in case of individual policies, the premiums are debited to the respective Drawings Accounts of the partners. But if the premiums are debited to the Profit and Loss Account the surrender value of the joint life policy or of the individual policies should be ascertained. This amount should be credited to the Revaluation Account and debited to "Surrender Value of Policy (ies) Account." Thus the retiring partner will automatically receive benefit of the policy or policies. The Surrender Value of Policy Account will be shown in the balance sheet. Of course, it may be written off by debiting the capital accounts of the remaining partners in the new profit sharing ratio.

Death of a partner

The problems arising on the death of a partner are similar to those arising on retirement. Assets and liabilities have to be revalued and the resultant profit or loss has to be transferred to the capital accounts of all the partners including the deceased partner. Goodwill is dealt with exactly in the way already discussed in case of retirement. Treatment of joint life policy or individual policies has been given above. The only additional point is that as death may occur on any day, the representatives of the deceased partner will be entitled to the partner's share of profits from the beginning of the year to the date of death. After ascertaining the amount due to the deceased partner, it should be credited to his Executor's Account. On payment, this account will be debited.

The amount due to the deceased partner carries interest at the mutually agreed upon rate. In absence of agreement, the representatives of the deceased partner can receive, at their option, interest at the rate of 6% p.a. or the share of profits earned with the use of the amount due to the deceased partner.

Illustration The balance sheet of Seed, Plant and Flower as at 31st December, 1978 was as under :

Liabilities		Rs.	*Assets*	Rs.
Sundry Creditors		20,000	Fixed Assets	40,000
General Reserve		5,000	S. Debtors	10,000
Capitals :			Bills Receivable	4,000
Seed	25,000		Stock	16,000
Plant	15,000		Joint Life Policy	6,000
Flower	15,000	55,000	Cash at Bank	4,000
		80,000		80,000

The joint life policy was for Rs. 30,000 and the premium was payable every year on 1st August. The profit sharing ratio was: Seed 5/10, Plant 3/10 and Flower 2/10. On 1st May, 1969 Plant died. It was agreed that

(*a*) Goodwill should be valued at 3 years' purchase of the average profits for 4 years. The profits were :

1975	Rs. 10,000	1977	Rs. 12,000
1976	Rs. 13,000	1978	Rs. 15,000

(*b*) The deceased partner to be given share of profits up to the date of death on the basis of the profits for the previous year

(*c*) Fixed Assets were to be depreciated by 10%. A bill for Rs. 1,000 was found to be worthless. These are not to affect goodwill.

(*d*) A sum of Rs. 24,950 was to be paid immediately, the balance was to remain as a loan with the firm at 9% p. a.

Seed and Flower agreed to share profits and losses in future in the ratio of 3 : 2. They also agreed that goodwill should not continue to appear in books.

Give journal entries and prepare the balance sheet of Seed and Flower.

Solution :

Journal *Dr.* *Cr.*

Date		Particulars		Dr. Rs.	Cr. Rs.
1979 May	1	Bank Account	Dr.	30,000 —	
		To Joint Life Policy Account			30,000 —
		Amount received against joint life policy on the death of Plant			
	1	Joint Life Policy Account	Dr.	24,000 —	
		To Seed's Capital Account			12,000 —
		To Plant's Capital Account			7,200 —
		To Flower's Capital Account			4,800 —
		Amount standing to the credit of Joint Life Policy Account (Rs. 30,000 less Rs. 6,000) transferred to the credit of capital accounts in the ratio of 5 : 3 : 2.			
	1	General Reserve Account	Dr.	5,000 —	
		To Seed's Capital Account			2,500 —
		To Plant's Capital Account			1,500 —
		To Flower's Capital Account			1,000 —
		General Reserve transferred to capital accounts on the death of Plant			
	1	Goodwill Account	Dr.	37,500 —	
		To Seed's Capital Account			18,750 —
		To Plant's Capital Account			11,250 —
		To Flower's Capital Account			7,500 —
		Goodwill raised at Rs. 37,500 and credited to Capital Accounts Value— $\frac{3(10,000+13,000+12,000+15,000)}{4}$			

Date		Particulars		Rs.		Rs.	
1979 May	1	Revaluation Account	Dr.	5,000	—		
		To Fixed Assets A/c				4,000	—
		To Bills Receivable Account				1,000	—
		Depreciation of fixed assets @ 10% and writing off one bill for Rs. 1,000 on Plant's death					
	1	Seed's Capital Account	Dr.	2,500	—		
		Plant's Capital Account	Dr.	1,500	—		
		Flower's Capital Account	Dr.	1,000	—		
		To Revaluation Account				5,000	—
		Loss on Revaluation transferred to capital accounts					
	1	P. & L. Suspense Account	Dr.	1,500	—		
		To Plant's Capital Account				1,500	—
		Plant's share of four months' profit based on 1978's profits, *i.e.*, Rs. 5,000 credited to his Capital Account.					
	1	Plant's Capital Account	Dr.	34,950	—		
		To Plant's Executors' Accounts				34,950	—
		The amount standing to the credit of Plant's Capital A/c transferred to the credit of his Executors' Account					
	1	Plant's Executors' Account	Dr.	24,950	—		
		To Bank Account				24,950	—
		The amount paid to Plant's Executors					
	1	Seed's Capital Account	Dr.	22,500	—		
		Flower's Capital Account	Dr.	15,000	—		
		To Goodwill Account				37,500	—
		Goodwill written off to Capital Accounts of Seed and Flower in the ratio of 3 : 2, the new ratio					

Balance Sheet of Seed and Flower as at May 1, 1979

Liabilities		Rs.	*Assets*	Rs.
Sundry Creditors		20,000 —	Fixed Assets	36,000 —
Plant's Executors Account—Loan		10,000 —	Sundry Debtors	10,000 —
Capital Accounts:			Bills Receivable	3,000 —
Seed	32,250		Stock	16,000 —
Flower	12,300		Cash at Bank	9,050 —
	———	45,550 —	Profit & Loss Suspense A/c (to be adjusted at the end of the year)	1,500 —
		75,550 —		75,550 —

Note : The student is advised to prepare ledger accounts.

Annuity. Annuity means an annual payment. It may be settled between the remaining partners on the one hand and the retiring partner or the representatives of the deceased partner on the other hand that the claim of the outgoing partner or the deceased partner will be settled in the form of an annual payment as long as the retiring partner lives or say, the widow of the deceased partner lives. If death occurs of these people, payment of annuity will stop and there will be no further claim on the firm. The amount to be paid annually will be usually determined by reference to the prevailing rate of interest and the number of years the person concerned is expected to live according to the mortality tables. This matter can be dealt with in three ways by the remaining partners.

The first method is that the amount due to the retiring or deceased partner is transferred to Annuity Account. The amount paid is debited to this account which is credited with interest at the proper rate (as determined by the partners). The credit balance in this account is treated as a liability and shown in the balance sheet. Should the person receiving the annuity (known as annuitant) die before this account is exhausted, the balance will be a profit to be shared by the partners in their profit sharing ratio. Should the account be exhausted and the annuitant continue to live, the payments made in future will be treated as loss and debited to the Profit and Loss Account.

Illustration Rose, Lily and Marigold were partners sharing profits and losses in the ratio of 2/5, 2/5 and 1/5. Marigold died on 1st January, 1972. The total of his claim upon the firm came to Rs. 40,000. It was decided by mutual agreement that Mrs. Marigold should receive an annuity, taking her future life to be 5 years and taking 5% p.a. as interest. (Annuity Tables show that Re. 1 @ 5% is equal to Re. ·230975 per year for 5 years). The first payment is to be made on 31st December, 1972.

Prepare Annuity Account assuming (1) that Mrs. Marigold died on 1st January, 1966 and (2) that she was still alive on 1st January, 1979.

Solution :

[The annual payment to be made is 40,000 × ·230975 or Rs. 9,239]

Case (I)

Mrs. Marigold's Annuity Account

Dr.		Rs.				Rs.	Cr.
1972				1972			
Dec. 31	To Bank Account	9,239	—	Jan. 1	By Marigold's Capital A/c	40,000	—
"	To Balance c/d	32,761	—	Dec. 31	By Interest Account (5% on Rs. 40,000)	2,000	—
		42,000	—			42,000	—
1973				1973			
Dec. 31	To Bank Account	9,239	—	Jan. 1	By Balance b/d	32,761	—
"	To Balance c/d	25,160	05	Dec. 31	By Interest A/c	1,638	05
		34,399	05			34,399	05
1974				1974			
Dec. 31	To Bank Account	9,239	—	Jan. 1	By Balance b/d	25,160	05
"	To Balance c/d	17,179	05	Dec. 31	By Interest A/c	1,258	—
		26,418	05			26,418	05
1975				1975			
Dec. 31	To Bank Account	9,239	—	Jan. 1	By Balance b/d	17,179	05
"	To Balance c/d	8,799	—	Dec. 31	By Interest A/c	858	95
		18,038	—			18,038	—
1976				1976			
Jan. 1	To Transfer to Capital A/cs—			Jan. 1	By Balance b/d	8,799	—
	Rose (1/2)	4,399	50				
	Lily (1/2)	4,399	50				
		8,799	—			8,799	—

In Case (2), up to 31st December, 1975, the Annuity Account will be as shown above. After that date it will be as under :

Case (II) :

Mrs. Marigold's Annuity Account

Dr.			Cr.		
		Rs.			Rs.
1976 Dec.31	To Bank Account	9,239 —	1966 Jan. 1	By Balance b/d	8,799 —
			Dec.31	By Interest A/c	440 —
		9,239 —			9,239 —
1967 Dec.31	To Bank Account	9,239 —	1967 Dec.31	By Profit & Loss A/c	9,239 —
		9,239 —			9,239 —
1968 Dec.31	To Bank Account	9,239 —	1968 Dec.31	By Profit & Loss A/c	9,239 —

It will be noted that the credit balance in the Annuity Account was exhausted on 31st December, 1966. After that date, the payments are debited to the Annuity Account, but are then transferred to the Profit and Loss Account as a loss.

The second method is to close the capital account of the partner concerned by transfer to the capital accounts of the remaining partners in their profit sharing ratio. In the above illustration, the entry would have been—

		Rs.	Rs.
Marigold's Capital Account	Dr.	40,000	
To Rose's Capital Account			20,000
To Lily's Capital Account			20,000

The annual payment is then debited to the Profit and Loss Account ; thus the remaining partners will automatically be charged with the annuity. If this method is followed care should be taken to bring the liability for future payments into books if there is any charge in the composition of the firm. Suppose, to continue the illustration, Mrs. Marigold is still alive on 1st January, 1969 when the firm admits Petal as a partner, The firm must estimate how many more payments are likely to be made to Mrs. Marigold (by reference to the mortality tables) and discount them at the proper rate of interest so as to find out the liability in terms of 1st January, 1969. A liability should be created for the annuity. The entry will be:

Revaluation Account Dr.
To Liability for Annuity to Mrs. Marigold

This point will also apply if the capital account was transferred to the Annuity Account but if it has been exhausted and the annuitant is still alive.*

The third method is to hand over the necessary amount to a life insurance company who will then assume the liability for the annuity. On payment, the capital account of the partner concerned will be debited. Any balance in the capital account will be treated as profit or loss to be shared by the remaining partners. But the firm will not be concerned at all in future as regards payment to the annuitant.

Amalgamation of Firms

Firms carrying on similar business may join together and set up a new firm to own and run the businesses. This is done with a view to avoiding competition and to securing economies in production and management. When firms join together it is known as amalgamation. If two firms amalgamate. it will necessitate the following treatment in accounts :—

(*a*) Revalue assets and liabilities of each firm separately. Each firm will open a Revaluation Account which will be closed by transfer to the capital accounts of the partners of the firm.

(*b*) Goodwill will be valued and raised in the books of each firm. Naturally the capital accounts of the partners will be credited.

(*c*) If the amalgamated firm is not to take over any asset, it should either be realised in cash or it should be taken over by the partners. The capital accounts of the partners will be debited in the ratio of the capitals (unless otherwise stated) and the asset account credited.

Note : *It is considered proper by many authorities that shares in companies should be taken over by partners in their profit sharing ratio.*

Similarly, if any liability is not to be taken over by the new firm, it will be paid off. If a partner agrees to discharge the liability, his account will be credited and the liability account debited.

(*d*) The new firm will be debited and assets taken over by it credited. Similarly, the accounts of liabilities taken over by the new firm will be debited and the new firm will be credited. This will close the accounts of the assets and liabilities.

(*e*) The capital accounts of the partners (as finally ascertained) will be closed by being debited, the new firm being credited.

These steps will close the books of the old firms. In the books of the new firm, assets taken over will be debited, liabilities

* If pensions are paid to employees, the treatment will be similar in respect of pensions payable in future.

taken over will be credited and capital accounts (as per books of the old firms) will be credited. This will open the books of the new firm.

Illustration The following are the balance sheets of two firms, M/s A and B and M/s X and Y, as on 31st Dec., 1978.

Liabilities	*A & B*	*X & Y*	*Assets*	*A & B*	*X & Y*
	Rs.	Rs.		Rs.	Rs.
Sundary Creditors	16,000	23,000	Land and Buildings	—	50,000
Reserve	10,000	—	Plant and Machiney	20,000	30,000
Capitals :			Patents	10,000	5,000
A 40,000			Stock	25,000	20,000
B 10,000	50,000		Debtors	10,000	16,000
			Invest-ments	5,000	—
X 50,000			Cash	6,000	2,000
Y 50,000		1,00,000			
	76,000	1,23,000		76,000	1,23,000

A and B shared profits and losses in the ratio of 3 : 2 and X and Y shared them equally. The two firms decided to amalgamate. The terms agreed upon were :

(*a*) Investments of A and B were not to be taken over by the new firm but were to be distributed among A and B in the profit sharing ratio.

(*b*) Goodwill of A and B was Rs. 20,000 and that of X and Y Rs. 40,000. Goodwill was not to remain in the books of the new firm.

(*c*) Patents of A and B were valued at Rs. 15,000 and stock at Rs. 30,000. A provision of 8% was to be created on Debtors.

(*d*) The Plant and Machinery of X and Y was to be written down to Rs. 25,000. Stock of X and Y was found over-valued by Rs. 2,000. A book debt of Rs. 1,000 was bad and had to be written off. Patents of X and Y were to be valued at Rs. 8,000.

(*e*) The new profit sharing ratio was to be : A 2/10, B 2/10, X 3/10 and Y 3/10.

(*f*) The total capital of the new firm was to be Rs. 200,000, partners paying in or withdrawing cash as the case may be.

Give journal entries to close books of the old firms and open those of the new one. Also prepare balance sheet after amalgamation.

Solution:

Journal of A and B

Date		Particulars		Dr. Rs.	Cr. Rs.
1978 Dec.	31	Reserve A/c	Dr.	10,000 —	
		To A's Capital Account			6,000 —
		To B's Capital Account			4,000 —
		Reserve transferred to Capital Accounts in the profit sharing ratio			
	31	Goodwill Account	Dr.	20,000 —	
		To A's Capital Account			12,000 —
		To B's Capital Account			8,000 —
		Goodwill raised in books of A & B before amalgamation			
	31	Patents Account	Dr.	5,000 —	
		Stock Account	Dr.	5,000 —	
		To Revaluation Account			10,000 —
		Values of assets raised			
	31	Revaluation Account	Dr.	800 —	
		To Provision for Bad Debts A/c			800 —
		8% provision against debtors raised			
	31	Revaluation Account	Dr.	9,200 —	
		To A's Capital Account			5,520 —
		To B's Capital Account			3,680 —
		Profit on revaluation of assets transferred to Capital Accounts in the ratio of 3 : 2			

Date		Particulars		Dr. Rs.	Cr. Rs.
1978 Dec.	31	A's Capital Account	Dr.	3,000 —	
		B's Capital Account	Dr.	2,000 —	
		To Investments Account			5,000 —
		Investments transferred to he Capital Accounts because A and B have taken them in the ratio of 3 : 2			
	*31	New Firm	Dr.	1,01,000 —	
		To Plant and Machinery			20,000 —
		To Patents A/c			15,000 —
		To Stock A/c			30,000 —
		To Debtors A/c			10,000 —
		To Cash A/c			6,000 —
		To Goodwill A/c			20,000 —
		Assets Transferred to the New Firm at changed values			
	*31	Sundry Creditors	Dr.	16,000 —	
		Provision for Bad Debts A/c	Dr.	800 —	
		To New Firm			16,800 —
		Liabilities and Provision for Bad Debts transferred to New Firm			
	31	A's Capital A/c	Dr.	60,520 —	
		B's Capital A/c	Dr.	23,680 —	
		To New Firm			84,200 —
		Capital accounts of partners closed by transfer to the New Firm			

*The student is advised to first prepare the balance sheet of M/s A & B after revaluation before making the last three entries.

Books of M/s. X and Y

Journal

Date		Particulars		Dr. Rs.		Cr. Rs.	
1978 Dec.	31	Goodwill Account	Dr.	40,000	—		
		To X's Capital Account				20,000	—
		To Y's Capital Account				20,000	—
		Goodwill raised in the books prior to amalgamation					
	31	Revaluation A/c	Dr.	8,000	—		
		To Plant and Machinery A/c				5,000	—
		To Stock A/c				2,000	—
		To Sundry Debtors A/c				1,000	—
		Recording of decrease in value of assets					
	31	Patents A/c	Dr.	3,000	—		
		To Revaluation A/c				3,000	—
		Increase in the value of patents recorded					
	31	X's Capital A/c	Dr.	2,500	—		
		Y's Capital Account	Dr.	2,500	—		
		To Revaluation A/c				5,000	—
		Loss on revaluation transferred to the Capital Accounts					
	31	New Firm	Dr.	1,58,000	—		
		To Land & Buildings A/c				50,000	—
		To Plant & Machinery A/c				25,000	—
		To Patents A/c				8,000	—
		To Stock A/c				18,000	—
		To Debtors A/c				15,000	—
		To Cash A/c				2,000	—
		To Goodwill A/c				40,000	—
		Assets transferred to the New Firm					
	31	Sundry Creditors	Dr.	23,000	—		
		To New Firm				23,000	—
		Sundry creditors transferred to the New Firm					
	31	X's Capital Account	Dr.	67,500	—		
		Y's Capital Account	Dr.	67,500	—		
		To New Firm				1,35,000	—
		Capital Accounts of partners closed by transfer to the New Firm					

Books of the New Firm

Date		Particulars		Dr. Rs.	Cr. Rs.
1978 Dec.	31	Plant & Machinery A/c	Dr.	20,000 —	
		Patents A/c	Dr.	15,000 —	
		Stock A/c	Dr.	30,000 —	
		Debtors A/c	Dr.	10,000 —	
		Cash A/c	Dr.	6,000 —	
		Goodwill A/c	Dr.	20,000 —	
		To Sundry Creditors			16,000 —
		To Provision for Bad Debts A/c			800 —
		To A's Capital A/c			60,520 —
		To B's Capital A/c			23,680 —
		Various assets and liabilities taken over from A & B			
	,,	Land & Building A/c	Dr.	50,000 —	
		Plant & Machinery A/c	Dr.	25,000 —	
		Patents A/c	Dr.	8,000 —	
		Stock A/c	Dr.	18,000 —	
		Debtors A/c	Dr.	15,000 —	
		Cash A/c	Dr.	2,000 —	
		Goodwill A/c	Dr.	40,000 —	
		To Sundry Creditors			23,000 —
		To X's Capital A/c			67,500 —
		To Y's Capital A/c			67,500 —
		Various assets and liabilities taken over from X & Y			
	,,	A's Capital A/c	Dr.	12,000 —	
		B's Capital A/c	Dr.	12,000 —	
		X's Capital A/c	Dr.	18,000 —	
		Y's Capital A/c	Dr.	18,000 —	
		To Goodwill A/c			60,000 —
		Goodwill Account written off to all partners in the new profit sharing ratio			
	,,	Cash A/c	Dr.	28,320 —	
		To B's Capital A/c			28,320 —
		Cash brought in by B to bring up his capital to Rs. 40,000 *i.e.*, 2/10 of Rs. 2,00,000			
	,,	A's Capital Account	Dr.	8,520 —	
		To Cash Account			8,520 —
		Cash paid to bring down his capital to Rs. 40,000, *i.e.*, 2/10 of Rs. 2,00,000			

				Rs.		Rs.	
1978 Dec.	31	Cash Account	Dr.	21,000	—		
		To X's Capital A/c				10,500	—
		To Y's Capital A/c				10,500	—
		Cash brought in by X and Y to make up capital to Rs. 60,000 each, *i.e.*, 3/10 of Rs. 2,00,0000					

Balance Sheet of the New Firm as at Dec. 31, 1968

Liabilities		Rs.		*Assets*		Rs.	
Sundry Creditors		39,000	—	**Fixed Assets :**			
Capital Accounts :				Land & Buildings		50,000	—
A	40,000			Plant & Machinery		45,000	—
B	40,000			Patents		23,000	—
X	60,000			**Current Assets :**			
Y	60,000			Stock		48,000	—
		2,00,000	—	Debtors	25,000		
				Less Provision	800		
						24,200	—
				Cash		48,800	—
		2,39,000	—			2,39,000	—

DISSOLUTION OF FIRMS

A partnership is dissolved or comes to an end on —

(*a*) the expiry of the term for which it was formed;

(*b*) the completion of the venture for which it was entered, into;

(*c*) the death of a partner;

(*d*) the insolvency of a partner; and

(*e*) the retirement of a partner.

However, the partners or remaining partners (in case of death, insolvency or retirement) may continue to do the business. In such a case there will be a new partnership but the firm will continue. When the business also comes to an end then only will it be said that the firm has been dissolved.

A firm stands dissolved in the following cases :—

(*i*) the partners agree that the firm should be dissolved;

(*ii*) all partners except one become insolvent;

(*iii*) the business becomes illegal;

(*iv*) in case of partnership at will, a partner gives notice of dissolution; and

(*v*) the court orders dissolution.

The court has the option to order dissolution of a firm in the following circumstances :—

(*a*) where a partner has become of unsound mind;

(*b*) where a partner suffers from permanent incapacity;

(*c*) where a partner is guilty of misconduct affecting the business;

(*d*) where a partner persistently disregards the partnership agreement;

(*e*) where a partner transfers his intrerest or share to a third party;

(*f*) where the business cannot be carried on except at a loss; and

(*g*) where it appears to be just and equitable.

Settlement of accounts. The assets of the firm have to be applied in the following order :

(1) in paying debts due to third parties;

(2) in paying rateably advances or loans made by partners (over and above the capitals contributed by them) to the firm; and

(3) in paying the partners of sums due to them on account of capital.

If there is still some surplus, it has to be distributed among the partners in the profit sharing ratio. The above means that the amount realised by sale of the firm's assets should be used first to pay outsiders, then to repay loans taken from partners and then only to repay capitals of the partners.

The losses of the firm on dissolution have to be made up,

(*a*) first out of past accumulated profits;

(*b*) then out of capitals of the partners; and

(*c*) if the loss is still not covered fully, out of contributions from the private estates of the partners in the profit sharing ratio.

The private property of a partner is to be used first to pay his private debts and only the surplus, if any, can be used to pay firm's liabilities. Similarly, firm's assets are first used to pay firm's liabilities. A partner can use only his share of the surplus to pay his private liabilities.

Entries to close the books. We will illustrate the entries to be made for closing the books of a firm with the example given below.

Balance Sheet of Fast and Quick as at Dec. 31, 1978

Liabilities		Rs.	*Assets*		Rs.
Sundry Creditors		20,000	Plant and Machinery		40,000
Fast's Loan		10,000	Patents		6,000
General Reserve		10,000	Stock		25,000
Capitals :			Sundry Debtors		
				Rs. 19,000	
Fast	Rs. 30,000		*Less* Provision		
Quick	Rs. 25,000		for Bad Debts		
		55,000		Rs. 1,000	
					18,000
			Cash		6,000
		95,000			95,000

Fast and Quick shared profits in the ratio of 3 : 2. On 1st January, 1969 the firm was dissolved. Fast took over the patents at a valuation of Rs. 5,000. The other assets realised as under :

	Rs.
Goodwill	15,000
Plant & Machinery	30,000
Stock	22,000
Sundry Debtors	18,500
Total	85,500

The Sundry Creditors were paid off at a discount of 5%. The expenses amounted to Rs. 3,500.

The steps to close the books are given below :

I. Open a Realisation Account and transfer all assets except cash in hand or at bank *at book values*. Realisation Account is debited and the various asset accounts are credited and thus closed. It should be remembered that Sundry Debtors and Provision for Bad Debts Accounts are two separate accounts and the gross amount of debtors should be transferred. In the above example the entry will be :

		Rs.	Rs.
Realisation Account	Dr.	90,000	
To Plant & Machinery A/c			40,000
To Patents A/c			6,000
To Stock A/c			25,000
To Sundry Debtors			19,000
Transfer of various assets to the debit side of Realisation A/c			

II. Transfer liabilities to outsiders and provisions and reserves against assets (*e.g.*, Provision for Doubtful Debts) to the credit side of the Realisation Account. The accounts of the liabilities and provisions will be debited and thus closed. The entry should be made at *book figures*. Thus

Sundry Creditors Account	Dr.	20,000	
Provision for Bad Debts Account	Dr.	1,000	
To Realisation Account			21,000
Transfer of liabilities to outsiders and provision against debtors to Realisation Account.			

Note. Accounts denoting accumulated losses or profits should not be transferred to the Realisation Account.

III. (*i*) The Realisation Account should be credited with the actual amount realised by sale of assets. This should take no note of the book figures. Of course, Cash (or Bank) Account will be debited. Thus—

Cash Account	Dr.	85,500	
To Realisation Account			85,500
Amount realised by sale of various assets.			

(*ii*) If a partner takes over an asset, his capital account should be debited and Realisation Account credited with the *value agreed upon*. Thus—

Fast's Capital Account	Dr.	5,000	
To Realisation Account			5,000
Patents taken over by Fast at Rs. 5,000.			

IV. Expenses of dissolution or realisation of assets are debited to the Realisation Account and credited to Cash Account. Thus—

Realisation Account	Dr.	3,500	
To Cash Account			3,500
Payment of expenses			

V. (*i*) The actual amount paid to creditors should be debited to the Realisation Account. Cash Account is credited. Thus—

Realisation Account	Dr.	19,000	
To Cash Account			19,000
Payment to Sundry Creditors, Rs. 20,000 less 5%.			

(*ii*) If any liability is taken over by a partner, his Capital Account should be credited and Realisation Account debited with the amount agreed upon.

VI. At this stage, the Realisation Account will show profit or loss. If the debit side is bigger, there is a loss; if the credit side is bigger, there is a profit. Profit or loss is transferred to the Capital Accounts of partners in the profit sharing ratio. In case of profit, Realisation Account is debited and Capital Accounts credited. The entry for loss is, naturally, reverse of this. The Realisation Account in the example given above shows a loss of Rs. 1,000 (*see* account below). The entry is :

Fast's Capital Account	Dr.	600	
Quick's Capital Account	Dr.	400	
To Realisation Account			1,000
Transfer of loss to Capital Accounts in the ratio of 3 : 2.			

VII. Partner's Loans, if any, should now be paid. The entry is to debit the Loan Account and Credit Cash Account. Thus—

Fast's Loan Account	Dr.	10,000	
To Cash Account			10,000
Repayment of Fast's Loan.			

VIII. Any reserve or accumulated profit or loss lying in the books (as shown by the Balance Sheet) should be transferred to the Capital Account in the profit sharing ratios. Thus—

General Reserve	Dr.	10,000	
To Fast's Capital Account			6,000
To Quick's Capital Account			4,000
General Reserve transferred to Capital Accounts in the ratio of 3 : 2.			

IX. At this stage, the Capital Accounts will show how much amount is due to them or from them. A partner owing money to the firm will pay; Cash Account will be debited and his Capital Account credited and thus closed. Money owing to a partner will be paid to him; his Capital Account will be debited and the Cash Account credited. This will close the Capital Accounts as well as the

Cash Account. The entry in the above example is (*see* Capital Accounts below).

Fast's Capital Account Dr.	30,400	
Quick's Capital Account Dr.	28,600	
To Cash Account		59,000
Amounts paid to partners on capital account.		

Ledger Accounts

Plant and Machinery Account

Dr. *Cr.*

Date	Particulars	Rs.	Date	Particulars	Rs.
1979 Jan. 1	To Balance b/d	40,000 —	1979 Jan. 1	By Realisation A/c—Transfer	40,000 —

Patents Account

Date	Particulars	Rs.	Date	Particulars	Rs.
1979 Jan. 1	To Balance b/d	6,000 —	1979 Jan. 1	By Realisation A/c—Transfer	6,000 —

Stock Accounts

Date	Particulars	Rs.	Date	Particulars	Rs.
1979 Jan. 1	To Balance b/d	25,000 —	1979 Jan. 1	By Realisation A/c—Transfer	25,000 —

Sundry Debtors Account

Date	Particulars	Rs.	Date	Particulars	Rs.
1979 Jan. 1	To Balance b/d	19,000 —	1979 Jan. 1	By Realisation A/c—Transfer	19,000 —

Provision for Bad Debts Account

Date	Particulars	Rs.	Date	Particulars	Rs.
1979 Jan. 1	To Realisation A/c—Transfer	1,000 —	1979 Jan. 1	By Balance b/d	1,000 —

Sundry Creditors Account

Date	Particulars	Rs.	Date	Particulars	Rs.
1979 Jan. 1	To Realisation A/c—Transfer	20,000 —	1979 Jan. 1	By Balance b/d	20,000 —

Fast's Loan Account

Date	Particulars	Rs.	Date	Particulars	Rs.
1979 Jan. 1	To Cash Accoun	10,000 —	1979 Jan. 1	By Balance b/d	10,000 —

General Reserve Account

Dr. *Cr.*

Date	Particulars	Rs.	Date	Particulars	Rs.
1979 Jan. 1	To Capital A/c— Transfer to: Fast 6,000 Quick 4,000	10,000 —	1979 Jan. 1	By Balance b/d	10,000 —
		10,000 —			10,000 —

Realisation Account

Date	Particulars	Rs.	Date	Particulars	Rs.
1979 Jan. 1	To Sundry Assets—		1979 Jan. 1	By Sundry Creditors	20,000 —
	Plant and Machinery	40,000 —	"	By Provision for Bad Debts A/c	1,000 —
	Patents	6,000 —			
	Stock	25,000 —	"	By Cash Account—assets realised	85,500 —
	Sundry Debtors	19,000 —			
"	To Cash Account—Expenses	3,500 —	"	By Fast's Capital A/c—patents taken over	5,000 —
"	To Cash Account—Creditors paid	19,000 —	"	By Loss to: Fast 600 Quick 400	1,000 —
		1,12,500 —			1,12,500 —

Cash Account

Date	Particulars	Rs.	Date	Particulars	Rs.
1979 Jan. 1	To Balance b/d	6,000 —	1979 Jan. 1	By Realisation A/c—Expenses	3,500 —
"	To Realisation A/c	85,500 —	"	By Realisation A/c—Creditors	19,000 —
			"	By Fast's Loan A/c	10,000 —
			"	By Fast's Capital A/c	30,400 —
				By Quick's Capital A/c	28,600 —
		91,500 —			91,500 —

Fast's Capital Account

		Rs.				Rs.
1979 Jan. 1	To Realisation A/c—patents	5,000	1979 Jan. 1	By Balance b/d		30,000
	To Realisation A/c—loss	600	,,	By General Reserve		6,000
	To Cash Account	30,400				
		36,000				36,000

Quick's Capital Account

		Rs.			Rs.
1979 Jan. 1	To Realisation A/c—loss	400	1979 Jan. 1	By Balance b/d	25,000
	To Cash Account	28,600		By General Reserve	4,000
		29,000			29,000

Illustration Bat, Ball and Wicket were carrying on business as manufacturers of sports goods. The profit sharing ratio was 3 : 2 : 1 respectively. Their balance sheet on 31st December, 1977 was as under :

Liabilities		Rs.	*Assets*		Rs.
Sundry Creditors		15,000	Plant and Machinery		16,000
Mrs. Bat's Loan		13,000	Stock		15,000
Repairs & Renewals			Sundry Debtors	20,000	
Reserve		1,200	Less Provision	1,000	19,000
Capitals :					
Bat	10,000		Prepaid Insurance		400
Ball	15,000		Investments		3,000
Wicket	2,000	27,000	Cash		2,800
		56,200			56,200

On this date the firm was dissolved. The assets realised as under :

	Rs.
Plant & Machinery	10,000
Stock	12,000
Sundry Debtors	16,000

The investments were taken over by Bat at a value of Rs. 2,000. He also agreed to pay Mrs. Bat's Loan. During the course of realization it was found that a bill for Rs. 5,000 previously discounted by the firm was dishonoured and had to be paid. Expenses came to Rs. 800.

Give ledger accounts to close the books of the firm.

Solution :

Realisation Account

Dr. *Cr.*

1977			Rs.	1977			Rs.
Dec.31	To Sundry Assets—			Dec.31	By Sundry Crs.		15,000 —
	Plant and Machinery		16,000		By Mrs. Bat's Loan		13,000 —
	Stock		15,000 —		By Provision		1,000 —
	Sundry Debtors		20,000 —		By Cash A/c (assets realised)		38,000 —
	Prepaid Insurance		400 —		By Bat's Capital A/c (Investments)		2,000 —
	Investments		3,000 —		By Capital A/cs (Loss)		
	To Cash A/c				Bat	9,600	
	Creditors	15,000			Ball	6,400	
	Bill Dishonoured	5,000			Wicket	3,200	
			20,000 —				19,200 —
	To Cash A/c—expenses		800 —				
	To Bat's Capital A/c—(Mrs. Bat's Loan)		13,000 —				
			88,200				88,200 —

Cash Account

1977		Rs.	1977		Rs.
Dec.31	To Balance b/d	2,800 —	Dec.31	By Realisation A/c—Creditors	20,000 —
	To Realisation A/c : assets realised	38,000 —		By Realisation A/c—expenses	800 —
	To Wicket's Capital A/c (amount due from him)	1,000 —		By Bat's Capital A/c	12,000 —
				By Ball's Capital A/c	9,000 —
		41,800			41,800 —

Repairs and Renewals Reserve Account

1977		Rs.	1977		Rs.
Dec. 31	To Transfer to Capital A/cs— Bat 600, Ball 400, Wicket 200	1,200	Dec. 31	By Balance b/d	1,200
		1,200			1,200

Bat's Capital Account

1977		Rs.	1977		Rs.
Dec. 31	To Realisation A/c—Investments	2,000	Dec. 31	By Balance b/d	10,000
	To Realisation A/c—loss	9,600	,,	By Repairs & Renewals Reserve	600
	To Cash A/c	12,000	,,	By Realisation A/c—Mrs. Bat's Loan	13,000
		23,600			23,600

Ball's Capital Account

1977		Rs.	1977		Rs.
Dec. 31	To Realisation A/c—loss	6,400	Dec. 31	By Balance b/d	15,000
	To Cash A/c	9,000		By Repairs & Renewals Reserve	400
		15,400			15,400

Wicket's Capital Account

1977		Rs.	1977		Rs.
Dec. 31	To Realisation A/c—loss	3,200	Dec. 31	By Balance b/d	2,000
				By Repairs & Renewals Reserve	200
				By Cash Account	1,000
		3,200			3,200

Note. Since the firm is being dissolved, Repairs and Renewals Reserve will no longer be required and hence it is a profit to be credited to capital accounts of partners in the profit sharing ratio.

Illustration Akbar, Ali and Wahid commenced business on 1st January, 1978 sharing profits and losses in the ratio of 2 : 2 : 1. Capitals contributed were : Akbar, Rs. 40,000; Ali, Rs.30,000 ; and Wahid, Rs. 20,000. The partners were entitled to interest @ 6% p.a.

During the year the firm earned a profit (before interest) of Rs. 25,000. The partners had drawn : Akbar Rs. 10,000 ; Ali Rs. 8,000; and Wahid Rs. 5,000.

On 31st December, 1978 the firm was dissolved. The assets realised Rs. 1,00,000. The creditors which totalled Rs. 15,000 were paid at a discount of 3%. Expenses of realisation totalled Rs. 1,450.

Prepare accounts to close the books of the firm.

Solution :

Akbar's Capital Account

Dr. *Cr.*

Date	Particulars	Rs.	Date	Particulars	Rs.
1978 Dec.31	To Drawings	10,000	1978 Jan. 1	By Cash A/c	40,000
,,	To Balance c/d	40,240	Dec.31	By P. & L. A/c—Interest	2,400
			,,	By P. & L. A/c—Share of profit	7,840
		50,240			50,240
1978 Dec.31	To Realisation A/c—loss	3,200	1978 Dec.31	By Balance b/d	40,240
,,	To Cash A/c	37,040			
		40,240			40,240

Ali's Capital Account

Date	Particulars	Rs.	Date	Particulars	Rs.
1978 Dec.31	To Drawings A/c	8,000	1978 Jan. 1	By Cash A/c	30,000
,,	To Balance c/d	31,640	Dec.31	By P. & L. A/c—Interest	1,800
			,,	By P. & L. A/c—Profit	7,840
		39,640			39,640
1978 Dec.31	To Realisation A/c—loss	3,200	1978 Dec.31	By Balance b/d	31,640
	To Cash A/c	28,440			
		31,640			316.40

Wahid's Capital Account

		Rs.			Rs.
1978 Dec.31	To Drawings A/c	5,000 —	1978 Jan. 1	By Cash A/c	20,000 —
„	To Balance c/d	20,120 —	Dec.31	By P. & L. A/c—Interest	1,200 —
			„	By P. & L. A/c—Profit	3,920 —
		25,120 —			25,120 —
1978 Dec.31	To Realisation A/c—loss	1,600 —	1978 Dec.31	By Balance b/d	20,120 —
„	To Cash A/c	18,520 —			
		20,120 —			20,120 —

Profit and Loss Account

			Rs.			Rs.
1978 Dec.31	To Capital A/cs— Interest :			1978 Dec.31	By Net Profit	25,000 —
	Akbar	2,400				
	Ali	1,800				
	Wahid	1,200	5,400 —			
	To Profit transferred to :					
	Akbar	7,840				
	Ali	7,840				
	Wahid	3,920	19,600 —			
			25,000 —			25,000 —

Balance Sheet as at 31st Dec. 1978

		Rs.		Rs.
Sundry Creditors		15,000 —	Sundry Assets	1,07,000 —
Capital A/cs :				
Akbar	40,240			
Ali	31,640			
Wahid	20,120	92,000 —		
		1,07,000		1,07,000 —

Realisation Account

1978		Rs.	1978		Rs.
Dec.31	To Sundry Assets	1,07,000	Dec.31	By Sundry Creditors	15,000
	To Cash A/c —Expenses	1,450		By Cash A/c	1,00,000
	To Cash A/c—Creditors (Rs. 15,000 less 3%)	14,550		By Loss transferred to: Akbar 3,200; Ali 3,200; Wahid 1,600	8000
		1,23,000			1,23,000

Cash Account

1978		Rs.	1978		Rs-
Dec.31	To Realisation A/c (assets realised)	1,00,000	Dec.31	By Realisation A/c—Expenses	1,450
				By Realisation A/c—Creditors	14,550
				By Capital A/cs :	
				Akbar	37,040
				Ali	28,440
				Wahid	18,520
		1,00,000			1,00,000

Sale to a company. Often partners form a joint stock company to take over their business or they may sell their business to an existing company. The partners usually receive shares and cash as purchase consideration. Shares are divided among partners in the ratio of their final claims. There is really no new problem in closing the books of the firm in case of sale to a company. The steps are :—

1. Transfer assets to Realisation Account. If the company takes over cash, it will also be transferred to this Account.

2. Transfer liabilities to the Realisation Account.

3. Debit Shares Account (with the value of shares received) from the company and Cash Account (with cash received) and credit the Realisation Account.

4. If any asset is to be realised by the firm itself (*i.e.*, not take over by the company), debit Cash Account and credi Realisation Account with the amount realised. If an asse is taken over by a partner, his Capital Account should b debited and Realisation Account credited with the valu agreed upon.
5. Expenses payable by the firm should be debited to th Realisation Account and credited to Cash Account Expenses payable by the company should be ignored in th books of the firm.
6. If any liability is to be paid by the firm (*i.e.*, not take over by the company), the Realisation Account should b debited and Cash Account credited with the amoun actually paid.
7. Profit or loss on realisation should be transferred to th Capital Accounts in the profit sharing ratio. Similarly an accumulated profit or reserve lying in the books of th firm should be transferred to the Capital Accounts in th profit sharing ratio. This will determine the amount du to each partner.
8. Shares received from the company should be distribute among partners in the ratio of amounts due. Thus if A and B have to get Rs. 10,000 and Rs. 5,000 respectivel and if their profit sharing ratio is 3 : 2, they will divid the shares in the ratio of 10 : 5*. Further, care should b taken to give whole numbers of shares. Fractions of share cannot be issued. If a partner's share comes to 116 shares, he should be given 117 shares. The amount involve should be debited to Capital Accounts and credited t Shares Account.
9. Final settlement will be made in cash. Debit Capita Accounts and credit Cash Account.

These steps should close all accounts and books of the firm.

Illustration Following is the Balance Sheet of Vikram an Hanif as at 1st January, 1978.

Liabilities		Rs.	*Assets*		R
Sundry Creditors		16,000	Stock		20,00
General Reserve		6,000	Furniture		5,00
Capitals :	Rs.		Sundry Debtors	15,000	
Vikram	20,000		Less Provision	750	14,25
Hanif	15,000	35,000	Cash		2,75
Mrs. Hanif's Loan		3,000	Plant & Machinery		18,00
		60,000			60,00

*It should be noted that many authorities believe and recommend th partners should divide the shares among themselves in the profit sharing ratio.

The business was taken over by a joint stock company. It issued 3,000 shares of Rs. 10 each (fully paid) and paid Rs. 10,000, in cash. Close the books of the firm by giving ledger accounts. Assume that there were no expenses. The company did not take over Mrs. Hanif's Loan; it was paid by the firm.

Solution :

Realisation Account

Dr. *Cr.*

Date	Particulars	Rs.		Date	Particulars	Rs.	
1978 Jan. 1	To Sundry Assets—			1978 Jan. 1	By Provision A/c	750	—
	Stock	20,000	—	„	By Sundry Creditors	16,000	—
	Furniture	5,000	—	„	By Mrs. Hanif's Loan	3,000	—
	Sundry Debtors	15,000	—	„	By Shares A/c	30,000	—
	Cash	2,750	—	„	By Cash A/c	10,000	—
	Plant and Machinery	18,000	—	„	By Loss to Capital A/c: Vikram 2,000 Hanif 2,000	4,000	—
	To Cash A/c— Mrs. Hanif's Loan	3,000	—				
		63,750	—			63,750	—

Cash Account

Date	Particulars	Rs.		Date	Particulars	Rs.	
1978 Jan. 1	To Balance b/d	2,750	—	1978 Jan. 1	By Transfer to Realisation A/c	2,750	—
„	To Realisation A/c (cash received from company)	10,000	—	„	By Realisation A/c — Mrs. Hanif's Loan	3,000	—
				„	By Vikram's Capital A/c	4,420	—
				„	By Hanif's Capital A/c	2,580	—
		12,750	—			12,750	—

General Reserve

1978		Rs.		1978		Rs.	
Jan. 1	To Transfer to Capital A/cs—			Jan. 1	By Balance b/d	6,000	—
	Vikram	3,000	—				
	Hanif	3,000	—				
		6,000	—			6,000	—

Vikram's Capital Account

1978		Rs.		1978		Rs.	
Jan.	To Realisation A/c—loss	2,000	—	Jan. 1	By Balance b/d	20,000	—
"	To Shares A/c	16,580	—	"	By General Reserve	3,000	—
"	To Cash A/c	4,420	—				
		23,000	—			23,000	—

Hanif's Capital Account

1978		Rs.		1978		Rs.	
Jan. 1	To Realisation A/c—Loss	2,000	—	Jan. 1	By Balance b/d	15,000	—
"	To Shares A/c	13,420	—	"	By General Reserve	3,000	—
	To Cash A/c	2,580	—				
		18,000	—			18,000	—

Shares Account

1978		Rs.		1978		Rs.	
Jan. 1	To Realisation A/c	30,000	—	Jan. 1	By Vikram's Capital A/c	16,580	—
					By Hanif's Capital A/c	13,420	—
		30,000	—			30,000	—

Notes. (1) In absence of agreement, both partners are equal.

(2) 3,000 shares will be divided among Vikram and Hanif in the ratio of final claims, *viz.*, Rs. 21,000 and Rs. 17,000 (for instance, for Vikram 15,000+3,000−2,000). The number of shares comes to 1,658 for Vikram and 1,342 for Hanif. The amount is Rs. 16,580 and Rs. 13,420 respectively.

Illustration Parker and Pelican, sharing profits in the ratio of 2 : 1, sold their business to a joint stock company Swan Ltd. on 1st July, 1979. On this date the Balance Sheet of the firm was as follows :

	Rs.		Rs.
Creditors	20,000	Plant	20,000
Capital :		Furniture	3,000
Parker	50,000	Investments	15,000
Pelican	30,000	Stock	25,000
		Debtors	30,000
		Cash at Bank	7,000
	1,00,000		1,00,000

The company did not take over investments which were distributed among the partners in the profit sharing ratio. The valuation put was :

	Rs.
Goodwill	15,000
Plant	18,000
Furniture	3,000
Stock	28,000
Debtors	27,000
Creditors	18,000

The company issued 6,000 shares of Rs. 10 each fully paid and paid the balance in cash. The firm's bank balance was not taken over. Expenses of Rs. 2,500 were paid by Swan Ltd. Close the books of the firm, journal entries are not required.

Solution :

Note. The total value of assets taken over by Swan Ltd. is Rs. 91,000. The amount of liabilities is Rs. 18,000. Hence the purchase consideration is Rs. 73,000. The company will give shares worth Rs. 60,000 and will pay Rs. 13,000 in cash.

Realisation Account*

Dr.							*Cr.*
		Rs.				Rs.	
1978 July 1	To Sundry Assets— Plant	20,000	—	1979 Ju y 1	By Sundry Creditors	20,000	—
	Furniture	3,000	—		By Shares in Swan Ltd.	60,000	—
	Stock	25,000	—		By Bank A/c	13,000	—
	Debtors	30,000	—				
"	To Profit transferred to Capital A/cs— Parker 10,000 Pelican 5,000	15,000	—				
		93,000	—			93,000	—

Investments Account

		Rs.				Rs.	
1979 July 1	To Balance b/d	15,000	—	1979 July 1	By Capital A/cs— Parker (2/3)	10,000	—
					Pelican (1/3)	5,000	—
		15,000	—			15,000	—

Bank Account

		Rs.				Rs.	
1979 July 1	To Balance b/d	7,000	—	1979 July 1	By Parker's Capital A/c	12,500	—
"	To Realisation A/c	13,000	—	"	By Pelican's Capita A/c	7,500	—
		20,000	—			20,000	—

*Investments Account has not been transferred to the Realisation Account because investments have been divided specially among partners at book value.

Shares in Swan Ltd.

Date	Particulars	Rs.		Date	Particulars	Rs.	
1979 July 1	To Realisation A/c	60,000	—	1979 July 1	By Parker's Capital A/c (5/8)	37,500	—
					By Pelican's Capital A/c (3/8)	22,500	—
		60,000	—			60,000	—

Parker's Capital Account

Date	Particulars	Rs.		Date	Particulars	Rs.	
1979 July 1	To Investments A/c	10,000	—	1979 July 1	By Balance b/d	50,000	—
"	To Shares in Swan Ltd.	37,500	—	"	By Realisation A/c—Profit	10,000	—
	To Bank A/c	12,500	—				
		60,000	—			60,000	—

Pelican's Capital Account

Date	Particulars	Rs.		Date	Particulars	Rs.	
1979 July 1	To Investments A/c	5,000	—	1979 July 1	By Balance b/d	30,000	—
"	To Shares in Swan Ltd.	22,500	—	"	By Realisation A/c—Profit	5,000	—
"	To Bank A/c	7,500	—				
		35,000	—			35,000	—

Insolvency of a partner. If there are two partners and one of them is insolvent, then the solvent partner will have to bear all the loss that there might be because of the insolvency of the other partner. Suppose the position after realisation of assets is :

	Rs.		Rs.
A's capital	15,000	Loss on Realisation	10,000
B's capital	2,000	Cash	7,000
	17,000		17,000

A and B share in the ratio of 3 : 2. In that case the loss on realisation will be debited to A, Rs. 6,000 and to B, Rs. 4,000 converting B's credit balance into a debit balance of Rs. 2,000. If B is solvent he will pay Rs. 2,000 and thus A will get Rs. 9,000. But if B is insolvent, the Rs. 2,000 payable by B will be a loss and will have to be transferred to the debit of A's Capital Account. This will reduce his credit balance to Rs. 7,000 and thus he will get Rs. 7,000 only.

The position is more complicated when there are two or more solvent partners and the others are insolvent. If the capital accounts of the insolvent partners show a debit balance (and thus loss to the firm), the question arises as to whether this loss is like the other losses to be borne in the profit sharing ratio or whether it is a special loss to be dealt with differently. Before the decision in Garner *vs* Murray, it was thought that the loss due to insolvency of a partner was an ordinary loss and was to be borne by the other partners in the profit sharing ratio. Suppose, the position of a firm after realisation is :

	Rs.		Rs.
A's Capital	10,000	C's Capital	3,000
B's Capital	5,000	Cash	12,000
	15,000		15,000

All partners share equally. If C is unable to contribute anything, the amount of Rs. 3,000 owing from him will be a loss and this loss (*before Garner* vs. *Murray*) will be shared by A and B equally Thus A will get Rs. 8,500, *i.e*,, Rs. 10,000 minus Rs. 1,500 and B will get Rs. 3,500, *i.e.*, Rs. 5,000 minus Rs. 1,500.

Garner *vs.* Murray. The decision in Garner *vs.* Murray changed **the position outlined above.** The judgment laid down the following **rules** :—

(*a*) Solvent partners should bring cash equal to their share of the loss or realisation ;

(*b*) The loss on account of the insolvent partner should be borne in the ratio of capitals after (*a*).

The net result is that the loss due to the insolvency of a partner is not to be shared by the solvent partners in the ratio in which they share profits or losses but in the ratio of capitals *just before dissolution* In the above example, the loss on account of C's insolvency will be debited to A and B in the ratio of 10 : 5. Thus A will be debited with Rs. 2,000 and B with Rs. 1,000. A will get Rs. 8,000 and B will get Rs. 4,000.

It follows from the above that should a solvent partner's capital account show a debit balance he will not be responsible for loss due to an insolvent partner. This is so even if he is richer than the other solvent partners.

Fixed and fluctuating capitals. The loss on account of an insolvent partner has to be borne in the ratio of capitals just before dissolution. This raises another point. Often adjustments are to be made in the Capital Accounts, for example, for undistributed profits On dissolution, such profits must be distributed. This will change the capitals. If the capitals are fixed, the adjustments will be made in the current accounts really and hence the capitals will not be changed. Therefore, the ratio for distributing loss due to an insolvent partner will not change because of undistributed profits or reserves. If the capitals are fluctuating the undistributed profits or reserves (or other adjustments prior to dissolution) will change capitals and also the ratio for sharing the insolvent partner's loss. Suppose after realisation, the position is:

	Rs.		Rs.
A's Capital	10,000	C's Capital	5,000
B's Capital	5,000	Cash	16,000
Reserve	6,000		
	21,000		21,000

Reserve has to be credited to all partners (who are presumably equal). A's capital account becomes Rs. 12,000 ; B's capital account will be Rs. 7,000 and C's capital account will show a debit balance of Rs. 3,000. If the capitals are fixed, C's loss (Rs. 3,000) will be borne by A and B in the ratio of 10 : 5. But if the capitals are fluctuating, the ratio will be 12 : 7.

Illustration P, Q and R were sharing profits and losses in the ratio of 5 : 3 : 2. On 1st January, 1978 their balance sheet was as under :

Liabilities		Rs.	*Assets*		Rs.
Sundry Creditors		11,500	Furniture & Fixtures		3,000
General Reserve		5,000	Stock		13,000
Capital Accounts :			Debtors	20,000	
			Less Provision	1,000	19,000
P	10,000				
Q	8,000		Cash		1,000
R	1,500	19,500			
		36,000			36,000

The firm was dissolved on that date. The assets realised as under :

	Rs.
Furniture & Fixture	1,000
Stock	10,000
Debtors	12,000

Rs. 500 of the creditors were not to be paid and the remaining creditors were paid at a discount of 5%. It was found, however, that there was a liability for Rs. 3,050 for damages which had to be paid. The expenses came to Rs. 1,000. R could contribute only Rs. 100. Give ledger accounts to close the books of the firm.

Solution :

Realisation Account

Dr. *Cr.*

		Rs.			Rs.
1978			1978		
Jan. 1	To S. Assets : Furniture & Fixtures Stock Debtors	3,000 13,000 20,000	Jan. 1	By Provision against Debtors	1,000
"	To Cash A/c—Expenses	1,000	"	By Sundry Creditors	11,500
"	To Cash A/c—Liabilities (Rs. 11,000 less 5%)	10,450	"	By Cash Account (assets realised)	23,000
"	To Cash A/c—Damages	3,050	"	By Loss transferred to Capital A/cs— P 5/10 7,500 Q 3/10 4,500 R 2/10 3,000	15,000
		50,500			50,500

Cash Account

		Rs.			Rs.
1978			1978		
Jan. 1	To Balance b/d	1,000	Jan. 1	By Realisation A/c : Expenses Creditors Damages	 1,000 10,450 3,050
"	To Realisation A/c	23,000	"	By P's Capital A/c	12,273
"	To R's Capital A/c	100	"	By Q's Capital A/c	9,327
"	To P's Capital A/c (loss on realisation)	7,500			
"	To Q's Capital (loss on realisation)	4,500			
		36,100			36,100

P's Capital Account

		Rs.			Rs.
1978			1978		
Jan. 1	To Realisation A/c —loss	7,500	Jan. 1	By Balance b/d	10,000
"	To R's Capital A/c	227	"	By General Reserve	2,500
"	To Cash Account	12,273	"	By Cash Account	7,500
		20,000			20,000

Q's Capital Account

		Rs.			Rs.
1978 Jan. 1	To Realisation A/c —loss	4,500	1978 Jan. 1	By Balance b/d	8,000
"	To R's Capital A/c	173	"	By General Reserve	1,500
,,	To Cash Account	9,327	"	By Cash Account	4,500
		14,000			14,000

R's Capital Account

		Rs.			Rs.
1979 Jan. 1	To Realisation A/c —loss	3,000	1978 Jan. 1	By Balance b/d	1,500
			"	By General Reserve	1,000
				By Cash A/c	100
			"	By P's Capital A/c $400\times\frac{12,500}{22,000}$	227
			"	By Q's Capital A/c $400\times\frac{9,500}{22,000}$	173
		3,000			3,000

Notes : (1) Capitals have bean treated as fluctuating. Hence R's loss (Rs. 400) has to be borne by P and Q in the ratio of 12,500 : 9,500, *i.e.* capitals plus their share of reserve.

If the capitals are fixed, the loss would have been in the ratio of 10 : 8.

(2) Strictly speaking, it should not be necessary for solvent partners to bring cash for their share of the loss on realisation, because in practice they only pass notional entries—entries not backed by actual cash paid in.

All partners insolvent. Should all partners be insolvent the resultant loss will have to be borne by creditors. In such a case it is better not to transfer the creditors to the Realisation Account ; otherwise, the Realisation Account should be prepared in the usual way. All the available cash should be paid to the creditors ; the amount remaining unpaid should be transferred to the Profit and Loss Account. The capital accounts of partners will be closed by transfer to the Deficiency Account.

Illustration Stupid and Reckless were partners sharing profits in the ratio of 3 : 2. On 1st July, 1967 their balance sheet was as under :

Liabilities		Rs	*Assets*	Rs.
Sundry creditors		20,000	Stock	12 000
Capitals :			Debtors	15,000
Stupid	5,000		Furniture	600
Reckless	3,000	8,000	Cash	400
		28,000		28,000

The firm was dissolved on the above date. The assets realised only Rs. 16,000. Expenses came to Rs. 500. Stupid's private estate could pay only Rs. 1,000. Reckless had no surplus. Close the books of the firm by giving ledger accounts.

Solution :

Realisation Account

Dr. | | | | | *Cr.*

		Rs.			Rs.
1978 July 1	To Sundry Assets :		1978 July 1	By Cash Account	16,000
	Stock	12,000	,,	By Loss transferred to :	
	Debtors	15,000		Stupid 3/5 7,260	
	Furniture	600		Reckless 2/5 4,840	12,100
,,	To Cash A/c—expenses	500			
		28,100			28,100

Cash Account

		Rs.			Rs.
1978 July 1	To Balance b/d	400	1978 July 1	By Realisation A/c—expenses	500
,,	To Realisation A/c	16,000		By Sundry Creditors	16,900
,,	To Stupid's Capital Account	1,000			
		17,400			17,400

Sundry Creditors

		Rs.			Rs.
1978 July 1	To Cash A/c	16,900	1978 July 1	By Balance b/d	20,000
	To Deficiency A/c—amount unpaid	3,100			
		20,000			20,000

Deficiency Account

		Rs.			Rs.
1978 July 1	To Stupid's Capital A/c	1,260	1978 July 1	By S. Creditors —transfer	3,100
	To Reckless's Capital A/c	1,840			
		3,100			3,100

Stupid's Capital Account

		Rs.			Rs.
1978 July 1	To Realisation A/c—loss	7,260	1978 July 1	By Balance b/d	5,000
			,,	By Cash Account	1,000
			,,	By Deficiency A/c transfer	1,260
		7,260			7,260

Reckless's Capital Account

		Rs.			Rs.
1978 July 1	To Realisation A/c—loss	4,840	1978 July 1	By Balance b/d	3,000
				By (Deficiency A/c transfer	1,840
		4,840			4,840

Piece-meal Distribution. When a firm is dissolved, assets are gradually sold so as to realise the best price. The amounts thus realised are used, naturally, to first pay outsiders and then the available amounts are distributed among the partners—again first to pay off their loans, if any, to the firm and then their capitals. After paying the creditors, the amounts are paid proportionately to discharge the loans. When it comes to the turn of capitals, the monies should be so distributed that the ultimate loss, i.e. amounts left unpaid, should be in the profit sharing ratio. Obviously, the loss has to be shared by the partners in their profit sharing ratio.

For this, two methods are followed — either the proportionate capitals method or the maximum loss method. Suppose all creditors and partners' loans have been paid off and the partners' capitals are A Rs.30,000, B 25,000 and C Rs.20,000. The partners share profits and losses in the ratio of 5:3:2. If Rs.30,000 is available for distribution among the partners we can proceed in one of the following two ways :

(1) *Proportionate Capitals.* The total of capitals is Rs.75,000; had the capitals been in proportion to the profit sharing ratio, these would have been Rs.37,500, Rs.22,500 and Rs.15,000. A's capital is lower than that "required"; hence taking A's capital as the base, the capitals of B and C should have been :

B :	30,000 × 3/5	Rs. 18,000
C :	30,000 × 2/5	Rs. 12,000

It means that first of all the monies available should be so distributed as to bring down the capitals of B and C to Rs.18,000 and Rs.12,000 respectively.

As between B and C, taking B's capital as the base, C's capital should have been Rs.16,667 i.e. 25,000 × 2/3. Hence, first the capital of C should be reduced to Rs.16,667 by paying Rs.3,333. Once the capitals are in the profit sharing ratio, the available amounts can be distributed in the profit sharing ratio. The payment will, therefore, be as shown below :

	Capitals		
	A	B	C
	Rs.	Rs.	Rs.
Amount due	30,000	25,000	20,000
Amount paid to C (to bring the capital to Rs. 16,667)			3,333
		25,000	16,667

Amounts paid to B and C (to bring their capitals to Rs.18,000 and Rs. 12,000 respectively)		7,000	4,667
	30,000	18,000	12,000
Balance in proportion to the profit sharing ratio	7,500	4,500	3,000
Balance still due (or Loss if there are no further assets to realise)	22,500	13,500	9,000

(2) *Maximum Loss*. Comparing the total of amounts due to the partners as capital with the amount available, the loss can be ascertained on the assumption that no further amounts will be received. This is the maximum loss. It should be distributed among the partners in the profit sharing ratio—if a minus figure results, that should be dealt with according to Garner *vs*. Murray. The total of the balances in the capitals will be equal to the amount in hand and partners will be paid accordingly. In the example given above, the total of capitals is Rs.75,000 and the available amount is Rs.30,000. Hence the maximum loss is Rs.45,000.

The following shows how the Rs.30,000 should be distributed :

	Capitals		
	A	B	C
	Rs.	Rs.	Rs.
Capital	30,000	25,000	20,000
Less : Maximum Loss (in the profit sharing ratio)	22,500	13,500	9,000
Balance, and amount paid	7,500	11,500	11,000

(Though ultimately the total amount paid to each partner will be the same in both the methods, in the initial stages the amounts paid can differ.)

Illustration. The following was the balance sheet of X, Y & Z when the firm was dissolved :

Balance Sheet as at January 1, 1981

		Rs.		Rs.
Capitals :			Plant & Machinery	70,000
X	40,000		Stock in trade	35,000
Y	30,000		Sundry Debtors	20,000
Z	25,000	95,000	Cash	5,000
Loans: X	10,000			
Y	5,000	15,000		
Creditors		20,000		
		1,30,000		1,30,000

The partners shared profits and losses in the ratio of 3:2:1. The assets realised as follows :

		Rs.
January	1981	25,000
February	1981	45,000
March	1981	45,000

Show how the amount available each month will be distributed and confirm your results by computing the final profit or loss on realisation.

Solution :

Statement Showing Distribution

	Creditors Rs.	X's Loan Rs.	Y's Loan Rs.	Capitals X Rs.	Capitals Y Rs.	Capitals Z Rs.
Amount due	20,000	10,000	5,000	40,000	30,000	25,000
January: Amount available Rs. 30,000						
Paid: to Creditors 20,000 to Partners for Loans (ratio 10:5)		6,667	3,333	—	—	—
Balance due	—	3,333	1,667	40,00	30,000	25,000
February : Amount Rs. 45,000 Partners' Loans		3,333	1.667			
Amounts towards capital of Y and Z				—	3,333	11,667
		—	—	40,000	26,667	13,333
Balance of Rs.25,000 in the profit sharing ratio				12,500	8,333	4,167
Balance due				27,500	18,334	9,166
Amount available in March, distributed in profit sharing ratio				22,500	15,000	7,500
Balance, being loss				5,000	3,334	1,666

The total loss is Rs.10,000 i.e. Rs.5,000 + Rs.3,334 + Rs.1,666. The book value of assets sold is Rs.1,25,000 and the amount realised is Rs.1,15,000 in total. These being no expenses, the loss is Rs.10,000.

Note : Taking X's capital as the base, Y's capital should be Rs.26,667 and Z's Rs.13,333. First, payments should be made so as to reduce the capitals of Y and Z to these figures.

Alternatively (as regarding partners' capitals) :

			Capitals	
		X	Y	Z
		Rs.	Rs.	Rs.
Amounts due		40,000	30,000	25,000
Feb : Max. Loss : Total Capitals	95,000			
Amount available after paying off Loans	40,000			
Distributed in the profit sharing ratio	55,000	27,500	18,333	9,167
Amount paid		12,500	11,667	15,833
March : Balance Due		27,500	18,333	9,167
Loss: Total of capitals	55,000			
Amount available	45,000			
Loss	10,000	5,000	3,333	1,667
Amount Paid		22,500	15,000	8,000

Exercises

Division of Profits

1. There is no Partnership Deed among A, B and C who are carrying on manufacture of cycle parts. The following disputes arose at the end of the first year :—

(*a*) A wanted a salary of Rs. 6,000 p.m. for working as Production Manager and C wanted a commission of 5% on sales (which totalled Rs. 1,50,000). B objected and says no amount is due to either A or B.

(*b*) B wanted interest @ 9% on capital contributed by him, there being no capital contributed by A or C. A and C objected to this.

(*c*) B also wanted interest @ 12% on loan given by him to the firm. A and C objected to this also.

(*d*) B wanted 1/2 share of profits for himself; but A and C said B should get only 1/4 share; A wanted 3/8 and C also wanted 3/8.

(*e*) The whole work was carried on in A's building. A wanted rent for the building but B and C objected.

Resolve the disputes according to the law.

(*There should be no interest on capital or commission on sales or salary. Profits should be shared equally. Before dividing profits, A should be given reasonable rent for his building and B should be given interest on his loan @ 6% p.a.*).

2. Grass and Blade formed a partnership on 1st January, 1968. They agreed that out of profits :

(*i*) Grass should receive a salary of Rs. 500 per month;
(*ii*) Interest on capitals should be allowed on capitals @ 6% p.a.; and
(*iii*) Remaining profits be divided equally.

Grass contributed a capital of Rs. 50,000 on 1st January, 1968 but Blade brought in his capital of Rs. 1,00,000 on 1st April, 1968. During the year the drawings were : Grass, Rs. 15,000 and Blade, Rs. 20,000. Profits before the above noted salary and interest were Rs. 50,000. Prepare Profit and Loss Appropriation Account and Capital Accounts of the partners.

(*Capital Accounts : Grass, Rs. 62,250; Blade, Rs. 1,02,750*)

3. Tree, Bush and Hedge were partners sharing profits and losses in the ratio of 3 : 2 : 1 with the provision that Hedge's share of profits (including interest on capital) should not be less than Rs. 10,000 p.a. Partners were entitled to interest on capitals @ 9% p.a. but interest on drawings or current account balances was to be ignored. Tree was entitled to a rent of Rs. 500 p.m. because the business was carried on from his premises. On 1st Janurary, 1978 the balances were :

	Capital Accounts	*Current Accounts*
	Rs.	Rs.
Tree	50,000	5,600 (Cr)
Bush	30,000	3,100 (Cr.)
Hedge	20,000	1,100 (Dr.)

Drawings during 1978 were : Tree, Rs. 24,000; Bush Rs. 16,000 and Hedge, Rs. 5,800. Profits before any of the above mentioned matters were Rs. 45,000. Prepare ledger accounts to show amounts due to the partners at the end of 1978.

[*Current Account balances : Tree, Rs. 5,180 (Cr.); Bush Rs. 1,480 (Dr.) and Hedge Rs. 3,100 (Cr.)*]

4. Clever and Wise were partners. They had agreed that interest on capitals was to be allowed at 6% p.a. and charged on drawings at the same rate. Clever who was in charge of accounts presented the following Profits and Loss Appropriation Account relating to 1977 :

P. & L. Appropriation Account

	Rs.		Rs.
To Interest on Capitals :		By Profit earned	40,000
Clever 6% on Rs. 60,000	3,600	By Interest on Drawings :	
Wise 6% on Rs. 40,000	2,400	Clever 6% on Rs. 20,000	1,200
To Interest on Clever's		Wise 6% on Rs. 15,000	900
Loan @ 9% p.a.	1,800		
To Profit to : Clever 3/5	20,580		
Wise 2/5	13,720		
	42,100		42,100

Wise consults you whether he should accept the account. What do you advise ? If you do not accept the above account redraw it. Also pass the entry necessary to correct the Current Accounts which have been drawn up by Clever already. Interest on Clever's loan has also been credited to his Current Account.

(*Debit Clever and credit Wise Rs. 3,655*)

(*Hint* : Interest on drawings should be for 6 months; interest on Clever's loan should be at 6% p.a. and profits have to be divided equally. First prepare accounts of partners according to the figures given above; then prepare them as they should be. Entry should be passed for the difference.)

5. Swami and Rao were partners sharing profits and losses in the ratio of 3 : 2, having started business on 1st January, 1978. They employed Iyer as manager who deposited Rs. 10,000 as security carrying interest @ 8%. Iyer received a salary of Rs. 400 p.m. plus a commission of 5% on net profit (after such commission).

Swami's capital was Rs. 20,000 and Iyer's Rs. 15,000. They allowed interest on capitals @ 6% p.a. During 1968 they earned a profit (before allowing interest on capitals and Iyer's bonus) of Rs. 10,500.

After the profits were divided, it was decided to make Iyer a partner with effect from 1st January, 1978 and to give him 1/4 of profits. His deposit was converted into capital. His salary was reduced to Rs. 200 p.m.

Give the entries necessary to give effect to this arrangement.

(*Debit Iyer Rs. 250 and credit Swami, Rs. 150 and Rao, Rs. 100*)

(*Hints* : First work out what Iyer received as manager and then as partner. Interest on Iyer's capital will also be @ 6% p.a.

6. On 31st December, 1977 the capital accounts (bearing interest at 5%) of X, Y and Z sharing in proportion of 4/9, 1/3 and 2/9 stood at Rs. 18,000, Rs. 14,000 and Rs. 12,000 respectively. The profits for the year amounted to Rs. 7,600 before allowing interest on capital accounts. It was decided that the capital of the whole firm be Rs. 54,000 and that partners should bring in or withdraw cash to make their capitals in profit sharing ratio. Prepare Profit and Loss Account and Capital Accounts.

7. The trial balance of Wazir and Shah on 31st December, 1977 was as under :—

	Dr. Rs.	*Cr.* Rs.
Stock (1st Jan., 1967)	1,50,000	
Purchases and Sales	6,40 000	9,74,000
Goodwill	40,000	
Wages	67,500	
Wages and Expenses unpaid		14,000
Capitals :		
Wazir		1,20,000
Shah		80,000
Freehold Land	60.000	
Factory Buildings	34,500	
Plant	80,000	
Motor Vehicles	15,000	
6% Debentures in D Ltd. (purchased on 1st Jan., 1967)	1,00,000	
Interest received on above		3,000
Debtors and Creditors	50,000	68,500
Salaries	34,500	
Office Expenses	19,500	
Manufacturing Expenses	52,000	
Balance at Bank	36,500	
Drawings : Wazir	20,000	
Shah	10,000	
Loan @ 9% (taken on 31st Dec., 1966)		1,50,000
	14,09,500	14,09,500

Adjustments to be made are :

(1) Depreciate Buildings, Rs. 4,500; Plant Rs. 10,000 and Motor **Vehicles**, Rs. 3,000.

(2) A provision of 5% on Debtors is required for doubtful debts.

(3) Office Expenses include insurance premium, Rs. 1,000 paid for the year up to April 1, 1978.

(4) Stock on 31st December, 1977 was Rs. 1,20,000.

(5) Interest on capitals and drawings is to be @ 6% p.a.

(6) Shah is to get a salary of Rs. 1,000 p.m.

(7) Profits and losses are to be shared equally.

Prepare Trading and Profit and Loss Account for 1977 and Balance Sheet as on 31st Dec., 1977.

(*Gross Profit, Rs. 1,84,500; Net Profit before partners' interest and Salary Rs. 1,03,250; Total of Balance Sheet Rs 5,19,250*)

8. Boat and Oar were partners sharing profits and losses in the ratio of 3 : 1 after allowing interest on capitals @ 12% p.a. and charging interest on drawings @ 6% p.a. and after allowing Oar a salary of Rs. 500 p.m. Their trial balance on 30th June, 1978 was as under :—

	Rs.		Rs.
Capital—Boat	50,000	Discount Allowed	580
Oar	20,000	Discount Received	340
Stock (1st July 1977) :		Land and Buildings	16,000
Raw Materials	4,000	Plant and Machinery	59,000
Finished Goods	9,000	Furniture	600
Purchases	74,000	Debtors	42,000
Sales	1,74,080	Creditors	15,820
Returns of Materials	200	Cash in hand	1,600
Sales Returns	400	Cash at Bank	6,000
Wages and other manufacturing expenses	42,400	Electric Power	3,000
		Lighting, Office	500
Salaries	12,000	Provisions for Bed Debts	5[illegible]0
Insurance	400	Carriage	760
Postage	400	Office Expenses	4,000
Travelling	2,100	Drawings—Boat	9,000
Advertising	6,100	Oar	3,000
Bad Debts	300		
Reserve Fund	20,000		
Bills Payable	16,200		

After taking into account the following adjustments, prepare Manufacturing Account, Trading and Profiting and Loss Account for the year ended 30th June, 1978 and Balance Sheet as on that date :

(*a*) Stocks on 30th June, 1978 were :
Raw Materials 5,000
Finished Goods 10,000

(*b*) Depreciation—
Land and Buildings @ 3%;
Furniture and Plant and Machinery @ 10%; and

(*c*) Provision for Bad Debts is to be maintained @ 3% on Debtors.

(*d*) Goods taken by Oar for his private use were Rs. 2,000.

(*e*) Materials were received on 29th June. 1978 of the value of Rs. 2,000 and these were included in stock but not recorded in books

Land and Buildings were used wholly for production.

(*Cost of goods manufactured, Rs. 1,27,340; Gross Profit. Rs. 49,340; Net Profit before interest and salary of partners, Rs. 22,540; Total of Balance Sheet Rs. 1,32,560*)

Admission

9. Tanna and Desai are partners sharing profits and losses in the ratio of 3 : 2. They admit Mehta into partnership giving him 1/5 share. Mehta is to bring Rs. 10,000 as goodwill and Rs. 25,000 as his capital. Give journal entries to record these and show the new profit sharing ratio.

(*Tanna credited, Rs. 6,000 ; and Desai credited Rs. 4,000 ; New Ratio 12 : 8 : 5*)

10. Syed and Shah are two partners sharing profits and losses in the ratio of 3 : 1. They admit Khan as partner who pays Rs. 30,000 as capital. The new ratio is to be 3 : 1 : 1. The goodwill of the firm is to be based on 3 years' purchase of the average of 4 years' profits which were Rs. 15,000, Rs. 12,000, Rs. 18,000 and Rs. 19,000. Show journal entries if

(*a*) Khan pays for goodwill in cash ; and

(*b*) he is unable to bring cash for goodwill.

[(*a*) *Syed credited with Rs. 7,200 and Shah credited with Rs. 2,400 ; (b) Syed credited with Rs. 36,000 and Khan credited with Rs. 12,000*)]

11. Sheikh and Pandit are in partnership sharing profits and losses in the ratio of 5 : 3. Granthi is admitted as a partner who pays Rs. 40,000 as capital and the necessary amount for goodwill which is valued at Rs. 60,000 for the firm. His share of profits will be 1/5 which he takes 1/10 from Sheikh and 1/10 from Pandit. Give journal entries to record the admission and calculate the future profit sharing ratio.

(*Sheikh and Pandit each credited with Rs. 6,000 ; New ratio 21 : 11 : 8*)

12. Following is the Balance Sheet of Active and Sharp who shared profit and losses in the ratio of 3 : 2.

Balance Sheet

	Rs.		Rs.
Active's Capital	30,000	Goodwill	10,000
Sharp's Capital	25,000	Sundry Assets	50,000
Sundry Creditors	10,000	Cash	5,000
	65,000		65,000

Blunt was admitted as partner on the date of the Balance Sheet. The new ratio for sharing profits and losses will be 5 : 3 : 2. Blunt pays Rs. 20,000 as Capital but nothing for goodwill which has to be valued on the basis of 2 years' purchase of 3 years' profits. The profits for 3 years were Rs. 10,000, Rs. 12,000 and Rs. 14,000. Draw up the Balance Sheet after giving journal entries and ledger accounts relating to Blunt's admission.

(*Active's Capital, Rs. 38,400 ; Sharp's Capital, Rs. 30,600 ; Total of Balance Sheet, Rs 99,000*)

13. The following is the Balance Sheet of North and East as at Jan. 1, 1978:—

Liabilities		Rs.	*Assets*	Rs.
Sundry Creditors		21,000	Cash at Bank	15,000
General Reserve		9,000	Sundry assets	1,05,000
Capitals :				
North	50,000			
East	40,000	90,000		
		1,20,000		1,20,000

North and East were shaing profits and losses in the ratio of 2 : 1. On the above date West was admitted as partner on the conditions that

(*a*) he brings Rs. 30,000 as capital;

(*b*) he pays Rs. 15,000 as his share of goodwill;

(*c*) North and East withdraw half of their share of goodwill; and

(*d*) The new profit sharing ratio is to be 3/5 to North, 1/5 East and West each.

Give journal entries, ledger accounts and balance sheet after West's admission.

(*North Capital, Rs. 58,500 ; East's Capital, Rs. 48,000 ; Total of Balance Sheet, Rs. 1,57,500*)

14. The Balance Sheet of Ganga and Yamuna as on 31st December, 1978 was as under:

		Rs.		Rs.
Sundry Creditors		15,000	Cash	6,000
Capitals:			Sundary Assets (no goodwill)	44,000
Ganga	20,000			
Yamuna	15,000	35,000		
		50,000		50,000

Sutlej was admitted as partner and the new ratio was fixed as 4 : 3 : 2. Sutlej was unable to pay anything for goodwill but was to bring Rs. 16,000 as capital. Goodwill of the firm was fixed at Rs. 18,000. Give journal entries on the admission of Sultej assuming that partners do not want goodwill to appear in the books. Draw up the Balance Sheet of the newly constituted firm.

(*Capitals : Ganga, Rs. 21,000 ; Yamuna Rs. 18,000 ; Sutlej, Rs. 12,000; Total of Balancc Sheet, Rs. 66,000*)

15. (*a*) Foolchand and Ghelabhai with capitals of Rs. 75,000 and Rs. 1,00,000 respectively agree to admit Himatbhai into partnership as from 1st April, 1977, upon the terms that Himatbhai should bring in Rs. 80,000 of which Rs. 30,000 is to be regarded as a premium or goodwill and that he is to be given a fourth share in the future profits.

Draft the Journal Entries assuming that Himatbhai brings in the necessary amount and that the goodwill amount after being brought into record is withdrawn by the partners entitled thereto.

Show also the Capital Accounts of the Partners and Goodwill Account. State the future profit sharing proportions of Foolchand, Ghelabhai and Himabhai. (*Each of the existing partners credited with Rs. 15,000*)

(*b*) Suppose Himatbhai can bring only Rs. 50,000 as his capital and cannot pay cash for goodwill which has been valued on the same basis as in (*a*) above. What do you recommend so that the rights of the partners may be equitably adjusted? Assume there is no Goodwill Account in the books of Foolchand and Ghelabhai. Draft journal entries to give effect to your recommendation.

(*Foolchand and Ghelabhai each credited with Rs. 60,000*)

(*c*) Continuing (*b*) above, suppose the partners do not want goodwill to continue to appear in books. What entry will you pass ?

(*Debit : Foolchand, Rs. 45,000 : Ghelabhai. Rs. 45,000 ; Himatbhai, Rs. 30,000*)

16. The following was the balance sheet of C, D and E who were equal partners on 30th June, 1978:

Liabilities	Rs.	*Assets*	Rs.
Bills Payable	3,300	Cash	600
Creditors	6,000	Debtors	10,800
Capital :		Stock	11,400
C	16,800	Furniture	2,400
D	12,600	Building	19,500
E	6,000		
	44,700		44,700

They agreed to take F into partnership and to give him a fourth share of the profits on the following terms :—

(1) That F should bring in Rs. 9,000 as Goodwill and Rs. 15,000 as capital.

(2) That half the Goodwill shall be withdrawn by the old partners.

(3) The Stock and Furniture be depreciated by 10%.

(4) That a provision of 5% on Debtors be created to cover Doubtful Debts.

(5) That the value of the building, having appreciated, the Building Account should be raised to Rs. 27,000.

Give effect to the above arrangement, prepare the Profit and Loss Adjustment Account and the Balance Sheet of the newly constituted firm.

(*Profit on Revaluation, Rs. 5,580 ; Capitals : C, Rs. 20,160 ; D. Rs.15,960; E, Rs. 9,360 ; F, Rs. 15,000 ; Total of Balance Sheet, Rs. 69,780*)

17. A, B and C were in partnership sharing profits and losses in the ratio of 3 : 2 : 1. Their balance sheet as on 21st December, 1976 was as follows:

Liabilities	Rs.	*Assets*		Rs.
Creditors	11,000	Cash at Bank		4,000
Reserve	6,000	Debtors	12,000	
		Less Provision	600	11,400
Capitals : A	12,500	Stock		8,000
B	7,500	Investments		6,000
C	5,000	Furniture		2,000
		Machinery		10,600
	42,000			42,000

They admitted D into partnership as from 1st Jan., 1977. D was to have 1/7 share of profits and to contribute Rs. 5,000 as capital and Rs. 4,500 as goodwill (which was to remain in business). Investments were revalued at Rs. 5,000, stock was reduced by Rs. 680, and the provision against debtors was to be at 4% of the debtors. Machinery was revalued at Rs. 13,000.

Give journal entries and ledger accounts to give effect to the above and draw up the Balance Sheet after D's admission.

(*Capital : A, Rs. 18,170 ; B, Rs. 11,280 ; C, Rs. 6,890 ; D, Rs. 5,000 ; Total of Balance Sheet, Rs. 52,340*)

18. Yusuf and Raza were partners sharing profits and losses in the ratio of 4 : 3 Their Balance Sheet as on 1st July, 1978 was as under :

Liabilities		Rs.	*Assets*		Rs.
Sundry Creditors		16,000	Goodwill		10,000
Capital Accounts :			Plant & Machinery		45,000
Yusuf	50,000		Patents		5,000
Raza	40,000		Stock		15,000
		90,000	Debtors	12,000	
			Less Provision	300	11,700
			Cash at Bank		9,300
			Investments		10,000
		1,06,000			1,06,000

On the above date Mirza was taken into the partnership and given 2/9 share of profits. He was to bring Rs. 27,000 as his capital and the capital of the other partners was to be made proportionate to their share in profits by opening Current Accounts. Goodwill was valued at Rs. 17,000, Plant and Machinery at Rs. 40,000, Patents at Rs. 6,000 and Stock at Rs. 13,000. Provision against Debtors is to be @ 5%. A liability of Rs. 700 included in Sundry Creditors is not likely to arise and has to be removed from books. Give journal entries to record the above and Balance Sheet after Mirza's admission.

(*Current Accounts* ; *Yusuf, Rs. 3,200 (Dr.)* ; *Raza, Rs. 100 (Cr.)* ; *Total of Balance Sheet, Rs. 1,36,900*)

19. Basu and Das were partners sharing in the ratio of 3 : 2. On 1st Jan., 1979 their Balance Sheet was as follows:—

Liabilities	Rs.	*Assets*	Rs.
Bills Payable	5,000	Cash	4,000
Creditors	20,000	Stock	16,000
Reserve	10,000	Debtors	11,000
Capitals :		Building	35,000
Basu	30,000	Plant	24,000
Das	25,000		
	90,000		90,000

Chatterji was admitted as partner on the above date. The new profit sharing ratio was to be Basu 3/8, Das 3/8 and Chatterji 2/8. Chatterji paid Rs. 10,000 as his share of goodwill and is to bring in capital sufficient to make it proportionate to his share in profits. The other terms were :

(1) As between Basu and Das also, the capitals should be proportionate to the share of profits (for this purpose the capitals are to be aggregated first).

(2) Plant was to be valued at Rs. 23,000 and Building at Rs. 40,000 and a provision against a claim for damages, Rs. 1,000, is to be created.

Prepare Ledger accounts to record Chatterji's admission and Balance Sheet after completion of the above noted arrangements.

(*Basu receives Rs. 7,800* ; *Das pays, Rs. 7,800* ; *Chatterji's Capital, Rs. 26,000* *Total of Balance Sheet, Rs. 1,30,000*)

20. A and B share profits in the ratio of 3 : 1. On 31st December, 1977 their Balance Sheet was as under :—

Liabilities			Rs.	*Assets*	Rs.
Creditors			37,500	Cash at Bank	22,500
General Reserve			4,000	Bills Receivable	3,000
Capital Accounts :				Debtors	16,000
		Rs.		Stock	20,000
	A	30,000		Fixtures	1,000
	B	16,000	46,000	Land and Buildings	25,000
			87,500		87,500

On 1st January, 1978 C was admitted into the partnership on the following terms :—

(*a*) That C pays Rs. 20,000 at his Capital for a fifth share in future profits of the firm.

(*b*) That Stock and Fixtures be reduced by 10% and a 5% provision for Doubtful Debts be created on Debtors.

(*c*) That the value of Land and Buildings be appreciated by 20%.

(*d*) That the share of C in firm's goodwill be valued at Rs. 4,000 but that C will not be required to bring goodwill in cash.

(*e*) That the Capitals of the partners be in their profit sharing ratio, the necessary amounts being paid in or withdrawn.

Give the Profit and Loss Adjustment Account, Goodwill Account and Capital Accounts of the partners together with the Balance Sheet after the above noted arrangements have been put through.

(*A pays Rs. 10,425*; *B receives, Rs. 2,525*; *Total of Balance Sheet, Rs. 1,37,500*)

(*Hint* : Goodwill should be raised at Rs. 20,000)

21. Mehta and Sethi were in partnership, sharing profits and losses in the ratio of 3 : 2. Their Balance Sheet on 31st December, 1977 was as under :

Liabilities		Rs.	*Assets*		Rs.
Sundry Creditors		20,000	Cash		4,000
Bills Payable		6,000	Stock		15 000
Capitals :			Debtors	15,000	
Mehta	40,000		*Less* Provision	600	14,400
Sethi	30,000	70,000			
			Plant & Machinery		62,600
		96,000			96,000

On 1st January, 1978 Verma was admitted. He was to be given 1/6 share of profits and capitals were to carry interest @ 5% p.a. The terms of admission were :

(*a*) Verma was to pay Rs. 20,000 as capital;

(*b*) Goodwill was to be raised at Rs. 15,000;

(*c*) Plant and Machinery was to be written down to Rs. 60,000 and the provision against debtors was to be raised to Rs. 1,000.

On 30th June, 1978, it was found that the profit (before interest on capital) was Rs. 15,000. During the six months, Mehta had drawn Rs. 3,000; Sethi Rs. 4,000 and Verma Rs. 2,500.

(*Capital Accounts : Mehta Rs. 51,605*; *Sethi, Rs. 35,820*; *Verma, Rs. 20,075*; *Total of Balance Sheet, Rs. 1,33,500*)

(*Hint* : Assume profit has been realised in cash).

22. Slow and Sure who were in partnership sharing profits and losses in the ratio of 9 : 7 admitted Steady as a partner on 1st Jan., 1978. Steady paid in Rs. 60,000 of which Rs. 20,000 was to be for goodwill. The amount was credited to Steady's Account. Steady was entitled to 1/4 of profits which he acquired 3/16 from Slow and 1/16 from Sure On 31st Dec., 1978 their trial balance was :

		Rs.		Rs.
Sundry Assets		2,00,000	Slow's Capital	60,000
Drawings :			Sure's Capital	50,000
Slow	12,000		Steady	60,000
Sure	10,000		Creditors	20,000
Steady	8,000	30,000	Profit for 1968	40,000
		2,30,000		2,30,000

Profits are to be distributed after allowing 6% interest on capitals. Prepare the Profit and Loss Appropriation Account and the Balance Sheet as at 31st Dec., 1968.

(*Capital Accounts : Slow; Rs. 78,675; Sure, Rs. 59,475; Steady, Rs. 41,850*)

23. A and B admit C as a partner and give him 1/5 share of profits. C pays Rs. 20,000 as capital and Rs. 5,000 for goodwill. Already in the books of A and B, goodwill is appearing at a figure of Rs. 10,000. It is desired that goodwill should continue to appear at the figure. Give the necessary journal entries to record C's admission.

(*Credit A and B each with Rs. 2,000*)

(*Alternatively, Debit Goodwill Rs. 15,000, Credit A and B each, Rs. 7,500 and then Debit A, Rs. 6000; B, Rs. 6000, C, Rs. 3,000 and Credit Goodwill Rs. 15,000*)

(**Note** : The point to note is : Does Rs. 5,000 represent 1/5 share of *total goodwill* or *additional goodwill* ? Entries will depend upon answer to this question. If A and B are credited Rs. 2,500 each, it means that Rs. 5000 is 1/5 of additional goodwill).

Retirement and Death

24. A, B and C were partners sharing profits and losses in the ratio of 2 : 2 : 1. On 1st July, 1977 their goodwill was valued at Rs. 25,000, there being no account for it in the books. On this date B retired. Pass journal entries to record goodwill if

(*a*) it is allowed to remain in books;

(*b*) it is not allowed to remain in books;

(*c*) only B's share is recorded; and

(*d*) no account is raised for goodwill.

25. A and B are partners in a business sharing Profit and Loss as A, 3/5ths and B, 2/5ths. Their Balance Sheet as on 1st January, 1978, is given below :

Liabilities		Rs.	*Assets*	Rs.
Capital Accounts :			Plant and Machinery	19,500
A	20,000		Goodwill	6,000
B	15,000	35,000	Stock	10,000
Reserve Account		15,000	Debtors	15,000
Sundry Creditors		7,500	Closing Balance :	
			At Bank	6,000
			In hand	1,000
		57,500		57,500

B retires from the business owing to illness and A takes it over. The following revaluations are made :

(1) The Goodwill of the firm is valued at Rs. 15,000.

(2) Depreciation :
Plant and Machinery by 10% ; and
Stock by 15%; and

(3) A Bad Debts Provision is raised against Debtors at 5% and a Discount Reserve against Creditors at 2%.

(4) A liability of Rs. 500 included in Creditors is not likely to arise and should be written back.

You are asked to journalise the above transactions in the books of the firm and close the Partner's Accounts as on 1st January, 1968. Give also the Opening Balance Sheet of A.

(*B's Loan, Rs. 23,176; Total of Balance Sheet, Rs. 62,300*)

26. Chintamani, Dinker and Eknath were partners, sharing profits in the proportion of one-half, one-third and one-sixth respectively. The Balance sheet of the firm on 31st March, 1977 was as follows :—

		Rs.			Rs.
Sundry Creditors		1,90,000	Cash at Bank		25,000
Bills Payable		50,000	Debtors	1,60,000	
Reserve Fund		1,20,000	*Less* Reserve	5,000	1,55,000
Capital Accounts :—					
Chintamani	4,00,000		Stock		2,50,000
Dinker	3,00,000		Motor Vans		80,000
Eknath	2,00,000	9,50,000	Plant and Machinery		3,50,000
			Factory Building		4,50,000
		13,10,000			13,10,000

Dinker retires on that date subject to the following adjustments :—

(*a*) The Reserve for Doubtful Debts to be increased by Rs. 19,500;

(*b*) The goodwill of the firm to be valued at Rs. 1,80,000;

(*c*) Plant to be depreciated by 10% and Motor Vans by 15%;

(*d*) Stock to be appreciated by 20% and Building by 10%.

Pass journal entries, give the Capital Account of Dinker, the Profit and Loss Adjustment Account, the Goodwill Account and prepare the Balance Sheet of the continuing partners, as at 1st April, 1977. Chintamani and Eknath decide to write off goodwill.

(*Diaker's Loan, Rs. 4,09,500; Capital Accounts : Chintamani, Rs. 4,29,250; Eknath, Rs. 2,59,750; Total of Balance Sheet Rs. 13,38,500*)

27. A, B and C had the following Balance Sheet on 31st Dec., 1977 :

Liabilities	Rs.	*Assets*	Rs.
Sundry Creditors	4,500	Plant	8,000
A's Loan	6,000	Tools	1,500
Capitals :		Stock	10,000
A 12,000		S. Debtors	14,000
B 10,000		Cash	6,500
C 7,500	29,500		
	40,000		40,000

The profits were shared in the ratio of 2 : 2 : 1. On the above date A retired. He left his loan in the business but B and C contributed sufficient cash to pay off A's Capital. A cash balance of Rs. 4,500 was considered desirable. The following were the values placed on assets :

	Rs.	
Goodwill	5,000	Sundry Debtors, book figure subject to a Provision for Bad Debts at Rs. 1,100 and a Provision for Discount @ 5%.
Plant	7,200	
Tools	1,500	
Stock	9,000	

Sundry Creditors were subject to a reduction of Rs. 200. Give journal entries to record the above and Balance Sheet of B and C on A's retirement.

(*B's Capital, Rs. 17,770; C's capital, Rs. 11,385; Total of Balance Sheet Rs. 39,455*)

28. The Balance Sheet of A, B and C who shared profits in the ratio of 3 : 1 : 1 was as under on 31st December, 1978 :—

Liabilities		Rs.	*Assets*	Rs.
Sundry Creditors		15,000	Cash at Bank	6,000
Reserve		10,000	Sundry Assets (excluding Goodwill A/c)	69,000
Capitals :				
A	20,000			
B	10,000			
C	10,000	40,000		
Profit for 1968		10,000		
		75,000		75,000

The above Balance Sheet is wrong since C had retired with effect from 1st October, 1978. No adjustments had been made consequent on C's retirement. You are now required to make them and redraft the Balance Sheet. The goodwill of the firm was to be valued at Rs. 20,000 (but no goodwill account is to be raised).

(*C's Loan, Rs. 17,762·50; Capitals : A, Rs. 29,178·13; B, Rs. 13,059·37; Total of Balance Sheet, Rs. 75,000*)

(*Hints* : Apportion profits for first nine months and for later three months. C is entitled to his share in profits up to 30th Sep., 1968. Thereafter he will get interest @ 6% p.a.)

29. Gurtu, Raja and Nawab were partners sharing profits and losses in the ratio of 5 : 3 : 2. On 1st July, 1967 their Balance Sheet was as under :

Liabilities	Rs.	Rs.	*Assets*	Rs.
Sundry Creditors		16,000	Cash at Bank	2,000
Contingency Reserve		4,000	Debtors	5,000
Capitals :	Rs.		Stock	11,000
Gurtu	30,000		Plant & Machinery	39,000
Raja	15,000		Patents	3,000
Nawab	10,000	45,000	Investments	5,000
		65,000		65,000

On that date Raja retired and it was decided by Gurtu and Nawab to divide his share in the ratio of 1 : 2. Goodwill was valued at Rs. 10,000. Raja received the investments at a value of Rs. 4,000. Plant and Machinery was valued at Rs. 45,000 and Patents at Rs. 2,000. Rs. 500 is to be written off as a bad debt. It was decided not to raise any goodwill Account in the books. Make entries in the books of the firm and prepare Balance Sheet of Gurtu and Nawab. What is the new ratio for sharing profits ?

(*Capitals : Gurtu, Rs. 22,750 ; Nawab, Rs. 9,500 ; and Raja's Loan, Rs. 16,250 ; Total of Balance Sheet, Rs. 64,500*)

(*Hint* : Gurtu will take $\frac{1}{3} \times \frac{3}{10}$ and Nawab will take $\frac{2}{3} \times \frac{3}{10}$ of Raja's share. Gurtu's share will be $\frac{5}{10} + \frac{1}{10}$ and Nawab's share will be $\frac{4}{10}$. Goodwill should be credited Rs. 3,000 to Raja and debited to Gurtu, Rs. 1,000 and to Nawab Rs. 2,000).

30. Pappu, Kuku and Goloo were in partnership sharing losses in the ratio of 3 : 2 : 1. On 1st January, 1978 Kuku retired. On that date the Balance Sheet was as follows :—

Liabilities		Rs.	*Assets*		Rs.
Bills Payable		5,000	Plant and Machinery		30,000
Expenses Owing		2,000	Patents		3,000
Trade Creditors		10,000	Debtors	10,000	
Capitals :	Rs.		Less Provision	500	9,500
Pappu	15,000		Stock		11,000
Kuku	12,000		Cash		500
Goloo	10,000	37,000			
		54,000			54,000

The terms were :

(*i*) Goodwill was to be valued at Rs. 12,000 but no goodwill account was to be raised.

(*ii*) The new ratio between Pappu and Goloo will be 3 : 2.

(*iii*) Expenses owing it to be brought down to Rs. 1,500 ; Plant and Machinery is to be valued at 10% less than the book value and Patents at Rs. 4,000.

(*iv*) The total capital of the newly constituted firm was fixed at Rs. 25,000 to be contributed by the partners in the Profit sharing ratio.

Prepare ledger accounts to record the above and give the Balance Sheet after Kuku's retirement.

(*Kuku's loan, Rs. 15,500 ; Capitals : Pappu, Rs. 15,000 ; Goloo, Rs. 10,000 ; Cash paid : Rs. 1,950 by Pappu and Rs. 3,050 by Goloo. Total of Balance Sheet, Rs. 57,000*)

31. R, S and T were partners sharing profits and losses in the ratio of 2 : 2 : 1. On 30th June, 1978, S retired. Adjustments had to be made in respect of the following :

(*a*) On 1st January, 1976 a machine was purchased for Rs. 10,000 and had been included in Repairs and Renewals Account. The machine would have been subject to 10% depreciation on the diminishing balance.

(*b*) Goodwill which stood in the books at Rs. 10,000 was valued at Rs. 25,000.

(*c*) There was a joint life policy for Rs. 50,000 on which premiums totalling Rs. 20,000 had been paid; the surrender value is 45% of premiums paid.

(*d*) The firm pays an annual pension of Rs. 2,400 to a former manager. The present value of pensions payable in future is Rs. 20,000.

Give journal entries to record the above and also the decision of R and T not to keep accounts for goodwill and the liability for pensions in books.

(*S Credited with Rs. 4,678*)

32. Radha and Gopi took out a joint life policy on 1st May, 1974 for Rs. 30,000, the premium for which was Rs. 1,200. A joint life policy account was maintained on surrender value basis.

The surrender value was : nil in 1974, Rs. 600 in 1975 ; Rs. 1,500 in 1976 and Rs. 2,500 in 1977. Gopi died on October 15, 1967. Accounts are closed each year on 31st December. Prepare the relevant accounts.

(*Each partner credited with Rs. 13,650 on 15th Oct. 1977*)

33. (*a*) P, Q and R shared profits and losses of a business in the ratio of 4 : 3 : 3. On 31st December, 1973 their Balance Sheet was as follows :

Liabilities		Rs.	*Assets*		Rs.
Creditors		12,000	Cash		6,000
Reserve against Joint Life Policy		5,000	Joint Life Policy (for Rs. 20,000)		8,000
			Debtors	15,000	
Capitals :			*Less* Provision	750	14,250
P	30,000		Stock		20,000
Q	20,000		Plant		32,750
R	20,000	70,000	Goodwill		6,000
		87,000			87,000

On 1st May, 1974 Q died. The relevant clauses in the Partnership Deed provided that in case of a death of a partner his heirs should be entitled to :

(*a*) his capital on the date of the previous Balance Sheet;

(*b*) his share of goodwill based on 3 years' purchase of the profits for four years ;

(*c*) his share of Profits up to the date of death on the basis of the previous year's profit ;

The profits for the previous four years were :

1970	Rs.	15,000	1972	Rs.	15,000
1971	Rs.	16,000	1973	Rs.	18,000

Ascertain the amount due to Q's heirs and prepare the relevant accounts; assuming the surrender value of the Joint Life Policy to be Rs. 4,000.

(*Amount due to Rs. 39,500*)

(*b*) Continuing the above question, if it is decided to pay Rs. 3,500 immediately to Q's heirs and to pay the remaining amount over four years in equal instalments bearing interest at 9% p.a., show the account relating to Q's heirs till it is fully settled.

34. Black and Brown were partners. The profit sharing ratio was 3/6 to Black, 2/6 to Brown and 1/6 to Reserve. The Balance Sheet showed the following figures on 30th June, 1973 :

	Rs.
Black's Capital	40,000
Brown's Capital	30,000
Reserve	20,000

Black died on 1st October, 1973. His heirs were entitled to :

(*a*) his share of goodwill which was valued at Rs. 40,000.

(*b*) interest on his capital and his share of Reserve @ 20% p.a. up to the date of death in lieu of profits.

The firm had taken out a joint life policy for Rs. 50,000. The premiums had been charged to the Profit and Loss A/c up to the date of death. Black had drawn Rs. 3,000 for private use. Show by preparing ledger accounts the amount due to Black's Executors.

(*Rs. 1,05,600*)

35. Messrs. Gibson, Varma and Datta carry on a business in partnership sharing profits and losses in proportion of 7/16, 5/16 and 1/4 respectively. The Balance Sheet of the firm on 31st December, 1975 was as follows :

		Rs.		Rs.
Bills Payable		2,350	Cash in hand	250
Creditors		5,450	Cash at Bank	580
Loans		14,200	Bills Receivable	1,850
Capital :	Rs.		Stock	9,570
Gibson	22,750		Debtors	10,250
Varma	15,250		Goodwill	20,000
Datta	12,0.0	50,000	Furniture	2,100
			Joint Life Policy (for Rs. 30,000)	6,800
			Leasehold Building	20,600
		72,000		72,000

Profits for the year ended 31st December 1975 were Rs. 24,000. Mr Datta died on 30th April, 1976. The Partnership Deed provides that Goodwill of the Business is to be calculated on the basis of 3 times the average profits of the past 5 years. Profits for the previous years were as follows :

	Rs.
1971	28,600
1972	25,400
1973	20,000
1974	22,000

It is agreed between the surviving partners and the Executors of the deceased partner that the share of profits of the deceased from 1st January, 1966 till his death may be ascertained on the basis of the last year's profits. The Executor agrees to receive the amount due to the deceased as Rs. 8,800 on settlement (*i.e.*, on the date of death) and the balance with Interest at 9 per cent per annum in 4 six-monthly instalments.

Show the amount due to the deceased Partner's Estate and also show the Executor's Account till the full amount due is paid to him with interest.

(*Amount due Rs. 32,800*)

Amalgamation

36. The following are the Balance Sheets of two like businesses owned by Mr. Sarkar and Mr. Basu respectively who decide to amalgamate the businesses under the name of Messrs. Sarkar and Basu.

	Sarkar	*Basu*		*Sarkar*	*Basu*
	Rs.	Rs.		Rs.	Rs.
Capital	30,000	18,000	Premises	9,000	—
Reserve	4,500	—	Plant	19,500	6,600
Creditors	9,000	13,500	Stock	12,000	9,000
Bills Payable	7,290	—	Debtors	8,700	14,100
Bank Overdraft	3,000	—	Investments	4,500	—
			Cash	90	1,800
	53,790	31,500		53,790	31,500

It was mutually decided that the partnership should take over all the assets and liabilities subject to the following :

Mr. Sarkar's Premises, Investments and Debtors are to be valued at Rs. 15.C00, Rs. 3,000 and Rs. 8,265 respectively.

Mr. Basu's Stock and Debtors are to oe valued at Rs 10,500 and Rs. 12,690 respectively.

The Capitals of Mr. Sarkar and Mr. Basu should be Rs. 36,000 and Rs. 24,000 respectively and the profits and losses to be shared in the same proportions.

Prepare the partnership Balance Sheet after giving effect to the foregoing transactions. (*Sarkar is paid, Rs. 2,565 ; Basu pays, Rs. 5,910 ; Total of Balance Sheet, Rs. 89,790*)

37. The Balance Sheet of two firms, M/s. Orange and Apple and M/s. Mango and Banana, on 1st January, 1978 were as under :

Liabilities	*Orange & Apple* Rs.	*Mango & Banana* Rs.	*Assets*	*Orange & Apple* Rs.	*Mango & Banana* Rs.
Creditors	10,000	8,000	Building	15,000	—
Reserve	6,000	—	Plant	20,000	—
Capitals :			Stock	10,000	26,000
Orange	20,000		Debtors	5,000	15,000
Apple	15,000		Cash	1,000	7,000
Mango		30,000			
Banana		10,000			
	51,000	48,000		51,000	48,000

Mango and Banana shared profits in the ratio of 3 : 2 and Orange and Apple's profit sharing ratio was 5 : 3. The two firms decided to amalgamate. The profit sharing ratio was to be Orange $\frac{3}{10}$, Apple $\frac{2}{10}$, Mango $\frac{3}{10}$ and Banana $\frac{2}{10}$. The other terms were :

(*a*) Goodwill of Orange and Apple was valued at Rs. 20,000 and that of Mango and Banana at Rs. 15,000. The new firm was not to retain goodwill in the books.

(*b*) Stock of Mango and Banana was valued at Rs. 25,000 and a provision of 5% was required against their debtors.

(*c*) In case of Orange and Apple, Rs. 600 of the debtors was to be written off ; Buildings were valued at Rs. 20,000 and Plant at Rs. 18,000.

(*d*) The total capital of the firm was fixed at Rs. 80,000 to be contributed by partners in profit sharing ratio, adjustments to be made in cash.

Close the books of the two firms and open the books of the new firm styled as All Fruits.

(*Amounts received by : Orange, Rs. 2,250 ; Apple, Rs. 3,650 ; and Mango, Rs. 3,450, Banana pays Rs. 7,700 ; Total of Balance Sheet, Rs. 98,000*)

Dissolution

38. The Balance Sheet of A, B and C sharing profits and losses in the ratio of 3 : 2 : 1 was as follows on 1st Jan. 1977 :—

Liabilities		Rs.	*Assets*		Rs.
Sundry Creditors		12,000	Machinery		25,000
Contingency Reserve		3,000	Stock		11,000
Capitals :			Debtors	10,000	
	Rs.		Less Prov.	500	9,500
A	20,000		Patents		5,000
B	15,000				
C	10,000	45,000	Goodwill		8,000
			Cash		1,500
		60,000			60,000

On the above date the firm was dissolved. The assets except cash realised Rs. 50,000. The Creditors were paid Rs. 11,500 in full settlement. Expenses of dissolution came to Rs. 1,000. Give journal entries and ledger accounts to close the books of the firm.

(*A receives Rs. 17,000 ; B Rs. 13,000 and C Rs. 9,000. Loss on Realisation Rs. 9,000*)

39. E, F and G were in partnership and decided to dissolve. Their position at 31st December, 1978 was as follows :

Balance Sheet

Liabilities		Rs.	*Assets*	Rs.
Creditors		11,200	Debtors	12,500
Bills Payable		2,000	Goodwill	1,500
Loans from Bank		12,000	Bills Receivable	1,250
Capitals :			Plant	21,250
E	6,000		Furniture	1,200
F	4,000		Cash on hand	500
G	3,000	13,000		
		38,200		38,200

They shared profits and losses in the proportion of 2 : 2 : 1 respectively.

Goodwill realised Rs. 7,500. 10% of book debts proved bad and the Bills Receivable realised only Rs. 1,200 ; Plant was sold for Rs. 17,750 and Office Furniture was taken over by E at the book value. Bills Payable were met before due dates, earning a discount of Rs 100. The Bank Loan was paid off including interest of Rs. 200. The Creditors were settled for Rs. 10,700.

Show the Realisation Account, the Bank Account and the Capital Accounts of the Partners.

(*Profit on Realisation, 1,600, E receives, Rs. 5,440, F, Rs. 4,640 and G, Rs. 3 320*)

40. P, Q and R dissolved their firm on 1st July, 1979. On that date their Balance Sheet was :

Liabilities		Rs.	*Assets*	Rs.
Creditors		21,000	Goodwill	10,000
Reserve		9,000	Machinery	30,000
Capitals :			Debtors	15,000
P	30,000		Stock	22,000
Q	20,000		Patents	10,000
R	10,000	60,000	Cash	3,000
		90,000		90,000

P agreed to take over the business and for this purpose the value of the entire business was fixed at Rs. 81,000. P paid in cash the amount due from him. Close the books of the firm by giving journal entries and give the Balance Sheet of P.

(*P pays Rs. 44,000 and Q receives Rs. 27,000 and P receives Rs. 17,000*)

(*Hint* : The price of Rs. 81,000 includes cash also. Cash will be transferred to the Realisation Account).

41. X and Y were carrying on partnership as publishers. They shared profits in the ratio of 3 : 2. On 1st Jan. 1978 they dissolved the firm. Their Balance Sheet on that date was as follows :

Liabilities		Rs.	Assets		Rs.
Sundry Creditors		15,000	Stock of books		40,000
Royalties Payable		2,000	Debtors	10,000	
Capitals :			*Less* Provision	500	9,500
X	20,000		Investments		5,000
Y	20,000	40,000	Cash at Bank		2,500
		57,000			57,000

The stock realised Rs. 35,000; Rs. 8,700 was collected from debtors. It was found that a sum of Rs. 800 was owing to a supplier of paper. This sum was not included in the creditors given above. The Royalties were settled for Rs. 1,500. Copyrights were sold for Rs. 2,600. Expenses of realisation were Rs. 500, Investments were divided equally by the two parties.

(*Loss on Realisation Rs. 4,000 ; X receives Rs. 15,000 and Y receives, Rs. 15,900*)

42. Gupta and Aggarwal were partners sharing profits and losses in the ratio of 5 : 3. On 31st Oct., 1978 their Balance Sheet was as under :

Liabilities		Rs.	Assets	Rs.
Creditors		18,000	Patents	10,000
Capitals :			Machinery	30,000
Gupta	40,000		Stock	20,000
Aggarwal	10,000	50,000	Debtors	6,000
			Cash	2,000
		68,000		68,000

The firm also had a joint life policy for Rs. 30,000 of which the surrender value was Rs. 3,000. The firm was dissolved on the above date. Patents were found useless Machinery realised Rs. 14,000, Stock Rs. 15,000 and Debtors proved bad to the extent of 50%. Creditors allowed a discount of 5%. The expenses came to Rs. 1,900. Give ledger accounts to close the books of the firm.

(*Loss on Realisation, Rs. 32,000; Aggarwal pays, Rs 2,000; Gupta receives, Rs. 20,000*)

43. Lal and Ratan started business as equal partners (after allowing interest on capitals @ 6% p.a.) on 1st January, 1977. Their capitals were Rs. 50,000 and Rs. 30,000. During 1967 they earned a profit (before charging interest) of Rs. 24,800. Their drawings were Rs. 8,000 for Lal and Rs. 7,000 for Ratan. On 31st December, 1967 their liabilities were Rs. 12,000. On this date they dissolved the firm. The assets realised Rs. 95,000 and the expenses came to Rs. 1,200. Close the books of the firm by giving ledger accounts.

(*Lal receives, Rs. 51,000; Ratan receives, Rs. 30,800; Loss on Realisation, Rs. 8,000*)

(*Hint :* Prepare capital accounts for 1977. Total assets will be liabilities plus capitals. The figure thus ascertained should be transferred to Realisation Account).

44. Black and White shared profits and losses in the ratio of 3 : 2. They dissolved their firm on 31st December, 1973. Their capitals on this date were : Black Rs. 40,000 and White Rs. 30,000. There was a general reserve of Rs. 10,000 and a joint life policy for Rs. 50,000; the annual premiums was charged to the Profit and Loss Account. The total premium paid were Rs. 15,000 and the surrender value of the policy was 40% of the premiums paid. White took over the business. He paid Rs. 10,000 as goodwill to Black who also took over the joint life policy. Prepare Accounts to close the books of the firm and give the Balance Sheet of White.

(*Black receives Rs 53,600 in cash*)

45. O, P and Q are partners in a firm sharing profits and losses as 6 : 3 : 1. Their Balance Sheet as on 31st December, 1978, is given below :

Liabilities		Rs.	*Assets*	Rs.
O	8,000		Plant & Machinery	7,500
P	3,000	11,000	Stock-in-trade	2,500
			Sundry Debtors	6,000
Bank Overdraft		3,500	Cash in hand	500
O's Advance		500	Q Overdrawn	1,000
Sundry Creditors		2,500		
		17,500		17,500

The partners decide on dissolution of the firm and the assets realised as follows :

Plant and Machinery 20% less. Stock-in-trade 25% less, Sundry Debtors 30% less. Expenses of dissolution amounted to Rs. 250.

Q became bankrupt and his private estate yielded Rs. 100. You are requested to close the books of the firm.

(Loss on Realisation, Rs. 4,175; O receives, Rs. 7,041·82 and P receives, Rs. 2,640·68)

46. Sharma, Verma and Dharma were partners sharing profits and losses in the ratio of 4 : 3 : 3. On 1st July, 1979 they dissolved the firm. The Balance Sheet on this date was as follows :

Liabilities	Rs.	*Assets*		Rs.
Capital Accounts :		Land & Buildings		30,000
Sharma	40,000	Plant & Machinery		60,000
Verma	30,000	Patents		10,000
Dharma	30,000	Stock		30,000
Sharma's Loan	20,000	Debtors	20,000	
Reserve	10,000	*Less* Provision	1,000	19,000
Creditors	25,000			
Current A/cs :		Cash		1,500
Sharma	1,000	Dharma's Current		
Verma	2,500	Account		8,000
	1,58,500			1,58,500

The assets realised as under :

	Rs.
Land & Buildings	32,000
Plant and Machinery	40,000
Patents	3,000
Stock	20,000
Debtors	17,500

It was found that there was a liability for compensation to workers injured in an accident, amounting to Rs. 5,000. The expenses of liquidation totalled Rs. 4,000. The firm had to pay Rs. 60,000 loss suffered in a speculative deal. Dharma was insolvent and unable to contribute anything from his private estate.

Give ledger accounts to close the books of the firm.

(Loss on Realisation, Rs. 1,05,500 ; Sharma receives (including loan and contribution for loss on realisation), Rs. 61,200 ; Verma receives Rs. 32,650)

47. Dumb and Mutt were partners sharing profit and losses in the ratio of 5 : 3. Their Balance Sheet was as follows on 31st December, 1978 when they dissolved the firm.

Liabilities		Rs.	*Assets*	Rs
Sundry Creditors		20,000	Cash at Bank	1,000
Capitals :			Sundry Assets	37,000
Dumb	15,000			
Mutt	3,000	18,000		
		38,000		38,000

The sundry assets realised Rs. 12,000 only. The estate of Mutt could not contribute anything but Dumb contributed Rs. 2,000. The expenses of realisation were Rs. 600.

Close the books of the firm.

(*Sundry Creditors receive Rs. 14,400; Loss on Realization Rs. 25,600*)

48. The Balance Sheet of Sarkar, Basu and Mirza showed as follows on 31st March 1977 :—

		Rs.		Rs.
Creditors		1,10,000	Cash at Bank	12,500
Capitals :			Debtors	25,000
Sarkar	65,000		Stock	75,000
Mirza	10,000	75,000	Investments	65,000
Reserve		15,000	Furniture	3,500
			Basu—Overdrawn	19,000
		2,00,000		2,00,000

The firm was dissolved as on that date. For the purposes of dissolution, the Investments were realised at Rs. 60,000 and Stock at Rs. 40,000 Sarkar took over the furniture at book value. The Debtors realised Rs. 18,000. The Creditors were paid Rs. 1,07,000 in full satisfaction of their claims. Expenses of realisation came to Rs. 400. In addition, Mirza is entitled to commission of 10% on amounts waived by creditors.

Assuming that Basu is insolvent and is unable to bring in anything in respect of his debt to the firm, show the Realisation and Capital Accounts of all the Partners. The final adjustments are to be made in accordance with the decision in Garner *vs.* Murray. Assume the capitals are not fixed.

(*Loss on Realisation, Rs. 44,700; Sarkar receives, Rs. 42,700 ; Mirza receives Rs. 10,200*)

49. The Balance Sheet of Mirza, Varma and Basu stood as follows on 31st December, 1975 :—

		Rs.			Rs.
Creditors		17,000	Cash at Bank		6,200
Bills Payable		1,200	Sundry Debtors	20,000	
Capital Accounts :			*Less* Provision for Doubtful		
Mirza	20,000				
Basu	20,000		Debts	1,000	19,000
Varma	10,000	50,000			
			Stock-in-trade		22,000
			Machinery & Plant		15,000
			Fixtures & Fittings		1,500
			Goodwill		4,500
		68,200			68,200

It was decided to sell the business to the Calcutta Commercial Corporation Limited, on the Company agreeing to allot 6,000 fully paid shares of Rs. 10 each in full satisfaction of the purchase consideration. The Company assumed the liabilities except Bills Payable and took over all the assets excepting the Bank Balance. The partners shared profits and losses in proportions of one-half to Mirza, one-third to Basu and one-sixth to Varma. Pass Journal Entries and prepare accounts showing the final settlement as regards the partners, assuming that the shares were duly allotted.

(*Profit on Realisation, Rs. 15,000; Mirza receives Rs. 25,380 in shares and Rs. 2,120 in cash ; Basu receives; Rs. 23,080 in shares and Rs. 1.920 in cash and Varma receives Rs. 11,540 in shares and Rs. 960 in cash*)

Note : Shares have been divided in the ratio of final claim, *viz.*, Rs. 27,500; Rs. 25,000; Rs. 12,500; but they could also be divided in the profit sharing ratio. Fractions of shares cannot be given.)

50. Grass and Seed were partners sharing profits and losses in the ratio of 3 : 2. On 1st July 1978 their Balance Sheet was as under :

Liabilities		Rs.	*Assets*		Rs.
Sundry Creditors		20,000	Plant & Machinery		50,000
Reserve		15,000	Stock		20,000
Capitals :			Debtors	18,000	
Grass	40,000		*Less* Provision	900	17,100
Seed	30,000	70,000			
			Cash at Bank		17,900
		1,05,000			1,05,000

The partners sold the business (entire including Cash at Bank) to Plants Ltd. The valuation put on the various assets was :

	Rs.
Goodwill	30,000
Plant	45,000
Stock	18,000
Debtors	17,500

It was found that the liabilities contained Rs. 1,600 which was not to be paid. The company issued 8,250 shares of Rs. 10 each fully paid and paid the remaining amount in cash.

Close the books of the firm.

(*Purchase consideration Rs. 1,10,000 ; Grass receives, Rs. 48,000 in shares and Rs. 16,000 in cash ; Seed receives, Rs. 34,500 in shares and Rs. 11,500 in cash.*)

Alternatively Grass would receive Rs. 49,500 and Seed Rs. 33,000 in shares and the balances in cash.)

CHAPTER XIII

JOINT STOCK COMPANIES

Introduction

Definition. A company is a voluntary association of persons formed for the purpose of some business for profit with common capital, divisible into transferable shares, having a corporate legal entity and a common seal. It is created by a process of law, and is sometimes called an artificial person. It is invisible and intangible ; yet it is capable of doing business, through its directors. It is something distinct from the persons who are its members. A member can both be a shareholder in it and its creditor at the same time. A shareholder cannot be held liable for acts of the company even if he holds virtually the entire share capital. The company is not bound by the acts of its members. A company has a right to sue and can be sued. It can own property, have a banking account in its own name, owe money and be a creditor. The company has perpetual succession ; its life is not affected by the life of its members. New members succeed old members. Since a company exists only in contemplation of law and has no physical personality, it must function through agents, *viz*., the directors. Shareholders or members as such do not carry on the business of the company.

Kinds of joint stock companies. In the beginning joint stock companies came into being in England only through the grant of a royal charter. Such companies are known as chartered companies. In India no chartered companies can be formed now. Some companies in India are formed by a special Act of the Parliament, *e.g.*, the Industrial Finanace Corporation, the State Bank of India, the Life Insurance Corporation of India, Air India International, etc. Such companies are known as statutory companies. They are not governed by the Companies Act. The great majority of companies, however, are floated by following the provisions of the Companies Act, 1956 (this act having consolidated and amended the previous laws on the subject). Such companies are the ordinary joint stock companies and we shall deal with only such companies.

From the point of view of the liability of the shareholders or members, companies can be divided into three types. These are :

(*a*) *Companies limited by shares*. In this case the liability of the members does not exceed the unpaid amount, if any, on the shares held by them. Thus a shareholder cannot be called upon to pay anything if he has already paid the full face value of the share to the company. This is so even if the creditors of the company cannot be paid in full. By far the largest number of companies engaged in business fall within this class.

(*b*) *Companies limited by guarantee.* In this case the liability of the members is limited to the amount which shareholders undertake to contribute in the event of winding up of the company, if necessary. Such companies are permitted only if the object is not to earn a profit but to promote social and cultural activity, etc.

(*c*) *Unlimited companies.* In this case the liability of the members is not restricted at all. They have to contribute the necessary amounts in order to pay off the creditors of the company in full.

It is the Memorandum of Association (see below) which declares whether the iability of the members will be limited, or limited up to the amount guaranteed or unlimited.

A company, the liability of whose members is limited, must include 'Limited' as the last word of its name. But companies whose purpose is not to pay dividends but to promote art, science, culture etc. by devoting all its income for such objectives may be allowed by the Central Government (under Section 25) to get themselves registered without the word 'Limited'.

The Central Government has the power to exempt by general or special order an association not for profit from any of the provisions of the Act as may be specified in the order. In granting such exemption, the Government may impose restrictions or vary the conditions of the licence.

From another point of view the companies may be divided into two classes : private and public. The Companies Act defines a private company as a company which by its articles—

(*a*) restricts the right to transfer its shares ;
(*b*) limits the number of its members (excluding employees who are members and ex-employees who were and continue to be members) to fifty ; and
(*c*) prohibits any invitation to the public to subscribe for any of its shares and debentures.

A private limited company must use "Private Limited" as the last two words of its name. A company which is not private, that is to say which does not observe any of the above three restrictions, is known as a public company. But where 25% or more of the paid-up share capital of a private company is held by one or more bodies corporate which does not mean cooperative societies), the private company will automatically become a public company from the date the capital is so held. For this purpose shares held by a bank under a trust under certain conditions are not to be reckoned. The above also does not apply in certain other cases.

If the paid-up capital held by bodies corporate falls below 25%, the company will again become private provided consent of the Central Government has been obtained and other provisions of the Act observed.

Also, when a "private" company holds 25% of the paid up share capital of a public company, it will become a public company. This will also be the result if the annual turnover (sales) of a private company is Rs. one crore or more—it will become public after the expiry of three months of the year in which its turnover totalled Rs. one crore or more.

Partnerships and public limited companies differ from one another. The point of distinction may be tabulated as follows :—

S. No.	*Particulars*	*Partnerships*	*Public Limited Companies*
1	Legislation	Indian Partnership Act, 1932.	Companies Act, 1956.
2	Numbers	Not more than 20 in a general business and not more than 10 in a banking business.	Minimum 7, no maximum limit.
3	Entity	Not a legal entity.	Legal entity.
4	Liability	Unlimited.	Depends upon Memorandum of Association—generally limited to the face value of shares.
5	Capital	As the partners agree. Capital changed by profits, losses and drawings.	Authorised capital as laid down in the Memorandum. Capital once subscribed by members cannot be altered or reduced without legal formalities. Capital kept distinct from profits or losses.
6	Profits	Divided amongst partners according to agreement.	Division among shareholders depends upon the Articles and the decision of the Directors and members.
7	Management	Minor dec n by majority vote, but major decisions require unanimous approval of partners. All partners can inspect accounts.	Shareholders elect directors (at least 3) who carry on the day-to-day business. Usually, a company has a managing director or general manager working under the Directors. Certain matters reserved for shareholders. Shareholders have the right of receiving only the Balance Sheet and the Profit & Loss Account.
8	Transfer of Share	No partner can transfer his share to another person without the consent of all the partners. In case of death, the heir does not automatically become partner.	Shares are transferred to other persons without the consent of the company generally. In case of death etc., the heirs automatically become members. Shares may be converted into warrants.

S. No.	*Particulars*	*Partnerships*	*Public Limited Companies*
9	Audit and Accounts	Not compulsory. Auditor's duties and responsibilities and powers depend upon the agreement with the auditor.	Compulsory. Duties, powers and responsibilities laid down by law. Auditor must be a qualified person under the Act. Proper books of account must be kept. In addition, certain other books known as "Statutory Books" must be kept. Also, an industrial company may be required to keep costing books and get the cost accounts audited, if the Central Government so orders.
10	Powers	Can carry on any business or trade agreed upon unless prohibited by law.	Only the business or trade covered by the objects clause of the Memorandum of Association can be carried on.
11	Winding up	Can be wound up voluntarily by agreement among partners or by court order. If insolvent, the Insolvency Act applies.	Can be wound up in various ways under the Companies Act. Insolvency Act also applies unless it is in conflict with the Companies Act.
12	Tax	If registered, individual partners pay tax on their share of the profit. If unregistered, firm pays tax itself on its profits. Profits are earned income for active partners.	The company pays tax on the whole of its profits. (Super tax is known as corporation tax). For shareholders, dividends are unearned income.
13	Managerial Remuneration	No restriction.	Total managerial remuneration cannot exceed 11% of profits, but in case of inadequacy of profits, up to Rs. 50,000 can be paid with the consent of the Central Government.
14	Publicity	No compulsion to file returns. No publicity.	Certain statements (for example Balance Sheet and Profit and Loss Account) must be filed with the Registrar. They are open for public inspection.

A private limited company, for practical purposes, is the same as a public limited company but it enjoys certain advantages over the latter, but not if the private company is the subsidiary of a public limited company.

Privileges of a private company. The privileges and exemptions are as follows :

1. Only two members are sufficient to form a private company.
2. It is not required to, nor it can, issue prospectus or file a statement in lieu of prospectus.
3. It may commence business immediately after obtaining certificate of incorporation.
4. It may allot shares as soon as it receives the Certificate of Incorporation as provisions with regard to "minimum subscription" do not apply to it.
5. It is not required to file a statutory report or hold a statutory meeting.
6. It may issue any kinds of shares (not only preference and equity). There are no restrictions on voting rights.
7. Subject to articles, only two members make a quorum.
8. The restrictions relating to the appointment of any person to an office of profit for more than 5 years at a time do not apply to it.
9. Only two directors are sufficient.
10. Director's consent to act as director and his contract to take up qualification shares need not be filed with the Registrar.
11. Directors of private companies need not retire by rotation.
12. Directors can be appointed by a single resolution.
13. New shares need not be issued to the existing shareholders of the company in the first instance.
14. It can grant loans to its directors without the sanction of the Central Government.
15. Provisions regarding managerial remuneration do not apply.
16. A person can be a managing director or a manager of more than two private companies.
17. Restrictions on investments in the same group of companies do not apply.
18. Changes in the directorate of a private company, even if prejudicial, can be made and the Government cannot interfere.
19. The Profit and Loss Account, though filed with the Registrar, cannot be examined by the public.

Floatation of companies. The person who thinks up the idea of a business to be run by a company is known as the promoter. He makes detailed investigations to find out whether the idea is really practicable or profitable. If he thinks that the proposed company can run successfully, he takes such steps as will ensure its smooth running. He then gets the following documents prepared and sends them to the Registrar of Joint Stock Companies :—

(*a*) *The Memorandum of Association.* It contains six clauses : (*i*) the name of the company with Limited as the last word if the liability of the members is limited ("Private Limited" has to be used by private limited companies) ; (*ii*) the State in which the registered office is to be situate ; (*iii*) the objects of the company divided into (*a*) main objects and (*b*) others ; (*iv*) a statement that the liability of the members is limited ; (*v*) the amount of authorised share capital and its division into shares; and (*vi*) the declaration of association. The memorandum must be printed, divided into paragraphs numbered consecutively and must be signed by at least seven persons who each agree to take one share at least. In case of a private company two signatures are enough. Signatures must be witnessed.

(*b*) *The Articles of Association.* It contains the rules and regulations for the conduct of the company's business or internal working. If special articles are not prepared, Table A. the articles framed as a model under the Companies Act, will apply.

(*c*) *A statement of nominal capital*, and where it exceeds Rs. 50 lakhs, a certificate from the Central Government permitting the issue of capital.

(*d*) A statutory declaration by an advocate or an attorney or a Chartered Accountant engaged in the formation of the company, or by a director or any other officer of the company that all requirements of the Companies Act and the Rules thereunder in respect of registration have been complied with.

(*e*) *A list of persons who have consented to be directors* of the company.

(*f*) If directors are appointed by articles or named in the prospectus, *their written consent* to act as directors and *written undertaking to take up and pay for qualification shares* (if any).

Note : If a separate list of directors is not filed, the subscribers to the memorandum will be deemed to be the first directors of the company.

(g) Notice of the address of the Registered Office (this may be given within 28 days after registration).

(*h*) Particulars regarding directors (may be filed later).

Note : (e) and (*f*) above do not apply to private companies.

On payment of the necessary fees, the Registrar will issue the Certificate of Incorporation if he is satisfied that the requirements of the Companies Act have been complied with. He will enter the company's name in the Register. The company comes into existence upon the issue of the Certificate of Incorporation.

Prospectus. A public limited company cannot commence business till the Registrar grants to it a Certificate of Commencement of Business. For this purpose the company has to issue a Prospectus (or prepare a statement in lieu of prospectus) signed by every director before its publication and file a copy with the Registrar. Section 2(36) defines a prospectus as "any document described or issued as a prospectus and included any notice, circular, advertisement or other document inviting offers from the public for the subscription or purchase of any shares in, or debentures of, a body corporate."

The main purpose of the Prospectus is to invite the public to take up the shares and debentures of the company so that the company collects the necessary funds. Whenever a public company makes a public issue of its shares or debentures, it will be required to publish a prospectus. It must be dated and that date, *prima facie,* will be the date of its issue. The prospectus must be issued within 90 days of its date by newspaper advertisements or otherwise.

The Prospectus is the basis of contract between the company and the person who buys the shares on the strength of the Prospectus. Therefore, if the Prospectus contains any misleading statement or if there is a material non-disclosure, the shareholder is entitled to rescind the contract within a reasonable time but before winding up of the company. In addition to the right of rescission, the allottee of shares is entitled to claim compensation from any director, promoter or any other person who authorised the issue of the Prospectus unless the court is satisfied otherwise. Further, according to Section 63, where a Prospectus contains an untrue statement, every person responsible for its issue is liable to imprisonment up to two years and/or fine up to Rs. 5,000, unless he proves that the statement was immaterial or that he believed it to be true and had reasonable ground for doing so. Section 68 provides imprisonment up to five years and/or fine up to Rs. 10,000 for fraudulently inducing any person to invest money in a company.

If the prospectus contains a statement made by an expert, he must not be a person who is or has been engaged or interested in the formation or promotion or in the management of the company. Further, the expert's written consent to the inclusion of the statement (in the form and context in which it is included) must be obtained.

A copy of every contract, or a memorandum giving full particulars of a contract not reduced to writing, and if any adjustment of figures has been made in any auditor's and accountant's report, then a written statement signed by the person making the report have to accompany the prospectus.

It is necessary to send a copy of the prospectus along with an application form for subscription of shares.

Certificate of Commencement of Business. Public companies having share capital cannot commence business unless they obtain a certificate for commencement of business. This certificate will be granted if the following conditions have been fulfilled :—

(1) The company has issued a Prospectus and has filed a copy with the Registrar or, if it has not issued a Prospectus, a

statement in lieu of Prospectus has been prepared and filed with the Registrar.

(2) The minimum number of shares which have to be paid for in cash has been subscribed and allotted (see p. 466 below);

(3) Every director has paid, in respect of shares for which he is bound to pay an amount equal to what is payable on shares offered to the public on application and allotment ;

(4) No money is, or may become liable to be repaid to applicants for any shares or debentures offered for public subscription by reason of any failure to apply for, or to obtain permission for the shares or debentures to be dealt with on any recognised stock exchange ; and

(5) A statutory declaration by the secretary or one of the directors that the aforesaid requirements have been complied with is filed with the Registrar.

Note : Suitable provisions from amongst the above will also apply to companies limited by guarantee but not having a share capital.

Objects listed as "main" can be pursued as soon as the certificate of commencement of business is obtained. But the "other" objects can be pursued normally only if a special resolution is passed by the shareholders.

Effect of irregular allotment. If a company, without complying with any of the conditions contained in Sections 69 and 71 of the Companies Act (these relate to minimum subscriptions, etc.), makes an allotment, the applicant of the shares may avoid the allotment within 2 months after the statutory meeting. If the company is not required to hold a statutory meeting or if the allotment is made after such a meeting, the allotment can be avoided within 2 months of the allotment. The directors are liable to compensate the company or the allottee for any loss, damage, or costs suffered through irregular allotment.

Classes of shares. The Companies Act provides that the shares or other interests of any member in a company shall be movable property, transferable in the manner provided by the articles of the company, and that each share in a company having a share capital shall be distinguished by its appropriate number. Previously there used to be three classes of shares : preference, ordinary and deferred. But now two classes of shares only are permitted, *viz.*, preference and equity (or ordinary). The law defines *preference share capital* as that part of the share capital which fulfils both the following conditions :—

(*a*) that it carries preferential right in respect of dividends ; and

(*b*) that it carries preferential right in regard to repayment of capital.

Preference shares participating in surplus profits, or participating in surplus assets on a winding up can also be issued.

In short, preference shareholders have by law the following two rights : (*i*) to receive, before the equity shareholders, dividend at a fixed rate ; and (*ii*) to get back the capital contributed by them before the equity shareholders receive any amount by way of repayment of capital. In addition, they may get the following rights depending upon the memorandum or articles of association : (*a*) to participate in the profits remaining after the equity shareholders have received dividend at a fixed rate ; (*b*) to receive arrears of dividend at the time of winding up ; (*c*) to receive premium on repayment of capital ; and (*d*) to participate in the surplus remaining after the equity share capital has been repaid in winding up.

It should be noted that if the articles of the company are silent the preference shareholders shall not have any of the above additional rights.

Equity share capital is the share capital other than the preference share capital. This is to say, if the share capital is not entitled to a fixed dividend in preference to others or if there is no prior right for the capital to be repaid, the share capital will be treated as equity share capital.

Voting rights. Holders of preference share capital have a right to vote only on resolutions placed before the company which directly affect the rights attached to the preference shares. But holders of preference share capital have the right to vote on any resolution for winding up of the company or for the reduction or repayment of share capital. In addition, they are entitled to vote on any resolution, if (*a*) the dividend in case of cumulative preference shares has remained unpaid for not less than two years preceding the date of the meeting, or (*b*) the dividends in case of non-cumulative preference shares have been in arrears for not less than two years preceding the meeting or for 3 out of 6 years preceding the meeting.

Holders of equity share capital have right to vote on any resolution placed before the company. The voting rights, on a poll, of every holder of equity capital shall be proportionate to his share of the paid up equity capital.

Classes of preference shares :

(*i*) *Cumulative Preference Shares*. The holders of this class of shares are entitled to arrears of dividends. If in any year the dividend on the preference shares has not been paid, the dividend will be payable out of the profits of the subsequent years. For example, there are 10,000 preference shares of Rs. 10 each carrying dividend at the rate of 6%, and say, dividend is not paid for 1966 and 1967. In 1968 dividend for the three years—1966, 1967 and 1968—*viz*., Rs. 18 000 will be payable (if 1968 profits are sufficient).

(*ii*) *Non-cumulative Preference Shares*. In this case if for any years dividend is not paid, the right to receive dividend for that year lapses. Arrears are not payable. In the above example, in 1968 only the dividend for 1968 will be paid and not for 1966 or 1967.

(iii) *Participating Preference Shares* are those which, in addition to receiving dividend at a fixed rate (prior to any dividend to equity shareholders), also have the right to share profits remaining after a dividend at a fixed rate has been paid to equity shareholders.

(iv) *Redeemable Preference Shares* are those which, in accordance with the terms of issue, will be repaid on or after a certain date. Normally shares cannot be redeemed unless the campany follows a special legal procedure or is wound up. But the law allows redemption of preference shares on certain conditions. These conditions are discussed later.

(v) *Guaranteed Preference Shares* are those which carry the right to a fixed dividend even if the company makes no or insufficient profits. The company itself cannot pay but the vendors or some outsider may undertake to pay the dividend if the company is unable to do so.

Whether the preference shares belong to one class or the other will depend on the articles or memorandum of association and the terms of issue as contained in the Prospectus.

Debentures. If a loan raised by a company is divided into regular parts (each part being serially numbered) and the loan is raised by enabling people to buy as many parts as they wish, each part will be known as a debenture. A debenture. therefore, is an acknowledgement under seal* of debt or loan. A debenture-holder differs from a shareholder. The following are the points of distinction between a debenture-holder and a shareholder :

(a) A shareholder or member is a joint owner of the company, but a debenture-holder is a creditor.

(b) The debenture-holder will receive the interest due to him whether or not the company has made a profit, but the shareholder cannot receive any dividend unless the company has made a profit. Even if the company has made a profit, the payment of dividend normally depends on the discretion of the directors. The directors, however, have no option as regards interest on debentures; it must be paid.

(c) The amount of debentures can be or must be repaid in accordance with the terms of issue, but except in case of redeemable preference shares, the share capital cannot be repaid without legal formalities.

(d) In case of winding up, the amount of debentures must be repaid before any amount is paid to preference or equity shareholders.

(e) There are no restrictions regarding the terms of issue of the debentures, but shares can be issued at a discount only subject to certain conditions contained in the Companies Act.

*When a seal is affixed under the witness of authorised persons, it evidences an act done by the company.

Different classes of debentures.

From the point of view of redemption :

(1) **Redeemable Debentures** are those that will be repaid by the company at the end of a specified period or by instalments during the existence of the company.

(2) **Irredeemable Debentures** are those that are not repayable during the life time of the company and hence will be repaid only when the company goes into liquidation.

From the point of view of security :

(3) **Mortgage Debentures** are those that are secured. The security may be some particular asset (fixed charge) or it may be the assets in general (floating charge). A regular mortgage deed is entered into between the company and the representatives or trustees of the debenture-holders.

(4) **Simple or Naked Debentures** are those that have no security.

From the point of view of recording:

(5) **Registered Debentures** are those in respect of which the names, addresses and particulars of holdings of the debentureholders are entered in a register kept by the company. The transfer of debentures in this case requires the execution of regular transfer deed.

(6) **Bearer Debentures** are transferable by mere delivery. The company keeps no record of the debenture-holders. Payment of interest is made on the production of coupons attached to the debentures.

From the point of view of priority:

(7) **First Debentures.** The debentures which have to be repaid before other debentures are known as First debentures.

(8) **Second Debentures.** The debentures, which will be paid after the First Debentures are redeemed are known as Second Debentures.

Management. The internal management of companies is carried on according to the Articles of Association. The articles define the relationship between members and between members and the company. Members are bound to each other but neither the company nor the members are bound to outsiders on the basis of the articles.

The memorandum and articles of association constitute a notice to persons dealing with the company, and persons contracting with the company are presumed to know their contents. If a contract is entered into by the company contrary to the terms of the memorandum or the articles, the company is not bound by it. But outsiders are entitled to assume that the provisions of the articles have been observed. This is known as the doctrine of "indoor management" or the rule in Royal British Bank *v.* Turquand. For example, outsiders need not enquire into the validity of the election of directors.

Subject to the provisions of the law and the memorandum, articles define the powers of the shareholders, directors, managing director etc. If directors exceed their powers as laid down in the articles, the shareholders can ratify the act provided they are entitled to exercise the power themselves.

Powers of shareholders. Annually, in general meeting, the shareholders consider the annual accounts and the balance sheet and the directors' report and adopt them if the shareholders think fit. Also they declare a dividend (not more than that recommended by the Board of Directors), elect directors in place of those who are due to retire and appoint auditors. In case of a public company and its subsidiary the consent of the company in general meeting is necessary to enable directors to—

(*a*) sell, lease or otherwise dispose of company's undertaking or substantial part of the undertaking;

(*b*) remit or give time for payment of any debt due by a director ;

(*c*) invest, otherwise than in trust securities, the amount of compensation received by the company in respect of the compulsory acquisition after the commencement of the Act or of any premises or property used for any such undertaking;

(*d*) borrow in excess of the aggregate paid up capital plus reserves (temporary loans from company's bankers in the ordinary course of the business of the company being left out of account for this purpose) ; and

(*e*) contribute to charitable and other funds not relating to the business of the company amounts exceeding Rs. 50,000 or 5% of its average net profits during the three preceding financial years whichever is greater in the course of any financial year. No contribution can be made to a political party or for a political purpose.

In respect of (*d*) and (*e*) above, the necessary resolution passed by the company in general meeting must specify the total amounts concerned. Temporary loans are defined as loans repayable on demand or within six months from the date of the loan, but not loans raised for the purpose of financing capital expenditure. If the Board of Directors acts in the above mentioned matters without the consent of the company, the third parties will be protected.

Further, the following should be kept in mind:—

(*a*) The appointment of the sole selling agents by the Board must be approved by the company in general meeting within 6 months of the appointment, otherwise it will cease to be valid. The appointment of selling agents after the commencement of the Amendment Act shall cease to be valid unless it is approved by the company in the first general meeting held after the date of the appointment.

(*b*) Issues of bonus shares or debentures can be made only with the consent of the company in general meeting.

(*c*) Reorganisation of capital, amendment of the Articles or Memorandum of association. requires the consent of the shareholders.

(*d*) Winding up, unless ordered by the court, can be commenced only with the approval of the company in general meeting.

Directors. The minimum number of directors is two for a private and three for a public company. Directors are elected by the shareholders except that casual vacancies can be filled by the Board of Directors.

Only individuals can be appointed as directors. Directors must have in their own name shares equal to the number specified by the articles' as qualification shares. A period of two months is allowed for a director to acquire qualification shares. In case of a public company or its subsidiary, one-third of the directors can be permanent. Of the remaining, one-third must retire every year by rotation. The retiring directors can be re-elected. The total number of directors can be varied within the limits set by the Articles or the Memorandum, but any increase beyond such limits requires the consent of the Central Government in case the company is public or subsidiary of a public company. A person cannot hold office at the same time as director in more than 20 public companies or their subsidiaries.

A company may, by ordinary resolution after special notice, remove a director other than a director appointed by the Central Government or a director of a private company holding office for life on April 1, 1957 or a director appointed in case of proportional representation. A director can resign his office but cannot withdraw his resignation even if the company does not accept it.

The following persons cannot be appointed as directors :

(*a*) a person found by court to be of unsound mind;

(*b*) an undischarged insolvent ;

(*c*) a person who has applied to be adjudged an insolvent and whose application is pending;

(*d*) a person who has been convicted of on offence involving moral turpitude and sentenced to 6 months' imprisonment (such a person may be appointed director after 5 years have passed after the expiry of the sentence) ;

(*e*) a person who has failed to pay calls for 6 months ; and

(*f*) a person who has been disqualified by the court under section 203.

In the following circumstances a director automatically ceases to be a director :—

(*a*) he fails to acquire qualification shares within two months or he ceases to hold the share qualification;

(*b*) he is found by the court to be of unsound mind;

(*c*) he applies to the court to be adjudged an insolvent;

(*d*) he is adjudged an insolvent;

(*e*) he is convicted of an offence involving moral turpitude and is sentenced to imprisonment for not less than six months;

(*f*) he fails to pay calls within 6 months (unless the Central Government grants exemption) ;

(*g*) he absents himself without obtaining leave of absence from the Board from three consecutive meetings of the Board or from all Board meetings for 3 months (whichever period is longer) ;

(*h*) he or any firm of which he is a partner or private company of which he is a director receives a loan or guarantee or security for a loan from the company, unless provisions of section 295 are complied with;

(*i*) he fails to disclose his interest in any contract with the company;

(*j*) he is debarred by the court from being a director;

(*k*) he is removed from directorship ; and

(*l*) he occupies an office of profit unless excused

Directors must act as a Board, *i.e.*, decisions arrived at only at meetings of the directors will be binding except that, depending upon articles, written resolutions signed by all the directors will also be effective. Individual directors have no power unless specific powers are delegated at a properly held meeting of the Board of Directors. The Board also has the power to appoint sub-committees to deal with specific matters. A meeting of the Board of Directors must be held once in every three calendar months. The Central Government has the power to exempt any class of companies from this provision. The quorum is two directors or one-third of the total number whichever is higher (not counting interested directors).

The directors are the trustees for the company's property and it is their duty to apply the property for company's benefit alone. Any director using it for his personal benefit is guilty of breach of trust. The Board is also in the position of an agent. Contracts signed by directors on behalf of the company may be ratified unless they are beyond the powers of the company itself. The directors are not responsible for any loss suffered by the company if they exercise reasonable care and skill in the exercise of their powers and discharge of their duties. But if the directors are guilty of gross negligence or of breach of trust they must compensate the company for damage suffered by it and any provision in the articles absolving the directors from such liability is invalid.

The directors have the duty of general supervision of the affairs of the company even if there is a managing director or manager.

The following powers must be exercised only by the Board at its meetings :—

(*i*) the power to make calls ;

(*ii*) the power to issue debentures ;

(*iii*) the power to borrow moneys otherwise than on debentures ;

(*iv*) the power to invest company's funds ; and

(*v*) the power to make loans.

The powers specified in (*iii*), (*iv*) and (*v*) may be delegated by resolution at a Board meeting up to specified limits. The above does not cover the ordinary transactions of a bank.

Managing Director. The directors may appoint one of themselves as Managing Director. A managing director is "a director who, by virtue of an agreement with the company or of a resolution passed by the company in general meeting or by its Board or, by virtue of its memorandum or articles of association, is entrusted with any powers of management which would not otherwise be exerciseable by him, and includes a director occupying the position of a managing director, by whatever name called." In the case of a public company and its subsidiary, amendment of any provision relating to the appointment or re-appointment of a managing director, whole-time director, or a director not liable to retirement by rotation will not be effective unless approved by the Central Government. A new managing director can be appointed only with the approval of the Central Government. Reappointment also requires the sanction of the Central Government. A managing director cannot act as such for more than two companies and, in the case of the second company, unanimous approval of the board of directors is necessary. The following cannot be appointed as managing director :-- (*i*) an undischarged insolvent ; (*ii*) one who has at any time been adjudged an insolvent ; (*iii*) one who suspends or has suspended payment to his creditors ; (*iv*) one who makes or has at any time within the preceding five years made, a composition with the creditors ; and (*v*) one who has been within the preceding five years, convicted of an offence involving moral turpitude.

Manager. A manager means "an individual (not being the managing agent) who subject to the superintendence, control and direction of the Board of Directors, has the management of the whole, or substantially the whole of the affairs of the company, and includes a director or any other person occupying the position of a manager, by whatever name called, and whether under a contract of service or not." A manager must be an individual. He is usually appointed by the Board of Directors. He cannot be appointed for more than five years at a time. The disqualifications and restrictions attaching to the managing director also apply to the manager.

A company may have either a managing director or a manager but not both but it may have two managing directors.

BOOKS & ACCOUNTS

Statutory Books. Apart from books required to record the company's transactions, the Companies Act requires some other books to be maintained mainly with a view to safeguard the interests of the shareholders and the public. Such books are known as 'Statutory

Books. The following is the list of these books to be maintained by a company :—

1. Register of investments not held in company's name (open to members and debenture-holders).
*2. Register of charges.
*3. Register of members.
*4. Index of members where the number is more than fifty, unless the register of members itself affords an index.
*5. Register of debenture-holders.
*6. Index of debenture-holders where the number is more than fifty, unless the register of debenture-holders itself affords an index.
*7. Foreign register (and a duplicate) of members and debenture-holders, if any.
8. Minute Books (Minute Books containing minutes of proceedings of general meetings open to members).
9. Register of contracts, companies and firms in which directors are interested directly or indirectly (open to members).
*10. Register of directors, managing director, managing agent, secretaries and treasurers, manager and secretary.
11. Register of directors' shareholdings (open to members and debentureholders during 14 days before and 3 days after the annual general meeting and to the Registrar and the Central Government).
12 Register of loans made, guarantees given or securities provided to companies under the same management.
13. Register of investments in shares and debentures of companies in the same group.

Nos. 12and 13are open for inspection to members. Those marked with an asterisk are to be open to the public also.

Books of Account. Section 209 requires a company to maintain such books as will give a true and fair view in respect of :

(*a*) all sums of money received and expended by the company and the matters in respect of which the receipt and expenditure take place ;

(*b*) all sales and purchases of goods by the company ; and

(*c*) all assets and liabilities of the company.

The Central Government now has also the power to require companies engaged in manufacturing, processing and mining to keep a record of particulars regarding utilisation of materials or labour or other items of cost. The Government prescribes the particulars the record of which is to be maintained; also it is up to the Government to decide which industry should be required to keep the desired record. The purpose of this power is to force companies (in the industry chosen by the Government) to keep proper cost records.

Sub-section (3) of Section 209 makes it clear that the books of account to be maintained should be such as will give a true and fair view of the state of affairs of the company and its transactions. The law does not expressly say so but the books have to be maintained on the double entry system. Also, the Actual System (or the Mercantile System) has to be followed.

If the company has a branch, proper books of account can be maintained there and quarterly statements summarising the position at the branch sent to the head office.

Books must be preserved for a minimum period of eight years.

These books are open to inspection of directors, the Registrar and officers authorised by the Central Government. The Board of Directors may decide to keep all or any of the books of account at a place other than the registered office (but in India); within seven days of the decision, the Registrar must be notified of the full address of the place where the books are kept.

Issue of Shares

It has been noted above that shares are usually issued by a public company on the basis of a prospectus. From the point of accounting entries the following points should be noted :—

(*a*) The prospectus mentions the number of shares issued, *i.e.*, the number of shares offered to the public. No company can allot a number of shares higher than the number of shares issued or offered. Thus if a company invites applications for 10,000 shares and if the public applies for, say, 15,000 shares, the company cannot allot more than 10,000 shares. Some applications will probably be rejected and others will be scaled down in order to see that the actual number of shares given to the members of the public does not exceed 10,000.

(*b*) The prospectus also mentions the minimum subscription. The minimum subscription may be defined as that number of shares which will enable the company to get enough cash for proper working. Under the Companies Act the directors have to estimate their requirements of cash and thus determine the minimum number of shares which will have to be subscribed by the public in order to enable the company to function. While determining the minimum subscription the directors will have to make an estimate for each of the following separately :—

(*i*) The purchase price of any property purchased or to be purchased which is to be met out of the proceeds of the issue of shares ;

(*ii*) any preliminary expenses payable by the company and any commission payable in connection with the issue of shares ;

(*iii*) the repayment of any money borrowed by the company in respect of the above two matters ;

(*iv*) working capital ; and

(*v*) any other expenditure.

It must be noted that if the public fails to apply for shares equal to the minimum subscription within 120 days of the issue of the prospectus, no allotment can be made. Any deposits which the public may have sent with the applications must be refunded within the next 10 days. If the company fails to make this refund the directors will be jointly and severally liable for the amount together with interest at 6 per cent per annum from the expiry of 130th day after the date of the prospectus.

(*c*) **In case the Prospectus states that application is being made to a stock exchange or more than one stock exchanges for permission so that the shares of the company will be traded on the stock exchange (s) *and* such permission is not granted within four weeks of the closure of the subscription lists or such application was not made with in 10 days of the prospectus, any allotment made will be void.**

(*d*) It is up to the directors to ask for the whole of the amount on the shares along with applications. But usually this is not done. A certain deposit (known as application money) is asked for with the applications. This must not be less than 5 per cent of the nominal value of the shares. Another instalment is payable when the applicant is informed of the acceptance of the application. This instalment is known as allotment money. The remaining amount is usually called according to the discretion of the directors but subject to the provisions of the articles. When the remaining amount is called up it is known as making a call.

(*e*) Moneys received along with the applications must be deposited in a scheduled bank and must be kept so deposited until the company (if it is new) obtains the certificate of commencement of business (or, if the company is already working until the entire amount payable on applications in respect of the minimun subscription has been received). This means the directors of the company have no authority to deal with the amount unless the certificate of commencement of business is issued to the company.

The student must remember these points in order to deal with the issue of shares effectively.

Accounting entries. It should be remembered that after the issue of the prospectus it would not be known as to how many applications would be received. The applications and application moneys are continuously received and deposited in bank for a number of days. The directors have to wait for a minimum of four clear days. After this if the public has applied for shares equal to the minimum subscription the directors will consider the application.

The first entry to be made is regarding the receipt of application money. The entry is :

Bank Account	Dr.	with the actual amount received by the company.
To Share Applications A/c		

Suppose a company invites applications for 10,000 shares of Rs. 100 each on which Rs. 20 are payable on application. The public applies for 11,000 shares. The entry for application money will be :

		Rs.	Rs.
Bank Account	Dr.	2,20,000	
To Share Applications Account			2,20,000
Application money on 11,000 shares at Rs. 20 per share.			

If the applications had amounted only to 9,000 shares, the entry would have been made only for Rs. 1,80,000.

The next step is for the directors to consider the applications* and to decide which applications will be accepted in full, which applications will be partially accepted and which applications will be rejected. If a company decides to give shares to an applicant it is said to allot so many shares to the person concerned. The person is informed through what is known as the Letter of Allotment. A specimen letter of allotment is given on the next page :—

*This process is known as "Allotment".

Ganesh Company Ltd.
(Incorporated under the Companies Act, 1956)
Letter of Allotment

18-C, Connaught Circus,
New Delhi.
December 20, 1978

No. 115
Shri J.D. Verma,
G-22, Defence Colony,
New Delhi

Dear Sir,

In respect of your application dated 15th December, 1978, for *250* equity shares, I have to inform you that the Board of Directors have allotted to you *200* equity shares of Rs. 10 each in the Ganesh Company Ltd.

	Rs.
The amount payable by you on application (Rs. 2) and allotment (Rs. 3), *viz.*, Rs. 5 per share on 200 equity shares is	1,000.00
You have already paid on *250* equity shares @ Rs. 2 per share	500.00
Leaving the amount due from you on allotment	500.00

This amount is now due from you and should be paid on or before the 15th January, 1979 to the company's bankers, Central Bank of India Janpath, New Delhi, by a crossed cheque.

Yours faithfully,
By Order of the Board
C. Ramaswamy
Secretary.

This should be sent entire to the company's bankers.

.................Perforated.........................

*Banker's Receipt for Allotment Money
Ganesh Company Ltd.

Received this *Fifth* day of *January*, 1979, the sum of Rs. *Five hundred* only due in respect of allotment letter No. 115.

Rs. *500·00* Stamp

N.B. The Share Certificate will be delivered only against production of this Banker's receipt.

Signatures

.................Perforated................

To be detached and retained by bankers
Ganesh Company Ltd.

No. 115. Name *J.D. Verma.* Amount received Rs. 500.00.
Date Received *5th January*, 1979

Signatures

II. On allotment the following accounting entries are necessary :—

1. *Transfer of the application money on the number of shares allotted.* The entry is :

Share Applications Account	Dr.	application money on the actual number of shares allotted.
To Share Capital A/c		

If, continuing the above example, when 11,000 shares are applied for and when 10,000 shares are allotted, the entry will be :

		Rs.	Rs.
Share Applications Account	Dr.	2,00,000	
To Share Capital A/c			2,00,000
Application money on 10,000 shares @ Rs. 20 each transferred to Share Capital A/c.			

2. *Recording the amount due on allotment.* Suppose Rs. 30 per share are demanded by the directors on allotment (in the above example). This means that Rs. 3,00,000 will be due by the persons to whom shares have been allotted. The entry is :

		Rs.	Rs.
Share Allotment Account	Dr.	3,00,000	
To Share Capital A/c			3,00,000
Amount due on 10,000 shares @ Rs. 30 per share on allotment.			

The nature of the Share Allotment Account is that of a collective account for all shareholders. It means that this is the sum due from the various shareholders on account of allotment.

3. *Transfer of application money to Allotment Account in case of partially accepted applications.* It happens often that a person applies for, say, 100 shares but is given only 40 shares. It means that the application money sent by him on 60 shares becomes surplus. Usually, this surplus money is not refunded to the applicant but is kept by the company against the money due on allotment. This is recorded by the following entry :

Share Applications Account	Dr.
To Share Allotment Account	

Suppose in the above example applicants for 700 shares are given only 300 shares. In that case the application money on 400 shares will become surplus and at the rate of Rs. 20 per share the amount will be transferred from the Share Application Account to Shares Allotment Account. The entry is :

		Rs.	Rs.
Share Application Account	Dr.	8,000	
To Share Allotment A/c			8,000
Surplus application money on partially accepted application transferred to Share Allotment A/c.			

4. *Refund of application money on rejected applications.* Some of the applications are rejected. In that case naturally a letter of regret is written and along with the letter a cheque for the application money is enclosed. At the time of refund, the entry is :

Share Application Account Dr.
To Bank Account

5. *Receipt of money on allotment.* When the allotment money is received the entry naturally is :

Bank Account Dr.) with the actual amount
To Share Allotment A/c) received.

It may happen, of course, that some people may not pay the money due on allotment. In that case the Allotment Account will show a debit balance. It should be remembered that normally a person does not become a shareholder and his name is not put on the Register of Members unless he has paid the allotment money.

III. On making calls, two entries become necessary :

(1) Whenever a call is made the Call Account is debited and the Share Capital Account is credited. The entry is :

Call Account Dr.) with the total amount
To Share Capital A/c) due on the call.

(2) As and when the money due on the call is received, the following entry will be passed :

Bank Account Dr.) with the actual
To Share Call Account) amount received.

Some shareholders may not pay the amount due on the call and to that extent the Call Account will show a debit balance. This amount is known as calls in arrear. In some cases, the call account is closed by transfer to Calls in Arrear Account. In that case the entry will be :

Calls in Arrear Account	Dr.	with the amount still remaining uncollected on the call.
To the Call Account		

Note : In the balance sheet the amount of the calls in arrear must be shown by way of deduction from the share capital.

Illustration A limited company issued 10,000 shares of Rs. 10 each payable as under :

Rs. 2 on application;

Rs. 3 on allotment;

Rs. 3 on first call; and

Rs. 2 on final call.

The public applied for 9,000 shares. These were allotted. The final call was not made. All the money due on the shares was received except the first call on 400 shares.

Give journal entries, ledger accounts and the balance sheet.

Solution :

Journal

	Particulars		Dr. Rs.		Cr. Rs.	
	Bank Account	Dr.	18,000	--		
	To Share Applications A/c				18,000	–
	Application money received on 9,000 shares applied for by the public					
	Share Applications Account	Dr.	18,000	–		
	To Share Capital Account				18,000	–
	Application money on 9,000 shares allotted transferred to Share Capital Account					
	Share Allotment Account	Dr.	27,000	–		
	To Share Capital Account				27,000	–
	Amount due from the members on allotment of shares					

	Particulars		Rs.		Rs.	
	Bank Account Dr. To Share Allotment Account Amount due on Allotment received		27,000	—	27,000	—
	Share First Call Account Dr. To Share Capital Account Amount due on 9,000 shares at Rs. 3 per share on first call as per director's resolution No......dated.........		27,000	—	27,000	—
	Bank Account Dr. To Share First Call Account Amount received on First Call Account		25,800	—	25,800	—

LEDGER ACCOUNTS

Bank Account

Dr. *Cr.*

		Rs.				Rs.	
	To Share Application Account	18,000	—		By Balance c/d	70,800	—
	To Share allotment A/c	27,000	—				
	To Share First Call A/c	25,800	—				
		70,800	—			70,800	—
	To Balance b/d	70,800	—				

Share Applications Account

		Rs.				Rs.	
	To Share Capital A/c—transfer	18,000	—		By Bank A/c	18,000	—
		18,000	—			18,000	—

Share Allotment Account

	Rs.			Rs.	
To Share Capital A/c	27,000	—	By Bank A/c	27,000	—

Share First Call Account

	Rs.			Rs.	
To Share Capital A/c	27,000	—	By Bank A/c	25,800	—
			By Balance c/d	1,200	—
	27,000	—		27,000	—
To Balance b/d	1,200	—			

Share Capital Account

	Rs.			Rs.	
To Balance c/d	72,000		By Share Application A/c	18,000	—
			By Share Allotment A/c	27,000	—
			By Share First Call Account	27,000	—
	72,000	—		72,000	—
			By Balance b/d	72,000	—

Balance Sheet of.............

Liabilities	Rs.		*Assets*	Rs.	
*Authorised Capital	?		Bank	70,800	—
*Issued Capital : 10,000 Shares of Rs. 10 each	1,00,000	—			
*Subscribed Capital : 9,000 Shares of Rs. 10 each, Rs. 8 Called Rs. 72,000 Less Calls in Arrear 1,200	70,800	—			
	70,800	—		70,800	—

* It is compulsory for this information to be given in case of companies. Authorised Capital means the maximum capital which the company is allowed to have. This is fixed by the Memorandum of Association.

Illustration X Limited having an authorised capital of Rs. 15,00,000 in share of Rs. 10 each issued 1,00,000 shares of Rs. 10 each payable as under :

On Application	Rs. 2
On Allotment	Rs. 3
On First Call	Rs. 2
On Final Call	Rs. 3

Applications received from the public totalled 1,50,000 shares. The directors decided to allot as follows :—

To the applicants for 70,000 shares	—	full
To the applicants for 50,000 shares	—	30,000 shares
To the applicants for 30,000 shares	—	nil

The directors did not make the final call. All moneys due on shares were received with the exception of the first call on 4,000 shares.

Give journal entries, ledger accounts and the balance sheet.

Solution :

Journal

	Particulars		Dr. Rs.		Cr. Rs.	
	Bank Account To Share Applications A/c Application money of Rs. 2 per share received on 1,50,000 shares	Dr.	3,00,000	—	3,00,000	—
	Share Applications Account To Share Capital Account Application money on 1,00.000 shares allotted by the directors transferred to Share Capital Account	Dr.	2,00,000	—	2,00,000	—
	Share Allotment Account To Share Capital Account Amount due on 1,00,000 shares on allotment @ Rs. 3 per share	Dr.	3,00,000	—	3,00,000	—
	Share Applications Account To Bank Account Application money on 30,000 shares refunded because no allotment was made	Dr.	60,000	—	60,000	—

			Rs.	Rs.
	Share Applications Account Dr. To Share Allotment A/c Surplus application money on partially accepted applications transferred to Allotment Account		40,000 —	40,000 —
	Bank Account Dr. To Share Allotment A/c Amount due on allotment received		2,60,000 —	2,60,000 —
	Share First Call Account Dr. To Share Capital Account A call of Rs. 2 per share made on 1,00,000 shares as per director's resolution no....... dated...........		2,00,000 —	2,00,000 —
	Bank Account Dr. To Share First Call A/c Amount received against first call		1,92,000 —	1,92,000 —

LEDGER ACCOUNTS

Bank Account

Dr. *Cr.*

			Rs.				Rs.
	To Share Applications Account		3,00,000 —		By Share Applications Account		60,000 —
	To Share Allotment A/c		2,60,000 —		By Balance c/d		6,92,000 —
	To Share First Call A/c		1,92,000 —				
			7,52,000 —				7,52,000 —
	To Balance b/d		6,92,000 —				

Share Applications Account

	Rs.			Rs.	
To Share Capital A/c	2,00,000	—	By Bank A/c	3,00,000	—
To Share Allotment A/c	40,000	—			
To Bank A/c—refund	60,000	—			
	3,00,000	—		3,00,000	—

Share Allotment Account

	Rs.			Rs.	
To Share Capital Account	3,00,000	—	By Share Applications A/c—Surplus	40,000	—
			By Bank A/c	2,60,000	—
	3,00,000	—		3,00,000	—

Share First Call Account

	Rs.			Rs.	
To Share Capital A/c	2,00,000	—	By Bank A/c	1,92,000	—
			By Balance c/d	8,000	—
	2,00,000	—		2,00,000	—
To Balance b/d	8,000	—			

Share Capital Account

	Rs.			Rs.	
To Balance b/d	7,00,000	—	By Share Applications Account	2,00,000	—
			By Share Allotment A/c	3,00,000	—
			By Share First Call A/c	2,00,000	—
	7,00,000	—		7,00,000	—
			By Balance b/d	7,00,000	—

Balance Sheet of X Ltd.

	Rs.			Rs.	
Share Capital— Authorised : 1,50,000 Shares of Rs. 10 each	15,00,000	—	Bank	6,92,000	—
Issued and Subscribed : 1,00,000 Shares of Rs. 10 each, Rs. 7 called Rs. 7,00,000 Less Calls in arrear Rs. 8,000	6,92,000	—			
	6,92,000	—		6,92,000	—

Application and Allotment Account (joint). These days it is becoming popular to open only one account in respect of applications and allotment and not two separate accounts. In such a case all entries in respect of application and allotment should be made in the account called 'Application and Allotment Account'. If this method is followed there will be a saving in the number of entries to be passed. Only one entry will do for crediting the Capital Account in respect of both the application money and the allotment money. Further the entry for surplus application money on partially accepted applications need not be passed. If the above illustration has to be worked out in the manner, the journal entries will be as follows :—

Journal

				Rs.		Rs.	
		Bank Account To Share Applications and Allotment Account Application money on 1,50,000 shares @ Rs. 2 per share	Dr.	3,00,000	—	3,00,000	—
		Share Applications and Allotment Account To Share Capital Account Application money, Rs. 2 and allotment money, Rs. 3 per share credited to Capital Account on the allotment of 1,00,000 shares	Dr.	5,00,000	—	5,00,000	—

		Rs.		Rs.	
Share Applications and Allotment Account To Bank Account Refund of application money on rejected applications	Dr.	60,000	—	60,000	—
Bank Account To Share Applications and Allotment Account Amount received on allotment of shares	Dr.	2,60,000	—	2,60,000	—
Share First Call Account To Share Capital Account Amount due on first call @ Rs 2 per share on 1,00,000 shares	Dr.	2,00,000	—	2,00,000	—
Bank Account To Share First Call A/c Receipt of money due on first call except on 4,000 shares	Dr.	1,92,000	—	1,92,000	—

The balance sheet will be naturally the same as shown already. Instead of the Share Applications Account and Share Allotment Account there will be only one account. The Share Applications and Allotment Account which will be as shown below :

Share Applications and Allotment Account

Dr. *Cr.*

	Rs.			Rs.	
To Share Capital A/c	5,00,000	—	By Bank A/c	3,00,000	—
To Bank A/c—refund	60,000	—	By Bank A/c	2,60,000	—
	5,60,000	—		5,60,000	—

Calls in Arrear Account. In the above example Share First Call Account shows a debit balance of Rs. 8,000. This represents calls in arrear. If desired, the Share First Call Account and such other calls on which the amount may remain unpaid may be closed by transferring the debit balance to a newly opened account called "Calls in Arrear Account". The directors may insist upon interest if the amount is not paid on the due date. The rate of interest is generally laid down in the articles of association. But if the articles are silent it should be taken that the directors will charge interest at 5 per cent per annum.

Entries under the Practical System. The student knows already that under the Practical System cash entries are made in the cash book directly. Therefore, if the company is following this system as it is likely it will, entries in respect of receipt of money will all be made in the cash book directly. No journal entry may be passed for these transactions. Journal entries will be passed only in respect of other transactions, for instance, for transfer of application money or allotment money to the Share Capital Account or to bring into books the amount due from the shareholders in respect of the first call, second call, etc. If the above Illustration were to be worked out under this system it will be as follows :

Cash Book (Bank Columns only)

Dr. *Cr.*

		Rs.				Rs.	
	To Share Applications A/c—application money Rs. 2 on 1,50,000 shares	3,00,000	—		By Share Applications A/c—refund of application money on 30,000 shares	60,000	—
	To Share Allotment A/c—money due received	2,60,000	—		By Balance c/d	6,92,000	—
	To Share First Call A/c—First Call Rs. 2, on 96,000 shares	1,92,000	—				
		7,52,000	—			7,52,000	—
	To Balance b/d	6,92,000	—				

Journal

		Dr. Rs.		Cr. Rs.	
	Share Applications Account Dr. To Share Capital Account Application money on 1,00,000 shares allotted, transferred to Share Capital A/c	2,00,000	—	2,00,000	—
	Shares Allotment Account Dr. To Share Capital Account Amount due on 100,000 Shares on allotment @ Rs. 3 per share	3,00,000	—	3,00,000	—
	Share Applications Account Dr. To Share Allotment Account Surplus application money on partially accepted applications transferred to Allotment A/c	40,000	—	40,000	—
	Share First Call Account Dr. To Share Capital Account Amount due on First Call on 1,00,000 shares @ Rs. 2 per share	2,00,000	—	2,00,000	—

Calls in Advance. Usually a company is authorised by its articles of association to receive from the shareholders the amount which has not yet been called on shares. If such an amount is received, it should not be credited to Share Capital Account but should be credited to a separate account called "Calls in Advance Account" A company may pay interest on the amount received in advance according to its articles of association. If the articles are silent it should be taken that the company can pay interest upto 6 per cent per annum.

The question of calls in advance may also arise if only a small number of shares is allotted against an application for a very large number. Suppose a person applies for 100 shares and pays Rs. 2 per share, *i.e.*, Rs. 200 in all. He is given only 30 shares on which Rs. 3 per share is due as allotment money. In this case his surplus application money will be Rs. 140. The amount due on allotment is only Rs. 90. After keeping the money against allotment, Rs. 50 will still be left. This money may either be refunded to the shareholder or, if he has authorised the company in this behalf, the money may be kept against further calls to be made. In such a case such an amount will be credited to Call in Advance Account. When the particular call is made, naturally, no amount will be received from the shareholder who has already paid the amount in advance. In respect of such amounts the Call in Advance Account should be debited and the particular call account credited.

Illustration Goodluck Ltd. issued 10,000 shares of Rs. 100 each payable as under :—

Rs. 20 on application ;

Rs. 25 on allotment ;

Rs. 30 on first call ; and

Rs. 25 on final call.

The public applied for 18,000 shares. The allotment was made on 1st July, 1977 as follows :—

To the applicants of 9,000 shares	—	full
To the applicants of 4,000 shares	—	25%
To the remaining applicants	—	nil

The directors made the first call on 1st October, 1977 and the second call on 1st December, 1977. Under the terms of issue the surplus application money could be kept by the directors against money due on allotment and against subsequent calls. One shareholder to whom 1,000 shares were allotted on 100% basis paid, on allotment, the full amount due on shares. On 1st December the directors paid the interest due on calls in advance at 6 per cent per annum.

Give entries in the cash book and the journal of the company assuming that all moneys due have been received.

Solution :

Cash Book (Bank Columns only)

Dr. *Cr.*

Date	Particulars	Rs.	Date	Particulars	Rs.
1977 ?	To Share Applications & Allotment A/c—Application money on 18,000 shares @ Rs. 20 per share	3,60,000	1977 July 1	By Share Applications & Allotment A/c—refund of application money on 5,000 shares	1,00,000
July 1	To Share Applications & Allotment Account—Allotment money on 9,000 shares	2,25,000	Dec. 1	By Interest A/c : 6% on Rs. 60,000 for 3 months 900; 6% on 30,000 for 5 months 750	1,650
"	To Calls in Advance Account—First and Second Calls received on 1,000 shares	55,000		By Balance c/d	9,98,350
Oct. 1	To Share First Call Account—First Call received on 8,000 shares	2,40,000			
Dec. 1	To Share Final Call Account Call received on 9,000 shares less Rs. 5,000	2,20,000			
		11,00,000			11,00,000
Dec. 1	To Balance b/d	9,98,350			

Journal

				Dr		Cr.	
1977				Rs.		Rs,	
July	1	Share Application & Allotment Account To Share Capital Account Application money Rs. 20, and allotment money, Rs. 25 per share transferred to Share Capital Account on allotment of 10,000 shares	Dr.	4,50,000	—	4,50,000	—
	,,	Share Application and Allotment Account To Call in Advance Account Surplus application money on allotment of 1,000 shares to applicants of 4,000 shares transferred to Calls in Advance Account : Total application money received Rs. 80,000 Less application and allotment money on 1,000 shares Rs. 45,000 Surplus Rs. 35,000	Dr.	35,000	—	35,000	—
Oct.	1	Share First Call Account To Share Capital Account Amount due from various members at Rs. 30 per share on first call as per directors' resolution No.........dated......	Dr.	3,00,000	—	3,00,000	—
,,	,,	Calls in Advance Account To Share First Call Account Amount already received from shareholders previously credited to Calls in Advance Account now transferred to First Call Account	Dr.	60,000	—	60,000	—
Dec.	1	Share Final Call Account The Share Capital Account Amount due on second call on 10,000 shares as per directors' resolution no......dated......	Dr.	2,50,000	—	2,50,000	—

				Rs.		Rs.	
Dec.	1	Calls in Advance Account To Share Final Call Account Amount already received against final call previously credited to Calls in Advance Account credited to the Final Call Account now	Dr.	30,000	—	30,000	—

(The student is advised to prepare ledger account and Balance Sheet.)

Different classes of shares. If a company issues two calls of shares simultaneously there should be separate Share Applications Account, one each for equity shares and for preference shares. Similarly, there should be separate accounts to record money due on allotment, on first call, second call etc.

Illustration Ashoka Limited issued 1,000 equity shares of Rs. 100 each and 1,000 6% preference shares of Rs. 100 each. The amounts were payable as follows :—

	Equity Shares	*Preference Shares*
	Rs.	Rs.
On application	20	25
On allotment	30	50
On first call	25	25
On final call	25	—

These shares were applied for and allotted. All the money due were received except the final call on 200 equity shares.

Give entries in the Cash Book and the journal of the company and also show the balance sheet.

Solution :

Cash Book (Bank Columns only)

Dr.		Rs.			Rs. Cr.
	To Preference Shares Application and Allotment A/c (Rs. 25 on 1,000 shares)	25,000		By Balance c/d	1,95,000
	To Equity Shares Applications and Allotment A/c (Rs. 20 on 1,000 shares)	20,000			
	To Equity Shares Applications and Allotment A/c (Rs. 30 on 1,000 shares)	30,000			
	To Preference Shares Application and Allotment A/c (Rs. 50 on 1,000 shares)	50,000			
	To Equity Shares First Call A/c (Rs. 25 on 1,000 shares)	25,000			
	To Pref. Shares First & Final Call A/c (Rs. 25 on 1,000 shares)	25,000			
	To Equity Shares Final Call A/c (Rs 25 on 800 shares)	20,000			
		1,95,000			1,95,000
	To Balance b/d	1,95,000			

		Rs.	Rs.
Equity Shares Application and Allotment Account Dr. To Equity Share Capital A/c Application money Rs. 20 and allotment money Rs. 30 on 1,000 equity shares transferred to Equity Share Capital Account		50,000 —	50,000 —
Preference Shares Applications and Allotment Account Dr. To 6% Preference Share Capital Account Application money Rs. 25 and allotment money Rs. 50 per share on 1,000 preference shares transferred to Preference Share Capital Account		75,000 —	75,000 —
Equity Shares First Call A/c Dr. To Equity Share Capital A/c Amount due on 1,000 equity shares as first call as per directors' resolution no...... dated............		25,000 —	25,000 —
Preference Share First and Final Call Account Dr. To Preference Share Capital A/c Amount due on 1,000 shares as first and final call as per directors' resolution no...... dated............		25,000 —	25,000 —
Equity Share Final Call Account Dr. To Equity Share Capital A/c Amount due on 1,000 equity shares on final call		25,000 —	25,000 —

Balance Sheet of Goodluck Ltd. as at..............

	Rs.			Rs.	
Share Capital—			Cash at Bank	1,95,000	—
Authorised	?				
Issued and subscribed : 1,000 6% Preference Shares of Rs. 100 each, fully paid	1,00,000	—			
1,000 Equity Shares of Rs. 100 each fully called Rs. 1,00,000 Less Calls in arrear Rs. 5.000	95,000	—			
	1,95,000	—		1,95,000	—

Issue of shares at a premium. A successful company or a company which is likely to be very successful sometimes asks people to pay even more than the face value of the shares. A company may ask the people to pay Rs. 120 for every share of Rs. 100. In this case the company will be said to have issued the shares at a premium of Rs. 20. There are no legal restrictions upon the issue of shares at a premium but section 78 of the Companies Act puts certain restrictions on the company as regards the disposal of the amount collected as share premium. This amount must be credited to Share Premium Account and it can be used for issue of fully paid bonus shares, *i.e.*, shares for which no payment will be required from the shareholders. The company can also use the Share Premium Account for the following other purposes :—

1. Writing off the preliminary expenses of the company.
2. Writing off the expenses or the commission paid or discount allowed on shares or debentures issued by the company.
3. Providing for the premium payable on the redemption of any redeemable preference shares or debentures of the company.

If the company wishes to use the Shares Premium Account for any other purpose it will have to first obtain the sanction of the Court.

Entries. The premium may be collected by a company along with application or on allotment or on first call or second call, as the company may wish. Usually, the company collects the premium along with allotment. Suppose, the amount due on allotment by way of capital is Rs. 25 and by way of premium Rs. 20, it is clear then that on allotment the total amount due is Rs. 45. Therefore, the following entry can be passed :—

	Rs.	Rs.
Share Allotment Account	Dr. 45	
To Share Capital Account		25
To Share Premium Account		20

When the amount is received it should be credited to the Share Allotment Account and, therefore, the entry will be :—

Bank Account	Dr.	45	
To Share Allotment Account			45

In this manner the proper amount will be credited to Share Capital Account and to Share Premium Account. However, an alternate method is possible. At first the entry for allotment may record only the amount due on account of share capital. Continuing the above example the entry will be :—

Share Allotment Account	Dr.	25	
To Share Capital Account			25

In fact, Rs. 45 will be received including Rs. 20 for premium. This amount will now be credited to Share Premium Account. The entry will be :—

Bank Account	Dr.	45	
To Share Allotment Account			25
To Share Premium Account			20

If the premium is to be collected along with the applications only the first method should be used. This is because when applications are received the money is in the nature of a deposit and it is not known for certain whether the money will be kept or returned. Therefore, if premium is received on applications the two entries will be :

1. Bank Account Dr. } with the total amount received
   To Share Applications A/c
2. Shares Applications A/c Dr.
   To Share Capital A/c
   To Share Premium A/c

Illustration Good Pictures Ltd. invited applications for 10,000 shares of Rs. 100 each at a premium of Rs. 20 per share. The shares were payable as follows :—

On application	Rs. 20 ;
On allotment	Rs. 50 including premium ;
On first call	Rs. 30 ; and
On final call	Rs. 20.

The public applied for 20,000 shares. Allotments were made as follows :—

To applicants of 8,000 shares	—full ;
To applicants of 8,000 shares	—2,000 shares ; and
To applicants of 4,000 shares	—nil.

The company was authorised to retain all sums over-paid for adjustment against money due on allotment and on calls. The company exercised this power. The directors made the allotment on 1st April, 1973, and 1st call on 1st July, 1973. By the end of 1973 no further call had been made. All the moneys due on allotment were collected and against first call the directors had received Rs. 2,65,000.

Give journal entries and the balance sheet of the company on 31st December, 1973 assuming that the directors had paid interest due to shareholders in cash at the proper date at the rate of 6 per cent per annum.

Solution :

Journal

Date		Particulars		Dr. Rs.		Cr. Rs.	
?		Bank Account Dr. To Share Applications A/c Application money on 20,000 shares at Rs. 20 per share		4,00,000		4,00,000	—
1973 Apr.	1	Share Applications A/c Dr. To Share Capital Account Application money on 10,000 shares transferred to Share Capital Account, on allotment vide Director's Resolution dated		2,00,000	—	2,00,000	—
1973 Apr.	1	Share Allotment Account Dr. To Share Capital Account To Share Premium Account Amount due on allotment at Rs. 50 per share out of which Rs. 20 are for premium		5,00,000	—	3,00,000 2,00,000	— —
1973 Apr.	1	Share Applications Account Dr. To Share Allotment A/c To Calls in Advance A/c Surplus application money on partially accepted applications transferred to Share Allotment Account (Rs. 1 lakh, *i.e.*, Rs. 50 due on 2,000 shares allotted) and Calls in Advance Account		1,20,000	—	1,00,000 20,000	— —
1973 Apr.	1	Share Applications Account Dr. To Bank Account Application money refunded on rejected applications		80,000	—	80,000	—
1973 Apr.	1	Bank Account Dr. To Share Allotment A/c Moneys due on allotment received, *i.e.*, Rs. 5 lakhs minus Rs. 1 lakh already adjusted		4,00,000	—	4,00,000	—

				Rs.		Rs.	
1973 July	1	Share First Call Account To Share Capital Account Amount due on first call made by directors at Rs. 30 per share	Dr.	3,00,000	—	3,00,000	—
	1	Bank Account To Share First Call Account Amount received against first call	Dr.	2,65,000	—	2,65,000	—
	1	Calls in Advance Account To First Call Account Amount previously credited to Calls in Advance Account adjusted against the amount due on first call	Dr.	20,000	—	20,000	—
	1	Interest on Calls in Advance Account To Bank Account Interest paid for three months, *i.e.*, from 1st April to 1st July for amount received in advance at 6% per annum	Dr.	300	—	300	—

Balance Sheet of Good Pictures Ltd. as at....................

	Rs.			Rs.	
Share Capital			**Bank**	9,84,700	—
Authorised	?		**Interest Paid (awaiting adjustment)**	300	—
Issued and Subscribed—10,000 shares of Rs. 100 each.					
Rs. 80 called	8,00,000	—			
Less Calls in arrear	15,000	—			
	7,85,000	—			
Share Premium Account	2,00,000	—			
	9,85,000	—		9,85,000	—

Forfeiture of shares. If a shareholder fails to pay the amount due on his shares as called upon by the directors his shares may be forfeited by the directors if they are so authorised by the articles of association. This means that the shares held by the shareholder can be 'cancelled' and the amount already paid by him may be forfeited. The directors have to, first of all, give a notice to the shareholder giving him at least 14 clear days to pay the amount due and interest on it, stating that if he fails to pay the amount and th interest on it, if any, the shares will be forfeited. If the shareholder still fails to pay the amount, the case will be put up before the Board of Directors who may then decide to forfeit the shares. Without proper notice the shares cannot be forfeited. It should be noted that the power to forfeit shares should be taken by the company by inserting a suitable clause in the articles of association. If the articles of association do not authorise the directors to forfeit shares they will not be able to do so. Surrender of shares operates in the same way but here the move is made by the shareholder himself. The shareholder, finding that he cannot pay for the calls, may give up the shares by giving intimation to the company in writing. The directors will then 'cancel' the shares and forfeit the amount actually paid by that shareholder.

The effect of both forfeiture and surrender of shares is that the share capital is reduced. This is naturally recorded in the books by a suitable entry. Share Capital Account is debited at the amount called up or credited to Share Capital Account. In the Illustration given above Rs.15,000 has not been paid on account of first call. The first call is for Rs. 30. Therefore, it is clear that first call has not been received on 500 shares. Suppose these shares have to be forfeited. The student has seen that the Share Capital Account has been credited at the rate of Rs. 80, *i.e.*, Rs. 20 on application, Rs. 30 on allotment and Rs. 30 on first call. (For this purpose Share Premium must not be counted.) If the 500 shares have been forfeited, Share Capital Account should be debited with Rs. 40,000, *i.e.*, Rs. 80 on 500 shares. The accounts to be credited are : firstly, the Call Account that may be in arrear with the amount in arrear and, secondly, the Shares Forfeited Account with the amount actually paid by the shareholder on the shares (not counting the share premium). In the illustration Rs. 15,000 are lying to the debit of Share First Call Account. The shareholder has paid Rs. 50, *i.e.*, Rs. 20 on application and Rs. 30 on all allotment or Rs. 25,000 in all. Therefore, on forfeiture of these 500 shares, Share First Call Account will be credited with Rs. 15,000 and Shares Forfeited Account will be credited with Rs. 25,000. The entry therefore is summarised as :

(1) debit share capital with the amount called up on the forfeited shares ;

(2) credit the call accounts with the amount in arrears in respect of forfeited shares ; and

(3) credit Shares Forfeited Account with the amount actually paid.

In the above example the entry is :		Rs.	Rs.
Share Capital Account	Dr.	40,000	
To Share First Call A/c			15,000
To Shares Forfeited A/c			25,000

This entry may also be split up into two. Firstly, the total amount debited to Share Capital Account in respect of forfeited shares is transferred to Shares Forfeited Account. The entry, using the above figures, is :

Share Capital Account	Dr.	40,000	
To Shares Forfeited A/c			40,000

Then the amount standing to the debit of the call account is transferred to the Shares Forfeited Account and thus the call account is closed. The entry for the above illustration is :

Shares Forfeited Account	Dr.	15,000	
To Share First Call A/c			15,000

Whatever the method followed the Shares Forfeited Account will show a credit equal to the amount actually received on shares. This is a special profit but is not to be disposed of by the company until the shares are re-issued. This amount is shown in the Balance Sheet along with share capital. In the above example after forfeiture the Balance Sheet will appear as under :—

Balance Sheet (after forfeiture)

	Rs.			Rs.	
Share Capital— Authorised	?		Bank Account	9,84,700	—
Issued & Subscribed —9,500 Shares of Rs. 100 each, Rs. 80 paid	7,60,000	—	Interest (awaiting adjustment)	300	—
Shares Forfeited A/c	25,000	—			
Share Premium Account	2,00,000	—			
	9,85,000	—		9,85,000	—

The student is advised to prepare ledger accounts relating to forfeiture.

The student should note that if premium has been received on the shares it should remain intact and, on forfeiture, no entry is to be made in respect of share premium. But in some cases Share Premium Account is credited when a call is made ; if the call is not received in cash, it would be necessary to debit the Share Premium Account also in respect of the amount not received. It is emphasised again that this procedure will be followed only if the amount has been already credited to Share Premium Account but has not been received.

Re-issue of forfeited shares. Forfeited shares can be re-issued by the directors and they can issue them at a price lower than the paid up value or, in other words, at a discount. But the discount must not be more than the actual amount already received on shares. Continuing the above Illustration, where 500 shares have been forfeited and on which Rs.50 had already been received, the directors are at liberty to issue these 500 shares at any price above Rs. 30 for a paid up value of Rs. 80. In other words, the directors can allow a discount up to Rs. 50 but not more than this. Suppose the directors re-issue the 500 shares at Rs. 60 per share. It means that there will be a discount of Rs. 20 per share. The share capital will be credited with the full amount already credited as paid, *i.e.*, Rs. 80 per share. Cash received will be Rs. 30,000, *i.e.*, Rs. 60 on 500 shares. This will naturally be debited to the Bank Account. The remaining Rs. 10,000, *i.e.*, the discount of Rs. 20 on 500 shares is a loss and will be debited to Shares Forfeited Account. Therefore, the entry on re-issue of share is :—

(1) debit bank with the amount received ;

(2) debit Shares Forfeited Account with the discount allowed ; and

(3) credit Share Capital Account with the amount credited as paid.

The entry for the above illustration is :

		Rs.	Rs.
Bank Account	Dr.	30,000	
Shares Forfeited Account	Dr.	10,000	
To Share Capital Account			40,000

The Shares Forfeited Account now stands at a credit of Rs. 15,000. The shares have been re-issued. Therefore, this Rs. 15,000 represents profit for the company and, according to the Companies Act, it has to be transferred to Capital Reserve. For this the entry is :

Shares Forfeited Account	Dr.	15,000
To Capital Reserve Account		

The ledger accounts and balance sheet after re-issue of the 500 shares will now appear as follows :—

Share Capital Account

Dr.		Rs.		Cr.		Rs.
To Balance c/d		8,00,000	By Balance b/d			7,60,000
			By Sundries—			
			Bank	30,000		
			Shares Forfeited A/c	10,000		
						40,000
		8,00,000				8,00,000
			By Balance b/d			8,00,000

Shares Forfeited Account

	Rs.		Rs.
To Share Capital A/c—loss on reissue of shares	10,000	By Balance b/d	25,000
To Capital Reserve A/c—transfer	15,000		
	25,000		25,000

Capital Reserve Account

	Rs.		Rs.
		By Shares Forfeited Account	15,000

Balance Sheet of Good Pictures Ltd.

	Rs.		Rs.
Share Capital :		Bank	10,14,700
Authorised	?	Interest (awaiting adjustment)	300
Issued & subscribed—10,000 shares of Rs. 100 each Rs. 80 paid	8,00,000		
Share Premium	2,00 000		
Capital Reserve A/c	15,000		
	10,15,000		10,15,000

It should be noted that if some forfeited shares remain unissued the forfeited amount in respect of such shares should remain in the

Forfeited Shares Account. Only when the shares are re-issued, the profit remaining after the re-issue should be transferred to Capital Reserve.

Illustration Better Farms Ltd. issued 1,00,000 shares of Rs. 10 each at a premium of Re. 1 per share. The amount was payable as follows :—

Rs. 2 on application ;
Rs. 4 on allotment including premium ;
Rs. 2·50 on first call ; and
Rs. 2·50 on second call.

The public applied for 90,000 shares and these shares were allotted. The directors made both the calls. The first call was not received on 1,000 shares and the second call on 1,500 shares. The directors forfeited the shares on which the first call was not paid. 800 of these shares were re-issued as fully paid at Rs. 8 per share.

Give journal entries and balance sheet of the company.

Solution :

Journal

			Dr. Rs.	Cr. Rs.
	Bank Account	Dr.	1,80,000 —	
	To Share Applications and Allotment Account			1,80,000 —
	Rs. 2 on 90,000 shares received as application money			
	Share Applications and Allotment Account	Dr.	5,40,000 —	
	To Share Capital Account			4,50,000 —
	To Share Premium Account			90,000 —
	Amount transferred to Share Capital Account at Rs. 5 per share and to Share Premium Account at Re. 1 per share on 90,000 shares, on allotment as per Director's Resolution dated			
	Bank Account	Dr.	3,60,000 —	
	To Share Applications and Allotment Account			3,60,000 —
	Amount received on allotment on 90 000 shares at Rs. 4 per share			
	Share First Call Account	Dr.	2,25,000 —	
	To Share Capital Account			2,25,000 —
	Amount due on 90,000 shares at Rs. 2·50 per share as first call			

		Rs.		Rs.	
Bank Account	Dr.	2,22,500	—		
To Share First Call Account				2,22,500	—
Amount received against first call on 89,000 shares					
Share Final Call Account	Dr.	2,25,000	—		
To Share Capital Account				2,25,000	—
Amount due on final call at Rs. 2·50 per share					
Bank Account	Dr.	2,21,250	—		
To Share Final Call Account				2,21,250	—
Amount received against final call on 88,500 shares					
Share Capital Account	Dr.	10,000	—		
To Share First Call Account				2,500	—
To Share Final Call Account				2,500	—
To Share Forfeited Account				5,000	—
Forfeiture of 1,000 shares on which both first call and final call have not been received. These calls credited with amount due					
Bank Account	Dr.	6,400	—		
Shares Forfeited Account	Dr.	1,600	—		
To Share Capital Account				8,000	—
Reissue of 800 shares as fully paid for Rs. 8 per share					
Share Forfeited Account	Dr.	2,400	—		
To Capital Reserve Account				2,400	—
Profit remaining after reissue on 800 forfeited shares transferred to Capital Reserve; the amount forfeited on 200 shares, not yet reissued remains in the Forfeited Shares Account. (See Forfeited Shares Account below)					

Forfeited Shares Account

Dr.	Rs.			Cr. Rs.	
To Share Capital Account (Loss @ Rs. 2 per share on 800 shares)	1,600	—	By Share Capital A/c (Rs. 5 on 1,000 shares)	5,000	—
To Capital Reserve Account (Profit remaining on 800 shares @ Rs. 3 per share)	2,400	—			
To Balance c/d (Rs. 5 per share on 200 shares not yet re-issued)	1,000	—			
	5,000	—		5,000	—
			By Balance b/d	1,000	—

Balance Sheet of Better Farms Ltd.

	Rs.			Rs.	
Share Capital :			Bank	9,90,150	—
Authorised :					
Issued : 1,00,000 Shares of Rs. 10 each	10,00,000	—			
Subscribed : 89,800 shares of Rs. 10 each fully called Rs. 8,98,000 Less Calls in arrear 1,250	8,96,750	—			
Forfeited Shares A/c	1,000	—			
Share Premium A/c	90,000	—			
Capital Reserve	2,400	—			
	9,90,150	—		9,90,150	—

The student should prepare ledger accounts.

Issue of shares at a discount. A company can always issue forfeited shares at a discount provided the discount does not exceed the amount actually received. But otherwise the company can issue shares at a discount only subject to the legal restrictions placed by the

Companies Act. Section 79 governs issue of shares at a discount. The following points must be noted in this regard :—

(*a*) The issue of the shares at a discount is authorised by a resolution passed by the company in general meeting and sanctioned by the Company Law Board.

(*b*) The resolution specifies the maximum rate of discount at which the shares are to be issued. (The rate may exceed 10 per cent only if the Company Law Board is of the opinion that in view of the circumstances of the company concerned a higher percentage of discount should be allowed.)

(*c*) Not less than one year has, at the date of the issue, elapsed since the date on which the company was entitled to commence business.

(*d*) The shares are of a class which has already been issued.

(*e*) The shares are issued within 2 months of the date on which the issue is sanctioned by the Company Law Board or within such extended time as the court may allow.

It follows from the above that no new company can issue shares at a discount and a new class of shares also cannot be issued at a discount. The discount allowed to shareholders has to be debited to an account called Discount on Issue of Shares Account. This represents loss of a special nature and it has to be shown in the balance sheet until it is written off. In the absence of any other instructions the student will do well to raise the debit against the Discount on Issue of Shares Account at the time of allotment.

If shares issued at a discount have to be forfeited, it would be better to credit the Discount on Issue of Shares Account with the proportionate amount (at the time of the forfeiture). This will ensure that the Discount on Issue of Shares Account will represent discount on the shares actually at issue. Subsequently, if the forfeited shares are re-issued, it will again be better to debit the amount of the original discount to Discount on Issue of Shares Account.

Illustration Fair Practice Limited invited applications for 10,000 shares of Rs. 100 each at a discount of Rs. 4 per share. The amount was to be paid as follows :—

On application	Rs. 20 ;
On allotment	Rs. 30 ; and
On first and final call	Rs. 46.

The public applied for 9,000 shares and these were allotted. All moneys due were collected with the exception of the first and final call on 400 shares. 200 of these shares were re-issued as fully paid for a payment of Rs. 80 per share.

Make entries in the cash book of the company and in its journal assuming that all legal requirements have been complied with. Give also the balance sheet of the company relating to these transactions.

Solution :

Cash Book (Bank Columns only)

Dr. *Cr.*

		Rs.				Rs.	
	To Share Applications A/c (Rs. 20 on 9,000 shares)	1,80,000	—		By Balance c/d	8,61,600	—
	To Share Allotment A/c (Rs. 30 on 9,000 shares)	2,70,000	—				
	To Share First and Final Call A/c (Rs. 46 on 8,600 shares)	3,95,600	—				
	To Share Capital A/c (Rs. 80 on 200 shares)	16,000	—				
		8,61,600	—			8,61,600	—
	By Balance b/d	8,61,600	—				

Journal

	Dr.	Cr.
	Rs.	Rs.
Share Applications Account Dr. To Share Capital Account Transfer of application money on 9,000 shares on which Rs. 20 per share have been received as application money	1,80,000 —	1,80,000 —
Share Allotment Account Dr. Discount on Issue of Shares A/c Dr. To Share Capital Account Amount due on Allotment, Rs. 30 per share, and discount allowed, Rs. 4 per share on 9,000 shares	2,70,000 — 36,000	3,06,000 —
Share First and Final Call A/c Dr. To Share Capital Account Amount due on first and final call at Rs. 46 per share on 9,000 shares	4,14,000 —	4,14,000 —
Share Capital Account Dr. To Share First & Final Call A/c To Discount on Issue of Shares A/c To Shares Forfeited Account Forfeiture of 400 shares on which the call has not been received. Discount on Issue of Shares Account credited at Rs. 4 per share	40,000 —	18,400 — 1,600 — 20,000 —
Discount on Issue of Shares A/c Dr. Shares Forfeited Account Dr. To Share Capital Account Discount on shares at Rs. 4 per share and the loss on issue of shares debited to Shares Forfeited Account	800 — 3,200 —	4,000 —
Shares Forfeited Account Dr. To Capital Reserve Account Profit remaining on re-issued shares transferred to Capital Reserve (see note below the Balance Sheet)	6,800 —	6,800 —

Balance Sheet of Fair Practice Ltd.

	Rs.			Rs.	
Share Capital 8,800 shares of Rs. 100 each fully paid	8,80,000	—	Bank	8,61,600	—
Shares Forfeited A/c	10,000	—	Discount on Issue of Shares A/c (Rs. 4 on 8,800 shares)	35,200	—
Capital Reserve A/c	6,800	—			
	8,96,800	—		8,96,800	—

Note : Since 200 shares have not been reissued the forfeited amount in respect of these must remain in the Forfeited Shares Account.

Issue of shares to vendors. Vendors are often shares given in exchange for properties or assets handed over by them to the company. Such shares are not paid for in cash. On acquisition of the assets the entry will be :

Sundry Assets Account Dr.) with the price put
) on the assets taken
To Vendors' Acccount) from the vendor.

On allotment of shares to the vendor, the entry will be :

Vendors' Account Dr.
To Share Capital Account
To Share Premium Account (if any).

In the balance sheet of the company the number of shares issued like this to vendors has to be given by way of a note.

Issue of shares to promoters. Very often promoters are given shares as remuneration for bringing the company into existence. On allotment of such shares the amount should be debited to Formation Account and credited to Share Capital Account. The entry is :

Formation Costs Account Dr.
To Share Capital Account

Issue of Debentures

As the students already know debentures are uniform parts of a loan raised by the company. The public will be invited to purchase as many parts as they wish. Debentures are issued just like shares, that is to say on the basis of the prospectus. The public will apply for debentures just as they apply for shares. After receipt of applications the directors will consider them and will make the allotment according to their discretion. The entries to be passed are more or less like the issue of shares :

1. *On receipt of applications.* Applications will be accompanied by a deposit or application money. The entry will be :

Bank Account Dr.
To Debenture Applications A/c

2. (*a*) *On allotment.* Application money on debentures is transferred to debentures. The entry is :

Debentures Applications A/c Dr.
To Debentures

(*b*) Further, on allotment another instalment is payable. Sometimes even the whole of the remaining amount is payable on allotment. The amount due is recorded by the following entry :

Debenture Allotment Account Dr.
To Debentures

(*c*) On receipt of the amount bank will be debited and Debenture Allotment Account will be credited.

If any amount still remains uncalled, the directors will have the right to make calls. If a call is made, Debenture Call Account will be debited and Debentures Account will be credited. On receipt of money against the call, Bank Account will be debited and Debentures Call Account will be credited.

It is usual to put the rate of interest before debentures. If the debentures carry interest at the rate of 9% per annum, the account will be headed as 9% Debentures Account.

Illustration A company issued 5,000 13·5% debentures of Rs. 100 each payable at Rs. 20 on application and the remaining amount on allotment. The public applied for 4,000 debentures and these debentures were allotted. All moneys were received.

Solution :

Journal

		Dr. Rs.	Cr. Rs.
Bank Account Dr. To Debenture Applications Account 4,000 applications received for debentures of Rs. 100 accompanied by the application money of Rs. 20 per debenture		80,000 —	80,000 —
Debenture Applications A/c Dr. To 13.5% Debenture Account Allotment of 4,000 debentures; application money transferred to Debentures Account		80,000 —	80,000 —

		Rs.	Rs.
	Debenture Allotment Account Dr. To 13.5% Debentures Account Amount due on 4,000 debentures on allotment at Rs. 80 per debenture	3,20,000 —	3,20,000 —
	Bank Account Dr. To Debentures Allotment Account Amount received against allotment	3,20,000 —	3,20,000 —

Balance Sheet

Liabilities	Rs.	*Assets*	
9% Debentures	4,00,000	Bank	4,00,000

Summary entries. If the whole of the amount is received from people to whom, it is definitely sure, debentures will be allotted, it is better to pass just one entry debiting Bank Account and crediting Debentures Account. Thus if 1,000 debentures of Rs. 100 each are allotted to people who pay the whole amount in lump sum, the entry will be :

		Rs.	Rs.
Bank Account	Dr.	1,00,000	
To Debentures Account			1,00,000

Terms of issue of debentures. A company is free to issue the debentures on any term it likes. For instance, the following possibilities are there :

1. Debentures are issued at par also to be redeemed at par. This means a debenture of Rs. 100 will be issued at Rs. 100 and will also be repaid at this figure. The entry is :

Bank Account	Dr.	Rs. 100	
To Debentures Account			Rs. 100

2. Debentures may be issued at a discount but may be redeemable at par. This means that the company will receive less than the face value, say, Rs. 95 against Rs. 100 but at the time of repayment full Rs. 100 will be paid. The loss which is suffered by the company is debited to an account called Discount on Issue of Debentures Account. Suppose debentures of Rs. 100 each are issued at Rs. 95. The entry will be :

Bank Account	Dr.	Rs. 95	
Discount on Issue of Debentures Account	Dr.	Rs. 5	
To Debentures			Rs. 100

*Redemption means repayment.

Discoun on Issue of Debentures Account should be shown in the balance sheet until it is written off.

3. The debentures may be issued at a premium but may be redeemable at par. Suppose a debenture of Rs. 100 is issued at Rs. 105. In this case the extra Rs. 5 received is a capital profit and is to be credited to Premium on Debentures Account. This account will be shown in the balance sheet. The entry for issue of debentures at a premium is :

Bank Account	Dr.	Rs. 105	
To Debentures			Rs. 100
To Premium on Debentures Account			Rs. 5

4. Debentures may be issued at a discount but may be redeemable at a premium. This means that while issuing the debentures the company will receive less than the face value but at the time of repayment the company will have to pay more. Suppose a debenture of Rs. 100 is issued at Rs. 95 but is to be redeemed at Rs. 105. This means that there is a loss of Rs. 10. This will be debited to an account called Loss on Issue of Debentures. The entry in this case will be :

Bank Account	Dr.	Rs. 95	
Loss on Issue of Debentures A/c	Dr.	Rs. 10	
To Debentures			Rs. 100
To Premium on Redemption of Debentures A/c			Rs. 5

Premium on Redemption of Debentures is a liability and has to be shown in the balance sheet. The Loss on Issue of Debentures is a capital loss and is shown in the balance sheet until it is written each off.

The student will have seen in the above cases that Debentures have always been credited with the face value. This is because the interest will always be calculated with reference to this figure.

Illustration Newways Limited issues 1000 11% debentures of Rs. 100 each. Give journal entries and the balance sheet in each of the following cases :

1. The debentures are issued and are redeemable at par.
2. They are issued at a discount of 6% but redeemable at par.
3. They are issued at a premium of 5% but redeemable at par.
4. They are issued at a discount of 4% but are redeemable at a premium of 5%.

Solution :

Journal

	Particulars		Dr. Rs.		Cr. Rs.	
1	**Issue at par :**					
	Bank Account	Dr.	1,00,000	—		
	To 11% Debentures				1,00,000	—
	Issue of 1,000 6% debentures of Rs. 100 each					
2	**Issue at discount :**					
	Bank Account	Dr.	94,000	—		
	Discount on Issue of Debentures Account	Dr.	6,000	—		
	To 11% Debentures				1,00,000	—
	Issue of 1,000 Debentures of Rs. 100 at a discount of Rs. 6 *i.e.*, at Rs. 94					
3	**Issue at premium :**					
	Bank Account	Dr.	1,05,000	—		
	To 11% Debentures				1,00,000	—
	To Premium on Debentures Account				5,000	—
	Issue of 1,000 debentures of Rs. 100 each at Rs. 105					
4	**Debentures issued at discount but redeemable at par :**					
	Bank Account	Dr.	96,000	—		
	Loss on issue of Debentures	Dr.	9,000	—		
	To 11% Debentures				1,00,000	—
	To Premium on Redemption of Debentures				5,000	—
	Issue of 1,000 Debentures @ 96 but redeemable at 105					

Balance Sheet

Liabilities	Rs.		Assets	Rs.	
(1) 11% Debentures	1,00,000	—	Bank	1,00,000	—
(2) 11% Debentures	1,00,000	—	Bank	94,000	—
			Discount on Issue of Debentures	6,000	—
	1,00,000	—		1,00,000	—
(3) 11% Debentures	1,00,000	—	Bank	1,05,000	—
Premium on Debentures	5,000	—			
	1,05,000	—		1,05,000	—

Balance Sheet

		Rs.			Rs.	
(4)	6% Debentures	1,00,000	—	Bank	96,000	—
	Premium on Redemption of Debentures	5,000	—	Loss on Issue of Debentures	9,000	—
		1,05,000	—		1,05,000	—

Debentures issued as collateral security. Sometimes a loan is taken from a bank and, in addition to any other security that may be given, the company may sign and deliver debentures to the bank. The understanding is that these debentures will not be used by the bank as long as the company fulfils its obligations regarding payment of interest and repayment of loan. Such debentures will be returned by the bank and cancelled by the company when the bank loan is paid off. If debentures are issued in such a manner they are known as debentures issued as collateral security. No entry is passed in the books of the company; only in the balance sheet a note will be given along with the bank loan indicating that such debentures have been issued. If, however, it is desired that an entry should be passed, the following entry may be there :

Debentures Suspense Account Dr.
 To Debentures Issued as Collateral Security.

Writing off loss and discounts on the issue of Debentures. There is no legal provision regarding the writing off the loss or discounts on the issue of debentures, but a company should write them off as quickly as possible. Such loss may also be written off against premium on debentures, or premium on shares but usually they are written off against the Profit and Loss Account. The entry for writing off is simple. It is :

Profit & Loss Account Dr.
 To Discount (or Loss) on Issue of Debentures Account.

If the debentures are to be paid off by annual instalment, the loss or discount on debentures should be written off in each year taking into account the use made of the funds. Suppose Debentures of the face value of Rs. 50,000 have been issued at a discount of 6%. These debentures have to be redeemed by annual instalments of Rs. 10,000. This means that in the first year the company will use Rs. 50,000, in the next year Rs. 40,000, in the third year Rs. 30,000 and so on. The ratio of the amounts in use for each year is as follows :—

First year	50,000	Third year	30,000
Second year	40,000	Fourth year	20,000
		Fifth year	10,000

The discount of Rs. 3,000 should be written off in the ratio of 5 : 4 : 3 : 2 : 1 (making a total of 15) for the respective years. In he first year the discount to be written off will be $\frac{3,000 \times 5}{15}$ or Rs. 1,000. In the second year it will be $\frac{3,000 \times 4}{15}$ or Rs. 800.

Nature of Premium or Discount on Issue of Debentures. If a company issues debentures but offers less than the market rate of interest, it will have to issue the debentures at a discount, depending upon the difference between the rate of interest prevailing in the market and the interest offered by the company. In the reverse case, when the company offers a rate of interest higher than the market rate it will issue the debentures at a premium. Suppose in the market debentures normally carry 9% interest per annum. A company offering 9½% interest p.a. will issue the debentures at a premium and a company offering only 8½% interest will have to issue the debentures at a discount. The premium or the discount is therefore only the capitalised value of the difference between the market rate and the actual rate of interest. In the example given above the amount will be equal to 50 P. per annum capitalised at 9% for the period after which the debentures will be redeemed. If the debentures are redeemable after 25 years, the premium or the discount will be Rs. 4·91 or say Rs. 5.

Underwriting. Underwriters are firms which undertake the responsiblity that the shares or debentures issued by the company will be taken up by the public. If the public does not take up the debentures or shares the underwriters will have to take them up at the same terms as those offered to the public. Suppose 1,000 Debentures of Rs. 500 each have been offered to the public at a discount of 10%. These debentures are underwritten. The public takes up only 800 debentures. In that case, 200 debentures will have to be taken up by the underwriters at Rs. 450 which is the issue price for the public. If the public takes up the whole of the issue the underwriters will have no liability.

For this responsibility the underwriters get a commission. Under the law the commission cannot exceed 2½% of the *issue price* of debentures and 5% of the issue price of shares. Of course, the commission may be lower than this. It is essential that the Articles should permit payment of the underwriting commission; otherwise it will not be valid to do so. The prospectus must disclose particulars of the underwriting arrangements. It must also contain a statement by the Directors that, in their opinion, the underwriters have the resources to fulfill their obligation. It should be noted that underwriting commission can be paid only on shares offered to the public at large and not on shares for which private arrangement has been made.

As against underwriters there are some firms which act as brokers; they do not undertake any obligation. They merely try to procure subscriptions and they get commission only to the extent of shares or debentures applied through them. The applications which are received through brokers or underwriters are known as marked applications. But if the whole of the issue has been underwritten, the underwriters will also get the benefit of unmarked applications or applications applied for directly by the public.

Illustration. Goodluck Limited issued 1,000 Equity Shares of Rs.100 each and 1,000 12% Debentures of Rs. 100 each. The Debentures were issued at a discount of 6%. The whole of the issue was underwritten by M/s Wise and Co. for a commission of 4% on the issue price of Shares and 2% on the issue price of Debentures. The public applied for 900 shares and 800 debentures. These were immediately paid for. The underwriters fulfilled their obligations.

Pass journal entries and give ledger accounts and balance sheet.

Solution :

Journal

		Dr.	Cr.
		Rs.	Rs.
	Bank Account Dr. To Equity Share Capital Allotment of 900 shares to the public at Rs. 100, payment being received in full	90,000 —	90,000 —
	Bank Account Dr. Discount on Issue of Debentures Dr. To 12% Debentures Allotment of 800 debentures on Rs. 100 each at a discount of 6% payment being received in fu ll	75,200 — 4,800 —	80,000 —
	M/s Wise & Co. Dr. To Equity Share Capital The Allotment of 100 shares not applied for by the public to the underwriters	10,000 —	10,000 —
	M/s Wise & Co. Dr. Discount on Issue of Debentures Dr. To 12% Debentures Allotment of 200 debentures not applied for by the public to the underwriters	18,800 — 1,200 —	20,000 —
	Underwriting Commission on Shares A/c Dr. Underwriting Commission on Debentures A/c Dr. To M/s Wise & Co. Commission due to the underwriters as follows : On shares at 4% on Rs. 1,00,000 =4,000 At 2% on Rs. 94,000 =1,880	4,000 -- 1,800 —	5,880 --
	Bank Account Dr. To M/s Wise & Co. Amount due from them received	22,920 —	22,920 —

			Rs.		Rs.	
	*Cost of Issue of Debentures Dr.		7,880	—		
	To Discount on Issue of Debentures A/c				6,000	—
	To Underwriting Commission on Debentures A/c				1,880	—
	Transfer of the discount and underwriting commission on debentures, to the Cost of Issue of Debentures					

LEDGER ACCOUNTS

Dr. **Bank Account** *Cr.*

		Rs.					Rs.	
	To Equity Share Capital Account	90,000	—		By Balance c/d		1,88,120	—
	To 6% Debentures	75,200	—					
	To M/s Wise & Co.	22,920	—					
		1,88,120	—				1,88,120	—
	To Balance b/d	1,88,120	—					

Equity Share Capital Account

		Rs.					Rs.	
	To Balance c/d	1,00,000	—		By Bank A/c		90,000	—
					By M/s Wise & Co.		10,000	—
		1,00,000	—				1,00,000	—
					By Balance b/d		1,00,000	—

*Strictly speaking this entry is not necessary but it is better to transfer the Discount and Underwriting Commission to one account because both represent loss.

6% Debentures

	Rs.			Rs.
To Balance c/d	1,00,000 —		By Bank A/c	75,200 —
			By Discount on Issue of Debentures A/c	4,800 —
			By Wise & Co.	18,800 —
			By Discount on Issue of Debentures A/c	1,200 —
	1,00,000 —			1,00,000 —
			By Balance b/d	1,00,000 —

Wise & Co.

	Rs.			Rs.
To Equity Share Capital A/c	10,000 —		By Underwriting Commission on Shares A/c	4,000 —
To 6% Debentures A/c	18,800 —		By Underwriting Commission on Debentures A/c	1,880 —
			By Bank A/c	22,920 —
	28,800 —			28,800 —

Underwriting Commission on Shares Account

	Rs.			
To M/s Wise & Co.	4,000 —			

Underwriting Commission on Debentures A/c

	Rs.			Rs
To M/s. Wise & Co.	1,880 —		By Cost of Issue of Debentures A/c—transfer	1,880 —

Discount on Issue of Debentures Account

	Rs.			Rs.
To 6% Debenture A/c	4,800 —		By Cost of Issue of Debentures A/c—transfer	6,000 —
To 6% Debentures A/c	1,200 —			
	6,000 —			6,000 —

Cost of Issue of Debentures Account

	Rs.			Rs.	
To Underwriting Commission on Debentures A/c	1,880	—	By Balance c/d	7,880	—
To Discount on Issue of Debentures A/c	6,000	—			
	7,880	—		7,880	—
To Balance b/d	7,880	—			

Balance Sheet of Goodluck Ltd.

	Rs.			Rs.	
Share Capital :			Bank	1,88,120	—
1,000 Equity Shares of Rs. 100 each fully paid	1,00,000	—	Underwriting Commission on Shares	4,000	—
6% Debentures	1,00,000	—	Cost of Issue of Debentures	7,880	—
	2,00,000	—		2,00,000	—

Redemption of debentures. Redemption of debentures means repayment. The entry for repayment is very simple. It is the reverse of the entry made at the time of issue. When the debentures are to be redeemed the entry is :

Debentures Account Dr.
To Bank

This will hold good if the debentures have to be redeemed at par. If, however, the debentures were to be redeemed at premium the entry is :

Debentures Account Dr.
Premium on Redemption of Debentures A/c Dr.
To Bank

Premium on Redemption of Debentures should have been credited at the time of the issue of the debentures. In that case it would appear in the books. But if a company does not create this liability at the time of issue, it will have to now write off the Premium on Redemption of Debentures to Profit and Loss Account or to Share Premium Account.

Another method of redemption of debentures is to pay them off by instalments. Debentures to be redeemed will be selected by drawing lots. Slips containing all the numbers of debentures are put in a box. The requisite number of slips is then drawn. The debentures bearing the numbers so drawn out are then redeemed.

The entry is not different from what has been given above. It will be:

Debentures Account	Dr.		
To Bank			

The third method of redeeming debentures is to purchase them in the market. When this is done the market price may be lower than or higher than the face value. If the market price is lower, the entry will be :

Debentures Account	Dr.		
To Bank			
To Profit on Redemption of Debentures A/c			

Suppose 100 debentures of Rs. 100 each are purchased in the market at Rs. 94. This means that there is a profit of Rs. 6 per debenture because by paying Rs. 94, the liability of Rs. 100 will be cancelled. The entry will be :

		Rs.	Rs.
Debentures Account	Dr.	10,000	
To Bank Account			9,400
To Profit on Redemption of Debentures A/c			600

If, however, the market price is higher than the face value the extra amount paid will represent a loss and will be debited to Loss on Redemption of Debentures Account. Suppose in the above case 100 debentures are purchased in the market at Rs. 102, the Rs. 2 paid extra is a loss and the entry will be :

Debentures Account	Dr.	10,000	
Loss on Redemption of Debentures A/c	Dr.	200	
To Bank Account			10,200

The Loss on Redemption of Debentures Account should be written off to the Profit and Loss Account.

Own Debentures. It is not necessary that a company should cancel debentures on purchase from the market. The company has the option to keep such debentures alive and to re-sell them in the market. Of course, such debentures may also be cancelled later on. If the debentures are purchased not for cancellation, but for keeping, they should be treated like an investment and the entry should be as if somebody else's debentures have been purchased. This means that the exact amount paid will be debited to "Own Debentures Account" and credited to Bank Account. In the above case the entries will be :

Firstly, when purchase is at Rs. 94—

Own Debentures Account	Dr.	9,400	
To Bank Account			9,400

Secondly, when the debentures are purchased at Rs. 102—

Own Debentures Account	Dr.	10,200	
To Bank Account			10,200

"Own Debentures" will be shown in the balance sheet as an asset, it is an investment.

If later the debentures are cancelled the entries will be :

		Rs.	Rs.
In the first case :			
Debentures Account	Dr.	10,000	
To Own Debentures A/c			9,400
To Profit on Redemption of Debentures A/c			600
In the second case :			
Debentures Account	Dr.	10,000	
Loss on Redemption of Debentures A/c	Dr.	200	
To Own Debentures A/c			10,200

The student will have noted from the above that the profit on redemption or loss on redemption arises only when the debentures are cancelled.

Sinking Fund. We have already discussed the sinking fund device in connection with depreciation. The device is a general one and can be used for collecting funds for the purpose of paying off liabilities, replacing assets or expansion. It consists of setting aside every year a certain sum of money, investing it in outside securities and re-investing the interest whenever received. In this manner the investments will accumulate to the desired figure at the end of the desired period. The amount to be invested every year will have to be ascertained from the Sinking Fund Tables. The rate of interest which is expected to be earned will have to be determined and, of course, the period at the end of which the amount is required will be known. The Sinking Fund Tables will show how much has to be invested every year to get Re. 1 at the end of the stated period at the expected rate of interest. An extract from the sinking fund table has been given on page 290. For example, it shows that if we want Re. 1 at the end of 15 years at 5% interest per annum, we will have to invest every year **·046342** and also reinvest the interest to be received on investments. This figure will be multiplied by the amount which is required. If the amount set aside every year is provided out of profits it would be an ideal way. What is done is that the annual amount is debited to the Profit and Loss Appropriation Account (that is the account showing the division of profits). It should not be debited to the Profit and Loss Account proper because there is no loss or expense involved in paying off a liability. If previously Rs. 1 lakh were obtained on issue of debentures and now Rs. 1 lakh have to be paid, there is no loss or expenses. Merely debiting the Profit and Loss Account will not provide ready funds. For getting ready funds, money must be invested in outside securities. The entries for creating a sinking fund are as under :

In the first year (at the end) :—

1. Profit and Loss (Appropriation) A/c ...Dr. } The annual instalment to be invested.
   To Sinking Fund A/c

This entry represents the intention to make an investment.

2. Sinking Fund Investments A/c ...Dr. To Bank	}	the actual amount invested.

This entry represents the carrying out of the intention to invest.

In all subsequent years (at the end) :—

1. Bank ...Dr. To Interest on Sinking Fund Investments A/c	}	the amount of interest received.
2. Interest on Sinking Fund Investments A/c Dr. To Sinking Fund A/c	}	transfer of the amount received as interest to the Sinking Fund.
3. Profit and Loss (Appropriation) A/c ...Dr. To Sinking Fund A/c	}	the annual instalment to be invested.
4. Sinking Fund Investments A/c ...Dr. To Bank	}	the annual investment plus the interest received invested.

Note. In the year in which redemption has to be carried out, entry No. 4 should not be made because, then, to repay the debentures, investments will have to be sold. There is no point in making investments and then immediately realising them.

When the debentures fall due for payment, investments will be realised and debenture-holders paid off. The entries are :

1. Bank ...Dr. To Sinking Fund Investments A/c	}	actual amount realised on sale of investments.
2. Debentures Account ...Dr. To Bank	}	the amount paid to debenture-holders.

3. Sinking Fund investments A/c ...Dr. To Sinking Fund	}	transfer of profit on sale of Investments.

This entry will be reversed if there is a loss on sale of investments.

4. Sinking Fund ..Dr. To General Reserve	}	the balance in the Sinking Fund transferred to General Reserve.

Entry No. 4 shows that the accumulation of profits in the Sinking Fund by debiting the Profit and Loss (Appropriation) Account is really an appropriation. The sole purpose of the Sinking Fund Account is to ensure that amounts required to build up investments for paying the debentures are not utilised in any other manner, say, paying dividends.

Illustration B Ltd. issued 6% Debentures for Rs. 60,000 on 1st January, 1960. These Debentures were to be redeemed on 31st December, 1963. For this purpose a sinking fund was established. The investments were expected to earn 5% net per annum. Sinking Fund Tables show that ·232012 invested annually at 5% amounts to Re. 1 in four years. Give journal entries and ledger accounts to deal with the redemption, assuming investments realise Rs. 44,000 on 31st December, 1963 and that the bank balance on that date was Rs. 24,500 before receipt of interest on Sinking Fund Investments.

Solution :

The annual investments (excluding interest) required is Rs. 13,920·72 *i.e.*, ·232012 × 60,000 = (The student is requested to watch preparation of ledger accounts while making journal entries.)

Journal

				Dr. Rs.		*Cr.* Rs.	
1960 Jan.	1	Bank Account To 6% Debentures Issue of 6% Debentures for Rs. 60,000	Dr.	60,000	—	60,000	—
Dec.	31	Profit & Loss (Appropriation) A/c To Sinking Fund Annual instalment necessary for redemption of debentures debited to P. & L. (App) A/c	Dr.	13,920	72	13,920	72

Date		Particulars		Dr. Rs.		Cr. Rs.	
1960 Dec.	31	Sinking Fund Investments A/c To Bank Account Investments purchased to represent Sinking Fund	Dr.	13,920	72	13,920	72
1961 Dec.	31	Bank Account To Interest on S.F. Investments A/c Interest received @ 5% on S.F. Investments	Dr.	696	04	696	04
	"	Interest on S.F. Investments A/c To Sinking Fund Interest on S.F. Investments transferred to Sinking Fund	Dr.	696	04	696	04
	"	Profit and Loss (Appropriation) A/c To Sinking Fund Annual Instalments to be invested	Dr.	13,920	72	13,920	72
	"	S.F. Investments A/c To Bank Account Investments purchased for the annual instalment and the interest received	Dr.	14,616	76	14,616	76
1962 Dec.	31	Bank Account To Interest on S.F. Investments A/c Interest received on S.F. Investments 5% on Rs. 28,537.48 *i.e.*, Rs. 1,426.87	Dr.	1,426	87	1,426	87
	"	Interest on S.F. Investments A/c To Sinking Fund Interest received transferred to the Sinking Fund	Dr.	1,426	87	1,426	87
	"	Profit & Loss (App.) A/c To Sinking Fund Annual instalment to be invested	Dr.	13,920	72	13,920	72

Date		Particulars		Dr. Rs.		Cr. Rs.	
1962 Dec.	31	Sinking Fund Investments A/c To Bank Account Investments purchased for the annual instalment and the interest received	Dr.	15,347	59	15,347	59
1963 Dec.	31	Bank Account To Interest on S.F. Investments A/c Interest received on Sinking Fund Investments—5% on Rs. 43,885·07	Dr.	2,194	25	2,194	25
	"	Interest on S.F. Investments Account To Sinking Fund Interest transferred to the Sinking Fund	Dr.	2,194	25	2,194	25
	"	Profit and Loss (App.) A/c To Sinking Fund Annual instalment appropriated	Dr.	13,920	72	13,920	72
	"	Bank Account To S.F. Investments A/c Sale of investments for redemption of debentures	Dr.	44,000	—	44,000	—
	"	S.F. Investments A/c To Sinking Fund Profit on S.F. Investments transferred to the Sinking Fund	Dr.	114	93	114	93
	"	6% Debentures To Bank Account Redemption of 6% Debentures	Dr.	60,000	—	60,000	—
	"	Sinking Fund To General Reserve Transfer of the balance in Sinking Fund to General Reserve after redemption of Debentures	Dr.	60,114	97	60,114	97

Ledger Accounts
6% Debentures

Date	Particulars	Rs.		Date	Particulars	Rs.	
1960 Dec. 31	To Balance c/d	60,000	—	1960 Jan.	By Bank A/c	60,000	—
1961 Dec. 31	To Balance c/d	60,000	—	1961 Jan.	By Balance b/d	60,000	—
1962 Dec. 31	To Balance c/d	60,000	—	1962 Jan.	By Balance b/d	60,000	—
1963 Dec. 31	To Bank A/c	60,000	—	1963 Jan.	By Balance b/d	60,000	—

Sinking Fund

Date	Particulars	Rs.		Date	Particulars	Rs.	
1960 Dec. 31	To Balance c/d	13,920	72	1960 Dec. 31	By P. & L. (App.) A/c	13,920	72
1961 Dec. 31	To Balance c/d	28,537	48	1961 Jan. 1	By Balance b/d	13,920	72
				Dec. 31	By Interest on S.F. Investments A/c	696	04
				,,	By P. & L. (App.) A/c	13,920	72
		28,537	48			28,537	48
1962 Dec. 31	To Balance c/d	43,885	07	1962 Jan. 1	By Balance b/d	28,537	48
				Dec. 31	By Interest on S.F. investments A/c	1,426	87
				,,	By P. & L. (App.) A/c	13,920	72
		43,885	07			43,885	07
1963 Dec. 31	To General Reserve—transfer	60,114	97	1963 Jan. 1	By Balance b/d	43,885	07
				Dec. 31	By Interest on S.F. Investments A/c	2,194	25
				,,	By P. & L. (App.) A/c	13,920	72
				,,	By S.F. Investments A/c—profit	114	93
		60,114	97			60,114	97

Sinking Fund Investments A/c

		Rs.				Rs.	
1960 Dec. 31	To Bank Account	13,920	72	1960 Dec. 31	By Balance c/d	13,920	72
1961 Jan. 1	To Balance b/d	13,920	72	1961 Dec. 31	By Balance c/d	28,537	48
Dec. 31	To Bank Account	14,616	76				
		28,537	48			28,537	48
1962 Jan. 1	To Balance b/d	28,537	48	1962 Dec. 31	By Balance c/d	43,885	07
Dec. 31	To Bank Account	15,347	59				
		43,885	07			43,885	07
1963 Jan. 1	To Balance b/d	43,885	07	1963 Dec. 31	By Bank A/c —sale proceeds	44,000	—
Dec. 31	To Sinking Fund—profit transferred	114	93				
		44,000	—			44,000	—

Interest on Sinking Fund Investments Account

		Rs.				Rs.	
1961 Dec. 31	To P. & L. A/c—transfer	696	04	1961 Dec. 31	By Bank A/c	696	04
1962 Dec. 31	To P. & L. A/c—transfer	1,426	87	1962 Dec. 31	By Bank A/c	1,426	87
1963 Dec. 31	To P. & L. A/c—transfer	2,194	25	1963 Dec. 31	By Bank A/c	2,194	25

Bank Account

		Rs.				Rs.	
1963 Dec. 31	To Balance b/d	24,500	—	1963 Dec. 31	By 6% Debentures—Redemption	60,000	—
"	To Interest on S.F. Investments A/c	2,194	25	"	By Balance c/d	10,694	25
"	To Sinking Fund Investments A/c	44,000	—				
		70,694	25			70,694	25
1964 Jan. 1	To Balance b/d	10,694	25				

General Reserve

						Rs.	
				1963 Dec. 31	By Sinking Fund	60,114	97

The student will do well to note the following :—

(*a*) Sinking Fund to redeem debentures may also be termed "Debenture Redemption Reserve Fund."

(*b*) Investments may be made in multiples of Rs. 100. This will be so if securities are purchased directly from the Government.

(*c*) If securities are purchased in the market, the face value is likely to be different from the amount paid. The Sinking Fund Investments Account will be debited with the actual amount paid and profit or loss on sale of investments will be ascertained with reference to the book figure or the amount paid. But interest will be calculated on the face value.

Illustration On 1st January, 1978 the following balances appeared in the books of X Ltd.

	Rs.
6% Debentures	1,00,000
Debenture Redemption Reserve Fund	80,000
D.R. Reserve Fund Investments	80,000

The investments consisted of 4% Government securities of the face value of Rs. 90,000. The annual instalment was Rs. 16,400. On 31st December, 1973 the balance at Bank was Rs. 26,200 (after receipt of interest on D.R. Reserve Fund Investment). The investments were realised at 92 and the Debentures were redeemed. The interest for the year had already been paid. Show ledger accounts affecting redemption.

Solution :

6% Debentures

Dr. *Cr.*

		Rs.				Rs.
1978 Dec. 31	To Bank Account	1,00,000	1978 Jan. 1	By	Balance b/d	1,00,000

Debenture Redemption Reserve Fund Account

		Rs.				Rs.
1978 Dec. 31	To General Reserve—transfer	1,02,800	1978 Jan. 1	By	Balance b/d	80,000
			Dec. 31	By	Interest on D.R.R. Fund Investments A/c—4% on Rs. 90,000	3,600
			„	By	P. & L. (App.) A/c	16,400
			„	By	D. R. R. F. Investments A/c—profit	2,800
		1,02,800				1,02,800

Debenture Redemption Reserve Fund Investments Account

		Rs.			Rs.
1978 Jan. 1	To Balance b/d	80,000	1978 Dec. 31	By Bank A/c—$\frac{92 \times 90,000}{100}$	82,800
„	To D.R. Reserve Fund profit transferred	2,800			
		82,800			82,800

Bank Account

1978		Rs.	1978		Rs.
Dec. 31	To Balance b/d	26,200	Dec. 31	By 6% Debentures	1,00,000
„	To D.R. Reserve Fund Investments A/c—sale proceeds	82,800	„	By Balance c/d	9,000
		1,09,000			1,09,000
1979 Jan. 1	To Balance b/d	9,000			

General Reserve

					Rs.
			1978 Dec. 31	By D.R. Reserve Fund	1,02,800

Sinking fund to replace a wasting asset and sinking fund to redeem a liability. In the chapter on Depreciation, the student has seen the Depreciation Fund accompanied by the Depreciation Fund Investments. The purpose, of course, is to provide ready funds for replacement of an asset at the expiry of its life. Such a fund may also be called "Sinking Fund to Replace a Wasting Asset".

The student has also seen, above, the operation of a Sinking Fund to pay off debentures. Such a sinking fund is called "Sinking Fund to Redeem a Liability". Both types of sinking funds operate similarly but the careful student must have noted the following differences in the two types of sinking funds :—

(*a*) The annual instalment in case of the Sinking Fund to replace a wasting asset is really a depreciation and is, therefore, a charge against profits. In case of sinking fund to redeem a liability, the annual instalment is really an appropriation of profits. For this point to be clear, let the student realise that in Illustration No. 85, what was debited to the Profit and Loss (Appropriation) Account during the four years, 1970 to 1973, has been ultimately credited to General Reserve, of course, via the Sinking Fund Account. See below the meaning of "Redemption of Debentures out of Profits".

(*b*) At the end of the stipulated period the proceeds of the investments are used, in case of sinking fund to redeem liability, to pay off the liability, debiting liability account and crediting Bank. In case of sinking fund to replace an asset, the proceeds are used to acquire a new asset. The old asset account is closed by transfer to the Depreciation (or Sinking) Fund A/c thus closing the two accounts. The sinking fund to redeem a liability remains after redemption and is transferred to General Reserve. It represents accumulation of profits.

Suppose there is a lease costing Rs. 1,00,000 to be replaced and Rs. 1,00,000 of debentures to be redeemed, both having the necessary sinking funds. The two sinking funds will stand as follows :

Lease Account

	Rs.			Rs.	
To Balance b/d	1,00,000	—	By transfer to Dep. Fund A/c	1,00,000	—

Depreciation Fund A/c

To Lease A/c—transfer	1,00,000	—	By Balance b/d	1,00,000	—

Dep. Fund Investments A/c

To Balance b/d	1,00,000	—	By Bank	1,00,000	—

(New) Lease A/c

To Bank	1,00,000	—			

Debentures A/c

To Bank	1,00,000	—	By Balance b/d	1,00,000	—

Sinking Fund A/c

To General Reserve—transfer	1,00,000	—	By Balance b/d	1,00,000	—

S.F. Investments A/c

To Balance b/d	1,00,000	—	By Bank	1,00,000	—

General Reserve

			By Sinking Fund	1,00,000	—

Redemption of Debentures out of Profits. Often this phrase is used. The sinking fund device, illustrated above (in the two preceding illustrations) really is a device showing how profits are used to redeem debentures. What it really means is that the funds generated By profits are collected and temporarily invested in government securities sometimes, and then used to pay off the claims of the debentureholders. Care is exercised, by transferring the profits to appropriately named accounts, to see that cash dividends are not paid out of profits previously used to redeem debentures—a transfer to General Reserve also serves this purpose. The whole process is illustrated below by balance sheets showing the result of various steps and processes involved. For sake of simplicity, it is assumed that assets consist only of cash.

(*i*) Position, say, on 1st January, 1967

Balance Sheet

	Rs.		Rs.
Share Capital	5,00,000	Cash	7,00,000
Debentures	2,00,000		
	7,00,000		7,00,000

(*ii*) Profit earned during 1967 and 1968 Rs. 2,60,000; no dividends paid :

Share Capital	5,00,000	Cash	9,60,000
Debentures	2,00,000	(increase due	
Profit and Loss		to profit earned)	
Account	2,60,000		
	9,60,000		9,60,000

(*iii*) Debentures redeemed on 31st Dec. 1968

Share Capital	5,00,000	Cash	7,60,000
Debentures	—	(decrease due	
Profit & Loss		to repayment of	
Account	2,60,000	debentures)	
	7,60,000		7,60,000

(*iv*) Amount equal to the amount of debentures transferred to General Reserve :

Share Capital	5,00,000	Cash	7,60,000
General Reserve	2,00,000		
Profit and Loss			
Account	60,000		
	7,60,000		7,60,000

Step (iii) and (iv) together make "redemption of debentures out of profits". As a result, only Rs. 60,000 is left in the Profit and Loss Account and dividends exceeding this figure cannot be paid. Even if the whole amount is paid, the total cash in hand will not be less than Rs. 7,00,0C0 and the position will be no worse than the starting position as shown in (i) above.

If steps (iv) is not taken, the Profit and Loss Account standing as Rs. 2,60,000 may be used to pay dividends. Suppose Rs. 1,50,000 is paid out. The position then will be :

	Rs.		Rs.
Share Capital	5,00,000	Cash	6,10,000
Profit and Loss A/c (Rs. 2,60,000 *Less* Rs. 1,50,000)	1,10,000		
	6,10,000		6,10,000

The company does not have as much cash as to begin with. In fact, there is danger that the company will also pay out Rs. 1,10,000 as dividend reducing the cash in hand to Rs. 5,00,000. The assets can be preserved only if step (iv) is taken. That is what is meant by "redemption out of profits."

Redemption of preference shares. Ordinarily, no company is allowed to repay the amount of share capital unless a special legal procedure is followed or unless the company is wound up. But the Companies Act allows a company to issue redeemable preference shares, that is to say, preference shares which can be redeemed or repaid without obtaining sanction of the court or without the company having to be wound up. The fact that the shares are redeemable and the terms according to which redemption will be carried out must be disclosed in the prospectus. Naturally, redemption can be carried out only according to these terms. But this is also subject to legal restrictions contained in Section 80 of the Companies Act. These restrictions are as follows :—

(*i*) Shares can be redeemed only if they are fully paid :

(*ii*) Redemption is possible only out of profits which would be otherwise available for paying dividends to shareholders or out of proceeds of the fresh issue of shares *made for the purpose.* This means that the funds necessary for redeeming the preference shares should be collected either through earning revenue profits or by issuing new shares with the specific purpose of redeeming the preference shares.

(*iii*) If the shares are redeemed out of profits, a sum equal to the face value of the shares thus redeemed must be transferred to "Capital Redemption Reserve Account" by debiting Profit and Loss Account or other accounts containing revenue profits (such as General Reserve).

(*iv*) If any premium is payable to the shareholders on the redemption of shares, it must be provided out of profits or out of Share Premium Account.

(*v*) The Capital Redemption Reserve Account can be used to issue fully paid bonus shares. Otherwise, sanction of the court will be necessary to dispose of it.

Illustration On 30th June, 1978 the Balance Sheet of Y Ltd. stood as follows :—

Liabilities	Rs.	*Assets*	Rs.
Equity Share Capital	5,00,000	Sundry Assets	7,60,000
Redeemable Preference Share Capital	2,00,000	Bank	1,90,000
General Reserve	1,50,000		
Sundry Creditors	1,00,000		
	9,50,000		9,50,000

On the above date, the Preference Shares had to be redeemed. For this purpose 1,000 Equity Shares of Rs. 100 each were issued at 110. The shares were immediately subscribed and paid for. The preference shares were duly redeemed. Give journal entries and Balance Sheet after redemption.

Solution :

Journal

Date		Particulars		Dr. Rs.	Cr. Rs.
1968 June	30	Bank Account To Equity Share Capital Account To Share Premium Account Issue of 1,000 Equity Shares of Rs. 100 each at a premium of Rs. 10	Dr.	1,10,000 —	 1,00,000 — 10,000 —
	"	General Reserve To Capital Redemption Reserve A/c Total amount required to redeem preference shares being Rs. 2,00,000 and amount of new shares being Rs. 1,00,000 Rs. 1,00,000 transferred to Capital Redemption Reserve A/c (being redemption out of profits)	Dr.	1,00,000 —	 1,00,000 —
	"	Redeemable Preference Shares Capital A/c To Bank Account Repayment of Redeemable Preference Shares.	Dr.	2,00,000 —	 2,00,000 —

The student is advised to first prepare ledger accounts before preparing the Balance Sheet.

Balance Sheet of Y Ltd as at June 30, 1968

Liabilities	Rs.	*Assets*	Rs.
Equity Share Capital	6,00,000 —	Sundry Assets	7,60,000 —
Share Premium Account	10,000 —	Bank	1,00,000 —
Capital Redemption Reserve Account	1,00,000 —		
General Reserve	50,000 —		
Sundry Creditors	1,00,000 —		
	8,60,000 —		8,60,000 —

Illustration Exe Ltd. had to redeem the 5,000 6% Redeemable Preference shares of Rs. 100 each at a premium of 4% on 31st December, 1978. The company made the following issues in the latter half of December :—

(*i*) 2,000 equity shares of Rs. 100 each @ Rs. 130 per share; and

(*ii*) 6% Debentures of Rs. 2,00,000 at a discount of 5%.

The issues were successful and all the cash against them was received. The company carried out the redemption, satisfying all the requirements of the law. However, holders of 200 shares had not yet claimed the amount due to them. Expenses in this respect came to Rs. 5,000.

State the journal entries covering the issue of shares and debentures and the redemption of preference shares.

Solution :

Journal of Exe Ltd.

Date		Particulars		Dr.	Cr.
1968 Dec.	?	Bank Account	Dr.	2,60,000 —	
		To Equity Share Capital Account			2,00,000 —
		To Share Premium Account			60,000 —
		Issue of 2,000 equity shares of Rs. 100 each at a premium of Rs. 30 per share			
"		Bank Account	Dr.	1,90,000 —	
		Discount on issue of Debentures A/c	Dr.	10,000 —	
		To 6% Debentures			2,00,000 —
		Issue of Rs. 2,00,000 6% Debentures at a discount of 5%			
"	"	Expenses of issue, Redemption etc. A/c	Dr.	5,000 —	
		To Bank Account			5,000 —
		Expenses relating to issue of shares and debentures and redemption of preference shares.			
"	31	6% Redeemable Preference Share Capital A/c	Dr.	5,00,000 —	
		Premium on Redemption of Preference Shares Account	Dr.	20,000 —	
		To Sundry Preference Shareholders			5,20,000 —
		Amount due to Preference Shareholders in respect of capital and premium @ 4%			

1978				Dr. Rs.		Cr. Rs.	
Dec.	31	Profit and Loss Account	Dr.	3,00,000	—		
		To Capital Redemption Reserve Account				3,00,000	—
		Amount transferred to Capital Redemption Reserve Account: Face value of shares redeemed Rs. 5,00,000 Less face value of new shares issued 2,00,000 3,00,000					
,,	,,	Sundry Preference Shareholders	Dr.	5,20,000	—		
		To Bank				5,20,000	—
		Amount due to the preference shareholders paid					
,,	,,	Share Premium Account	Dr.	35,000	—		
		To Discount on issue of Debentures A/c				10,000	—
		To Expenses of Issue, Redemption etc. A/c				5,000	—
		To Premium on Redemption of Preference Shares A/c				20,000	—
		Various accounts resulting from the issue and redemption written off against Share Premium Account as permitted by law					

Notes : (1) Instead of the Profit and Loss Account, General Reserve could be debited but a debit to either of these would be necessary. It has to be assumed that there is sufficient credit balance in either of these accounts—otherwise the redemption would be unlawful.

(2) It is safer to credit the Capital Redemption Reserve Account with the difference between (i) the face value of shares redeemed and (ii) the face value of shares newly issued; but some people transfer only such an amount as equals the difference between the face value of shares redeemed and the actual proceeds of the new shares. In such a case, the credit to the capital Redemption Reserve Account would have been Rs. 2,40,000 *i.e.*, Rs. 5,00,000—Rs. 2,60,000.

(3) If the credit to the capital Redemption Reserve Account is Rs. 2,40,000 (the alternative indicated in note (2), the expenses on the issue of shares, etc. Discount on issue of debentures and redemption of preference shares cannot be written off against Share Premium Account; these would have to be written off against Profit and Loss Account.

In fact, it is compulsory to write off the Premium on Redemption of Preference Shares but *not* the Discount on Issue of Debentures or the Expenses of Issue, Redemption etc. The latter two accounts can be shown in the Balance Sheet if it is so desired.

(4) The student will have noted that for the purpose of ascertaining the amount to be transferred to the Capital Redemption Reserve Account, the amount raised by the issue of debentures has been entirely ignored. This is because the law requires redemption out of profits or out of the proceeds of a new issue of shares, not debentures.

Purchase of business. A company often purchases a running business. The purchase consideration is usually determined by deducting liabilities taken over by the company from the assets taken over. The purchase consideration may be discharged in the form of shares, cash or debentures. Shares or debentures will be issued in the names of the partners (if a partnership business is taken over) or in the name of the shareholders of the outgoing company. The entries to record the purchase of business are as under :—

(*a*) Debit Business Purchase Account) with the purchase
Credit Vendors) consideration agreed
) upon.

(*b*) Debit the various assets taken over at the value placed upon them by the company.

Credit the liabilities taken over.

Credit Business Purchase Account with the amount of purchase consideration.

If debits exceed the credits, the difference should be credited to Capital Reserve.

If credits exceed the debits, the difference should be debited to Goodwill Account.

Note: In case of purchase of business, goodwill or capital reserve should be ascertained only in the manner given above.

(*c*) Debit Vendors with the purchase consideration.
Credit Share Capital Account) with their respective
Credit Share Premium Account,) amounts.
(if the issue price exceeds the face)
value of the share))
Credit Debentures)
Credit Cash, etc.)

Illustration 90. The Balance Sheet of Ram and Mohan was as under as at December 31, 1968 : —

Liabilities		Rs.	*Assets*	Rs.
Sundry Creditors		20,000	Goodwill	10,000
Ram's Loan		10,000	Plant & Machinery	30,000
General Reserve		5,000	Premises	35,000
			Stock	24,000
Capitals :			Sundry Debtors	20,000
Ram	50,000		Investments	5,000
Mohan	40,000	90,000	Bank	1,000
		1,25,000		1,25,000

On 1st January, 1979 a new company, Fair Deals Ltd., took over the business. It did not take over Investments and Bank balance.

It agreed to assume the liabilities except Ram's Loan. The purchase consideration was fixed at Rs. 1,20,000 to be paid in the form of 8,000 shares of Rs. 10 each issued at Rs. 12 and the balance in cash.

The company issued 5,000 shares to the public at Rs. 12.

The shares were subscribed and immediately paid for. The company valued Plant and Machinery at Rs. 40,000 and Premises at Rs. 30,000.

Give journal entries in the books of Fair Deals Ltd. and its Balance Sheet.

Solution :

Fair Deals Ltd.
Journal

Date		Particulars		Rs.	Rs.
1979 Jan	1	Business Purchase Account	Dr.	1,20,000 —	
		To M/s Ram & Mohan			1,20,000 —
		Purchase of business of Ram & Mohan for Rs. 1,20,000			
	,,	Plant & Machinery A/c	Dr.	40,000 —	
		Premises Account	Dr.	30,000 —	
		Stock Account	Dr.	24,000 —	
		Sundry Debtors	Dr.	20,000 —	
		Goodwill Account	Dr.	26,000 —	
		To Sundry Creditors			20,000 —
		To Business Purchase Account			1,20,000 —
		Assets and liabilities taken over from Ram & Mohan Goodwill ascertained by deducting debits from credits			
	,,	Bank Account	Dr.	60,000 —	
		To Share Capital Account			50,000 —
		To Share Premium Account			10,000
		Issue of 5,000 shares of Rs. 10 each at Rs. 12 each, Rs. 2 per share credited to Share Premium Account			
	,,	M/s Ram & Mohan	Dr.	1,20,000 —	
		To Share Capital Account			80,000 —
		To Share Premium Account			16,000 —
		To Bank Account			24,000 —
		Issue of 8,000 shares of Rs. 10 each @ Rs. 12 each to Ram & Mohan and the balance paid in cash (Rs. 2 per Share credited to Share Premium A/c)			

Balance Sheet of Fair Deals Ltd. as at January 1, 1979

Liabilities	Rs.		*Assets*	Rs.	
Share Capital			Goodwill	26,000	—
13,000 Shares of Rs. 10			Plant & Machinery	40,000	—
each fully paid	1,30,000	—	Premises	30,000	—
Share Premium A/c	26,000	—	Stock	24,000	—
Sundry Creditors	20,000	—	Sundry Debtors	20,000	—
			Bank	36,000	—
	1,76,000	—		1,76,000	—

Debtors collected and creditors paid on behalf of vendors. Sometimes the purchasing company does not take over debtors and creditors of the vendor (and, therefore, does not settle for them in cash). But the company may collect the debts and pay the creditors on behalf of the vendors, any loss or profit being that of the vendors. The company may not record the vendors' debtors and creditors in its books. When cash is received from debtors, the amount will be credited to the vendors and, on payment to creditors, the vendors will be debited. But it is better to make a proper record in the books. The entries will be as follows :—

(*a*) Debit Vendors' Debtors with their total.
Credit Vendors' Creditors with their total.
Credit Vendors' Suspense A/c with the difference.

(*b*) On receipt of cash from the debtors :—
Debits Cash Account.
Credit Vendors' Debtors.
Any loss on collection of debts will be debited to Vendors' Suspense A/c and credited to Vendors' Debtors*

(*c*) On payment to creditors :—
Debit Vendors' Creditors.
Credit Cash Account.
Any profit on payment to creditors will be credited to Vendors' Suspense Account and debited to Vendors' Creditors. The entry will be reversed in case the amount paid is more than the book figure.

(*d*) If any commission is to be charged from the vendors for doing the work of collection of debts and payment of liabilities, Vendors' Suspense Account will be debited and Commission Account credited.

The amount actually collected less amount paid to creditors and less commission, if any, should be paid to the vendors and debited to the Vendors' Suspense Account. The balance in the Vendors' Suspense Account should be equal to the difference between the Vendors' Debtors still uncollected and Vendors' Creditors still unpaid.

*Any profit will be credited to Vendors' Suspense Account.

Illustration Wye Ltd. took over the business of M/s North and East but not their debtors and creditors which were respectively Rs. 35,000 and Rs. 15,000. The company agreed to collect the debts and pay the creditors on behalf of the vendors for a commission of 3% on amount collected and 2% on the amount paid to the creditors. The company collected Rs. 32,000 and paid Rs. 14,500 in full settlement. Give journal entries in the books of Wye Ltd.

Solution :

Journal of Wye Ltd.

			Dr. Rs.	Cr. Rs.
	Vendors' Debtors Account	Dr.	35,000 —	
	To Vendors' Creditors A/c			15,000 —
	To Vendors' Suspense A/c			20,000 —
	Debtors to be collected and creditors to be paid on behalf of the vendors			
	Bank Account	Dr.	32,000 —	
	Vendors' Suspense Account	Dr.	3,000 —	
	To Vendors' Debtors A/c			35,000 —
	The amount collected from Vendors' Debtors, the loss debited to Vendors' Suspense Account			
	Vendors' Creditors A/c	Dr.	15,000 —	
	To Bank Account			14,500 —
	To Vendors' Suspense A/c			500 —
	Amount paid to Vendors' Creditors, the gain credited to Vendors' Suspense A/c			
	Vendors' Suspense A/c	Dr.	1,250 —	
	To Commission Account			1,250 -
	Commission due from vendors— 3% on Rs. 32,000 960; 2% on Rs. 14,500 290; —— 1,250			
	Vendors' Suspense Account	Dr.	16,250 —	
	To Bank Account			16,250 —
	Amount paid to vendors in respect of their debtors and creditors			

Final Accounts

Every company is required to prepare every year a Profit and Loss Account* (this term includes Trading Account also) and Balance Sheet at the end of the year. A year is, of course, of twelve months usually but a company may choose to prepare a Profit and Loss

*The term also includes Income and the Expenditure Account.

Account for fifteen months and even for eighteen months (with the permission of the Registrar). The general principles for preparing the Profit and Loss Account are the same as already explained. But in addition, a company must also keep in mind the provisions of the Companies Act.

The Profit and Loss Account must exhibit a true and fair view of the profit earned or loss suffered by the company during the year concerned. It means that profits or losses must not be inflated or suppressed. The Profit and Loss Account must be so made out as to disclose clearly the result of the working of the company during the year concerned and must disclose every material feature, including credits or debits in respect of non-recurring or exceptional transactions. The Profit and Loss Account must disclose the following*:—

(*i*) total sales or gross income derived from services rendered ;
(*ii*) purchase of raw materials or goods ;
(*iii*) opening and closing stocks of goods produced or purchased ;
(*iv*) work in progress at the commencement and at the end of the year.
(*v*) consumption of stores and spare parts ;
(*vi*) power and fuel ;
(*vii*) salaries, wages and bonus ;
(*viii*) contribution tc provident fund and other funds ;
(*ix*) workmen's welfare expenses ;

(1) income tax relating to previous years.
(2) amount provided for repayment of share capital and loans ;
(3) the amount (if material) set aside as reserves ;
(4) dividends paid and proposed

(*a*) commission, brokerage and discounts on sales to selling agents ;
(*b*) depreciation provided on the company's fixed assets ;
(*c*) interest on the company's debentures and other fixed loans ;
(*d*) amounts set aside for meeting specific liabilities, contingencies or commitments (if material) and amounts withdrawn from such provision when no longer needed (if material) ;
(*e*) rent :
(*f*) repairs to buildings ;
(*g*) repairs to machinery ;
(*h*) insurance ;
(*i*) rates and taxes (excluding taxes on income) ;
(*j*) miscellaneous expenses ;
(*k*) income from investments ;
(*l*) income by way of interest ;
(*m*) profits or losses on investments ;
(*n*) profits or losses in respect of transactions of a kind not usually undertaken or undertaken in circumstances of an exceptional or non-recurring nature (if material in amount) ;

*Items numbered (*i*) to (*ix*) will usually be entered in the Trading Account. Items numbered (1) to (4) are items of appropriation or distribution of profit and items numbered (*a*) to (*r*) are usually found in the P. & L. A/c. The items have been arranged in these orders by the author.

(o) miscellaneous income ;

(p) dividends from subsidiary companies ;

(q) the amount (if material) by which any items shown in the the profit and loss account are affected by any change in the basis of accounting.

(r) income-tax relating to current year.

Amounts paid to directors have to be shown in the Profit and Loss Account or shown by way of a note. Similarly, information must be given regarding remuneration received by the auditor as auditor and in other capacity. The P. & L. Account should have a note to show how the commission paid to directors or manager has been arrived at. Profit and Loss Accounts, except for the first year, must contain figures relating to the previous year.

The Profit and Loss Account must also contain the following additional information either by means of a note appended to the Profit and Loss Account or in the account itself in respect of the financial year covered :

(i) Sales, separately, of each class of goods dealt with by the company together with quantities of such sales.

(ii) Value of the basic raw materials concerned together with the quantities for each item. In case intermediates or components are procured from outside may be grouped suitably but information for all items (value and quantities) accounting for 10% or more of the total of the raw material concerned must be given separately.

(iii) Opening and closing stocks of goods produced together with a break up in respect of each class of goods along with quantities.

(iv) In the case of trading companies, purchases, opening stocks and closing stocks of each class of goods traded in by the company together with quantities.

(v) In the case of companies rendering services, the gross income derived from services rendered.

(vi) In the case of a company which is a manufacturing and a trading company and also renders service, it will be sufficient if the total amounts are shown in respect of the opening and closing stocks, purchases, sales and consumption of raw material with value and quantitative break-up and the gross income from services rendered is shown.

(vii) In the case of other companies, the gross income derived under different heads.

[*Note* : The quantities to be shown should be in units in which normally the material concerned is sold or purchased in the market.]

(*viii*) Break-up of expenditure incurred on employees having remuneration of Rs. 3,000/- p.m. or more (the remuneration is to be calculated in accordance with the Income-tax Act) ; the number of such employees must also be given. In addition, the names of the employees concerned have also to be disclosed in a separate statement.

(*ix*) All expenses which are more than 1% of the total revenue of the company or Rs. 5,000 (whichever is higher) must be stated separately and not grouped under "Miscellaneous Expenses."

(*x*) The extent of the profits earned or losses incurred on account of membership of a partnership firm.

(*ix*) In the case of manufacturing companies, in respect of each class of goods :—

(*a*) the licensed capacity (where licence is in force) ;

(*b*) the installed capacity.

(*c*) the actual production separately for goods produced for sale and for semi-processed goods.

(*xii*) The value of imports calculated, on C.I.F. basis by the company in respect of

(*a*) raw material ;

(*b*) components and spare parts ; and

(*c*) capital goods.

(*xiii*) (*a*) Expenditure in foreign currency on account of royalty, know-how, professional consultation fees, interest and other matters.

(*b*) Value of all imported raw materials, spare parts and components consumed during the year and the value of all indigenous raw materials, spare parts and components similarly consumed and the percentage of each to the total consumption.

(*c*) Amount remitted in foreign currencies on account of dividends with a specific mention of the number of non-resident shareholders, the number of shares held by them on which the dividends were due and the year to which the dividend related.

(*d*) Earnings in foreign exchange classified under :

1. export of goods calculated on F.O.B. basis ;
2. royalty, know how professional and consultation fees ;
3. interest and dividends ; and
4. other income, indicating the nature thereof.

The aim of all the requirement of disclosure of the information mentioned above undoubtedly is to enable a significant analysis of the economic factors operating in the company concerned and to ascertain the extent to which a company is a source of foreign exchange and to which it draws upon them. It should be now possible to measure the efficiency of operation of a company on the basis of quantitative analysis and to isolate the effect of price charges.

Special points. While preparing the final accounts of joint stock companies the student will do well to remember the following points :—

(*a*) Cost of issue of debentures or shares, underwriting commission and discount on issue of shares and debentures should continue to appear in the balance sheet unless there are instructions to write them off. A prudent policy is to write them off as quickly as possible but this is a matter for management. However, if debentures or preference shares are due to be redeemed, the cost of and underwriting commission paid on issue of such debentures or preference shares together with the discount allowed thereon should be written off by the time of redemption. Suppose Discount on Issue of Debentures stands at Rs. 20,000 and the Debentures are to be redeemed in five years. The student will do well to write off one-fifth of Discount on Debentures. Rs. 4,000 will be transferred to the Profit and Loss Account and the remaining balance will remain in the Discount on Debentures Account and will appear in the Balance Sheet.

(*b*) Preliminary Expenses should be written off only if the student has been instructed to do so. Preliminary Expenses are those expenses which are incurred to establish the company and include expenses for the preparation, printing and publishing of Memorandum and Articles of Association and the Prospectus and also include registration expenses.

(*c*) Interest for the full year should be debited to the Profit and Loss Account in respect of Debentures. Suppose the company has at issue 6% Rs. 3,00,000 Debentures. The annual interest comes to Rs. 18,000. If the books show that Rs. 12,000 has been paid, it means that Rs. 6,000 is still due for payment. A liability for this amount should be created by debiting Debenture Interest Account and crediting Debenture Interest Outstanding Account. The latter account will appear in the Balance Sheet.

This treatment also applies to public deposits, a new source of finance for companies. Under the law, a company can receive deposits from the public up to 25% of its paid up capital and reserves and an additional 10% from the shareholders. The minimum period is 6 months and the maximum is 3 years.

Note. If the due date of payment of interest has already arrived, the amount unpaid will be "Due and Outstanding". But if the due date falls in the next financial year, the amount due up to the close of the present financial year will be "accrued".

(*d*) Treatment as recommended in (*c*) above is also necessary in respect of investments held by the company (excluding shares).

(*e*) Since the Companies Act requires all interest income of the company to be shown in the Profit and Loss Account, interest received on Sinking Fund Investments should be credited to the Profit and Loss Account (and not directly to the Sinking Fund). Then the amount should be debited to the Profit and Loss A/c and credited to the Sinking Fund together with the annual instalment.

(*f*) Any unusual item should be shown separately in the Profit and Loss Account. For example, if the company suffered a loss on speculation, or earned a profit through speculation (speculation not being its usual business), the loss or profit should be shown separately in the Profit and Loss Account and not merged in any other amount or figure.

(*g*) Special attention should be paid to *managerial remuneration.* The law lays down certain maximum limits beyond which the remuneration can be paid only with the permission of the Central Government. Total remuneration for all managerial personnel (directors) managing director or manager cannot exceed 11% of net profit. With the permission of the Central Government it may be Rs. 50,000 in case profits are not adequate. For manager or managing director, the maximum remuneration is 5% of net profit.

Part time directors get only 1% of profits if the Company has a managing director (or whole time director), manager, managing agent or secretaries and treasurers. If the company does not have any of these managerial personnel, part time directors may get 3%.

Net profits have been defined in sections 349, 350 and 351 of the Companies Act. Broadly speaking, the definition conforms to the accountancy meaning of profits. Profits will not include—

(*a*) premium on shares or debentures issued by the company;

(*b*) profit on reissue of forfeited shares ;

(*c*) profit of a capital nature including profit from the sale of the immovable property* or undertaking of the company.

But profit on sale of fixed asset above its written down value will be included up to the original cost of the asset—amount realised above the original cost is not to be treated as profit.

The following are not to be treated as expenses for determining the profit (for calculating managerial remuneration) :—

*Unless the company's business is to buy and sell immovable property.

loss or profit should be shown separately in the Profit and Loss Account and not merged in any other amount or figure.

(i) remuneration payable to the managerial personnel concerned ;

(ii) income tax and super tax payable on profits (unless the tax is on excess profits) ;

(iii) any compensation, damages or payments made voluntarily ; and

(iv) loss of capital nature; but loss on fixed assets (the difference between amount realised and the written down value) should be deducted from profits.

N.B. The P & L A/c. must show by way of a note, the amount of profit on which managerial remuneration is based if it is paid as a percentage of profits.

(h) **Depreciation,** strictly speaking, need not be written off although no prudent company will adopt the course of not providing for depreciation. A note must be given in the Profit & Loss Account if depreciation is not provided for, stating the amount of the depreciation. A company need not provide for depreciation if it does not wish to pay any dividend.

However, the Companies Act prohibits a company from declaring dividends unless depreciation is provided for on fixed assets. Depreciation should be provided for (a) according to the provisions of the Income Tax Act or (b) by dividing 95% of the amount of the asset by its life or (c) according to a method approved by the Central Government. The Central Government has so far not indicated its approval for a method other than the two methods covered by (a) and (b) above. It must be noted that if a company wishes to adopt the straight-line method, it must compute the life of the asset concerned on the basis of the rates prescribed under the income-tax law. The life will be the number of years in which, on applying the prescribed rates and using the diminishing value method, the balance in the asset account would be reduced to 5% of the original cost (which is the estimated scrap value according to the Companies Act). Roughly, the rates, applicable in the diminishing value method is a little less than 3 times the rate to be used in the straight line method, the life being the same. If life is 10 years, the rate will be 10% on the straight line basis but about 30% on the other basis.

This has an interesting aspect. Suppose two companies start business in the same industry in the same year and instal a plant costing Rs 10 lakh, having an estimated life of 10 years. The annual depreciation on the straight line basis every year will be Rs.95,000, *i.e.*, (10,00,000 — 50,000 *i.e.*, 5% of Rs.10,00,000) ÷ 10. The depreciation according to the other method will be:

First year Rs.3,00,000 *i.e.*, 30% of Rs.10,00,000
Second year Rs.2,10,000 *i.e.*, 30% of Rs.7,00,000
Third year Rs.1,47,000 *i.e.*, 30% of Rs.4,90,000 and so on.

One can see that the first company will report a higher profit and the second company will report a much lower profit simply because of the difference in depreciation. This will be so for the first half of the life of the asset; later the second company will report a higher profit and the first company will show lower profit. The method of depreciation chosen, thus, has an important influence on the profit disclosed by the profit and loss account.

The Companies Act does not require disclosure of the method chosen but, if a company later changes the method (or the basis of accounting as is the term used), it must disclose the fact of the change and also the amount of depreciation according to the previous method. This is required by the consistency concept as well as the Companies Act. It should be noted that income-tax authorities allow full year's depreciation even if the asset is used for a single day. But while drawing up the Profit and Loss Account, depreciation should be computed on the basis of the time actually used. If an asset is used for only 4 months, the deciation to be charged should be 1/3 of the annual depreciation.

If an asset is sold during the year for an amount less than the book value, the difference is loss and should be charged to the Profit and Loss Account; income-tax authorities also will treat this as a loss for tax purposes. If there is a profit, then the profit upto the original cost is revenue profit and should be shown as income; any profit above the original cost is capital profit and should be credited to Capital Reserve. Suppose a building which cost Rs.20,00,000 and on which depreciation provided comes to Rs.6,00,000 is sold for Rs.18,00,000. The book value is Rs.14,00,000; the profit of Rs.4,00,000 is revenue profit, being in the nature of reimbursement of depreciation. If the building had been sold for Rs.22,00,000, Rs.2,00,000 would have been capital profit and Rs.6,00,000 revenue profit. Tax authorities follow the same principle.

A point to note is that if depreciation according to Section 205 is not provided or is provided only partially, then in future the arrears first must be provided before any dividend is declared. If depreciation is provided for and then there is a loss, in future (before declaring dividend) either the amount of the depreciation or the loss (after depreciation), whichever is less, must first be adjusted out of the available profits.

For calculating managerial remuneration and provision required for income-tax, depreciation only as per Income-tax Act and Rules is to be considered.

(*i*) *Adjustment of items relating to previous years.* Often, it is necessary to take into account in the current year amounts that really pertain to previous years. This may be necessary because of mistakes committed in the past or because relevant information becomes available only in the current year. Examples of mistakes would be the following:—

(*a*) Omission to record a purchase or a sale of goods;
(*b*) Errors in valuation of inventories; and
(*c*) Wrong treatment of expenditure, say, when revenue expenditure is capitalised.

Examples of the other type are as follows:—

(*a*) Provision made for some purpose, say, taxation being found short or in excess;

(*b*) Payments that arise out of agreements, say, with workers regarding wages having retrospective effect;

(*c*) Settlement of claims raised in previous years but not accounted for, such as railway claims.

The general rule is that if the amount involved is not material or substantial, there is no need for any special treatment of the adjustment involved in respect of previous years. This is to say, the amount can be merged with the amounts pertaining to the current year. Suppose it was only a small purchase invoice that was omitted from the books last year—the amount can very well be added to the current year's purchases. As regards what amount is material or substantial, there is no hard and fast rule. An amount will be considered material if separate information about it is essential for proper appraisal of the profit or loss or the financial position. A broad rule is that materiality should be judged by considering both the amount of the item and the amount of the profit or loss disclosed by the Profit and Loss Account. Suppose it is a case of last year's inventory sheets being totalled wrong. Whether the mistake was material will be considered by considering the amount of the opening stock and the profit, both. Thus, an amount may be material for one company but not for a bigger company.

If the amount pertaining to previous years is material or substantial, it must be shown separately, preferably in the appropriation section. Suppose the provision for taxation was Rs.4,60,000 on 1st January, 1981 but the settlement for tax liability was for Rs. 4,90,000 and the provision required for 1981 was Rs.5,05,000. It would be wrong to debit the Profit and Loss Account in respect of the provision by Rs.5,35,000 as one item. Rs.5,05,000 should be shown separately as the amount concerning 1981; Rs.30,000, the excess amount required to settle the liability as in the beginning of the year, should be shown separately; better if it is shown in the appropriation part of of the Profit and Loss Account. To continue the example, if the liability upto Jan. 1, 1981 is settled for Rs.4,40,000, the saving of Rs.20,000 has to be shown on the credit side of the Profit and Loss Account, there being a separate debit of Rs.5,05,000 in respect of the current year's provision.

To take another example, suppose some goods, costing Rs.50,000 were lost in transit in 1979 and a claim was lodged with the railways but, because of the various uncertainties involved, no entry was passed. Suppose the railways paid Rs.38,000 in 1981. This amount should not be merged with other incomes relating to 1981; it should be shown separately. This may not be necessary for a big company, say Tata Iron and Steel Co. Ltd.—it may be merged with current year's income since, for that company, the amount is not material.

This treatment of previous or prior year adjustments results from the character of the Profit and Loss Account—it must give a true and fair view of the profit earned or loss suffered by the company during the year as well as of the factors that resulted in the profit (or loss)

The Profit and Loss Account must disclose the current year's profit or loss; items relating to previous years will vitiate the picture unless they are shown separately.

The Appropriation Section or Below the Line. One can see that every firm first must ascertain what profit it has earned before the question of its distribution arises. The Profit and Loss Account proper has this function; unless all incomes, expenses and provisions are considered, one cannot determine the profit earned. Items to be considered for this purpose are said to be "Above the Line". The profit earned is transferred to the next section of the Profit and Loss Account where appropriations of the profit are shown—*e.g.*, transfer to reserves, dividends paid, etc. Such items arise only when there is a profit. This section of the Profit and Loss Account is termed as "Below the Line" or the Profit and Loss Appropriation Account. Besides items showing appropriations, this also is the proper place for showing adjustments relating to previous years, debit or credit. However, there is no legal requirement for such a treatment—the items can certainly be shown above the line separately or even within brackets along with the general items to which they pertain.

Below is an example of the Profit and Loss Appropriation Account with assumed figures.

Profit and Loss Appropriation Account

	Rs.		Rs.
To Expenses relating to previous year	31,800	By Balance b/d from previous year	28,500
To Adjustment in Depreciation on change of method in respect of previous years	45,300	By Profit for the year	2,07,300
To Transfer to General Reserve	80,000	By Incomes relating to previous years	21,400
To Proposed Dividend	60,000	By Excess Provision in repect of Taxation for the previous year	16,700
To Balance c/d	56,800		
	2,73,900		2,73,900

Next year, this account will begin with a balance of Rs.56,800; this year this amount will appear in the Balance Sheet under "Reserves".

Dividends to be paid by the company should be paid on the amount actually received by the company and for this purpose the period of time should also be taken into account. Suppose the company has issued 10,000 shares of Rs. 100 each, Rs. 80 paid. Rs. 20 was called and paid on 1st July, one shareholder holding 500 shares failing to pay. If 10% dividend is to be paid, the amount will be (accounts closed on 31st December—)

	Rs.
10% on Rs. 8,00,000 for 6 months up to 30th June	40,000
10% on Rs. 9,90,000 for 6 months after 1st July	49,500
	89,500

Dividends paid by the company are appropriation or distribution of profits. Dividends are declared by the company in general meeting on the recommendation of directors. At the time of closing the accounts, the amount as recommended is called "Proposed Dividend". This is debited to the Profit and Loss Account and credited to "Proposed Dividend Account" and shown in the Balance Sheet. Sometimes the directors pay a dividend for a year even before the year closes. Such a dividend is known as Interim Dividend. Later the company may declare an additional dividend. That will be known as Final Dividend.

Dividends are declared only at the annual general meeting of the shareholders. On declaration the dividend must be paid within 42 days – the posting of dividend warrants is enough in this regard. If such dividend warrants have not been posted or the amount not paid otherwise within 42 days, the unpaid amount has to be deposited in a scheduled bank in a special account entitled "Unpaid Dividend Account of... Co Ltd./Co (Private) Ltd." On the expiry of three years, any balance in this account must be transferred to the Central Government's general revenue account. The person concerned will then have to claim the amount from the Central Government. Thus companies can no longer forfeit any dividend.

Reserves are amounts set aside out of profits, that is to say, the company may decide not to use up part of its profits. The term "Retained Earnings", used in U.S.A., conveys the real meaning of the term 'reserve'. It means accumulated profits. It will debit the Profit and Loss Account and credit a "Reserve" Account. Reserves always denote accumulated profits at the disposal of the company. If a "provision" contains more than the proper amount, the excess will be "reserve". Suppose the Provision for Bad Debts shows a credit of Rs. 40,000. It is expected that only Rs. 15,000 is sufficient to meet expected bad debts. Then Rs. 25,000 will be treated as reserve and shown on the liability side of the Balance Sheet under "Reserves and Surplus" and only Rs. 15,000 will be deducted from Sundry Debtors.

Under powers given by the Companies Act, the Central Government has framed rules regarding amounts to be transferred to reserves and withdrawal from reserves for paying a dividend. Under the rules, if a company pays a dividend in excess of 10%, it must make transfers to reserves amounts stated below:

Rate of dividend	*Required Transfer to Reserve*
10%, or below	nil
In excess of 10% but not exceeding 12.5%	2.5% of the current profit after tax
In excess of 12.5% but not exceeding 15.0%	5% of the current profit after tax
In excess of 15% but not exceeding 20%	7.5% of the current profit after tax
In excess of 20%	10% of the current profit after tax

Higher amounts may also be transfered to reserves but this is subject to the following:—

(*i*) The dividend declared must not be less than the average of of the rate of dividend declared in the three immediately preceding years. (If current year's profits are 20% lower than the average of 2 previous years, it will not be necessary to maintain the dividend at the average for 3 years as stated above.)

(*ii*) If no dividend is declared, the transfer to reserves must be lower than the average amount of dividend paid in the 3 previous years.

If reserves are to be used for paying dividend, the following must be complied with:—

(*i*) The rate of dividend must not exceed the average rate for the 5 previous years or 10% whichever is lower;

(*ii*) Not more than 1/10 of paid up capital and free reserves can be drawn from reserves in a year and the amount so drawn must first be used for setting off losses incurred in the current year; and

(*iii*) The balance in reserves after such drawal must not be less than 15% of the paid up share capital.

Provisions, Reserves and Reserve Funds. If an amount is payable in future and the figure is exact, it is a liability. For instance, December's Wages, totalling Rs. 15,960, are payable on 31st December. The company will debit Wages Account and Wages Outstanding Account. It is a definite liability. If the amount in respect of a liability or expected loss is not certain an estimated amount will be set aside by debiting Profit and Loss Account. This will be a provision. Income tax will certainly be payable in respect of current year's profits but the exact amount will not be known for quite some time. In such a case the amount will be estimated and credited to "Provision for Income Tax Account". The debit will, of course, be to the Profit & Loss Account. Thus "provision" means an estimated amount to meet a loss or expense in future whose amount as yet is uncertain.

Reserves mean accumulated profits. The purpose of reserves may be :

(*a*) expansion:
(*b*) better financial position;
(*c*) redemption of liabilities;
(*d*) meeting unforeseen contingencies; and
(*e*) making dividends uniform from year to year.
(*f*) meeting legal requirements such as Investment Reserve required by the Income-tax law.

Reserves meant for a particular purpose, say paying off a liability, are called specific reserves; other reserves are called general reserves.

If reserves are invested in outside securities and such securities are earmaked for the particular purpose denoted by the reserve, the reserve will be called "Reserve Fund". A company will invest the funds outside only if (1) ready cash is necessary on a certain date or (2) the funds cannot be profitably invested in the business itself.

Secret Reserves are reserves which the company keeps secret. Such reserves are created only by deflating profits. The usual ways are:

(*i*) **undervaluing stock;**
(*ii*) **providing excess depreciation;**
(*iii*) **writing off capital expenditure as revenue expense;**
(*iv*) **not taking into account incomes earned but not yet received; and**
(*v*) **treating income as a liability.**

Secret reserves are not legal now because if these are secret reserves the company's Profit and Loss Account and Balance Sheet will not exhibit a true and fair view; the view will be much worse than what it really is.

Hidden Reserves are reserves which are created out of profits but are not clearly shown as such in the Balance Sheet. For example, General Reserve may be shown as "Miscellaneous Accounts". Hidden reserves are also not legal these days. Companies are required to prepare their Balance Sheets without hiding things.

Fundamental Accounting Assumptions and Accounting Policies : Through standards issued by the International Accounting Standards Committee and the Institute of Chartered Accountants of India, a distinction has been made between fundamental accounting assumptions, underlying the Profit and Loss Account and the Balance Sheet, and accounting policies. *Fundamental Accounting assumptions* are three:

(*i*) Going concern; (*ii*) Accrual; and (*iii*) Consistency

Unless otherwise stated, it will be assumed that the company is a going concern—that it will continue to operate in the foreseeable future and that that there is neither the intention nor the necessity to wind up the affairs wholly or substantially. It will also be assumed that the effect of all events and transactions, capable of being measured in monetary terms, even if partially, has been brought into the accounts and that there has been no departure from the accounting policies followed in the past, unless the change has been disclosed. If any of these assumptions is not valid, it is the duty of the company concerned to say so explicitly.

Accounting policies are the particular bases or methods adopted by the management in arriving at the amounts pertaining to areas where judgment is involved—for example whether the method of depreciation should be the diminishing value method or the straight line method and what the estimated life of the asset is. Other examples are: valuation of stock, whether on FIFO basis or LIFO bais or average basis; treatment of deferred revenue expenditure, accounting for the liability for gratuity to staff, etc. In all such cases, the management must necessarily make a choice out of many methods that are available and suitable; since circumstances change, no rigid formula will suit all cases and firms. It has been seen already that, for example, different methods of depreciation and valuation of stock lead to different figures of profit. Hence for proper understanding of final accounts of a company, it is desirable that the accounting policies adopted by the company should be disclosed as also any change that may have been made.

Both the International Accounting Standards Committee and the Institute of Chartered Accountants of India state that the choice of the particular accounting policies must be left to the management but that it should be made on the basis of:

(*i*) Prudence;

(*ii*) Materiality; and

(*iii*) Substance over form.

Prudence requires that the choice should be made on a rational basis and revenue should not be recognised unless it is realised. Prudence, however, does not permit creation of secret reserves; certainly it will not permit any window dressing. Materiality requires that accounting statements should not be made unwieldy or unintelligible due to a very strict adherence to accounting principles. For example, if an inkstand is purchased, strictly it should be capitalised since it will serve for many years. But, since the amount is very small, it will be better if it is written off as a revenue expense. Even income-tax authorities allow capital expenditure upto Rs.750 to be treated as an expense. 'Substance over form' demands that if there is a conflict between the real situation and the technical or legal situation, accounting treatment should be based on reality. As an instance, if an asset is acquired on hire-purchase basis, technically the instalments, until the last instalment is paid, are only hires; strictly, therefore, they should be treated as an expense. In reality, an asset is being acquired, hence the asset must come into the books.

To repeat, for the proper understanding of the Profit and Loss Account and the Balance Sheet, knowledge of the accounting policies followed is essential. One should be aware that different accounting policies will lead to different figures of profit.

The Companies Act permits a company to merge the Trading Account, the Profits and Loss Account and the Profit and Loss Appropriation Account into one account which will then be called Profit and Loss Account. All items of profit or loss including appropriation items except balance brought forward from the previous year will be shown in this account. The special points discussed above should all be properly treated. The balance in this account together with previous year's balance will be shown in the Balance Sheet.

If there is a loss, the Profit and Loss Account will show a debit balance. This has to be shown in the Balance Sheet (asset side) ; but if there is general reserve already created, the loss should be deducted from the general reserve and not shown separately in the Balance Sheet. Only the net difference between the General Reserve and the debit balance in the Profit and Loss Account is shown in the Balance Sheet.

Figures for the previous year have to be given alongside the figures for the current year. For the purpose, usually another column on the left hand side is provided on each side.

Illustration The Quick Ltd. had a nominal capital of Rs. 6,00,000 divided into shares of Rs. 10 each. The balances as per ledger of the company as at December 31, 1977 was as follows :—

	Rs.		Rs.
Calls in arrear	7,500	Stock (1st Jan. 1977)	75,000
Premises	3,00,000	Fixtures	7,200
Plant & Machinery	3,60,000	Sundry Debtors	87,000
Interim Dividend paid	7,500	Goodwill	25,000
Purchases	1,85,000	Cash in Hand	750
Preliminary Expenses	5,000	Cash at Bank	39,900
Freight	13,100	Wages	84,800
Directors' Fees	5,740	General Expenses	16,900
Bad Debts	2,110	Salaries	14,500
6% Debentures	3,00,000	Debentures Interest	9,000
P. & L. A/c (Cr.)	14,500	Share Capital (fully called)	4,60,000
Sundry Creditors	50,000	Bills Payable	38,000
General Reserves	25,000	Sales	4,15,000
4% Govt. Securities	60,000	Provision for Bad Debts	3,500

Prepare the Final Accounts and the Balance Sheet relating to 1977 from the figures given above after taking into account the following:—

1. Depreciate Plant & Machinery by 10% and Fixtures by 5% ;
2. Write off 1/5 of Preliminary Expenses;
3. Rs. 10,000 of wages were utilised in adding rooms to the premises; no entry has as yet been made for it;
4. Leave Bad Debts Provision at 5% of the Sundry Debtors;
5. Provide a final dividend @ 5% ;
6. Transfer Rs. 10,000 to General Reserve; and
7. Make a Provision for Income tax to the extent of Rs. 25,000.
8. The stock on 31st December, 1977 was Rs. 1,01,000.

Solution :

Trading and Profit and Loss Account of the Quick Ltd. for the year ended 31st December, 1977

Figures re at-ing to 31s i Dec. 1976	*Expenses*		*Figures for the current year* Rs.	*Figurss relat-ing to 31st Dec. 1976*	*Incomes*	*Figures for the current year* Rs.
?	To Stock		75,000 —	?	By Sales	4,15,000 —
	To Purchases		1,85,000 —		By Stock	1,01,000 —
	To Wages	84,800				
	Less charged to premises	10,0C0	74,800 —			
	To Freight		13,100 —			
	To Gross Profit c/d		1,68,100 —			
			5,16,000 —			5,16,000 —
	To General Expenses		16,900 —		By Gross Profit b/d	1,68,100 —
	To Salaries		14,500 —		By Interest due on Govt. Securities (4% on Rs. 60,0000)	2,400 —
	To Debenture Interest*					
	Paid	9,000				
	Add outstanding	9,000	18,000 —			
	To Directors' Fees		5,740 —			
	To Preliminary Expenses		1,000			
	To Depreciation—					
	Plant & Machinery	36,000				
	Fixtures	360	36,360 —			
	To Provision for Bed Debts—					
	Required	4,350				
	Add Bad Debts	2,110				
		6,460				
	Less Existing Provision	3,500	2,960 —			
	To Provision for Income Tax		25,000 —			
	To Net Profit c/d		50,040 —			
			1,70,500 —			1,70,500 —

*6% Interest on Rs. 3,00,000 of Debentures comes to Rs. 18,000. Rs. 9,000 has been paid. Hence Rs. 9,000 must be provided now.

(*Continued*)

Balance Sheet of the Quick Ltd. as at December 31, 1977

(not in prescrbied form)

Liabilities		*Amount* Rs.	*Assets*		*Amount* Rs.
Share Capital :			**Fixed Assets :**		
Authorised—60,000 Shares of Rs. 10 each		6,00,000	Goodwill		25,000
			Premises		3,10,000
Issued Subscribed & Paid-up Capital :		?	Plant and Machinery	3,60,000	
46,000 Shares of Rs. 10 each fully called	4,60,000		Less Depreciation	36,000	
					3,24,000
Less Calls in arrear	7,500		Fixtures	7,200	
		4,52,500	Less Depreciation	360	
					6,840
Reserves and Surplus :			**Current Assets :**		
General Reserve		35,000	Investments		60,000
P. & L. A/c		24,415	Interest Due		2,400
			Stock		1,01,000
Secured Loans :			Sundry Debtors	87,000	
6% Debentures		3,00,000	Less Provision for Bad Debts	4,350	
Interest Outstanding		9,000			82,650
Current Liabilities :			Cash in Hand		750
			Cash in Bank		39,900
Bills Payable		38,000	Preliminary Expenses		4,000
Sundry Creditors		50,000			
Provision for Income Tax		25,000			
Proposed Dividend		22,625			
		9,56,540			9,56,540

Alternatively, the Trading and Profit and Loss Account and the Profit and Loss Appropriation Account may be merged together and presented as follows:—

Profit and Loss Account of the Quick Ltd. for the Year ending Dec. 31, 1977

Figures relating to Dec. 31, 1976	*Expenses*	*Figures for the current year* Rs.		*Figures relating to Dec 31, 1976*	*Incomes*	*Figures for the current year* Rs.	
?	To Stock	75,000	—	?	By Sale	4,15,000	—
	To Purchases	1,85,000	—		By Stock	1,01,000	—
	To Wages	74,800	—		By Interest on Govt. Securities	2,400	—
	To Freight	13,100	—				
	To General Expenses	16,900	—				
	To Salaries	14,500	—				
	To Debenture Interest	18,000	—				
	To Directors' Fees	5,740	—				
	To Preliminary Expenses	1,000	—				
	To Depreciation— Plant & Machinery 36,000 Fixtures 360	36,360	—				
	To Provision for Bad Debts: Required 4,350 Add Bad Debits 2,110 6,460 Less Existing Provision 3,500	2,960	—				
	To Provision for Income-Tax	25,000	—				
	To General Reserve	10,000	—				
	To Interim Dividend	7,500	—				
	To Proposed Dividend	22,625	—				
	To Balance of Profit	9,915	—				
		5,18,400	—			5,18,400	—

Form of the Balance Sheet. A company must prepare the Balance Sheet in the form prescribed under the Companies Act. The main principle is that the Balance Sheet must exhibit a true and fair view of the financial position of the company at the close of the year concerned. This means that the position shown should not be better than or worse than the actual position. Assets and liabilities must be shown at their proper figures—neither inflated nor deflated. There is no room for secret reserves or inflated profits. Further, sufficient information must be given to enable one to judge the financial state of affairs. The form prescribed by the Act is given on the following pages along with the instrucuons under the Companies Act relating to the various items. but the following points should be noted by students:—

(*a*) Figures relating to the previous year should be given preferably on the left hand side.

(*b*) All assets have to be grouped under the main headings of :

(*i*) Fixed Assets;

) Investments;

(*iii*) Current Assets, Loans and Advances—

1. Current Assets;

2. Loans and Advances;

(*iv*) Miscellaneous Expenses (to the extent not written off);

(*v*) Profit and Loss Account (Dr.)

In the case of fixed assets, original cost, additions made during the year, cost of the asset sold during the year and depreciation written off against the asset to date have to be shown.

In case of investments, work in progress, stock and loose tools mode of valuation (cost or market price) is to be shown. In case of sundry debtors and loans and advances, amounts outstanding for more than six months must be shown separately. Also, the amounts which are secured and unsecured and which are doubtful aud amounts owed by directors and their business associates have to be given.

(*c*) 'Liabilities' have to be grouped under :

(*i*) Share Capital;

(*ii*) Reserves and Surplus;

(*iii*) Secured Loans;

(*iv*) Unsecured Loans; and

(*v*) Current Liabilities and Provisions—

1. Current Liabilities;

2. Provisions.

In addition, contingent liabilities (amounts which may become payable on the happening of a certain event) have to be shown by way of a note.

In case of Share Capital information has to be given regarding different classes of shares, right of redemption if any, shares issued for consideration other than cash and shares issued as bonus shares and the source from which these have been issued.

Capital reserves must be shown separately from revenue reserves. Additions to and withdrawals from reserves must be shown. In case of secured loans, there must be information regarding security and terms of redemption.

We now give the prescribed form with suitable adaptations consequent on the abolition of managing agents and secretaries and treasurers. Assets and Liabilities have to be given in one statement. For want of space, we have had to give liabilities first and then the assets. "Notes" at the end of the form apply to the whole of the Balance Sheet. On the right side. "instructions" given in the Companies Act regarding the various items have been given. These should be read carefully.

SCHEDULE VI

(*See* section 211)

(PART 1A)

FORM OF BALANCE SHEET

Balance Sheet of.....................................(here enter the name of the company)

As at...................................(here enter the date as at which the balance sheet is made out)

Liabilities			Instructions
Figures for the previous year		*Figures for the current year*	
Rs. (*b*)	***SHARE CAPITAL :**	Rs. (*b*)	
	Authorised...........shares of Rs...............each.		
	Issued distinguishing between the various classes of capital and stating the particulars specified below, in respect of each class)...........shares of Rs.................... . ...each.		Terms of redemption or conversion (if any) of any Redeemable Preference Capital to be stated. together with earliest date of redemption or conversion. Particulars of any option on unissued share capital to be specified.
	Subscribed (distinguishing between the various classes of capital and stating the particulars specified below, in respect of each class) (c) ....…shares of Rs.......,...each, Rs.......,...called up.		Particulars of the different classes of preference shares to be given.

Liabilities			Instructions
Figures for the previous year		Figures for the current year	
Rs. (b)	Of the above shares...............shares are allotted as fully paid up pursuant to a contract without payments being received in each.	Rs. (b)	
	Of the above shares...............shares are allotted as fully paid up by way of bonus shares or other shares by way of capitalisation of profits or reserves and/or from share premium account.		
	Less : Calls unpaid :		
	(i) By directors.		
	(ii) By others.		
	Add : Forfeited shares		

RESERVES AND SURPLUS :	
(1) Capital Reserves not available for dividend	*Additions and deductions since last balance-sheet to be shown under each of the specified heads.
(2) Capital Redemption Reserve.	
(3) Share Premium Account (cc)	The word "fund" in relation to any "Reserve" should be used only where such reserve is specifically represented by readily realisable and earmarked assets.
(4) Other Reserves specifying the nature of each reserve and the amount in respect thereof.	
Less : Debit balance in Profit and Loss Account (if any).	
(5) Any other Reserve created out of Net Profit.	
(6) Surplus that is balance in Profit and Loss Account after providing for proposed allocations, *viz.*, Dividend, Bonus or Reserves.	
(7) Proposed additions to reserves.	
(8) Sinking Funds.	
SECURED LOANS :	
(1) Debentures	The nature of the security to be specified in each case. Where loans have been guaranteed by managers and/or directors, a mention thereof shall also be made and also the aggregate amount of such loans under each head.
(2) Loans and Advances from Bankers	
(3) Loans and Advances from subsidiaries	
(4) Other Loans and Advances	Terms of redemption or conversion (if any) of debentures issued to be stated together with earliest date of redemption or conversion.

Figures for the previous year	Liabilities	Figures for the current year	Instructions
Rs. (*b*)		Rs. (*b*)	
	UNSECURED LOANS :		
	(1) Fixed Deposits.		Where loans have been guaranteed by managers, and/or directors a mention thereof shall also be made and also the aggregate amount of such loans under each head.
	(2) Loans and Advances from subsidiaries.		
	(3) Short Term Loans and advances : (*d*)		
	(*a*) From Banks. (*b*) From others.		
	(4) Other Loans and advances :		
	(*a*) From Banks. (*b*) From others.		
	CURRENT LIABILITIES AND PROVISIONS:		
	A. **Current Liabilities :**		
	(1) Acceptances		
	(2) Sundry Creditors.		
	(3) Subsidiary Companies.		

(4) Advance Payments and Unexpired Discounts for the portion for which value has still to be given, *e.g.*, in the case of the following classes of companies:
(Newspapers, Fire Insurance, Theatre, Clubs, Banking, Steamship Companies, etc.)

(5) Unclaimed Dividends.

(6) Other Liabilities (if any).

(7) Interest accrued but not due on loans.

B. Provisions :

(8) Provision for Taxation.

(9) Proposed Dividends.

(10) For contingencies.

(11) For Provident Fund scheme.

(12) For insurance, pension and similar staff benefits schemes.

(13) Other provisions.

A foot-note to the balance-sheet may be added to show separately:—

(1) Claims against the company not acknowledged as debts.

(2) Uncalled liability on shares partly paid.

The period for which the dividends are in arrear or if there is more than one class of shares, the dividends on each such class are in arrear, shall be stated.

Figures for the previous year	Liabilities	Figures for the current year	Instructions
Rs. (*b*)		Rs. (*b*)	
	(3) Arrears of fixed cumulative dividends.		The amount shall be stated before deduction of Income tax, except that in the case of tax free dividends the amount shall be shown free of income tax and the fact that it is so shown shall be stated.
	(4) Estimated amount of contracts remaining to be executed on capital amount and not provided for.		
	(5) Other money for which the company is contingently liable.)		The amount of any guarantees given by the company on behalf of directors or other officers of the company shall be stated and where practicable, the general nature and amount of each such contingent liability, if material shall also be specified.

Figures for the previous year	Assets	Figures for the current year	Instructions
Rs. (*b*)		Rs. (*b*)	
	FIXED ASSETS :		
	Distinguishing as far as possible between expenditure upon –		Under each head the original cost, and the addition, thereto and deductions therefrom during the years and the total depreciation written off or provided up to the end of the year to be stated.
	(*a*) goodwill,		
	(*b*) land,		In case where original cost cannot be ascertained, the valuation shown by the books shall be given and where any of the assets are sold and the original cost in respect thereof is not ascertainable, the amount of the sale proceeds shall be shown as deduction.
	(*c*) buildings,		
	(*d*) leaseholds,		
	(*e*) railway sidings,		
	(*f*) plant and machinery,		Where sums have been written off on a reduction of capital or a revaluation of assets, every balance-sheet, (after the first balance sheet) subsequent to reduction or revaluation shall show the reduced figures and with the date of the reduction in place of the original cost.
	(*g*) furniture and fittings,		
	(*h*) development of property,		
	(*i*) patents, trade marks and designs,		Each balance-sheet for the first five years subsequent to the date of the reduction, shall show also the amount of the reduction made.
	(*j*) live-stock, and		
	(*k*) vehicles, etc.		

Figures for the previous year	Assets	Figures for the Current year	Instructions
Rs. (b)		Rs. (b)	
			Similarly, where sums have been added by writing up the assets, every balance-sheet subsequent to such writing up shall show the increased figures with the date of the increase in place of the original cost. Each balance-sheet for the first five years subsequent to the date of writing up shall also show the amount of increase made.
			N.B. If a fixed asset is acquired out of a foreign currency loan and the rupee is devalued, the increase in the liability in respect of the foreign currency loan still remaining outstanding should be added to the cost of the asset concerned. It will not be a case of revaluation.
	INVESTMENTS :		
	Showing nature of investments and mode of valuation, for example cost or market value and distinguishing between—		
	(1) Investments in Government or Trust Securities.		
	(2) Investments in shares, debentures or bonds, showing separately shares, fully paid up and partly paid up and also distinguishing the different classes of shares and showing also in similar details investments in shares, debentures or bonds of subsidiary companies.		Aggregate amount of company's quoted investments and also the market value thereof shall be shown. Aggregate amount of company's unquoted investments shall also be shown.
	(3) Immovable properties.		
	(4) Investment in the capital of partnership firms.		

CURRENT ASSETS, LOANS AND ADVANCES :	
(A) Current Assets :	
(1) Interest accrued on Investments.	
(2) Stores and Spare Parts.	Mode of valuation of stock shall be stated and the amount in respect of raw materials shall also be stated separately where practicable.
(3) Loose Tools.	
(4) Stock-in-trade	
(5) Works in Progress.	Mode of valuation of works-in-progress shall be stated.
(6) Sundry Debtors	In regard to Sundry Debtors particulars to be given separately of (*a*) debts considered good and in respect of which the company is fully secured; (*b*) debts considered good for which the company holds no security other than the debtor's personal security; and (*c*) debts considered doubtful or bad.
(*a*) Debts outstanding for a period exceeding six months.	
(*b*) Other debts.	
Less : Provision.	Debts due by directors or other officers of the company or any of them either severally or jointly with any other person or debts due by firms or private companies respectively in which any director is partner or a director or a member to be separately stated.
(7A) Cash balance on hand.	
(7B) Bank Balances :	
(*a*) with Scheduled Banks.	Debts due from other companies under the same management to be disclosed with the names of the companies (*vide* section 370).
(*b*) with others.	
	The maximum amount due by directors or other officers of the company at any time during the year to be shown by way of a note.

Assets			Instructions
Figures for the previous year		*Figures for the current year*	
Rs. (*b*)		Rs. (*b*)	
			The Provision to be shown under this head should not exceed the amount of debts stated to be considered doubtful or bad and any surplus of such Provision, if already created, should be shown at every closing under "Reserves and Surplus" (in the Liabilities side) under a separate sub-head "Reserve for Doubtful or Bad Debts".
			The balance lying with Scheduled Banks on current accounts, call accounts and deposit accounts shall be shown separately.
			Names of the bankers other than Scheduled Banks and the balances lying with each such banker on current accounts, call accounts and deposit accounts and the maximum amount outstanding at any time during the year with each such banker shall be given.
			The nature of the interest, if any, of any Director or his relativc in each of the bankers (other than Scheduled Banks) shall aiso be given.

(B) Loans and Advances : **8(*a*)** Advances and Loans to subsidiaries. **8(*b*) Advances and Loans to partnership firms in which the company or any of its subsidiaries is a partner.** (9) Bills of Exchange (10) Advances recoverable in cash or in kind or for value to be received, *e.g.*, Rates, Taxes, Insurance, etc. (11) Balance with Customs, Port Trust, etc. (where payable on demand).	The above instructions regarding "Sundry Debtors" apply to "Loans and Advances" also.
MISCELLANEOUS EXPENDITURE (to the extent not written off) : (1) Preliminary Expenses. (2) Expenses including commission or brokerage on underwriting or subscription of shares or debentures. (3) Discount allowed on the issue of shares or debentures. (4) Interest paid out of capital during construction (also stating the rate of interest). (5) Development expenditure not adjusted. (6) Other items (specifying nature).	
PROFIT AND LOSS ACCOUNT : Loss brought forward. *Less* : Reserve set off.	

NOTES

General instructions for preparation of balance sheet.

(*a*) The information required to be given under any of the items or sub-items in this Form, if it cannot be conveniently included in the balance sheet itself. shall be furnished in a separate Schedule or Schedules to be annexed to and to form part of the balance sheet. This is recommended when items are numerous.

(*b*) Paise can also be given in addition to Rupees, if desired.

(*c*) In the case of subsidiary companies, etc , the number of shares held by the holding company as well as by the ultimate holding company and its subsidiaries must be separately stated.

The auditor is not required to certify the correctness of such shareholdings as certified by the management.

(*c*) The item "Share Premium Account" shall include full details of its utilization in the manner provided in Section 78.

(*d*) Short Term Loans will include those which are due for not more than one year as at the date of the balance sheet.

(*e*) Depreciation written off or provided shall be allocated under the different asset heads and deducted in arriving at the value of Fixed Assets.

(*f*) Dividends declared by subsidiary companies after the date of the balance sheet cannot be included unless they are in respect of period which closed on or before the date of the balance sheet.

(*g*) Any reference to benefits expected from contracts to the extent not executed shall not be made in the balance sheet but shall be made in the Board's report.

(*h*) The debit balance in the Profit and Loss Account shall be set off against the General Reserve, if any.

(*i*) As regards Loans and Advances. the amounts due from other companies under the same management should be given with the names of the companies *vide* section 370, the maximum amount due from every one of these at any time during the year must be shown.

(*j*) Particulars of any redeemed debentures which the company has power to issue should be given.

(*k*) Where any of the company's debentures are held by a nominee or a trustee for the company, the nominal amount of the debentures and the amount at which they are stated in the books of the company shall be stated.

(*l*) A statement of investments (whether shown under "Investments" or under "Current Assets" as stock-in-trade) separately classifying trade investments and other investments should be annexed to the balance sheet showing the names of the bodies corporate; indicating separately the names of the bodies corporate in the same group (with the name of the managing agent or secretaries and treasurers, if any, of every body corporate) in whose shares or debentures investments have been made (including all investments whether existing or not, made subsequent to the date as at which the previous balance sheet was made out) and the nature and extent of the investments so made in each such body corporate, provided that in the case of an investment company, that is to say, a company whose principal business is the acquisition of shares, stock, debentures or other securities, it shall be sufficient if the statement shows only the investments existing on the date as at which the balance-sheet has been made out: **In regard to the investments in the capital of partnership firms, the names of the firms (with the names of all their partners, total capital and the share of each partner) shall be given in the statements.**

A "Trade Investment" means an investment by a company in the shares or debentures of another company, not being its subsidiary; for the purpose of promoting the trade or business of the first company.

(*m*) If, in the opinion of the Board, any of the current assets have not a value on realisation in the ordinary course of business at least equal to the amount at which they are stated, the fact that the Board is of that opinion shall be stated.

(*n*) Except in the case of the first balance sheet laid before the company after the commencement of the Act, the corresponding amounts for the immediately preceding financial year for all items shown in the balance sheet shall also be given in the balace sheet. The requirements in this behalf shall in the case of companies preparing quarterly or half-yearly accounts, etc., relate to the balance sheet for the corresponding date in the previous year.

(*o*) The amounts to be shown under Sundry Debtors shall include the amounts due in respect of goods sold or services rendered or in respect of other contractual obligations but shall not include the amounts which are in the nature of loans or advances.

(*p*) Advances by Directors or Managers as also balances on current account with them whether they are in credit or debit shall be shown separately.

Vertical Form of Balance Sheet. Government have now permitted companies to prepare the balance sheet either in the horizontal form as given above, or in the vertical form. The vertical form is given below:

Name of the Company..........................

Balance Sheet as at..................................

I. Sources of Funds	*Schedule No.*	*Figures as at the end of the current year*	*Figures as at the end of the previous year*
(1) *Shareholders' Funds*			
(*a*) Capital	..	..	..
(*b*) Reserves and Surplus	..	..	..
(2) *Loan Funds*			
(*a*) Secured Loans	..	..	..
(*b*) Unsecured Loans	..	..	..
Total			

II. Application of Funds

(1) *Fixed Assets*

(*a*) Gross Block	..	..	..
(*b*) Less Depreciation	..	..	..
(*c*) Net Block	..	..	..
(*d*) Capital Work in Progress	..	..	..
(2) *Investments*	..	..	..
(3) *Current Assets, Loans and Advances*			
(*a*) Inventories	..	..	..
(*b*) Sundry Debtors	..	..	..
(*c*) Cash and Bank Balances	..	..	..
(*d*) Other current assets	..	..	..
(*e*) Loans and Advances	..	..	..
Less: *Current Liabilities and Provisions*			
(*a*) Liabilities	..	..	..
(*b*) Provisions	..	..	..
Net Current Assets	..	..	..
(4) (*a*) Miscellaneous Expenditure to the extent not written off or adjusted	..	..	..
(*b*) Profit and Loss Account	..	..	..
Total			

Notes: 1. Details under each of the above items shall be given in separate schedules. The schedules shall incorporate all the information required to be given under Part IA of Schedule VI read with Notes containing General Instructions for Preparation of Balance Sheet.

2. The Schedules, referred to above, accounting policies and explanatory notes that may be attached shall form an integral part of the balance sheet.

3. The figures in the balance sheet may be rounded off to the nearest "000" or "00" as may be convenient or may be expressed in terms of decimals of thousnads.

4. A footnote to the balance sheet may be added to show separately contingent liabilities.

Illustration The Trial Balance of Moonshine Ltd. (having an authorised capital of Rs. 8,00,000) as at 31st December, 197 was as under :

	Rs.	Rs.
Share Capital (shares of Rs. 100 each fully paid)		5,00,000
Share Premium Account		50,000
Land and Buildings (Cost Rs. 3,00,000)	2,50,000	
Plant and Machinery (Cost Rs. 4,00,000)	3,00,000	
Livestock	20,000	
Gross Profit earned during 1975,		1,30,000
General Reserve		2,00,000
6% Debentures (secured by mortgage on Land and Buildings, redeemable on 31st December, 1971)		1,00,000
Sundry Debtors and Creditors	60,000	30,000
Stock as at December 31, 1975 (at cost below market price)	50,000	
Provision for Income Tax		65,000
Income Tax paid during the year	59,000	
Salaries	25,000	
Directors' Fees	10,000	
General Expenses	15,000	
Cash in hand	600	
Cash at Bank	6,400	
Bills Receivable	20,000	
Discount on Issue of Debentures	4,000	
P. & L. A/c		10,000
Investments —		
4% Government Securities (face value Rs. 1,00,000)	95,000	
Equity shares (10 shares of Rs. 25 each, Rs. 20 paid)	1,70,000	
	10,85,000	10,85,000

Further information is supplied to as follows :—

(*a*) Of the shares allotted, Rs. 2,000 shares were allotted as fully paid to vendors from whom a running business was acquired.

(*b*) During the year a building costing Rs. 60,000 (depreciation written off Rs. 8,000) was sold for Rs. 75,000. The profit was credited to General Reserve.

(*c*) Of the debtors, Rs. 10,000 were outstanding for more than six months. All debts are unsecured but are considered good except a debt of Rs. 5,000.

(*d*) There was no further liability in respect of income tax for the previous years. For 1975, a provision of 50% is desired.

(*e*) The Government securities have a market value of Rs. 93,000 and the market value of shares is Rs. 1,60,000. It is not desired to write down the value of securities on shares.

(*f*) Auditors' Fee, Rs. 3,000, should be provided for. Included in General Expenses is six months' insurance up to 30th June, 1976 @ Rs. 1,500 p.a.

(*g*) Depreciation is to be provided for @ 6% on original cost of machinery and 2% on the original cost of Land and Buildings. Under the Income-tax Rules, the depreciation allowable is Rs. 35,000.

(*h*) The managing director is entitled to a commission of 5% of the profit.

(*i*) Provide for a dividend of 5% on shares.

Solution :

Profit and Loss Account of the Moonshine Ltd for the Year ended Dec. 31, 1975

Figures for 31st Dec., 1974	*Expenses*	*Figures for the current year* Rs.		*Figures for 31st Dec., 1974*	*Incomes*	*Figures for the current year* Rs.	
?	To Salaries	25,000	—	?	By Gross Profit	1,30,000	—
	To Directors' Fees	10,000	—		By Interest on Government Securities (4% on Rs. 1,00,000)	4,000	—
	To General Expenses :	14,250			By Saving in the Provision for Income Tax	6,000	—
	To Auditor's Fees	3,000	—				
	To Depreciation— Plant & Machinery	24,000	—				
	Land & Buildings	6,000	—				
	To Discount on Issue of Debentures	1,000	—				
	To Interest on Debentures	6,000	—				
	To Commission due Mg. Director	2,038					
	To Provision for Income Tax	19,356	—				
	To Proposed Dividend	25,000	—				
	To Balance c/d	4,356	—				
		1,40,000	—			1,40,000	—

Commission to Managing Director

		Rs.	
Income (Gross Profit plus Interest received)			**1,34,000**
Less Expenses :	**Salaries**	**25,000**	
	Directors' Fees	**10,000**	
	General Expenses	**14,250**	
	Audit Fee	**3,000**	
	Depreciation (I.T. Rules)	**35,000**	
	Interest on Debentures	**6,000**	**93,250**
			40,750
Commission due to Mg. Director @ 5%			**2,038**

Income tax .

Profit after commission due to Mg. Director	**38,712**
Income tax @ 50%	**19,356**

Balance Sheet of the Moonshine Ltd. as at Dec. 31, *1975*

Figures for Dec. 31, 1974 Rs.	*Liabilities*		*Figures relating to the current year* Rs.	*Figures for 31st Dec. 1974* Rs.	*Assets*		*Figures for the current year* Rs.
	Share Capital :			?	**Fixed Assets :**	Rs.	
	Authorised – 8,000 shares of Rs. 100 each		8,00,000 —		Land & Bulidings – Cost	3,60,000	
			====== =		*Less* Cost of Building sold during the year	60,000	
	Issued,		?			3,00,000	
	Subscribed and Paid up Capital— 5,000 Shares of Rs. 100 each fully paid		5,00,000				
	(Of the above 2,000 shares were issued for consideration other than cash to the vendors)				*Less* Depreciation written off to date	56,000	2,44,000 —
	Reserves and Surplus :				Plant & Machinery—Cost	4,00 000	
	Share Premium Account		50,000		*Less* Depreciation written off to date	1,24,000	2,76,000 —
	Capital Reserve*		15,000 —		Livestock		20,000 —
	General Reserve :		—		**Investments :**		
	Balance as at 31st Dec., 1967	1 77,000					
	Addition during the year (Profit on sale of Building)*	8,000	1,85,000 —		Government Securities (4% Rs. 1,00,000, market value Rs. 93,000)		95,000 —
	Profit & Loss Account :				Partly paid Equity shares (market value Rs. 1,60,000)		1,70,000 —
	Balance as at 31st Dec., 1967	10,000					
	Balance of profit this year	4,356	14,356				

Liabilities	Rs.	P.	Assets	Rs.	Rs.	P.
Secured Loans :			**Current Assets, Loan and Advances :**			
			(A) *Current Assets* :			
6% Debentures (secured by mortgage on Land & Buildings and redeemable on 31st Dec., 1965)	1,00,000	—	Interest Due on Securities		4,000	—
Interest Outstanding	6,000	—	Stock (at cost or below market price)		50,000	—
Unsecured Loans	Nil		Sundry Debtors			
Current Liabilities and Provisions :			Outstanding for more than six months	10,000		
A. *Current Liabilities* :			Others	50,000		
					60,000	—
Sundry Creditors for goods	30,000	—	Debts, unsecured but good	55,000		
Creditors for expenses :		—	Debts considered doubtful	5,000		
				60,000		
Audit Fee and Commission to Mg Director	5,038		Cash in hand		600	—
B. *Provisions*			Cash in Bank (assumed scheduled)		6,400	—
Provision for Income Tax	19,356	—	(B) *Loans and Advances* :			
Proposed Dividend	25,000	—	Bills Receivable (details not available)		20,000	—
Contingent Liabilities :			Insurance prepaid		750	—
There is a liability of Rs. 5 per share on 10,000 partly paid equity shares			**Miscellaneous Expenses** (to the extent not written off or adjusted)			
			Discount on Issue of Debentures		3,000	—
*Of the total profit on sale of building, Rs. 15,000 *i.e.*, Rs. 75,000—Rs. 60,000 is special or capital profit to be credited to Capital Reserve.						
	9,49,750	—			9,49,750	—

In the vertical form the balance sheet would have appeared as shown below (the Schedules will have the details—these are not given):

Balance Sheet of Moonshine Ltd. as at 31st December, 1975

	Schedule No.		Figures as at 31st Dec. 1975 Rs.
I. Sources of Funds			
(1) Shareholders' Funds			
(*a*) Share Capital	1		5,00,000
(*b*) Reserves Surplus	2		2,64,356
(2) Loan Funds			
(*a*) Secured Loans	3		1,06,000
(*b*) Unsecured Loans	—		nil
Total			8,70,356
II. Application of Funds			
(1) Fixed Assets			
(*a*) Gross Block	4		7,20,000
(*b*) Less Depreciation	5		1,80,000
			5,40,000
(2) Investments	6		2,65,000
(3) Current Assets, Loans and Advances			
(*a*) Stock	7	50,000	
(*b*) Sundry Debtors	8	60,000	
(*c*) Cash and Bank Balances	9	7,000	
(*d*) Other current assets—Interest due	10	4,000	
(*e*) Loans and Advances	11	20,750	
		1,41,750	
Less Current Liabilities & Provisions			
(*a*) Liabilities	12	35,038	
(*b*) Provisions	13	44,356	62,356
		79,394	
(4) Miscelleneous Expenditure not yet written off or adjusted			3,000
Total			8,70,356

Illustration: The following Trial Balance has been extracted from the books of Cochin-Andaman Line Ltd., as on 31st December, 1973:

	Dr. Rs.		Cr. Rs.
Opening Stock of Stores and Provisions	2,000	Freight Earnings	7,50,000
Purchase of Stores and Provisions	28,000	Term Loan from Bank	6,50,000
Stevedoring Charges	1,45,000	Sundry Creditors	35,000
Fuel and Oil	60,000	Provisions for Income-tax for 1972	55,000
Port Charges and Dock Dues	12,000	Profit and Loss Account: Balance as on 31st December 1972	4,500
Interest and Bank Charges	75,000	Outstanding expenses	11,400
Establishment	40,000	Depreciation Provision:	
Rent, Rates and Taxes	8,600		
Freight and Commission	18,500	(Upto 31st December, 1972):	
Fixed Assets: Cost upto Last year		Ship	2,00,000
Ship	12,00,000	Furniture	
Furniture and Fittings	20,000	and Fittings	5,000
Motor Car	22,000	Motor Car	8,000
Survey Fee	5,000	Share Capital	2,00,000
Postage, Telegram and Telephones	9,500		
Sundry Debtors	86,000		
Preliminary Expenses	2,500		
Investments	6,500		
Call-in-arrear	3,000		
Advance Payment of Income-tax for 1973	44,000		
Cash in hand	6,450		
Cash at Bank	62,500		
Advance Payment of Income-tax for 1972	60,000		
Directors' Fees	900		
Audit Fees	1,000		
Law Charges	450		
Total	19,18,900	Total	19,18,900

The following further particulars are available:

(1) Stock of Stores and Provisions as on 31st December, 1973—Rs. 1,500

(2) Share Capital represents 20,000 equity shares of Rs.10 each fully called up.

(3) Depreciation to be charged on *w.d.v.* at the following rates:

(*i*) Ship	15%
(*ii*) Furniture and fittings	10%
(*iii*) Motor Car	20%

(4) Postage, Telegram and Telephone expenses include Rs.3,000 paid on 1st January, 1973 as 20 years' rental under Own Your Own Telephone Scheme.

(5) Investments represent 1,300 Equity Shares of Rs.10 each, Rs. 5 per share called-up of a Public Limited Company.

(6) No effect has been given for the Income-tax assessment of 1972 completed during the year resulting into a gross tax demand of Rs. 62,000.

(7) Directors are entitled to a remuneration of 3 per cent on the net profits of the Compnay.

(8) Term Loan is secured by charge on the Ship in addition to the personal guarantees of the Directors of the Company.

(9) Provision for Income-tax is to be made for Rs.1,08,800 for 1973.

You are required to prepare the Profit and Loss Account for the year ended 31st December, 1973 and also to draw up the Balance Sheet as on that date from the particulars. Ignore previous year's figures.

Solution:

COCHIN-ANDAMAN LINE LTD.

Profit and Loss Account for the year ended 31st December, 1973

Dr.		Rs.		Cr. Rs.
To Stores & Provisions consumed:	Rs.		By Freight earnings	7,50,000
Opening Stock	2,000			
Purchases	28,000			
	30,000			
Less: Closing Stock	1,500			
		28,500		

	Rs.		Rs.
To Stevedoring charges	1,45,000		
To Fuel & Oil	60,000		
To Port Charges & Dock Dues	12,000		
To Interest & Bank Charges	75,000		
To Establishment	40,000		
To Rent, Rates & Taxes	8,600		
To Freight & Commission	18,500		
To Postage, Telegrams & Telephone 9,500 *Less*: Prepaid 2,850	6,650		
To Audit Fee	1,000		
To Law Charges	450		
To Directors' fees	900		
To Directors' remuneration	5,823		
To Survey Fee	5,000		
To Depreciation	1,54,300		
To Provision for Taxation	1,08,800		
To Net Profit carried down	79,477		
	7,50,000		7,50,000
To Income-tax for 1972	7,000	By Balance from last year	4,500
To Balance carried down	76,977	By Net Profit f/d	79,477
	83,977		83,977

Balance Sheet as at 31st December, 1973

Liabilities		Rs.	*Assets*	Rs.	Rs.
Share Capital			Fixed Assets:		
Authorised		?	Ship: Cost	12,00,000	
Issued, Subscribed & Paid-up:			*Less* Depreciation	3,50,000	8,50,000
20,000 Equity shares of Rs. 10 each fully called up	2,00,000		Furniture & Fittings: Cost	20,000	
Less Call-in-arrear	3,000	1,97,000	*Less* Depreciation	6,500	13,500
			Motor car: Cost	22,000	
Reserves and Surplus					
Profit & Loss A c		76,977	*Less* Depreciation	10,800	11,200
Secured Loan :					
Term Loan from Bank (Secured by charge on					8,74,700

Liabilities	Rs.	Rs.	Assets	Rs.	Rs.
the ship in addition to personal guarantees of Directors)		6,50,000	*Investment*: (At Cost) Partly-paid Equity Shares (unquoted)		6,500
Current Liabilities and Provisions			*Current Assets, Loans and Advances* :		
A. Current Liabilities:			A. Current Assets:		
Outstanding Expenses	17,223		Stores & Provisions		1,500
Sundry Creditors	35,000		Sundry Debtors (Unsecured, good)		
Income-tax Payable	2,000	54,223	(*i*) Out-standing for more than 6 months	16,000	
B. Provision for Taxation		1,08,800	(*ii*) Others Rs.	70,000	86,000
			Cash in hand		6,450
			Cash at Bank (Scheduled Bank)		62,500
			B. Loans & Advances: (Unsecured, good)		
			Income-tax Advance payment		44,000
			Pre-paid Telephone Rent		2,850
			Miscellaneous Expenditure:		
			Preliminary Expenses		2,500
		10,87,000			10,87,000

Contingent Liabilities:

In respect of partly-called shares held as investment—Rs.6,500/-

Note Regarding Directors' Remuneration:

	Rs.
Net Profit carried down	79,477
Add: Provision for taxation	1,08,800
Directors' Remuneration	5,823
	1,94,100
Remuneration @ 3% of Rs. 1,94,100	5,823

Depreciation :

	W.D.V. Rs.	Rate	Depreciation Rs.
Ship	10,00,000	15%	1,50,000
Furniture & Fittings	15,000	10%	1,500
Motor Car	14,000	20%	2,800

Profit prior to incorporation. Sometimes a company takes over a running business as from a certain date even though the company may come into existence at a later date. The profit which the company may thus earn before its birth is a special profit and is known as "Profit Prior to Incorporation". It is a capital profit and not available for dividends. If there is a loss, it is a special loss and may be added to Goodwill.

Strictly speaking, a Profit and Loss Account should be prepared for the pre-incorporation period. But this involves stock taking and is inconvenient. Usually the Profit and Loss Account is prepared for the whole year and then allocation is made between the pre and post-incorporation periods. For this purpose the following may be noted :—

(*a*) Gross profit should be allocated in the ratio of sales for the two periods ;

(*b*) Expenses dependent on sales, for example, discount allowed, carriage on sales, etc., should be apportioned in the same ratio.

(*c*) Expenses dependent upon time, for example, salaries, rent, etc., should be allocated in the ratio of time.

(*d*) Expenses that arise only when the company comes into existence, for example, preliminary expenses, directors' fees, debenture interest, should be charged to the post-incorporation period wholly.

Difference between the gross profit and the total of expenses is naturally, profit.

Illustration New Ltd. was incorporated on 1st May, 1968 and was entitled to commence business on 1st June, 1968. It had acquired a running business as from 1st January, 1968. The Profit and Loss Account for 1968 was as under :

	Rs.		Rs.
To Salaries	40,000	By Gross Profits	2,00,000
To General Expenses	10,000		
To Carriage	15,000		
To Advertising	20,000		
To Debenture Interest	6,000		
To Directors' Fees	4,000		
To Audit Fees	5,000		
To Depreciation	20,000		

(*Continued*

To Interest to Vendor (up to 30th June)	10,000		
To Net Profit	70,000		
	2,00,000		2,00,000

Ascertain the profit prior to incorporation. Sales up to 1st May, 1968 were Rs. 2,00,000 and after 1st May, 1968 Rs. 8,00,000.

Solution :

	Prior to Incorporation	*After Incorporation*
	Rs.	Rs.
Gross Profit (ratio 1 : 4)	40,000	1,60,000
Expenses :		
Salaries (4 : 8 or 1 : 2)	13,333	26,667
General Expenses (1 : 2)	3,333	6,667
Carriage (1 : 4)	3,000	12,000
Advertising („)	4,000	16,000
Debentures Interest		6,000
Directors' Fees		4,000
Audit Fees (1 : 2)*	1,667	3,333
Depreciation (1 : 2)	6,667	13,333
Interest to vendors (4 : 2)	6,667	3,333
Total Expenses	38,667	91,333
Profit	1,333	68,667

Profit prior to incorporation comes to Rs. 1,333. The entry to be passed is :

		Rs.	Rs.
Profit and Loss Account ...	Dr.	1,333	
To Profit prior to Incorporation A/c			1,333

* Strictly speaking audit fees may arise only if the company is formed and hence these may be charged wholly to the post-incorporation period. But since audit will cover the pre-incorporation period also, audit fees should be apportioned over the two periods.

Issue of bonus shares. Bonus shares are shares issued without payment. They are issued only out of profits, both capital and revenue. The process of issue of bonus shares is also known as capitalisation of reserves. Only equity shareholders are given bonus shares usually. A company issues bonus shares in order to (*a*) conserve cash resources (instead of a cash dividend, shares are issued), (*b*) enable shareholders to have a capital gain and (*c*) present a proper figure of share capital with which the profit is to be compared. Suppose a company has a capital of Rs. 1,00,000 and reserve of Rs. 3,00,000. If it earns a profit of Rs. 40,000, the earning is not 40% *i.e.*, $\frac{40,000}{100,000} \times 100$ but only 10% *i.e.*, $\frac{40,000}{400,000} \times 100$.

It should, however, be remembered that a shareholder will gain *nothing* if there is no increase in the *total amount of dividend* received by him. This is because, in the market, the value of a share depends upon the dividend on the share. If after the issue of bonus shares, dividend per share is reduced proportionately, it amounts to no additional gain for the shareholder. But if the dividend per share is maintained, there will be a capital gain equal to the market value of additional shares received (as bonus shares). If the dividend per share is reduced but leaving a higher total amount, the shareholder will get a capital gain equal to the total market value of shares held by him now minus the total market value of shares held by him previously. Sometimes bonus is declared in the form of making partly paid shares fully paid. Since this extinguishes liability of the shareholders, it amounts to a real gain for him.

Fully paid bonus shares can be issued out of Share Premium Account or out of Capital Redemption Reserve Account or out of other reserves—capital or revenue. Only revenue reserves should be used for making partly paid shares fully paid.

The amount of the bonus involved is debited to the Reserve Account* concerned and credited to "Bonus to Shareholders Account". Then this latter account is debited and Share Capital Account is credited. Thus the Reserve Account will be reduced and Share Capital Account increased. The number of shares issued as bonus shares and their source must be disclosed in the Balance Sheet as a note.

In case partly paid shares are made fully paid the following entries will be necessary :

(*a*) Reserve Account ... Dr.
  To Bonus to Shareholders A/c

(*b*) Share Final Call Account ... Dr.
  To Share Capital Account

(*c*) Bonus to Shareholders Account ... Dr.
  To Share Final Call Account

* Or Share Premium Account, Capital Redemption Reserve A/c etc.

Illustration The Balance Sheet of X Y Ltd., as at 31st December, 1978 was as under :

Liabilities	Rs.	*Assets*	Rs.
5,000 shares of Rs. 100 each, Rs. 75 paid	3,75,000	Sundry Assets	10,25,000
Share Premium	1,00,000		
General Reserve	2,00,000		
Profit and Loss Account	1,50,000		
Sundry Creditors	2,00,000		
	10,25,000		10,25,000

The company decided to make the shares fully paid out of Profit and Loss Account and then to issue one fully paid bonus share for every two held. For this purpose the Share Premium Account was to be used fully and then the General Reserve. Journalise and prepare Balance Sheet after the arrangements are put through.

Solution :

Journal

			Dr. Rs.	Cr. Rs.
1978 Dec.	31	Share Final Call Account ...Dr. To Share Capital Account The amount due on 5,000 shares @ Rs. 25 per share; the call to be met out of P. & L. A/c	1,25,000 —	1,25,000 —
	,,	Profit and Loss Account ...Dr. To Bonus to Shareholders A/c The final call to be met as a bonus out of Profit and Loss A/c	1,25,000 —	1,25,000 —
	,,	Bonus to Shareholders A/c ...Dr. To Share Final Call Account Final call settled as a bonus out of P. & L. A/c	1,25,000 —	1,25,000 —
	,,	Share Premium Account ...Dr. General Reserve ...Dr. To Bonus to Shareholders Account 2,500 (one for every two held) fully paid shares to be issued out of Share Premium and General Reserve	1,00,000 — 1,50,000 —	2,50,000 —
	,,	Bonus to Shareholders Account...Dr. To Share Capital Account Bonus converted into shares	2,50,000 —	2,50,000 —

Balance Sheet of X Y Ltd. as at Dec. 31, 1978

Share Capital : 7,500 Shares of Rs. 100 each fully paid (of the above, 2,500 shares were issued as bonus shares out of Share Premium Rs. 1,00,000, and General Reserve, Rs. 1,50,000)	7,50,000	—	Sundry Assets	Rs. 10,25,000	—
Share Premium A/c Rs. 1,00,000 Utilised for Bonus Shares 1,00,000	—				
General Reserve 2,00,000 Less utilised for Bonus Shares 1,50,000	50,000	—			
Profit and Loss A/c	25,000	—			
Sundry Creditors	2,00,000	—			
	10,25,000	—		10,25,000	—

Reduction of Capital. It has been pointed out that the Profit and Loss Account cannot be adjusted in the Capital Account in case of joint stock companies. If a company has been suffering losses, these will be accumulated in the Profit and Loss Account itself and shown on the asset side of the Balance Sheet. There may be some other assets also which have no value. It becomes necessary to write them off. This can be done only with the sanction of the Court.* The method followed will be to reduce the value of each share and then to utilise the amount thus made available to write off the fictitious assets and Profit and Loss Account. The entries are:

(*i*) Share Capital Account ... Dr.) the total
To Capital Reduction A/c) amount
) reduced

(*ii*) Capital Reduction A/c ... Dr.
To Profit and Loss Account
To Discount on Issue of Debentures A/c
To Goodwill Account, etc.

The following points should be noted :—

(*a*) All fictitious assets should be written off even if there is no instruction.

(*b*) The amount written off the fixed assets should be shown for five years in the Balance Sheet.

(*c*) The words "And Reduced" should be added to the name of the company if the Court so orders.

(*d*) If after writing off all fictitious assets and writing down other assets to their proper values, a balance is

*Sometimes, a company having surplus funds may want to refund part of capital or extinguish liability on partly paid shares. This also amounts to reduction of capital and requires Court sanction.

left in the Capital Reduction A/c. it should be transferred to Capital Reserve.

(e) The amounts written off fixed assets should be disclosed in the balance sheet for five years.

Illustration . The Balance Sheet of Gloomy Ltd., was as follows on 30th June, 1978 :

Liabilities	Rs.	*Assets*	Rs.
4,000 Shares of Rs. 100 each fully paid	4,00,000	Goodwill	60,000
6% Debentures	2,00,000	Land and Buildings	1,00,000
Sundry Creditors	2,50,000	Plant & Machinery	4,00,000
		Stock	90,000
		Sundry Debtors	60,000
		Preliminary Expenses	10,000
		Profit & Loss Account	1,30,000
	8,50,000		8,50,000

In order to reconstruct the company, wiping off fictitious assets and writing down Plant & Machinery to its proper figure of Rs. 3,00,000, the shares were reduced to Rs. 20 each. Court approval was obtained. Give journal entries and show the Balance Sheet after the scheme is put through.

Solution :

Journal

			Dr.	Cr.
1978			Rs.	Rs.
June	30	Share Capital Account Dr.	3,20,000 —	
		To Capital Reduction A/c		3,20,000 —
		Reduction of 4,000 Shares of Rs. 100 each to shares of Rs. 20 each		
		Capital Reduction Account Dr.	3,20,000 —	
		To Profit and Loss A/c		1,30,000 —
		To Preliminary Expenses A/c		10,000 —
		To Goodwill A/c		60,000 —
		To Plant and Machinery A/c		1,00,000 —
		To Capital Reserve		20,000 —
		Utilisation of Capital Reduction A/c to write off Rs. 1,00,000 from the Plant and Machinery Account and to write off P.&L. Account and other fictitious assets ; the balance left transferred to Capital Reserve		

Balance Sheet of Gloomy Ltd. as at 30th June 1968

Liabilities	Rs.		*Assets*	Rs.	Rs.	
4,000 Shares of Rs. 20 each, fully paid	80,000	—	Goodwill	60,000		
Capital Reserve	20,000	—	Written off under reconstruction scheme dated ...	60,000		
6% Debentures	2,00,000			———		
Sundry Creditors	2,50,000	—	Land and Buildings		1,00,000	—
			Plant and Machinery	4,00,000		
			Written off under reconstruction scheme dated ...	1,00,000		
				———	3,00,000	—
			Stock		90,000	—
			Sundry Debtors		60,000	—
	5,50,000	—			5,50,000	—

Subdivision and consolidation of shares. If a share of Rs. 100 is converted into 10 shares of Rs. 10 each, it will be called subdivision. If 10 shares of Rs. 10 each are made into one share of Rs. 100, it will be a case of consolidation. A company is authorised to subdivide or consolidate shares subject to its articles. Usually, a journal entry is passed to record sub-division or consolidation. Thus—

Share Capital Account (Rs. 100 each)	Dr.	same amount
To Share Capital A/c (Rs. 10) each		

Stock. The aggregate of shares is called stock. Only fully paid shares can be converted into stock. Debentures can also be converted into Debenture Stock. If a person holds 1,000 shares of Rs. 10 each, then, after conversion he will be said to hold Rs. 10,000 of stock. Shares cannot be transferred in fractions. But any part of stock can be transferred. Stock can be reconverted into shares. All this is subject to the Article of Association.

Bearer Warrants. Subject to the Articles of Association, fully paid shares can be converted into bearer shares. The holders' names are then removed from the Shareholders Register. The shares can then be transferred by mere delivery. Holders can attend meetings only if they deposit the bearer warrants with the company for the duration of the meeting.

EXERCISES

1. New Ltd. invited applications for 10,000 shares of Rs. 100 each. The shares were payable :

	Rs.
on application	20;
on allotment	30;
on 1st call	25; and
on final call	25.

The public applied for 9,000 shares. All applications were accepted and all moneys were received. Give journal entries, ledger accounts and the Balance Sheet.

2. Fine Ltd. acquired Land costing Rs. 1,00,000 and in payment allotted 10,000 shares of Rs. 10 each as fully paid. Further, the company issued 4,000 shares to the public. The shares were payable as follows :—

On application Rs. 30; on allotment Rs. 30; on first and final call Rs. 40.

The public applied for all shares which were allotted. All moneys were received except the call on 200 shares.

Give journal entries and the Balance Sheet.

3. Newlite Ltd. issued 20,000 shares of Rs. 10 each, payable as under :

on application Rs. 2;
on allotment Rs. 3;
on first call Rs. 2; and
on final call Rs. 3.

The public applied for 15,000 shares which were allotted. The directors did not make the final call. All moneys called on shares were received except the first call on 500 shares. These shares were forfeited and then reissued, Rs. 7 paid, @ Rs. 5 per share. Give journal entries and Balance Sheet.

4. Brite Ltd. invited applications for 5,000 shares of Rs. 100 each at Rs. 110. The payment was to be received.

	Rs.
on application	30;
on allotment	50 (including premium); and
on call	30.

The public applied for 6,500 shares. Allotment was made :
100% to applicants for 4,000 shares;
50% to applicants for 2,000 shares; and
nil to applicants for 500 shares.

A shareholder holding 500 shares failed to pay the amount due on call. His shares were forfeited and 200 of these shares were subsequently reissued as fully paid @ Rs. 80 per share. Enter these transactions in the books of the company and prepare the Balance Sheet.

5. Clever Ltd. invited applications for 4,000 shares of Rs. 100 each at a discount of Rs. 5 per share. The payment was to be :

	Rs.
on application	25;
on allotment	45; and
on call	25 (three months after allotment).

Applications totalled 3,500 shares and these were all accepted. One shareholder holding 400 shares paid the call also on allotment. Another shareholder, holding 100 shares, failed to pay the call and these shares were forfeited. These shares were reissued as fully paid @ Rs. 80 per share. The company paid the interest on calls in advance @ 6% p.a.

Journalise these transactions and prepare the Balance Sheet.

6. Shine Ltd. had allotted 20,000 shares of Rs. 10 each. The amounts received were :

on 16,000 shares	full;
on 3,000 shares	Rs. 8 per share (due on Oct. 1, 1967);
on 500 shares	Rs. 5 " " ;
on 500 "	Rs. 2 " " .

On 31st December, 1967 the amount due on 3,000 shares was collected together with interest @ 5%. The other shares were forfeited. These shares were then reissued as fully paid @ Rs. 9 per share.

Give journal entries and show the Balance Sheet.

7. Blunt Ltd. invited applications for 10,000 shares of Rs. 10 each, payable as under :—

	Rs.
on application	4,
on allotment	3; and
on call	4.

The public applied for 15,000 shares. Applications for 1,000 shares were rejected and allotment was made among the remaining applicants proportionately.

One shareholder, holding 100 shares, failed to pay the money due on allotment and the call. His shares were forfeited and later reissued as fully paid @ Rs. 8 per share. Give entries in the books of the company and prepare its balance sheet.

(Hint : *There is a premium of Re. 1 per share.*)

8. A company invited applications for 5,000 Equity Shares of Rs. 100 each and 2,000 7% Preference Shares of Rs. 100 each. Rs. 25 was payable on application, Rs. 30 on allotment, Rs. 20 on first call and Rs. 25 on final call. The public applied for 6,000 Equity Shares and for 1,500 Preference Shares. The directors made the allotment but no application was rejected outright. The final call was not received on 500 equity shares and 100 preference shares. The shares were forfeited. Give entries in the books of the company and prepare Balance Sheet.

9. B Ltd. allotted 3,000 equity shares of Rs. 10 each as fully paid to the promoters.

The company forfeited 200 equity shares of Rs. 10 each on which the final call of Rs. 3 was not received. These shares were reissued as fully paid @ Rs. 7 per share. There was no entry on forfeiture or reissue except that the amount received was credited to Share Capital Account.

Give journal entries to record or rectify the above.

10. X Ltd. issued 2,000 6% Debentures of Rs. 100 each payable as under :

	Rs.
on application	30;
on allotment	20; and
on call	50 (three months after allotment).

One debentureholder holding 500 debentures paid the full amount on allotment. He was allowed interest @ 4% p.a. All moneys were received. Give entries to record the above.

11. J Ltd. invited applications for 3,000 6% Debentures and 4,000 Shares of Rs. 100 each. The debentures were issued at a discount of 5%. All moneys were immediately received (applications totalled exactly equal to the issue). Give journal entries.

12. Give entries to record the following issues of debentures :—

(*a*) 6% Debentures, Rs. 1,00,000, issued at a premium of 10%.

(*b*) 5% Debentures, Rs. 1,00,000, issued at a discount of 5% but redeemable at a premium of 5%.

(*c*) 6% Debentures, Rs. 1,00,000, issued to a supplier of machinery costing Rs. 90,000.

(*d*) 6% Debentures, Rs. 2,00,000, issued as collateral security to bank against loan of Rs. 1,50,000.

13. X Ltd. invited applications for 2,000 6% Debentures of Rs. 100 each @ Rs. 95 and 3,000 Equity Shares of Rs. 100 each at par. The whole of the issue was underwritten by M/s Bull and Bear for a commission of 2% on Debentures and 4% on Shares (nominal value). The public sent applications totalling 1,500 6% Debentures and 2,800 Equity Shares. All the amount due was received. Give journal entries and the Balance Sheet.

14. Z Ltd. invited applications for 5,000 6% Debentures of Rs. 100 each @ Rs. 95. Sixty per cent of the issue was underwritten by M/s Stag & Co. Applications totalled 3,500 Debentures. The whole of the amount due was received. Record the transactions in the books of the company.

15. Sure Ltd. issued (fully paid for) 3,000 6% Debentures of Rs. 100 each @ Rs. 110. The debentureholders had the right of getting the debentures converted into equity shares (a share being valued @ Rs. 120) within five years. At the end of the first year, a debenture holder holding 500 debentures exercised the option. The interest on debentures was not yet paid. Journalise.

16. A company issued Rs. 1,00,000 debentures at a discount of 10%. The debentures were to be redeemed by annual instalments of Rs. 10,000 each. How much discount should be written off each year?

(**Hint :** *The amount to be written off each year should be in the proportion of amount of debentures outstanding each year—Rs. 1,00,000 in the first year, Rs. 90,000 in the next year and so on*).

17. Sunlite Ltd. purchased its own 200 6% Debentures of Rs. 100 each at Rs. 96 and cancelled them immediately. Also, it purchased 100 6% Debentures (own) @ Rs. 97 but did not cancel them until one year later. Journalise these transactions.

18. Fairways Ltd. issued debentures of Rs. 1,00,000 on 1st January 1964 redeemable on 31st December, 1967. It was decided to establish a sinking fund for the purpose of redemption. Investments were expected to realise 4% net. Sinking Fund Tables show that Re. ·235490 invested annually @ 4% p.a. amounts to Re. 1 at the end of 4 years.

Before receiving interest on investments the bank balance stood at Rs. 31,600 on Dec. 31, 1967. On that date the investments were realised at Rs. 73,600 and the debentures were redeemed.

Show all the accounts relating to redemption.

19. On 1st January, 1967 Zest Ltd. had the following balances in its books :

	Rs.	
6% Debentures	1,00,000	
Sinking Fund	85,000	
Sinking Fund Investments (4%)	90,000	(face value)

The annual instalment was Rs. 11,400. On 31st Dec., 1967 the investments were realised @ Rs. 95 and the debentures were redeemed. On that date the Bank balance, before receiving interest on investments, was Rs. 18,300.

Give ledger accounts relating to the redemption.

20. Cautions Ltd. issued on 1st January, 1956 2,000 6% Redeemable Perference shares. The following redemptions were made :

	Rs.
on 31st Dec., 1964	50,000
on 31st Dec., 1966	50,000
on 31st Dec., 1967	1,00,000

Immediately before the last redemption 8,000 shares of Rs. 10 each were issued (and paid for) the purpose of redemption.

Journalise the redemptions.

21. The Balance Sheet of a company on 31st December, 1968 was as under :

Liabilities	Rs.	*Assets*	Rs.
4,000 Equity Shares of Rs. 100 each, fully paid	4,00,000	Sundry Assets	7,30,000
2,000 Redeemable Preference Shares of Rs. 100 each	2,00,000	Bank	2,80,000
General Reserve	1,60,000		
Profit & Loss A/c	1,00,000		
Sundry Creditors	1,50,000		
	10,10,000		10,10,000

On this date the preference shares were redeemed. Journalise and prepare Balance Sheet after redemption.

22. (*a*) The Balance Sheet of Quick Ltd. on 30th June, 1968 was as under :

Liabilities	Rs.	*Assets*	Rs.
3,000 Equity Shares of Rs. 100 each	3,00,000	Sundry Assets	6,20,000
2,000 Redeemable Preference Shares of Rs. 100 each	2,00,000	Sinking Fund Investments	1,00,000
6% Debentures	1,00,000	Bank	1,40,000
Sinking Fund (to redeem Debentures)	1,00,000		
Profit & Loss A/c	90,000		
Sundry Creditors	70,000		
	8,60,000		8,60,000

On the above date the Sinking Fund Investments were realised at a loss of 5%. The Debentures were redeemed. 1,500 new Redeemable Preference shares were issued at Rs. 90 (with proper legal formalities) for the purpose of redeeming the old Preference Shares. These shares were all taken up and paid for and the old preference shares were redeemed. Prepare the Balance Sheet after the redemptions.

(*b*) Fully paid bonus shares were issued to equity shareholders in the above case on the basis of one share for every three held. Give the journal entries and prepare the changed Balance Sheet.

23. A company had its Land and Buildings revalued. It was found that it should be increased by Rs. 50,000. Also it was found that in previous years excessive depreciation had been provided to the extent of Rs. 75,000. The new values were adopted and with the money thus made available, Rs. 25,000 was written off the patents. The balance of the amount was utilised to issue fully paid bonus shares.

Give journal entries.

24. Gold and Silver were partners sharing profits and losses in the ratio of 3 : 2. On 31st Dec., 1968, their Balance Sheet was as under :

Liabilities		Rs.	*Assets*	Rs.
Sundry Creditors		15,000	Land & Premises	25,000
General Reserve		3,000	Machinery	10,000
Capitals :			Stock	12,000
Gold	20,000		Sundry Debtors	5,000
Silver	15,000	35,000	Bank	1,000
		53,000		53,000

Fine Metals Ltd. was formed with an authorised capital of Rs. 1,00,000 divided into shares of Rs. 10 each. It acquired the whole of the business of Gold and Silver for a payment of Rs. 45,000 to be paid for as to Rs. 40,000 in the form of fully paid shares and as to the balance in cash. The company issued 5,000 shares to the public for cash. It acquired further machinery costing Rs. 25,000. It had to pay Rs. 6,000 as preliminary expenses.

Record the above in the Cash Book and Journal of the company and show its Balance Sheet.

25. V.J. Ltd. acquired the business of M/s White and Black whose Balance Sheet as at Dec., 31, 1968 was as under :

Liabilities	Rs.	*Assets*	Rs.
Sundry Creditors	21,000	Goodwill	10,000
Mrs. Black's Loan	10,000	Plant and Machinery	30,000
Capitals :		Patents	6,000
White 30,000		Sundry Debtors	11,000
Black 20,000		Stock	15,000
	50,000	Bank	9,000
	81,000		81,000

The values put on the assets taken over were :

Goodwill	25,000
Plant & Machinery	35,000
Patents	2,000
Sundry Debtors	10,500
Stock	14,500

The company did not take over Mrs. Black's Loan but agreed to pay the sundry creditors. The company issued 5,000 shares of Rs. 10 each valued at Rs. 12 each and the balance in cash. Record the acquisition entries in the books of the company.

26. V.C. Ltd. acquired the business of M/s Green and Red, agreeing to collect debts and pay creditors on their behalf. The debtors were Rs. 25,000 and the creditors totalled Rs. 10,000. The company was entitled to a commission of 5% on the amount collected and 2% on the amount paid. The company paid Rs. 7,500, receiving a discount of Rs. 500 from the creditors of the vendors. It collected Rs. 18,000 from the debtors, allowing them discount of Rs. 700. In addition a debt previously written off as bad was also collected. The amount was Rs. 600. The vendors were paid the amount due to them.

Give journal entries.

(*Vendors receive Rs. 10,020*)

27. New Industries Ltd. present you with the following Trial Balance as at 30th June, 1977.

Debit Balances	Rs.	*Credit Balances*	Rs.
Land and buildings (cost Rs. 4,00,000)	3,10,000	Share Capital (fully paid)	4,00,000
		Share premium	40,000
Plant & Machinery (cost Rs. 4,50,000)	3,40,000	General Reserve	1,00,000
		P. & L. A/c	25,000
Preliminary Expenses	15,000	Bank Loan @ 6% taken on 1st Jan., 1977	2,00,000
Stock, 1st July, 1976	65,000		
Purchases	3,30,000	Sundry Creditors	35,000
Salaries	50,000	Sales	6,00,000
General Expenses	15,000		
Directors' Fees	3,000		
Auditors' Fees	2,000		
Wages	60,000		
Manufacturing Expenses	20,000		
Carriage	5,000		
Advertising	20,000		
Sundry Debtors	60,000		
Goodwill	90,000		
Bank Balance	15,000		
	14,00,000		14,00,000

The company had an authorised capital of Rs. 10,00,000 divided into shares of Rs. 100 each. The company had issued 2,000 shares to vendors as fully paid.

The closing stock on 30th June, 1977 was Rs. 55,000. The managing director is entitled to a commission of 5% on net profits before income tax and his commission. General Expenses include prepaid rates totalling Rs. 300. A provision for income tax to the extent of Rs. 15,000 is desired and the directors recommend a dividend @ 5%. Depreciation should be written off Plant and Machinery at 10% and @ 2% on Land and buildings at cost.

Prepare Trading and Profit and Loss Account for the year ended 30th June, 1967 and Balance Sheet as at that date.

(*Gross Profit, Rs. 1,75,000; Net Profit (after tax), Rs. 9,980; Total of Balance Sheet, Rs. 8,32,300*)

28. Criticise the following Profit and Loss Account :

	Rs.		Rs.
To Purchases and Stock	2,80,000	By Balance b/d	21,300
To Wages & Salaries	1,15,000	By Sales and Closing and Stock	4,65,000
To Rent, Advertising, Carriage, etc.	20,000	By Interest and prepaid expenses	7,500
To Income Tax	50,000		
To Dividends paid less dividends received on investments	20,000		
To Balance—net profit	8,800		
	4,93,800		4,93,800

29. From the following trial balance of Goodways Ltd. as at 31st December, 1967 prepare the Profit and Loss A/c relating to 1977 and the Balance Sheet as at the end of the year.

Debit Balances	Rs.	*Credit Balances*	Rs.
Opening Stock	60,000	Sundry Creditors	45,000
Purchases	3,20,000	Provision for Income Tax	45,000
Wages	90,000	P. & L. A/c	38,000
Power	15,000	General Reserve	1,00,000
Manufacturing Expenses	35,000	Share Capital (fully paid) :	
Carriage outwards	20,000	Equity	3,00,000
Carriage inwards	10,000	6% Redeemable Preference (to be redeemed on 31st Dec., 1971)	2,00,000
Salaries	60,000		
Insurance	10,000		
Sundry Debtors	90,000	6% Debentures (secured by mortgage on fixed assets)	2,00,000
Bank Balance	6,000		
S. Fund Investments (4% Govt. securities of face value of Rs. 1,00,000)	90,000	Salaries and Wages unpaid	25,000
Debenture Interest	6,000	Sales	7,70,000
Land & Buildings	3,00,000	Interest received on Government securities (Sinking Fund)	2,000
Plant & Machinery	4,50,000		
Directors' Fees	10,000		
Audit Fees	6,000	Sinking Fund	90,000
Income Tax paid	41,000		
Dividends paid :			
Preference	6,000		
Interim on Equity Shares	30,000		
Preliminary Expenses	20,000		
Goodwill	1,40,000		
	18,15,000		18,15,000

The closing stock on 31st Dec., 1977 was Rs. 58,000. There was no further liability for income tax except for 1977 for which a provision of Rs. 50,000 should be made. The directors recommned that Rs. 25,000 be transferred to General Reserve and that a final dividend of 10% on Equity Shares be paid, Rs. 10,000 have to be added to the Sinking Fund. Depreciation is to be provided @ 2% on Land and Buildings and 10% on Plant and Machinery. Write off Rs. 5,000 from Preliminary Expenses.

(*Gross Profit, Rs. 2,98,000; Net Profit (after tax), Rs. 82,000; Total of Balance Sheet, Rs. 11,00,000*)

Hints : *Provide Rs. 6,000 interest due on Debentures and Rs. 2,000 interest receivable on S.F. Investments : Credit whole of interest on S.F. Investments to the Profit and Loss A/c. Transfer Rs. 14,000 i.e. Rs. 10,000 plus Rs. 4,000 interest to the Sinking Fand as an item of appropriation. Provide six months' dividend on Preference Shares—dividend on Equity Shares cannot be paid unless preference dividend is paid).*

30. The following trial balance of Nuts Ltd. as at 30th June, 1968 is given to you :

Debits	Rs.	*Credits*	Rs.
Calls in arrear	10,000	Sundry Creditors	50,000
Sales Returns	15,000	General Reserve	40,000

Debits	Rs.	*Credits*	Rs.
Stock, 1st July, 1977	40,000	6% Debentures	1,00,000
Purchases	3,86,000	Share Capital, 4,000 Shares of Rs. 100 each, Rs. 75 paid	3,00,000
Wages	54,000		
Establishment	30,000		
General Expenses	20,000	Sales	5,00,000
Insurance	2,000	Purchase Returns	10,000
Land & Buildings	1,50,000	P. & L. A/c	6,000
Plant & Machinery	2,00,000		
Discount on issue of Debentures	5,000		
Sundry Debtors	40,000		
Bills Receivable	15,000		
Insurance Prepaid	200		
Bank	8,800		
Patents	30,000		
	10,06,000		10,06,000

The stock on 30th June, 1978 was Rs. 37,000. Wages unpaid totalled Rs. 5,000. A provision of 5% is required on Sundry Debtors for doubtful debts. Depreciate Plant & Machinery @ 7½% and Land & Buildings @ 4% and Patents @ 10%.

(*Gross Profit, Rs 47,000; Net Loss, Rs. 37,000; Total of Balance Sheet, Rs. 4,60,000*)

31. Criticise the following Balance Sheet of X Ltd.

	Rs.		Rs.
Authorised Capital (shares of Rs. 100 each)	10,00,000	Fixed Assets	11,00,000
Reserves & Provisions (including Share Premium, and Provision for Income Tax, P. & L. A/c and General Reserve)	3,50,000	Investments in Government securities, shares of other companies and interest due on the securities	2,56,000
		Stock	60,000
		Sundry Debtors	1,00,000
		Bank Balance	24,000
Loans, secured and unsecured	3,00,000	Preliminary Expenses	10,000
Sundry Creditors	40,000	Shares not yet issued to the public	3,00,000
Amount not yet called on partly paid shares held by the company (Rs. 6 per share)	60,000		
Depreciation on Fixed Assets	90,000		
Provision for Bad Debts	10,000		
	18,50,000		18,50,000

32. The following is the Trial Balance of the Ganges Co., Ltd., as at 31st December, 1976, with an Authorized Capital of Rs. 3,00,000 in 30,000 shares of Rs. 10 each of which 20,000 shares have been issued and fully paid up :—

		Rs.	Rs.
Freehold Premises	...	1,50,000	
Plant & Machinery	...	1,65,000	
Find Furniture axtures	...	3,600	

		Rs.	Rs.
Stock, 1st January, 1976	...	37,500	
Sundry Debtors	...	43,500	
Interim Dividend paid 1st November, 1976	...	18,750	
Purchases	...	92,500	
Cash in hand	...	375	
Cash at Bank	...	23,700	
Wages	...	42,432	
Carriage	...	5,334	
Fuel and Power	...	1,225	
Preliminary Expenses	...	2,500	
Repairs and Renewals	...	2,150	
Salaries	...	10,437	
Directors' Fees	...	2.862	
General Charges	...	3.080	
Debenture Interest paid	...	4.500	
Bad Debts	...	1,055	
Subscribed and fully paid up Capital	...		2,00,000
6 per cent Debentures	...		1,50,000
Profit and Loss Account Balance at 1-1-76	...		7,250
Sundry Creditors	...		44,000
Sales	...		2,07,500
Bad Debts Provision	...		1,750
TOTAL	...	6,10,500	6,10,500

Stock at 31st December, 1976, was Rs. 47,000.

Prepare Trading and Profit and Loss Account for the year ended 31st December, 1976, after making the following adjustments :—

(*a*) Provide 10 per cent Depreciation on the cost of Plant and Machinery.

(*b*) Write off Rs. 500 from Preliminary Expenses.

(*c*) Create a Provision for Bad Debts @ 5% on Sundry Debtors.

(*d*) During the year a machine whose book value was nil was sold for Rs. 7,000; the amount is included in Sales.

(*e*) Included in Plant and Machinery is newly acquired machine (on 30th June) costing Rs. 30,000. The cost of the remaining machinery is Rs. 2,00,000.

(*Gross Profit, Rs. 68,509 ; Net Profit, Rs. 24,500 ; Total of Balance Sheet, Rs. 4,11,500*)

33. The Calcutta Chemicals Ltd. was registered with a capital of Rs. 8,00,000 divided into 5% preference shares of Rs. 20 each and 30,000 equity shares of Rs. 20 each. The following balances were extracted from the books of the company as on 31st December, 1977 :—

Debit Balances	Rs.	*Credit Balances*	Rs.
Calls in arrear	3,000	5 per cent Preference Shares Capital : 10,000 Preference Shares of Rs. 20 each	2,00,000
Purchases	4,50,000		
Wages	1,16,400		
Salaries	25,300		
Factory Power Lighting, Heating, etc.	28,500	Equity Share Capital 30,000 Equity Shares of Rs. 20 each Rs. 15 called up	4,50,000
Machinery (at beginning)	5,80,000		

Debit Balances	Rs.	Credit Balances	Rs.
Machinery, purchased on 1st July, 1977.	20,000	Reserve Fund	50,000
Manufactured stock (at beginning)	22,520	Sundry Creditors	15,200
Raw Materials (at beginning)	8,950	Sales	7,05,900
Stationery and Printing	5,500	Dividend Unpaid	1,650
Postage and Office Expenses	6,730	Provision for Doubtful Debts	6,500
Directors' and Auditors' Fees	3,000	Profit and Loss Account — Balance brought forward	40,500
Advertising Suspense (beginning of year)	18,000		
Advertising Expenditure during the year	3,500		
Preliminary Expenses	4,200		
Dividend Paid—			
On Preference Shares	10,000		
On Equity Shares	18,000		
Upkeep of Motor Lorries	17,700		
Cash at Bank and on hand	27,850		
Sundry Debtors	50,600		
Motor Lorries	45,000		
Furniture and Fittings	5,000		
Total	14,69,750		14,69,750

You are required to prepare the final accounts of the company, taking into consideration the following information and instructions :

(*a*) Manufactured stock on hand at end of year was valued at Rs. 40,500 and Raw materials were valued at Rs. 7,500.

(*b*) Provide depreciation on machinery, Motor Lorries and Furniture and Fittings at 5 per cent per annum.

(*c*) Unused Office Stationery was valued at end of year at Rs. 1,500.

(*d*) Office Expenses remaining unpaid at end of year amounted to Rs. 750.

(*e*) Provide for doubtful Debts at 5 per cent on Sundry Debtors.

(*f*) One-third of the total expenditure on Advertisement Account is to be written off.

(*Gross Profit, Rs. 1,27,030; Net Profit, Rs. 34,520; Total of Balance sheet, Rs. 7,61,620*)

34. Reckless Ltd. had the following Balance Sheet as at Dec. 31, 1977 :—

Liabilities	Rs.	*Assets*	Rs.
6% Preference Shares of Rs. 100 each	2,00,000	Goodwill	60,000
Equity shares of Rs. 100 each	4,00,000	Fixed Assets	3,00,000
Debentures	1,00,000	Stock	1,50,000
Sundry Creditors	1,50,000	S. Debtors	60,000
		Discount on Debentures	10,000
		Bank	1,000
		P. & L. A/c	2,69,000
	8,50,000		8,50,000

The following reconstruction scheme was approved :

(*a*) Preference shares be reduced to 8% Preference Shares of Rs. 60 each.

(*b*) Equity Shares to be reduced by Rs. 80 each.

(*c*) The amount made thus available be utilized to write off fictitious assets including goodwill and Rs. 50,000 from fixed assets.

Journalise the arrangements and prepare Balance Sheet.

35. Zed Ltd. had a capital of Rs. 10,00,000 consisting of 2,000 6% Preference Shares of Rs. 100 each and 8,000 Equity Shares of Rs. 100 each. Its reserves consisted of the following :—

(*i*) Share Premium, Rs. 40,000;

(*ii*) Capital Redemption Reserve Account, Rs. 1,00,000;

(*iii*) General Reserve, Rs. 3,50,000; and

(*iv*) Profit and Loss Account, Rs. 78,000.

It was decided to (*i*) issue fully paid bonus shares to the equity shareholders at the rate of 2 shares for five already held; and (*ii*) to utilise revenue profits for the purpose only to the necessary extent.

State the journal entries required to implement the decision. Also show how the various items will appear in the Balance Sheet after the bonus issue.

(General Reserve will show a balance of Rs. 1,70,000 and Profit and Loss Account Rs. 78,000)

36. Wye Ltd. decided to revalue its Land and Buildings at Rs. 15,00,000 against Rs. 6,00,000 which was the book figure. It also had to the credit of the Profit and Loss Account, Rs. 2,40,000. The capital of the company consisted of 6,000 shares of Rs. 100 each, Rs. 80 paid. The company decided to make the shares fully paid (without requiring the shareholders to pay cash) and to issue bonus shares (fully paid) at the rate of one for one.

Give the journal entries to be passed by the company and show how the Balance Sheet will show the various items.

(Profit and Loss Account will show a balance of Rs. 1,20,000 and Capital Reserve, Rs. 3,00,000)

37. The capital of Exe Ltd. consisted of the following :—

(*i*) 20,000 6% Preference Shares of Rs. 10 each; and

(*ii*) 5,000 Equity Shares of Rs. 100 each.

The company decided to (*a*) consolidate the preference shares into shares of Rs. 100 each; and (*b*) to subdivide the equity shares into shares of Rs. 10 each.

What journal entries should be passed to put this decision into effect ?

CHAPTER XIII

BRANCH AND DEPARTMENTAL ACCOUNTS

Branches and departments are divisions of a business. Branches are situated at different geographical locations whereas departments are under the same roof.

A firm which has branches would like to know the profit or loss made by each branch. The method will, naturally, differ for different types of branches. The various types are the following :—

(*a*) a branch which receives goods only from the head office, sells goods only for cash, remits all cash to the head office ; and the expenses of the branch are met by remittance from head office ;

(*b*) a banch similar to the above except that goods are sold on credit also ;

(*c*) a branch similar to (*b*) except that the head office invoices the goods at selling price or cost plus profit ;

(*d*) "independent branch", that is, a branch which carries on its own purchase or manufacture and sales ; such branches also, usually, keep own books of account ; and

(*e*) a foreign branch.

The first three types of branches do not themselves keep books of account ; the head office does that. But if a branch sells goods on credit, accounts of credit customers will be kept by the branch. Branches are required to send regular stock statements to the head office so that it knows the requirements of the branches and controls the stocks there.

For the first type of branch, the accounting is really simple. Suppose, the head office sends goods worth Rs. 20,000 to a newly opened branch and sends Rs. 5,000 for expenses. The branch remits Rs. 27,000 to the head office as sale proceeds. If the whole of the goods are sold, there is a profit of Rs. 2,000, *i.e.*, Rs. 27,000 less Rs. 25,000. If there are goods still lying unsold at the branch, this will increase the profit. Suppose, in the above case, goods worth Rs. 3,000 are still with the branch, the profit will be Rs. 5,000. The above means that the head office should debit the branch with whatever is sent there and credit it with whatever is received from it. Therefore :—

(*a*) when goods are sent to the branch—
Debit Branch Account ; and
Credit Goods sent to Branch A/c.

(*b*) when cash is sent to the branch for expenses—
Debit Branch Account ; and
Credit Cash Account.

(*c*) when cash is received from the branch—
Debit Cash Account ; and
Credit Branch Account.

(*d*) if goods are lying unsold with the branch—
Debit Branch Stock Account ; and
Credit Branch Account.

At this stage the Branch Account will show profit or loss. This is transferred to the Profit and Loss Account. The entry is :

Debit Branch Account)
Credit Profit and Loss) with the profit.

Reverse entry will be passed if there is a loss.

The Goods Sent to Branch Account is closed by transferring the amount to the credit of Trading Account in case of manufacturing concerns or Purchases Account (in case of trading concerns). Next year, the Branch Account will be debited with the opening stock.

If the branch sells goods for credit also, the only additional entry to be passed is in respect of debtors at the end of the year. The total amount due will be debited to Branch Debtors Account and credited to Branch Account. To sum up, a newly opened branch will be debited with goods and cash sent to the branch. It will be credited with cash remitted to the head office, value of closing stock of goods and the amount of the debtors at the branch at the end of the year. An existing branch will also be debited with the opening stock of goods and the amount of the debtors at the branch in the beginning.

The student should note that the branch account should be credited with actual cash remitted to the head office (both in respect of cash sales and cash received from debtors). Credit sales, as such, discount, etc., allowed to debtors will not be entered in the branch account. However, this information may be needed to ascertain the amount due from the branch customers.

Illustration Fancy Clothes Ltd., opened a branch in 1977 at Delhi. The figures for 1977 and 1978 are given below :

	1977	*1967*
	Rs.	Rs.
Goods sent to Branch	25,000	35,000
Sales—Cash	10,000	16,000
Credit	18,000	25,000
Cash received from debtors	16,000	20,000
Discount allowed to them	300	500
Cash sent to Branch for expenses	3,500	5,000
Stock on 31st December	4,000	7,000

Give journal entries and ledger account for 1977 and only the Branch Account for 1978.

Solution :

Journal

Date		Particulars		Dr. Rs.	Cr. Rs.
1977		Delhi Branch Account To Goods Sent to Branch A/c Goods sent to the Branch	Dr.	25,000 —	25,000 —
		Delhi Branch Account To Cash Account Cash sent to Branch for expenses	Dr.	3,500 —	3,500 —
		Cash Account To Delhi Branch Account Cash received from Delhi : Cash Sales Rs. 10,000 from Debtors 16,000 26,000	Dr.	26,000 —	26,000 —
1977 Dec.	31	Delhi Branch Stock A/c Delhi Branch Debtors A/c To Delhi Branch Account The stock of goods at Delhi and the amount of debtors at the end of the year*	Dr. Dr.	4,000 — 1,700 —	5,700 —
"	"	Delhi Branch Account To Profit and Loss A/c Profit at the Delhi Branch transferred to the Profit and Loss Account	Dr.	3,200 —	3,200 —
"	"	Goods Sent to Branch A/c To Trading Account Goods sent to Branch A/c transferred to the Trading Account	Dr.	25,000 —	25,000 —

*The amount of debtors will be ascertained by preparing the Branch Debtors A/c. This account will be debited with credit sales; cash received and discount showed will be credited.

Ledger Accounts

Delhi Branch Account

Dr.		Rs.			Cr. Rs.
1977			1977		
	To Goods sent to Branch A/c	25,000 —		By Cash—received from Branch	26,000 —
	To Cash—Expenses	3,500 —	Dec. 31	By Delhi Branch Stock A/c	4,000 —
Dec. 31	To Profit and Loss A/c—transfer	3,200 —	,,	By Delhi Branch Debtors A/c	1,700 —
		31,700 —			31,700 —

Goods Sent to Branch A/c

		Rs.			Rs.
1977 Dec. 31	To Trading A/c—transfer	25,000 —	1977	By Delhi Branch A/c	25,000 —

Cash Account

		Rs.			Rs.
1977	To Delhi Branch A/c	26,000 —	1977	By Delhi Branch A/c	3,500 —

Delhi Branch Stock Account

		Rs,			Rs,
1977 Dec. 31	To Delhi Branch A/c	4,000 —	1977 Dec. 31	By Balance c/d	4,000 —
1968 Jan. 1	By Balance b/d	4,000			

Delhi Branch Debtors Account

1977 Dec. 31	To Delhi Branch A/c	1,700 —	1977 Dec. 31	By Balance c/d	1,700 —
1968 Jan. 1	To Balance b/d	1,700 —			

Profit and Loss Account

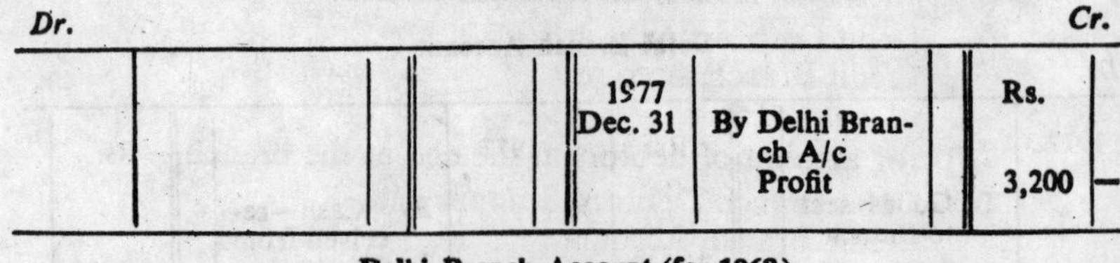

Dr.							*Cr.*
				1977		Rs.	
				Dec. 31	By Delhi Branch A/c Profit	3,200	—

Delhi Branch Account (for 1968)

		Rs.				Rs.	
1978				1978			
Jan. 1	To Opening Balances :				By Delhi Branch A/c—Cash received	36,000	—
	Stock	4,000	—				
	Debtors	1,700	—				
	To Goods sent to Branch A/c	35,000	—	Dec. 31	By Delhi Branch Stock A/c	7,000	—
	To Cash A/c—expenses	5,000	—	"	By Delhi Branch Debtors A/c* (closing balances)	6,200	—
Dec. 31	To Profit & Loss A/c—Profit transferred	3,500	—				
		49,200	—			49,200	—

*Branch Debtors Account should be prepared.

Goods invoiced at selling price or inflated price. Some firms choose to "invoice" goods to its branches at selling price. This presupposes that there will be a fixed selling price. The purpose of making out the invoice at selling price is to control stocks at the branch easily. We shall see how this is done later. But at the moment we must remember that to ascertain profit we must compare the sale proceeds only with the cost. If the Branch Account is debited with more than the cost, the difference must be credited to the Branch. Stock at the end will also be valued according to the "invoiced" value. This will be more than the cost. The difference between the cost of the stock and its "invoiced" or loaded price must be put right. The Branch Account is debited and Stock Reserve Account is credited with the difference. Both Branch Stock Account and Stock Reserve Account are carried forward to the next year and then transferred to the Branch Account.

To recapitulate, the entries to be made are :

(*a*) when goods are sent to the branch—
Debit Branch Account) at the invoiced
Credit Goods sent to Branch Account) figure.

(*b*) when cash is sent to the branch for expenses—
Debit Branch Account and
Credit Cash Account.

(*c*) when cash is received from the branch—
Debit Cash Account and
Credit Branch Account.

(*d*) for amount of debtors at the end at the branch—
Debit Branch Debtors Account and
Credit Branch Account.

(*e*) for value of stock at the branch—
Debit Branch Stock Account) according to the invoiced
Credit Branch Account) price.

(*f*) to remove the loading (or inflation) from goods sent to the branch—
Debit Goods Sent to Branch Account) with the amount
Credit Branch Account) added to the cost.

(*g*) to "correct" the amount of the stock—
Debit Branch Account and
Credit Stock Reserve Account.

The Branch Account will now reveal profit and loss which is transferred to the Profit and Loss Account. The balance in the Goods sent to Branch Account is transferred to the Trading Account or Purchases Account.

Illustration. Good Shoes Ltd. opened in 1977 a branch at Nagpur. It invoiced goods to the Branch at cost plus 25%. Information about 1977 and 1978 is given below :

	1977 Rs.	*1978* Rs.
Goods sent to the Branch (invoice price)	50,000	80,000
Cash sent to the Branch for expenses	8,000	10,000
Sales—		
Cash	22,000	33,000
Credit	23,000	48,000
Cash received from debtors	20,000	47,000
Bad Debts written off	600	400
Stock on 31st December (invoice price)	4,800	4,000

Journalise the entries to be made in the Head Office books for 1967 and give ledger accounts for both the years.

Solution :

Journal

Date		Particulars		Dr. Rs.	Cr. Rs.
1977		Nagpur Branch Account To Goods sent to Branch A/c Goods sent to the Nagpur Branch (invoice value)	Dr.	50,000 —	50,000 —
		Nagpur Branch Account To Cash Account Cash remitted to the Branch for expenses	Dr.	8,000 —	8,000 —
		Cash Account To Nagpur Branch Account Cash received from the Branch Cash Sales 22,000 from Debtors 20,000 ——— 42,000	Dr.	42,000 —	42,000 —
Dec.	31	Branch Debtors Account To Nagpur Branch Account The balances due from Branch Debtors, Rs. 23,000—(Rs. 20,000 plus Rs. 600)	Dr.	2,400 —	2,400 —
"	"	Branch Stock Account To Nagpur Branch Account Invoice value of the stock lying at the Branch	Dr.	4,800 —	4,800 —
"	"	Goods sent to Branch Account To Nagpur Branch Account Leading in the goods sent to Branch credited to Nagpur Branch A/c— $50{,}000 \times \frac{25^*}{125} = 10{,}000$	Dr.	10,000 —	10,000 —

*The cost being 100, 25 was added, making invoice value to be 125. Loading, therefore, is 25/125 of invoice price.

			Rs.	Rs.
1977 Dec.	31	Nagpur Branch Account Dr. To Stock Reserve Account Reserve against stock created equal to the loading in the Closing Stock	960 —	960 —
"	"	Goods sent to Branch Account Dr. To Trading Account The balance in the former account transferred to the Trading Account	40,000 —	40,000 —
"	"	Nagpur Branch Account Dr. To Profit and Loss Account Profit at Nagpur Branch transferred to the Profit and Loss Account	240 —	240 —

Nagpur Branch Account

Dr. *Cr.*

1977		Rs.	1977		Rs.
	To Goods sent to (Branch) A/c	50,000 —	Dec, 31	By Cash A/c	42,000 —
	To Cash—expenses	8,000 —	"	By Branch Debtors A/c	2,400 —
Dec. 31	To (Branch) Stock Reserve Account—loading	960 —	"	By Branch Stock A/c	4,800 —
"	To Profit & Loss A/c—transfer of profit	240 —		By Goods sent to Branch A/c—loading	10,000 —
		59,200 —			59,200 —

Goods Sent to Branch Account

1967		Rs.	19		Rs.
Dec. 31	To Nagpur Branch A/c —loading	10,000 —		By Nagpur Branch A/c	50,000 —
	To Trading A/c —transfer	40,000 —			
		50,000 —			50,000 —

Nagpur Branch Debtors Account

Dr. *Cr.*

Date	Particulars	Rs	Date	Particulars	Rs.
1977 Dec. 31	To Nagpur Branch A/c	2,400 —	1977 Dec. 21	By Balance c/d	2,400 —
1978 Jan. 1	To Balance b/d	2,400 —	1968 Jan. 1	By Nagpur Branch A/c—transfer	2,400 —

Nagpur Stock Account

Date	Particulars	Rs.	Date	Particulars	Rs.
1977 Dec. 31	To Nagpur Branch A/c	4,800 —	1977 Dec. 31	By Balance c/d	4,800 —
1968 Jan. 1	To Balance b/d	4,800 —	1978 Jan. 1	By Nagpur Branch A/c —transfer	4,800 —

Stock Reserve Account

Date	Particulars	Rs.	Date	Particulars	Rs.
1977 Dec. 31	To Balance c/d	960 —	1977 Dec. 31	By Nagpur Branch Account	960 —
1978 Dec. 31	To Nagpur Branch A/c —transfer	960 —	1978 Jan. 1	By Balance b/d*	960 —

Nagpur Branch Account

Date	Particulars	Rs,	Date	Particulars	Rs.
1978 Jan. 1	To Opening Balances— Stock Debtors	 4,800 — 2,400 —	1978 Dec. 31	By Cash A/c	80,000
	To Goods Sent to Branch A/c	80,000 —	„	By Branch Debtors A/c	3,000 —
Dec. 31	To Cash—expenses	10,000 —	„	By Branch Stock A/c	4,000 —
„	To Stock Reserves A/c (required)	800 —	„	By Stock Reserve A/c (opening)	960 —
	To Profit & Loss A/c—profit transferred*	5,960 —	„	By Goods Sent to Branch A/c—loading	16,000 —
		1,03,960 —			1,03,960 —

*The student should note that if there is opening stock of inflated price, there will be a Stock Reserve A/c showing a credit balance equal to the loading.

Goods Sent to Branch Account

Dr.		Rs.			Cr. Rs.
1978 Dec. 31	To Nagpur Branch A/c—loading	16,000	1978	By Nagpur Branch A/c	80,000
	To Trading A/c—transfer	64,000			
		80,000			80,000

Branch Debtors Account

		Rs.			Rs.
1978 Dec. 31	To Nagpur Branch A/c	3,000	1978 Dec. 31	By Balance c/d	3,000
1969 Jan. 1	To Balance b/d	3,000			

Branch Stock Account

		Rs.			Rs.
1978 Dec. 31	To Nagpur Branch A/c	4,000	1978 Dec. 31	By Balance c/d	4,000
1969 Jan. 1	To Balance b/d	4,000			

Stock Reserve Account

		Rs.			Rs.
1978 Dec. 31	To Balance c/d	800	1978 Dec. 31	By Nagpur Branch A/c	800
			1969 Jan. 1	By Balance b/d	800

Stock and debtors system. It was said above that if the branch is instructed to sell goods at a fixed price and if goods are invoiced to the branch at selling price, it will help in controlling the stocks at branch. The necessity of controlling stocks in this manner arises if the branch sells a number of articles.

The method is really quite simple. If the goods sent to the branch at selling price, total, say, Rs. 50,000, and if the branch sells goods totalling Rs. 42,000, there should be a stock of Rs. 8,000 (at selling price). If the value of the stock actually on hand is Rs, 7,500, there is a shortage of Rs. 500. This method of controlling stocks can also be used to find out the profit. Instead of the usual "Branch Account," Branch Stock Account, Branch Debtors Account, Branch Expenses Account and Branch Adjustment Account are opened. If such a system is followed, it will be known as "Stock and Debtors System".

Goods sent to the branch are debited to the Branch Stock Account. Total sales are credited to this account. Credit sales are debited to Branch Debtors Account. Cash sales are, of course, debited to Cash Account. The amount of the stock is put on the credit side of the Branch Stock Account (as Balance c/d). The two sides of this account are then totalled. If the debit side is bigger, there is a shortage and is put on the credit side. If the credit side is bigger, there is surplus and is put on the debit side.

Branch Debtors Account is prepared in the usual manner. Credit sales are debited, cash received from debtors, discount allowed to them, bad debts written off, etc. are credited. The balance of the account is carried down. Cash sent to branch for expenses is debited to Branch Expenses Account. Discounts allowed to debtors or bad debts written off are also debited to this account.

The loading in the goods sent to branch is credited to an account called "Branch Adjustment Account". Stock reserve in respect of closing stock is debited to this account and credited to Stock Reserve Account. Opening stock reserve (in respect of opening stock) is transferred to the Branch Adjustment Account. This account is debited with Branch Expenses (including discount allowed or bad debts written off). Shortage or surplus of stock is also transferred to this account. The balance of the Branch Adjustment Account represents profit or loss and is transferred to the Profit and Loss Account.

We illustrate below the working of this system by the figures of 1978 in the above Illustration below.

Branch Stock Account

Dr. *Cr.*

		Rs.			Rs.
1978 Jan. 1	To Balance b/d	4,800	1978	By Cash—cash sales	33,000
	To Goods Sent to Branch Account	80,000		By Branch Debtors A/c—credit sales	48,000
Dec. 31	To Surplus—transferred to Branch Adjustment A/c	200	Dec. 31	By Balance c/d	4,000
		85,000			85,000
1979 Jan. 1	To Balance b/d	4,000			

Goods Sent to Branch Account

Dr.		Rs.			Cr. Rs.
1978 Dec. 31	To Branch Adjustment A/c—loading	16,000	1978	By Branch Stock Account	80,000
,,	To Trading A/c—transfer	64,000			
		80,000			80,000

Branch Debtors Account

		Rs.			Rs.
1978	To Balance b/d	2,400	1978	By Cash	47,000
,,	To Branch Stock A/c—credit sales	48,000		By Branch Expenses A/c—bad debts	400
			Dec. 31	By Balance c/d	3,000
		50,400			50,400
1979 Jan. 1	To Balance b/d	3,000			

Branch Expenses Account

		Rs.			Rs.
1978	To Cash	10,000	1978 Dec. 31	By Branch Adjustment A/c—transfer	10,400
	To Branch Debtors A/c—bad debts	400			
		10,400			10,400

Stock Reserve Account

		Rs.			Rs.
1978	To Branch Adjustment A/c transfer	960	1978 Jan. 1	By Balance b/d	960
Dec. 31	To Balance c/d	800	Dec. 31	By Branch Adjustment A/c—reserve required	800
		1,760			1,760
			1979 Jan.	By Balance b/d	800

Branch Adjustment Account

Dr.		Rs.		Cr.		Rs.	
1978 Dec.31	To Stock Reserve A/c—required	800	—	1978 Dec.31	By Stock Reserve A/c—opening	960	—
" "	To Branch Expenses A/c	10,400	—	"	By Goods Sent to Branch A/c—loading	16,000	—
" "	To Profit and Loss A/c—profi	5,960	—	"	By Branch Stock A/c—surplus	200	—
		17,160	—			17,160	—

Independent branch or branch keeping own accounts. We have so far considered branches that do not maintain accounts themselves. The accounting is done at the head office. Now we shall consider the branch that keeps its own books of account.

The method of accounting is really simple ; in essence it means treating the branch as a sort of special customer. The branch keeps its accounts like anyone else. The head office will have a "Branch Account" in its books. All goods sent to the branch or cash sent to it will be debited to this account and cash received from the branch will be credited to it. Entries are made in the usual manner. The balance in this account will show the amount invested by the head office at the branch.

Similarly, the branch will open "Head Office Account" in its books. The balance shown by this account will usually be credit. The balance shown by the Branch Account (in head office books) will be debit. The amounts in both cases should be the same. But due to certain reasons there may be a difference. If there is a difference, the cause of it must be located and suitable entries passed at the end of the financial year.

Cash or goods in transit. One of the reasons for difference in the balances of the two accounts may be cash sent by branch but received by the head office after the close of the year. Similarly, goods sent by the head office may reach the branch after the close of the financial year. Entries are passed immediately by the branch when cash is sent by the branch but the head office will not pass entry for receipt until cash is actually received. So also for goods in transit. A record must be made for cash or goods in transit. The entry is usually made by the party which sent the cash or goods. If cash sent by the branch has not yet reached head office, the branch will pass the entry :

Cash in Transit A/c Dr.
    To Head Office Account.

If goods sent by the head office are in transit, the head office will record it as under :

Goods in Transit A/c Dr.
    To Branch Account.

But there is no hard and fast rule about it. In fact it is enough if either party makes a record of the items in transit.

Both the Cash in Transit and Goods in Transit are assets and shown in the balance sheet.

Note: In examination problems, cash or goods in transit may have to be inferred. This is done by comparing the balance of the Branch Account (in head office books) and of the Head Office Account (in branch books). Suppose the Branch Account shows a debit balance of Rs. 16,000 and the Head Office Account shows a credit balance of Rs. 11,000. The difference is Rs. 5,000 and can be taken to be either Cash in Transit or Goods in transit.

Accounts of branch fixed assets kept in H.O. books. Often the accounts of branch fixed assets are kept in head office books and not in branch books. Even if the branch pays for them the amount is debited to Head Office Account. The Head Office will debit the asset account and credit Branch Account. At the end of the year, the question of depreciation will arise. The entries to be passed are :

In Head Office Books—

Branch Account Dr.

To Branch Asset A/c

In Branch Books—

Depreciation Account Dr.

To Head Office A/c

Head Office expenses. The head office will always do some work for the branch. At the end of the year, the head office may charge the branch with an amount representing the value of the time devoted to the branch. The entries required are :

In Head Office Books—

Branch Account Dr.

To Salaries Account.

In Branch Books—

Head Office Expenses A/c Dr.

To Head Office A/c

Illustration Preliminary accounts made by the Kanpur Branch on 31st December, 1968 showed a profit of Rs. 9,500. It was found that the following items were not yet taken into account :

	Rs.
Cash remitted to H.O., not yet received there	5,000
Goods sent by the H.O., not yet received at Kanpur	4,000
Depreciation on Branch assets (accounts kept in H.O. books)	1,200
H.O. expenses charged to the branch	2,500

Journalise the above in the books of both the Head Office and the Branch. Also show how much is the real profit at Kanpur.

Solution :

H.O. Journal

				Dr.	Cr.
				Rs.	Rs.
1978 Dec.	31	Goods in Transit A/c To Kanpur Branch A/c Goods sent to Kanpur, not yet received there	Dr.	4,000	4,000
Dec.	31	Kanpur Branch A/c To Kanpur Branch Assets A/c. Depreciation on Kanpur Branch, assets charged to the Branch accounts of assets being kept in own books	Dr.	1,200	1,200
"		Kanpur Branch A/c To Salaries Account Amount of expenses charged to the Branch for work done on its behalf	Dr.	2,500	2,500

Branch Journal

				Rs.	Rs.
1978 Dec.	31	Cash in Transit A/c To Head Office Account The amount of the cash sent to the H.O. not yet received there	Dr.	5,000	5,000
"	"	Depreciation Account To Head Office Account Depreciation Branch assets whose accounts are in Head Office Books	Dr.	1,200	1,200
"	"	Head Office Expenses A/c To Head Office A c Amount charged to the branch in respect of work done at the H.O.	Dr.	2,500	2,500

The profit at the Branch is reduced by Rs. 1,200 and Rs. 2,50[illegible] It now stands at Rs. 5,800.

Incorporation of Branch accounts in H.O. books. The branch sends its trial balance to the Head Office which will then incorporate branch figures to prepare consolidated Profit and Loss Account and balance sheet. The entries to be passed in the Head Office Books are :

(*a*)	Debit Branch Trading Account Credit Branch Account	with the items debited to Trading A/c such as opening stock, purchases, wages, etc. at the branch.
(*b*)	Debit Branch Account Credit Branch Trading Account	with the sale and closing stock at the branch.
(*c*)	Debit Branch Trading Account Credit Branch Profit and Loss A/c	transfer of gross profit.
(*d*)	Debit Branch Profit and Loss Account Credit Branch Account	with the total of expenses at the branch.
(*e*)	Debit Branch Account Credit Branch Profit and Loss Account	with items of gain at the branch.
(*f*)	Debit Branch Profit and Loss Account Credit (General) Profit and Loss A/c	with the net profit at the branch, as disclosed by the Branch Profit and Loss A/c.

(This entry will be reversed in case of loss.)

With these six entries given above, the Branch Account will show a balance equal to net assets at the branch, *i.e.*, assets less liabilities. If it is desired to close the Branch Account two further entries will be required :

(*g*) Debit Branch Assets (individually)
Credit Branch Account ; and

(*h*) Debit Branch Account
Credit Branch Liabilities (individually).

Illustration A head office receives the following Trial Balance from its branch :

Debits	Rs.	*Credits*	Rs.
Opening Stock	21,800	Head Office A/c	21,000
Purchases	42,300	Sundry Creditors	5,600
Wages	10,200	Discount received	300
Salaries	6,300	Sales	81,000
General Expenses	8,300		
Sundry Debtors	18,200		
Cash at Bank	800		
	1,07,900		1,07,900

The closing stock at the branch was Rs. 19,700. The Branch Account (in Head Office books) stood at a debit of Rs. 26,500. Goods sent by the Head Office, Rs. 1,000, had not yet reached the Branch. Head Office expenses chargeable to the Branch were Rs. 3,100. Depreciation of Branch assets whose accounts are kept in Head Office books was Rs. 3,600. Record the above noted items and the incorporation of Branch figures in Head Office books by means of journal entries and show Branch Account.

***Solution :**

Head Office Journal

			Dr. Rs.		Cr. Rs.	
?	Goods in transit Account To Branch Account Adjustment for goods still in transit	Dr.	1,000	—	1,000	—
	Branch Account To Salaries Account Amount charged to the Branch in respect of work done on its behalf	Dr.	3,100	—	3,100	—
	Branch Account To Branch Assets Account Depreciation on Branch assets whose accounts are kept in H.O. Books	Dr.	3,600	—	3,600	—
	Branch Trading Account To Branch Account Total of items debited to the Branch Trading Account, *viz.*, opening stock, purchases and wages	Dr.	74,300	—	74,300	—

*The student is advised to first prepare Branch Trading and Profit and Loss Account and then to note the journal entries.

	Particulars		Rs.	Rs.
?	Branch Account To Branch Trading A/c Total of sales and closing stock to be credited to Branch Trading Account	Dr.	1,00,700 —	 1,00,700 —
	Branch Trading Account To Branch Profit and Loss Account Transfer of gross profit	Dr.	26,400 —	 26,400 —
	Branch Profit and Loss A/c To Branch Account Total of expenses to be debited to Branch Profit and Loss Account : Salaries Rs. 6,300 General Expenses 8,300 H.O. Expenses 3,100 Depreciation 3,600 21,300	Dr.	21,300 —	 21,300 —
	Branch Account To Branch Profit and Loss A/c Discount received credited to Branch Profit and Loss A/c	Dr.	300 —	 300 —
	Branch Profit and Loss A/c To General Profit and Loss Account Net Profit transferred to General Profit and Loss Account	Dr.	5,400 —	 5,400 —
	Branch Sundry Debtors A/c Branch Bank A/c Branch Stock A/c Cash in Transit A/c* To Branch Account Branch assets transferred to H.O. Books	Dr. Dr. Dr. Dr.	18,200 — 800 — 19,700 — 4,500 —	 43,200 —
	Branch A/c To Branch Sundry Creditors Branch Liabilities transferred to H.O. Books	Dr.	5,600 —	 5,600 —

Note : If the last two entries are not passed, the Branch Account will show a balance, showing the H.O. investment at the Branch at the end of the year. If the two entries are passed, the Branch Account will balance and accounts for various assets and liabilities will be opened in the H.O. Books.

*The difference between the Branch A/c balance and H.O. A/c balance is Rs. 5,500 (Rs. 26,500—21,000). Of this Rs. 1,000 is explained by goods in transit. The balance of difference is due to cash in transit.

Branch Account

Dr.	Rs.	Cr.	Rs.
To Balance b/d	26,500	To Goods in Transit A/c	1,000
To Balance A/c H.O. expenses	3,100	By Branch Trading Account	74,300
To Branch A/c depreciation	3,600	By Branch Profit and Loss A/c—	21,300
To Branch Trading Account	1,00,700	By S. Assets : Debtors 18,200, Bank 800, Cash in Transit 4,500, Stock 19,700	43,200
To Branch P. & L. A/c	300		
To Branch Sundry Creditors	5,600		
	1,39,800		1,39,800

Alternatively, only one entry in respect of revenue items may be passed. This is passed after preparing the Branch Profit and Loss Account on memorandum basis. If there is net profit, the Branch Account is debited and the (General) Profit and Loss Account is credited. In case of loss, this entry is reversed. If we do the above illustration in this manner, only the following entry (for net profit) will be necessary :

		Rs.	Rs.
Branch Account	Dr.	5,400	
To (General) Profit and Loss A/c			5,400
Being the net profit at the Branch during the year.			

(Note : The first three entries in respect of goods in transit, head office expenses and depreciation of Branch assets will still be necessary).

The Branch Account will appear as under :

Branch Account

Dr.	Rs.	Cr.	Rs.
To Balance b/d	26,500	By Goods in Transit A/c	1,000
To Salaries A/c—H.O. expenses	3,100	By Balance c/d	37,600
To Branch Assets A/c—depreciation	3,600		
To Profit and Loss A/c	5,400		
	38,600		38,600
To Balance b/d	37,600		

The balance in the Branch Account represents what the branch owes to the Head Office; what any firm owes to its proprietor is the difference between assets and liabilities Capital is always assets — liabilities. Therefore, the accuracy of the branch balance can be checked by ascertaining net assets. In Illustration 99, the balance in the Branch Account, Rs. 37,600, tallies with the net assets at the Branch as shown below :—

	Rs.
Stock	19,700
Debtors	18,200
Bank	800
Cash in Transit	4,500
	43,200
Less Creditors	5,600
Net Assets	37,600

If the Branch Account is to be closed, two entries are necessary:—

Branch Stock A/c	...	Dr.	19,700	
Branch Debtors A/c	...	Dr.	18,200	
Branch Bank A/c	...	Dr.	800	
Cash in Transit	...	Dr.	4,500	
To Branch Account				43,200
Branch Account	...	Dr.	5,600	
To Branch Creditors A/c				5,600

Foreign Branch.

A foreign branch keeps its own books of account. It will send a trial balance to the head office but in foreign currency and the one additional problem is to convert the foreign currency into own currency. Once the trial balance is converted, the treatment is exactly like the one for "independent branch" already discussed above. The rules for conversion of the trial balance are as follows :—

(*a*) Fixed assets (and fixed liabilities, if any) should be converted at the rate prevailing on the date of acquisition. The same rate will be used always in future. (In examination problems, in absence of information, fixed assets should be converted at the rate prevailing on the first day of the year).

(*b*) Current assets and current liabilities should be converted at the rate prevailing on the last day of the year.

(*c*) Revenue items, that is items appearing in the trading and profit and loss account, should be converted at the average rate. (But opening stock should be converted at the opening rate and closing stock should be at the closing rate).

Also, if goods have been received from the H... Office, the Goods Received from H.O. Account should be converted at the same figure as is shown by the Goods sent to Branch Account (in H.O. books).

Further, if during the year there has been a devaluation revenue items should be converted at the rate prevailing at the end of the year and not at the average rate.

(*d*) Head Office Account and connected accounts (like Remittances to H.O. A/c etc.) are **not converted** by caiculation. The relevant accounts in the Head Office Books should be seen and their balances should be used to convert Head Office and similar accounts. Suppose Branch Trial Balance shows a credit balance in the Head Office Account as £3,000 and the Branch Account (in H.O. books) stands at Rs. 54,200. The Head Office Account will be converted at Rs. 54,200.

(*c*) The trial balance will now disagree. The difference should be put on the shorter side as "Difference in Exchange Account". If the amount is small, it should be transferred to the Profit and Loss Account. If the amount is big and credit, it may be carried forward to the next year. A debit balance by the Difference in Exchange Account should be transferred to the P. & L. A/c.

Illustration Delhi Textiles Ltd. have a branch in London. On 31st December, 1978 the Trial Balance of the Branch was as given below :—

	Dr.	*Cr.*
	£	£
Head Office Account	...	18,000
Sales	...	1,20,000
Goods from Head Office Account	90,000	
Stock, 1st January 1968	15,000	
Furniture & Fixtures	20,000	
Cash in hand	100	
Cash at Bank	1,900	
Owing for Expenses	...	2,000
Salaries	6,000	
Taxes, Insurance, etc.	500	
Rent	2,000	
Sundry Debtors	4,500	
	1,40,000	1,40,000

The Branch Account in the Head Office showed a debit balance of Rs. 2,25,000 and "Goods Sent to Branch Account" a credit balance of Rs. 16,15,000.

Furniture and Fixtures were acquired in 1965 when £ 1= Rs. 13.50. The exchange rates were :

January	1, 1978	£ 1 = Rs. 17.50
December	31, 1978	£ 1 = Rs. 18.50
Average		£ 1 = Rs. 18.00

The stock at branch on 31st December 1968 was valued at £ 9,000.

Convert the Branch Trial Balance into rupees and prepare the Branch Trading and Profit and Loss Account for 1978 and the Branch Account in Head Office Books. Depreciation is to be written off the furniture and fixtures @ 10%.

Solution :

London Branch Trial Balances as at December 31, 1978.

Item	*Rate* Rs.	*Dr.* £	*Cr.* £	*Dr.* Rs.	*Cr.* Rs.
H. O. Account	—		18,000		2,25,000
Sales	18.00		1,20,000		21,60,000
Goods from H.O. A/c	—	90,000		16,15,000	
Stock 1st Jan., 1968	17.50	15,000		2,62,500	
Furniture & Fixtures	13.50	20,000		2,70,000	
Cash in hand	18.50	100		1,850	
Cash in Bank	18.50	1,900		35,150	
Owing for Expenses	18.50		2,000		37,000
Salaries	18.00	6,000		1,08,000	
Taxes, Insurance etc.	18.00	500		9,000	
Rent	18.00	2,000		36,000	
Sundry Debtors	18.50	4,500		83,250	
		1,40,000	1,40,000	24,20,750	24,22,000
Difference in Exchange				1,250	
				24,22,000	24,22,000
Closing Stock	18.50	9,000		1,66,500	

London Branch Trading and Profit & Loss Account for the year ended December 31, 1978

	Rs.		Rs.
To Stock opening	2,62,500	By Sales	21,60,000
To Goods from H.O.	16,15,000	By Closing Stock	1,66,500
To Gross Profit c/d	4,49,000		
	23,26,500		23,26,500
To Salaries	1,08,000	By Gross Profit b/d	4,49,000
To Taxes, Insurance etc.	9,000		
To Rent	36,000		
To Difference in Exchange	1,250		
To Depreciation	27,000		
To Net Profit	2,67,750		
	4,49,000		4,49,000

London Branch Account

		Rs.			Rs.
1978 Dec. 31	To Balance b/d	2,25,000	1978 Dec. 31	By Branch Trading A/c Opening Stock 2,62,500 Goods from H.O. 16,15,000	18,77,500
	To Branch Trading A/c Sale 21,60,000 Stock 1,66,500	23,25,500	"	By Branch Profit & Loss A/c (various expenses)	1,81,250
			"	By Balance c/d	4,92,750
		25,51,500			25,51,500
1979 Jan. 1	To Balance b/d	4,92,750			

Alternatively :

London Branch Account

		Rs.			
1978 Dec. 31	To Balance b/d	2,25,000	1978 Dec. 31	By Balance c/d	4,92,750
	To Profit & Loss A/c—net profit	2,67,750			
		4,92,750			4,92,750
1979 Jan. 1	To Balance b/d	4,92,750			

The alternative treatment of the Branch Account assumes that the Branch Trading and Profit and Loss Account was prepared on a memorandum basis.

The accuracy of the balance shown by the London Branch Account is proved below :

Assets at the Branch :—

	Rs.
Stock	1,66,500
Sundry Debtors	83,250
Cash at Bank	35,150
Cash in hand	1,850
Furniture (Rs. 2,70,000 *less* Depreciation Rs. 27,000)	2,43,000
Total of assets	5,29,750
Less Liabilities, expenses unpaid	37,000
Net assets	4,92,750

Departmental Accounts

If a business is divided into broad divisions—known as departments - it becomes desirable to know the profit or loss for each department separately. Suppose a retailer has two departments, cloth and shoes. Accounts should be prepared in such a manner as to disclose profit (or loss) earned on cloth and shoes separately. This merely involves making out a separate trading and profit and loss account for each department. To facilitate this, subsidiary books will be provided with suitable columns to disclose purchases and sales of each department. If there are two departments, two more columns (one for each department) should be added to the Purchase and Sales Books. Sometimes goods are transferred from one department to another. In such a case, the trading account of the transferring department should be credited and that of the transferee department debited. The main problem in preparing departmental accounts is that of allocation of common expenses. For this purpose the following may be noted :—

(*a*) Expenses that relate to premises—rent, rates, etc., should be allocated in the ratio of area occupied by the various departments.

(*b*) Expenses that relate to sales—carriage outwards, bad debts, discounts allowed, etc.—should be allocated according to the sales of each department. Preferably internal transfers should be ignored for this purpose.

(*c*) Other expenses should be treated individually. If an expense can be allocated properly it should be apportioned. For example, carriage inward should be allocated in the ratio of purchases. But if a proper allocation is not convenient, the expenses concerned should b debited to the common profit and loss account. Prof or loss as disclosed by the separate accounts should b transferred to this common account.

While presenting accounts, it will be better to have a colum for each department and an additional one for totals.

Illustration From the following figures prepare accoun to disclose total profit and the profit of the two departments, and *B* :—

		Rs.			Rs.
Opening Stock :	A	15,200	Sales :	A	1,00,00
	B	10,800		B	80,00
Purchases :	A	75,100	Purchase		
	B	69,800	Returns :	A	1,10
Carriage inwards		2,860		B	80
Salaries :	A	9,000	Discount Received		1,43
	B	8,500			
General		11,600			
Rent and Rates		6,000			
Advertising		8,100			
Insurance		1,000			
General Expenses		5,400			
Discount Allowed		1,800			
Accountancy Charges		500			

The following further information is supplied :

(*a*) Goods transferred from department A to B wer Rs. 5,000. This has not yet been recorded.

(*b*) General Salaries are to be allocated equally.

(*c*) The area occupied is in the ratio of 3 : 2.

(*d*) Insurance premium is for a comprehensive policy, allo cation being inconvenient.

(*e*) The closing stocks of the two departments were : A Rs. 17,800 and B, Rs. 15,600.

Solution :

Departmental Trading and Profit and Loss Account

	Deptt. A Rs.	Deptt. B Rs.	Total Rs.		Deptt. A Rs.	Deptt. B Rs.	Total Rs.
To Opening Stock	15,200	10,800	26,000	By Sales	1,00,000	80,000	1,80,000
To Purchases (Less Returns)	74,000	69.000	1,43,000	By Transfer to B	5,000		5,000
To Carriage Inwards	1,480	1,380	2,860	By Closing Stock	17,800	15,600	33,400
To Transfer from A		5,000	5,000				
To Gross Profit c/d	32,120	9,420	41,540				
	1,22,800	95,600	2,18,400		1,22,800	95,600	2,18,400
To Salaries :				By Gross Profit b/d	32,120	9,420	41,540
Departmental	9,000	8,500	17,500	By Discount Received	740	690	1,430
General	5,800	5,800	11,600	By Loss		13,390	7,430
To Rent and Rates	3,600	2,400	6,000				
To Advertising	4,500	3,600	8,100				
To General Expenses	3,000	2,400	5,400				
To Discount Allowed	1,000	800	1,800				
To Net Profit	5.960						
	32,860	23,500	50 400		32,860	23,500	50,400
To (Net) Loss b/d			7,430	By Net Loss c/d			8,930
To Insurance			1,000				
T Accountancy Charges			500				
			8,930				8,930

Notes : (1) Carriage inward and Discount Received have been allocated in the ratio of net purchases.

(2) Advertising, General Expenses and Discount Allowed have been allocated in the ratio of sales.

EXERCISES

1. A new branch was opened in 1973 at Patna by the New Era, Ltd. From the following figures ascertain the profit earned there :

	Rs.
Goods Sent to Branch	25,000
Sales at Branch :	
Cash	8,000
Credit	18,500
Stock at the end of the year at the Branch	5,000
Cash received from debtors	16,200
Cash sent to the Branch for expenses	3,800

(Profit Rs. 2,700)

2. The following information is supplied to you for 1978 relating to the Surat Branch :

		Rs.
Stock 1st Jan., 1978		11,200
Branch Debtors 1st Jan., 1978		6,300
Goods Sent to Branch		51,000
Cash sent to Branch for :		
Rent	1,500	
Salaries	3,000	
Petty Cash	500	5 000
Sales at Branch :		
Cash		25,000
Credit		39,000
Cash received from debtors		41,200
Debtors at the Branch, 31st Dec.		4,100
Stock " " " "		13,600

(Profit Rs. 10,400)

3. Finewear Ltd. opened a branch at Calcutta in 1977. Goods are invoiced to the branch at cost plus 20%. From the following figures ascertain the profit or loss made at the Branch :

	Rs.
Goods sent to the Branch (invoice price)	30,000
Cash sent to Branch for expenses	5,000
Sales :	
Cash	18,000
Credit	14,000
Cash received from debtors	10,500
Discount allowed	200
Goods returned by the debtors	300
Stock on 31st December, 1977 (invoice price)	4 200
Petty cash Balance on 31st Dec. 1977	50

(Profit Rs. 5,050)

(Hint : *Ignore Discount and Goods returned by customers while preparing Branch Account; but for ascertaining amount due from customers at the end of the year, these two items should be taken into account. Entry for petty cash on hand is like that of closing stock).*

4. Good Trade Ltd. had a branch at Kanpur to which goods were invoiced at cost plus 25%. The following information is supplied to you for 1978.

	Rs.
Stock (invoice value) on 1st Jan.	15,000
Debtors, 1st Jan.	10,000
Petty Cash, 1st Jan.	80
Goods sent to the Branch (cost)	40,000
Sales :	
Cash	26,000
Credit	36,000
Cash received from debtors	34,200
Discount allowed to them	800
Cash remitted to Branch for expenses	8,000
Petty cash at the Branch, 31st Dec.	90
Stock 31st Dec., (invoice price)	12,000
Liability for expenses, 31st Dec.	250

(*Profit Rs. 10,560*)

(**Hint** : *For liability in respect of expenses debit Branch Account*).

5. Edible Oils Ltd. opened a branch at Jamshedpur in 1967. Goods were invoiced at cost plus 33⅓%. From the following information ascertain the profit or loss made at the Branch using the Stock and Debtors system :

	Rs.
Goods invoiced to the Branch (cost)	30,000
Cash sent for expenses	5,100
Sales :	
Cash	25,200
Credit	9,300
Cash received from debtors	7,100
Bad Debts written off	200
Stock at Branch on 31st Dec. (invoice price)	5,200

(*Profit Rs. 3,100*)

6. Using the Stock and Debtors system, find out the profit or loss made at the Kotah Branch in 1978 :

	Rs.
Stock (1st Jan.), invoice price	12,000
Debtors (,,)	6,200
Goods sent to the Branch (invoice price)	35,000
Goods returned by the Branch (invoice price)	1,000
Sales :	
Credit	21,000
Cash	20,000
Goods returned by customers	600
Cash received from debtors	19,800
Discount allowed to them	300
Cash sent for expenses at the branch	6,100
Shortage of goods at the Branch (invoice price)	400

Goods are invoiced to the Branch so as to show a profit of 30% on invoice price.

(*Profit Rs. 5,440*)

(**Hint** : *Put shortage on the credit side of Stock Account ; the balance in this account will be closing stock at the Branch*).

7. Mohan & Co. Ltd. have a branch at Madras to which goods are invoiced at cost plus 25%. Of the cash collected by the Branch, Rs. 8,000 was retained by it for expenses and the rest was remitted to the head office. From the following information prepare Branch Stock, Branch Debtors, Branch Expenses and Branch Adjustment Account to show profit or loss made at the Branch during 1978 :

	Rs.
Stock (invoice price), 1st Jan.	11,400
Debtors ,, ,,	9,300
Goods sent to the Branch (invoice price)	62,000
Sales : Cash	30,000
Credit	34,000
Cash collected from Debtors	32 000
Goods returned by them	700
Discount allowed to them	800
Surplus at the Branch in stock (invoice price)	300
Petty Cash balance, 31 Dec.	60

(*Profit Rs. 2,160*)

8. The following trial balance of a branch is given to you :

Debit Balances	Rs.	*Credit Balances*	Rs.
Stock (opening)	8,300	Sales	44,100
Purchases	20,100	Sundry Creditors	5,200
Goods Received from Head Office	15,600	Head Office A/c	14,100
Carriage	1,800		
Salaries	6,100		
General Expenses	3,600		
Debtors	6,800		
Balance at Bank	1,100		
	63,400		63,400

The closing stock at the Branch was Rs. 7,600. Branch has to be charged Rs. 1,500 in respect of depreciation of Branch Assets whose accounts are kept in Head Office Books. In the Head Office Books, Branch Account stands at Rs. 20,400 (Dr.).

(*a*) Prepare the Branch Trading and Profit and Loss Account and Balance Sheet.

(*b*) Give journal entries for incorporation of the figures in Head Office books. (*Loss at Branch Rs. 5,300*)

9. Give journal entries to rectify or adjust the following in the books of both the Head Office and the Branch :

(*a*) Goods purchased by Branch, but payment made by Head Office, Rs. 800. The Head Office has debited its own Purchases Account.

(*b*) Branch paid salary, Rs. 1,500, to a Head Office official visiting the Branch temporarily. The Branch debited Salaries Account.

(*c*) Goods, Rs. 900, returned by the Branch to the Head Office.

(*d*) Depreciation, Rs. 2,500, in respect of Branch Assets whose accounts are kept in H.O. books.

(*e*) Expenses, Rs. 3,500 to be charged to the Branch for work done on its behalf.

10. From the following trial balances of an Head Office and its Branch as at 31st Dec., 1978 prepare Final Accounts in tabular form and combined Balance Sheet :

	Head Office		*Branch*	
	Dr. Rs.	*Cr.* Rs.	*Dr.* Rs.	*Cr.* Rs.
Capital	—	1,00,000	—	—
Fixed Assets—				
Branch	30,000	—	—	—
H.O.	60,000	—	—	—
Debtors	15,000	—	4,000	—
Creditors	—	3,000	—	2,500

	Head Office Dr. Rs.	Head Office Cr. Rs.	Branch Dr. Rs.	Branch Dr. Rs.
Purchases	80,000	—	10,000	—
Sales	—	1,10,000	—	35,000
Goods to Branch/ from H.O.	—	30,000	28,000	—
Head Office A/c	—	—	—	15,000
Branch A/c	18,000	—	—	—
Expenses	30,000	—	7,500	—
Bank Balance	10,000	—	3,000	—
	2,43,000	2,43,000	52,500	52,500

The stocks were Rs. 8,100 at the Head Office and Rs. 11,400 at the Branch. Depreciation is to be charged at 10% on fixed assets for full year.

(Profit at Head Office, Rs. 32,100; Loss at Branch, Rs. 2,100; Total of Balance Sheet, Rs. 1,35,500)

(Hint : *Ascertain goods and cash in transit*).

11. A firm has two departments, X and Y. From the following figures prepare the Departmental Trading and Profit and Loss Accounts and Balance Sheet :—

Debits	Rs.	*Credits*	Rs.
Opening Stock : X	15,000	Transfer to X	5,000
Y	20,000	Sales : X	1,00,000
Carriage : In	3,000	Y	60,000
Out	5,000	Sundry Creditors	15,000
Advertising	10,000	Capital	30,000
Salaries : X	6,000	Loan	30,000
Y	7,000		
General	12,000		
Rent and Rates	9,000		
Lighting	900		
Fixtures	15,000		
Sundry Debtors	20,000		
Bad Debts	1,600		
Purchases : X	60,000		
Y	40,000		
Bank Balance	6,500		
Bank Interest	4,000		
Transfer from Y	5,000		
	2,40,000		2,40,000

Area occupied by the two departments is in the ratio of 2 : 1. General Salaries are to be divided in the ratio of 5 : 3. The closing stocks were : X, Rs. 14,000 and Y, Rs. 15,000. Depreciation of fixtures is 10% to be allocated in the ratio of space occupied. *(Profit on X, Rs. 725; Loss on Y Rs. 2,725; Total Loss Rs. 6,000; Total of Balance Sheet, Rs. 69,000)*

CHAPTER XV

SELF-BALANCING LEDGERS.

If the number of credit customers and of credit suppliers is large, the ledger becomes bulky. The trial balance is too long and if there is an error, it becomes difficult to locate it. The Self-Balancing Ledgers system is a way to condense the trial balance and thus help in locating the area in which the error lies. The method is simply to divide up the main ledger and to prove the accuracy of each part separately. The main divisions are as follows :

(*a*) A ledger containing accounts of credit customers, known as the Sales Ledger, Debtors Ledger, etc.

(*b*) A ledger containing accounts of suppliers of goods on credit, known as Bought Ledger or Creditors Ledger.

(*c*) A ledger containing all other accounts (assets, liabilities, expenses, incomes, etc.), known as the Principal Ledger or General Ledger or Nominal Ledger.

In other words, from the principal ledger, accounts of credit customers and credit suppliers are removed. But this will naturally leave a void. In the principal ledger double entry will not be complete. To complete the double entry and for other purposes, one account to represent all debtors (known as Total Debtors Account) and another account to represent all creditors (known as Total Creditors Account) are introduced. The trial balance will thus be possible and will be quite small.

Sales and bought ledgers are known as subsidiary ledgers. In very big firms there may be more than one Sales Ledger. In that case there will be as many "Total Debtors Accounts" as there are Sales Ledgers. Sales Book and Cash Book will have to be ruled with additional columns to provide information for sales to and cash received from each set of customers.

We will now show by a small example how the system works. Suppose the following information is supplied for May, 197V.

Customer	*Opening Balance*	*Sales*	*Cash Received*	*Discount allowed*	*Goods Returned*
	Rs.	Rs.	Rs.	Rs.	Rs.
A	680	910	650	30	—
B	820	730	400	—	200
C	1,040	580	850	20	—
D	530	1,120	410	—	100
	3,07	3,340	2,310	50	300

In this Sales Ledger the accounts of the customers will appear as follows :—

A

1979		Rs.	1979		Rs.
May 1	To Balance b/d	680 —	May 1	By Cash	650 —
	To Sales	910 —		By Discount	30 —
			May 31	By Balance c/d	910 —
		1,590 —			1,590 —
June 1	To Balance b/d	910 —			

B

1979		Rs.	1979		Rs.
May 1	To Balance b/d	820 —	May 1	By Cash	400 —
	To Sales	730 —		By Returns Inwards	200 —
			May 31	By Balance c/d	950 —
		1,550 —			1,550 —
June 1	To Balance b/d	950 —			

C

1979		Rs.	1979		Rs.
May 1	To Balance b/d	1,040 —	May 1	By Cash	850 —
	To Sales	580 —		By Discount	20 —
		—	May 31	By Balance c/d	750 —
		1,620 —			1,620 —
June 1	To Balance b/d	750 —			

D

1979		Rs.	1979		Rs.
May 1	To Balance b/d	530 —	May	By Cash	410 —
	To Sales	1,120 —		By Returns Inwards	100 —
			May 31	By Balance c/d	1,140 —
		1,650 —			1,650 —
June 1	To Balance b/d	1,140 —			

Total Debtors Account

1979		Rs.	1979		Rs.
May 1	To Balance b/d	3,070 —	May 1	By Cash	2,310 —
	To Sales	3,340 —		By Discount	50 —
				By Return Inwards	300 —
			May 31	By Balance c/d	3,750 —
		6,410 —			6,410 —
June 1	To Balance b/d	3,750			

The student will have seen that the Total Debtors Account is prepared exactly like that of a customer. Posting is done in totals. Accuracy of the individual accounts in the Sales Ledger is proved by totalling the balances of individual accounts and comparing the total with the balance of the Total Debtors Account. If the two figures differ, there is a mistake. If the two figures agree it may be taken that there is no error in the Sales Ledger or in the Total Debtors Account. In the above case the balance in the Total Debtors Account agrees with the total of individual balances, thus—

	Rs.
A	910
B	950
C	750
D	1,140
	3,750

We know then that the Sales Ledger and the Total Debtors Account are both correct. This is how the system works. Creditors Accounts are prepared in the same way.

Advantages. The advantages of the self-balancing system of ledgers may be summed up as under :

1. Errors are localised and thus quickly located and rectified.
2. Figures for the total amounts owing by the debtors and owing to the creditors will be readily available (from the Total Debtors and Total Creditors Accounts).
3. The Total Debtors Account and the Total Creditors Accounts are posted in totals and are kept in the main ledger. This will show up inaccuracies and mischiefs, if any, in the Sales or Bo ht Ledgers.
4. Work can be done simultaneously on all the ledgers and thus completed soon.

Illustration From the following figures relating to April, 1979 prepare the Total Debtors and Total Creditors Accounts :

	Rs.
Balances, 1st April, 1979 :	
Total Debtors	21,600
Total Creditors	8,200
Purchases, credit	25,300
Credit Sales	39,400
Cash paid to creditors	19,100
Cash received from customers	37,200
Bills Payable issued	5,000
Bills Receivable received	4,000
Bills Receivable dishonoured	500
Bad Debts written off	600
Cash Sales	6,300
Discount received from supplies	900
Discount allowed to customers	1,100

Solution :

Total Debtors Account

Dr. *Cr.*

		Rs.			Rs.
1979 April 1	To Balance b/d	21,600	1979 April 1	By Cash	37,200
	To Sales	39,400		By Bills Receivable	4,000
	To Bills Receivable Dishonoured	500		By Bad Debts	600
				By Discount Allowed	1,100
			April 1	By Balance c/d	18,600
		61,500			61,500
May 1	To Balance b/d	18,600			

Cash Sales have not been entered because these do not concern credit customers.

Total Creditors Account

Dr. *Cr.*

		Rs.			Rs.
1979 April 1	To Cash	19,100	1979 April 1	By Balance b/d	8,200
	To Bills Payable	5,000		By Purchases	25,300
	To Discount Received	900			
April 30	To Balance c/d	8,500			
		33,500			33,500
			May 1	By Balance b/d	8,500

Sectional *vs.* Self-Balancing ledgesr. The student will have noted that in the Sales Ledger only one-sided entries are made and that the double entry is not completed. For instance in the ledger containing accounts of A, B, C, D (given above on pages 581), these are only debit balances. No trial balance of this ledger is possible. Strictly speaking, it is not necessary because we have been able to prove its accuracy. A system maintained like this is called "Sectional Ledgers System".

Some people maintain that if there is a ledger there must be a trial balance. Only then can the system be called "Self-Balancing". In fact that the possibility of a trial balance for each ledger is the only distinguishing feature of Self-Balancing System as compared to the Sectional System. If the system is to be made self-balancing in the strict sense, one additional account will have to be introduced in each of the subsidiary ledgers. In each case it will be called General Ledger Adjustment Account. The account would have appeared like the following in the examples given above :

Dr. **General Ledger Adjustment Account** *Cr.*

			Rs.				Rs.	
1979					1979			
May	To Cash		2,310	—	May 1	By Balance c/d	3,070	
	To Discount		50	—		By Sales	3,340	—
	To Returns Inwards		300	—				
May 31	To Balance c/d		3,750	—				
			6,410	—			6,410	—
					June 1	By Balance b/d	3,750	

This account, introduced *in* the Sales Ledger, will enable a trial balance to be taken of that ledger. The student will have noted that this account is exactly the reverse of the Total Debtors Account. Similarly, in the Bought Ledger there will be a General Ledger Adjustment Account. This will be the reverse of Total Creditors Account. In such a system, the Total Debtors Account is renamed as Sales Ledger Adjustment Account and the Total Creditors Account is renamed as Bought Ledger Adjustment Account.

Making entries. *At first* entries are made in the usual manner. For instance in case of sales, individual customers are debited and Sales Account is credited. In case of cash received from them, Cash Book is debited and the customers are credited. In case of discount received from suppliers, their accounts are debited and the Discount Account credited. *Then* the various Adjustment Accounts are prepared with mutual double entry. Debit Sales Ledger Adjustment Account (in other words Total Debtors Account) and credit General Ledger Adjustment Account (in the Sales Ledger) for Sales, Bills Receivable dishonoured, charges debited to customers etc. Debit

General Ledger Adjustment Account and credit Sales Ledger Adjustment Account for cash received, discount allowed, goods returned, Bills Receivable received, Bad Debts written off, etc.

Similarly, for credit purchases debit General Ledger Adjustment Account (in the Bought Ledger) and Credit Bought Ledger Adjustment Account (in other words, Total creditors A/c). For cash paid, discount received, Bills Payable issued and goods returned to supplier debit the Bought Ledger Adjustment Account and credit General Ledger Adjustment Account.

Illustration The following information is supplied to you for March, 1978 :

	Rs.
Balances 1st March, 1978 :	
Debtors	20,600
Creditors	11,500
Credit Sales	40,300
Credit Purchases	19,800
Cash received from customers	28,400
Discount allowed to them	1,400
Bad Debts written off	700
Bills Receivable received	9,600
Charges debited to customers	150
Amount received from customers whose accounts were previously written off	400
Cash paid to suppliers	15,600
Bills Payable issued	6,100
Discount received	400

Prepare the various adjustment accounts.

Solution :

In the General Ledger

Bought Ledger Adjustment Account

Dr.		Rs.			*Cr.* Rs.
1978 Mar.	To General Ledger Adjustment A/c:		1978 Mar.	By Balance b/d	11,500 —
	Cash	15,600 —		By General Ledger Adjustment A/c: —Purchase	19,800 —
	Bills Payable	6,100 —			
	Discount	400 —			
Mar. 31	To Balance c/d	9,200 —			
		31,300 —			31,300 —
			April 1	By Balance b/d	9,200 —

Sales Ledger Adjustment Account

		Rs.			Rs.
1978 Mar. 1	To Balance b/d	20,600 —	1978 Mar.	By General Ledger Adjustment A/c:	
	To General Ledger Adjustment A/c :			Cash Received	28,400 —
	Sales	40,300 —		Discount	1,400 —
	Charges	150 —		Bad Debts	700 —
				Bills Receivable	9,600 —
			Mar. 31	By Balance c/d	20,950 —
		61,050 —			61,050 —
April 1	To Balance b/d	20,950 —			

Will the student say why the figure of Rs. 400 received against previously written off bad debts has not been entered ?

In the Sales Ledger

General Ledger Adjustment Account

		Rs.			Rs.
1978 Mar. 1	To Sales Ledger Adjustment A/c:		1978 Mar. 1	By Balance b/d	20,600 —
	Cash	28,400 —		By Sales Ledger Adjustment A/c :	
	Discount	1,400 —		Sales	40,300 —
	Bad Debts	700 —		Charges	150 —
	Bills Receivable	9,600 —			
Mar. 31	To Balance c/d	20,950 —			
		61,050 —			61,050 —
			Apr. 1	By Balance b/d	20,950 —

In the Bought Ledger

General Ledger Adjustment Account

1978		Rs.		1978		Rs.	
Mar. 1	To Balance b/d	11,500	—	Mar.	By Bought Ledger Adjustment Account :		
	To Bought Ledger Adjustment A/c: Purchases	19,800	—		Cash	15,600	—
					Bills Payable	6,100	—
					Discount	400	—
				Mar. 31	By Balance c/d	9,200	—
		31,300	—			31,300	—
April 1	To Balance b/d	9,200	—				

Transfers. Sometimes a purchase is made from a person to whom previously goods were sold. The person's account will appear in the Sales Ledger (as debtor) and also in the Bought Ledger (as creditor). He will pay or be paid only the difference. To square up accounts, his credit balance will have to be transferred from the Bought Ledger to the Sales Ledger. Transfers of this nature will not only affect the two personal accounts, *but also all the four adjustment accounts.* Suppose Ram's Account has been transferred in this manner. The journal entries required will be:

1.	Ram ...Dr. (In Bought ledger) To Ram (In Sales Ledger)	To transfer his credit balance to his account in the Sales Ledger.
2.	Bought Ledger Adjustment A/c ...Dr. (In General Ledger) To General Ledger Adjustment A/c (In Bought Ledger)	To correct the two adjustment accounts in respect of creditors.
3.	General Ledger Adjustment A/c ...Dr. (In Sales Ledger) To Sales Ledger Adjustment A/c (In General Ledger)	To correct the two adjustment accounts in respect of customers.

Illustration Exe Ltd. located the undermentioned error in its books of account :

(*i*) The total of the Purchase Book was undercast by Rs. 10

(*ii*) Amount paid, Rs. 450, to M. Madan, a creditor, wa debited to the account of N. Madan, a customer.

(*iii*) The total of discount column on the receipts side of th Cash Book was undercast by Rs. 10.

(*iv*) The sale of Rs. 430 to N. Mohan was debited t N. Madan's Account as Rs. 340.

(*v*) Sale of Rs. 840 to A. Ali was entered in the Sales Book a Rs. 480.

Give the necessary correcting journal entries if the books ar maintained on (*a*) sectional-balancing basis ; and (*b*) self-balancin basis.

Solution :

Journal

			Dr Rs.	Cr Rs
	(a) Sectional Balancing System :			
(*i*)	Purchases Account	Dr	100	
	To Total Creditors Account			100
	The under-debit to Purchases Account and under-credit to Total Creditors Account,as a result of the undercasting of the Purchase Book, now corrected.			
(*ii*)	M. Madan (In Creditors' Ledger)	Dr	450	
	To N. Madan (In Debtors' Ledger)			450
	Correction of the error resulting from wrong debit to N. Madan and omission of debit to M. Madan			
(*iii*)	Discount Account	Dr	10	
	To Total Debtors Account			10
	Correction of the error resulting from undercasting the Discount column (Dr) in the Cash Book			
(*iv*)	Debit N. Mohan Rs. 430			
	Credit N. Madan Rs. 340			
	(To rectify the omission of debit to N. Mohan and wrong debit to N. Madan).			

	Particulars	Dr Rs.	Cr Rs.
(*v*)	Debit A. Ali Rs. 360 (To rectify short debit		
	Total Debtors Account Dr	360	
	To Sales Account		360
	Rectification of the result of entry in the Sales Book Rs. 480 instead of Rs. 840, sale to A. Ali		
	(b) Self-Balancing System		
(*i*)	Debit Purchases Account Rs. 100 (To rectify short debit because of a undercasting the Purchase Book)		
	General Ledger Adjustment A/c— Dr (In the Bought Ledger)	100	
	To Bought Ledger Adjustment A/c (In the General Ledger)		100
	The two accounts affected by the undercasting of the Purchase Book, corrected.		
(*ii*)	Same entry as in (*a*) above.		
(*iii*)	Debit Discount Account Rs. 10 (To rectify the short debit to Discount Account because of undercasting the Discount Column		
	Sales Ledger Adjustment Account—(Dr) (In the Sales Ledger)	10	
	To General Ledger Adjustment Account (In the General Ledger)		10
	The two accounts affected by the undercasting of the Discount Column (Dr) now corrected		
(*iv*)	Same as in (*a*) above		
(*v*)	A. Ali Dr	360	
	To Sales Account		360
	Correction of the error of sale of Rs. 840 being entered as Rs. 480		
	Sales Ledger Adjustment Account Dr (In the Sales Ledger)	360	
	To General Ledger Adjustment Account (In the Sales Ledger)		360
	The two accounts affected by the error and now corrected		

Illustration From the following information relating to July, 1978 prepare the Sales Ledger Adjustment Account and the Bought Ledger Adjustment Account:

			Rs.
Opening Balances:			
Sales Ledger:		(Dr.	25,600
		(Cr.)	700*
Bought Ledger:		(Dr.)	400*
		(Cr.)	14,700
Credit Sales			31,800
Credit Purchases			19,100
Cash received from customers			26,300
Discount allowed to ,,			800
Goods returned by ,,			1,200
Cash paid to ,,			400
Cash paid to creditors			17,300
Discount allowed by creditors			500
Transfer from Bought Ledger to Sales Ledger			1,100
Closing Balances:	Bought Ledger	(Dr.)	300
	Sales Ledger	(Cr.)	600

Solution :

General Ledger

Sales Ledger Adjustment Account

Dr. *Cr.*

		Rs.			Rs.
1968			1968		
July 1	To Balance c/d	25,600	July 1	By Balance b/d	700
	To General Ledger Adjustment A/c:			By G.L. Adjustment A/c	
				Cash	26,300
				Discount	800
	Sales	31,800		Returns	1,200
	Cash paid	400		Transfer	1,100
July 31	To Balance c/d**	600		By Balance c/d	28,300
			July 31		
		58,400			58,400
Aug. 1	To Balance b/d	28,300	Aug. 1	By Balance b/d	600

Bought Ledger Adjustment Account

		Rs.			Rs.
1968			1968		
July 1	To Balance b/d	400	July 1	By Balance b/d	14,700
	To General Ledger Adjustment Account:			By General Ledger Adjustment A/c:	
	Cash paid	17,300		Purchases	19,100
	Discount	500	July 31	By Balance c/d	300
	Transfer	1,100			
July 31	To Balance c/d	14,800			
		34,100			34,100
Aug. 1	To Balance b/d	300	Aug. 1	By Balance b/d	14,800

*Such balances usually arise because of goods returned or special discounts (or rebates) allowed after payment.

** The closing credit balance has to be put on the debits side before totalling.

Illustration: A firm maintains a subsidiary ledger for its credit customers on sectional-balancing basis. On March 1, 1981 the total of the amounts due was Rs.58,950. The transactions in March 1981 were the following as per records:

	Rs.
Sales: Cash	20,400
Credit	75,300
Sales Returns	1,150
Cash Received from customers	62,060
Discount allowed	1,050
Bill Receivable (received in January) dishonoured	2,320
Bad Debts written off	570
Transfers from Creditors' Accounts	430
Bad Debts recovered	675

The list of customers' balances on March 31, 1981 totalled Rs.71,670; the trial balance as on that date was out by Rs.360, excess credit. Prepare the control account in the general ledger. Have you any comment to offer ?

Solution:

Total Debtors Account

1981		Rs.	1981		Rs.
March 1	To Balance b/d	58,950	March 31	By Cash	62,060
31	To Credit Sales	75,300		By Discount	1,050
	To B/R Dis-honoured	2,320		By Returns	1,150
				By Bad Debts	570
				By Transfer from creditors Accounts	430
				By Balance c/d	71,310
		1,36,570			1,36,570
April 1	To Balance b/d	71,310			

Comment: The amount entered in the trial balance must have been Rs.71,310 which has resulted in the debit column in the trial balance being short by Rs.360. The total of the customers' balances is Rs.71,670 which is Rs.360 in excess of the balance in the Total Debtors Account. Probably, therefore, the correct amount is Rs. 71,670 since with this figure the trial balance will also agree; the mistake lies in the Total Debtors Account. The difference of Rs.360 is such that probably it has been caused by transposing the figures (the total of all the digits is 9). Possibly, the figures for Returns is Rs.1,510 and not Rs.1,150.

EXERCISES

1. (*a*) Prepare Total Debtors Account from the following figures for January, 1978 :—

	Rs.
Balance of Debtors on 1st January, 1978	15,300
Credit Sales	41,200
Cash received from customers	37,400
Discount allowed to them	900
Bad Debts written off	600
Bills Receivable received	4,100
Bills Received dishonoured	800

(*Balance Rs. 14,300*)

(*b*) Prepare Sales Ledger Adjustment Account and the General Ledger Adjustment Account from the figures given above.

2. From the figure relating to June 1977 given below prepare the Bought Ledger Adjustment Account and General Ledger Adjustment Account :

	Rs.
Creditors on 1st June, 1977	11,800
Credit Purchases	19,300
Cash paid to Creditors	16,500
Discount allowed by them	700
Bills payable issued	5,300
Transfer to Sales Ledger	1,100
Cash Purchases	8,200

(*Total Creditors, Rs. 9,700*)

(**Hint**: Unless otherwise stated, it should be assumed that the transfer from the Bought Ledger is that of a credit balance. Therefore the Total Creditors Account or Bought Ledger Adjustment Account should be debited.)

3. You are supplied the following figures relating to July, 1978 :—

	Rs.
Debtors on 1st July, 1978—(Dr.)	23,400
(Cr.)	800
Credit Sales	45,700
Cash Sales	9,200
Cash paid to debtors	500
Cash received from debtors	36,400
Bills Receivable received	7,500
Charges debited to customers	600
Transter from Bought Ledger	900
Goods Returned by customers	1,600
Credit balance in Sales Ledger	600

Prepare the Sales Ledger and General Ledger Adjustment Accounts.

(*Dr. Balance Rs. 23,600*)

4. The Total Debtors Account shows a balance of Rs. 37,400. The schedule of debtors totals Rs. 37,250. The trial balance of the firm is out by Rs. 150 excess debit. What conclusion do you draw ?

(**Hint** : In the trial balance, the figure in respect of Sundry Debtors would be Rs. 37,400).

5. Prepare the various adjustment accounts from the following : —

	Rs.
Debtors, 1st January, 1978	35,500
Creditors, " "	19,600
Credit Purchases	26,700
Credit Sales	41,200
Cash received from customers	32,100
Cash paid to creditors	20,500
Bills Payable issued	7,200
Bills Receivable received	8,500
Discount allowed	1,600
Discount received	500
Bad Debts written off	1,700
Transfer from Bought Ledger To Sales Ledger	800
Credit balance in the Sales Ledger (31st January, 1978)	1,200
Debit balance in Bought Ledger (31st January, 1978)	700

[*Sales Ledger (Dr.) Rs. 33,200*; *Bought Ledger (Cr.), Rs. 18,000*]

6. State what conclusion you draw from following figures relating to March 1979 :

	Rs.
Debtors 1st March, 1979	16,700
Credit Sales	29,400
Cash Sales	7,500
Cash received from debtors	21,700
Bills Receivable received	6,900
Bills Receivable dishonoured	800
Transfer from Bought Ledger	900
Discount allowed	1,100
Bad Debts written off	600
Bad Debts previously written off now recovered	250
Total of Debtors, 31st March, 1979 (as per schedule)	16,600

7. By an error an amount, Rs. 840, paid by Shri M. Ali, a customer, was credited to the account of Shri N. Ali, a supplier. Also it was found that Sales Book for December was overcast by Rs. 1,000.

You are required to pass journal entries in case the firm maintains the personal ledgers on (*i*) self-balancing basis and (*ii*) sectional balancing basis.

CHAPTER XVI

HIRE PURCHASE, INSTALMENTS AND ROYALTIES

Goods are often purchased on the basis that payment will be made in instalments. Sometimes the instalments are treated as mere hire so that the ownership or property does not pass to the "buyer" unless he pays all the instalments. Even if the last instalment remains unpaid, the seller can take away the goods. The "purchaser" can also return the goods at any time without having to pay further instalments. This system is known as Hire-Purchase. Under the Hire-Purchase Act, the purchaser has certain rights, the chief of which is that, if a certain proportion of the total amount due is paid, the goods cannot be repossessed without sanction of the court. There is also a ceiling on the interest that can be charged. The purchaser can also demand, on payment of a small sum, an account from the vendor.

If the property passes immediately, the payment to be made by instalments, the only right the seller has, if the buyer defaults, is to sue for the amount unpaid. He has no right to take possession of the goods,

In case of both Hire Purchase and Instalments systems, the buyer has to pay more than the cash price—interest has to be paid. Obviously, the buyer cannot debit the whole amount paid to the cost of the asset acquired. *Only the cash price should be so debited. The extra amount paid is by way of interest and should be debited to Interest Account.* Since accounts are prepared annually, interest must be calculated for each year separately. It should be remembered that interest will be the same under the Hire Purchase and Instalments systems.

To calculate interest, one should prepare the account of, say, the supplier on ordinary lines. The cost price should be credited; cash paid to him should be debited and interest should be calculated on the balance. In the last year, the difference between the amount paid and the balance standing in the account will be the interest. This is so because instalments are generally in round figures. Suppose Y acquires from X a machine on the hire purchase system. The cash price is Rs. 6,000. Payment is to be made as to Rs. 1,000 down and Rs. 2,100 annually for three years. Interest is to be charged @12% p.a. In this case the interest for the three years will be calculated by making out the account of X. Thus*—

*It should be noted that this account is only on memorandum basis.

X

		Rs.			Rs.
Year 1	To Cash	1,000	Year 1	By Machinery A/c	6,000
	To Cash	2,100		By Interest A/c—12% on Rs. 5,000	600
	To Balance c/d	3,500			
		6,600			6,600
Year 2	To Cash	2,100	Year 2	By Balance b/d	3,500
	To Balance c/d	1,820		By Interest A/c —12% on Rs. 3,500	420
		3,920			3,920
Year 3	To Cash	2,100	Year 3	By Balance b/d	1,820
				By Interest A/c (balancing figure)	280
		2,100			2,100

Calculation of interest if rate is not given. If the rate of interest is not given, the interest will be in the ratio of amount outstanding for each year. In the above example, the total amount to be paid is Rs. 7,300 and the cash price is Rs. 6,000. Interest for the three years is Rs. 1,300. Out of the total sum due, Rs. 1,000 was paid immediately. In the first year the amount outstanding was Rs. 6,300, *i.e.*, Rs. 7,300 minus Rs. 1,000. In the second year it was Rs. 4,200, *i.e.*, Rs. 6,300 minus Rs. 2,100. In the third year it was Rs. 2,100, *i.e.*, Rs. 4,200 minus Rs. 2,100. The interest of Rs. 1,300 will be divided in the ratio of 6300 : 4200 : 2100 or 3 : 2 : 1. Interest for the first year is $1,300 \times \frac{3}{6}$ or Rs. 650. For the second year it is Rs. 433 and for the third year it is Rs. 217.

Entries in books—Hire Purchase System. *The purchaser* makes entries as and when he pays the instalments. He debits the amount paid for interest to the Interest Account and the *balance of the instalment* to the asset account. In the above example, the amount paid in the very beginning contains no interest. Hence the whole of it will be debited to the Machinery Account. The amount paid at the end of the first year contains Rs. 600 as interest. This will be debited to the Interest Account. The remaining amount, Rs. 1,500 (Rs. 2,100—Rs. 600), will be debited to the Machinery Account. *Depreciation will be written off on the basis of the full cash price.* Taking the above example we give journal entries for the first year and ledger accounts for all the three years. Depreciation is taken at 15% of cash price on diminishing value.

Books of Purchaser

Journal

			Dr.	Cr.
			Rs.	Rs.
Year 1 beginning	Machinery Account To Cash Account Amount paid towards machinery purchased on hire purchase	Dr.	1,000 —	1,000 —
Year 1 (end)	Machinery Account Interest Account To Cash Account Of the amount paid, Rs. 600 debited to Interest A/c (being first year's interest) and the balance debited to Machinery A/c	Dr. Dr.	1,500 — 600 —	2,100 —
" "	Depreciation Account To Machinery Account Depreciation @ 15% on Rs. 6,000, the cash price	Dr.	900 —	900 —

Ledger

Machinery Account

Dr.		Rs.		Cr.		Rs.
Year 1	To Cash Account	1,100 —	Year 1	By Depreciation A/c		900 —
	To Cash Account	1,500 —		By Balance c/d		1,600 —
	(Rs. 2,100 – Rs. 600)	2,500 —				2,500 —
Year 2	To Balance b/d	1,600 —	Year 2	By Depreciation A/c —15% on Rs. 5,100 *i.e.,* Rs. 6,000—Rs. 900		765 —
	To Cash Account (Rs. 2,100 – Rs. 420)	1,680 —		By Balance c/d		2,515 —
		3,280 —				3,280 —
Year 3	To Balance b/d	2,515 —	Year 3	By Depreciation A/c		650 25
	To Cash Account	1,820 —		By Balance c/d		3,684 75
		4,335 —				4,335 —
	To Balance b/d	3,684 75				

Interest Account

		Rs.			Rs.
Year 1	To Cash A/c	600 —	Year 1	By P. & L. A/c	600 —
Year 2	To Cash A/c	420 —	Year 2	By P. & L. A/c	420 —
Year 3	To Cash A/c	280 —	Year 3	By P. & L. A/c	280 —

Depreciation Account

			Rs.				Rs.	
Year 1	To	Machinery A/c	900	—	Year 1	By P. & L. A/c	900	—
Year 2	To	„ „	765	—	Year 2	By P. & L. A/c	765	—
Year 3	To	„ „	650	25	Year 3	By P. & L. A/c	650	25

Cash Account

						Rs.	
				Year 1	By Machinery A/c	1,000	—
					By Sundries— Machinery Interest	 1,500 600	 — —
				Year 2	By Sundries	2,100	—
				Year 3	By Sundries	2,100	—

An alternate treatment. It is permissible to make entries in respect of the hire purchase transactions as if it is case of an ordinary purchase, involving payment of interest on outstanding balance due to the seller. But in such a case care should be exercised to describe the item properly in the Balance Sheet; one should know on reading the Balance Sheet that the asset concerned has been "purchased" on hire purchase basis. The purchase of the machinery, as per example given above, will be recorded in the ledger as shown below.

Machinery Account

Dr. *Cr.*

		Rs.				Rs.	
Year 1	To Vendor	6,000	—	Year 1 (end)	By Depreciation	900	—
					By Balance c/d	5,100	—
		6 000	—			6,000	—
Year 2	To Balance b/d	5,100	—	Year 2 (end)	By Depreciation	765	—
					By Balance c/d	4,335	—
		5,100	—			5,100	—
Year 3	To Balance b/d	4,335	—	Year 3 (end)	By Depreciation	650	—
					By Balance c/d	3,685	—
		4,335	—			4,335	—
Year 4	To Balance b/d	3,683	—				

Hire Vendor's Account

		Rs.			Rs.
Year 1 (beginning)	To Cash	1,000	Year 1	By Machinery Account	6,000
(end)	To Cash	2,100	(end)	By Interest A/c	600
(end)	To Balance c/d	3,500			
		6,600			6,600
Year 2 (end)	To Cash	2,100	Year 2	By Balance b/d	3,500
(end)	To Balance c/d	1,820	(end)	By Interest Account	420
		3,920			3,920
Year 3 (end)	To Cash	2,100	Year 3	By Balance b/d	1,820
			(end)	By Interest Account	280
		2,100			2,100

Accounts in respect of interest and depreciation will be the same as already given. In the Balance Sheet, the items will be shown as follows:—

(Extract from) **Balance Sheet**

End of year 1

	Rs.		Rs.
Vendor (amount due against machinery as per contra, exclusive of interest)	3,500	Machinery	6,000
		less Depreciation	900
		(Subject to payment of two annual instalments of Rs. 2,100 each)	5,100

End of Year 2

	Rs.		Rs.
Vendor (amount due in respect of machinery as per contra, exclusive of interest)	1,820	Machinery	6,000
		Less Depreciation	1,655
		(Subject to payment of one instalment of Rs. 2,100).	4,335

End of Year 3

	Rs.
Machinery	6,000
Less Depreciation	2,315
	3,685

Books of the seller. The seller passes entries only in the usual way. He debits the purchaser with the full cash price and the interest as and when due. He credits him with the amount received. The balance is due from him and is shown in the balance sheet. The first year's journal entries will be made as under (taking the above example):

Books of Hire Vendor—Journal

			Rs.	Rs.
Year 1	Y To Sales Account Machinery sold to Y, payment to be received in instalments.		6,000 —	6,000 —
	Cash Account To Y Amount received from Y on the beginning of the agreement	Dr.	1,000 —	1,000 —
(end)	Y To Interest Account Interest due from Y for one year	Dr.	600 —	600 —
	Cash Account To Y Amount received from Y	Dr.	2,100 —	21,00 —

Y's account and the Interest Account will appear as follows.

Y

		Rs.			Rs.
Year 1	To Sales A/c	6,000 —	Year 1	By Cash A/c	1,000 —
	To Interest A/c	600 —		By Cash A/c	2,100 —
				By Balance c/d	3,500 —
		6,600 —			6,600 —
Year 2	To Balance b/d	3,500 —	Year 2	By Cash A/c	2,100 —
	To Interest A/c	420 —		By Balance c/d	1,820 —
		3,920 —			3,920 —
Year 3	To Balance b/d	1,820 —	Year 3	By Cash A/c	2,100 —
	To Interest A/c	280 —			
		2,100 —			2,100 —

Interest Account

Year 1	To P. & L. A/c	600 —	Year 1	By Y	600 —
Year 2	To P. & L. A/c	420 —	Year 2	By Y	420 —
Year 3	To P. & L. A/c	280 —	Year 3	By Y	280 —

Instalments System. As pointed out above ownership passes immediately on purchase of goods on the instalment's system. Therefore, on purchase, the cash price of the goods is debited to the asset account, the amount to be paid as interest (total) is debited to the Interest Suspense Account and the vendor is credited with the total amount due to him. Thus (continuing the above example)—

		Rs.	Rs.
Machinery Account	...	Dr. 6,000	
Interest Suspense Account	...	Dr. 1,300	
To Vendor			7,300

As and when payment is made, the vendor's account is debited. At the end of each year, the interest for the year is transferred to Interest Account by crediting Interest Suspense Account. Thus—

			Rs.
Interest Account	...	Dr. 600	
To Interest Suspense Account			600

The balance in the Interest Suspense Account is carried forward and is shown in the Balance Sheet. Depreciation is written off in the usual way. We show below the Machinery Account, Interest Suspense Account and the account of X (in the books of Y).

Machinery Account

Dr.		Rs.				Rs.	*Cr.*
Year 1	To X	6,000	—	Year 1	By Depreciation Account	900	—
					By Balance c/d	5,100	—
		6,000	—			6,000	—
Year 2	To Balance b/d	5,100	—	Year 2	By Depreciation A/c	765	—
					By Balance c/d	4,335	—
		5,100	—			5,100	—
Year 3	To Balance b/d	4,335	—	Year 3	By Depreciation A/c	650	25
					By Balance c/d	3,684	75
		4,335	—			4,335	—
Year 4	To Balance b/d	3,684	75				

Interest Suspense Account

		Rs.			Rs.
Year 1	To X	1,300	Year 1	By Interest A/c	600
				By Balance c/d	700
		1,300			1,300
Year 2	To Balance b/d	700	Year 2	By Interest A/c	420
				By Balance c/d	280
		700			700
Year 3	To Balance b/d	280	Year 3	By Interest A/c	280

X

		Rs.			Rs.
Year 1	To Cash Account	1,000	Year 1	By Sundries—Machinery	6,000
end	To Cash Account	2,100		Int. Suspense	1,300
,,	To Balance c/d	4,200			
		7,300			7,300
Year 3	To Cash Account	2,100	Year 2	By Balance b/d	4,200
(end)	To Balance c/d	2,100			
		4,200			4,200
Year 3	To Cash Account	2,100	Year 3	By Balance b/d	2,100

The seller debits the purchaser with the total amount due from him, credits sales with the cash price and credits Intersst Suspense Account with the total interest due. Thus—

	Rs.	Rs.
Y ... Dr	7,300	
To Sales Account		6,000
To Interest Suspense A/c.		1,300

The purchase is credited as and when cash is received from him. At the end of each year, the interest for the year is transferred to Interest Account by debiting Intesest Suspense Account.

Continuing the above example, the Interest Suspense Account and the account of Y are shown below in the books of X.

Dr. **Y** *Cr.*

		Rs.			Rs.
Year 1	To Sundries— Machinery	6,000	Year 1	By Cash A/c	1,000
	Interest Suspense	1,300		By Cash A/c	2,100
				By Balance c/d	4,200
		7,300			7,300
Year 2	To Balance b/d	4,200	Year 2	By Cash A/c	2,100
				By Balance c/d	2,100
		4,200			4,200
Year 3	To Balance b/d	2,100	Year 3	By Cash A/c	2,100

Interest Suspense Account

		Rs.			Rs.
Year 1	To Interest A/c	600	Year 1	By Y	1,300
	To Balance c/d	700			
		1,300			1,300
Year 2	To Interest A/c	420	Year 2	By Balance b/d	700
	To Balance c/d	280			
		700			700
Year 3	To Interest A/c	280	Year 3	By Balance b/d	280

Hire Purchase Trading Account

A firm which sells a large number of small items to a number of customers will probably treat the hire purchase sales differently from its other sales. A systematic record will be kept in respect of each customer so that it is readily known how much is due from him and when, whether the amount due has been received or not, and if not, whether the goods in his possession have been recovered and so on. To ascertain the profit or loss on hire purchase sales, such sales are treated as if made by a separate department or branch. The method employed to ascertain the profit of a branch to which goods are invoiced at cost plus profit (See pp. 5 -5 above), is also used in case of "hire purchase department". In a nutshell, the method is the following:—

(*i*)	Debit Hire Purchase Trading Account Credit Goods Sold on Hire Purchase Account	with the selling price of goods sold on hire purchase.
(*ii*)	Debit Bank Credit Hire Purchase Trading Account	with the cash received from hire purchase customers
(*iii*)	Debit Goods Returned Account Credit Hire Purchase Trading Account	with the value place on goods recovered from customers who cease to pay
(*iv*)	Debit Goods Sold on Hire Purchase Account Credit Hire Purchase Trading Account	with the profit included in goods sold i.e. selling price minus cost
(*v*)	Debit Instalment Due Credit Hire Purchase Trading Account	with the instalments that are due but not yet received from *those customers who are still paying*

(*vi*) The amount of instalments not yet due is carried down as a balance—a sort of closing stock; it is put on the credit side of the Hire Purchase Trading Account and then carried down to the next year.

(*vii*)	Debit Hire Purchase Trading Account Credit Stock Reserve Account	with the 'profit' included in the instalments not yet due from customers as in (vi) above.

"Goods Sold on Hire Purchase Account" is transferred to the Trading Account. The Hire Purchase Trading Account will now reveal profit or loss. Instalments Due and Stock Reserve Account will be carried down to the next year and then transferred to the Hire Purchase Trading Account of that year. The assets of the firm at the end of the year consist of, in this respect, (i) instalments due and (ii) instalments not yet due less the Stock Reserve as per step (vii) above,

Illustration Fast Traders started selling goods on hire purchase basis in 1977—the hire purchase price was cost plus 50%. Following are the particulars pertaining to 1977 and 1978.

	19	1978
	Rs.	Rs.
Goods Sold on Hire Purchase (selling price)	30,000	50,100
Cash Received from h.p. customers	18,000	39,000
Instalments due, customers paying, on 31st Dec.	1,000	1,500
Instalments not yet due	11,000	20,100
Value of goods recovered from defaulting customers		200

Prepare the ledger accounts for the two years and show how various items will appear in the Balance Sheets as at 31st December 1977 and 1978.

Solution :

BOOKS OF FAST TRADERS

Hire Purchase Trading Account

Dr.					*Cr.*
		Rs.			Rs.
1977	To Goods Sold on Hire Purchase Account	30,000	1977	By Cash	18,000
Dec. 31	To Stock Reserve A/c—Reserve required for unrealised profit on instalments not yet due	3,667	Dec.31	By Instalments Due A/c	1,000
„	To Profit & Loss A/c—Profit transfered	6,333	„	By Goods sold on Hire Purchase A/c: loading	10,000
			„	By Balance c/d: instalments not yet due	11,000
		40,000			40,000
1978 Jan 1	Balance b/d	11,000			
	To				

Goods Sold on Hire Purchase Account

1977			1977		Rs.
Dec.31	To Hire Purchase Trading A/c—loading	Rs. 10,000		By Hire Purchase Trading Account	30,000
	To Trading A/c—transfer	20,000			
		30,000			30,000

Instalments Due Account

1977		Rs.	1977		Rs
Dec.31	To Hire Purchase Trading A/c	1,000	Dec.31	By Balance c/d	1,000
1978 Jan. 1	To Balance b/d	1,000			

Stock Reserve Account

		Rs.			Rs.
1977 Dec.31	To Balance c/d	3,667 —	1977 Dec.31	By Hire Purchase Account	3,667 —
			1968 Jan. 1	By Balance b/d	3,667

(Extracts from) Balance Sheet as at December 31, 1977

		Assets		Rs.
		Instalments Due		1,000 —
		Instalments not yet due	11,000	
		Less Reserve for Unrealised Profit	3,667	7,333 —

1978 Accounts
Instalments Due Account

		Rs.			Rs.
1978 Jan. 1	To Balance b/d	1,000 —	1978 Jan. 1	By Hire Purchase Trading A/c – transfer	1,000 —
Dec.31	To Hire Purchase Trading A/c	1,500 —	Dec.31	By Balance c/d	1,500 —
		2,500. —			2,500
1979 Jan. 1	To Balance b/d	1,500 —			

Stock Reserve Account

		Rs.			Rs.
1978 Dec.31	To Hire Purchase Trading A/c—transfer	3,667 —	1978 Jan. 1	By Balanced b/d	3,667 —
"	To Balance c/d	6,700 —	Dec.31	By Hire Purchase Trading Account	6,700 —
		10,367 —			10,367 —
			1979 Jan. 1	By Balance b/d	6,700 —

Goods Sold on Hire Purchase Account

1978		Rs.	1978		Rs.
Dec. 31	To Hire Purchase Trading A/c—loading	16,700		By Hire Purchase Trading Account	50,100
"	Trading Account—transfer	33,400			
		50,100			50,100

Hire Purchase Trading Account

1978		Rs.	1978		Rs.
Jan. 1	To Balance b/d: Instalments not yet due	11,000		By cash	39,000
"	To Instalments Due—opening balance	1,000	Dec.31	By Instalments Due A/c	1,500
"	To Goods sold on Hire Purchase A/c	50,100		By Goods Recovered A/c	200
Dec. 31	To Stock Reserve A/c Reserve required	6,700	"	By Stock Reserve A/c—Opg. Balance	3,667
"	Profit & Loss A/c - profit	12,367	"	By Goods Sold on H.P. A/c	16,700
			"	By Balance c/d	20,100
		81,167			81,167
1979 Jan. 1	To Balanced b/d	20,100			

(Extracts from) Balance Sheet as at December 31, 1978

Assets		Rs.
Instalments Due		1,500
Instalments Not Yet Due	20,100	
Less Reserve for unrealised profit	6,700	13,400

The student should note that if in the beginning of a year certain instalments were not due (i.e., there is an opening balance in the Hire Purchase Trading Account), there will be an amount lying to the credit of Stock Reserve Account. The amount will be equal to the (unrealised) profit included in the instalments not yet due.

ROYALTIES

"Royalty" is the payment made by a person who exploits. for business purposes, rights belonging to another Thus a publisher pays royalties to authors of books ; a manufacturer pays royalties to the owners of patents and the owner of a mine receives royalties from the person or firm which actually works the mine. Lumpsums paid for the right do not come under the term royalty because then the ownership of the right is transferred. Royalty is usually calculated as so much per unit of output or unit of sale.

Usually the contract stipulates a minimum (often called minimum rent or dead rent). The excess of the amount of minimum royalty over the amount actually earned is called "Shortworking". Contracts mostly provide for the recovery of shortworkings out of subsequent royalties (if they exceed the minimum figure). There is often a date line for recovery beyond which shortworkings will not be recovered.

Suppose S develops a patent to make a new type of sewing machine. He authorises Y to manufacture the machines by using his patent on the conditions that (1) he will receive Rs. 10 per machine produced, (2) there will be a minimum annual payment of Rs. 5,000 and (3) shortworkings, if any, will be made good out of royalties of the first four years. The output of the first four years is 300 machines, 450 machines and 600 machines and 900 machines respectively. We will illustrate the entries to be made using the above figures.

If royalties are less than the minimum amount, Royalties Account should be debited with the amount earned by the owner as royalties, shortworking should be debited with the "excess" amount paid and the owner of the right should be credited with the minimum amount due. In the first year, the entry is :

		Rs.	Rs.
Royalties Account ...	Dr.	3,000 (i.e., 300 × 10)	
Shortworkings Account ...	Dr.	2,000	
To S			5,000

The entry may also be passed as follows :

(i) Minimum Rent Account	Dr.	5,000	
To S			5,000

(ii) Royalties Account ...	Dr.	3,000	
Shortworkings Account ...	Dr.	2,000	
To Minimum Rent Account			5,000

The Shortworkings Account is carried forward as an asset. Royalties Account, being an expense, is transferred to the Profit and Loss Account.

When actual royalties exceed the minimum amount *and* when there is shortworking to be recouped, actual Royalties Account should be debited with the actual amount of the royalties, Shortworkings Account should be credited with the amount that can be recovered and the balance should be credited to the owner of the right. In the above example, in the third year the actual royalties come to Rs. 6,000. Toal shortworking is Rs. 2,500. Minimum rent being Rs. 5,000, Y can recover only Rs. 1,000. Next year actual royalties being Rs. 9,000, he can recover the full Rs. 1,500 and he will have to pay Y Rs. 7,500, *i.e.*, Rs. 9,000 minus Rs. 1,500, The entries for the two years in this respect are :

		Dr. Rs.	Rs.
3rd year	Royalties Account ...	6,000	
	To Shortworking Account		1,000
	To S		5,000
4th year	Royalties Account ... Dr.	9000	
	To Shortworking Account		1,500
	To S		7,500

Suppose in the 4th year actual output was only 550 machines. In that case Y would have recovered only Rs. 500. Since shortworking can be recovered, according to the agreement, only in 4 years, the balance in the Shortworkings Account, Rs. 1,000 would have to be written off by debiting Profit and Loss Account. This point should be noted by the student.

We now give journal entries for the four years and the relevant ledger accounts.

Journal

				Dr. Rs.	Cr. Rs.
		Alternatively : Minimum Rent Account To S The amount payable to S	Dr.	5,000	5,000
Year (end)	1	Royalties Account Shortworkings Account To S Amount due to S, Rs. 5,000 : actual royalties being only Rs. 3,000.	Dr. Dr.	3,000 — 2,000 —	5,000 —
"	"	S To Bank Account Amount paid to S.	Dr.	5,000 —	5,000 —
"	"	Profit & Loss Account To Royalties Account Royalties Account transferred to the P. & L. Account.	Dr.	3,000 —	3,000 —
		Royalties Account Shortworking Account To Minimum Rent Account The amount of royalties and short-working	Dr.	3,000 2,000	5,000

				Rs	Rs.
Year	2	Royalties Account Dr. Shortworkings Account Dr. To S Royalties on 4,500 machines subject to a minimum of Rs. 5,000.	Dr. Dr.	4,500 — 500 —	 5,000 —
"	"	S Dr. To Bank Account Amount paid to S.	Dr.	5,000 —	5,000 —
"	"	Profit and Loss Account To Royalties Account Royalties Account transferred to P. & L. Account.	Dr.	4,500 —	4,500 —
Year	3	Royalties Account To Shortworkings Account To S Royalties due on 600 machines, Rs. 1,000 recovered from S on account of shortworkings.	Dr.	6,000 —	 1,000 — 5,000 —
	"	S To Bank Account Amount paid to S.	Dr.	5,000 —	5,000 —
	"	Profit and Loss Account To Royalties Account Royalties Account transferred to P. & L. A/c.	Dr.	6,000 —	6,000 —
Year	4	Royalties Account To Shortworkings Account To S Amount due to S for 900 machines; Rs. 1,500 recovered for shortworkings.	Dr.	9,000 —	 1,500 — 7,500 —
"	"	S To Bank Account Amount due to S paid.	Dr.	7,500 —	7,500 —
"	"	Profit and Loss Account To Royalties Account Royalties Account transferred to P. and L. A/c.	Dr.	9,000 —	9,000 —

Ledger

S

Dr.		Rs.			Cr. Rs.
Year 1	To Bank A/c	5,000	Year 1	By Sundries— Royalties Shortworkings	 3,000 2,000
					5,000
Year 2	To Bank A/c	5,000	Year 2	By Sundries	5,000
			Year 3	By Royalties A/c	5,000
Year 3	To Bank A/c	5,000			
			Year 4	By Royalties A/c	7,500
Year 4	To Bank A/c	7,500			

Royalties Account.

		Rs.			Rs.
Year 1	To S	3,000	Year 1	By P. & L. A/c	3,000
Year 2	To S	4,500	Year 2	By P. & L A/c	4,500
Year 3	To Sundries— S 5,000 Shortworkings 1,000	 6,000	Year 3	By P. & L. A/c	6,000
Year 4	To Sundries	9,000	Year 4	By P. & L. A/c	9,000

Shortworkings Account

		Rs.			Rs.
Year 1	To S	2,000	Year 1	By Balance c/d	2,000
Year 2	To Balance b/d To S	2,000 500	Year 2	By Balance c/d	2,500
		2,500			2,500
Year 3	To Balance b/d	2,500	Year 3	By Royalties A/c By Balance c/d	1,000 1,500
		2,500			2,500
			Year 4	By Royalties A/c	1,500
Year 4	To Balance b/d	1,500			

EXERCISES

1. M/s A and B purchased on 1st Jan., 1966 from X & Co. a machine whose cash price was Rs. 7,450. Payment was to be made in four instalments of Rs 2,000 each, the first payment to be made immediately and the other three at the end of 1976, 1977 and 1978. Interest was taken to be 5% p.a. Depreciation is 10% p.a. on the diminishing value.

Give journal entries and ledger accounts in the books of both the parties under both the Hire Purchase and Instalments systems.

2. A new firm purchased a printing machine on 1st January, 1975 on the hire purchase system. The cash price was Rs. 15,000; payment was to be in

four half yearly instalments of Rs. 4 000 each, the first payment to be made on 30th June, 1975. Interest is to be taken at 5% p.a. The machine is to be depreciated at 15% p.a. on the diminishing value.

Record the transactions in the books of the purchaser.

3. Newman & Co. purchased on 1st July, 1973 a machine whose cash price was Rs. 12,000. Rs. 3,000 was to be paid immediately and similar amounts were to be paid annually for three years together with interest @ 9% p.a. The machine is to be depreciated at 10% on the original cost.

Give the Machinery Account for the three years.

4. Black purchased on 1st October, 1974 a machine on the hire purchase system. The cash price was Rs. 20,000. Payment was to be made as to Rs. 5,000 down and Rs. 4,000 annually for five years. The machine was depreciated @ 15% p.a. on the diminishing value. The third annual instalment could not be paid and the vendors seized the machine. Record the above transactions in the books of Black.

(**Hint** : *Interest will be in the ratio of amounts outstanding from year to year. On seizure write off Machine Account.*)

5. North Coal Co. leased a mine from K on the basis of royalties @ Rs. 2 per tonne of coal raised subject to a minimum of Rs. 10,000 per annum. Short-workings, if any, could be recovered out of royalties of the first four years. The output was as follows :—

	Tonnes
First year	2,000
Second year	4,500
Third year	5,600
Fourth year	6,500

Give journal entries in the books of the North Coal Co.

6. New Publishers Ltd. published a book written by S. The arrangement was that S will get a royalty of Rs. 3 per copy sold subject to a minimum of Rs. 5,000 per annum. Shortworking of each year could be recovered out of royalties for the subsequent three years.

Number of copies sold was :—

	Rs.
First year	800
Second year	1,500
Third year	2,000
Fourth year	2,000
Fifth year	3,000

Record the above in the books of the publishers.

7. Dee Ltd. sell goods on hire purchase basis, the price being cost plus 60%. From the following particulars relating to 1978 ascertain the profit or loss on hire purchase transactions :—

		Rs.
Instalments Due, customers paying	on Jan. 1,	2,000
Instalments not yet due	1978	25,000
Goods sold during the year or line purchase (cost)		60,000
Cash Received from H.P. customers		90,000
Instalments Due on 13th December, 1961 customers paying		3,000

(Profit, Rs. 34,125)

(**Hint** : Ascertain the amount of instalments not yet due on December 3, 1968)

CHAPTER XVII

ACCOUNTS FROM INCOMPLETE RECORDS

(Or the Single Entry System)

The Single Entry System is really no system at all for keeping accounts. Under this system, only such accounts are kept as seem to be absolutely necessary. Usually the accounts that are kept are those relating to cash, credit customers and creditors. One may not find accounts relating to fixed assets, purchases, sales, expenses, incomes, etc. Thus one may find that some transactions are not recorded at all, some transactions are recorded only in one of their aspects while, for some others, both the aspects are recorded. Goods sold on credit will be recorded only in the account of the customer concerned. Cash received from him will be recorded both in the Cash Account and in the account of the customer. Purchase of machinery on credit will not be recorded at all till payment is made.

This system of recording transactions is very defective. No trial balance can be taken out and hence accuracy of books cannot be proved. Chances of mischief or fraud remaining undetected are high. Trading and Profit and Loss Account cannot be prepared and, hence, the proprietor will have no firm idea of profit earned or loss suffered. Balance Sheet, called statement of affairs here, is prepared in an unsatisfactory manner. The assets and liabilities are not proved from records but are put down by physical inspection and on an estimated basis. In spite of all the defects, the system is quite popular with small firms which cannot afford to spend money on proper accounting.

Ascertaining profit or loss. Under the Single Entry System profit or loss is ascertained on a commonsense basis. If Y starts a business with a capital of Rs. 10,000 and finds that his capital at the end of the year is Rs. 14,000, he is entitled to believe that he made a profit of Rs. 4,000 during the year. Capital normally grows on account of profit. This is subject to two things. If Y brought in a further Rs. 1,500 as capital, the profit must have been only Rs. 2,500, i.e., Rs. 4,000 minus Rs. 1,500. But if Y took Rs. 250 every month for domestic use, he must have taken Rs. 3,000 in all. Had he not withdrawn this sum, his capital at the end would have been Rs. 17,000 and, therefore, his profit should be increased by Rs. 3,000. His profit comes to Rs. 5,500. Therefore, to ascertain profit under the Single Entry System :

Take capital at the end, add drawings, deduct fresh capital introduced during the year and deduct capital in the beginning.

Capital at any date can be always ascertained by deducting liabilities from assets. Remember that always

Capital = Assets—Liabilities

Illustration Wali commenced business on 1st January, 1977 with a capital of Rs. 15,000. On 1st July, 1977 he introduced a further capital of Rs. 8,000. During the year he withdrew Rs. 500 p.m. for domestic use. On 31st December, 1977 his assets and liabilities were :

	Rs.
Stock	21,000
Debtors	10,000
Furniture	3,500
Cash at Bank	2,100
Expenses Unpaid	700
Sundry Creditors	8,300

Solution :

Statement of Affairs of Wali as at 31 Dec. 1977*

Liabilities	Rs.	*Assets*	Rs.
Expenses Unpaid	700	Stock	21,000
Sundry Creditors	8,300	Sundry Debtors	10.000
Capital (balancing figure)	27,600	Furniture	3,500
		Cash at Bank	2,100
	36,600		36,600

Profit or Loss :

	Rs.
Capital on 31st Dec., 1977	27,600
Add Drawings	6,000
	33,600
Less fresh capital introduced	8,000
	25,600
Less Capital on 1st Jan., 1977	15,000
Profit	10,600

Illustration Shah and Rao are partners sharing profits and losses in the ratio of 3 : 2 after charging interest on capitals @ 6% p.a. Interest on Drawings is ignored. On 1st July. 1978 their position was as under :

Liabilities		Rs.	*Assets*	Rs.
Sundry Creditors		14,300	Machinery	20,000
Capitals :			Stock	12,000
Shah	20,000		S. Debtors	11,000
Rao	15,000	35,000	Cash at Bank	4,000
			Furniture	2,000
			Prepaid Insurance	300
		49,300		49,300

*The "Balance Sheet" under the Single Entry System is called "Statement of Affairs."

During the year ended 30th June, 1979 Shah had drawn Rs. 5,000 and Rao had drawn Rs. 3,500 for their private purposes. On 30th June, 1979 the assets and liabilities were :

	Rs.	
Sundry debtors	12,000	(subject to a provision of 5% for doubtful debts)
Stock	18,000	
Cash at Bank	4,500	
Prepaid Insurance	200	
Sundry Creditors	13,700	
Expenses Owing	600	

Machinery and Furniture were the same as previously but a depreciation @ 10% p.a. was to be written off. Prepare the Statement of Affairs as at 30th June, 1979.

Solution :

Statement of Affairs as at 30th June, 1979.

Liabilities	Rs.	*Assets*		Rs.
Sundry Creditors	13,700	Machinery	20,000	
Expenses unpaid	600	Less Depreciation	2,000	18,000
Combined Capitals : (bolancing figure)	39,600	Stock		18,000
		Sundry Debtors	12,000	
		Less Provision for Doubtful Debts	600	11,400
		Cash at Bank		4,500
		Prepaid Insurance		200
		Furniture	2,000	
		Less Depreciation	200	1,800
	53,900			53,900

Profit or Loss :	Rs.	Rs.
Capital on 30th June, 1979		39,600
Add Drawings :		
Shah	5,000	
Rao	3,500	8,500
		48,100
Less Capitals on 1st July, 1978		35,000
Profit		13,100

Division of Profit

Profit and Loss (Appropriation) Account

		Rs.		Rs.
To Interest on Capitals :			By Profit	13,100 —
Shah	1,200			
Rao	900	2,100 —		
To Profit transferred—				
Shah 3/5	6,600			
Rao 2/5	4,400	11,000 —		
		13,100 —		13,100 —

Statement of Affairs of Shah and Rao as at 20th June, 1969

Liabilities		Rs.	*Assets*		Rs.
Sundry Creditors		13,700 —	*Fixed Assets*		
Expenses Unpaid		600 —	Machinery	20,000	
Capitals :	Rs.		Less Depreciation	2,000	18,000 —
Shah—					
Balance on 1st July, '68	20,000		Furniture	2,000	
Add Interest	1,200		Less Depreciation	200	1,800 —
Profit	6,600		*Current Assets* :		
	27,800		Stock		18,000 —
Less Drawings	5,000	22,800 —	Sundry Debtors	12,000	
Rao—			Less Provision for Bad Debts	600	11,400 —
Balance on 1st July, '68,	15,000		Cash at Bank		4,500 —
Add : Interest	900		Prepaid Insurance		200 —
Profit	4,400				
	20,300				
Less Drawings	3,500	16,800 —			
		53,900 —			53,900 —

Preparing Final Accounts from incomplete (or single entry) records. If a summary of cash transactions during the year is available together with opening and closing balances of sundry debtors and sundry creditors, it is possible to prepare Trading and Profit and Loss Account. The real problem is to find out sales and purchases for the year. This can be done by preparing accounts of Sundry Debtors and Sundry Creditors. Suppose total debtors on 1st Jan., 1968, were Rs. 15,000; during the year Rs. 81,000 were received from the customers; and the amount due from them on 31st December, 1968 was Rs. 11,000. It is clear that the total sales to customers must have been Rs. 77,000. Out of Rs. 81,000 received, Rs. 15,000 is for the previous year, leaving Rs. 66,000 for 1968. Rs. 11,000 is still due.

Thus total sales must be Rs. 77,000. These figures can be presented in account from, like this—

Sundry Debtors Account

			Rs.				Rs.	
1978 Jan.	1	To Balance b/d	15,000	—	1978 Dec. 31	By Cash	81,000	—
		To Credit Sales (balancing figure)	77,000	—		By Balance c/d	11,000	—
			92,000	—			92,000	—

The Total Debtors Account should be prepared in the usual manner putting opening balance on the debit side and the closing balance on the credit side. Also cash received, discount allowed, bad debts written off, etc. should be put on the credit side. The debit side will be short. The difference will be credit sales. Cash sales will be found in the summary of cash transactions. Thus total sales can be found. Similarly, if Total Creditors Account is prepared credit purchases can be ascertained.

Cash summary will indicate expenses (on the credit side) and incomes (on the debit side). These items will represent actual payments or receipts. To make them suitable for entry in the Trading and Profit and Loss Account, the amounts will have to be adjusted for outstanding or prepaid items. Suppose cash summary shows the payment of salaries as Rs. 15,300. It may be that Rs. 1,800 is still unpaid. Total salaries will be Rs. 17,100, *i.e.*, Rs. 15,300 + Rs. 1,800. Rs. 17,100 will be debited to the Profit and Loss Account. Rs. 1,700 will be a liability to be shown in the Balance Sheet.

Cash summary will also contain "capital" items, *e.g.*, payments for assets acquired or liabilities redeemed. Such items affect the Balance Sheet.

Illustration Bose supplies to you the following information :

	1st Jan., 1978	31st Jan., 1978
	Rs.	
Sundry Debtors	18,100	19,300
Stock	15,000	14,000
Machinery	25,000	
Furniture	4,000	
Sundry Creditors	11,000	12,500

Summary of cash transactions for 1978 :

Receipts	Rs.	*Payment*	Rs.
Opening Balance	500	Payments to Creditors	35,000
Cash Sales	6,100	Wages	16,000
Received from Debtors	75,300	Salaries	15,000
Miscellaneous receipts	200	Drawings	4,000
Loan from Dass		Expenses	11,000
(@ 9% on 1st July)	10,000	Machinery purchased (1st July)	9,500
		Closing Balance	1,600
	92,100		92,100

Discounts allowed were Rs. 700 and discounts received were Rs. 400. Bad Debts written off were Rs. 800. Depreciation is to be written off Furniture @ 5% and Machinery @ 10%. Expenses include insurance @ Rs. 500 p.a. paid up to 31st March, 1979, Wages. Rs. 2,000, are still due.

Prepare Trading and Profit and Loss Account and Balance Sheet relating to 1978.

Solution :

Total Debtors Account (to ascertain credit sales)

Dr. *Cr.*

		Rs.				Rs.	
1978 Jan. 1	To Balance b/d	18,100	–	1978 Dec. 31	By Cash	75,300	–
	To Credit Sales (balancing figure)	78,000	–		By Discount	700	–
					By Bad Debts	800	–
					By Balance c/d	19,300	–
		96,100	–			96,100	–

Total Creditors Account
(to find out credit purchases)

		Rs.				Rs.	
1968 Dec.31	To Cash	35,000	—	1978 Jan. 1	By Balance b/d	11,000	—
	To Discount	400	—		By Credit Purchases (balancing figure)	36,900	—
	To Balance c/d	12,500	—				
		47,900	—			47,900	—

Balance Sheet on 1st Jan. 1978
(to find out Capital)

Liabilities	Rs.		*Assets*	Rs.	
Sundry Creditors	11,000	—	Cash	500	—
Capital (balancing figure)	51,600	—	Stock	15,000	—
			Sundry Debtors	18,100	—
			Machinery	25,000	—
			Furniture	4,000	—
	62,600	—		62,600	—

Trading and Profit and Loss Account of Bose for the year ended Dec. 31, 1978

		Rs.				Rs.
To Opening Stock		15,000	—	By Sales :		
To Purchases		36,900	—	Credit	78,000	
To Wages : Paid	16,000			Cash	6,100	
Add outstanding	2,000					84,100
		18,000	—	By Closing Stock		14,000
To Gross Profit c/d		28,200	—			
		98,100	—			98,100
To Salaries		15,000	—			
To Expenses :	11,000			By Gross Profit b/d		28,200
Less prepaid	125					
		10,875	—			
To Interest on Loan : 9% for 6 mos. on Rs. 10,000		450	—	By Miscellaneous Receipts		200
To Depreciation :				By Discount Received		400
Machinery	2,975			By Loss		2,200
Furniture	200					
		3,175	—			
To Discount allowed		700	—			
To Bad Debts		800	—			
		31,000	—			31,000

Balance Sheet of Bose as at December 31, 1978

Liabilities			Rs.		*Assets*		Rs.	
Sundry Creditors			12,500	—	***Fixed Assets :***			
Wages unpaid			2,000	—	Machinery			
Loan :		10,000			Balance on 1st Jan.,	25,000		
Add Interest unpaid		450	10,450	—	Addition	9,500		
Capital :		Rs.				34,500		
Balance on 1st Jan. 1968		51,600			Less Depreciation	2,975	31,525	—
Less. Loss	2 200				Furniture :			
Drawing	4,000	6,200	45,400	—	Balance on 1st Jan.	4,000		
					Less Dep.	200	3,800	—
					Current Assets :			
					Stock		14,000	—
					Debtors		19,300	—
					Cash		1,600	—
					Prepaid Insurance		125	—
			70,350	--			70,350	—

Note : Depreciation on machinery has been calculated as under :

	Rs.
10% on Rs. 35,000 for full year	2,500
10% on Rs. 9,500 for six months	475
	2,975

Illustration Surya does not keep a systematic record of his transactions. He is able to give you the following information regarding his assets and liabilities :—

	1977 Dec. 31	1978 Dec. 31
Creditors for goods	21,000	19,000
Creditors for expenses	1,500	1,800
Bills Payable	8,700	11.500
Sundry Debtors	35,000	34,000
Stock (at cost)	28,000	25,000
Furniture & fittings	10,000	12,000
Cash	5,100	?

The following additional information is also available relating to 1978 :—

	Rs.
Bills Payable Issued	20,800
Cash Sales	15,000
Payment to Sundry Creditors	31,000
Expenses paid	6,600
Drawings	8,000

Bad Debts during the year were Rs. 900. As regards sales, Surya tells you that he always sells goods at cost plus 25%. Furniture & fittings is to be depreciated at 10% of the value in the beginning of the year.

Prepare Surya's Trading and Profit and Loss Account for 1978 and his Balance Sheet as at the end of that year.

Solution :

Notes : Information about a number of items is missing and has to be ascertained. An obvious item is sales. Since sales are 25% above cost of goods sold, we must find the figure of cost of goods sold which is purchases plus stock in the beginning less stock at the end. Hence we must find what the purchases were. Therefore the following two accounts :

Sundry Creditors Account

		Rs.				Rs.	
1978	To Cash	31,000	—	1978 Jan. 1	By Balance b/d	21,000	—
	To Bills Payable, issued	20,800	—		By Purchases (balancing figure)	49,800	—
Dec. 31	To Balance c/d (as given)	19,000	—				
		70,800	—			70,800	—
				1979 Jan. 1	By Balance b/d	19,000	—

Bills Payable Account

		Rs.				Rs.	
1978	To Cash (balancing figure)	18,000	—	1978 Jan. 1	By Balance b/d	8,700	—
Dec. 31	To Balance b/d (as given)	11,500	—		By Sundry Creditors	20,800	—
		29,500	—			29,500	—
				1979 Jan. 1	By Balance b/d	11,500	—

Cost of Goods Sold & Credit Sales :	Rs.
Opening Stock	28,000
Add Purchases	49,800
	77,800
Less Closing Stock	25,000
Cost of Goods sold	52,800
Add Gross Profit @ 25%	13,200
Sales (Total)	66,000
Cash Sales	15,000
Credit Sales	51,000

(*ii*) We do not know the amount paid by Sundry Debtors. Their account will reveal this figure :

Sundry Debtors Account

		Rs.				Rs.	
1978 Jan. 1	To Balance b/d	35,000	—	1978	By Bad Debts	900	—
	To Credit Sales (See above),	51,000	—		By Cash (balancing figure)	51,100	—
				Dec. 31	By Balance c/d (as given)	34,000	—
		86,000	—			86,000	—
1979 Jan. 1	To Balance b/d	34,000	—				

(*iii*) The cash balance in hand on Dec. 31, 1978 is also not known. Therefore the summarised Cash Account :

Cash Account

		Rs.				Rs.	
	To Balance b/d	5,100	—		By Bills Payable (see Bills Payable A/c)	18,000	—
	To Cash Sales	15,000	—		By Sundry Creditors	31,000	—
	To Sundry Debtors	51,100	—		By Expenses	6,600	—
					By Furniture & Fittings*	2,000	—
					By Drawings	8,000	—
					By Balance c/d	5,600	—
		71,200	—			71,200	—

(*iv*) To ascertain capital on 31st Dec. 1977, the Balance Sheet as on that date is necessary.

Balance Sheet

	Rs.			Rs.	
Creditors for goods	21,000	—	Sundry Debtors	35,000	—
Creditors for Expenses	1,500	—	Stock	28,000	—
Bills Payable	8,700	—	Furniture & Fittings	10,000	—
Capital (balancing figure)	46,900	—	Cash	5,100	—
	78,100	—		78,100	—

*The increase in this asset must have been due to additional furniture purchased.

Now the final accounts can be prepared.

Trading and Profit and Loss Account of Surya

for the year ended December 31, 1978

		Rs.			Rs.
To Stock, opening		28,000	By Sales		66,000
To Purchases		49,800	By Closing Stock		25,000
To Gross Profit c/d		13,200			
		91,000			91,000
To Expenses :			By Gross Profit b/d		13,200
Paid	6,600				
Add due on 31/12	1,800				
	8,400				
Less due on 1/1	1,500	6,900			
To Bad Debts		900			
To Depreciation		1,000			
To Net Profit		4,400			
		13,200			13,200

Balance Sheet of Surya as at December 31, 1978

Liabilities		Rs.	*Assets*		Rs.
Creditors for goods		19,000	Furniture & Fittings	12,000	
Creditors for Expenses		1,800	Less Depreciation	1,000	11,000
Bills Payable		11,500	Stock, at cost		25,000
Capital :	Rs.		Sundry Debtors		34,000
As on 1/1/68	46,900		Cash		5,600
Add Profit	4,400				
	51,300				
Less Drawings	8,000	43,300			
		75,600			75,600

Illustration Mehta's Balance Sheet as on 31st December, 1977 was as follows :

Liabilities		Rs.	*Assets*	Rs.
Sundry Creditors		15,300	Cash	2,200
Loan @ 9%			Sundry Debtors	28,500
Principal	10,000		Bill Receivable	8,100
Interest due	300	10,300	Stock	24,700
Capital		84,200	Prepaid Expenses	300
			Machinery	40,000
			Furniture & Fittings	6,000
		1,09,800		1,09,800

Mehta inform you that his transactions during the year 1978 were :—

	Rs.		Rs.
Sales, credit	51,300	Expenses paid	9,300
Cash	9,600	Interest paid on Loan	750
Purchases	21.600	Drawings	3,000
Payment to Creditors	20,000	Machinery Purchased	10,000
Discount allowed by them	300	Wages paid	25,000
		Cash received :	
Discount allowed to customers	900	from Sundry Debtors	36,000
Bills Receivable dishonoured	1,500	Against Bills Receivable	13,000

The Bills Receivable on hand on 31st December 1978 totalled Rs. 7,800. Machinery is to be depreciated @ 10%. The closing stock valued at cost was Rs. 26,300, and expenses included insurance paid Rs. 900 for the year ended 30th June, 1979.

Prepare the Trading and Profit and Loss Account of Mehta for 1968 and his Balance Sheet at the end of it.

Solution :

The following accounts are prepared to ascertain missing items of information. The items are in italic :-

Sundry Creditors Account

		Rs.				Rs.	
1978	To Cash	20,000	—	1978			
	To Discount	300	—	Jan. 1	By Balance b/d	15,300	—
Dec. 31	*To Balance c/d*	*16,600*	—	1978	By Purchases	21,600	—
		36,900	—			36,900	—
				1979 Jan. 1	By Balance b/d	16,600	—

Bills Receivable Account

		Rs.				Rs.	
1968 Jan. 1	To Balance b/d	8,100	—	1968	By Cash	13,000	—
	To Sundary Debtors : Bills Received (balancing figure)	14,200	—		By Sundry Debtors : Bills Dishonoured	1,500	—
				Dec. 31	By Balance c/d	7,800	—
		22,300	—			22,300	—
1969 Jan. 1	To Balance b/d	7,800	—				

Sundry Debtors Account

		Rs.				Rs.	
1968 Jan. 1	To Balance b/d	28,500	—	1968	By Cash	36,000	—
	To Sales	51,300	—		By Discount	900	—
	To Bills Receivable, dishonoured	1,500	—		By Bills Receivable, received during the year	14,200	—
				Dec. 31	*By Balance c/d*	*30,200*	—
		81,300	—			81,300	—
1969 Jan. 1	To Balance b/d	30,200	—				

(Summarised) Cash Account

		Rs.				Rs.	
	To Balance b/d	2,200	—		By Sundry Creditors	20,000	—
	To Cash Sales	9,600	—		By Expenses	9,300	—
	To Sundry Debtors	36,000	—		By Interest	750	—
	To Bills Receivable	13,000	—		By Machinery	10,000	—
	To Balance c/d (Bank overdraft)	7,250	—		By Wages	25,000	—
					By Drawings	3,000	—
		68,050	—			68,050	—

Now the final accounts can be prepared.

Trading and Profit & Loss Account of Mehta for the year ended December 31, 1978

		Rs.			Rs.	
To Opening Stock		24,700	—	By Sales : Cash 9,600 Credit 51,300	60,900	—
To Purchases		21,600	—	By Closing Stock	26,300	—
To Wages		25,000	—			
To Gross Profit c/d		15,900	—			
		87,200	—		87,200	—
To Expenses : Paid	9,300			By Gross Profit	15,900	—
Add Prepaid on 1/1	300			By Discount received	300	—
	9,600					
*Less Prepaid on 31/12	450	9,150	—			
To Interest on Loan (9% for full year on Rs. 10,000)		900	—			
To Discount allowed		900	—			
To Depreciation*		4,500	—			
To Net Profit		750	—			
		16,200	—		16,200	—

*For one year on Rs. 40,000 and six months on Rs. 10,000.

Balance Sheet of Mehta on 31st December, 1978

Liabilities		Rs.		*Assets*		Rs.	
Bank Overdraft		7,250	—	Bills Receivable		7,800	—
Sundry Creditors		16,600		Sundry Debtors		30,200	—
Loan @ 9%				Stock		26,300	—
Principal	10,000			Prepaid Insurance		450	—
Interest	450	10,450	—	Machinery :			
				As on 1/1/68	40,000		
Capital :				Addition	10,000		
As on 1/1/68	84,200				50,000		
Add Profit	750		—	Less Depreciation	4,500		
	84,950						
Less Drawings	3,000	81,950	—			45,500	—
				Furniture & Fittings		6,000	—
		1,16,250	—			1,16,250	—

Illustration. Khan gives you some of the balances as per his records as on January 1, 1981 and 31st December, 1981:

	January 1, 1981	Dec. 31, 1981
	Rs.	Rs.
Cash and Bank Balances	4,500	3,650
Sundry Debtors	?	37,800
Sundry Creditors	19,600	21,700
Stock in trade	11,000	13,400
Furniture & fixtures	16,000	?
Expenses outstanding	4,100	5,300

He informs you that he always sells goods at a margin of 25% on Sales but one lot costing Rs.1,500 had to be sold for Rs.1,400 due to damage. The Cash Book summary, inter alia, showed the following items:

	Rs.		Rs.
Paid to Creditors	57,000	Received from Sundry Debtors	76,000
Paid for Expenses	20,300	Misc. Receipts	900
Paid for Furniture	2,500	Drawings	6,000
Cash Purchases	6,000		

Discounts allowed and received were Rs.650 and Rs.300.

Depreciation on Furniture was @ 10%.

Prepare Khan's Trading and Profit and Loss Account for 1981 and his Balance Sheet as at the end of that year.

Solution:

Notes : Again good deal of information is not available—it will have to be ascertained. Hence the following workings:

(1) To ascertain credit purchases :

Sundry Creditors Account

	Rs.		Rs.
To Cash	57,000	By Balance b/d	19,600
To Discount Received	300	By Purchases (balancing figure)	59,400
To Balance c/d	21,700		
	79,000		79,000

		Rs.
(2) Total Purchases:	Credit	59,400
	Cash	6,000
		65,400

(3) Cost of goods sold and Sales :

	Rs.
Purchases	65,400
Add Opening Stock	11,000
	76,400
Less Closing Stock	13,400
Cost of goods sold	63,000
Less: Item sold below cost	1,500
	61,500
Gross Profit @ 33 1/3% which is the same as 25% on Sales	20,500
	82,000
Add Sale below cost	1,400
	83,400

(4) Cash Sales :

Cash Book

	Rs.		Rs.
To Balance b/d	4,500	By Sundry Creditors	57,000
To Sundry Debtors	76,000	By Cash Purchases	6,000
To Misc. Receipts	900	By Expenses	20,300
To Cash Sales (balancing figure)	14,050	By Furniture	2,500
		By Drawings	6,000
		By Balance c/d	3,650
	95,450		95,450

(5) Credit Sales :

	Rs.
Total Sales	83,400
Less Cash Sales	14,050
	69,350

(6) Opening Balance of Sundry Debtors

Sundry Debtors Account

	Rs.		Rs.
To Balance b/d (balancing figure)	45,100	By Cash	76,000
		By Discount	650
To Credit Sales	69,350	By Balance c/d	37,800
	1,14,450		1,14,450

(7) **Opening balance of capital**

Balance Sheet

	Rs.		Rs.
Sundry Creditors	19,600	Cash & Bank Balance	4,500
Expenses Outstanding	4,100	Sundry Debtors	45,100
Capital	52,900	Stock in Trade	11,000
(Balancing figure)		Furniture & Fixtures	16,000
	76,600		76,600

Trading and Profit and Loss Account of Khan for the year ended 31st December, 1981

	Rs.		Rs.
To Opening Stock	11,000	By Sales	83,400
To Purchases	65,400	By Closing Stock	13,400
To Gross Profit c/d	20,400		
	96,800		96,800
To Expenses	21,500	By Gross Profit b/d	20,400
To Depreciation	1,725*	By Discount Received	300
To Discount allowed	650	By Misc. Receipts	900
		By Loss	2,275
	23,875		23,875

Balance Sheet of Khan as at 31st December, 1981

Liabilities		Rs.	*Assets*		Rs.
Capital:			Cash & Bank Balances		3,650
As on Jan., 1, 1980		52,900	Stock in Trade		13,400
Less: Drawings	6,000		Sundry Debtors		37,800
Loss	2,275	8,275	Furniture		
		44,625	As on 1, Jan., 1981	16,000	
Sundry Creditors		21,700	Addition during the year	2,500	
				18,500	
Expenses Outstanding		5,300	*Less* Depreciation	1,725	16,775
		71,625		(625)	71,625

*On the addition, depreciation has been allowed for half year on the assumption that the purchase was made in the middle of the year.

1. Murty started a firm on 1st January, 1978 with a capital of Rs. 8,000 On 1st April, 1978, he borrowed from his wife a sum of Rs. 4,000 @ 9% p.a. On 31st December, 1978 his assets and liabilities (besides the above) were :

	Rs.
Cash	600
Stock	9,400
Sundry Debtors	7,100
Sundry Creditors	4,200

Ascertain the profit or loss of Murty during 1978. Murty had drawn Rs. 2,500 for his domestic use. *(Profit, Rs. 3,130)*

2. Ali keeps his books by Single Entry. He gives you the following information from which he requires you to ascertain his profit or loss during 1968 :

	1st January, 1978 Rs.	31st Dec. 1978 Rs.
Bank Balance	740 (Cr.)	400 (Dr.)
Cash in hand	...	10
Sundry Debtors	5,300	8,800
Sundry Creditors	1,500	1,950
Stock	1,700	1,900
Plant	2,000	2,000
Furniture	140	140

Ali had withdrawn Rs. 3,000 during the year but had introduced fresh capital of Rs. 600 on 1st July, 1978. A provision of 5% on Sundry Debtors is necessary. Write off depreciation on Plant @ 5%. Interest on capital is to be allowed @ 5% p.a. *(Profit after interest on capital, Rs. 5,900)*

3. Akbar did not keep proper books of account. However, he gives you the following information relating to 1977 :—

Assets and Liabilities :

	1st January 1977 Rs.	31st December, 1977 Rs.
Cash at Bank	1,000	1,800
Stock	20,000	19,500
Sundry Debtors	15,000	16,000
Machinery	40,000	
Sundry Creditors	20,000	18,500

Summary of Cash Transactions :

Receipts	Rs.	*Payments*	Rs.
Opening Balance	1,000	Payment to Creditors	35,000
Received from Debtors	76,500	Wages	15,100
Cash Sales	8,200	Salaries and Expenses	11,600
Sale of old newspapers	200	Building Purchased	20,000
Loan from Mrs. Akbar		Drawings	8,400
(@ 9% on 1st Oct. 1967)	6,000	Closing Balance	1,800
	91,900		91,900

During the year Rs. 600 had to be written off as bad. Machinery is to be depreciated @ 15% p.a. Expenses owing are Rs. 800.

Prepare Akbar's Trading and Profit and Loss Account and Balance Sheet relating to 1977.

(Gross Profit, Rs. 37,200; Net Profit, Rs. 18,265; Total of Balance Sheet, Rs. 91,300).

4. Mohan's books, kept on the Single Entry System, reveal the following :—

Assets nad Liabilities :	1st July, 1976	30th June, 1977
	Rs.	Rs.
Stock	18;000	17,300
Debtors	16,000	14,800
Bills Receivable	6,200	4,800
Bills Payable	5,000	5,600
Sundry Creditors	10,000	9,300
Cash at Bank	2,500	1,800

Summary of Cash Transactions

Receipts	Rs.	*Payments*	Rs.
Opening Balance	2,500	Payment to Creditors	20,000
Received from Debtors	35,000	Payment against Bills Payable	15,000
Received against Bills Receivable	15,600	Office Expenses	6,000
Miscellaneous	300	Domestic Expenses	4,000
		Investments	6,600
		Closing Balance	1,800
	53,400		53,400

Investments consisted of 4% Government Bonds of the face value of Rs. 8,000 and were purchased on 1st Jan., 1977. Prepare Trading and Profit and Loss Account and Balance Sheet from the above figures.

(*Gross Profit, Rs. 12,400*; *Net Profit, Rs. 6,860*; *Total of Balance Sheet, Rs. 45,460*)

[Hint : Prepare Bills Receivable and Bills Payable Accounts. This will reveal Bills Receivable received (which should be credited to Debtors) and Bills Payable issued to be debited to creditors).

5. The Balance Sheet of Bose and Dass was as under on 31st Dec. 1977: —

Liabilities		Rs.	*Assets*	Rs.
Sundry Creditors		11,600	Stock	15,000
Bills Payable		4,300	Debtors	16,100
Capitals :				
Bose	20,000		Furniture	4,000
Dass	15,000	35,000	Delivery Van	13,000
			Cash at Bank	2,800
		50,900		50,900

The transactions during 1978 were :

	Rs.		Rs.
Purchases	30 000	Bills Payable Issued	7,000
Sales	50,000	Discount Received	500
Bills Receivable received	6,000	Discount allowed	800

The stock on 31st Dec., 1978 was Rs. 18,200. Cash transactions were as follows :

	Rs.
Received from Debtors	45,000
Received against B/R	4,500
Received from sale of old gunny bags	200
Payment to Creditors	21,500
Payment against B/P	8,000
Expenses (including salaries)	10,000

The Balance at Bank on 31st Dec. 1978 was Rs. 4,500. Delivery van is to be depreciated @ 15%. During the year both partners had withdrawn an equal sum of money. Allowing a commission of 10% of net profits to the manager, prepare Trading and Profit and Loss Account and Balance Sheet relating to 1968.

(Gross Profit, Rs. 23,200; Net Profit, Rs. 10,035; Total of Balance Sheet Rs. 53,550)

[Hint : Prepare Cash Book and accounts relating to Sundry Debtors Sundry Creditors, Bills Receivable and Bills Payable. The difference in the Cash Book may be treated as drawings.]

6. The Balance Sheet of Kye, Tai and Chung on 31st December, 1967 was as follows :—

Balance Sheet as at 31st December, 1977

		Rs.			Rs.
Sundry Creditors		25,300	Cash		5,400
Expenses Payable		800	Stock at Cost		41,000
Loan from Tai		10,000	Sundry Debtors		27,900
Capitals :	Rs.		Furniture & Fixtures		6,100
Kye	20,000		Current Assets :		
Tai	15,000		Kye	1,500	
Chung	10,000	45,000	Chung	1,100	2,600
Tai's Current Account		1,900			
		83.000			83,000

Profits were shared by the partners in the ratio of Kye 4/10, Tai 3/10 and Chung 3/10. On 31st December, 1978 the various assets and liabilities of the firm were as follows :

	Rs.		Rs.
Cash	4,700	Sundry Creditors	27,000
Stock	45,200	Expenses Prepaid	240
Sundry Debtors	31,400	Loan from Tai	10,000
Furniture & Fixtures	5,660		

The partners had drawn : Rs. 6,000 by Kye, Rs. 5,000 by Tai and Rs. 4,000 by Chung. Prepare the Balance Sheet of the firm at the end of 1978.

(Current Accounts : Kye Rs. 620 (Cr.); Tai Rs. 3,590 (Cr.) and Chung Rs. 990 (Cr.); Total of Balance Sheet, Rs. 87,200)

7. Desai wants to ascertain the profit he earned during 1968 and his balance sheet at the end of the year. He does not keep systematic books of

account and can give you only the following information :—

(*i*) *Assets and Liabilities* :

	Dec. 31, 1967	Dec. 31, 1968
	Rs.	Rs.
Sundry Debtors	45,000	48,600
Sundry Creditors	24,000	?
Cash	6,300	?
Furniture and Fixtures	11,000	13,600
Stock at cost	25,000	30,000

(*ii*) *Transactions during 1968* :

	Rs.
Cash received from Debtors	80,000
Discount allowed to them	1,400
Bad Debts written off	1,800
Cash paid to creditors	64,000
Goods returned by customers	3,000
Goods returned to suppliers	2,000
Expenses paid	5,200
Drawings	9,000

He still owes Rs. 800 for expenses and the depreciation on furniture & Fixtures is @ 5%. He affirms that he always sells goods at cost plus 40%. A provision of 2½% on debtors is required against bad debts. Help Desai.

(*Gross Profit, Rs. 24,800; Net Profit, Rs. 13,770; Total of Balance Sheet, Rs. 95,870*)

[Hint : First ascertain net sales (*i.e.* total sales less returns) by preparing Sundry Debtors Account. Then find out cost of goods sold—gross profit is 40/140 of sales. Purchases made will be. Cost of goods sold and closing stock less opening stock. Prepare account for Sundry Creditors and Cash.]

8. Sethi had declared an income of Rs. 26,000 during 1967 and 1968. The Income Tax Officer thinks that Sethi has not disclosed his income fully. He asks for your assistance to find out whether his impression is correct.

Sethi owned, on December 31, 1966, a dwelling house valued at Rs. 50,000 and had in his firm, a capital of Rs. 60,000. He also had Rs. 5,000 in his (private) Savings Bank Account. He owed Rs. 10,000 to his brother.

It is established that besides the dwelling house, Sethi's assets and liabilities on 31st December, 1968 were :

	Rs.
Cash at Bank (firm's)	1,700
Savings Bank Account, private	7,800
Stock	25,000
Sundry Debtors	35,000
Furniture & Fixtures	6,000
Motor Car	16,000
Sundry Creditors	20,000
Expenses Payable	600

The loan to his brother is no longer outstanding. His living expenses have been @ Rs. 1,000 p.m. Besides, he reported that he had made a gift of Rs. 1,500 to his niece on her marriage.

What advice will you give to the Income Tax Officer ?

(*Sethi's total income for the two years was Rs. 40,400*)

[Hint : Compare Sethi's total wealth on 31st Dec. 1968 and 31st Dec. 1966; make adjustment for drawings.]

9. A new trader who commenced business on 1st July, 1980 with a capital of Rs. 50,000 (out of which Rs. 10,000 had been borrowed @ 20%) reported that he had the following assets and liabilities on 30th June, 1981 :—

	Rs.
Bank Balance as per Pass Book	4,500
Sundry Debtors	26,700
Stock in trade at selling price which is cost plus 25%	40,000
Furniture & Fixed (cost as on 1st July, 1980 ; estimated life 10 years)	10,000
Creditors for goods and expenses	15,000

You find that a customer had paid Rs. 1,500 directly into the bank which was not yet recorded in the trader's books ; also a cheque for rent, Rs. 800, was issued in June 1981 but it had not yet been presented for payment. Household drawings totalled Rs. 15,000. No payment was made to the loan creditors whatever.

Ascertain the profit earned or loss suffered by the trader during the year

(Profit Rs. 17,900)

10. A small trader does not maintain proper books of account From the following information, prepare Trading and Profit and Loss Account for the year ended 31st Dec., 1977 and a Balance Sheet, as on that date.

	on 31-12-1976	*on 31-12-1977*
	Rs.	Rs.
Debtors	9.000	12,500
Stock	4,900	6,600
Furniture	500	750
Creditors	3,000	2,250

Analysis of other transactions are :

	Rs.
Cash Collected from Debtors	30,400
Cash Paid to Creditors	22,000
Salaries	6,000
Rent	750
Office Expenses	900
Drawings	1.500
Fresh Capital Introduced	1,000
Cash Sales	750
Cash Purchases	2 500
Discount Received	350
Discount Allowed	150
Returns Inwards	500
Returns Outwards	400
Bad Debts	100
New Furniture Purchased	250

He had Rs. 2,500 cash at the beginning of the year.

(B. Com Pass Delhi)

[Gross Profit, Rs. 12,500 ; N.P. Rs. 4,950 ; Total of B/s Rs. 20.600]

CHAPTER XVIII

ACCOUNTS OF NON-PROFIT ORGANISATIONS

(Receipts and Payments Account, Income and Expenditure Account and Balance Sheet)

There is really nothing special about the accounts of non-profit organisations such as hospitals, schools, clubs, etc., except that often they do not keep a full set of books and do not extract a trial balance from their books. If they do keep the usual books of account and prepare a trial balance at the end of the year, they can easily present their final accounts as already shown.

However, usually they maintain a Cash Book only and, on the basis of entries made in it, prepare a summary of the cash transactions. When presented in an account form, this summary is called Receipts and Payments Account.

Features of the Receipts and Payments Account. This account has the undermentioned features :—

(*a*) The account starts with the opening balance of cash in hand and at bank.

(*b*) All receipts, irrespective of the period to which the transaction may pertain and of nature (whether it is revenue or capital) are entered. The account will, for instance, contain both cash received on account of tuition fees and on sale of an asset. There will be an entry even if the tuition fee relates to the previous year or the next year.

(*c*) All payments, irrespective of nature and period, are entered in this account.

(*d*) Only actual receipts and payments are entered.

(*e*) The balance in the account will show closing balance on hand (including cash in hand and at bank).

The following is a specimen :

Receipts and Payments Account of the Delhi Cricket Club for the year ended Dec. 31, 1978

Receipts		Rs.	Payments	Rs.
To Opening Balances :				
On hand		700	By Rent	2,000
At Bank		9,700	By Upkeep of Grounds	3,000
To Subscriptions :			By Materials Purchased	4 000
1967	500		By Salaries	8,000
1968	15,000		By Office Expenses	1,800
1969	800		By Land Purchased	15,000
		16,300	By Closing Balances :	
To Entrance Fees		1,000	In hand	400
To Donation for Pavilion		5,000	At Bank	5,000
To Sale of old sports materials		1,500		
To Investments realised		5,000		
		39,200		39,200

By itself the Receipts and Payments Account does not indicate the financial position of the institution since a large cash balance can result from the sale of an asset; the balance will quickly disappear if current expenses exceed current income. For the purpose of knowing the financial position of the institution, it is necessary to compare *current expenses* with *current incomes* and to compile assets and liabilities. For this, what is required is Income and Expenditure Account and Balance Sheet.

The Income and Expenditure Account has the following characteristics :--

(i) It is concerned with only revenue items—expenses and incomes. If a school pays Rs. 25,000 for a cinema projector, it will not be entered in the Income and Expenditure Account; it is an asset and will appear in the Balance Sheet. Salaries, Stationery used, etc., will figure in the Income and Expenditure Account.

(ii) It does not start with any opening balance. This is because the purpose of preparing the Income and Expenditure Account is to ascertain the revenue deficit or surplus for the year concerned; previous year's deficit or surplus is not relevant for this year's Income and Expenditure Account.

(iii) Expenses and income are so adjusted as to:

(*a*) exclude figures relating to previous or future years; and,

(*b*) include all figures relating to the current year, even if the items are not fully settled in cash.

Suppose salaries actually paid this year amount to Rs. 83,000 but, of these, Rs. 6,000 relate to the previous year. Only Rs. 77,000 will be debited to the Income and Expenditure Account. But if Rs. 4,000 are still payable for the current year, the amount will be increased to Rs. 81,000. To take another example, suppose subscriptions, Rs. 1,23,000, received actually include Rs. 5,000 for the next year and Rs. 8,000 for the previous year. Both these amounts will be deducted from Rs. 1,23,000 and only Rs. 1,10,000 will be credited to the Income and Expenditure Account. (See below for another illustration).

(iv) The difference between two sides of the Income and Expenditure Account is either surplus (showing that revenue income exceeds the revenue of expenses) or deficit (showing that the total of revenue expenses is more than the total of incomes). Surplus or deficit should not be confused with cash balance in hand.

(v) The surplus or deficit affects the capital fund at the disposal of the institution : surplus increases it and deficit reduces it.

To give a complete picture, the Income and Expenditure Account should be accompanied by the Balance Sheet. The careful student will have noted remarkable similarity between Profit and Loss Account and the Income and Expenditure Account. The principles involved are the same; only, the former is prepared by business houses and the latter by non-profit organisations, like schools, clubs, ete.

The treatment of items received (or paid) in advance or still not received (or remaining unpaid) is important and is again taken up below.

Suppose during 1968 actal subscriptions received as Rs. 21,000. These include Rs. 800 for 1977 and Rs. 300 for 1979. Also Rs. 1,500 have still to be received for 1968. Then the amount to be entered in the Income and Expenditure Account in respect of subscriptions is Rs. 21,400. Thus—

		Rs.
Amount received		21,000
Add Outstanding on 31st Dec., 1978		1,500
	Rs.	22.500
Less : Received on account of 1977	8C0	
Received on account of 1979	300	1,100
		21,400

The entry for outstanding subscriptions for 1978 will be passed on 31st Dec., 1978. Thus*—

		Rs.	Rs.
Subscriptions Outstanding Account	Dr.	1,500	
To Subscriptions Account			1,500

*The student should supply narrations.

For subscriptions received in advance (on account of 1979) the entry is :

Subscriptions Account	Dr.	300	
To Subscriptions Received in Advance A/c			300

At the end of 1977 an entry must have been passed for subscriptions outstanding, as shown above. Subscriptions Outstanding Account must have shown a debit balance. *This year* it will be closed by transfer to the Subscriptions Account. The entry is :

Subscriptions Account	Dr.	800	
To Subscriptions Outstandings Account			800

The various accounts will appear as under :

Subscription Outstandings Account

		Rs.			Rs.
1978 Jan. 1	To Balance b/d	800	1978 Dec. 31	By Subscriptions A/c—transfer	800
Dec. 31	To Subscriptions A/c	1,500	"	By Balance c/d	1,500
1979 Jan. 1	To Balance b/d	1,500			

Subscriptions Accounts

		Rs.			Rs.
1978 Dec. 31	To Subscriptions Outstanding A/c—transfer	800	1978 Dec. 31	By Cash	21,000
Dec. 31	To Subscriptions Received in Advance A/c	300	"	By Subscriptions Outstanding Account	1,500
"	To Transfer to Income and Expenditure Account	21,400			
		22,500			22,500

Subscription Received in Advance Account

		Rs.			Rs.
1978 Dec. 31	To Balance c/d	300	1978 Dec. 31	By Subscriptions A/c	300
			1979 Jan. 1	By Balance b/d	300

Subscriptions Outstanding, Rs. 1,500, and Subscriptions Received in Advance, Rs. 300, will be shown in the Balance Sheet on the assets and liabilities sides respectively. Next year these will be transferred to the Subscriptions Account.

Similar treatment is necessary for expenses. Suppose expenses paid during 1978 were Rs. 11,500. The following further information is available.

	Rs.
Expenses unpaid on 31st Dec., 1977	700
Expenses prepaid on ,, ,, ,,	200
Expenses ,, ,, ,, 1978	300
Expenses unpaid on ,, ,, ,,	900

In respect of expenses unpaid and prepaid on 31st Dec., 1977 there must be opening balances—the unpaid expenses account showing a credit balance and the prepaid expenses account showing a debit balance. First, these accounts will be transferred to Expenses Account. The entries are (without narration) :

		Rs.	Rs.
Expenses Account	Dr.	200	
To Expenses Prepaid Account			200
Expenses Outstanding Account	Dr.	700	
To Expenses Account			700

The entries to record outstanding and prepaid expenses on 31st Dec., 1978 are :

		Rs.	Rs.
Expenses Account	Dr.	900	
To Expenses Outstanding Account			900
Prepaid Expenses Account	Dr.	300	
To Expenses Account			300

Expenses Outstanding Accounts is a liability and Prepaid Expenses Account is an asset.

The relevant accounts will be as follows :—

Expenses Account

Dr.					*Cr.*
1978		Rs.	1978		Rs.
Dec. 31	To Cash	11,500 —	Dec. 31	By Expenses Outstanding A/c (1967)	700 —
„	To Expenses Prepaid Account (1967)	200 —	„	By Expenses Prepaid A/c (1969)	300 —
„	To Expenses Outstanding A/c (1969)	900 —	„	By Transfer to Income and Expenditure Account	11,600 —
		12,600 —			12,600 —

Expenses Outstanding Account

1978		Rs.	1978		Rs.
Dec. 31	To Expenses A/c—transfer	700 —	Jan. 1	By Balance b/d	700 —
„	To Balance c/d	900 —	Dec. 31	By Expenses A/c	900 —
			1969		
			Jan. 1	By Balance b/d	900 —

Expenses Prepaid Account

1978		Rs.	1978		Rs.
Jan. 1	To Balance b/d	200 —	Dec. 31	By Expenses A/c transfer	200 —
Dec. 31	To Expenses A/c	300 —	„	By Balance c/d	300 —
1969					
Jan. 1	To Balance d/d	300 —			

Besides the above, the following points should be remembered while preparing Income and Expenditure Account :

(*a*) Receipts of non-recurring nature (*e.g.*, life memberships) should be added to the capital fund and not credited to the Income and Expenditure Account.

(*b*) Entrance fees may be credited to this account. If the amount of entrance fee is large, considering the annual subscription, it means the entrance fee is meant as a capital receipt. In that case entrance fees should be added to the capital fund directly and not credited to the Income and Expenditure Account.

(*c*) Depreciation on various assets should be provided.

(*d*) Donatious and receipts for special purposes should not be credited to the Income and Expenditure Account ; these should be credited to special accounts ; the balances of these accounts will appear in the balance sheet. Any income from moneys thus received, is also credited to the concerned accounts (and not to the Income and Expenditure Account): similarly any expenditure for the particular purpose is debited to the concerned account (and not to the Income and Expenditure Account). Examples :

(*i*) Donation received for instituting a prize. The amount should be credited to the Prize Fund Account. Interest received on investment of the money is also credited to the Prize Fund Account and the cost of the prize or prizes is debited to this account, the balance in this account appearing in the balance sheet.

(*ii*) Endowment (or donation) received for conducting a tournament. The treatment is similar to (*i*) above.

(*iii*) Endowment for a building. The amount received is credited to Building Fund Account ; any interest received on the investment of the amount is also credited to the Building Fund Account. On construction of the building, of course Building Account will be debited.

Donations meant for meeting day to day expenses or costs should be credited to the Income and Expenditure Account. Suppose a school receives a donation or a grant for its running expenses: the amount will be credited to the Income and Expenditure Account. But a grant received, say for setting up a laboratory in the school, will be credited to Laboratory Fund Account.

(*e*) The account reveals 'deficit' (if the debit side is bigger) or 'surplus' (if the credit side is bigger). Surplus is added to the capital fund and deficit is deducted.

Preparation of Balance Sheet. In absence of a trial balance, the points to be noted for preparing the balance sheet are as follows :—

(*a*) Assets appearing in the previous balance sheet should be adjusted for (*a*) additions, (*b*) sale and (*c*) depreciation during the year.

(*b*) New assets acquired (for which payment must have been entered on the credit side of the Receipts and Payments Account) will be entered in the Balance Sheet. This also applies to new liabilities incurred, *e.g.*, loans taken. The debit side of the Receipts and Payments Account will show this.

(*c*) Oustanding and prepaid expenses, subscriptions, etc. will be shown in the Balance Sheet. This also applies to incomes received in advance.

(*d*) The closing balances of cash on hand or at bank (as shown by the Receipts and Payments Account) will be entered in the Balance Sheet.

(*e*) Previous year's liabilities should be adjusted for payments made.

(*f*) Special receipts (as shown by the Receipts and Payments Account) will be shown in the Balance Sheet.

(*g*) Capital fund (as disclosed by the previous Balance Sheet) should be adjusted for surplus or deficit and then shown in the Balance Sheet. Capital fund at any date can be ascertained by deducting liabilities from assets.

Illustration The South Sports Club gives you the following Receipts and Payments Account for the year ended 31st December, 1978 :

Receipts	Rs.	*Payments*	Rs.
Cash in hand	150	Grounds men's Fees	1,500
Cash at Bank	2,100	Mowing Machine	1,100
Subscriptions	5,800	Rent	500
Tournament Fund	1,500	Salaries to coaches	3,600
Life Memberships	2,000	Tournament Expenses	900
Entrance Fees	200	Office Expenses, postage etc.	2,400
Donations for Pavilion	3,000	Sports Equipment Purchased	1,200
Sale of grass	100	Cash in hand	350
		Cash at Bank	3,300
	14,850		14,850

Subscriptions due on 31st December, 1977 and on 31st December, 1978 were Rs. 900 and Rs. 800 respectively. Subscriptions received also include subscription for 1979, Rs. 200. Sports Equipment on hand on 31st December, 1977 was Rs. 1,100. The value placed on the equipment on hand on 31st December, 1978 was Rs. 1,300. The mowing machine was purchased on 1st July, 1978 and is to be depreciated @ 20% p.a. Office Expenses include Rs. 300 for 1977 and Rs. 400 are still due for payment. Tournament receipts and expenses are to be separated from general incomes and expenses.

The South Sports Club

Income and Expenditure Account for the year ended Dec. 31, 1978

Expenses		Rs.	*Income*		Rs.
To Groundsmen's Fees		1,500 —	By Subscriptions :		
To Rent		500 —	Received :	5,800	
To Salaries to Coaches		3,600 —	Add Outstanding	800	
To Office Expenses :				6,600	
Paid	2 ,400		Less Received for 1967	900	
Less for 1967	300			5,700	
	2,100		Received for 1969	200	5,500 —
Add more for 1968	400	2,500 —	By Entrance Fees		200 —
To Sports Equipment—Depreciation*		1,000 —	By Sale of grass		100 —
To Mowing Maching—Depreciation		110 —	By Deficit—transferred to Capital Fund		3,410 —
		9,210 —			9,210 —

Balance Sheet as at 31st Dec. 1978

		Rs.			Rs.
Expenses Outstanding		400 —	Cash in hand		350 —
Subscriptions Received in Advance		200 —	Cash at Bank		3,300 —
Tournament Fund :			Sports Equipment		1,300 —
Received	1,500		Subscriptions Outstanding		800 —
Spent	900	600 —	Mowing Machine :	1,100	
Donation for Pavilion		3,000 —	Less Depreciation	110	990 —
Capital Fund :					
Balance on 1st Jan., 1968	3,950				
Add Life Memberships	2,000				
	5,950				
Less Deficit	3,410	2,540 —			
		6,740 —			6,740 —

*Rs. 1,200 added to Rs. 1,100 (the opening balance) is Rs. 2,300. The value of equipment on hand is Rs. 1,300, Rs. 1,000, must be the depreciation

Prepare Income and Expenditure Account and Balance Sheet relating to 1978.

Solution : First the Balance Sheet for 1977 should be prepared to ascertain Capital Fund on 31st December, 1977. Thus—

Liabilities	Rs.	*Assets*	Rs.
Office Expenses Due	300	Cash in hand	150
Capital Fund		Cash at Bank	2,100
(balancing figure)	3,950	Subscriptions Due	900
		Sports Equipment	1,100
	4,250		4,250

Illustration The following is the Trial Balance as at 31st December, 1978, of the Delhi Education Society :—

Debit Balances		Rs.	*Credit Balances*	Rs.
Cash in hand		500	Capital Fund	45,600
Cash at Bank—Current Account		2,100	Subscriptions Received :	
Fixed Deposit @ 6%		10,000	1977	2,400
Government Securities :			1978	32,300
Prize Fund	10,000		1979	1,700
Others	40,000	50,000	Grants from Government	24,000
Scholarships awarded		48,000	Prize Fund	10,000
Prizes awarded		300	Interest on Government Securities	2,000
Salaries		9,100	Life Memberships Received	6,000
Rent		2,100	Entrance Fees	500
Miscellaneous Expenses		1,900	Salaries Outstanding 1st Jan., 1978	1,500
Stationery on hand		500	Subscriptions Received in advance 1st Jan. 1978	600
Subscriptions Outstanding, 1st Jan., 1978		2,100		
		1,26,600		1,26,600

Subscriptions still receivable for 1978 total Rs. 3,600. Salaries due but not yet paid totalled Rs. 1,300 on 31st Dec., 1978. Rs. 2,100 are still payable for scholarships for 1978. The Fixed Deposit was made on October 1, 1978.

Prepare the Society's Income and Expenditure Account for 1978 and the accompanying Balance Sheet.

Solution :

The Delhi Education Society
Income and expenditure Account for the year ended December 31, 1978.

Expenditure	Rs.	*Income*	Rs.
To Scholarships awarded	50,100	By Subscriptions	36,800
To Salaries	8,900	By Grant from Government	24,000
To Rent	2,100	By Interest	1,750
To Miscellaneous Expenses	1,900	By Deficit, excess of expenditure over income	450
	63,000		63,000

Balance Sheet of the Delhi Education Society as at December 31, 1978.

Liabilities		Rs.	*Assets*		Rs.
Scholarships Payable		2,100	Cash in hand		500
Subscriptions Received in Advance		1,700	Cash at Bank, current Account		2,100
Salaries Outstanding		1.300	Fixed Deposit at Bank		10,000
Prize Fund :	10,000		Interest accrued on above		150
Interest	400				
	10,400				
Less Prizes	300	10,100	Government Securities :		
Capital Fund :	45,600		Prize Fund	10,000	
Add : Life Memberships	6,000		Others	40,000	50,000
Entrance Fees	500		Subscriptions : Outstanding		3,600
	52,100				
Less Deficit	450	51,650	Stationery on hand		500
		66,850			66,850

Notes : (i) Subscriptions have been calculated as shown below :

	Rs.
Received for 1978	32,300
Still receivable	3,600
Received in 1977 in respect of 1978	600
Excess of 1977 subscriptions received over the figure appearing in books (Rs 2,400 less Rs. 2,100)	300
	36,800

(ii) Salaries have been put at Rs. 8,900 since out of Rs. 9,100, the trial balance figure, Rs. 1,500 pertains to 1967 and Rs. 1,300 is still payable.

(iii) Interest received :

Total Interest on Rs. 50,000 is Rs. 2,000 or 4%. This means that Rs. 400 is for Prize Fund and Rs. 1,600 is on general investments. To Rs. 1,600 should be added 3 months' interest accrued on the Fixed Deposit.

Illustration The Bombay Sports Club has prepared the undermentioned accounts :

(i) Income and Expediture Account for 1978

	Rs.			Rs.
To Salaries	1,500	By Subscriptions		15,600
To Printing and Stationery	2,200	By Rents		4,000
		By Sale of Old Sports Equipment (book value Rs. 1,100)		700
To Advertising	1,600			
To Audit Fees	500	By Tournament Reciepts	15,000	
		Less Expenses	13,100	
				1,900
To Life Insurance	1,000			
To Depreciation on Sports Equipment	9,000			
To Surplus	6,400			
	22,200			22,200

(ii) Receipts and Payments Accounts for 1978

		Rs.		Rs.
To Balance b/d		4,200	By Salaries	1,000
To Life Memberships		10,500	By Sports Equipment	11,100
To Tournament Receipts		14,600	By Printing and Stationery	2,600
To Subscriptions :			By Advertising	1,600
1977	600		By Fire Insurance	1,200
1978	15,000		By Tournament Expenses	10,300
1979	400			
		16,000		
To Rent Received		3,000	By Investments (made on 31.12.68)	20,000
To Sale of Old Equipment		1,800	By Balance c/d	2,300
		50,100		50,100

The club owned on Jan. 1, 1978 a pavilion valued at Rs. 25,000 Sports Equipment valued at Rs. 20,000 and furniture valued at Rs. 2,000.

Prepare the Balance Sheet as at 31st December, 1978.

Solution :

Notes : (i) First the Balance Sheet as on 31st December, 1977 should be prepared to ascertain the capital fund on that date. Hence:

Balance Sheet as at December, 1977

	Rs.		Rs.
Printing and Stationery Payable*	400	Subscriptions Outstanding	600
		Cash	4,200
Capital Fund (balancing figure)	51,400	Pavilion	25,000
		Sports Equipment	20,000
		Furniture	2,000
	51,800		51,800

* Amount paid is Rs. 2,600 whereas the amount pertaining to 1968 (as per Income and Expenditure Account) is Rs. 2,200. Since Stationery bills are usually paid after stationery is received, the difference of Rs. 400 must be for 1977.

(ii) The amount outstanding for subscriptions for 1978 :

	Rs.
Full amount for 1978	15,600
Less Received (as per Receipts & Payments Account)	15,000
	600

	Rs.
(iii) **Fire Insurance :**	
Amount paid	1,200
Amount relating to 1978	1,000
Amount prepaid	200

		Rs.
(iv) **Sports Equipment :**		
Amount as on 1st Jan., 1978		20,000
Add Purchased during the year		11,100
		31,100
Less . Book Value of equipment sold	1,100	
Depreciation written off	9,000	10,100
		21,000

(v) Tournament Receipts Still receivable Rs. 400 i.e., Rs. 15,000—Rs. 14,600.

(vi) Tournament Expenses Still Payable Rs. 2,800 i.e., Rs. 13,100—Rs. 10,300.

(vii) Rent Receivable Rs. 1,000, i.e., Rs. 4,000 less Rs. 3,000.

Now the Balance Sheet can be prepared.

Balance Sheet of the Bombay Sports Club
as at December 31, 1978

Liabilities		Rs.	*Assets*	Rs.
Expenses Payable :	Rs.		Cash	2,300
Tournament	2,800		Investments	20,000
Salaries	500			
Audit Fees	500	3,800	Subscriptions Outstanding	600
Subscriptions Received in Advance		400	Pavilion	25,000
			Furniture	2,000
Capital Fund :			Sports Equipment	21,000
Balance on 1st Jan.,	51,400		Prepaid Insurance	200
Add :			Rent Receivable	1,000
Life Memberships	10,500		Tournament Receipts Due	400
Surplus	6,400	68,300		
		72,500		72,500

Illustration The Charitable Dispensary of Agra had the following Balance Sheet on 31st December 1978.

Balance Sheet as at December 31, 1978

		Rs.		Rs.
Salaries Payable		3,000	Cash	1,500
Subscriptions Received in Advance		500	Equipment	8,000
			Stock of Medicines	1,600
			Furniture and Fittings	6,000
Capital Fund :				
As on 1st Jan., 1977	11,200		Subscriptions, Due and Receivable	2,000
Add : Life Memberships	2,500			
Surplus	1,900	15,600		
		19,100		19,100

The accompanying Income and Expenditure Account was the following :—

Income and Expenditure Account for 1978

	Rs.		Rs.
To Salaries	35,000	By Entrance Fees	300
To Cost of Medicines used	6,700	By Subscriptions	36,100
To Depreciation of equipment	600	By Miscellaneous Receipts	150
To Miscellaneous Expenses	1,500	By Profit on Sale of Old Furniture (Book value Rs. 1,500)	200
To Surplus	1,900	By Grant from Municipal Corporation	8,950
	45,700		45,700

You learn that on 31st December, 1977 equipment stood at Rs. 6,000; subscriptions due and receivable totalled Rs. 2,500 whereas subscriptions already received for 1978 were Rs. 700. Stock of medicines on December 31, 1978 was Rs. 1,100.

Prepare the Receipts and Payments Account of the Dispensary for 1978.

Solution :

Notes : (i) The figure for subscriptions has been calculated as follows ;—

			Rs.
Subscriptions as per Income & Exp. A/c			36,100
Add : Subscriptions for 1977 (received in 1968)			2,500
,, ,, 1979 (,, ,,)			500
			39,100
Less :	1968 subscription not yet received	2,000	
	1968 subscriptions received in 1977	700	2,700
	Amount actually received		36,400

(ii) Proceeds of the sale of old furniture is Rs. 1,700, i.e., Rs. 200 (profit) plus book value, Rs. 1,500.

(iii) Payments for medicines is Rs. 6,700 (expended) plus Rs. 1,600 stocks on hand on 31st December, 1978 less stock on hand in the beginning of the year, Rs. 1,100.

(iv) Equipment purchased during the year :

		Rs.
As per Balance Sheet		8,000
Less Book Value of Equipment on 1st Jan.	6,000	
Less Depreciation	600	5,400
Addition during the year		2,600

Receipts and Payments Account for the year ended December 31, 1978

Receipts	Rs.	*Payments*	Rs.
To Subscriptions	36,400	By Balance b/d*	5,200
To Entrance Fees	300	By Salaries	32,000
To Grant from Municipal Corporation	8,950	By Medicines	7,200
		By Miscellaneous Expenses	1,500
To Life Memberships	2,500		
To Miscellaneous Receipts	150	By Equipment	2,600
To Sale of Old Furniture	1,700	By Balance c/d	1,500
	50,000		50,000

* Balancing Figure.

Can you prepare the Balance Sheet as on December 31, 1977 ?

EXERCISES

1. From the figures given below prepare an Income and Expenditure Account for 1977 :

Receipts		Rs.	*Payments*		Rs.
Opening Balance : In hand		200	Salaries		4,800
at Bank		1,600	Rent		500
Subscriptions :			Stationery & Postage		200
1976	500		Bicycle Purchased		300
1977	8,300		National Savings Certificates		3,000
1978	600	9,400	Help to needy students		2,000
Sale of Investments		2,000	Balance		
Sale of old Furnitures (Book value Rs. 400)		300	In hand	300	
			at Bank	2,400	2,700
		13,500			13,500

Subscriptions for 1978 still receivable were Rs. 700, interest due on Savings certificates, Rs. 100 and Rent unpaid but due was Rs. 60.

(*Excess of Income over Expenditure, Rs. 1,440*)

2. The U club gives you its Receipts and Payments Account for 1977. Prepare its Income and Expenditure Account for the year.

Receipts and Payments Account

	Rs.		Rs.
To Balance b/d	1,200	By Sports Equipment	3,500
To Subscriptions	15,300	By Rent	1,000
To Sale of old newspapers	300	By Cost of Entertainments	10,100
To Donations for Building	10,100	By Miscellaneous Expenses	800
To Sale of furniture	600	By Investments	10,000
		By Balance c/d	2,100
	27,500		27,500

Investments consisted of 4% Government Loan and were purchased on 1st July, 1977. Subscriptions included Rs. 700 for 1976 and Rs. 200 for 1978. Subscriptions for 1977 still receivable were Rs. 1,500 but of these Rs. 200 were considered doubtful. (*Excess of income over Expenditure Rs. 4,300*)

3. From the following prepare Income and Expenditure Account for the year ended 31st March, 1977 and also a Balance Sheet as on that date.

Receipts and Payments Account far the year ended March 31, 1977.

	Rs.		Rs.
To Balance b/d :		By Salaries	3,600
In Hand	55	By Rent	600
At Bank	455	By Printing and Stationery	145
To Subscriptions (including Rs. 200 for 1977-78)	3,000	By Postage	25
To Interest on Investments	1,500	By Bicycle Purchased	95
To Bank Interest	10	By Govt. Bonds	680
To Sale of Old Car	250	By Balance c/d :	
		In Hand	12
		At Bank	113
	5,270		5,270

Subscriptions include Rs. 120 for 1975-76, Rent includes Rs. 50 paid for March, 1976. Rent for March, 1977, Rs. 50, is still unpaid. Subscriptions amounting to Rs. 150 have still to be collected for 1976-77. Rs. 25 are payable against a bill for stationery. The book value of the car was Rs. 320. The cost of the investments (acquired on 1st October 1975) was Rs. 40,000; the interest was @ 5% of cost, interest is paid each year on 30th September.

(*Surplus Rs. 375 : Total of Balance Sheet, Rs. 42,550*)

(**Hint :** *Ascertain opening capital fund by preparing opening Balance Sheet Interest accrued on investments is Rs. 1,000*).

4. The following was the Receipts and Payments Account of a Club for the year ended Dec. 31, 1976.

Receipts	Rs.	*Payments*	Rs.
Cash in hand	100	Groundsman's Fee	750
Balance at Bank as per Pass Books ;		Mowing Machine	1,500
Deposit Account	2,230	Rent of Ground	250
Current Account	600	Cost of teas	250
Bank Interest	30	Fares	400
		Printing & Office Expenses	280
Donations and Subscriptions	2,600	Repairs to equipment	500
Receipts from teas	300	Honoraria to Secretary and Treasurer for 1975	400
Contributions to fares	100	Balance at Bank as per Bass Book :	
Sale of Equipment	80	Deposit Account	3,090
Net Proceeds of Variety Entertainment	780	Current Account	150
Donations for forthcoming Tournament	1,000	Cash in hand	250
	7,820		7,820

You are given the following additional information :–

	Jan. 1., 1976 Rs.	Dec. 31, 1976 Rs.
Subscriptions Due	150	100
Amount due for printing, etc.	100	80
Cheques unpresented being payment for repairs	300	260
Interest not yet entered in Pass Book	—	20
Estimated value of machinery and equipment	800	1,750

For the year ended Dec. 31, 1976, the honoraria to the Secretary and Treasurer are to be increased by a total of Rs 200. The groundsman is to receive a bonus of Rs. 300.

Prepare the Income and Expenditure Account for 1976 and the relevant Balance Sheet.

(*Excess of income over expenditure, Rs. 40 ; Total of Balance Sheet, Rs. 5,210*)

(**Hint :** *Unpresented cheques should be deducted from the bank balance and the amount added to repairs*).

5. **The Madras School Society gives you the following information :—**

(i) *Income and Expenditure Account for 1978*

	Rs.		Rs.
To Salaries	8,300	By Subscriptions	47,800
To Scholarships	41,300	By Govt. Grant	5,300
To Rent	2,800	By Proceeds of Tickets for Entertainment	8,300
To General Expenses	3,100	By Advertisements in Souvenir	5,100
To Audit Fees	600	By Interest (for full year @ 5%)	1,500
To cost of Printing tickets and souvenir	1,500		
To Cost of Entertainment	3,500		
To Loss on Sale of Furniture (Book value 800)	300		
To Depreciation on furniture	600		
To Surplus	6,000		
	68,000		68,000

(ii) *Receipts and Payments Account for 1978*

	Rs.		Rs.
To Balance b/d	3,800	By Salaries	9,400
To Subscriptions	46,000	By Scholarships	40,100
To Govt. Grant	5,300	By Rent	2,600
To Sale of tickets	8,300	By General Expenses	3,100
To Advertisements in souvenir	4,600	By Printing of tickets and Souvenir	1,200
To Interest	1,000	By Cost of Entertainment	3,500
To Sale of Furniture	500	By Furniture	2,000
		By Balance c/d	7,600
	69 500		69,500

On 31st Dec., 1977 subscriptions due were Rs. 1,500; furniture on that date was Rs. 6,000. Prepare the Balance Sheet as at 31st Dec., 1978.

(*Total of Balance Sheet Rs. 48,500*)

6. The Balance Sheet as at 31st Dec., 1977 of the Salem Sports Club was the following :

Balance Sheet as at 31st Dec. 1977

	Rs,		Rs.
Salaries Unpaid	1,500	Cash	500
Subscriptions Received in advance	400	Cash at Bank	2,100
Capital Fund (including Life Memberships Rs. 1,000)	14,300	Sports Equipment	10,300
		Subscriptions Due	3,100
		Prepaid Expenses	200
	16,200		16,200

The Income and Expenditure Account for the year was as under :—

Expenditures		Rs.	*Receipts*	Rs.
To Salaries		5,500	By Subscriptions	21,700
To Cost of Entertainment		5,300	By Profit on Sale of Equipment (book value Rs. 800)	300
To Audit Fee		400		
To Depreciation		1,000	By Deficit excess of expenditure over income	1,500
To Tournament Expenses and prizes		2,100		
To Insurance		600		
To Restaurant :				
Expenses	30,300			
Takings	21,700	8,600		
		23,500		23,500

You are informed that on 31st Dec., 1976 subscriptions in arrear and received in advance were respectively, Rs. 1,800 and Rs. 800. On that date the Sport Equipment stood in the books at Rs. 8,000. Cash in hand on that date was Rs. 400.

You are required to prepare the club's Receipts and Payments Account for 19 7 and its Balance Sheet as at 31st Dec., 1976.

(*Total of Balance Sheet on 31st Dec. 1976, Rs. 15,600 ; Cash at Bank Rs. 5,400*).

7. The following is the Receipts and Payments Account of Mehruli Club for the year ended 31st Dec., 1978 :

		Rs.		Rs.
Cash in hand (1—1—78)		350	Bank Overdraft (1—1—78)	180
Subscription			Salaries	670
1977	400		Printing and Stationery	50
1978	2,200		Furniture	1,000
1979	100	2,700	Investment in Securities	1,500
Income from Entertainment		230	Balance on 31-12-78	
			Cash in Hand	170
Entrance Fee		450	Cash at Bank	900
Interest on Securities		560		
Sale of Old Furniture (Book Value 150)		180		
		4 470		4 470

Prepare Income and Expenditure Account for the year ended 31st Dec., 1978 and the Balance Sheet, as on that date, having due regard to the following additional information :

(*i*) The Club has 250 members paying an annual subscription of Rs. 10 each. (During the year 5, new members joined).

(*ii*) Salary Rs. 50 was outstanding on 1-1-78 and Rs. 60 is still payable for the year 1978.

(*iii*) The Club had furniture Rs. 2 650, Building Rs. 5,000 and Investments Rs. 7,000, as on 1-1-78.

(*iv*) Depreciate Building and Furniture by 5% of their closing balances.

(*Adapted from B. Com. Pass. Delhi*)

[*Excess of Income over Expenditive, Rs. 2,165 ; Total of B/s Rs. 17 945.*]

CHAPTER XIX

AMALGAMATION, ABSORPTION, AND RECONSTRUCTION OF JOINT-STOCK COMPANIES

There are a number of advantages which accrue if two or more companies doing similar or complimentary business join together. The chief advantages are :

(*i*) avoidance of competition and maintenance of prices ;

(*ii*) ready marketability of products or availability of raw materials at reasonable prices ; if a steel company acquires a coal company, there will be no problem of selling coal (for the colliery) and no problem regarding availability of coal (for the steel company) ; and

(*iii*) reduction in costs of production and selling costs through economy of large-scale operations.

Companies may join together through amalgamation or absorption. *When a new company is set up to acquire the businesses of existing companies, it is amalgamation. When one of the existing companies acquires the businesses of other companies, it is a case of absorption.* Suppose there are three companies, Big Ltd., Medium Ltd. and Small Ltd. If a new company, Giant Ltd., is formed to take over the businesses of the three companies there will be amalgamation. If Big Ltd. takes over the other two companies, the term used will be absorption.

There is another term—Reconstruction. In this case only one company is involved and there is no case of two or more companies joining together. A company, usually unsuccessful, is reorganised, the business and the shareholders being the same. The purpose is to write off accumulated losses and over-valuation of assets and to begin on a new slate. The company may be liquidated and a new company may be floated to take over the business. The company will have the same shareholders. This is a case of external reconstruction.

There is an alternative course open to the company. It may go to the Court and ask for reduction of capital—a reduction in the paid up value of each share of the company and thus to write off past losses and over-valuation of assets. The company is not liquidated and there is no new company. This is internal reconstruction.

The accounting problem is common to amalgamation, absorption and external reconstruction. A company buys business (assets and liabilities) ; some companies sell their business. We must know how to close the books of a company selling its business and to record the purchase of business in the books of the purchasing company. Entries in case of internal reconstruction will be different.

Before we discuss the entries to be passed, the student should know how to calculate purchase consideration. *Purchase consideration* is, of course, the amount which the purchasing company will pay to the selling company ; it should not include any payment that the purchasing company has to make directly to the creditors of the selling company. Purchase consideration is usually calculated by adding the values (to the purchasing company) of the assets taken over and deducting the liabilities taken over. Consider the following balance sheet of X Ltd.

Liabilities	Rs.	*Assets*	Rs.
10,000 shares of Rs. 100 each	10,00,000	Goodwill	2,00,000
6% Debentures	4,00,000	Land and Buildings	2,50,000
Sundry Creditors	2,30,000	Plant and Machinery	3,60,000
Profit Prior to Incorporation	20,000	Stock	2,50,000
		Sundry Debtors	2,00,000
		Cash at Bank	10,000
		Profit and Loss Account	3,80,000
	Rs. 16,50,000		Rs. 16,50,000

Y Ltd. agrees to take over the assets except bank balance and liabilities to sundry creditiors, the goodwill being valued at Rs. 50,000. The purchase consideration will be :

		Rs.
Assets taken over :	Goodwill	50,000
	Land and Buildings	2,50,000
	Plant and Machinery	3,60,000
	Stock	2,50,000
	Sundry Debtors	2,00,000
	Total	11,10,000
Less liabilities taken over—Sundry Creditors		2,30,000
Purchase consideration		8,80,000

Sometimes, the agreement states what amount has to be paid to shareholders and debentureholders. Suppose, in the above case, it is agreed that (*i*) for debentures in X Ltd., Y Ltd. will issue its own debentures at the rate of Rs. 90 for every Rs. 100 ; and (*ii*) shareholders will be given five shares of Rs. 5 each as fully paid at an agreed value of Rs. 6 each and Rs. 3 in cash for each share held in X Ltd. The purchase consideration in this case would be :

	Rs.
Amount to be paid to Debentureholders $(4,00,000 \times \frac{90}{100})$ (in the form of debentures)	3,60,000
For shareholders—Shares $(10,000 \times 5 \times 6)$	3,00,000
—Cash $(10,000 \times 3)$	30,000
Total	6,90,000

Entries in the books of the selling company. The selling company will pass entries to close its books. The following are the steps :—

(*i*) Open a Realisation Account and transfer *all* assets to it at *book value*. The entry is :

Realisation Account ... ... Dr.
To various assets (individually)

The accounts of assets will then be closed.

Notes. (1) If the purchasing company (say P Ltd.) does not take over cash or bank balance, these should not be transferred. Other assets should be transferred even if they are not taken over by P Ltd. ; this is because such assets will have to be realised.

(2) The term asset does not include accounts representing losses (Profit and Loss Account, debit balance) or expenses not yet written off such as Underwriting Commission on Shares or Debentures or Preliminary Expenses.

(*ii*) Transfer those liabilities which P Ltd. agrees to take over to the Realisation Account by the entry—

Liabilities Accounts ... ... Dr.
To Realisation Account

This entry will close the account of the liabilities.

Notes. (1) The term "liability" should not be taken to mean accumulated profits or reserves such as General Reserve, credit balance of Profit & Loss Account, Contingency Reserve, etc.

(2) Those liabilities which P Ltd. is not taking over should not be transferred to the Realisation Account.

(*iii*) Debit P Ltd. with the agreed amount of purchase consideration and credit Realisation Account.

(iv) On receipt of cash, debentures or shares from P Ltd. in discharge of the purchase consideration :

Debit Cash, debentures in P Ltd., or shares in P Ltd. with the respective amounts ; and

Credit P Ltd.

(v) The treatment of expenses depends upon as to which company is to bear them. If the selling company is to bear them,

Debit Realisation Account, and
Credit Cash Account

If the purchasing company is to bear them, the matter can be dealt with in the following ways :—

Either, (a) ignore the expenses ;

Or, (b) Debit P Ltd.
Credit Cash Account } on payment made on behalf of P Ltd.

and

Debit Cash Account
Credit P Ltd. } on reimbursement of the expenses.

It is also possible that the amount of expenses to be borne by the purchasing company is added to the purchase consideration. The amount will then be taken into account while passing entries as explained in steps (iii) and (iv). On payment of the expenses, then, the Realisation Account should be debited and Cash Account credited.

(vi) The liabilities not taken over by the purchasing company have to be paid. The actual amount paid should be debited to the liability account ; the difference between the book figure and the amount paid should be transferred to the Realisation Account. Suppose Debentures of Rs. 1,00,000 are paid Rs. 1,05,000. The entries will be :

		Rs.	Rs.
Debentures Account	Dr.	1,05,000	
To Cash Account			1,05,000
To record payment.			
Realisation Account	Dr.	5,000	
To Debentures Account			5,000
Loss because of extra payment, transferred to Realization Account.			

Or		Rs.	Rs.
Debentures Account	Dr.	1,00,000	
Realisation Account	Dr.	5,000	
To Bank Account			1,05,000
Rs. 1,05,000 paid against book figure of Rs. 1,00,000.			

(vii) (a) Transfer Share Capital Account to Shareholders Account. The entry is :

Share Capital Account Dr.
To Shareholders Account

(b) Transfer all accumulated losses or profits (capital or revenue) or expenses not yet written off to Shareholders Account. For example

Profit and Loss Account (Cr.) Dr.
General Reserve A/c Dr.
Share Premium A/c Dr.
To Shareholders Account

Or

Shareholders Account Dr.
To Profit and Loss Account (Dr.)
To Preliminary Expenses A/c
To Discount on Issue of Debentures A/c

(c) Prepare Realisation Account ; the difference in the two sides will be profit or loss ; it must be transferred to Shareholders Account, the entry being (in case of profit) :

Realisation Account Dr.
To Shareholders Account

The entry will be reversed in case of loss.

Step no. (vii) determines the amount due to shareholders.

(viii) The available cash or shares (or anything else) should be distributed among shareholders. The entry is :

Shareholders Account Dr.
To Cash Account
To Shares in P Ltd. etc.

There should be no balance left in the Shareholders Account. If it still shows a balance, it means that there is some error.

Illustration Blue Ltd. and Star Ltd. whose balance sheets on 1st Jan. 1974 are given below decided to amalgamate under the name of Blue Star Ltd. which was floated for the purpose with an authorised capital of 20,000 shares of Rs. 100 each.

Balance Sheet of Blue Ltd.

Liabilities	Rs.	*Assets*	Rs.
50,000 shares of Rs. 10 each fully paid	5,00,000	Land and Buildings	3,00,000
Sundry Creditors	50,000	Plant and Machinery	2,00,000
6% Debentures	50,000	Goodwill	50,000
P. & L. A/c	50,000	Stock	20,000
		Sundry Debtors	20,000
		Cash at Bank	60,000
	6,50,000		6,50,000

Balance Sheet of Star Ltd.

Liabilities	Rs.	*Assets*	Rs.
1,00,000 shares of Rs. 10 each fully paid	10,00,000	Land and Buildings	4,00,000
Sundry Creditors	80,000	Goodwill	50,000
		Plant and Machinery	3,00,000
		Patents	10,000
		Stock	1,00,000
		Sundry Debtors	1,20,000
		Cash at Bank	50,000
		Profit and Loss Account	50,000
	10,80,000		10,80,000

Blue Star Ltd. took over all assets except cash at bank but considered goodwill of Star Ltd. as valueless. It also agreed to take over trade creditors. For the purpose, it agreed to issue fully paid shares to the liquidators of the two companies. Give journal entries in the books of the two companies to close their books.

Solution :

Purchase consideration :	*Blue Ltd.* Rs.	*Star Ltd.* Rs.
Land and Buildings	3,00,000	4,00,000
Plant and Machinery	2,00,000	3,00,000
Goodwill	50,000	—
Patents	—	10,000
Stock	20,000	1,00,000
Sundry Debtors	20,000	1,20,000
Total	5,90,000	9,30,000
Less Creditors	50,000	80,000
Purchase Consideration	5,40,000	8,50,000

5,400 shares will be issued to shareholders of Blue Ltd. and 8,500 shares will be issued to shareholders of Star Ltd. Thus, shareholders of Blue Ltd. will receive 54 shares in Blue Star Ltd. for every 500 held (5,400 : 50,000), or 27 for 250 shares held. Similarly, shareholders of Star Ltd. will receive 85 shares for every 1,000 shares held or 17 for every 200 shares (8,500 : 1,00,000).

Journal of Blue Ltd.

				Dr.	Cr.
				Rs.	Rs.
1974 Jan.	1	Realisation Account To Land and Buildings To Plant and Machinery To Goodwill To Stock To Sundry Debtors Transfer of various assets to Realisation on amalgamation with Star Ltd.	Dr.	5,90,000	3,00,000 2,00,000 50,000 20,000 20,000
	,,	Sundry Creditors Account To Realisation Account Liability to Sundry Creditors transferred to Realisation Account, this being taken over by Blue Star Ltd.	Dr.	50,000	50,000
	,,	Blue Star Ltd. To Realisation Account The amount of Rs. 5,40,000 receivable from the purchasing company as purchase consideration	Dr.	5,40,000	5,40,000
	,,	Shares in Blue Star Ltd. To Blue Star Ltd. Shares received in discharge of amount due from Blue Star Ltd.	Dr.	5,40,000	5,40,000
	,,	6% Debentures To Bank Account Amount paid to Debenture-holders	Dr.	50,000	50,00
	,,	Share Capital Account Profit and Loss Account To Shareholders Account Transfer of Share Capital and Profit and Loss Account to Shareholders Account	Dr.	5,00,000 50,000	5,50,00
	,,	Shareholders Account To Shares in Blue Star Ltd. To Bank Account Available shares and cash distributed among shareholders	Dr.	5,50,000	5,40,0 10,0

Note. There is no profit or loss in Realisation Account.

Journal of Star Ltd.

Date		Particulars		Dr.	Cr.
1974				Rs.	Rs.
Jan.	1	Realisation Account	Dr.	9,80,000	
		To Land and Buildings			4,00,000
		To Goodwill			50,000
		To Plant and Machinery			3,00,000
		To Patents			10,000
		To Stock			1,00,000
		To Sundry Debtors			1,20,000
		Transfer of assets except cash at bank to Realisation Account on transfer of business to Blue Ltd.			
	"	Sundry Creditors	Dr.	80,000	
		To Realisation Account			80,000
		Liability to Sundry Creditors transferred to Realisation A/c on being taken over by Blue Star Ltd.			
		Blue Star Ltd.	Dr.	8,50,000	
		To Realisation Account			8,50,000
		Amount due from Blue Star Ltd.			
	"	Shares in Blue Star Ltd.	Dr.	8,50,000	
		To Blue Star Ltd.			8,50,000
		Shares received in discharge of purchase consideration			
	"	Share Capital Account	Dr.	10,00,000	
		To Sharesholders Account			10,00,000
		Transfer of Share Capital to Shareholders			
	"	Shareholders Account	Dr.	1,00,000	
		To Profit and Loss Account			50,000
		To Realisation Account			50,000
		Debit balance on Profit and Loss Account and loss on Realistion Account transferred to Shareholders			
	"	Shareholders Account	Dr.	9,00,000	
		To Sbares in Blue Star Ltd.			8,50,000
		To Bank Account			50,000
		Available cash and shares distributed among shareholders			

We can present the balance sheet of Blue Star Ltd., putting the assets taken over on one side and amount of shares issued and liabilities taken over on the other. Thus—

Liabilities	Rs.	*Assets*	Rs.
13,900 shares of Rs 100		Land and Buildings	7,00,000
each fully paid	13,90,000	Plant and Machinery	5,00,000
Sundry Creditors	1,30,000	Goodwill	50,000
		Patents	10,000
		Stock	1,20,000
		Sundry Debtors	1,40,000
Total	15,20,000	Total	15,20,000

Entries in the books of the purchasing cnmpany. The purchasing company passes the following entries: —

(*i*) Debit Business Purchase Account }
Credit Vendor Company } with the purchase consideration.

(*ii*) Debit tangible assets taken over at the value assigned to them by the purchasing company;

credit liabilities taken over at agreed amounts;

credit Business Purchase Account with the purchase consideration;

if the debits exceed credits, credit the difference to Capital Reserve ; or,

if the credits exceed debits, debit the difference to goodwill.

Goodwill or capital reserve should be ascertained only in this manner; the figure of goodwill appearing in the books of the vendor company should be ignored.

(*iii*) Debit Vendor Company ;

credit Share Capital (face value only) ;

credit Share Premium (if shares have been issued at a price higher than face value) ; and

credit Cash, etc.

Note : If the purchasing company has to pay expenses of liquidation of the selling company, the amount should be debited to Goodwill Account or Capital Reserve, as the case may be.

Illustration The balance sheet of Old Ltd. on June 30, 1974 was as under:—

Liabilities	Rs.	*Assets*	Rs.
5,000 shares of Rs. 100 each fully paid	5,00,000	Goodwill	1,00,000
5% Debentures	2,00,000	Land and Buildings	2,50,000
General Reserve	1,00,000	Plant and Machinery	3,00,000
Profit and Loss Account	50,000	Stock	80,000
Employees Provident Fund	80,000	Sundry Debtors	1,10,000
Sundry Creditors	1,00,000	Investments	1,00,000
		Cash at Bank	90,000
	10,30,000		10,30,000

New Ltd. was formed to take over the business. It had an authorised capital of 10,000 shares of Rs. 100 each. It took over all assets and liabilities, valuing Land and Buildings at Rs. 3,00,000 and Plant and Machinery at Rs. 2,70,000. It agreed to:

(*i*) issue its own debentures in exchange for debentures in Old Ltd. at the rate of Rs. 105 for every Rs. 100;

(*ii*) pay Rs. 20, cash, and issue one share, fully paid, at an agreed value of Rs. 130 per share for each share in Old Ltd.

Expenses of liquidation of Old Ltd., Rs. 10,000, were to be paid by New Ltd. New Ltd. offered 5,000 shares to the public at Rs. 130 per share. All the shares were subscribed and immediately paid for.

Give journal entries to close the books of Old Ltd. and to open the books of New Ltd.

Solution :

		Rs. *Amount*	*Form*
Purchase considerations :			
Debentures	$2,00,000 \times \frac{105}{100}$	2,10,000	Debentures
Shares :	5,000 × 20	1,00,000	Cash
	5,000 × 130	6,50,000	Shares
	Total	9,60,000	

Journal of Old Ltd.

Date		Particulars	Dr. Rs.	Cr. Rs.
1974 June	30	Realisation Account ... ... Dr.	10,30,000	
		To Goodwill		1,00,000
		To Land and Buildings		2,50,000
		To Plant and Machinery		3,00,000
		To Stock		80,000
		To Sundry Debtors		1,10,000
		To Investments		1,00,000
		To Bank Account		90,000
		Various assets taken over by New Ltd. transferred to Realisation Account		
„	„	Sundry Creditors Account ... Dr.	1,00,000	
		Employees Provident Fund ... Dr.	80,000	
		To Realisation Account		1,80,000
		Transfer of liabilities taken over by New Ltd. to Realisation Account		
„	„	New Ltd. ... ... Dr.	9,60,000	
		To Realisation Account		9,60,000
		Amount due from New Ltd. as purchase consideration		
„	„	Shares in New Ltd. ... Dr.	6,50,000	
		Cash Account ... Dr.	1,00,000	
		Debentures in New Ltd. ... Dr.	2,10,000	
		To New Ltd.		9,60,000
		Shares, debentures and cash received in discharge of purchase consideration.		
„	„	New Ltd. ... Dr.	10,000	
		To Cash Account		10,000
		Expenses paid on behalf of New Ltd.		
„	„	Cash Account ... Dr.	10,000	
		To New Ltd.		10,000
		Account received from New Ltd. to reimburse expenses.		
„	„	6% Debentures ... Dr.	2,00,000	
		Realisation Account ... Dr.	10,000	
		To Debentures in New Ltd.		2,10,000
		Debentures in New Ltd. worth Rs. 2,10,000 distributed among debenture holders with a book figure of Rs. 2,00,000.		
„	„	Share Capital Account ... Dr.	5,00,000	
		General Reserve ... Dr.	1,00,000	
		Profit and Loss Account ... Dr.	50,000	
		Realisation Account ... Dr.	1,00,000	
		To Shareholders Account		7,50,000
		Transfer of share capital, accumulated profits and profit on Realisation to shareholders.		

Date		Particulars		Dr. Rs.	Cr. Rs.
1974 June	30	Shareholders Account	Dr.	7,50,000	
		To Cash Account			1,00,000
		To Share in New Ltd.			6,50,000
		Available cash and share distributed among shareholders.			

Journal of New Ltd.

Date		Particulars		Dr. Rs.	Cr.
1974 June	30	Business Purchase Account ...	Dr.	9,60,000	
		To Liquidator of Old Ltd.			9,60,000
		The amount to be paid for the business of Old Ltd.			
"	"	Land and Buildings Account ...	Dr.	3,00,000	
		Plant and Machinery Account	Dr.	2,70,000	
		Stock Account ...	Dr.	80,000	
		Sundry Debtors ...	Dr.	1,10,000	
		Investments Account ...	Dr.	1,00,000	
		Bank Account ...	Dr.	90,000	
		Goodwill Account ...	Dr.	1,90,000	
		To Sundry Creditors			1,00,000
		To Employees Provident Fund			80,000
		To Business Purchase Account			9,60,000
		Various assets and liabilities taken over; Goodwill is the balancing figure.			
"	"	Bank Account	Dr.	6,50,000	
		To Share Capital Account			5,00,000
		To Share Premium Account			1,50,000
		5,000 shares of Rs. 100 each issued to the public (and taken up by it) at Rs. 130 each.			
"	"	Liquidator of Old Ltd.	Dr.	9,60,000	
		To Debentures			2,10,000
		To Bank Account			1,00,000
		To Share Capital Account			5,00,000
		To Share Premium Account			1,50,000
		Purchase consideration satisfied by issue of debentures for Rs. 2,10,000, 5,000 shares of Rs. 100 each @Rs. 130 and payment of cash.			
"	"	Goodwill Account	Dr.	10,000	
		To Bank Account			10,000
		Expenses of liquidation of Old Ltd. paid.			

Balance Sheet of New Ltd. as at June 30, 1974

Liabilities	Rs.	*Assets*	Rs.
Share Capital :		**Fixed Assets**	
Authorised, issued and subscribed, 10,000 shares of Rs.100 each fully paid (of the above 5,000 shares were issued to vendors for consideration other than cash)	10,00,000	Goodwill	2,00,000
		Land and Buildings	3,00,000
		Plant and Machinery	2,70,000
		Investments	1,00,000
		Current Assets	
		Stock	80,000
		Sundry Debtors	1,10,000
		Cash at Bank	6,30,000
Share Premium	3,00,000		
Debentures	2,10,000		
Sundry Creditors	1,00,000		
Employees Provident Fund	80,000		
Total	16,90,000	Total	16,90,000

Illustration Notsowell Ltd. had the following Balance Sheet as at December 31, 1974:—

Liabilities	Rs.	*Assets*	Rs.
Capital (in shares of Rs. 100 each)	10,00,000	Land and Buildings	3,00,000
		Plant and Machinery	4,00,000
6% Debentures	5,00,000	Stock	1,50,000
Sundry Creditors	1,00,000	Sundry Debtors	1,20,000
		Cash	10,000
		Profit and Loss Account	6,20,000
	16,00,000		16,00,000

Good Prospects Ltd. was formed on 1st January, 1975 to take over the assets of Notsowell Ltd., the purchase consideration being:

(*a*) $7\frac{1}{2}\%$ Debentures of the value of Rs. 4,00,000 (to be issued to Debentureholders in Notsowell Ltd.);

(*b*) Rs. 1,20,000 in cash; and

(*c*) Rs. 4,00,000 in shares of the face value of Rs. 25 each, credited at Rs. 10 each.

Good Prospects Ltd. valued Land and Buildings at Rs. 4,00,000 and Plant and Machinery at Rs. 3,50,000.

Before the above scheme is put through, existing shareholders of Notsowell Ltd. have to apply for the shares, paying Rs. 7·50 on application and Rs. 7·50 on allotment.

The expenses of liquidation of Notsowell Ltd. came to Rs. 10,000. Give ledger accounts in the books of the vendor company and journal entries of the purchasing company and also the balance sheet of that company after completion.

Solution :

Books of Notsowell Ltd.

Ledger

Realisation Account

Dr. *Cr.*

		Rs.			Rs.
1975 Jan. 1	To Sundry Assets:		1975 Jan. 1	By Good Prospects Ltd. (Purchase consideration)	9,20,000
	Land and Buildings	3,00,000		By 6% Debentures (Profit on redemption)	1,00,000
	Plant and Machinery	4,00,000			
	Stock	1,50,000			
	Sundry Debtors	1,20,000			
	Cash	10,000			
	To Cash—Expenses	10,000			
	To Sundry Shareholders—Profit	30,000			
		10,20,000			10,20,000

Land and Buildings

		Rs.			Rs.
1975 Jan. 1	To Balance b/d	3,00,000	1975 Jan. 1	By Realisation A/c—Transfer	3,00,000

Cash

		Rs.			Rs.
1975 Jan. 1	To Balance b/d	10,000	1975 Jan. 1	By Realisation A/c—Transfer	10,000
	To Good Prospects Ltd.	1,20,000	"	By Realisation A/c—Expenses	10,000
			"	By Sundry Creditors	1,00,000
			"	By Sundry Shareholders	10,000
		1,30,000			1,30,000

Good Prospects Ltd.

		Rs.			Rs.
1975 Jan. 1	To Realisation A/c	9,20,000	1975 Jan. 1	By Debentures in G.P. Ltd.	4,00,000
			"	By Shares in G.P. Ltd.	4,00,000
			"	By Cash	1,20,000
		9,20,000			9,20,000

Debentures in G.P. Ltd.

		Rs.			Rs.
1975 Jan. 1	To Good Prospects Ltd.	4,00,000	1975 Jan. 1	By 6% Debentures	4,00,000

Shares in G.P. Ltd.

		Rs.			Rs.
1975 Jan. 1	To Good Prospects Ltd.	4,00,000	1975 Jan. 1	By Sundry Shareholders	4,00,000

6% Debentures

		Rs.			Rs.
1975 Jan. 1	To Debentures in G.P. Ltd.	4,00,000	1975 Jan. 1	By Balance b/d	5,00,000
"	To Realisation A/c—transfer	1,00,000			
		5,00,000			5,00,000

Sundry Creditors

		Rs.			Rs.
1975 Jan. 1	To Cash	1,00,000	1975 Jan. 1	By Balance b/d	1,00,000

Share Capital Account

		Rs.			Rs.
1975 Jan. 1	To Sundry Shareholders—Transfer	10,00,000	1975 Jan. 1	By Balance b/d	10,00,000

Profit and Loss Account

		Rs.			Rs.
1975 Jan. 1	To Balance b/d	6,20,000	1975 Jan. 1	By Sundry Shareholders—Transfer	6,20,000

Sundry Shareholders Account

		Rs.			Rs.
1976 Jan. 1	To Profit loss A/c—Transfer	6,20,000	1975 Jan. 1	By Share Capital —Transfer	10,00,000
„	To Share in G.P. Ltd.	4,00,000	„	By Realisation A/c—Profit	30,000
	To Cash	10,000			
		10,30,000			10,30,000

Books of G.P. Ltd.

Journal

			Dr. Rs.	Cr. Rs.
1975 Ja.1n.	1	Bank Account Dr.	3,00,000	
		To Share Applications and Allotment A/c		3,00,000
		Application money on 40,000 shares received @ Rs. 7·50 per share.		
„	„	Share Application and Allotment A/c Dr.	6,00,000	
		To Share Capital Account		6,00,000
		Rs. 7·50 on application and Rs. 7·50 on allotment credited to Share Capital A/c in respect of 40,000 shares applied for and allotted.		
„	„	Bank Account Dr.	3,00,000	
		To Share Applications and Allotment Account		3,00,000
		Amount due on allotment received.		
„	„	Business Purchase Account Dr.	9,20,000	
		To Liquidator of Notsowell Ltd.		9,20,000
		Amount to be paid for assets of Notsowell Ltd.		
„	„	Land and Buildings Dr.	4,00,000	
		Plant and Machinery Dr.	3,50,000	
		Stock Dr.	1,50,000	
		Sundry Debtors Dr.	1,20,000	
		Cash Dr.	10,000	
		To Business Purchase Account		9,20,000
		To Capital Reserve		1,10,000
		Various assets taken over, excess of assets over purchase consideration credited to Capital Reserve.		
„	„	Liquidator of Notsowell Ltd. Dr.	9,20,000	
		To 7½% Debentures		4,00,000
		To Share Capital Account		4,00,000
		To Bank Account		1,20,000
		Discharge of purchase consideration as per terms of agreement.		

Balance Sheet of Good Prospects Ltd. as at Jan. 1, 1975

Liabilities	Rs.	*Assets*	Rs.
Share Capital		**Fixed Assets**	
Authorised		Land and Buildings	4,00,000
Issued, Subscribed		Plant and Machinery	3,50,000
Paid up :			
40,000 shares of Rs. 25 each fully paid (Rs. 10 per share being received in a form other than cash)	10,00,000	**Current Assets**	
		Stock	1,50,000
		Sundry Debtors	1,20,000
		Cash in hand	10,000
Capital Reserve	1,10,000	Cash at Bank	4,80,000
7½% Debentures	4,00,000		
Total	15,10,000	Total	15,10,000

Illustration Wye Ltd. had the following Balance Sheet as at June 30, 1974:—

Liabilities	Rs.	*Assets*	Rs.
5,000 shares of Rs. 100		Land and Buildings	1,00,000
each fully paid	5,00,000	Plant and Machinery	2,00,000
6% Debentures	2,00,000	Goodwill	90,000
Profit Prior to Incor-		Patents	30,000
poration	10,000	Cash	5,000
Sundry creditors	1,50,000	Sundry Debtors	1,00,000
		Stock	95,000
		Profit and Loss Account	2,20,000
		Preliminary Expenses	20,000
	8,60,000		8,60,000

The following scheme of reconstruction was adopted:—

(*i*) Each share was to be reduced to a share of Rs. 20 each;

(*ii*) Each shareholder was to subscribe for half the number of shares already held by him and pay immediately in cash for the new shares acquired;

(*iii*) All fictitious assets including Goodwill and Patents were to be eliminated;

(*iv*) A provision of 5% on debtors in respect of doubtful debts was to be created ; and

(*v*) Plant and Machinery was to be written down by Rs. 40,000.

Give Journal entries to record the above, assuming the scheme has been implemented, and the Balance Sheet immediately afterwards.

Journal

Date		Particulars		Dr.	Cr.
1974				Rs.	Rs.
June	30	Share Capital Aceount	Dr.	4,00,000	
		Profit Prior to Incorporation A/c.	Dr.	10,000	
		To Capital Reduction Account			4,10,000
		Reduction of shares to shares of Rs. 20 each; Profit prior to Incorporation also transferred to Capital Reduction Account.			
	,,	Bank Account	Dr.	50,000	
		To Share Capital Account			50,000
		2,500 shares of Rs. 20 each taken up by the shareholders			
	,,	Capital Reduction Account	Dr.	4,10,000	
		To Profit and Loss Account			2,20,000
		To Preliminary Expenses Account			20,000
		To Goodwill			90,000
		To Patents			30,000
		To Plant and Machinery			40,000
		To Provision for Doubtful Debts A/c			5,000
		To Capital Reserve A/c			5,000
		Capital Reduction Account utilised to write off fictitious assets and losses, to create Provision for Doubtful Debts @ 5% of Debtors and to write off Rs 40,000 from Plant and Machinery; balance credited to Capital Reserve.			

Balance Sheet of Wye Ltd. as at June 30, 1974

Liabilities	Rs.	*Assets*		Rs.
Share Capital		**Fixed Assets :**		
Authorised		Land and Buildings		1,00,000
Issued, subscribed and paid up :		Plant and Machinery	2,00,000	
7,500 shares of Rs. 20 each fully paid	1,50,000	Less written off under Reconstruction Scheme	40,000	1,60,000
Capital Reserve	5,000	Goodwill	90,000	
6% Debentures	2,00,000	Less written off under Reconstruction Scheme	90,000	
Sundry Creditors	1,50,000			

(*Contd.*)

	Rs.			Rs.
		Patents	30,000	
		Less written off under Reconstruction Scheme	30,000	—
		Current Assets :		
		Stock		95,000
		Sundry Debtors	1,00,000	
		Less Provision for Doubtful Debts	5,000	95,000
		Cash		55,000
Total	5,05,000	Total		5,05,000

Illustration Exe Ltd. decides to sell its business to Zed Ltd. as on 30th Sept., 1974 on which date its balance sheet was as under :

Liabilities	Rs.	*Assets*	Rs.
Share Capital : 50,000 shares of Rs. 10 each	5,00,000	Goodwill	60,000
$7\frac{1}{2}$% Debentures	1,00,000	Property	1,50,000
Sundry Creditors	1,50,000	Plant	2,10,000
Reserve	50,000	Stock	2,00,000
Profit and Loss Account	40,000	Sundry Debtors	1,50,000
		Cash at Bank	70,000
	8,40,000		8,40,000

Zed Ltd. took over all assets except Cash at Bank at their book values except that Goodwill was valued at Rs. 1,00,000 and property at Rs. 1,80,000. Zed Ltd. also undertook to discharge the liability to creditors. Zed Ltd. agreed to pay Rs. 90,000 in cash and the balance in the form of fully paid shares @ Rs. 150 each, the par value being Rs. 100. Expenses of liquidation were Rs. 15,000. Record the above noted transactions in the journal of the two companies.

Solution :

	Rs.
Purchase consideration—	
Value of assets taken over:	
Goodwill	1,00,000
Property	1,80,000
Plant	2,10,000
Stock	2,00,000
Sundry Debtors	1,50,000
	8,40,000
Less liabilities taken over (creditors)	1,50,000
	6,90,000
To be discharged as to : Cash	90,000
Shares	6,00,000

Number of shares to be issued Rs. $\frac{6,00,000}{150} =$

Books of Exe Ltd.

Journal

Date		Particulars		Dr.	Cr.
1974				Rs.	Rs.
Sept.	30	Realisation Account	Dr.	7,70,000	
		To Goodwill			60,000
		To Property			1,50,000
		To Plant			2,10,000
		To Stock			2,00,000
		To Sundry Debtor			1,50,000
		Transfer of various assets to Realisation Account at book values.			
	"	Sundry Creditors	Dr.	1,50,000	
		To Realisation Account			1,50,000
		Transfer of liabilities taken over by Zed Ltd.			
	"	Zed Ltd.	Dr.	6,90,000	
		To Realisation Account			6,90,000
		Amount to be paid by Zed Ltd.			
	"	Cash Account	Dr.	90,000	
		Shares in Zed Ltd.	Dr.	6,00,000	
		To Zed Ltd.			6,90,000
		Cash and shares received from Zed Ltd. in discharge of purchase consideration			
	"	Realisation Account	Dr.	15,000	
		To Cash Account			15,000
		Expenses paid.			
	"	7½% Debentures	Dr.	1,00,000	
		To Cash Account			1,00,000
		7½% Debentures redeemed.			
	"	Share Capital Account	Dr.	5,00,000	
		Reserve	Dr.	50,000	
		Profit and Loss Account	Dr.	40,000	
		Realisation Account	Dr.	55,000	
		To Sundry Shareholders Account			6,45,000
		Transfer of Share Capital Reserve, P. and L. and profit on Realisation A/c to shareholders to determine amount due to them.			
	"	Sundry Shareholders Account	Dr.	6,45,000	
		To Cash Account			45,000
		To Shares in Zed Ltd.			6,00,000
		Amount due to Shareholders paid in the form of available cash and shares.			

Books of Zed Ltd.
Journal

				Dr.	Cr.
				Rs.	Rs.
1974 Sept.	30	Business Purchase Account To Liquidator of the Exe Ltd. Amount due to Exe Ltd. for taking over their business	Dr.	6,90,000	6,90,000
	"	Goodwill Account	Dr.	1,00,000	
		Property	Dr.	1,80,000	
		Plant	Dr.	2,10,000	
		Stock	Dr.	2,00,000	
		Sundry Debtors	Dr.	1,50,000	
		To Sundry Creditors			1,50,000
		To Business Purchase Account Various assets and liabilities taken over from Exe Ltd.			6,90,000
	"	Liquidator of Exe Ltd.	Dr.	6,90,000	
		To Cash			90,000
		To Share Capital			4,00,000
		To Premium on Shares Payment of Rs. 90,000 in cash and issue of 4,000 shares of Rs. 100 each @ Rs 150 in discharge of the purchase consideration.			2,00,000

EXERCISES

1. A Co. Ltd. and B. Co., Ltd. agree to amalgamate. A new company, C Ltd. has been formed to take over the two companies as on 31st December, 1974 on which date the balance sheets of the two companies were as follows :—

A Co. Ltd.

Liabilities	Rs.	*Assets*	Rs.
50,000 shares of Rs. 10 each, fully paid	5,00,000	Land and Buildings	3,00,000
Sundry Creditors	50,000	Plant and Machinery	3,00,000
Provident Fund	50,000	Goodwill	50,000
Profit and Loss Account	50,000	Stock	20,000
Reserve	50,000	Sundry Debtors	20,000
		Cash at Bank	10,000
	7,00,000		7,00,000

B Co. Ltd.

Liabilities	Rs.	*Assets*	Rs.
100,000 shares of Rs. 10 each, fully paid	10,00,000	Land and Buildings	4,50,000
Sundry Creditors	1,30,000	Plant and Machinery	2,00,000
		Patents	1,10,000
		Stock	1,50,000
		Sundry Debtors	1,20,000
		Cash at Bank	50,000
		Profit and Loss Account	50,000
	11,30,000		11,30,000

The authorised capital of C Ltd. is Rs. 20,00,000 divided into shares of Rs. 10 each. Fully paid shares were sued to the liquidators of A Co. Ltd. and B Co. Ltd. for the business, taken over.

You are required to :

(*i*) give entries to close the books of A Co. Ltd.,

(*ii*) show how shares received from C Ltd. will be distributed among shareholders of A Co. Ltd. and B Co. Ltd.

(*iii*) balance sheet of C Ltd. after competition.

(*Total of Balance Sheet, Rs. 17,80,000*)

2. The following is the Balance Sheet of R Co. Ltd. as at 31st Dec., 1978 :—

Liabilities	Rs.	*Assets*	Rs.
12,000 shares of Rs. 10 each	1,20,000	Goodwill	10,000
Sundry Creditors	30,000	Plant and Machinery	90,000
Profit Prior to Incorporation	2,000	Stock	15,000
Bank Overdraft	36,000	Plant and Machinery	40,000
		Sundry Debtors	22,000
		Profit and Loss Account	11,000
	1,88,000		1,88,000

M Co. Ltd. took over the assets of R Co. Ltd. for Rs. 1,20,000 payable as to half in fully paid shares and half in cash. The expenses of liquidation were Rs. 3,000. A creditor for Rs. 5,000 agreed to take shares in M Co. Ltd. The available cash was just sufficient to statisfy the claims of creditors.

Give entries to close the books of R Co. Ltd. and to record the purchase in the books of M Co. Ltd. (*Loss on Realisation, Rs. 56,000*)

4. With a view to effect economy in working, United India Ltd. agrees to take over the business of Asian Traders Ltd., from 30th September, 1979. The following is the Balance Sheet of Asian Traders Ltd. as on that date :—

Liabilities	Rs.	*Assets*	Rs.
Paid up Capital :		Land and Buildings	1,80,000
12,000 shares of Rs. 50 each	6,00,000	Plant and Machinery	1,25,000
Reserve	1,20,000	Stock	2,50,000
Provision for Doubtful Debts	10,000	Debtors	2,90,000
Creditors	75,000	Cash at Bank	25,000
Profit and Loss Account	65,000		
Total	8,70,000		8,70,000

The purchasers took over all the assets and liabilities of the vendor company excepting a sum of Rs. 10,000 to provide for cost of liquidation and payments to any dissentient shareholders.

The purchase price was to be discharged by the allotment to the sharesholders of the vendor company of one share of Rs. 100 (Rs. 90 paid up) of the United India Ltd. for every two shares in the Asian Traders Ltd.

The market value of the United India Ltd.'s Shares is Rs. 110 per hare on the date of sale. The expenses of liquidation amount of Rs. 3,000. Dissentient shareholders of 100 shares are paid out at Rs. 70 per share, *viz.*, Rs. 7,000.

Pass the necessary journal entries in the books of the respective companies to give effect to the above transactions.

(*Loss on Realisation, Rs. 1,23,500, Purchase consideration, Rs. 6,54,500 for 11,900 Shares in A.T. Ltd.*)

(*B. Com. Bombay*)

4. A Co. Ltd. sells its business to B Co. Ltd. as on 31st December, 1978 on which date its Balance Sheet was as under :—

Liabilities	Rs.	*Assets*	Rs.
Paid up Capital :		Goodwill	50,000
2,000 shares of Rs. 100 each	2,00,000	Freehold Property	1,50,000
Debentures	1,00,000	Plant and Tools	83,000
Trade Creditors	30,000	Stock	35,000
Reserve Fund	50,000	Bills Receivable	4,500
Profit and Loss Account	20,000	Sundry Debtors	27,500
		Cash at Bank	50,000
	4,00,000		4,00,000

The B Co. Ltd. agreed to take over the assets except cash at 10 per cent less than the book values, except that goodwill was valued at Rs. 75,000 and to take over the creditors.

The purchase consideration was to be discharged by the allotment to the A Co. Ltd. of 1,500 shares of Rs. 100 each at a premium of Rs. 10 per share and the balance in cash.

The cost of the liquidation amounted to Rs. 3,000. Show the necessary accounts in the books of A Co. Ltd. and pass the entries recording the transactions in the books of the B Co. Ltd.

(*Loss on Realisation, Rs. 8,000*)

5. On 31st Dec. 1978, the Balance Sheet of Records Ltd. was as under :—

		Rs.		Rs.
Capital :			Sundry Assets	1,57,000
75,000 6% Cumulative Preference Shares of Re. 1 each fully paid		75,000	Profit and Loss Account	52,000
1,00,000 Ordinary Shares of Re. 1 each full paid		1,00,000		
5% Debentures	20,000			
Accrued Interest	2,000			
		22,000		
Sundry Creditors		12,000		
		2,09,000		2,09,000

No dividend has been paid on the preference shares for the past two years. It is proposed that a new company, Stores Ltd., be formed to take over the whole of the assets. The capital of the new company is to consist of ordinary shares of Re. 1 each.

The following scheme has been duly adopted and sanctioned :—

(1) Shares in the new company to be issued in exchange for shares in the old company on the following basis :—

Ordinary shareholders to receive one new share for every five shares held by the them ;

Preference shareholders to receive three new shares for every five shares held and a further one-half new share for every twenty-five shares held in satisfaction of the arrears of preference dividend.

(2) The debenture-holders to be paid by the new company the amount due to them in respect of principal; any claim for arrears of interest was to be waived.

(3) The other creditors to be paid 25% of their claims by the new company in cash and to be allotted shares in the new company to the extent one-half of the balance.

You are required to close the books of the old company assuming that the cost of winding up is to be borne by the new company and that no fractional holdings results from the scheme. Your answer should show the losses sustained by each class of shareholder by reason of the reconstruction.

Also give the balance sheet of the Stores Ltd.

(*Loss on Realisation, Rs. 56,500*)

(*Adapted from B. Com., Bombay*)

6. The following are the balances of Jai Hind Ltd., as at 31st December, 1978 :—

	Rs.
Capital :—	
10,000 6% Cumulative Preference Shares of Rs. 10 each	1,00,000
16,000 Ordinary Shares of Rs. 10 each	1,60,000
Share Premium Account	30,000
Creditors	26,000
Goodwill	10,000
Patents and Trade marks	21,000
Freehold property at cost	70,000
Depreciation thereon	14,000
Plant and Machinery	1,40,000
Depreciation thereon	30,000
Stock on 31st December, 1978	24,000
Debtors	15,000
Profit and Loss Account	55,000
Preliminary Expenses	25,000

A scheme for reduction of capital by the Court was passed on the following terms :—

(1) Preference Shares to be reduced to Rs. 9 per share.

(2) Ordinary Shares to be reduced to Rs. 1.25 per share.

(3) The intangible assets (including Patents and Trade Marks) to be written off.

(4) Plant and Machinery to be revalued at Rs. 50,000.

(5) One Ordinary Share of Rs. 1·25 to be issued for each Rs. 10 of gross preference dividend arrears, which is in arrears since January, 1965.

Draft journal entries and the revised Balance sheet.

(*Total of Balance Sheet, Rs. 1,45,000*)

(*Adapted from B. Com., Bombay*)

7. On 1st July 1978, the Balance Sheet of Satish and Desai Limited was as under :—

	Rs.		Rs.
Issued Share Capital :—		Goodwill	55,000
5,000 6% Cumulative Preference Shares of Rs. 10 each	50,000	Sundry Assets	1,64,500
15,000 ordinary shares of Rs. 10 each fully paid	1,50,000	Cash	500
5% Debentures	30,000	Profit and Loss Account	30,000
Creditors	20,000		
	2,50,000		2,50,000

A scheme of Reconstruction was agreed upon as follows :—

(*i*) A new company to be formed called Satish Limited with authorised capital of Rs. 32,500 Ordinary Shares of Rs. 10 each.

(*ii*) One Ordinary Share, Rs. 5 paid in the new company to be issued for each Ordinary Share in the old company.

(*iii*) Two Ordinary Shares, Rs. 5 paid in the new company to be issued for each preference share in the old company.

(*iv*) Debentureholders to receive 3,000 Ordinary Shares in the new company credited as fully paid.

(*v*) Creditors to be taken over by the new company.

(*vi*) The remaining unissued shares to be taken up and paid for in full by the Directors.

(*vii*) The new company to take over the assets of the old company subject to :—

(*a*) Writing down sundry assets by Rs. 35,000.

(*b*) Adjusting Goodwill as required.

You are required to prepare :—

(*i*) Realization Account and Shareholders Account of the old company.

(*ii*) Opening Enteries of the new company.

(*iii*) Balance Sheet of the new company.

(*Loss on Realisation, Rs, 45,000*)
(*B. Com., Bombay and Delhi*)

8. Bright Ltd. agreed to acquire the goodwill and assets, other than cash, of Master Ltd. as on 31st December, 1966.

The summarised Balance Sheet of Master Ltd. on that date was as under :—

	Rs.		Rs.
Share Capital :		Goodwill	1,20,000
9.00 Shares of Rs. 100 each	9,00,000	Land and Buildings	3,00,000
		Plant	6,00,000
General Reserve	1,50,000	Stock	2,40,000
Profit and Loss A/c	37,000	Debtors	52,000
6% Debentures	2,00,000	Balance at Bank	45,000
Creditors	70,000		
	13,57,000		13,57,000

Bright Ltd. agreed to pay the consideration as follows :—

(1) The issue of 15,000 shares of Rs. 100 each, fully paid, in Bright Ltd. at a premium of Rs. ?0 per share.

(2) Cash payment of Rs. 10 per share for every share in Master Ltd.

(3) The issue of such an amount of fully paid 5% Debentures of Bright Ltd., at a discount of 10%. as is sufficient to discharge 6% debentures of Master Ltd. at a premium of 8%. All the debenture-holders of Master Ltd. agreed to the exchange.

The liabilities of Master Ltd., other than debentures, were to be discharged by that company.

While computing the purchase consideration, the Directors of Bright Ltd. valued land and buildings at Rs. 4,30,000, plant at Rs. 8,70,000, stock at Rs. 2,10,000 and the Debtors at their book value subject to an allowance of 5% to cover doubtful debts.

You are required to pass journal entries including those relating to cash, (*a*) in the books of Bright Ltd to record the acquisition, and (*b*) in the books of Master Ltd. to close the books assuming that the company is liquidated and the assets distributed *pro rata* to its shareholders.

(*Profit on Realisation, Rs. 7,78,000*)
(*B. Com., Bombay*)

9. The following is the Balance Sheet of Ashok Limited as at 31st December, 1968 :—

	Rs.		Rs.
Subscribed Capital :		Fixed Assets :	
36,000 Equity Shares of Rs. 10 each, fully paid	3,60,000	Goodwill	50,000
Reserves and Surplus :		Lend and Buildings	1,40,000
General Reserve	70,000	Plant and Machinery	2,20,700
Accident Insurance Fund	14,500	Furniture	20,800
Profit and Loss Account	1,500	Current Assets :	
Secured Loans :		Stock	72,800
5% Debentures	1,00,000	Debtors	60,000
Current Liabilities and Provisions :		Cash at Bank	16,700
Sundry Creditors	40,000	Miscellaneous Expenses :	
		Discount on issue of Debentures	5,000
	5,86,000		5,86,000

Bharat Limited, a newly formed company took over the assets of Ashok Limited with the exception of book debts. It took over no liabilities. However, it agreed to collect the book debts and pay the liabilities on behalf of Bharat Limited. The purchase consideration was to be discharged as follows :—

(a) To the ordinary shareholders of Ashok Limited were to be allotted six ordinary shares of Rs. 10 each in Bharat Limited for every five held.

(b) The Debenture holders of Ashok Limited were to be allotted 6% Debentures in Bharat Limited so as to give them a premium of 10 per cent.

The expenses of liquidation amounted to Rs. 3,250.

Of the debtors, Rs. 3,000 proved bad and a cash discount of 2 per cent was allowed on settlement. The creditors were paid subject to a discount of 3 per cent. The Bharat Limited were allowed a commission of one per cent on gross debtors collected by it.

Show the ledger accounts necessary to close the books of Ashok Ltd. and give journal entries to record the purchase of business in the books of Bharat Ltd.

(Profit on Realisation, Rs. 4,240)
(Adapted from B. Com., Bombay)

10. The following are the Balance Sheets of two companies A Ltd. and B Ltd. on 31st December, 1978 :—

A Ltd.

	Rs.		Rs.
Ordinary Shares of Re. 1 each fully paid	1,50,000	Goodwill	10,000
Forfeited Shares Account	150	Building at cost	45,000
Reserve Fund	10,000	Machinery at cost less depreciation	35,000
6% Debentures	35,000	Sundry Debtors	25,850
Sundry Creditors	5,785	Stock	68,276
Profit and Loss Account	16,865	Cash at Bank	33,674
	2,17,800		2,17,800

B Ltd.

	Rs.		Rs.
Ordinary Shares of Re. 1 each fully paid	39,000	Goodwill	10,000
5% Debentures	7,000	Building at cost	13,000
Sundry Creditors	25,700	Machinery at cost less depreciation	11,000
Bank Overdraft	600	Sundry Debtors	9,500
		Stock	15,200
		Profit and Loss A/c	13,600
	72,300		72,300

The two companies decided to amalgamate as on 31st December, 1968 and a new company called CY Ltd. was formed with an authorised capital of Rs. 2,50,000 in shares of Re. 1 each.

The following terms were agreed upon :—

A Ltd.

(1) The consideration was 6 shares of Re. 1 each fully paid in the new company in exchange for every five shares in A Ltd., and Rs. 1,000 in cash.

(2) The debentureholders were to be allotted 7% debentures in the new company.

(3) The new company to take over all assets and liabilities at their book values.

B Ltd.

(1) The consideration was one share of Re. 1 each fully paid in the new company in exchange for every 3 shares in B Ltd. and Rs. 500 in cash.

(2) The debentureholders were to be allotted such debentures in the new company bearing interest at 7% per annum as would bring them the same amount of interest.

(3) The new company to take over all the assets and liabilities at book value.

Each company to pay its own cost of winding up.

You are requested to draw up the Balance Sheet of XY Ltd. giving effect to the above scheme.

(*Total of Balance Sheet, Rs. 2,64,485*)
(*Adapted from B.Com., Bombay*)

11. The following is the rough Balance Sheet of X-Ray Trading Co. Ltd. at 31-12-1974 :—

Liabilities	Rs.	*Assets*	Rs.
2,00,000 6% Cumulative Preference Shares of Re. 1 each	2,00,000	Goodwill	2,39,935
1,00,000 Ordinary Shares of Re. 1 each	1,00,000	Buildings	90,970
7% First Mortgage debentures	1,00,000	Machinary	1,13,000
Sundry Creditors	64,300	Furniture	1,800
Reserve Fund	90,000	Stock	33,200
		Cash at Bank	18,950
		Sundry Debtors	30,445
		Profit and Loss A/c	26,000
	5,54,300		5,54,300

A scheme of reconstruction has been approved by members and sanctioned by the High Court which provides for the reduction of the authorised capital to Rs. 1,94,000 divided into 1,00,000 7%. Cumulative Preference Shares of Re. 1 each, 80,000 6% Non-cumulative Preference Shares of Re. 1 each, and 14,000 Ordinary Shares of Re. 1 each. Debentureholders receive one 7% Cumulative Preference Share and one-twentieth (1/20th) Ordinary Share (through fractional certificates) for each Re. 1 of Debenture held. Preference Shareholders receive two Non-cumulative Preference Shares and 1/10th Ordinary Shares for every 5 Shares held, and Ordinary Shareholders receive 1/20th Ordinary Share for every Ordinary Share held. The deficit on Profit and Loss Account and Goodwill Account to be completely written off. Rs. 20,970 and Rs. 9,095 to be written off Buildings and Machinery, respectively.

You are requested to prepare (*a*) Journal entries recording these transactions and (*b*) Reconstructed Balance Sheet of the Company, after giving full effect to the scheme. Prepare the Balance Sheet as far as practicable in the form laid down under Companies Act, 1956.

(*Total of Balance Sheet*; *Rs. 2,58,300*)
(*B.Com., Bombay*)

CHAPTER XX

INSOLVENCY ACCOUNTS

A person is called insolvent when he cannot pay his debts. A company can also be insolvent, but a company is governed almost wholly by the Companies Act. Strictly speaking, therefore, the term of insolvency applies only to an individual, a partnership firm or a Hindu Undivided Family. It may be noted that the terms bankrupt and insolvent are synonymous ; the word bankrupt is used in England and insolvent in India.

When a person (or a firm or a Hindu Joint Family) is unable to pay liabilities, in full, he may make a petition to the Court to be adjudged insolvent. One of the creditors may also submit a similar petition. The Court, after hearing the parties, decides whether the debtor is to be adjudicated as insolvent or not. If so, an officer called 'Official Receiver' is appointed by the Court to take charge of the entire property of the debtor, to realise it and to distribute the proceeds amongst the various creditors according to their claims. It is the duty of the debtor to surrender all his property to the Official Receiver and to give him all information relating to his property, assets and debts.

When the property has been realised and distributed, the Court may decide to discharge the debtor. On obtaining the discharge (to which certain conditions may be attached), the debtor becomes completely free again and he has no obligation to pay the previous debts, even if part of the debts remains unsatisfied.

Individuals and Partnerships. There is one important difference in the position of individuals and that of partnership firms. In case of an individual, there is no difference between the private liabilities and business liabilities and between private assets and business assets. Both are aggregated. Suppose, the business assets of a person are Rs. 30,000 and the private assets Rs. 5,000. The business liabilities are Rs. 45,000 and private liabilities Rs. 3,000. For all purposes, the total property will be Rs. 35,000 to be distributed amongst the creditors having a claim of Rs. 48,000. It is not permissible that the private creditors should claim a full payment of Rs. 3,000 out of the private assets.

In case of partnership, however, a distinction is made between firm's assets and private assets of partners on the one hand and firm's liabilities and private liabilities of partners on the other hand. The rule is that first the private assets of a partner should be used to pay his private liabilities. Only if there is a surplus, it can be used for paying the firm's liabilities. Similarly, the firm's assets must first be used to pay the firm's liabilities. If there is a surplus, then a partner's share of that surplus can be used to pay his private liabilities.

In India there are two Insolvency Acts. One is the Presidency Towns Insolvency Act which applies only to the Presidency towns of Bombay, Calcutta and Madras. The other is the Provincial Insolvency Act which is applicable to the rest of the country. There are certain minor differences in the two Acts.

Preferential Creditors. Out of the creditors who look to the assets of the debtor generally for satisfaction of their claims, certain creditors must be paid first. Such creditors are known as preferential creditors. Under the Presidency Towns Insolvency Act the following are the preferential creditors :—

1. All debts due to the Government or Local authorities.
2. Salary of each clerk for 4 months not exceeding Rs. 300. Suppose a clerk has worked for 5 months at a salary of Rs. 100. He will be preferential creditor to the extent of Rs. 300 and for the remaining balance of Rs. 200 he will be like other creditors.
3. Wages of each servant for 4 months not exceeding Rs. 100.
4. Rent for one month.

Under the provincial Insolvency Act the preferential creditors are the following :—

1. All debts due to Government or local authorities.
2. Salary of each clerk and wages of each servant for 4 months not exceeding Rs. 20 per clerk or servant.

If the amount available is not sufficient to pay all the preferential creditors fully, the amount has to be distributed proportionately amongst such creditors.

Statement of Affairs. Under the Insolvency Acts, the debtor has to prepare a statement of affairs showing the amounts which are expected to be paid and the amount which is expected to be realised from assets. Usually, the amount to be paid to creditors is more than the amount expected to be received by disposal of assets; the difference is known as deficiency. The statement of affairs has to set out the various liabilities and assets in a particular manner. In its essence, however, the statement of affairs is like the Balance Sheet with two important differences :

(1) The liabilities have to be shown at the amount at which they have to be paid and the assets have to be shown not at their book values but at their realisable values.

(2) The statement of affairs shows no capital. On the other hand, there is a deficit or deficiency.

Liabilities have to be grouped under four heads. These are:

(*a*) Unsecured creditors;
(*b*) Fully secured creditors;
(*c*) Partly secured creditors; and
(*d*) Preferential creditors.

Preferential creditors have already been explained. They are really unsecured since there is no particular asset in their hands which they can realise to pay themselves. But by law they have been put in a separate category. Unsecured creditors will be all those who have no claim on a particular asset belonging to the debtor. They will look to the Official Receiver for payment of their claims. Fully secured creditors are those whose claims are fully covered by the security held by them (*i.e.*, asset mortgaged in their favour). Partly secured creditors are those whose claims are not fully covered by the security held. They will be like the unsecured creditors for the amount left unpaid after the security has been realised. Both the fully secured and partly secured creditors can themselves realise the security in their hands, *i.e.*, sell the assets which have been mortgaged in their favour. If the amount realised by them is more than the amount of their claim they have to hand over the surplus to the Official Receiver. If the amount received is less they will prove their claim to the Official Receiver for the balance. A fully secured creditor up to the amount of his claim and a partly secured creditor up to the amount realised by the sale of asset under his charge has a better claim than even the preferential creditors.

The **unsecured creditors** in an ordinary trading firm would consist of the following :—

1. Amounts due to sundry creditors for supplies of the goods or other expenses (except amounts due for rates, taxes, wages, salaries and rent).
2. Creditors for expenses including the amounts due over and above the limits laid down for preferential creditors in respect of wages, salaries, and rent.
3. Bills payable.
4. Amount expected to be paid in respect of bills receivable already discounted. It should be noted that if the debtor received a bill and has kept it, it will be an asset in his hand; but if he has discounted it, there is a contingent liability. If the bill is dishonoured, the bank will call upon the debtor to pay. Usually, in such a case nothing is recoverable from those who have dishonoured the bill. Therefore, the amount to be paid is both a liability and a loss.
5. In case of individuals only, the amounts due to private creditors.

There is a small difference between gross liabilities and the amount expected to be paid or expected to rank. The difference is only in respect of contingent liabilities like bills discounted where the total contingent liability may be much more than the amount likely to be demanded. In the gross liabilities the total possible amount is included; for liabilities expected to rank only the amount likely to be demanded by the bank or other creditors is to be added.

Note. Loan from the wife of the insolvent will rank for payment like sums due to other creditors *unless* the loan was given out of funds provided by the insovent.

The debtor has to make lists of all creditors separately for the four categories mentioned. The list containing the names of unsecured creditors is named as list A. The list containing the names of secured creditors is called list B and the list of unsecured creditors is called list C. List D is the name for the list containing names of preferential creditors.

Properties and Assets. The properties and assets are divided into three main categories :—

1. Property.
2. Book debts.
3. Bills of exchange.

Under the head property details have to be given for the various assets like cash, stock in trade, furniture and fixtures, plant and machinery, land and buildings, etc. All these amounts have to be listed showing the book figure and the amount expected to be realised. The name given to this list is list E.

Two points should be noted :

1. In case of individuals, the private property of the debtor should be included.
2. Assets in the possession of secured or partly secured creditors should not be included.

Book debts are all listed under three categories :

(1) Good, *i.e.*, those from whom the full amount will be received ;

(2) Doubtful, *i.e.*, those from whom the amount may or may not be received; and

(3) Bad *i.e.*, those from whom nothing can be recovered.

Here also the book figure and the amount expected to be realised is to be given. The list is headed as list F. Bills of exchange in hand, *i.e.*, bills receivable in possession of the debtor are listed in list G. Information must be given for book value and amount expected to be realised.

The broad scheme for preparation of the statement of affairs is as under :—

1. On the left hand side, firstly, the total amount of unsecured creditors is entered.
2. In the inner column the amount due to fully secured creditors is put and, immediately below, the estimated realisable value of securities in their hands is given. Usually there is a surplus. The surplus is transferred to the other side of the statement of affairs. Sometimes, there may be a second charge created in favour of some partly secured creditor. In that case, the surplus is to

be added to the estimated realisable value of securities in the hands of such creditors.

3. The amount due to partly secured creditors is entered in the inner column and below that is given the estimated realisable value of securities in their hands (including any surplus to be transferred from fully secured creditors if there is a second charge). The excess of the amount to be paid over the estimated realisable value of security is entered in the outer column.

4. Total amount due to preferential creditors is entered in the inner column. It is not extended to the outer column because it will be deducted from the total of assets.

On the right hand side :

Firstly, the various assets under the head property should be entered giving the book figure and then the realisable value in the column headed 'estimated to produce'. Similarly, in case of book debts and bills of exchange book figures are to given and estimated to produce figures are entered in the outer column. Surplus, if any, left in the hands of fully secured creditors (if it is not to be transferred to partly secured creditors) is then entered in the outer column. The outer column is totalled for all assets. From this the amount due to preferential creditors is deducted. Then the outer column of the left hand side is totalled and compared with the remaining amount of assets; the difference will be deficiency and this will be put on the right hand side The statement is then totalled.

There is a prescribed form for the preparation of the statement of affair which will be given along with the illustration given below.

Illustration Gilra of Calcutta is insolvent. From the following figures prepare his statement of affairs as on 30th June, 1974 :—

Liabilities		*Assets*	*Book value*	*Realisable Value*
	Rs.		Rs.	Rs.
Trade Creditors	26,000	Furniture		
Bills Payable	3,000	business	3.000	1,000
Loan from Bank		private	2,000	1,000
against lien on stock	10,000	Stock	20,000	15,000

	Rs.		Rs.	Rs.
Mortgage on Building	15,000	Building	18,000	12,000
Creditors for taxes	600	Machinery	20,000	10,000
Salaries due to clerks for 5 months	1,000	Debtors—		
		Good	6,000	6,000
Gross amount of bills discounted (of these two bills for Rs. 2,000 are expected to be dishonoured)	6,000	Doubtful	7,000	3,000
		Bad	1,000	—
		Bills Receivable	2,500	2,000
		Cash	100	100
Private liabilities	2,000			

Solution :

Working Notes

	Rs.
Unsecured Creditors are the following :—	
Trade Creditors	26,000
Bills Payable	3,000
Salary to clerks for one month (four months' salary being preferential)	200
Amount payable on bills discounted	2,000
Private liabilities	2,000
	33,200

Fully Secured Creditor :

Bank Loan, Rs. 10,000, value of security (Stock) being Rs. 15,000.

Partly Secured Creditor :

Mortgage on Building, Rs. 15,000, value of security (Building) being Rs. 12,000.

Preferential creditors :

	Rs.
Taxes due	600
Salary to clerks for 4 months	800
	1,400

Statement of Affairs of Gilra as at June 30, 1964

Gross Liabilities Rs.	*Liabilities*	Rs.	*Expected to Rank* Rs.	*Property and Assets*	*Book Value* Rs.	*Estimated to Produce* Rs.
37,200	Unsecured creditors as per list A		33,200	Property as per list E :		
				Cash	100	100
				Furniture	5,000	2,000
10,000	Fully secured creditors as per list B	10,000		Machinery	20,000	10,000
	Estimated value of security	15,000	—	Book Debts as per list F :		
				Good	6,000	6,000
				Doubtful	7,000	
	Surplus carried to contra	5,000		Bad	1,000	
				Estimated to produce		3,000
15,000	Partly secured creditors as per list C	15,000		Bills of Exchange as per list G :	2,500	2,000
	Estimated value of security	12,000	3,000	Surplus as per contra		5,000
					41,600	28,100
1,400	Preferential creditors for taxes, salaries as per list D	1,400		Preferential creditors as per list D, deducted as per contra		1,400
	Deducted as per contra	1,400				26,700
				Deficiency as explained in list H		9,500
63,600	Total		36,200	Total		36,200

Deficiency Account (List H). Deficiency Account is meant to explain how various losses and domestic expenses come to absorb the proprietor's capital and the profits earned and leave a deficit to be borne by creditors. The Official Receiver or Assignee fixes a date and the insolvent person has to give information regarding profits and losses and withdrawals for private use since that date. The account is divided into two sides: the left hand side starts with the capital (excess of assets over liabilities) on the date fixed by the Official Receiver and records all profits earned after that date including the profit, if any, expected to be realised by sale of assets. The right hand side records all losses and withdrawals and starts with the deficit, if any, on the date fixed by the Official Receiver. The right hand side total is usually bigger than the total of the items on the left hand side—the difference is deficiency and agrees with the deficiency as shown in the Statement of Affairs. The order in which various items are put down is shown by the form given below.

Deficiency Account

	Rs.		Rs.
Excess of assets over capital on......		Excess of liabilities over assets on	
Net profit arising from carrying on business from..... to date of the Receiving Order after deducting usual trade expenses		Net loss arising from carrying on business from... ...to the date of the Receiving Order after accounting for the usual trade expenses.	
Income or profit from other sources since..... to the date of the Receiving Order		Bad Debts	
Deficiency as per Statement of Affairs		Expenses incurred since ......other than the usual business expenses (*e.g.*, household expenses)	
		Other Losses (loss expected on realisation of assets, for example)	
	————		————
	====		====

Illustration Reckless of Calcutta is insolvent. From the figures given below prepare his Statement of Affairs as at Dec. 31, 1963 and the Deficiency Account.

	Book Value	*Expected to Realise*
	Rs.	Rs.
(*i*) Business Assets :		
Land and Buildings	1,00,000	90,000
Book Debts—Good	60,000	60,000
—Doubtful	5,000	2,500
—Bad	19,000	

	Rs.	Rs.
Plant and Machinery	40,000	30,000
Stock in Trade	20,000	14,000
Shares	3,000	4,000

(*ii*) Private Assets :

Life Policy	10,000	5,000
Furniture	—	3,600

(*iii*) Business Liabilities :

Bank Loan	Rs.	50,000	(with a first mortgage on Land and Buildings)
Loan from the estate of Mrs. Reckless	Rs.	60,000	(with a second mortgage on Land and Buildings)
Trade Creditors	Rs.	1,25,000	
Wages (100 workers)	Rs.	26,000	

(*iv*) Private Liabilities :

Loan from L.I.C.	Rs.	3,000	(against surrender value of policy)
Creditors for supplies	Rs.	1,900	

In addition to above, he had got bills discounted to the extent of Rs. 6,000 out of which, it was expected, those for Rs. 2,500 would be dishonoured.

On 1st January, 1970 he had a capital of Rs. 1,20,000. After allowing 6% interest on the capital, he earned a profit of Rs. 20,000 in 1970 and Rs. 22,800 in 1971. In 1962 and 1973 he suffered losses of Rs. 22,550 and Rs. 37,200 similarly computed. His total withdrawals for domestic purposes were Rs. 1,45,850 in the four years.

Solution :

Workings

Unsecured Creditors :—	Amount	Security
	Rs.	Rs.
Trade Creditors	1,25,000	—
Wages (over Rs. 100 per worker)	16,000	—
Creditors for Supplies (Private)	1,900	—
Bills Discounted	2,500	—
	1,45,400	—
Fully Secured Creditors :		
Bank Loan	50,000	90,000
Loan From L.I.C.	3,000	5,000
	53,000	95,000
Partly Secured Creditor :		
Loan from the estate of Mrs. Reckless	60,000	40,000 (surplus from Land and Buildings)
Preferential Creditors :		
Wages of 100 workers @ Rs. 100	10,000	

Profit earned from business :

	Rs.	Loss	
In 1960	20,000	In 1962	22,550
In 1961	22,800	In 1963	37,200
Add interest or capital for two years	14,400		59,750
		Less Interest on capital for 2 years	14,400
	57,200		45,350

Surplus of Household assets :

	Rs.
Total assets	8,600
Less Private liabilities	4,900
	3,700

Statement of Affairs of Reckless as at December 31, 1963

Gross Liabilities Rs.	Liabilities		Expected to Rank Rs.	Property and Assets	Book value Rs.	Estimated to Produce Rs.
1,48,900	Unsecured Creditors as per list A		1,45,400	Property as per list E :		
				Stock	20,000	14,000
53,000	Fully Secured Creditors as per list B	53,000		Shares	3,000	4,000
				Plant and Machinery	40,000	30,000
	Estimated value of security	95,000	—	Furniture	—	3,600
				Book Debts as per list F :		
	Surplus	42,000		Good	60,000	60,000
	Surplus carried to contra	2,000		Doubtful	5,000	
				Bad	19,000	
	Surplus carried to list C	40,000		Estimated to produce		2,500
				Surplus as per contra		2,000
60,000	Partly Secured Creditors as per list C	60,000				1,16,100
	Estimated value of Security	40,000	20,000	Preferential Creditors as per list D, deducted as per contra		10,000
10,000	Creditors for wages being preferential as per list D	10,000				1,06,100
	Deducted as per contra		—	Deficiency as explained in list H		59,300
2,71,900		Total	1,65,400	Total		1,65,400

Deficiency Account—List (H)

	Rs.		Rs.	Rs.
Excess of assets over capital as at 1st Jan, 1960	1,20,000	Loss arising from carrying on of business from 1st Jan., 1960 to the date of Receiving Order		45,350
Net Profit arising from carrying on of business from 1st Jan. 1960 to the date of Receiving Order	57,200	Bad Debts		21,500
Incomes or Profits from other sources—surplus of household assets over liabilities	3,700	Expenses other than the usual business expenses—household expenses		1,45,850
Profit on Shares	1,000	Other Losses :—		
Deficiency as per Statement of Affairs	59,300	Land and Buildings	10,000	
		Plant and Machinery	10,000	
		Stock	6,000	
		Bills Discounted	2,500	28,500
Total	2,41,200	Total		2,41,200

Illustration A and B are in partnership and file their petition in bankruptcy. From the following particulars, prepare the Statement of Affairs of the firm as to December 31, 1964 :—

	Firm Rs.	*A* Rs.	*B* Rs.
Mortgage on freehold	3,000	—	—
Bank Overdraft	3,000	—	—
Sundry Creditors	12,400	1,500	2,900
Preferential Creditors	100	—	—
Capitals —A	3,000	—	—
—B	2,000	—	—
Surplus	—	5,000	1,100
	23,500	6,500	4,000
Freehold	6,000	—	—
Plant	6,500	—	—
Furniture	400	1,000	1,200
Debtors	5,000	—	—
Stock	5,500	—	—
Investments	—	2,500	800
Cash	100	—	—
Capitals in the firm	—	3,000	2,000
	23,500	6,500	4,000

The Bank overdraft was secured by a second mortgage on freeholds and on B's investments.

The amounts expected to be realised were :

	Firm Rs.	A Rs.	B Rs.
Freeholds	4,500	—	—
Plant	3,000	—	—
Furniture	150	600	800
Stock	3,100	—	—
Debtors	3,075	—	—
Investments	—	2,000	300

Solution :

Statement of Affairs of M/s. A and B as at 31st Dec. 1974

Gross Liabilities Rs.	*Liabilities*		*Expected to Rank* Rs.	*Property and Assets*	*Book Value* Rs.	*Estimated to Produce* Rs.
12,400	Unsecured Creditors as per list A		12,400	Property as per list E :—		
3,000	Fully secured creditors as per list A	3,000		Cash	100	100
	Estimated value of security	4,500		Stock	5,500	3,100
				Furniture	400	150
	Surplus to list C	1,500	—	Plant	6,500	3,000
				Surplus from A's estate		1,100
3,000	Partly secured creditors as per list C	3,000		Book Debts as per list F :— Good, Doubtful, Bad	5,000	
	Estimated value of security	1,500	1,500	Estimated to produce		3,075
						10,525
100	Preferential creditors as per list D, deducted as per contra	100	—	Preferential creditors as per list D, deducted as per contra		100
						10,425
				Deficiency as explained in list H		3,475
18'500	Total		13,900	Total		13,900

Deficiency Account—List (H)

	Rs.		Rs.
Excess of assets over liabilities as at 31st Dec. 1974	5,000	Losses :	
Surplus from A's estate	1,100	Freeholds	1,500
Deficiency as per Statement of Affairs	3,475	Plant	3,500
		Furniture	250
		Stock	2,400
		Debtors	1,925
	9,575		9,575

The Bank will get whatever it can from the firm and then prove for the balance for payment out of B's investments.

EXERCISE XX

1. Mr. Unlucky filed his petition on 31st December, 1973 and his Statement of Affairs was made from the following figures :

	Rs.
Creditors fully secured by lien on stock	20,000
Creditors partly secured by lien on shares	80,000
Creditors unsecured	1,50,000
Mortgage on building	20,000
Creditors payable in full	6,000
Liability on Bills Discounted (estimated to rank Rs. 7,000)	12,000
Bills of Exchange	2,800
Building	22,000
Machinery (estimated to realise Rs. 24,000)	30,000
Furniture & Fixtures (estimated to realise Rs. 3,000)	6,000
Sundry Assets (estimated to realise Rs. 6,000)	7,000
Book debts, good	40,000
Book debts, doubtful and bad (estimated to produce Rs. 4,000)	20,000
Consignments (realizable value)	10,000
Stock (estimated to realise Rs. 80,000)	1,20,000
Shares (cost and estimated to realise)	32,000
Cash	200

On 1st January, 1948, six years ago, Mr. Unlucky had a capital of Rs. 1,00,000. From 1948 to 1953 he made a profit of Rs. 41,000 after allowing interest on capital Rs. 20,000; his withdrawals amount to Rs. 77,200. He suffered a loss in speculation amounting to Rs. 69,800.

Prepare the Statement of Affairs and Deficiency Account.

(Deficiency, Rs. 59,000)
(Adapted from B. Com., Bombay)

2. Shri Bankrupt of Bombay filed his petition for being declared insolvent on 31st December, 1970. From the following information prepare his Statement of Affairs and Deficiency Account :

	Rs.
Creditors (including Rs. 10,000 due to Mrs. Bankrupt)	50,000
Buildings and Land (mortgaged)	35,000
Due to Government and Employee	1,000
Rent due to Landlord for four months	2,000
Cash	200
Due to Bank on Cash Credit Account against hypothecation of stock-in-trade	25,000
Investments	5,000
Stock-in-trade	40,000
Loan against pledge of Investments	10,000
Bills Receivable	7,000
Bills Payable	4,200
Sundry Debtors	45,000
Bills Receivable Discounted (of which Rs. 2,000 may be dishonoured)	7,000
Mortgage Creditors	40,000

The assets were expected to realise the following values :—

	Rs.
Buildings and Land	45,000
Investments	2,000
Debtors	26,000
Stocks	32,000
Bills Receivable	5,000

He had started business on 1st July 1956 with a capital of Rs. 50,000; up to 31st December 1959 he made profits of Rs. 22,000 and thereafter losses of Rs. 39,600. His drawings were at the rate of Rs. 600 per month throughout.

(Deficiency Rs. 24,000)
(Adapted from B. Com., Bombay)

3. Shri Scarce Finance finding himself unable to pay off his liabilities filed his petition in bankruptcy on 31st December 1954. His books showed the following position :

Liabilities :—

	Rs.
Trade Creditors (including a Creditor for Rs. 19,200 who held as security stock costing Rs. 6,000 estimated to realise 80%)	1,40,000
Loan Creditors	2,400
Creditors for Income-tax, Salaries and Rent of which Rs. 300 are not preferential	2,304
Bills Payable	1,000
Creditors secured against mortgage of Buildings	29,358
Bank overdraft the Bank holding a second charge on Buildings)	31,500

Assets :—

	Book value Rs.	*Estimated to Realise* Rs.
Stock on hand (excluding stock in the hand of the creditor)	51,900	28,200
Plant and Machinery	12,000	4,800
Furniture	2,400	600
Sundry Debtors—Good,	41,400	41,400
Bad and Doubtful	51,000	4,500
Surplus from Private Estate	...	3,000
Buildings	36,000	32,400
Cash on hand	240	240

There is a contingent liability for Rs. 480 on Bills discounted by him for Rs. 2,700.

On 1st January, 1953, the books showed excess of assets over liabilities of Rs. 15,000 and the business resulted in profit of Rs. 3,450 for the first year and in a loss of Rs. 7,272 in the second year. He had his drawings amounting to Rs. 16,800 in course of the two years.

From the above particulars prepare the Statement of Affairs and Deficiency Account.

(Deficiency Rs 87,102)
(Adapted from B.Com., Bombay)

4. A Receiving Order was made against Desai on 31st December, 1955. He commenced business on 1st January 1950 with a capital of

Rs. 30,000. From the following particulars prepare his Statement of Affairs and Deficiency Account.

Assets	*Book Value* Rs.	*Estimated to produce* Rs.
Freehold Premises (subject to an annual rental of Rs. 3,600 paid up to 30th June, 1955)	32,000	32,000
Cash in hand	400	400
Book Debts	28,700	21,160
Bills Receivable	1,000	800
Private Residence (mortgaged in respect of a loan of Rs. 20,000 with interest at 6% per annum paid to 30th September, 1955)	25,000	25,000
Household Furniture	—	2,600
Machinery	38,000	18,000
Stock-in-Trade	18,000	13,500
Investments	2,600	3,200
Liabilities	*Gross value*	*Expected to Rank*
On Bills Discounted	11,000	4,000
Unsecured Creditors	61,600	61,600
Preferential Creditors	2,000	2,000
Private Creditors		12,000
Bank Overdraft (Secured by leasehold)	30,100	30,100
Mortgage of Private Residence	20,000	20,000 (plus interest to date)
Outstanding Expenses	70	70
Loan Account (Secured by Machinery)	20,000	20,000

Desai made a total profit of Rs. 14,880 in his business during the above period. His drawings amounted to Rs. 2,000 each year. During 1953 he had received gifts from relatives of Rs. 4,000 and this amount has been invested by him in the business. He had also lost Rs. 31,750 during this period due to speculation.

(*Deficiency Rs. 35,210*)

(*Adapted from B.Com., Bombay*)

5. A and B carrying on business in partnership shared profits and losses in the ratio of 2 : 3. They filed their petition in bankruptcy on 30th June, 1957, when their Balance Sheet was as follows :—

	Rs.		Rs.
A's Capital	17,000	Cash on hand	100
B's Capital	10,100	Goodwill	3,000
Loan Secured on Plant and Machinery	28,000	Plant and Machinery	30.000
		Furniture	5,000
		Investments	5,000
Bills Payable	10,000	Debtors (including Rs. 5,000 for dishonoured bill and Rs. 1,500 bad)	36,000
Bank overdraft	15,000	Stock	15.000
Sundry creditors	60,000	Loss in forward contracts	20,000
		Profit and Loss	8,000
		A's Drawings	10,000
		B's Drawings	8,000
	1,40,100		1,40,100

The assets of the firm are estimated to realise as under:—

Plant and Machinery Rs. 20,000 ; Stock Rs. 12,000; Investments Rs. 2,000 and Furniture Rs. 1,200.

The Loan secured was further secured by a charge on B's house.

Sundry creditors include Rs. 1,500 preferential ; Rs. 2,000 due to wife of A and Rs. 3,000 in respect of claim against the firm which is not expected to rank.

It is expected that A's private estate would show a surplus of Rs. 2,000.

Besides the house which was expected to realise Rs. 4,000, B owned furniture worth Rs. 1,000. He owed Rs. 4,500 to his private creditors.

Prepare the Statement of Affairs and the Deficiency Account of the firm.

(Deficiency, Rs. 43,200)

(Adapted from B.Com., Bombay)

6. Bhutto of Calcutta gives you the following figures :

	Rs.
Total assets on 31st December, 1964	1,20,000
Total creditors on 31st December, 1964	80,000
Estimated Deficiency on 31st December, 1964	30,000

The estimated deficiency and the other figures did not include the following :—

(*i*) Interest on capital on Rs. 50,000 (as at 1st Jan., 1964) @ 6% p.a.

(*ii*) Liability on bills discounted, total Rs. 5,000 out of which Rs. 2,000 was likely to rank.

(*iii*) Salary to two clerks for 5 months @ Rs. 125 p.m.

Prepare Bhutto's Statement of Affairs and Deficiency Account.

(Deficiency, Rs. 33,250)

CHAPTER XXI

BANK ACCOUNTS

The Banking Regulation Act, 1949, defines banking as "the accepting, for the purpose of lending or investment, of deposits of money from the public, repayable on demand or otherwise and withdrawable by cheque, draft or otherwise". Companies carrying on a banking business are also subject to the Companies Act, 1956 besides the Banking Regulations Act, 1949. Among other things the Banking Regulation Act prescribes forms for the final accounts of a bank. The relevant provisions of the Companies Act, 1956 do not apply to bank. 14 of the largest Indian banks were nationalised in 1969.

Restrictions on Business. Section 6 of the Banking Regulation Act lays down that in addition to the usual banking business, the following business may also be carried on by a banking company :

(*a*) agency business (except managing agency) and being an attorney on behalf of customers;

(*b*) contracting, negotiating and issuing public or private loans;

(*c*) work in respect of issue of shares, bonds, loans, etc.;

(*d*) guarantee and indemnity business;

(*e*) managing and selling property which the bank acquires in satisfaction of claims or which may be given to the bank as security;

(*f*) undertaking and executing trusts; and

(*g*) administration of estates.

A bank is allowed to do whatever is necessary for efficient conduct of its business such as welfare work for employees or ex-employees, acquisition of property necessary for its work, etc.

Other types of business are prohibited for a banking company. A bank cannot directly or indirectly deal in the buying or selling or bartering of goods, except in connection with the realisation of security given to or held by it, or engage in any trade or buy or sell or barter goods for others otherwise than in connection with bills of exchange. Immovable property, except that required for its own use, however acquired, must be disposed of within seven years from the date of acquisition. Such assets are also called non-banking assets.

Non-banking assets are those which are acquired by a bank in satisfaction of claims, *i.e.*, when a borrower does not pay and the bank acquires rights over the security lodged.

Management. A banking company cannot employ or be managed by :—

(*a*) a managing agent;

(*b*) a person who is, or at any time has been adjudicated insolvent, or has suspended payment or has compounded with his creditors, or who is or has been convicted by a criminal court of an office involving moral turpitude;

(*c*) a person who is a director of any other company not being a subsidiary company of the banking company or a company registered under Section 25 of the Companies Act, 1956. (This restriction does not operate for periods up to 3 months or such further period not exceeding 9 months as the Reserve Bank may allow);

(*d*) a person who is engaged in any other business or vocation.

The Board of Directors has to be so considered as to represent different interests – agricultural, industrial, etc. The chairman has to be a whole-time servant of the bank.

Remuneration cannot be fixed on the basis of a commission on profits. The Reserve Bank may also fix maximum limit of remuneration for the managerial personnel. The contract of service, except in case of directors, cannot be for more than five years at a time. The Reserve Bank can also order the removal of the chairman, director or chief executive officer if the person concerned has been found by any tribunal or other authority (other than a criminal court) to have contravened the provision of any law.

Minimum Capital and Reserve. Section 11 lays down the following as the minimum limit of paid up capital and reserves :—

(*a*) Banking companies incorporated outside India :—

If it has a place of business in Bombay or Calcutta.	Rs. 20 lakhs
If the places of business are elsewhere.	Rs. 15 lakhs
The sum must be kept deposited with the Reserve Bank either in cash or in the form of unencumbered securities.	

(*b*) Banking companies incorporated in India :—

(*i*) If the places of business are in more than one State and if any places of business are in Bombay or Calcutta.	Rs. 10 lakhs
(*ii*) If the places of business are in more than one State but none of the places of business are in Bombay or Calcutta.	Rs. 5 lakhs
(*iii*) If the places of business are only in one State, none of the places of business being in Bombay or Calcutta.	Rs. 1 lakh for the principal place plus Rs. 10,000 for each additional place of business in the same district and Rs. 25,000 for a place of business outside the district. The total capital need not exceed Rs. 5 lakhs.

		A new banking company must have a minimum paid up capital of Rs. 5 lakhs.
(*iv*)	If the places of business are only in one State and if the places of business are also in Bombay or Calcutta.	Rs. 5 lakhs plus Rs. 25,000 for each place of business situated outside Bombay and Calcutta. (The total capital need not exceed Rs. 10 lakhs).

In case of banking companies carrying on business in India :

(*a*) the subscribed capital cannot be less than half the authorised capital;

(*b*) the paid up capital cannot be less than half the subscribed capital; and

(*c*) the capital of the company must consist only of ordinary or equity shares and such preference shares as may have been issued before July 1, 1944.

Underwriting commission or brokerage on shares issued by a banking company cannot exceed 2½% of the paid up value of the shares. A charge on unpaid capital is illegal.

A shareholder cannot exercise more than one per cent of the total voting rights of the company. A chairman, managing director or chief executive of a banking company must declare his full holdings in the capital of the company.

Floating Charge on Assets. A banking company is not allowed to create a floating charge on the undertaking or any property of the company or any part thereof except upon a certificate from the Reserve Bank that such a charge is not detrimental to the interests of the depositors of the company.

Restrictions on Dividends. A banking company must not pay dividends unless all of its capitalised expenses (including preliminary expenses, organisation expenses, share selling commission, brokerage, amounts of losses incurred and any other item of expenditure not represented by tangible assets) have been completely written off.

Statutory Reserve. Section 17 of the Act lays down that 20 per cent of the profits prior to declaration of dividend must be transferred to the Reserve Fund unless the Reserve Bank has granted exemption to the bank.

Cash Reserves. A scheduled bank (*i.e.*, a bank included in the schedule maintained by the Reserve Bank of India) has to maintain with the Reserve Bank a balance equal to 3 per cent of its time liabilities (*i.e.*, deposits received for fixed terms) as well as of its demand liabilities. A non-scheduled bank has to maintain similar balances either in cash or as deposit with the Reserve Bank. In addition every banking company must continuously maintain in cash, gold or unencumbered approved securities valued at a price not exceeding the current market price, an amount not less than 25 per cent of the total of its time and demand liabilities in India. The Reserve Bank of India has powers to require larger proportions of cash and securities being maintained by banks.

Restrictions on Loans and Advances. A bank cannot now grant loans or advances against its own shares or to any of its Directors, to a firm in which any of its directors is interested as partner, manager or guarantor, to a company in which any of its directors is a Director, manager, employee or guarantor or in which he holds a substantial interest or to any individual who is a partner of any of the directors of the bank or for whom any director has provided a guarantee. But advances or loans to subsidiaries of the bank, Government companies or companies registered under Section 25 of the Companies Act (for promotion of science, culture etc. and prohibiting dividend to shareholders) will not be affected.

Control. The Reserve Bank of India has the authority to exercise general supervision on the working of banks and to conduct investigation into the affairs of any bank. The Reserve Bank may also order a bank not to accept further deposits. Every bank has to obtain a licence from the Reserve Bank and permission to open a branch.

Special type of service. One should note that in addition to the usual business of receiving deposits and making loans, banks render the following main types of service :—

(1) collection of bills and bills of exchange on behalf of clients;

(2) giving guarantees on behalf of its clients for loans raised by them or credit received by them; and

(3) accepting bills of exchange and making endorsements on their behalf.

In the first case, the bank keeps the bill of exchange till maturity; on realization it credits the account of the client concerned. To keep track of the numerous bills, the bank treats this as both an asset and a liability of equal amount—an asset because it will receive cash and liability because the amount must be credited to the account of the client. Bills for collection appear on both sides of the Balance Sheet.

Note. *Bills for Collection should not be confused with Bills Discounted and Purchased. The latter is an outright asset of the bank and is to be shown in the Balance Sheet as part of Advances.*

In the second and third cases the bank agrees to incur a liability on behalf of the client but, as soon as the bank is called upon to pay, the client will be debited. Liabilities and assets in this respect are, therefore, again equal. Entries are made on that basis. Suppose A makes a purchase from B and wants credit. B wants A to furnish proper security. A may—

(*a*) request his bank to stand as a guarantor;

(*b*) request the bank to send its own acceptance to B; and

(*c*) send a promissory note in favour of the bank and the bank may then endorse it in favour of B.

Guarantee and endorsements have the same effect and will stand cancelled when A makes the payment. If A does not pay, the bank will pay to B and debit A. In case the bank accepts a bill of exchange, the bank will have to pay in the first instance and then recover the amount from A. The bank's balance sheet will show Acceptances. Endorsements and Guarantees on behalf of clients on the liabilities side and an equal amount on the assets side. Entries are made on this basis to ensure that no item will be overlooked.

It should be noted that for all this service, the bank charges a commission.

An item of similar nature may arise in the case of nationalised banks. Under the Income-tax Act, people who pay income-tax and are below the age of 70 have to make a compulsory deposit, depending on their income, with any of the nationalised banks. These are refundable in 5 annual instalments after the initial two years. The bank immediately remits the money so received to the Central Government but will handle the refunds when due. This total amount of compulsory deposits received and outstanding should be shown on both sides of the Balance Sheet since the amount is payable by the bank to the depositors. But, on payment, the amount will be reimbursed by the Government; hence, it should be treated like Acceptance on behalf of customers.

Books of Account. A bank generally requires the following subsidiary books :—

(*a*) Receiving Cashier's Counter Cash Book;
(*b*) Paying Cashier's Counter Cash Book;
(*c*) Current Accounts Ledger;
(*d*) Savings Bank Accounts Ledger;
(*e*) Fixed Deposit Accounts Ledger;
(*f*) Investments Ledger;
(*g*) Loans Ledger;
(*h*) Bills Discounted and Purchased Ledger;
(*i*) Customers' Acceptances, Endorsements and Guarantee Ledger.

The principal books are : (1) The Cash Book into which are entered the analysed totals from the Receiving Cashier's Counter Cash Book and the Paying Cashier's Counter Cash Book; and (2) the General Ledger which will contain control accounts for the subsidiary ledgers listed above and accounts for expenses and assets not covered by the subsidiary ledgers.

The system of posting is the slip system, Accountants see to it that the accounts to be debited and credited are listed on separate vouchers. For example, cheques issued by customers, pay-in-slips made out by them, etc. are the basis of entry in the ledgers. Control accounts are prepared on the basis of analysis of these slips. Machine accounting helps control very much. *Accounts in a bank must be kept up-to-date*, or rather up to the hour. Accounts are closed on 31st December, each year.

Besides the above, the following chief registers and memorandoms book are kept :—

1. Bills for Collection Register.
2. Demand Draft Register.
3. Share Security Register.
4. Jewellery Register.
5. Safe Custody Register.

Final Accounts

The accounts of a bank must be made up annually to December 31.

The income of a bank consists chiefly of interest earned on loans, investments and advances and discounts earned on bills discounted and purchased. The bank also earns commission on bills for collection, remittance of money, circular notes or letters of credit, etc. A bank pays interest on deposits. The following should be noted :

Rebate on Bills Discounted. This means unearned discount for those bills that will mature after 31st December, the date of closing of accounts. On discounting a bill the bank :

debits the Bill Discounted with its full value,

credits the Customer's Account with its present cash value, and

credits the Discount Account with the difference.

The credit to the Discount Account represents the bank's income. If a bill matures after the final closing, the discount on the bill *from the date of closing to its date of maturity* is unearned. The unearned discount is known as "Rebate on Bills Discounted" and is brought into books by debiting Discount Account and crediting Rebate on Bills Discounted Account. This account appears in the Balance Sheet on the liabilities side.

Suppose a bill for Rs. 20,000 discounted in November, 1974, at 9% matures on March 14, 1975.

Then on 31st Dec., 1964 the unearned discount will be the discount for 73 days (1st January, 1975 to 14th March, 1975). The amount is :-

$$\frac{20,000 \times 9 \times 73}{365 \times 100} \text{ or Rs. 360.}$$

Bad Debts and Bad Debts Provision. For bad debts the usual entry is passed. Similarly, a proper provision to meet possible bad debts is also necessary. *But in the Profit and Loss Account, no mention at all is made of bad debts or provision for bad debts.* The requisite amount is deducted from interest and discounts. Suppose Interest and Discounts Account stands at Rs. 20,00,000; bad debts amount to Rs. 15,000 and a provision of Rs. 25,000 is required. Then the Profit and Loss Account will be credited with Rs. 19,60,000 (*i.e.*, Rs. 20,00,000 minus Rs. 40,000) *without any details.* The banking business depends upon public confidence and hence the actual or possible losses on account of bad debts are not shown. In the Balance Sheet also no information about Provision for Bad Debts is given. It is quietly deducted from Advances.

Interest on Doubtful Debts. Interest on doubtful debts should not be treated as income until the amount is actually received in cash. Therefore, the interest should be debited to the loan account concerned but the credit should be to Interest Suspense Account. To the extent the interest is received in cash, the Interest Suspense Account should be transferred to Interest Account; the remaining amount should be closed by transfer to the loan account.

Illustration Kapadia stands indebted to X Bank Ltd. for a sum of Rs. 1,00,000 on 1st January, 1974. The bank charges **interest @ 9% p.a. with annual rests. The loan is a doubtful one.**

In January, 1975 the bank receives 70% of the amount due on 31st December, 1974 in full and final settlement. Give ledger accounts in the books of the bank for 1964 and 1965.

Solution :

LEDGER

Dr. **Kapadia** **Cr.**

Date	Particulars	Rs.	Date	Particulars	Rs.
1974 Jan.1	To Balance b/d	1,00,000	1974 Dec. 31	By Balance c/d	1,09,000
Dec. 31	To Interest Suspense A/c	9,000			
		1,09,000			1,09,000
1975 Jan.1	To Balance b/d	1,09,000	1975 Jan.	By Cash (70% of Rs. 1,09.000)	76,300
				By Interest Suspense A/c	2,700
				By Bad Debts A/c	30,000
		1,09,090			1.09,000

Interest Suspense Account

Date	Particulars	Rs.	Date	Particulars	Rs.
1974 Dec. 31	To Balance c/d	9,000	1974 Dec. 31	By Kapadia	9,000
1975 Jan.	To Interest A/c (70% of Rs. 9,000)	6,300	1975 Jan.1	By Balance b/d	9,000
	To Kapadia	2,700			
		9,000			9,000

Note: The student should prepare the Interest Account and the Bad Debts A/c.

Income-Tax & Provision for Income-Tax are also not disclosed; these are quietly deducted from interest and discount. The Provision for Income-Tax is included in the item "Current Accounts and Contingency Accounts" in the Balance Sheet.

Loss on sale or revaluation of investments, gold and silver is also not disclosed in the final accounts of a bank; it is deducted from interest and discount quietly.

The Profits and Loss Account and the Balance sheet of a bank must be drawn up in prescribed form. These are given below.

FORM B

Form of Profit and Loss Account

Profit and Loss Account for the year ended 31st December, 19

Expenditure	Rs.	*Income* (Less Provision made during the year for Bad and Doubtful Debts and other usual or necessary provisions)*	Rs.
1. Interest paid on deposits, borrowings, etc.		1. Interest and Discount.	
2. Salaries and Allowances (showing separately salaries and allowances to managing director, manager, chief executive officer).		2. Commission, Exchange and Brokerage.	
Contribution to Provident Fund.		3. Rents.	
3. Directors' Fees and Local Committee Members' fees and allowances.		4. Net profit on sale of investments, gold and silver, land, premises and other assets.	
4. Rent, Taxes, Insurance, Lighting, etc.		5. Net profit on revolution of investments, gold and silver, land, premises and other assets.	
5. Law Charges.		6. Income from non-banking assets, and Profit from sale of or dealing with such assets.	
6. Postage Telegrams and Stamps.		7. Other receipts.	
7. Auditors' Fees.		8. Loss (if any).	
8. Depreciation on Bank's Property. Repair to Bank's Property.			
9. Stationery, Printing, Advertisement, etc.			
10. Loss from sale of or dealing with non-banking assets.			
11. Other Expenditure.			
12. Balance of profit			
Total		Total	

*Net loss on sale or revaluation of investments, gold and silver, land, premises and other assets if any, may be deducted from income.

The corresponding figures (to the nearest rupee, if so desired) for the year immediately preceding the year to which the profit and loss account donates should be shown in separate columns.

THE THIRD SCHEDULE

(See Section 29)

FORM A

Form of Balance Sheet

Capital and Liabilities	Rs.	*Property and Assets*	Rs.
1. *Capital* (*a*) Authorised Capital : ...Shares of Rs....... each Issued Capital : ...Share of Rs....... each Subscribed Capital : ...Shares of Rs...... each Amount called up at Rs......per share *Less* : Calls unpaid *Add*: Forfeited Shares.		1. *Cash* : *In hand and with Reserve Bank* (including foreign currency notes).	
2. *Reserve Fund and other Reserves*		2. *Balance with other Banks* (showing whether on deposit or current accounts) : (*i*) in India (*ii*) outside India.	
3. *Deposits and other accounts*: Fixed Deposits Saving Bank Deposits Current Accounts and Contingency Accounts		3. *Money at call and short notice*	
4. *Borrowing from other Banks, Agents etc.* (*i*) in India (*ii*) outside India Particulars : (*i*) Secured (stating the nature of security) (*ii*) Unsecured		4. *Investments* (stating mode of valuation, *e.g.*, cost or market value (*f*) (*i*) Securities of the Central and State Governments and Trustee Securities including Treasury Bills of the Central and State Governments. (*ii*) Shares (classifying into preference, ordinary, deferred and other classes of shares and showing separately shares fully paid up and partly paid up). (*iii*) Debentures or Bonds (*iv*) Other investments (to be classified under proper heads) (*v*) Gold.	
5. *Bills Payable*			
6. *Bills for Collection being Bills Receivable* (As per contra) (*i*) payable in India (*ii*) payable outside India.		5. *Advances* (other than bad and doubtful debts for which provision has been made to the satisfaction of the auditors)	

(*Contd.*)

Capital and Liabilities	Rs.	*Property and Assets*	Rs.
7. *Other Liabilities to be specified* (*c*) : Pension or Insurance Fund, Unclaimed Dividend, Advance Payments Rebate on Bills Discounted, etc.		(*i*) Loans, cash credit and overdrafts (*a*) in India (*b*) outside India	
8. *Acceptances, Endorsements and other Obligations per contra*		(*ii*) Bills discounted and purchased (excluding Treasury Bills of the Central and State Governments). (*a*) payable in India. (*b*) payable outside India.	
9. *Profit and Loss Account* Profit as per last Balance Sheet *Less* : Appropriations thereof *Add* : Profit for year brought forward from P. and L. A/c.		Particulars : (*i*) Debts considered good in respect of which the banking company is fully secured.	
10. *Contingent Liabilities* (*d*).		(*ii*) Debts considered good for which the banking company holds no other security than the debtor's personal security. (*iii*) Debts considered good, secured by the personal liabilities of one or more parties in addition to the personal security of the debtors. (*iv*) Debts considered doubtful or bad not provided for. (*v*) Debts due by directors or officers of the banking company or any of them either severally or jointly with any other persons. (*vi*) Debts due by companies or firms in which the directors of the banking company are interested as directors, partners or managing agents or, in the case of private companies, as members. (*vii*) Maximum total amount of advances including temporary advances made at any time during the year to directors or managers or officers of the banking company (ff).	

(*Contd.*)

Capital and Liabilities	Rs.	*Property and Assets*	Rs.
		(*viii*) Maximum total amount of loans including temporary advancing granted during the year to the companies or firms in which the directors of the banking company are interested as directors, partners or managing agents or, in the case of private companies as members (ff).	
		(*ix*) Due from banking companies.	
		6. *Bills Receivable being Bills for collection as per contra*:	
		(*i*) payable in India	
		(*ii*) payable outside India.	
		7. *Constituents' Liabilities for Acceptances, Endorsements and other obligations per contra.*	
		8. *Premises* less Depreciation (*g*)	
		9. *Furniture and Fixtures* less Depreciation (*g*).	
		10. *Other Assets* including Silver (to be specified) (*h*).	
		11. *Non-banking assets* acquired in satisfaction of claims (stating mode of valuation) (*i*)	
		12. *Profit and Loss.*	
Total		Total	

Notes : (*a*) *Capital* :

(*i*) The various classes of capital, if any, should be distinguished;

(*ii*) Shares issued as fully paid-up pursuant to any contract without payments being received in cash should be stated separately.

(*iii*) Where circumstances permit, issued and subscribed capital may be shown as one item, *e.g.*, issued and subscribed capital ......shares of Rs......paid up.

(*iv*) In case of banking companies incorporated outside India, the amount of deposit kept with the Reserve Bank of India under sub-section (2) of Section 11 of the Banking companies Act. 1949, should be shown under this head the amount, however should not be extended to the outer column.

(*c*) Under this heading are to be included such items as the following, to be shown under separate headings suitably described; pension or insurance funds, unclaimed dividends, advance payments and unexpired discounts, liabilities to subsidiary companies and other liabilities.

(*d*) These should be classified under the following categories :

(*i*) Claims against the banking company not acknowledged as debts.

(*ii*) Money for which the bank is contingently liable showing separately the amount of any guarantee given by the banking company on behalf of directors or officers.

(*iii*) Arrears of cumulative preference dividends.

(*iv*) Liability on Bills of Exchange re-discounted.

(*v*) Liability on account of outstanding Forward Exchange Contracts.

(*vi*) Partly-paid shares—uncalled amount.

(*f*) Where the value of the investments shown in the outer column of balance sheet is higher than the market value, the market value shall be shown separately in brackets.

(*ff*) Maximum total outstanding balance in all such accounts as a unit on any day during the year should be given under this heading.

(*g*) Premises wholly or partly occupied by the banking company for the purposes of business should be shown against "Premises less depreciation". In the case of fixed capital expenditure, the original cost and additions thereto and deductions therefrom during the year should be stated, as also the total depreciation written off. Where sums have been written off on a reduction of capital or revaluation of assets, every balance sheet after the first balance sheet subsequent to the reduction or revaluation should show the reduced figures with the date and amount of the reduction made. Furniture, fixtures and other assets which have been completely written off need not be shown in the balance sheet.

(*h*) Under this heading may be included such items as the following, which must be shown under headings suitably described, preliminary formation and organisation expenses, development expenditure, commission and brokerage on shares, interest accrued on investments but not collected, investments in shares of subsidiary companies and any other assets.

(*i*) Value shown shall in no case exceed market value and in cases where the market value is not ascertainable, the estimated realisable value.

The corresponding figures (to the nearest rupee, if so desired) for the year immediately preceding the year to which the balance sheet relates should be shown in separate columns.

Illustration: From the following figures relating to 1980, prepare the Profit and Loss Account of Zed Bank Ltd.

	Rs.
Interest (net after interest paid Rs.86,540)	1,37,460
Discount Received	94,580
Rebate on Bills Discounted as on Jan. 1, 1980	15,340
Salaries (including salary to managing director Rs.16,000)	64,670
Directors' Fees	1,510
Postage, Telegrams and Stamps	2,070

Audit Fees	3,000
Bad Debts	4,000
Stationery and Printing	6,200
Loss on sale of investments	5,100
Rent, Rates and Taxes	6,890
Dividend paid for 1979	20,000
Commission and Brokerage	4,130

The Bank had Rs.6,50,000 as Bills Discounted and Purchased on 31st December 1980; these were all discounted @ 16%; they had an average maturity date of March 14. The Bank wants to make a provision of Rs.11,000 for bad and doubtful debts and of Rs.25,000 for taxation.

Solution:

Zed Bank Ltd

Profit and Loss Account for the year ended 31st December, 1980

Expenditure	Rs.	Income (Less Provision made during the year for Bad and Doubtful Debts and other usual or necessary provisions)	Rs.
Interest paid on deposits, borrowings, *etc.*	86,540	Interest and Discount*	2,68,020
Salaries and Allowances (Salaries and Allowances for Managing Director Rs.16,000)	64,670	Commission and Brokerage	4,130
Directors' Fees	1,510		
Rent, Rates and Taxes	6,890		
Postage, Telegrams and Stamps	2,070		
Auditor's Fee	3,000		
Stationery and Printing	6,200		
Balance of Profit	1,01,270		
	2,72,150		2,72,150

*Interest received (Rs.1,37,460 + Rs.86,540)		2,24,000
Discount Received		94,580
Rebate on Bills Discounted—opening balance		15,340
		3,33,920
Less: Bad Debts	4,000	
Loss on Sale of Investments	5,100	
Provision required for bad and doubtful debts	11,000	
Provision required for Taxation	25,000	
Rebate on Bill Discounted Required $\left(6,50,000 \times \frac{16}{100} \times \frac{73}{365}\right)$	20,800	65,900
		2,68,020

Note : Dividend paid will not figure in the Profit and Loss Account, it will be shown in the Profit and Loss Appropriation Account.

Illustration The following Trial Balance was extracted from the books of the Small Security Bank of Bombay Ltd. as on 31st December 1978 :

	Dr. Rs.	*Cr.* Rs.
Share Capital		3,00,000
Cash on hand and with Reserve Bank	75,000	
Investments in Govt. of India Bonds	1,94,370	
Other Investments	1,55,630	
Gold Bullion	15.130	
Interest accrued on Investments	24,620	
Security Deposits of employees		15,000
Savings Account Balances		7,420
Current Account Ledger Control A/c		97,000
Fixed Deposits		23,050
Share Premium Account		90,000
Statutory Reserve		1,40,000
Silver Bullion	2,000	
Buildings	65,000	
Furniture	5,000	
Borrowings from Banks		77,230
Money at Call and Short Notice	26,000	
Advances	2,00,000	
Profit and Loss Account Balance		6,500
Bills Discounted and purchased	12,500	
Bills for collection		43,500
Interest	7,950	72,000
Commission and Brokerage		25,300
Discounts		42,000
Bills Receivable being bills for collection	43,500	
Audit Fees	5,000	
Loss on Sale of Furniture	1,000	
Directors' fees	1,200	
Salaries	21,200	
Postage	50	
Rents		600
Profit on Bullion		1,200
Managing Director's Remuneration	12,000	
Miscellaneous Income		2,700
Loss on sale of Investments	30,000	
Deposits with other banks	46,350	
	9,43,500	9,43,500

You are required to prepare a Profit and Loss Account for the year ended 31st December, 1978 and Balance Sheet as at that date after considering the following:—

(*i*) Provide Rebate on bills discounted, Rs. 5,000.

(*ii*) A scrutiny of the Current Account Ledger reveals that there are account overdrawn to the extent of Rs. 25,000 and the total of the credit balances is 1,22,000.

(*iii*) Claims by employees for Bonus Rs. 15,000 is pending arbitration.

(*iv*) The Directors state that the assets are over-depreciated.

(*v*) Acceptances on behalf of customers are Rs. 56,500.

(*vi*) A provision for doubtful debts to the extent of Rs. 12,500 is required.

(*vii*) Provision for taxation required is Rs. 10,000.

(*vii* Charge depreciation @ 5% on Building and 20% on Furniture.

(*viii*) Deposits made by income-tax payers totalled Rs.40,000

Solution: *(Adapted from B. Com., Bombay)*

The Small Security Bank of Bombay Ltd.
Profit and Loss Account for the year ended December 31, 196

Expenditure		*Amount*	*Income (Less Provision made during the year for Bad and Doubtful Debts and other usual or necessary provisions)*	*Amount*
		Rs.		Rs.
To Interest paid on deposits		7,950	By Interest and Discounts	56,500
To Salaries : Managing Director	12,000		By Commission and Brokerage	25,300
Others	21,200		By Rents	600
		33,200	By Profit on Bullion	1,200
To Directors' Fees		1,200	By Miscellaneous Income	2,700
To Postage		50		
To Audit Fees		5,000		
To Depreciation :				
Building	3,250			
Furniture	1,000			
		4,250		
To Loss on sale of furniture		1,000		
To Profit		33,650		
Total		86,300	Total	86,300

Note. Interest and Discounts have been ascertained as under :

	Rs.
Interest	72,000
Discounts	42,000
	1,14,000

Balance Sheet of the Small Security Bank of Bombay Ltd. as at December 31 19

Capital and Liabilities	Rs.	Amount Rs.
1. Capital—Authorised ?		
Issued ?		
Subscribed...shares of Rs...each		
Rs...paid up.		3,00,000
2. Reserve Fund and other Reserves		
Statutory Reserve (See P. & L. A/c below)		1,46,730
Share Premium Account		90,000
3. Dep sits and other accounts :		
Fixed Deposits	23,050	
Savings Bank Deposits	7.420	
Current Accounts	1,32,000	
		1, 2.470
4. Borrowings from other banks		77,230
5. Bills Payable		nil
6. Bills for Collection being Bills Receivable as per contra		43,500
7. Other Liabilities		
Rebate on Bills Discounted	5,000	
Security Deposits of employees	15,000	
		20,000
8. Acceptances, Endorsements and other obligations per contra		56,500
Deposits Received from Income-tax Payers as per contra		40,000
9. Profit and Loss Account :		
as per last Balance Sheet	6,500	
Add Profit for the year	33,650	
	40,150	
Less Transfer to Reserve	6,730	
		33,420
10. Contingent Liability : Employees' Claim for Bonus pending Arbitration, Rs. 15,000		
Total		9,69,850

Property and Assets	Rs.	Amount Rs.
1. Cash in hand and with Reserve Bank		75,000
2. Balance with other banks		46,350
3. Money at Call on Short Notice		26,000
4. Investments : Government of India		
Bonds	1,94,370	
Other Investments	1,55,630	
Gold	15,130	
		3,65,130
5. Advances :		
(i) Loans, cash credits and overdrafts	2.12,500	
(ii) Bills Discounted and purchased	12,500	
		2,25,000
6. Bills Receivable being Bills for collection per contra		43,500
7. Constituents' Liability for Acceptances, Endorsements and obligations per contra		56 500
Deposits Recoverable from Government as per contra		40,000
8. Building	65.000	
Less Depreciation	3,250	
		61,750
9. Furniture and Fixtures	5 000	
Less Depreciation	1,000	
		4,000
10. Other Assets : Silver	2,000	
Interest Accrued on Investments	24,620	
		26.620
11. Non-banking assets		nil
12. Profit and Loss Account		nil
Total		9,69,850

Less Loss on Investments and Rebate on Bills Discounted	35,000
	79,000
Less Provision for Doubtful Debts and for taxation	22,500
	56,500

The Provision for Doubtful Debts is also deducted from Advances which also include Rs. 25,000 (debit or balances or overdrafts in Current Accounts). The Provision for Taxation is added to Current Accounts and Contingency Accounts.

Particulars of Advances. Usually a bank invests more than half of its funds in the form of advances or loans including bills discounted and purchased. It is extremely important that the public which deposits money with a bank should know the quality of advances made by it. Hence. by law, a bank must give particulars about the advances (*see* pp. 752-53 above).

The particulars are meant to show whether the debts owing to the bank are good or not, together with the type of security that the bank has obtained from the borrowers. The first four particulars are meant to show this and the amount shown in the balance sheet as advances must be fully analysed into the first four particulars.

The next two are meant to show the amount due by officers and directors of the bank and firms in which directors are interested. (These amounts must already be included in the first four particulars, as regards security. The two particulars, VII and VIII. are meant to show even those amounts which the officers, directors and firms in which directors are interested borrowed during the year but were repaid during the year, wholly or partially. Particular IX shows amount lent to other banks. This must also be included in one of the first four particulars.

Taking imaginary figures, the particulars for the Illustration given above will be as follows:

Particulars of Advances	Rs.
(*i*) Debts considered good in respect of which the banking company is fully secured.	1,80,000
(*ii*) Debts considered good in respect of which the banking company holds no other security other than the debtors' personal security.	15,000
(*iii*) Debts considered good, secured by the personal liabilities of one or more parties in addition to the personal security of the debtors.	30,000
(*iv*) Debts considered doubtful or bad, not provided for	Nil
	2,25,000
(*v*) Debts due by Directors or Officers of the banking company or any of them either severally or jointly with any other person.	6,000

(*vi*) Debts due by companies or firms in which the directors of the banking company are interested as directors, partners or managing agents, or in case of private companies, as members.	11,000
(*vii*) Maximum total amount of loans, including temporary advances. made at any time during the year to directors, or managers or officers of the banking company or any of them either severally or jointly with any other person.	10,000
(*viii*) Maximum total amount of loans, including temporary advances made at any time du - ing the year to companies o firms in which the directors of the banking company are interested as directors, partners or managing agents or in the case of private companies, as members.	
(*ix*) Due from Banks.	Nil

Illustration. On 31st December, 1981 Wye Bank Ltd. showed in its balance sheet Advances after deducting Rs.1,50,000, provision for bad and doubtful debts. The gross amounts were:

(*i*) Bills Discounted and Purchased	46,50,000
(*ii*) Loans, Cash credits and overdrafts	85,70,000

Amounts shown against (*i*) were all good but out of (*ii*) Rs.1,95,000 was considered doubtful of recovery. The Bank held goods and securities of the value of Rs.41,00,000 against (*i*) and Rs.71,50,000 against (*ii*). Rs.3,80,000 out of (*ii*) were loans *etc*., granted only on the personal security of the borrowers but this amount was good. Officers of the Bank owed Rs.68,000 (good); the maximum amount owed by them during 1981 was Rs.1,12,000. Loans granted to other banks were Rs.3,00,000.

Give the particulars required under the Banking Regulations Act.

Solution:

Particulars of Advances	Rs.
(*i*) Debts considered good in respect of which the Bank is fully secured.	1,12,50,000
(*ii*) Debts considered good in respect of which the Bank holds no security other than the debtors' personal security	3,80,000
(*iii*) Debts considered good, secured by the personal liabilities of one or more parties in addition to the personal security of the debtors (balancing figure).	13,95,000
(*iv*) Debts considered doubtful or bad, not provided for*	45,000
	1,30,70,000**

*Rs.1,95,000 less Rs.1,50,000 (the existing provision).

**The total, Rs.1,32,20,000 less Rs.1,50,000 (provision for bad and doubtful debt).

(*v*)	Debts due by Directors or Officers of the Bank or any of them either severally or jointly with any other person.	68,000
(*vi*)	Debts due by companies or firms in which the Directors of the Bank are interested as directors, partners or managing agents or, in case of private companies, as members.	nil
(*vii*)	Maximum total amount of loans, including temporary advances, made at any time during the year to directors, or managers or officers of the Bank or any of them either severally or jointly with any other person.	1,12,000
(*viii*)	Maximum total amount of loans, including temporary advances made any time during the year to companies or firms in which the directors of the Bank are interested as directors, partners or managing agents or in the case of private companies, as members.	nil
(*ix*)	Due from Banks	3,00,000

EXERCISE XXI

1. The New Bombay Bank Ltd. was incorporated in 1956 with an Authorised Capital of Rs 25,00,000 divided into 25,000 shares of Rs. 100 each. From the balance extracted from its books on 31st December, 1967 prepare a Profit and Loss Account and a Balance Sheet as required under the Banking Regulation Act :—

	Rs.
Share Capital—Issued—10,000 shares of Rs. 100 each, Rs. 50 paid	5,00,000
Reserve Fund	3,50,000
Fixed Deposit Accounts	9,50,000
Savings Bank Deposits	30,00,000
Current Accounts	80,00,000
Money at call and short notice	3,00,000
Investments (at cost)	30,00,000
Interest accrued and paid	2,00,000
Salaries (including salary to General Manager Rs. 18,000 and Directors' Fees Rs. 5,000)	80 000
Rent paid	20,000
General Expenses (including stationery Rs. 5,000 and Auditors' fees Rs. 2,000)	10,000
Profit and Loss Account (Cr.) on 1st Jan., 1967	2,10,000
Dividend for the year 1969	50,000
Premises (after depreciation up to 31st December, 1966 Rs. 1,00,000)	12,00 000
Cash in hand	60.000
Cash with Reserve Bank of India	15,00.000
Cash with other Banks	13.00,000
Borrowings from Banks	7,00.000
Interest and Discounts	6,50,000
Bills Discounted and Purchased	5,00.000
Bills Payable	8,00.000

Loans Overdrafts and Cash Credits	70,00,000
Unclaimed Dividends	30,000
Sundry Creditors	30,000
Bills for Collection	1,40,000
Acceptances and Endorsements on behalf of customers	2,00,000

Rebate on bills discounted and purchased for unexpired terms amounted to Rs. 5,000. Allow 5% depreciation on premises on original cost. A provision for doubtful debts amounting to Rs. 30,000 has to be made. Transfer Rs. 50,000 to Reserve Fund and provide for Taxes Rs 1,10,000.

(*Profit before tax, Rs. 2,40,000 ; Total of Balance Sheet, Rs 1,51,05,000*)
(*B. Com., Bombay*)

2. The following particulars as at 31st December 1965 are furnished in respect of "The Credit-Worthy Bank Ltd." :—

	Rs.
Cash and Reserve Bank Balances	8,00,000
Statutory Reserve	35,00,000
Bills discounted and purchased	9,00,000
Acceptance and Endorsements on behalf of Constituents	15,00,000
Investments in Government Securities	28,00,000
Investments in fully paid shares of companies	30,00,000
Investments in partly paid shares of companies	10,00,000
Profit and Loss Account (Cr.) (subject to appropriations)	30,00,000
Bills for collection	7,00,000
Bills Payable	3,00,000
Branch adjustments (Dr.)	3,00,000
Premises	15,00,000
Current Accounts	50,00,000
Savings Bank Accounts	25,00,000
Fixed Deposits	15,00,000
Loans, Advances, Cash credits, etc.	93,00,000
Provision for Taxation	2,00,000
Money at Call	25,00,000
Gold	9,00,000
Silver	5,00,000
Borrowings	30,00,000

(*i*) The Provision for Taxation should stand at Rs. 12,00,000.

(*ii*) The Directors had paid an Interim Dividend of Rs. 5,00,000 which has not as yet been adjusted against profits.

(*iii*) In respect of some of its investments, a dividend of Rs. 3,00,000 was declared which was paid during the year by cash of Rs. 1,00,000 and by the allotment of fully paid shares for Rs 2,00,000 The Bank had only credited Rs. 1,00,000 to its Dividends Account in respect of this. No entry was passed in respect of the said Rs. 2,00,000.

(*iv*) An award on the employees' claim for Bonus of Rs. 1,00,000 for 1965 was passed on 20th January 1966 in favour of the employees after the above balances had been drawn out.

(*v*) The entry of unexpired discounts of Rs. 1,00,000 as at 31st December 1965 was not passed through oversight.

(*vi*) The liability in respect of Accrued Staff Gratuity was indeterminate.

You are required to prepare a Balance Sheet as at 31st December 1965 in the statutory form after making the necessary adjustments in respect of the above items.

(*P. and L. Account Balance Rs. 13,00,000; Total of Balance Sheet Rs. 2,57,00,000*)

(*Adapted from B Com., Bombay*)

(*The Student should prepare trial balance to ascertain share capital*).

3. The provisional Profit and Loss Account for 1964 of a bank showed a profit of Rs. 15,00,000. It was necessary to adjust the profit for matters arising out of the following :—

(*i*) Included in loans was a loan for Rs. 50,000 (principal). This loan was doubtful. For the year the interest of Rs. 4,500 was debited to the loan and credited to the Interest Account.

(*ii*) Bills Discounted totalled Rs. 40,00,000 all maturing on the average date of 14th March, 1965 and all discounted @ 9% p.a. The bank's books show a balance of Rs. 60,000 in the Rebate on Bills Discounted Account, brought forward from 1963.

(*iii*) One of the non-banking assets standing in the books at Rs. 50 000 was sold during the year for Rs. 55,000. The amount was credited to Non-banking Assets Account.

Ascertain the true profit of the bank, giving the necessary journal entries for adjustments.

(*Profit, Rs. 14,38,500*)

4. The total advances made by a bank outstanding on 31st December, 1964 were Rs. 2 10,50,000 including Rs. 40,60,000 bills discounted and purchased. There was no tangible security against bills discounted and purchased. Clear loans against the debtor's own personal security only amounted to Rs. 3,00,000. Rs. 1,50,000 were doubtful against which a provision of Rs. 1,00,000 was created. Loans totalling Rs. 1,50,00,000 were granted against tangible security whose value on 31st December, 1964 was Rs. 1,80,00,000.

During the year officers of the bank had borrowed Rs. 25,000 (all fully secured) against which a sum of Rs. 10,000 was still outstanding. Similarly, firms in which the officers were interested had borrowed Rs. 80,000 (all fully secured) out of which Rs. 55,000 was repaid.

Prepare the particulars required under the Banking Regulation Act for inclusion in the balance sheet.

CHAPTER XXII

ACCOUNTS OF INSURANCE COMPANIES

A contract of insurance is one of indemnity. Under it, one party, the insurer, agrees to make good loss suffered by the other party, the insured. The insured has to pay an amount called "premium" as consideration. Usually it is paid in advance. The contract lays down the risks which are covered—loss occurring due to other causes is not made good by the insurer. The document which embodies the insurance contract is called Insurance Policy ; it has to be properly stamped. Insurance affords excellent protection against unforeseen losses at a small price. The annual premium for getting a building insured against fire worth Rs. 1,00,000 may be only Rs. 150. By paying this sum annually to the insurer the owner can rest assured that if the building does get destroyed by fire, he will not suffer a loss.

Mainly, insurance is of two types—life and general. Life insurance (also known as Life Assurance) contracts cover risks to human life—for an annual premium, the insurer agrees to pay a certain sum when the person dies or when he reaches a stipulated age. General insurance con racts cover other types of risk which a business firm or a person has to face like fire, burglary, accidents and losses on the seas. General insurance contracts fall into the following chief categories :—

Fire (covering losses occasioned by a fire)

Marine (covering risks connected with a sea voyage)

Burglary (covering loss through theft, etc.)

Accidents (covering loss through mishaps, specially on the road)

Fidelity (covering loss through acts of dishonest employees)

Workmen's Compensation (covering liability to workers who receive injuries or who contact occupational diseases while at work)

Third Party (covering liability to outsiders who may suffer damage or loss through acts of the insured)

Consequential Loss, or Loss of Profit (covering loss suffered by the insured because of stoppage of business due to an unforeseen cause like fire or earthquake)

Life insurance has two main categories—annuity business and the ordinary life business. Under an annuity contract, the person concerned, called annuitant, pays a lump sum of money (called consideration for annuities granted) in return of a promise that the insurer will pay a certain sum of money each year as long as the annuitant lives or for an agreed period. **The annual payment is called** annuity. For the insurer the annuities are **an expenditure and the** consideration for annuities granted is income.

Some Terms. Besides the terms mentioned above, the following other terms should be noted :

Policy means the document which embodies the insurance contract, that is the contract between the insurer and the insured.

Whole Life Policy is one under which the amount of policy will be paid only on the death of the insured. Premiums may be payable throughout life or for a limited period.

Endowment Policy entitles the insured to receive the amount of the policy on his reaching a certain age when premiums also stop. If death occurs earlier, the amount of the policy will be paid at that time and payment of premiums will also stop then.

Without Profit Policies are those against which the insurer will pay only the amount stated—the policy holder will not be entitled to anything more or less.

With Profit Policies are those which also entitle the policy holder to a share of profits of the insurer. The amount of the policy is guaranteed. The premium on with profit policies is usually higher than those without profits.

The share of profit which a policy holder gets is called *Bonus*.

Reversionary Bonus is that bonus which is paid along with the amount of the policy and not earlier. It is then included in the claim against the policy.

Bonus in Cash is paid immediately. It is always much less than the reversionary bonus.

Bonus in Reduction of Premium is that bonus in cash which a policy holder gets adjusted against the premium due from him. The entry to be passed by the insurer is :

Bonus in Reduction of Premiums A/c ... Dr.
To Premiums Account

Both Premiums and Bonus in Reduction of Premiums are revenue items.

Interim Bonus is the bonus paid when a policy matures but when final rates of bonus are not available.

First Year's Premium is the premium paid in case of life insurance for the first year. This term is not applicable for other types of insurance.

Renewal Premium is also a term used only in case of life insurance and denotes premiums payable for years after the first.

Single Premium is a premium which arises only in case of life insurance ; the policy holder pays only one premium in the beginning and does not have to pay again.

Claim means the amount which an insurer has to pay against a policy. The amount includes reversionary bonus. If a claim arises on the death of the policy holder. it is called "claim by death" otherwise, "claim by maturity or survivance".

Surrender Value means the amount which the insurer is willing to pay in case the policy holder is not willing to pay further premiums and is willing to give up the policy. This arises only in case of life insurance.

Paid up Value means the amount which the insurer will pay at the date of maturity of the policy in case the policy holder is unable to pay further premiums. The paid up amount is calculated by the formula :

$$\text{Amount of Policy} \times \frac{\text{Number of premiums paid}}{\text{Total number of premiums payable}}$$

Reinsurance means placing of part of the risk by an insurer with an another insurer. The object is to reduce the possible loss to be borne by the original insurer, who must pay premiums at the ordinary rates to the reinsurer. The reinsurer will pay commission to the original insurer. For the reinsurer, the commission is an expense and is named "*Commission on Reinsurance Accepted*". For the original insurer, the commission is an income and is called "*Commission on Reinsurance Ceded*".

LIFE ASSURANCE

From the point of view of accounts of a company doing life insurance business, one has to remember that a life insurance contract is a long term one. At any time *in respect of policies in force*, a life insurance company will, *in future*, receive a much smaller sum by way of premiums than the sum payable by it. For instance, against a policy issued in 1955 for 20 years for Rs. 10,000, the annual premium being Rs. 500, the position at the end of 1969 is that :

(*a*) the company will receive only 5 more premiums of Rs. 500 each or Rs. 2,500 in all; the number may even be less if the policy holder dies earlier ; and

(*b*) the company will have to pay Rs. 10,000 in 1975 (or earlier if death occurs earlier).

If all goes well, there will still be a gap of Rs. 7,500 between what the company will have to pay and what it will receive. This is so in case of all policies that are in force. In case of annuity contracts, the company will receive nothing in future but still will be required to pay the stipulated amount as long as the annuitant lives. Therefore, it is clear that, at any time, a life insurance company will have a very big gap between what it will have to pay in future and what it will receive in future in respect of existing contracts. This gap is known as "net liability". Unless a company's present reserves exceed the net liability, it cannot be said to have earned a profit.

The calculation of net liability is complicated* because of possibilities of death and of rate of interest. The figure of net liability is arrived at only by actuaries and the work involved is such that at one time this figure was ascertained every five years. The Life Insurance Corporation of India, which alone can carry on life insurance business in India, ascertains the net liability evey two years. This

*The process is called "Valuation."

means that the Life Insurance Corporation can know its profit or loss only every two years. What is done is to compare the net liability with the reserve known as Life Fund; if the latter exceeds the net liability. the excess is the profit earned in the two year period. Life Fund is arrived at by preparing a revenue account for life insurance business—the excess of the credit side of the revenue account over its debit side is Life Fund.

A revenue account is prepared each year. The Life Fund in the beginning of the year (or at the end of the previous year) is put on the credit side to start with. Other main items on the credit side are the following :—

Premiums (net, that is, premiums received less reinsurance premiums paid)
Consideration for annuities granted
Dividends, rent, and interest (net, after tax deducted at source)

The items on the debit side, that is 'expenses', are chiefly :

Claims
Annuities
Surrenders
Bonus in Cash
Bonus in Reduction of Premiums
Commission to agents
Expenses of management
Income tax on Profits
Dividend paid to shareholders.

The excess of the credit side over the debit side is Life Fund and is shown in the balance sheet.

Note. The usual accountancy rules of bringing into account outstanding items apply here also. Following are some of the adjusting entries that may have to be passed :—

1. Claims intimated and still unpaid—
   Claims Account ... Dr.
   To Claims Outstanding Account*
2. Claims covered under reinsurance—
   Reinsurance Co* ... Dr.
   To Claims Account
3. Premiums outstanding—
   Premiums Outstanding Account* ... Dr.
   To Premiums Account
4. Bonus utilised for reduction of Premiums—
   Bonus in Reduction of Premiums A/c ... Dr.
   To Premiums Account
5. Interest Outstanding (or Accrued)
   Interest Outstanding (or Accrued) A/c* ... Dr.
   To Interest Account

Accounts marked with an asterisk will appear in the balance sheet ; others will affect revenue.

The balance sheet is prepared on the usual principles. But for both the revenue account and the balance sheet, there are forms prescribed by law, the Insurance Act, 1938. These are given below. It should be noted that all insurance companies must make up their accounts every year on 31st December. Another point to note is that in case of mutual (cooperative) life insurance companies, there is no share capital.

FORM D

Form of Revenue Account Applicable to Life Insurance Business

Revenue Account of.........for the year ended...in respect of Life Business

	Business within India	*Business out of India (a)*	*Total*		*Business within India*	*Business out of India*	*Total*
	Rs.	Rs.	Rs.		Rs.	Rs-	Rs.
Claims under Policies (including provision for claims due or intimated), less re-insurances.				**Balance of Fund at the beginning of the year.**			
By death.				**Premiums, less Reinsurances :—**			
By maturity.				First year's premiums.			
Annuities, less Reinsurances.				Where the maximum premiums paying period is (g)			
Surrenders including surrenders of Bonus less reinsurances.				two years...			
Bonuses in Cash, less reinsurances.				three years			
Bonuses in Reduction of Premiums, less reinsurances.				four years			
Expenses of management (h)				five years			
1. (a) **Commission to Insurance agents** less that on re-insurances.				six years			
				seven years			
(b) Allowances and Commission other than commission included in sub-item (a) preceding.				eight years...			
				nine years			
				twelve years or over including throughout life.			

(Contd.)

2. Salaries, etc. other than to agents and those contained in Item No. 1.

3. Travelling expenses.

4. Directors' fees.

5. Auditors' fees.

6. Medical fee.

7. Law Charges.

8. Advertisements.

9. Printing and Stationery.

10. Other expenses of management (accounts to be specified).

11. Rents for offices belonging to and occupied by the insurer.

Rents of other offices occupied by the insurer.

12. Bad debts.

13. United Kingdom, Indian, Dominion and Foreign Taxes.

14. Other Expenditure to be specified.

Profit transferred to Profit and Loss Account.

Balance of Fund at the end of the year as shown in the Balance Sheet.

Renewal premiums.

Single premiums.

Consideration for Annuities granted, less reinsurances (c).

Interest, Dividends and Rents. less Income-tax thereon (d).

Registration fees.

Other Income to be specified (c).

Loss transferred to Profit and Loss Account.

Transferred from Appropriation Account.

Notes. (*a*) These columns apply only to business, the premiums in respect of which are ordinarily paid outside India. If any question arises whether any premiums are ordinarily paid outside India, the Controller shall decide the question and his decision shall be final.

(*b*) If any sum has been deducted from this item and entered on the assets side of the balance sheet, the amount so deducted must be shown separately. Under this item the salary paid to the managing agent or managing director shall be shown separately from the total amount paid as salaries to the remaining staff.

(*c*) All single premiums for annuities, whether immediate or deferred, must be included under this heading.

(*d*) Indian, United Kingdom, Foreign and Dominion income-tax on Interest, Dividends and Rents must be shown under this heading, less any rebates of income-tax recovered from the revenue authorities in respect of expenses of management. The separate heading on the other side of the account is for United Kingdom, Indian, Foreign and Dominion taxes, other than those shown under this item.

(*e*) Under the head Other Incomes, fines, if any, realised from the staff must be shown separately. All the amounts received by the insurer directly or indirectly whether from his head office or from any other source outside India shall also be shown separately if the revenue account except such sums as properly appertain to the capital account.

(*f*) In the case of an insurer having his principal place of business outside the States, the expenses of management for business out of India and total business need not be split up into the several sub-heads, if they are not so split up in his own country.

(*g*) Where the maximum-paying period includes a fraction of a year, such fraction shall be ignored for the purposes of this revenue account.

FORM A

Form of Balance Sheet

Balance Sheet of as at... 19

	Life and Annuity Business (1)	Other Classes of Business (2)	Total		Life and Annuity Business (1)	Other Classes of Business (2)	Total
	Rs.	Rs.	Rs.		Rs.	Rs.	Rs.
Shareholders Capital				**Loans :**			
(each class to be stated separately).				On Mortgages of property within the States.			
Authorised Rs. ......Shares of Rs......each ——				On Security of municipal and other public rates.			
Subscribed : ......Shares of Rs.......each ——				On Stocks and Shares.			
Called up : ......Shares of Rs......each				On Insurers' Policies within their surrender value.			
Less unpaid calls ——				On Personal security.			
				To Subsidiary Companies (other than Reversionary) (f).			
				Reversions and life interests Purchased.			

(Contd.)

Reserve for Contingency Accounts (a) :	Loans on Reversions and Life Interests.
Investment Reserve Account	Debenture Stocks of Subsidiary Companies (f).
Profit and Loss Appropriation Account.	Ordinary Stocks and Shares of Subsidiary Reversionary Companies (f).
Balance of Funds and Accounts :	Loans to Subsidiary Reversionary Companies (f).
Life Insurance Funds	Investments :
(*i*) Business in India,	Deposit with the Reserve Bank of India (securities to be specified).
(*ii*) Business outside India.	Indian Government Securities
Fire Insurance Business Account.	State Government Securities.
Marine Insurance Business Account.	British, British Colonial and British Domination Government Securities.
Miscellaneous Insurance Business Account (m).	Foreign Government Securities.
Other Accounts, if any, to be specified (l).	Indian Municipal Securities
Pension or Superannuation Accounts (b).	British and Colonial Securities.
	Foreign Securities.

(*Contd.*)

Debenture Stock per cent

Loans and Advances (c).

Bills payable (c).

Estimated Liability in respect of outstanding claims, whether due or intimated (d).

Annuities due and unpaid (d).

Outstanding Dividends.

Amounts due to other Persons or Bodies carrying on Insurance Business.

Sundry Creditors including outstanding and accruing expenses and Taxes (c).

Bonds, Debentures, Stocks and other Securities whereon interest is guaranteed by the Indian Government or a State Government.

Bonds, Debentures, Stocks and other Securities whereon interest is guaranteed by the British or any Colonial Government.

Debentures of any railway in India.

Debentures of any Railway out of India.

Preference or guaranteed Shares of any Railway in India.

Preference or guaranteed Shares of any Railway out of India.

Railway Ordinary Stocks
(*i*) in India
(*ii*) out of India.

Other Debentures and Debenture Stocks of companies incorporated, (*i*) in India, (*ii*) out of India.

Other guaranteed and preference Stocks and Shares of companies incorporated, (*i*) in India, (*ii*) out of India.

(*Contd.*)

Liabilities	Assets
Other sums owing by the Insurer (particulars to be given. (c).	Other Ordinary Stocks and Shares of companies incorporated (*i*) in India, (*ii*) out of India.
	Holdings in Subsidiary Companies (f).
	House property, (*i*) in India, (*ii*) out of India.
	Freehold and Leasehold ground rents and rent charges.
Contingent Liabilities (to be specified).	**Agents' Balances.**
	Outstanding Premiums (g) (d).
	Interest, Dividends and Rents outstanding (d).
	Interest, Dividends and Rents accruing but not due (d).
	Amounts due from other persons or bodies carrying on Insurance Business (b).
	Sundry Debtors (*i*).
	Bills Receivable
	Cash
	At Bankers on Deposit Account.
	At Bankers and Current Account and in hand.
	At call and short notice (j).
	Other Accounts (to be specified) (k).

Assets and Liabilities, Shareholder's Capital and Reserves not allotted to any class of business specified in column (1) must be shown in column (2).

Notes. (*a*) The Reserves or Contingency Accounts must be separately stated.

(*b*) If the insurer has not full and unrestricted control of the assets constituting the Pension or Superannuation Accounts, either those Accounts, and the assets and liabilities relating thereto must be omitted from the balance sheet or the assets of which the insurer has not such control must be clearly indicated on the face of the balance sheet.

(*c*) If the insurer has deposited security as cover in respect of any of these items the amount and nature of the securities so deposited must be clearly indicated on the face of the balance sheet.

(*d*) These items are or have been included in the corresponding items in the Revenue or Profit and Loss Account. Outstanding and accruing interest, dividends and rents must be shown after deduction of income tax or the income tax must be provided for amongst the liabilities on the other side of the balance sheet.

(*e*) Such items as amount of liability in respect of bills discounted, uncalled capital of subsidiary companies, uncalled capital of other investments, etc., must either be shown in their several categories under the heading "Contingent Liabilities" or the appropriate items on the assets side must be set out in such details as will clearly indicate the amounts of the uncalled capital.

(*f*) As respects life and annuity business full particulars of holdings in and loans to subsidiary companies must be stated, giving the name of each company, the number and description of each class of shares held, the amounts paid up thereon, and the value at which the holdings in each company stand in the balance sheet.

(*g*) Either this item must be shown net or the commission must be provided for amongst the liabilities on the other side or the balance sheet.

(*h*) The aggregate amount owing by a subsidiary company or subsidiary companies is to be shown separately from all other assets and the aggregate amount owing to a subsidiary company or subsidiary companies is to be shown separately from all other liabilities.

(*i*) Amounts due from directors and officers must be shown separately.

(*j*) No amounts must be entered under this heading unless fully secured. If not fully secured, the amounts must be included under the heading "Sundry Debtors".

(*k*) Under the heading must be included such items as the following. which must be shown under separate headings suitably described ; Office furniture, goodwill, preliminary, formation and organisation expenses, development expenditure account, discount on debentures issued, other expenditure carried forward to be writien off in future years, balance being loss on Profit and Loss Appropriation Account etc. The amounts included in the balance sheet must not be in excess of cost.

(*l*) Under the head "Other accounts, if any to be specified" on the left hand side, fines realised from the staff and their contribution towards the provident fund, if any, should be shown under separate sub-heads.

(*m*) Where the insurer is required to maintain a separate account in respect of any sub-class of miscellaneous insurance business this heading is to be split up accordingly.

Illustration From the following figures of Hind Life Mutual Assurance Co. Ltd., as at 31st December, 1954, prepare a Revenue Account and Balance Sheet. The Assurance Fund Balance at 1st January, 1954 was Rs. 55,76,700.

	Rs.
Claims	1,68,990
Reserve	60,000
Surrender values paid	28,120
Renewal premiums	6,28,362
Single premiums	8,585
Claims admitted but not paid	68,081
First year's premiums	1,36,042
Bonus in reduction of premiums	2,710
Endowment Assurance Matured	84,153
Annuities paid	3,415
Interest received	1,90,627
Cash on Fixed Deposit	4,68,000
Rent, rates and taxes	17,848
Furniture and Fittings	4,630
Commission paid to Agents	15,975
Salaries and allowances	55,650
Government loans	15,50,000
Medical fees	10,800
Freehold premises	2,32,250
Loans on mortgage	29,05,655
Agents' balances	4,200
Cash on Current Account with bank	7,17,660
Bonus paid in cash	30,240
Expenses payable	2,838
Loans on policies	3,47,947
Consideration for annuities	28,536
Outstanding interest	10,400
Interest Accrued	9,040
General charges, travelling expenses, etc.	27,838
Depreciation on furniture	250

Outstanding Premium was **Rs. 7,060**; Further **bonus utilised** for reduction of premiums was **Rs. 2,400.** Claims covered **under reinsurance** amounted **to Rs. 15,000.**

Hind Life Mutual Assurance Co. Ltd.

Life Revenue Account for the year ended December 31, 1954

	Rs.			Rs.
To Claims less reassurance		By Life Fund as at		
by death	1,53,990	Jan. 1, 1954		55,76,700
by maturity	84,153	By Premiums—		
To Annuities	3,415	First Year's	Rs.	
To Surrenders	28,120	Premiums	1,36,042	
To Bonus in Cash	30,240	Renewal „	6,37,822	
To Bonus in Reduction		Single „	8,585	
of Premiums	5,110			7,82,449
To Expenses of Management		By Consideration for annuities		
Commission	19,975	granted		28,536
Salaries and allowances	55,650	By Interests, Dividends and Rents		1,90,627
General charges, Travelling etc	27,838			
Medical fees	10,800			
Rents, Rates and Taxes	17,848			
Depreciation	250			
To Life Fund at the end of the year	61,40,923			
	65,78,312			65,78,312

Balance Sheet of Hind Life Mutual Assurance Co. Ltd. as at Dec. 31, 1954

	Rs.		Rs.
Share Capital	nil	Loans :	
Reserve or Contingency		On Mortgages	29,05,655
Accounts	60,000	On Company's Policies	3,47,947
Balance of Funds :		Investments	15,50,000
Life fund	61,40,923	Freehold Premises	2,32,250
Claims Admitted but not		Agents' Balances	4,200
paid	68,081	Outstanding Premiums	7,060
Expenses Payable	2,838	Interest Outstanding	10,400
		Interest Accruing	9,040
		Amounts due from other persons or bodies carrying on Insurance business	15,000
		Cash on Fixed Deposit	4,68,000
		Cash on Current Account	7,17,650
		Furniture and Fittings	4,630
Total	62,71,842	Total	62,71,842

Note. Outstanding Premium and further bonus utilised in reduction of premiums have been added to Renewal Premiums. The bonus has also been added to the figure already given in the trial balance.

Valuation Balance Sheet. It has already been pointed out that a life insurance company ascertains its profit by comparing the net liability (as determined by the actuary) and the Life Fund on the particular date. The comparison is done in a statement known as "Valuation Balance Sheet". It is only a statement and not a balance sheet. It appears as follows (figures assumed) :

Valuation Balance Sheet......as at December 31, 19...

	Rs.		Rs.
To Net Liability as per Actuary's Valuation	45,00,000	By Life Assurance Fund as per Balance Sheet (Form A)	50,00,000
To Surplus, if any	5,00,000	By Deficiency, if any	—
Total	50,00,000	Total	50,00,000

The figures show that the company has made a profit of Rs. 5,00,000 for the period covered by valuation. The company must pay income tax on this.

The present law is that the Life Insurance Corporation must distribute 95% of the profits earned by it, after taxes, amongst the policyholders. A policyholder's share is, of course, known as "Bonus".

GENERAL BUSINESS

General insurance covers all types of insurances except life insurance. The chief forms of general insurance have been stated on page 764.

A common characteristic of all types of general insurance is that a policy covers only one year; the premium payable affords protection to the policyholder for one year commencing with the date of payment of the premium. If there is no damage or loss during the year, there is no claim. course, the premium is not refundable even if the insurer remaii under risk for a very short time, say, a day. A policy may be rei wed from year to year but, for all purposes, a renewal in general ir .urance means entering into a fresh contract. This is in contrast to life insurance where the policy covers a long period of time.

In general insurance, revenue accounts prepared for each year disclose profit or loss of the company. The essential feature is that against net premiums received, the claims paid and expenses incurred, including commission to agents, are compared. If premiums received exceed claims and expenses, there is profit; otherwise a loss.

This would be quite valid except that since policies are issued throughout the year and there may be claims after the close of accounts in respect of policies already issued. It is necessary to provide against the possibility. The rule is to make a provision of 100% of the net premiums in respect of marine insurance on hull (ships) and 40% of net premium in respect of other types of general insurance. Suppose, a new company starts fire insurance business in 1964 and receives Rs. 5,00,000 as premiums. Claims are Rs. 80,000 and expenses, including commission, are Rs. 1,60,0C0. After deducting claims and expenses from premiums, Rs. 2,60,000 remains. But a provision of Rs. **2,00,000** (i.e., **40%** on Rs. 5,00,000) is required for claims that may arise next year. Hence the company makes a profit of Rs. **60,000** i.e., Rs. 2,60,000 minus Rs. **2,00,000** In 1965, the company would add the provision brought forward from 1964 to th premiums received and then proceed as outlined above to ascertain the profit or loss.

Illustration From the following particulars relating to the Delhi Fire Insurance Co. Ltd. for 1963, ascertain the profit or loss of the company for the year.

	Rs.
Provision against unexpired risk on 1st Jan., 1963	1,80,000
Premiums received	6,20,000
Reinsurance Premiums paid	80,000
Claims, paid and outstanding	1,60,000
Claims covered under reinsurance	15,000
Commission to chief agents	1,05,000
Commission on reinsurance ceded.	12,000
Expenses on Management, including Rs. 6,000 in connection with claims	2,10,000

Solution

Delhi Fire Insurance Co. Ltd.
Fire Revenue Account for the year ended December 31, 1963

		Rs.			Rs.
To Claims : Paid	1,66,000*		By Provision against unexpired Risk on 1st Jan., 1963		1,80,000
Less covered under reinsurance	15,000	1,51,000			
To Commission		105,000	By Net Premiums Received	6,20,000	
To Expenses of Management		2,04,000	Reinsurance Premiums Paid	80,000	5,40,000
To Provision against Unexpired Risk required (40% of net premiums)		2,16,000	By Commission on Reinsurance ceded		12,000
To Profit and Loss A/c—Profit		56,000			
		7,32,000			7,32,000

Additional Reserve. Good companies are not content with the usual reserve of 40% of net premiums against unexpired risk be-

*Expenses in connection with claims have been added to claims.

cause if there is a disaster leading to heavy claims, this reserve would be inadequate. Therefore, it is desirable to create an additional reserve to be increased each year. *Additional Reserve brought forward from the previons year is credited to Revenue Account and that required at the end of the year is debited to this account.*

Both the provision against unexpired risk and additional reserve as at the end of the year will appear in the Balance Sheet.

Separate Revenue Account for each type of business, Marine, Fire, etc. should be prepared. Only expenses and incomes directly allocated to a business should be entered in the relevant Revenue Account. Common expenses and losses should be entered in the Profit and Loss Account. Profit or loss disclosed by a Revenue Account is transferred to the Profit and Loss Account. The following forms prescribed by law should be strictly followed.

FORM F

Form of Revenue Account applicable to Fire Insurance Business, Marine Insurance Business and Miscellaneous Insurance Business.

Revenue Account of for the year ended 19

In respect of Business

	Rs.		Rs.
*Claim under policies, reinsurances paid during the year (*a*) (*d*).		Balance of Account at beginning of the year : Reserve for unexpired Risks.	
Total estimated liability in respect of outstanding claims at the end of the year whether due or intimated.		Additional Reserve, if any.	
		*Premiums, less re-insurance (*d*).	
Total		Interest, Dividends and Rents.	
Less outstanding at the end of previous year (*b*).		Less Income-tax thereon.	
*Commission :— Commission on direct business.		Commission on re-insurances ceded	
Commission on Reinsurance.		*Other Income to be specified (*e*).	
Commission on Reinsurances accepted		Loss transferred to Profit and Loss Account.	
*Expenses of Management (*c*).		Transferred from Appropriation Account.	
*Bad Debts.			
*United Kingdom, Indian Dominion and Foreign Taxes.			
*Other Expenditure to be specified.			
Profit transferred to Profit and Loss Account.			
Balance of account at the end of the year as shown in the balance sheet. Reserve for unexpired Risks, being...per cent of premium income of year.			
Additional Reserve, if any.			

Notes. (*a*) This heading must include all expenses directly incurred in settling claims.

(*b*) If in any year the claims actually paid and those still unpaid at the end of that year in respect of the previous year or years are in excess of the amount included in the previous year's Revenue Account as provision for outstanding claims, then the amount of such excess must be shown in the Revenue Account.

(*c*) If any sum has been deducted from this item and entered on the assets side of the balance sheet the amount so deducted must be shown separately.

(*d*) Where the account is furnished under the provisions of section 11 of the Insurance Act, 1938, separate figures for claims paid to claimants in India and claimants outside India and for premiums derived from business effected in India and effected outside India must be given.

(*e*) All the amounts received by the insurer directly or indirectly whether from his head office or from any other source outside India shall also be shown separately in the revenue account except such sums as properly appertain to the capital account.

Where the account is furnished under the provision of clause (*b*) of sub-section (2) of section 16 of the Insurance Act, 1938, by an insurer to whom that section applies separate figures for business within India and business out of India must be given against the items marked with an asterisk. Against all other items the total amount for the business as a whole may be given.

FORM B

Form of Profit and Loss Account

Profit and Loss Account of for the year ended

	Rs.		Rs.
Indian Central Taxes on the Insurer's Profits not applicable to any particular Fund or A/c.		Interest, Dividends and Rent, not applicable to any particular Fund or Account.	
Expenses of Management not applicable to any particular Fund or A/c.		Less Income-tax thereon—	
Loss on Realisation of Investments not charged to Reserves or any particular Fund or A/c.		Profit on realisation of Investments not credited to Reserves or any particular Fund or Account.	
Depreciation of Investments not charged to Reserves or any particular Fund or Account.		Appreciation of Investments not credited to Reserves or any particular Fund or Account.	
Loss transferred from Revenue Accounts (details to be given).		Profit transferred from Revenue Accounts (details to be given).	
		Transfer Fees.	
Other Expenditure to be specified.		Other income to be specified.	
Balance for the year carried to Appropriation Account.	——	Balance being loss for the year carried to Appropriation Account.	——
	==		==

FORM C

Form of Profit and Loss Appropriation Account

Profit and Loss Appropriation Account for the year ended 19

	Rs.		Rs.
Balance being loss brought forward from the last year.		Balance brought forward from last year Rs............ Less Dividends since paid in respect of last year (to be specified and, if free of tax, to be so stated).	
Balance being loss for the year brought from Profit and Loss Account as in Form B.		Balance for the year brought from Profit and Loss Account as in Form B.	
Dividends paid during the year on account of the current year to be specified and, if free of tax, to be so stated.		Balance being loss at end of the year as shown in the Balance Sheet.	
Transfers to any particular Funds or Account (details to be given).			
Balance at end of the year as shown in the Balance Sheet.	——		——
	==		==

Note. The form of balance sheet already given for life insurance is also applicable to companies doing general insurance business.

Illustration From the following trial balance of the Ideal Insurance Co. Ltd. as at December 31, 1964, prepare the final accounts of the company for 1964 :—

Debit Balances	Rs.	*Credit Balances*	Rs.
Government Securities	10,50,000	Capital	3,00,000
Claims Paid :		Provision against unexpired risk on 1/1/64.	
Marine	2,00,000		
Fire	1,60,000	Marine	6,00,000
Commission :		Fire	2,50,000
Marine	1,10,000	Additional Reserve	
Fire	1,20,000	(Fire)	1,00,000
Expenses :		Claims unpaid on 1/1/64.	
Marine	2,10,000	Marine	30,000
Fire	2,05,000	Fire	25,000
General Expenses	1,50,000	Due to other Insurance	
Premiums Outstanding :		Companies	35,000
Marine	20,000	Interest on Securities	65,000
Fire	15,000	General Reserve	50,000
Dividend Paid	30,000	P. & L. A/c	18,000
Premises	5,00,000	Premiums Received :	
Furniture	50,000	Marine	7,50,000
Cash at Bank	1,03,000	Fire	7,00,000
	29,23,000		29,23,000

Claims Outstanding on 31st Dec. 1964 were :

Fire Rs. 25,000
Marine Rs. 25,000

A taxation reserve of Rs. 30,000 is required.

Depreciate Premises by 5% and Furniture by 10%.

Additional Reserve (Fire) is to be increased by 5% of net premiums.

Solution :

The Ideal Insurance Co. Ltd.

Fire Revenue Account for the year ended Dec. 31, 1964

		Rs.		Rs.
To Claims Paid	1,60,000		By Provision against Unexpired Risk as at 1st Jan., 1964	2,50,000
Add Outstanding on 31st Dec. 1964	25,000		By Additional Reserve	1,00,000
	1,85,000		By Premiums	7,00,000
Less Outstanding on 1st Jan. 1964	25,000	1,60,000		
To Commission		1,20,000		
To Expenses of Management		2,05,000		
To Profit carried to Profit and Loss (balancing figure) A/c.		1,50,000		
To Provision against Unexpired Risk (required) 40% of Rs. 7,00,000		2,80,000		
To Additional Reserve Required (Rs. 1,00,000 +5% of Rs. 7,00,000)		1,35,000		
		10,50,000		10,50,000

Marine Revenue Account for the year ended Dec. 31, 1964

	Rs.	Rs.		Rs.
To Claims Paid	2,00,000		By Provision against unexpired Risk as at 1st Jan., 1964	6,00,000
Add Outstanding on 31-12-64	25,000		By Premiums	7,50,000
	2,25,000			
Less Outstanding on 1-1-64	30,000	1,95,000		
To Commission		1,10,000		
To Expenses of Management		2,10,000		
To Profit transferred to P. & L. A/c.		85,000		
To Provision against Unexpired Risk required, 100% of Rs. 7,50,000		7,50,000		
		13,50,000		13,50,000

Profit and Loss Account for the year ended Dec. 31, 1964

		Rs.		Rs.
To Provision against taxation		30,000	By Interest on securities	65,000
To General Expenses		1,50,000	By Profit on :—	
To Depreciation—			Fire Business	1,50,000
Furniture	5,000		Marine Business	85,000
Premises	25,000			
		30,000		
To Balance transferred to P. & L. Appropriation A/c.		90,000		
		3,00,000		3,00,000

Profit and Loss Appropriation Account

	Rs.		Rs.
To Dividend paid	30,000	By Balance b/d	18,000
To Balance c/d.	78,000	By Profit transferred from P. & L. A/c.	90,000
	1,08,000		1,08,000
		By Balance b/d	8,000

The Ideal Insurance Co. Ltd.

Balance Sheet as at Dec. 31, 1964

Liabilities		Rs.	*Assets*		Rs.
Share Capital		3,00,000	Loans		nil
General Reserve		50,000	Investments—		
Profit and Loss Account		78,000	Government Securities		10,50,000
Balance of Accounts				Rs.	
Marine	7,50,000		Premises	5,00,000	
Fire	4,15,000	11,65,000	Less Depreciation	25,000	4,75,000
Claims Unpaid		50,000			
Amounts due to other Insurance Companies		35,000	Outstanding Premium		35,000
			Cash at Bank		1,03,000
Provision for Taxation		30,000	Furniture :	50,000	
			Less Depreciation	5,000	45,000
Total		17,08,000	Total		17,08,000

EXERCISE XXII

1. Given below is the Trial Balance abstracted from the books of the Gujarat Mutual Life Assurance Association Ltd. on 31st December, 1952 :—

	Rs.	Rs.	Rs.
Claims paid and outstanding	1,15,200		
Surrenders	3,300		
Reversionary bonus paid and outstanding	12,300		
		1,30,800	
Establishment charges	23,500		
Commission to Agents	48,500		
Medical Fees	10,100		
Directors' & Auditors' Fees	24,000		
Stationery & Printing	4,800		
Postage & Telegrams	1,050		
Office Rent	4,200		
Sundry Expenses	800		
Bank Charges and Commission	950		
		1,17,900	
Investments		40,47,000	
Loan on Policies		1,74,700	
Outstanding Interest		69,800	
Outstanding Premium		23,600	
Cash at Bank		29,600	
Fines and Fees received			300
Interest and Dividends received and accrued			2,25,300
Premium received and outstanding			3,30.800
Premium received in advance			9,000
Claims admitted but not paid			10,000
Claims intimated but not admitted			20.000
Sundry creditors			18,000
Funds :—			
Life Assurance Fund	33,80,000		
Reserve Fund	6,00,000		39,80,000
	Rs.	45,93,400	45,93,400

Prepare the Revenue Account of the Association for the year ended 31st December, 1952, and the Balance Sheet as on that date.

(*Life fund, Rs. 36,87,700 ; Total of Balance Sheet. Rs. 43,44,700*)

2. The quinquennial valuation of the Eastern Life Assurance Co. Ltd., disclosed a net liability of Rs. 5. .25,000 on all their Life, Endowment and annuity policies in force on 31st December, 1953.

From the figures given below you are to prepare the Revenue Account for the year ended 31st December, 1953 and a Valuation Balance Sheet as at that date showing the surplus for the Shareholders and Policyholders :—

	Rs.
Life Assurance Fund, 1-1-1953	50,00,000
Premiums	20;00.000
Reassurance Premiums	30,000
Claims	3,50,000
Bad Debts	1.500
Considerations for annuities granted	75,000
Surrenders	1,50,000
Commission	1,12,000
Annuities	1,23.000
Interest, Dividends and Rents	9,20,000
Income-tax thereon	1,85,000
Bonuses in Cash	1,85,000
Bonuses in reduction of premiums	6,700
Expenses of management	1,75,000
Fines for revival of lapsed policies	1,350
Surplus on revaluation of reversion purchased	10,000

(*Life fund, Rs. 66,88,150 ; Profit, Rs. 8,63,150*)

(*Adapted from B.Com., Bombay*)

3. On 31st December, 1962 the books of the Fire for Fast Insurance Co. Ltd. contained the following particulars in respect of fire insurance :—

	Rs.
Reserve for unexpired risks on 31st December, 1961	5,00,000
Additional Reserve on 31st December, 1961	1,00,000
Claims paid	3,40,000
Estimated liability in respect of outstanding claims :—	
on 31st December, 1961	65,000
on 31st December, 1962	90,000
Expenses of management (including Rs. 30,000 legal expenses paid in connection with claims)	2,80,000
Reinsurance Premiums	75,000
Claims covered by Reinsurance	20,000
Premiums	11,25,000
Interest and Dividends less income-tax	58,000
Profit on sale of investments	11,000
Commission	1,52,000

Prepare the Fire Insurance Revenue Account for the year 1962, reserving 50% of the premiums for unexpired risks and increasing the additional reserve by 10% of the net premiums. *(Profit, Rs. 2,12,000)*

4. A life insurance company arrived at its Life Assurance Fund of Rs. 72,35,000 without taking into consideration the following :—

(*i*) Claims intimated but not yet admitted, Rs. 50,000.
(*ii*) Outstanding Premiums, Rs. 20,000.
(*iii*) Bonus in Reduction of Premiums Rs. 2,000.
(*iv*) Accrued interest on securities Rs. 15,000.
(*v*) Claims covered by reinsurance, Rs. 15,000.

Give journal entries and ascertain the Life Assurance Fund. *(Rs. 72,35,000)*

5. The following balances appeared in the books of The National General Insurance Company Ltd. on 31st December, 1958 :—

	Rs.
Reinsurance Premiums Paid :	
Fire	1,00,000
Marine	50,000
Interest and Dividends	1,55,700
Directors' Fees	10,000
Claims received from Reinsurance Company :	
Fire	1,00,000
Reserves for unexpired risks as on 1st January 1958	
Fire	3,33,700
Marine	8,24,800
Expenses of Management :	
Fire	2,31,900
Marine	1,20,600
Premiums received :	
Fire	9,76,000
Marine	7,89,000
Commission :	
Fire	1,27,000
Marine	1,22,000
Share Transfer Fees	200
Expenses of Management (General)	1,47,500
Claims Paid :	
Fire	4,30,000
Marine	3,51,000
Loss on Exchange :	
Fire	5,000
Balance of Profit and Loss Appropriation Account on 1st January, 1958 :	1,89,500
Claims outstanding on 1st January, 1958 :	
Fire	1,20,000
Marine	81 000
Income-tax paid	1,67,700

You are required to prepare the Revenue Accounts, Profit and Loss Account and Profit and Loss Appropriation Account for the year ended 31st December 1958, after taking the following information into consideration :—

(*i*) Provide for unexpired risk at 50% of the net premiums for Fire business and at 100% for Marine business.

(*ii*) Create additional reserve of Rs. 25,000 against fire business.

(*iii*) Premiums outstanding at the end of the year were :—

Fire Rs. 20,000 ; Marine Rs. 50,000 (not yet taken into account).

(*iv*) At the Company's Annual General Meeting held in July 1958, a dividend of Rs. 1,50,000 (free of tax) was declared for the year 1957.

(*v*) On 31st December, 1958, the claims outstanding were :—

Fire Rs. 84,600 ; Marine Rs. 37,000.

(*Profit, Rs. 2,04,100 as per Profit and Loss A/c*)

6. The accountant of Marfir Insurance Company Ltd. has extracted a few items from the Trial Balance of the Company as at 31st December, 1959 and has requested you to prepare the necessary accounts in the statutory forms to disclose the profit or loss for the year 1959. The items extracted are as follows :—

	Rs.	Rs.
Income-tax on Investment Income		3,000
Directors' Fees and Remuneration		27,000
Dividends Received		25,000
Interest Received		6,000
Provision for Taxation as at January 1, 1959		75,000
Fixed Assets (1st January. 1959)		10,000
Income Tax Paid during the year		50,000

	Fire	*Marine*
	Rs,	Rs.
Outstanding claims (1st January, 1959)	13,000	3 000
Claims Paid	45,000	29,000
Reserve for Unexpired Risks	50,000	37,000
Outstanding Premiums (31st December, 1959)	12,000	8.000
Premiums (excluding above)	1,27,000	75 000
Reinsurance Premiums (Credit)	6,000	4,000
Commissions etc. to Agents	15,000	10,000
Expenses of Management	19,000	7,000
Reinsurance Premiums (Debit)	13,000	3,000

The following points are also to be taken into account :—

(1) Depreciation on Fixed Assets at 10% p.a. to be provided.

(2) Interest accrued Rs. 2,000.

(3) The Directors have decided that the Provisions for Taxation should stand at Rs. 40,000 as at 31st December 1959.

(4) Claims Outstanding as on 31st December, 1959 :—

Fire Rs. 5,000
Marine Rs. 1,000

(*Profit on Fire, Rs. 45,000 ; Loss on Marine, Rs. 7,000 ; Profit and Loss A/c Balance, Rs. 25,000*)
(*Adapted from B.Com., Bombay*)

CHAPTER XXIII

DOUBLE ACCOUNT SYSTEM

The Double Account System was prescribed for public utility concerns in England. It is the characteristic of public utilities that expenditure on fixed assets is very heavy and a large amount of capital has to be raised for the purpose. It is considered desirable te show the amount raised by way of shares and debentures and the fixed assets required.

The Double Account System must not be confused with the Double Entry System. The former is only a way of presentation of Final Accounts while the latter is the basis of writing up books of account to be followed whether the final accounts are to be presented in the ordinary way or according to the Double Account System. The trial balance extracted from books written up according to the Double Entry System is the basis on which "Double Accounts" are prepared just as the trial balance is the basis for preparing the Trading and Profit and Loss Account and the Balance Sheet.

The chief characteristics of the Double Account System are the following :—

1. The usual balance sheet is split into two parts :—

(*a*) one containing fixed assets and fixed liabilities known as "Receipts and Expenditure on Capital Account" ; and

(*b*) one containing all other items usually found in a balance sheet, called "General Balance Sheet". The General Balance Sheet also contains the balance of the Receipts and Expenditure on Capital Account, *but*, in case of electricity companies, the total of fixed assets is shown on the assets side of the General Balance Sheet and the total of fixed liabilities is shown on its liabilities side.

2. A revenue account on the lines of the Profit and loss Account or Income and Expenditure Account is prepared. This reveals profit or loss during a period. It is accompanied by a net revenue account which is more or less on the lines of the usual Profit and Loss Appropriation Account. The following points should be noted :—

(*a*) Depreciation debited to Revenue Account is credited to Depreciation Reserve and *not* the asset.

(*b*) **Interest**, paid or received, figures in the Net Revenue Account. In case of railway companies, rent paid for lines or the ground on which lines are laid is also debited to Net Revenue Account.

The Receipts and Expenditure on Capital Account is prepared in the form of an account, the debit side recording fixed assets (expenditure) and the credit side fixed liabilities (receipts). Each side has three columns for amount to show figures respectively :

(1) up to the beginning of the year ;

(2) during the year ; and

(3) total.

Note. In case of electricity companies "General Stores" maintained more or less on permanent basis is treated as a fixed asset. Preliminary expenses are to be shown in the General Balance Sheet.

Illustration The following Trial Balance is extracted from the books of Bijlee Electricity Co. Ltd. for the year ending 31st December, 1961. The items regarding Capital account, except where specifically stated to have been incurred during the year, represent expenditure incurred up to the end of the previous year.

	Rs.	Rs.
Share Capital :		
Ordinary Shares of Rs. 100 each		6,00,000
Ordinary Shares of Rs. 100 issued during the year		1,00,000
Preliminary expenses	10,000	
Buildings	87,500	
Buildings, additions during the year	60,000	
Plant	1,50,000	
Plant additions during the year	50,000	
Mains	1,82,000	
Mains extensions during the year	55,000	
Transformers	25,000	
Meters	9,000	
Meters purchased during the year	3,000	
General Stores	1,000	
Sale of energy for lighting		80,000
Sale of energy for power		40,000
Meter Rent		2,500

	Rs.	Rs.
Reconnection and disconnection fees		500
Fuel consumed	15,000	
Oil, waste and engine room stores	2,000	
Salaries of engineers, supervisors and officers	6,000	
Power house salaries and wages	3,000	
Distribution and street lighting wages	1,500	
Repair and maintenance	2,000	
Rents payable	600	
Directors' fees	600	
Management expenses	4,800	
Auditors' fees	500	
Dividend paid	24,000	
Revenue Account—balance b/f		10,000
Depreciation Fund		40,000
Income-tax paid	20,000	
Stock of stores	40,000	
Sundry Debtors	18,500	
Creditors		7,500
Investments at cost, including reserve fund and depreciation fund investments	59,500	
Interest accrued on Investments	3,000	
Fixed deposits with banks	50,000	
Cash on hand and at banks	4,000	
Interest on investments and on fixed deposits (including Rs. 2,000 on depreciation fund investments)		7,000
	8,87,500	8,87,500

You are required to prepare the Capital Account, Revenue Account, Net Revenue Account and General Balance Sheet of the Company from the above Trial Balance after transferring a sum of Rs. 5,000 to Reserve Fund from the surplus brought forward and after providing for depreciation on Buildings Rs. 2,000 on Plant, Rs. 10,000 and on Mains, Rs. 12,000. *(Bombay University)*

The Bijlee Electric Co. Ltd.

Revenue Account for the year ended Dec. 31, 1961

		Rs.		Rs.
To Fuel consumed		15,000	By Sale of energy—	
To Oil, waste, etc.		2,000	for lighting	80,000
To Salaries of engineers, supervisors and officers		6,000	for power	40,000
To Power house salaries and wages		3,000	By Meter Rent	2,500
To Distribution and street lighting wages		1,500	By Reconnection and disconnection fees	500
To Repairs & maintenance		2,000		
To Rents Payable		600		
To Directors' Fees		600		
To Management expenses		4,800		
To Auditors' Fees		500		
To Depreciation Reserve—				
Buildings	2,000			
Plant	10,000			
Mains	12,000			
		24,000		
To Net Profit to Net Reserve Account		63,000		
		1,23,000		1,23,000

Net Revenue Account

	Rs.		Rs.
To Income-tax	20,000	By Balance b/d	10,000
To Dividend	24,000	By Net Profit	63,000
To Balance c/d	34,000	By Interest	5,000
	78,000		78,000
		By Balance b/d	34,000

General Balance Sheet as at Dec. 31, 1961

		Rs.		Rs.
Receipts as per Receipts and Expenditure on Capital Account		7,00,000	Expenditure as per Receipts and Expenditure on Capital Account	6,22,500
Net Revenue Account		34,000	Stores on hand	40,000
Depreciation Fund :			Sundry Debtors	18,500
Balance on 1st Jan., 1961	40,000		Preliminary Expenses	10,000
Additions	24,000		Investments	59,500
Interest Received	2,000		Interest accrued on Investments	3,000
		66,000	Fixed deposits with banks	50,000
Sundry Creditors		7,500	Cash on hand and at banks	4,000
Total		8,07,500	Total	8,07,500

Receipts and Expenditure on Capital Account

Expenditure	*Expenditure up to the beginning of the year* Rs.	*Expenditure during the year* Rs.	*Total* Rs.	*Receipts*	*Receipts upto the beginning of the year* Rs.	*Receipts during the year* Rs.	*Total* Rs.
Buildings	87,500	60,000	1,47,500	Share Capital	6,00,000	1,00,000	7,00,000
Plant	1,50,000	50,000	2,00,000				
Mains	1,82,000	55,000	2,37,000				
Transformers	25,000	—	25,000				
Meters	9,000	3,000	12,000				
General Stores	1,000	—	1,000				
Total	4,54,500	1,68,000	6,22,500				
Balance			77,500				
	4,54,500	1,68,000	7,00,000		6,00,000	1,00,000	7,00,000

Replacement of Assets. Usually, when an asset is discarded, its book value is written off. The amount spent on the new asset is capitalised. But in the Double Account System, this principle is modified. *The account of the original asset, even if the asset is discarded, is maintained intact.* The amount spent afresh on the new asset is split into two parts, capital and revenue. Out of the new amount spent, an amount equal to what would have been spent, had the old asset been built now, is written off and the remaining amount is capitalised. Suppose, a building built in 1940 at a cost of Rs. 2,00,000 is replaced in 1960 at a cost of Rs. 7,00,000. It is estimated that between 1940 and 1960 costs have doubled. It means that the building would have cost Rs. 4,00,000 had it been built in 1960. Out of Rs. 7,00,000 spent now, Rs. 4,00,000 has to be written off ; the remaining Rs. 3,00,000 has to be capitalised. The total amount capitalised will be Rs. 5,00,000 that is, Rs. 2,00,000 in 1940 and Rs. 3,00,000 in 1960. The entry to be passed is :

Replacement Account ...	Dr.	Rs. 4,00,000	
New Works Account ...	Dr.	Rs. 3,00,000	
To Bank Account			Rs. 7,00,000

If old materials are sold, Replacement Account should be credited (debiting Bank Account) and if old materials are used in the new works, New Works Account should be debited and Replacement Account credited. The balance in the Replacement Account is written off by transfer to the Reserve Account.

Illustration 131. The Calcutta Gas Company Limited incurred an expenditure of Rs. 7,70,000 to re-build and re-equip a part of their works. The part of the old works thus superseded cost originally Rs. 60,000 but if erected at present time would cost 20% more. A sum of Rs. 60,000 is realised by the sale of old material ; and old materials of the value of Rs. 30,000 are used in the reconstruction (included in Rs. 7,70,000 mentioned above).

Give Journal entries for recording the above transactions in the books of the Company.

Solution :

Journal

		Dr.	Cr.
		Rs.	Rs.
Replacement Account ...	Dr.	6,00,000	
New Works Account ...	Dr.	1,40,000	
To Bank Account			7,40,000
Cost of old works if built now (Rs. 5,00,000 +20%) debited to Revenue Account and the balance out of money spent capitalised.			
New Works Account ...	Dr.	30,000	
To Replacement Account			30,000
Old materials used for new works.			
Bank Account ...	Dr.	60,000	
To Replacement Account			60,000
Amount realised by sale of old materials.			
Revenue Account ...	Dr.	5,10,000	
To Replacement Account			5,10,000
Balance in Replacement Account transferred to Revenue Account.			

EXERCISES

1. From the following particulars for the year ended December 31, 1952, prepare under the Double Account System, the (i) Receipts and Expenditure on Capital Account and (*ii*) General Balance Sheet of an Electric Supply Company :—

	Rs.	Rs.
Capital		
Authorised :—**10,000 Ordinary Shares of Rs. 1,000 each Rs. 100,00,000**		
Issued, Subscribed and Paid up :		
6,000 Ordinary Shares of Rs. 1,000 each Rs. 800 per share paid up		48,00,000
9% Debentures		14,00,000
Depreciation Fund		5,00,000
Building	12,00,000	
Freehold Lands	9,00,000	
Plant and Machinery	23,35,000	
Mains	4,60,000	
Sundry Machine Parts	50,000	
Meters	40,000	
Instruments and Appliances	64,000	
Stock and General Stores	3,76,000	
Office Furniture	30,000	
Fuel	45,000	
Sundry Machine Room Materials (Lubricants, Jute waste, etc.)	10,000	
Sundry Creditors		1,70,000
Sundry Debtors	3,50,000	
Investments	9,00,000	
Cash in hand and at Bank	7,90,000	
Balance transferred from Net Revenue Account		6,80,000
	75,50,000	75,50,000

(Balance in Capital Account, Rs. 7,45,000 (Cr.) ; Total of Balance Sheet, Rs. 75,50,000)

(B. Com., Calcutta)

The Bright Electric Light and Power Co. Ltd., December 31, 1952 :—

	Rs.	Rs.
Ordinary Shares		5,49,000
Debentures		2,00,000
Lands, to December 31st, 1951	1,50,000	
Lands, expended during 1952	5,000	
Machinery, to December 31, 1951	6,00,000	
Machinery, expended during 1952	5,000	
Mains, including cost of laying	2,00,000	
Mains, expended during 1952	51,000	
Sundry Creditors on Open Accounts		1,000
Depreciation Account		2,50,000
Sundry Debtors for current supplied	40,000	
Other Debtors	500	
Stores on hand	5,000	
Cash	5,000	
Cost of generation of electricity	30,000	
Cost of distribution of electricity	5,000	
Rent, Rates and Taxes	5,000	
Management	12,000	
Depreciation	20,000	
Sale of Current		1,30,000
Rent of Meters		5,000
Interest on Debentures	10,000	
Interim Dividend	20,000	
Balance Net Revenue Account, December 31, 1951		28,500
	11,63,500	11,63,500

From the above Trial Balance, prepare Capital Account, General Balance Sheet, Revenue Account and Net Revenue Account.

(Profit Rs. 63,000; Net Revenue Account Balance, Rs. 61,500; Balance in Capital Account Rs. 2,62,000; Total of Balance Sheet Rs. 10,61,500)

(B. Com., Bombay)

3. The Nominal Capital of Bharat Electricity Supply Company Ltd., was Rs. 5,00,000 consisting of 5,000 shares of Rs. 100 each. From the following balances and particulars prepare Revenue Account, Capital Account and General Balance Sheet as at 31st December 1955 :—

31st Dec. 1954 Rs.		31st Dec., 1955 Rs.
	Subscribed Capital :	
2,50,000	4,000 Shares of Rs. 100 each Rs. 75 called	3,00,000
50,000	5 per cent Debentures	50,000
75,000	Freehold Land	75,000
25,000	Buildings	40,000
45,000	Plant and Machinery	50,000
88,750	Mains, Transformers, Meters, etc.	1,62,500
2,500	Office Furniture	2,500
	Stores and Fuel used	22,975
	Stores and Fuel in Stock	4,525
	Wages	45,032
	Repairs and Replacement	6,718
	Rates and Taxes	4,327
	Office Salaries	12,173

	Rs.
Directors' Fees	2,500
Miscellaneous Expenses	19,600
Sales by Meter	1,03,248
Meter Rents	3,750
Sales by Contract	24,352
Sundry Creditors	13,650
Sundry Debtors	43,150
Calls in arrear	5,000
Bank Current Account	25,730
Depreciation Fund	25,000
Net Revenue Account Balance at Credit	13,760
Investments in Government Securities	50,500
Interest on Investments	1,750
Renewals Fund	27,720

Provide for depreciation at the following rates:—5% on Buildings, 10% on Plant and Machinery and Mains. Transformers, Meters, etc., and 6% on Furniture, all on opening balances.

Carry Rs. 2,000 to Renewals' Fund.

(*Balance in Net Revenue Account, Rs. 23,260; Total of General Balance Sheet, Rs. 4,53,905; Net Profit, Rs. 10,250*)

4. From the following Balance Sheet of Bombay Water Supply Co. Ltd., prepared according to ordinary commercial method, construct Balance Sheet and Capital Account according to the requirements of double account system.

Balance Sheet

(*as at 31st March 1954*)

		Rs.			Rs.
Ordinary Share Capital : 8,000 shares of Rs. 10 each fully paid		80,000	Land and Building :		
Preference Share Capital : 2,000 6% Cumulative pref. shares of Rs. 10 each fully paid		20,000	Balance as per last Balance Sheet	Rs. 85,330	
Premium on shares		20,000	Additions during the year	20,000	
Sundry Creditors		841			1,05,330
Reserve Fund		500	Mains and Service Pipes :		
Unclaimed Dividend		20	Balance as per last Balance sheet	10,000	
Revenue Account :			Additions during the year	1,920	
Balance as per last Balance Sheet	1,000				11,920
Add : Balance brought from Revenue A/c	7,674		Meters		1,050
	8,674		Preliminary expenses		1,000
Less :			Reserve Fund Investments		500
Interim dividend	3,000		Sundry Debtors		1,290
Transfer to reserve	242		Stores on hand		340
Dividend on Pref. shares	1,200		Cash and Bank Balances :		
			Cash in hand	1,060	
			Cash at bank	3,103	
		4,232			4,163
		1,25,593			1,25,593

(*B. Com., Bombay*)

5. The Koyna Electric Light & Power Co. Ltd., accounts show the following balances as on 31st March, 1958 :—

	Rs.	Rs.
Credits :		
Equity shares	5,49,000	
6% Debentures	2,00,000	
Sundry creditors on open accounts	1,000	
Depreciation Account	2,50,000	
Sale of Current	1,30,000	
Rent of Meters	3,000	
Balance Net Revenue Account, March 31st, 1957	28,500	
		11,63,500
Debits :		
Lands, to March, 31st, 1957	1,50,000	
Lands, expended during 1958	5,000	
Machinery, to March 31st, 1957	6,00,000	
Machinery, expended during 1957-58	5,000	
Mains, including cost of laying	2,00,000	
Mains, expended during 1957-58	51,000	
Sundry Debtors for current supplied	40,000	
Other Debtors	500	
Stores on hand	5,000	
Cash	15,000	
Cost of generation of electricity	30,000	
Cost of distribution of electricity	5,000	
Rent, Rates and Taxes	5,000	
Management Expenses	12,000	
Depreciation	20,000	
Interim Dividend	20,000	
		11,63,500

You are required to prepare .

(*a*) Capital Account;

(*b*) General Balance Sheet;

(*c*) Revenue Account; and

(*d*) Net Revenue Account.

(*Net Profit, Rs. 63,000; Balance in Net Revenue Account Rs. 61,500*)
(*B. Com., Bombay*)

6. A Gas Company laid down a Main at a cost of Rs. 10,00,000. A few years later, the company laid down an auxiliary Main for a quarter of the length of the old Main for Rs. 3,00,000 and replaced the rest of the Main at a cost of Rs. 15,00,000, the cost of laying Mains having increased by 25% in the meantime. A sum of Rs. 40,000 is realised by the sale of old materials and old materials of the value of Rs. 25,000 have been used in the new construction and included in the cost of Rs. 15,00,000 mentioned above.

Give the Journal entries for recording the above transactions.

(*Replacement Account Balance, Rs. 8,72,500; Amount capitalised, Rs. 8,62,500*)

CHAPTER XXIV

CASH AND FUNDS FLOW STATEMENTS

In his book "A Dictionary for Accountants," Eric L. Kohler defines cash flow statement as follows:

"A statement of cash income and outgo between two given dates, its components being identified with items appearing in balance sheets and intervening income statements......"

In reality, a cash flow statement will be a summary of receipts and disbursements (or payments), reconciling the opening cash (and bank) balance with the closing balance of the concerned period with information about the various items appearing in the balance sheet and the profit and loss account. It is Receipts and Payments Account with the difference that the form used is the statement form and not the account form. It can be easily prepared by noting the movement in various assets and liabilities and the entries made in the Profit and Loss Account.

It is useful to remember that:

(*i*) in the case of assets, apart from depreciation or loss, a decrease will result only from sale and an increase in assets will result only from additional expenditure; and

(*ii*) in the case of liabilities, a reduction will be the result of payment made and an increase will be because of money (or money's worth) received.

Also, since the various items appearing in the Profit and Loss Account will be taken note of, the assets and liabilities resulting therefrom can be ignored. For example, since the payment in respect of purchases will be shown, there is no need to take note of the inventories on hand. Therefore, the two points stated above concern assets other than current assets and liabilities that are not current ; in other words these two points concern fixed assets, advances, investments, long-term loans, deposits and share capital. To ascertain the amount involved, the account of the concerned item should be prepared. See the following example :

	Rs.
Plant and Machinery —Balance on Jan. 1, 1981	5,20,000
— „ „ Dec. 31, 1981	5,75,000
Depreciation provided during the year	55,000
Book value of an item disposed of	18,000
Amount received on sale	23,000

The plant and machinery account will appear as follows :

Plant and Machinery Account

1981		Rs.			Rs.
Jan. 1	To Balance b/d	5,20,000	Dec. 31	By Cash	23,000
,,	To Profit and Loss A/c—profit on sale	5,000	,,	By Depreciation	55,000
	To *Bank (additional plant purchased, balancing figure)*	1,28,000	,,	By Balance c/d	5,75,000
		6,53,000			6,53,000
1982					
Jan. 1	To Balance b/d	5,75,000			

The account shows that during 1981 Rs.1,28,000 was spent on acquiring new plant and machinery. This can also be ascertained by means of a statement, as shown below:

			Rs.
Plant and Machinery as at Dec. 31, 1981			5,75,000
Book value of Plant on Jan. 1, 1981		5,20,000	
Less : Book value of item sold	18,000		
Depreciation	55,000	73,000	4,47,000
Amount spent on acquiring new plant			1,28,000

Illustration: Wye Ltd. gives below the summarised balance sheets as at Dec. 31, 1980 and Dec. 31, 1981 and also the Profit and Loss Account for 1981. Prepare the cash flow statement of the company for 1981.

Balance Sheet as 31st Dec. 1980 and 31st Dec. 1981

Assets	31-12-1980	31-12-1981
	Rs.	Rs.
Fixed Assets, net	4,70,000	5,42,000
Investments	80,000	60,000
Stock in Trade	1,20,000	1,45,000
Sundry Debtors	2,10,000	2,40,000
Cash at Bank	60,000	35,000
Preliminary Expenses	20,000	15,000
	9,60,000	10,37,000
Share Capital	2,50,000	2,50,000
Reserves and Surplus	50,000	60,000
Profit and Loss Account	20,000	26,000
Loans	5,00,000	6,00,000
Sundry Creditors	1,30,000	86,000
Outstanding Expenses (Manufacturing)	10,000	15,000
	9,60,000	10,37,000

Profit and Loss Account for 1981

	Rs.		Rs.
To Opening Stock	1,20,000	By Sales : Cash	2,00,000
To Purchases	4,50,000	Credit	8,00,000
To Wages	2,20,000	By Profit on Sale of Investment	5,000
To Manufacturing Expenses	1,00,000	By Interest Received	3,000
To Loss on Sale of Plant	11,000	By Closing Stock	1,45,000
To Administration Expenses	65,000		
To Depreciation	60,000		
To Interest Paid	75,000		
To Preliminary Expenses	5,000		
To Discounts allowed	6,000		
To Net Profit	41,000		
	11,53,000		11,53,000
To Transfer to Reserve	10,000	By Balance b/d	20,000
To Dividend Paid	25,000	By Profit for the year	41,000
To Balance c/d	26,000		
	61,000		61,000

Note : The cost of plant sold was Rs.80,000 with depreciation provided to the extent of Rs.50,000.

Solution :

Cash Flow Statement of Wye Ltd. for the year ended 31st Dec. 1981

			Rs.
Balance in hand on Jan. 1, 1981			60,000
Receipts :	Cash Sales	2,00,000	
	Collections from customers	7,64,000	
	Interest Received	3,000	
	Sale of Investments	25,000	
	Sale of Plant	19,000	
	Loan raised	1,00,000	11,11,000
			11,71,000
Disbursements :			
	Payment for purchases	4,94,000	
	Wages	2,20,000	
	Manufacturing Expenses	95,000	
	Administration Expenses	65,000	
	Interest Paid	75,000	
	Dividend	25,000	
	Fixed assets acquired	1,62,000	11,36,000
Balance as on Dec. 31, 1981			35,000

Notes : (1) Collections from customers :

Sundry Debtors Account

	Rs.		Rs.
To Balance b/d	2,10,000	By Discounts (as per P. & L. A/c)	6,000
To Sales	8,00,000	By Cash (balancing figure)	7,64,000
		By Balance c/d	2,40,000
	10,10,000		10,10,000

(2) Sale of investments

Investments Account

	Rs.		Rs.
To Balance b/d	80,000	By Cash (balancing figure)	25,000
To P. & L. A/c—profit	5,000	By Balance c/d	60,000
	85,000		85,000

(3) Sale of Plant :

Cost	80,000
Depreciation Provided	50,000
Book Value	30,000
Loss as per P. & L. A/c	11,000
Amount realised	19,000

(4) Loan raised is apparent on comparing the amount of loans on 31-12-80 and 31-12-81—the increase is due to additional loans raised.

(5) Payment for purchases :

	Rs.
Purchases during the year	4,50,000
Add : amount due in the beginning	1,30,000
	5,80,000
Less : amount still outstanding	86,000
Amount paid	4,94,000

(6) Payment for manufacturing expenses has been computed like payment for purchases.

(7) No cash payment is involved for (*i*) Depreciation, (*ii*) Preliminary Expenses written off, (*iii*) Discounts allowed, and (*iv*) Transfer to Reserves. Also, cash is not strictly involved in respect of opening and closing stocks,

(8) Fixed assets acquired :

		Rs.
Book value of fixed assets on 31/12/80		4,70,000
Less : Book value of asset sold	30,000	
Depreciation provided	60,000	90,000
		3,80,000
Book value of fixed assets on 31/12/81		5,42,000
Fresh outlay		1,62,000

(9) The student should note that amounts written off do not affect cash; also in respect of sales of investments and plant, the amounts have been shown at the actual amounts received—the profit or loss as such does not figure in the cash flow statement. Further, Cash Sales, Interest Received, Wages, Administration Expenses, Interest Paid and Dividends have been entered in the statement at the figures shown in the Profit and Loss Account since no adjustment was required.

Illustration: You are given below the Balance Sheet of Zed Ltd. as at 30th June 1980 and its Profit and Loss Account for the year ended 30th June 1981.

Balance Sheet as at June 30, 1980

	Rs.		Rs.
Share Capital : Fully paid shares of Rs.100 each	10,00,000	Fixed Assets: Cost	36,00,000
		Depreciation	15,00,000
Reserves	6,00,000		21,00,000
Profit and Loss Account	1,10,000	Inventories	3,50,000
Loans from I.F.C.	2,70,000	Book Debts	3,20,000
Public Deposits	2,50,000	Cash at Bank	1,30,000
Creditors	3,80,000	Underwriting Commission	20,000
Provision for Taxation	2,30,000		
Proposed Dividend	80,000		
	29,20,000		29,20,000

Profit and Loss Account for the year ended June 30, 1981

	Rs.		Rs.
Opening Stock	3,50,000	Sales	52,00,000
Purchases	27,00,000	Profit on sale of machine	16,000
Wages and Salaries	8,60,000	Closing Stock	4,10,000
Production Expenses	3,70,000		
Administration Expenses	2,30,000		
Selling and Advertising Expenses	2,50,000		
Interest	65,000		
Depreciation	2,05,000		
Underwriting Commission written off	10,000		

Provision for Taxation	3,00,000		
Proposed Dividend	1,50,000		
Balance of profit for the year	1,36,000		
	56,26,000		56,26,000

You are also informed that during 1980-81

(*i*) Rs.90,000 was repaid to the I.F.C.;

(*ii*) Rs.1,00,000 was raised by way of public deposits;

(*iii*) new fixed assets, costing Rs.3,40,000, were acquired;

(*iv*) the machine sold had cost Rs.60,000 and the depreciation provided in this respect till 30-6-80 was Rs.20,000; and

(*v*) Rs. 2,10,000 was paid in full settlement of the tax liability existing as on 30th June, 1980.

You are also informed that on 30th June, 1981 Book Debts totalled Rs.4,00,000 and creditors were Rs.3,60,000.

Prepare (*i*) the Cash Flow Statement of the Company for 1980-81, and

(*ii*) its Balance Sheet as at June 30, 1981.

Solution :

(*i*) Cash Flow Statement of Zed Ltd for the year ended June 30, 1981

		Rs.	Rs.
Receipts:			
Opening balance at Bank			1,30,000
Receipts from operations—Collection of sale proceeds			51,20,000
Sale proceeds of a machine			56,000
Public Deposits received during the year			1,00,000
			54,06,000
Disbursements:			
Operational costs :	Purchases	27,20,000	
	Wages and Salaries	8,60,000	
	Production Expenses	3,70,000	
	Administration Exps.	2,30,000	
	Selling and Advg. Exps.	2,50,000	
		44,30,000	
Other costs :	Interest	65,000	
	Tax	2,10,000	
Dividend for 1979-80		80,000	
Fixed assets acquired		3,40,000	
Repayment to I.F.C.		90,000	52,15,000
Balance at Bank on June 30, 1981			1,91,000

(*ii*) Balance Sheet of Zed Ltd. as at June 30, 1981

	Rs.		Rs.
Share capital : Fully paid shares of Rs.100 each	10,00,000	Fixed Assets : Cost on 30-6-80	36,00,000
Reserves	6,00,000	Addition during the year	3,40,000
Profit and Loss A/c	2,66,000		39,40,000
Loan from I.F.C.	1,80,000	Cost of machine sold during the year	60,000
Public Deposits	3,50,000		
Creditors	3,60,000		
Provision for Taxation	3,00,000		38,80,000
Proposed Dividend	1,50,000	Depreciation provided till date	16,85,000
			21,95,000
		Inventories	4,10,000
		Book Debts	4,00,000
		Cash at Bank	1,91,000
		Underwriting Commission	10,000
	32,06,000		32,06,000

Notes :

		Rs.
(1) Collection of Sales proceeds :	Opening Book Debts	3,20,000
	Sales	52,00,000
		55,20,000
	Less Closing Book Debts	4,00,000
	Amount collected	51,20,000
(2) Sale proceeds of the machine :	Cost	60,000
	Depreciation	20,000
	Book Value	40,000
	Profit realised	16,000
	Amount realised	56,000
(3) Amount paid for purchases :	Opening Creditors	3,80,000
	Purchases	27,00,000
		30,80,000
	Less Closing Creditors	3,60,000
	Amount paid	27,20,000

(4) The proposed dividend as on June, 30, 1981 must have been paid.

(5) The Provisions for Taxation as on 30/6/80 was Rs.2,30,000. The liability has been fully discharged by paying Rs.2,10,000. The surplus of Rs.20,000 has to be added to the balance of the Profit and Loss Account. Hence the figure in the Balance Sheet is Rs.2,66,000, *i.e.*, Rs.1,10,000 (Opg. balance) plus Rs.1,36,000 (profit as per P.&L. A/c) and Rs. 20,000 (surplus in respect of the Provision for Taxation.)

(6) The Depreciation Provision as on June 30, 1981:

	Rs.
Opening Balance	15,00,000
Less: Amount in respect of the machine sold	20,000
	14,80,000
Amount provided during the year	2,05,000
	16,85,000

(7) The underwriting commission is shown in the Balance Sheet at Rs.10,000 since out of Rs.20,000, the opening balance, Rs.10,000 has been written off.

An alternative way to ascertain closing balance of cash: One can easily see from the above two illustrations how to ascertain the cash balance at the end of a period—by noting the various items of receipts and payments; there is another way to do so. It is a two stage operation—first, to ascertain the *addition* to the cash balance *that would have* resulted if all transactions were settled in cash, that is there are no outstandings in respect of sales, purchases, etc. and, second, to see how the resulting cash balance changes bacause of the movements in various assets and liabilities.

Inflow from operations : Let us take the first illustration in this chapter and ascertain the cash balance in another manner. First, let us see how much cash would have been added by operations, had all transactions been settled in Cash :

		Amount Rs.	Remarks
Receipts			
Sales		9,94,000	Rs. 6,000 deducted on account of discount allowed
Interest Received		3,000	Amount received
Closing Stock		1,45,000	Saleable—hence equal to cash.
		11,42,000	
Disbursements			
Opening Stock	1,20,000		Amount spent in the previous year

Purchases	4,50,000		Amount paid or payable
Wages	2,20,000		"
Manufacturing Exps.	1,00,000		"
Adm. Expenses	65,000		"
Interest	75,000		"
		10,30,000	
Cash accruing (net) from operations		1,12,000	

(*Note* : Profit on sale of investment and loss on sale of plant have been ignored for the time being, as the gross amount in these respects will be considered. Depreciation and Preliminary Expenses and Transfer to Reserve do not obviously involve payment of cash. Dividends are appropriations and have to be dealt with separately.)

The amount of Rs.1,12,000 can also be arrived at as shown below:—

Operating Profit:	Profit as per P. & L. A/c	41,000
	Add Loss on Sale of Plant	11,000
		52,000
	Less Profit on Sale of Investment	5,000
		47,000
Depreciation		60,000
Preliminary Expenses written off		5,000
		1,12,000

The student will thus see that cash accruing from operations, or cash inflow from operations, can be ascertained by adding operating profit and all write-offs (involving no payment or loss of cash) such as Depreciation, Underwriting Commission written off, etc. Thus if profit, after Depreciation of Rs.1,75,000, is Rs.2,10,000, operations must have yielded cash totalling Rs.3,85,000. If, after providing depreciation to the extent of Rs.2,60,000, the loss is Rs.90,000, operations must have resulted in cash inflow of Rs.1,70,000. This point is of great importance and should be firmly grasped.

, Let us resume the illustration. We find that operations have yielded Rs.1,12,000. Now let as ascertain the final cash balance. Thus:

	Rs.	Rs.
Opeing Balance of Cash		60,000
Receipts		
Cash inflow from operations	1,12,000	
Sale of Investment (as already shown)	25,000	
Sale of Plant (")	19,000	

(*Contd.*)

Increase in Outstanding Expenses*	5,000	
Loan raised	1,00,000	2,61,000
		3,21,000

Disbursements or Utilisation

Acquisition of fixed assets (as shown already)	1,62,000	
Payment of Dividend	25,000	
Increase in Stock } **	25,000	
Increase in Debtors }	30,000	
Decrease in Creditors, showing payment	44,000	2,86,000
Cash Balance at the end		35,000

*Increase in outstanding expenses is equivalent to receipt of cash since the working so far assumes that the full amount of manufaturing expenses was paid but, in reality, Rs. 5,000 was paid less because of outstanding.

**Reasoning similar to above will show that increase in stocks and debtors means non-receipt of cash as against the assumption made while working out the cash inflow from operations.

The following is merely another way of putting the above statement

Cash Flow Statement for the year ended Dec., 31, 1981

Sources	Rs.	*Utilisation*	Rs.
Opening Balance*	60,000	Acquisition of fixed assets	1,62,000
Inflow from operations	1,12,000	Payment of Dividend	25,000
Loan raised	1,00,000	Increase in Stock*	25,000
Sale of Investments	25,000	Increase in Sundry* Debtors	30,000
Sale of Plant	19,000	Decrease in Creditors*	44,000
Outstanding Expenses-* increase	5,000	Cash Balance on hand at the end*	35,000
	3,21,000		3,21,000

Funds Flow Statement

Students can see that the items marked with an asterisk concern the working capitai which is current assets minus current liabilities. The statement could he drawn up on the basis of showing the net movement in working capital instead of showing the movement in individual current assets and current liabilities. Let us see the movement in the working capital in total :

	Decrease Rs.	Increase Rs.
Change in Cash balance	25,000	
Change in Stock—increase		25,000
Change in Debtors—increase		30,000

Decrease in Creditors—increase in working capital		44,000
Increase in outstanding expenses	5,000	
	30,000	99,000
Net increase in working capital	69,000	
	99,000	99,000

This can be confirmed by comparing the working capital on the two dates as shown below:—

		31st Dec., 1980 Rs.		31st Dec., 1981 Rs.
Current Assets:				
Stock in Trade		1,20,000		1,45,000
Sundry Debtors		2,10,000		2,40,000
Cash at Bank		60,000		35,000
		3,90,000		4,20,000
Current Liabilities:				
Sundry Creditors	1,30,000		86,000	
Outstanding Expenses	10,000	1,40,000	15,000	1,01,000
Working Capital		2,50,000		3,19,000

The working capital thus on 31st Dec., 1981 was Rs.69,000 more than that a year earlier—Rs.3,19,000 compared with Rs.2,50,000. The statement which shows only the net movement in the working capital is called "Funds Flow Statement" or "Statement of Sources and Application of Funds". A recent name, given by the International Accounting Standrads Committee, is "Statement of Financial Changes". In the above case it will appear as given below:—

Funds Flow Statement for the year ended Dec., 31 1981

Sources	Rs.	*Application*	Rs.
Inflow from operations	1,12,000	Acquisition of fixed assets	1,62,000
Loan raised	1,00,000	Payment of Dividend	25,000
Sale of Investments	25,000	Increase in working capital	69,000
Sale of Plant	19,000		
	2,56,000		2,56,000

One can see that if the total amount utilised on acquirising fixed assets, repayment of loans, payment of dividend is *less* than the total of new funds acquired, the difference will go to augment working capital. In the reverse case, the working capital will be reduced and, then, the reduction will be shown on the side of sources.

An alternative presentation:

Statement of Sources and Application of Funds for the year ended Dec., 31, 1981

		Rs.
Sources		
Working capital as on 31st December, 1980		2,50,000
Inflow from operations during the year		1,12,000
Loans raised		1,00,000
Sale of Investments		25,000
Sale of Plant		19,000
		5,06,000
Application	Rs.	
Acquisition of fixed assets	1,62,000	
Payment of Dividend	25,000	1,87,000
Working Capital as at Dec., 31, 1981		3,19,000

The normal meaning of funds is working capital, *i.e.*, the difference between current assets and current liabilities. The Funds Flow Statement, therefore, is the Statement which sets out how funds were augmented during the period concerned and how they were utilised. Kohler defines it as

"A statement of funds received and expended; a statement of changes in financial position or sources and application of funds in which elements of net income and working capital contributing to an understanding of the whole of the financial operations during the reporting period replace totals of these items...."

The term, "Funds", however, also includes anything which enables, the firm to discharge its financial obligations. For example, a company may acquire valuable assets by issuing shares to the vendor concerned, if it is so agreed, without payment of cash. In this case, the value of the shares issued is a source of funds and the assets acquired is utilisation of funds.

It should be noted that a very good name given to the statement is "Statement of Changes in Financial Position."

Steps for Preparation of the Funds Flow Statement: The following steps will be found useful for preparation of the statement:—

(1) Ascertain the operating profit earned or loss suffered after tax but before appropriations *excluding* the profit or loss on sale of any item of fixed assets or investments. Thus, if the profit before dividend or transfer to reserves is Rs.1,65,000 after including a profit on sale of on old machine, Rs.8,000, the operating profit is Rs.1,57,000. The profit or loss considered should be after income-tax or provision for income-tax since tax is a necessary payment like other costs such as salaries, wages, etc.

If the Profit and Loss Account is available, it will not be difficult to ascertain the operating profit. But if only the balance in the Profit and Loss Account on two dates is given, it will require some working; all the available information should be taken into account to ascertain the operating profit. Consider the following:—

Balance Sheet of Ess Ltd.

	31-12-80	31-12-81		31-12-80	31-12-81
	Rs.	Rs.		Rs.	Rs.
Share Capital	10,00,000	10,00,000	Fixed Assets		
Reserves	6,00,000	7,00,000	Cost	25,00,000	29,00,000
P. & L. A/c	1,70,000	2,10,000	Depreciation	11,00,000	14,00,000
Loans	6,00,000	5,50,000		14,00,000	15,00,000
Creditors	4,50,000	5,60,000	Current Assets	16,00,000	17,00,000
Provision for Tax	1,50,000	1,15,000	Underwriting Commission	50,000	35,000
Proposed Dividend	80,000	1,00,000			
	30,50,000	32,35,000		30,50,000	32,35,000

Information is also available that a machine was sold for Rs.40,000 during 1981; the cost was Rs.80,000 and the depreciation provided on it was Rs.50,000.

The operating profit is Rs.2,30,000, as shown below:

	Rs.
The increase in Profit & Loss Account balance	40,000
The increase in Reserves (which must have been due to a transfer from the P. & L. A/c)	1,00,000
The proposed dividend for 1981*	1,00,000
	2,40,000
Less: Profit on sale of machine (Sale Proceeds Rs.40,000; book value Rs.30,000, *i.e.* cost less Depreciation)	10,000
	2,30,000

If we prepare the Profit & Loss Account, then also this figure will be available. Thus:

*The Proposed Dividend as on 31. 12. 80 must have been paid during 1981.

Profit and Loss Account

	Rs.		Rs.
To Transfer to Reserve	1,00,000	By Balance b/d	1,70,000
To Proposed Dividend	1,00,000	By Profit on Sale of machine	10,000
To Balance c/d (as given)	2,10,000	By Profit for the year—balancing figure	2,30,000
	4,10,000		4,10,000

Note: It is better to consider profits after tax; then the actual payment is like any other expense and the balance in the Provision for Tax can be treated like any other current liability.

(2) Ascertain the write-off or other non-cash charges, chiefly Depreciation. In the example given above, the depreciation provided during 1981 comes to Rs.3,50,000—

		Rs.
Provision at the end of 1981		14,00,000
Less: Provision already existing: As on 31-12-80	11,00,000	
Provision relating to the sold item	50,000	10,50,000
		3,50,000

Looking at the Underwriting Commission, shown in the Balance Sheet, it is apparent that Rs.15,000 was written off. Thus the total of write-off comes to Rs.3,65,000. (If the Profits and Loss Account is given, the write-off will have been shown in that account itself and no computation would be necessary.).

(3) Add the operating profit as per (1) and the total of write-off as per (2). The total is the "inflow from operations." In our example, it comes to Rs.5,95,000.

(4) Ascertain the change in the working capital by comparing the figures in the beginning and at the end. In our example, there is an increase of Rs. 25,000 as shown below:

		31-12-80 Rs.		31-12-81 Rs.
Current assets		16,00,000		17,00,000
Less: Creditors	4,50,000		5,60,000	
Provision for Tax	1,50,000	6,00,000	1,15,000	6,75,000
Working capital		10,00,000		10,25,000

Notes: (1) Since payment of dividends is shown separately, the Proposed Dividend should not be considered for ascertaining working capital.

(2) Provision for Bad and Doubtful Debts as per the Balance Sheet should be deducted from the Sundry Debtors; it is a cash loss since so much money will not be collected.

(5) By comparing various remaining assets and liabilities, find out the amounts realised or spent. In the example given above:

(*i*) There is a payment of **Rs.50,000** for Loans since the amount outstanding now is **Rs.5,50,000** as compared to Rs.6,00,000 previously.

(*ii*) As stated, sale of a machine has realised Rs.40,000; and

(*iii*) Rs.4,80,000 has been spent on new fixed assets as shown below:

		Rs.
Fixed assets as on 31-12-81—cost		29,00,000
Less: Fixed assets as at 31-12-80	25,00,000	
Less Cost of the item sold	80,000	24,20,000
		4,80,000

(6) The statement should include items which indicate change in liabilities or fixed assets, even if no cash was insolved, *e.g.* conversion of debentures in to shares.

We can now prepare the Funds Flow Statement for 1981:

Funds Flow Statement of ESS Ltd for 1981

Sources		Rs.	*Application*	Rs.
Inflow from operations			Loan Repaid	50,000
Profit	2,30,000		Fixed Assets acquired	4,80,000
Non-Cash			Dividend for 1980	80,000
charges	3,65,000	5,95,000	Increase in Working Capital	25,000
Sale of Machine		40,000		
		6,35,000		6,35,000

Illustration: The following summarised balance sheets are given to you by Dee Ltd.

	31-12-80 Rs.	31-12-81 Rs.
Share Capital	10,00,000	11,00,000
Reserves	3,50,000	3,00,000
Profit & Loss A/c	80,000	70,000
Loans @ 10%	6,00,000	8,00,000
Provision for Tax	2,10,000	2,40,000
Provision for Doubtful Debts	30,000	20,000
Sundry Creditors	3,10,000	2,90,000
Proposed Dividend	1,00,000	1,20,000
	26,80,000	29,40,000

Fixed Assets: Cost less Depreciation	11,70,000	16,90,000
Investments	2,00,000	1,50,000
Sundry Debtors	5,00,000	4,50,000
Stock in Trade	4,50,000	3,90,000
Cash at Bank	90,000	60,000
Goodwill	2,70,000	2,00,000
	26,80,000	29,40,000

The following information is also available :

(*i*) Investments were sold during 1981 at a loss of 20% on the cost.

(*ii*) An item of fixed assets, cost Rs.70,000, depreciation provided for Rs.66,000, had to be discarded in 1981 without any scrap value;

(*iii*) Depreciation provided during 1981 came to Rs.1,80,000.

(*iv*) The increase in Share Capital was because of issue of bonus shares out of Reserves.

Prepare the Funds Flow Statement for the year ended December 31, 1981.

Solution :

Working Notes :

	Rs.
(1) *Movements in Reserves* : Balance as at 31-12-80	3,50,000
Less : Utilised for Bonus Shares	1,00,000
	2,50,000
Balance as at 31-12-81	3,00,000
Addition during the year	50,000
(2) Operating Profit earned in 1981 :	
P. & L. A/c Balance as on 31-12-81	70,000
Add : Transfer to Reserves (as shown above)	50,000
Proposed Dividend for 1981	1,20,000
Loss on Investment : 20% of Rs. 50,000	10,000
Loss on fixed assets scrapped	4,000
	2,54,000
Less Opening Balance in P. & L. A/c	80,000
Profit earned during the year	1,74,000
(3) Non-cash charges	
Depreciation provided	1,80,000
Goodwill written off	70,000
	2,50,000

(4) Movement in Working Capital :

Working capital as on			31-12-80	31-12-81
			Rs.	Rs.
Sundry Debtors			5,00,000	4,50,000
Less Provision for Doubtful Debts			30,000	20,000
			4,70,000	4,30,000
Stock in Trade			4,50,000	3,90,000
Cash at Bank			90,000	60,000
			10,10,000	8,80,000
Less : Current Liabilities				
Provision for Tax	2,10,000	2,40,000		
Sundry Creditors	3,10,000	2,90,000	5,20,000	5,30,000
			4,90,000	3,50,000
Decrease : Rs.	1,40,000			

			Rs.
(5) Fixed assets acquired : Figure as on 31-12-81			16,90,000
Less : Figure as on 31-12-80		11,70,000	
Less : Book value of item scrapped	4,000		
Depreciation	1,80,000	1,84,000	9,86,000
New assets acquired			7,04,000

Funds Flow Statement of Dee. Ltd. for the year ended 31st Dec., 1981

Sourccs		Rs.	*Application*	Rs.
Inflow from operations :			Fixed assets acquired	7,04,000
Profit	1,74,000		Dividend paid	1,00,000
Non-cash charges	2,50,000	4,24,000		
Saie of Investments		40,000		
New Loans raised		2,00,000		
Decrease in Working Capital		1,40,000		
		8,04,000		8,04,000

Illustration : M/s Shah and Jahan give you the following Balance Sheet as at 30th June, 1981.

Balance Sheet of M/s Shah and Jahan as at June 30, 1981

Capital Accounts :	Rs.	Rs.	*Fixed assets*	Rs.
Shah: Balance as at 1-7-80	50,000		Cost	2,10,000
Add			Less Depreciation	90,000
Interest	6,000			1,20,000
Profit	30,000		Shares in X Ltd. (acquired on 1-10-80)	15,000
	86,000		Stock in Trade	70,000
Less Drawings	18,000	68,000	Sundry Debtors	45,000
Jahan : Balance as at 1-7-80	40,000		Advertising Suspense	17,800
Add :				
Salary	10,000			
Interest	4,800			
Profit	20,000			
	74,800			
Less Drawings	20,000	54,800		
Loan from Mrs. Shah (raised on 1-2-81)		80,000		
Outstanding Expenses		5,000		
Sundry Creditors		35,000		
Bank Overdraft		25,000		
		2,67,800		2,67,800

You are also informed that during 1980-81 a machine costing Rs.50,000 (depreciation provided Rs.30,000) was sold for Rs.25,000 and that the cost of the fixed assets on 1-7-80 was Rs.1,20,000 with the provision for depreciation standing at Rs.60,000. The current assets on 1-7-80 exceeded the current liabilities by Rs.40,000. Advertising carried out in 1979-80, costing Rs.53,400, was put to Suspense Account to be written off in 3 years. The firm repaid on 15-2-81 the bank loan of Rs. 45,600.

Prepare the Statement of Sources and Application of Funds of the firm for 1980-81.

Solution :

Statement of Sources ond Application of Funds of M/s Shah and Jahan for the year ended June, 30 1981.

Sources :			Rs.
Working capital as at July, 1, 1980			40,000
Add : Inflow from operations—			
Profit	65,800		
Non-cash charges	77,800	1,43,600	

Loan raised from Mrs. Shah	80,000	
Sale of machine	25,000	2,48,600
		2,88,600
Utilisation :		
Fixed assets acquired	1,40,000	
Bank Loan Repaid	45,600	
Investments acquired	15,000	
Drawings of partners	38,000	2,38,000
Working capital on June 30, 1981		50,000

Statement of Working Capital as on June 30, 1981

		Rs.
Current assets—Stock in Trade		70,000
Sundry Debtors		45,000
		1,15,000
Less Current liabilities : Outstanding Expenses	5,000	
Sundry Creditors	35,000	
Bank Overdraft	25,000	65,000
		50,000

Working Notes :

	Shah	Jahan	Total
(1) Profit earned :	Rs.	Rs.	Rs.
Interest credited to Capital	6,000	4,800	10,800
Salary " "	—	10,000	10,000
Profit " "	30,000	20,000	50,000
	36,000	34,800	70,800
Less Profit on sale of machine			5,000
			65,800

(2) Non-Cash Charges :

Advertising Suspense written off (1/3 of 53,400)		17,800
Depreciation : Balance as on 1-7-80	60,000	
Less on machine sold	30,000	
	30,000	
Balance as on 1-7-81	90,000	
New Provision (90,000 — 30,000)		60,000
		77,800

(3) Fixed assets acquired : cost as on 30-6-81		2,10,000
Less : Cost as on 1-7-80	1,20,000	
Less cost of item sold	50,000	70,000
New fixed assets acquired		1,40,000

Illustration: Zed Ltd. gives you the following summarised balance sheets :

	30-9-80 Rs.	30-9-81 Rs.
Fixed assets : Cost	15,50,000	16,80,000
Less Depreciation	9,30,000	10,00,000
	6,20,000	6,80,000
Investments	50,000	30,000
Inventories	2,10,000	2,40,000
Book Debts	1,60,000	1,80,000
Preliminary Expenses	40,000	40,000
Profit & Loss Account	1,70,000	1,90,000
	12,50,000	13,60,000
Share Capital	5,00,000	5,00,000
Capital Reserve	1,00,000	1,50,000
Loans	4,00,000	5,00,000
Sundry Creditors	2,50,000	2,10,000
	12,50,000	13,60,000

You are informed that during 1980-81

(1) a piece of land costing Rs.1,00,000 was sold; the resulting profit was added to Capital Reserve; and

(2) investments were sold at a profit of Rs.10,000.

Prepare the Statement of Sources and Application of Funds for the year ended Sept. 30, 1981.

Solution :

Statement of Sources and Application of Funds for the year ended September 30, 1981

Sources		Rs.	*Application*	Rs.
Inflow from operations :			Fixed assets acquired	2,30,000
Depreciation provided dur-ring the year	70,000		Increase in working capital	90,000
Less : Loss	30,000	40,000		
Sale of land		1,50,000		
Sale of Investments		30,000		
Loans raised		1,00,000		
		3,20,000		3,20,000

Statement of Working Capital

	31-12-80	31-12-81
Current assets	Rs.	Rs.
Inventories	2,10,000	2,40,000
Book Debts	1,60,000	1,80,000
	3,70,000	4,20,000
Less Current Liabilities	2,50,000	2,10,000
	1,20,000	2,10,000
Working capital		
Increase	90,000	
	2,10,000	2,10,000

Working Notes :

	Rs.
(1) Operating loss: Increase in P. & L. A/c (Dr.) Balance	20,000
Add : Profit on investments	10,000
	30,000
(2) Sale of investments : Reduction in book value	20,000
Add profit	10,000
	30,000
(3) Sale of Land : Cost	1,00,000
Profit added to Capital Revenue	50,000
	1,50,000

Advantages of Funds Flow Statements. The following are the chief advantages of preparing funds flow statements :

(1) For the continued financial health or well-being of a firm, it is necessary to use available funds carefully and properly. The Funds Flow Statement shows up boldly how the funds made available in a year were used. Thus, the wisdom or otherwise of management's decisions in this regard will be apparent.

(2) The Funds Flow Statement provides a link between the Profit and Loss Account and the Balance Sheet. The statement shows how various operations during the year led to the changes in the Balance Sheet. In other words, the statement explains how Balance Sheet items on two dates, the beginning and at the end of the year, can be reconciled.

(3) It is possible for the management to change the reported profit by changing the figure of depreciation and the amount

of other write-offs. This means that it is not easy to compare profits in two years or of two firms. But the "inflow from operations", the total of profit and the various write-offs, is quite reliable for comparison purposes. The Funds Flow Statement always shows prominently the inflow from operations and is thus useful.

(4) To judge whether a firm faces any danger of becoming sick, *i.e.*, of facing financial difficulties, it is essential to know the amount of cash generated by operations, *i.e.*, the inflow from operations. If the flow is not big enough, the firm will not enjoy good financial position; if it is minus, it will face great difficulties. The Funds Flow Statement thus may give early warning of coming financial dangers—if the inflow is small and the use of funds is not proper.

(5) The Funds Flow Statement can be used easily as a basis for preparing financial plans for the coming period. On an estimated basis, it beomces the financial budget for the next year. In fact, when large sums are borrowed and repayment is made by annual instalments, Funds Flow Statements, prepared in anticipation for future years, will help determine the amount that can be paid each year. Thus the Statement can serve as a tool for planning also.

Exercises

1. The following are the summarised Balance Sheets of ABC Co. Ltd. as on 31st Dec. 1978 and 1979.

Balance Sheets

	1978 Rs.	1979 Rs.		1978 Rs.	1979 Rs.
Capital			Fixed Assets	41,000	40,000
7% Redeemable			Less Depreciation	11,000	15,000
Preferecne Shares	—	10,000			
Equity Shares	40,000	40,000		30,000	25,000
			Current Assets		
	40,000	50,000	Debtors	20,000	24,000
General Reserve	2,000	2,000	Stock	30,000	35,000
P. & L. A/c	1,000	1,200	Prepaid Expenses	300	500
Debentures	6,000	7,000	Cash	1,200	3,500
Current Liabilities					
Creditors	12,000	11,000			
Provision for Taxation	3,000	4,200			
Proposed Dividend	5,000	5,800			
Bank Overdraft	12,500	6,800			
	81,500	88,000		81,500	88,000

You are required to prepare (1) a statement showing changes in the working capital and (2) a statement of sources and application of funds.

(B. Com. (Pass), Delhi)

2. American Universal Ltd. gives you two balance sheets as on 31st December 1979 and 31st December 1980 :

Balance Sheets

Liabilities	1979 Rs.	1980 Rs.	*Assets*	1979 Rs.	1980 Rs.
Share Capital	1,00,000	1,25,000	Plant	75,000	84,500
General Reserve	25,000	30,000	Land & Buildings	1,00,000	95,000
Profit & Loss Account	15,250	15,300	Debtors	40,000	32,100
Loan from Bank	35,000	—	Stock	50,000	37,000
Creditors	75,000	67,500	Cash	250	300
Provision for Taxation	15,000	17,600	Bank	—	4,000
			Patents	—	2,500
	2,65,250	2,55,400		2,65,250	2,55,400

Depreciation provided during 1980 was Rs.16,500 and the provision for taxation relating to 1980 was Rs.12,500. Dividend paid in 1980 was Rs.5,000.

You are required to prepare : (1) a statement of changes in working capital, and (2) Funds Flow Statement for the year ended Dec. 31, 1980.

(Adapted from B.Com. (Pass), Delhi)

3. From the following particulars, preapre the Funds Flow Statement :

	1st January Rs.	31st December Rs.
Cash	4,000	3,600
Debtors	35,000	38,400
Stock	25,000	22,000
Land	20,000	30,000
Buildings	50,000	55,000
Machinery	80,000	86,000
	2,14,000	2,35,000
Sundry Creditors	36,000	41,000
Bank Loan	30,000	45,000
Capital	1,48,000	1,49,000
	2,14,000	2,35,000

During the year the drawings of the proprietor for personal use amounted to Rs.26,000. Provision for depreciation on machinery stood at Rs.27,000 on 1st January and Rs.36,000 on 31st December. *(B.Com. (Pass), Delhi)*

4. S.T. Ltd gives you the following:—

(1) **Balance Sheet as at December 1980**

	Rs.		Rs.
Share Capital	5,00,000	Fixed Assets : Cost	20,00,000
Reserves	3,20,000	Less Depreciation	9,00,000
Loans	5,00,000		
Provision for Tax	1,50,000		11,00,000
Sundry Creditors	3,15,000	Stock in Trade	3,00,000
		Book Debts	2,50,000
		Cash at Bank	1,10,000
		Preliminary Expenses	25,000
	17,85,000		17,85,000

(2) **Profit and Loss Account for 1981**

	Rs.		Rs.
Opening Stock	3,00,000	Sales : Cash	2,00,000
Purchases	9,20,000	Credit	25,00,000
Wages and Mfg. Exps.	6,10,000	Closing Stock	3,60,000
Administrative & Selling Expenses	2,20,000		
Interest	95,000		
Depreciation	1,75,000		
Preliminary Expenses	5,000		
Provision for Tax	3,15,000		
Balance of Profit	4,20,000		
	30,60,000		30,60,000

(3) Information about some other matters :

(*i*) Sundry Debtors and Sundry Creditors as at 31st December, 1981, were respectively Rs.2,10,000 and Rs.2,00,000.

(*ii*) During 1981 payment of tax amounted to Rs.3,90,000.

(*iii*) Fixed assets acquired during the year cost Rs.4,50,000.

(*iv*) Half the loans were repaid.

(*v*) Dividend @ 20% was paid.

You are required to prepare the Cash Flow Statement and the Funds Flow Statement for 1981 and also the Balance Sheet as at the end of that year.

5. Gomti Ltd had the following summarised balance sheets :

	30-6-79 Rs.	30-6-80 Rs.	Fixed assets	30-6-79 Rs.	30-6-80 Rs.
Share Capital	10,00,000	10,00,000	Cost less depreciation	12,30,000	13,50,000
Capital Reserve	50,000	50,000	Stock in Trade	4,10,000	5,60,000
Loans	5,00,000	6,50,000	Sundry Debtors	3,40,000	210,000
Sundry Creditors	6,00,000	7,85,000	Cash at Bank	20,000	5,000
			Profit & Loss Account	1,50,000	3,60,000
	21,50,000	24,85,000		21,50,000	24,85,000

During 1979-80, Depreciation was provided to the extent of Rs.1,15,000.

Prepare the Funds Flow Statement of the company for the year ended June 30, 1980.

CHAPTER XXV

ANALYSIS OF FINANCIAL STATEMENTS OR RATIO ANALYSIS

An intelligent study of a firm's Profit and Loss Account and Balance Sheet will generally yield good results towards undertstanding the financial position in which the company is placed and the degree of efficiency with which its operations are being conducted. Ratios, the arithmetic relationship between two figures, are of great assistance in this regard. Before working out the required ratios, however, it is better to draw up the financial statements in single column form as shown below with assumed figures. These should be seen carefully.

Single column form Balance Sheet and Profit and Loss Account:

Balance Sheet of X Ltd. as at June 30, 1981

Fixed Assets	Cost Rs.	Depreciation Rs.	Net Rs.
Land	1,00,000	—	1,00,000
Buildings	2,50,000	30,000	2,20,000
Plant & Machinery	20,00,000	6,00,000	14,00,000
	23,50,000	6,30,000	17,20,000

Working Capital		
Current Assets: Stocks	3,50,000	
Book Debts	2,60,000	
Cash at Bank	1,30,000	
	7,40,000	
Current Liabilities:		
Sundry Creditors	2,80,000	
Provision for Taxes	1,60,000	3,00,000
Operating Capital Employed		20,20,000
Non-operating assets—Investments		80,000
		21,00,000
Less: Loans		8,00,000
Net Worth or Shareholders' Funds		13,00,000

Represented by:

	Rs.
10% Preference Share Capital	3,00,000
Equity Share Capital	6,00,000
Reserves	4,00,000
	13,00,000

Profit and Loss Account for the year ended 30*th June*, 1981

		Rs.
Sales, net		40,00,000
Cost of goods sold*		30,00,000
Gross Profit		10,00,000
Other Operating Costs:		
Administration Expenses	3,20,000	
Selling Expenses	2,80,000	6,00,000
Profit before Interest and Tax (Operating Profit)		4,00,000
Financial items: Interest Paid	1,20,000	
Less Interest Received	3,000	1,17,000
Profit before tax		2,83,000
Tax		1,50,000
Profit after Tax		1,33,000

*Cost of goods sold:	
Materials consumed	16,00,000
Wages	7,00,000
Production Expenses	4,50,000
Depreciation	2,10,000
Cost of Production during the year	29,60,000
Add: Cost of opening stock of finished goods	2,10,000
	31,70,000
Less : Closing stock of finished goods	1,70,000
Cost of goods sold	30,00,000

The main advantages of drawing up the statements as shown above are the following :—

(*i*) Figures for many years, say 5 or 10 years, can be put side by side easily and that makes comparison quite easy.

(*ii*) For working out ratios, figures will be available quite readily; for example, the figure of operating profit (profit before interest and tax) can be readily available and its ratio to sales can be readily worked out.

RATIO ANALYSIS

A ratio as indicated above is an arithmetic relationship of two figures. For instance, if sales total Rs.45,00,000 and the gross profit is Rs.9,00,000, the latter is 20 per cent, *i.e.* $\frac{9,00,000 \times 100}{45,00,000}$, of Sales—this is the ratio or relationship between gross profit and sales. A ratio may be expressed as a percentage or as a decimal figure. 20 percent is the same as .20; 6% is the same as .06.

Ratio analysis of financial statements is aimed at mainly two things: (*i*) assessing the financial position of the concerned firm, and (*ii*) ascertaining the profitability of the firm.

Advantages of Ratios. The real advantage of ratios flows from the fact that an absolute figure is generally not very meaningful. Suppose one says that a company has made a profit of Rs.20 lakh. Has the company done well or not so well ? The figure of profit by itself cannot enable one to answer this question—for answering it one must know how much capital has been employed. If, in the above case, the capital employed was Rs.10 crores, the ratio of profit to capital comes to only 2%, which is certainly a very low figure. If the capital employed was Rs.1 crore, then the profit earned is 20% of capital—this is certainly a respectable figure. A figure thus becomes meaningful only in the light of the other relevant data. A ratio portrays the relationship of two figures meaningfully related to one another and, hence, it is ratios which can help us to understand the financial affairs of a firm fully.

In addition to understanding the financial situation of a firm, ratios help us to predict the future also. Work in the U.S.A. has shown that it is possible to predict insolvency of firms on the basis of ratios. In India, an effort is being made to predict sickness of firms by using ratio analysis.

Ratio analysis is also useful for financial planning. Suppose a firm is planning a big increase in sales next year. It will have to know how much additional funds it will need, say, for inventories and book debts. Ratios for the current year will help the firm to compute the amounts concerned.

Ratios are of great importance in inter-firm comparison, that is for comparing two or more firms in an industry as regards their performance and financial position. Usually, this is done on the basis of ratios worked out by considering figures in the balance sheet and the profit and loss account. But ratios may also be worked out on the basis of quantitative figures. One of the most important ratio of this type is the input-output ratio, meaning the quantity of goods produced against the quantity of materials used. Another such ratio is the quantity of goods produced per man-day or man-hour. If a company has similar departments or divisions, they can also be compared similarly—the term used for this purpose is "intra-firm comparison".

Ratios are useful but the following should be kept in mind.

Precautions. Ratios obviously will be only as reliable as the basic data on which they are based. If the balance sheet figures are themsalves unreliable, it will be a mistake to put any reliance on the ratios worked out on the basis of that balance sheet. Therefore, the very first precaution is that the reliability of the balance sheet and the accompanying profit and loss account should be tested. However, ratio analysis may itself be useful in this regard.

Secondly, a ratio by itself may not be much meaningful. This is because circumstances attending different industries differ greatly. Some industries have a low turnover rate but a high margin on sales; others have a low margin on sales but a high turnover rate. Some industries are seasonal; in many cases even a year is too a short period for completion of the production cycle. Thus, ratios for a particular industry may not at all be suitable for others. Ratios yield their best advantage on comparison with other similar firms; also if ratios for a year are compared with ratios in previous years, it will be a useful exercise. Comparison is the essential requirement for using ratios for interpreting a given situation in a firm or industry.

Thirdly, ratios are nothing better than symptoms; they must be studied further to know the real cause of the situation. Suppose liabilities of a firm are mounting, leading to a difficult short-term financial situation. The immediate remedy may be to put in more money; but the real problem may be wrong pricing or lack of control over costs (giving rise to losses and loss of funds). If it is so, ignoring this problem will mean that the firm will be in greater trouble even if it is able to raise fresh funds. Ratios, thus, will indicate the area where further investigation is needed.

Assessing the financial position

The financial position of a firm has to be assessed on considering both the long-term aspect and the short-term aspect.

Long-term aspect. The long-term aspect of the financial position again has two parts: One, the long-term needs of the firm should be met out of long-term funds only. Short-term funds should not be used for, say, buying plant and equipment. The reason is quite simple: short-term funds may have to be repaid soon and, if they are invested in long-term assets, repayment will be very difficult. Second, the components of long-term funds have to be determined carefully.

Long-term funds consist of:

(1) Share Capital, both preference and equity,

(2) Reserves, and

(3) Debentures, loans from financial institutions such as the Industrial Finance Corporation of India, etc.

The long-term needs of an industrial concern consist of amounts required to acquire fixed assets *and* about half the current assets. The reason for the latter part is that a going industrial concern will always have certain amounts invested in inventories, book debts, etc. This amount will go on changing shape—raw material stocks into finished goods stock into book debts into cash—but it cannot be released.

On this basis a ratio can be developed, called the fixed assets ratio. It is calculated as : $\frac{\text{Fixed Assets}}{\text{Long-term funds}}$

The ratio should be substantially less than 1 since that will show that a part of the long-term funds is available for financing current assets. Suppose in a company the fixed assets total Rs.25,00,000 and the long-term funds total Rs.20,00,000. It means that Rs.5,00,000 out of short-term funds have been used for acquiring fixed assets whereas out of long-term funds a portion should have been left for current assets. The policy of the company may land it in trouble.

[Previously, this ratio was calculated as Fixed Assets/Net Worth but that was when borrowing was considered improper. The ratio properly is based on long-term funds.]

Generally long term funds will lie invested either as Fixed Assets or as Working Capital. Thus if total long term funds are Rs. 50,00,000 and fixed assets are Rs. 35,00,000 : to the working capital must be Rs. 15,00,000 (assuming no investments or miscellaneous expenditure). Also if the ratio of Fixed assets to long-term funds is 0.80 ; the ratio of working capital to long term funds must be 0.20 *i.e.* 1—0.80.

The other aspect of the long-term financial situation is regarding the composition of the long-term funds—what should be the proportion of long-term loans (or debt, as it is called) in the total long-term funds. Shareholders' funds or net worth is called "Equity." The relevant ratio is called "*Debt-Equity*" *Ratio.* It is measured in two ways:

(*i*) $\frac{\text{Debt}}{\text{Equity}}$ *or* (*ii*) $\frac{\text{Debt}}{\text{Equity + Debt}}$
(*i.e.* total long-term funds)

Suppose a company's balance sheet shows the following on the liability side:

	Rs.
11% Preference Capital	10,00,000
Equity Share Capital	25,00,000
Share Premium	2,00,000
Reserves	13,00,000
10% Debentures	20,00,000
Loan @ 12% from I.F.C.I.	10,00,000
Sundry Creditors	8,00,000
Provision for Taxation	3,00,000

The debt and equity are as stated below :

Debt	Rs.	*Equity*	Rs.
10% Debentures	20,00.000	11% Preference Capital	10,00,0000
Loan @ 12% from I.F.C.I.	10,00,000	Equity Share Capital	25.00,000
		Share Premium	2,00,000
		Reserves	13,00,000
Total	30,00,000	Total	50,00,00

The Debt-Equity Ratio can be calculated in two ways, as already stated:

$$(i)\ \frac{\text{Debt}}{\text{Equity}} \quad i.e. \quad \frac{30,00,000}{50,00,000} \text{ or } 0.60$$

Or

$$(ii)\ \frac{\text{Debt}}{\text{Equity plus Debt}} \quad i.e. \quad \frac{30,00,000}{80,00,000} \text{ or } 0.375$$

In India, it is accepted that normally Debt/Equity may be 2 or Debt/Equity plus Debt may be 0.67 meaning that, of the total long-term funds, 2/3rds may be raised by way of borrowing or that loans can be twice the shareholders' funds. Both ways will lead to the same figure of loan. A ratio higher than that stated above will indicate that the concerned firm is not following a proper financial policy—that it has borrowed too much which may lead to failure to pay interest if there is a large fall in profits.

Borrowing has an advantage since the interest payable on loans is fixed but these funds can and are certainly used to earn profits at a higher rate. Further, income-tax authorities treat interest as a deductible expense which means that, with tax rates being high, a large or major portion of interest is borne by Government; the real burden of interest, due to income-tax, is often low. Thus, loans mean a low annual cost—if the yield from them is quite high, the difference between the yield and the cost will augment the profit available for shareholders. This is called "Trading on Equity"; it is the main reason for the large-scale borrowing to which companies resort these days.

A useful ratio that compares the annual interest with the profit available for paying interest is called "Fixed Charges Cover" or, "Interest coverage Ratio". It is calculated as

$$\frac{\text{Profit before interest}}{\text{Interest}}$$

Suppose the profit after interest is Rs.4,00,000 and the interest is Rs.1,00,000. The profit before interest will be Rs.5,00,000; and the fixed charges cover will be 5 *i.e.* 5,00,000 ÷ 1,00,000. The Fixed Charges Cover should be about 4 or 5; a low figure will mean that the company has borrowed too much. Suppose, the Cover is only 2; it means that if profits fall by more than 50%, the company concerned will not be able to pay the interest.

Short-term aspect: During the short-period, which is considered to be one year, it is necessary that the company should be able to meet its obligations on time, *i.e.*, make payments to its creditors as amounts fall due to them *and* that funds should be available to enable the company to carry on its day-to-day operations. In the short period funds will be yielded by current assets and it is current liabilities that will have to be met. Current assets are those assets which can be and are meant to be converted into cash within one year. Security deposits and advances against supply of plant and equipment are not current assets since they will take longer than one year to be adjusted. Advances against supply of materials are current assets since it is likely that fresh supplies of materials are received shortly which, on conversion into finished goods, will yield cash.

Current liabilities are similarly liabilities that have to be settled within one year. The usual examples are: amounts due for purchases of materials, expenses outstanding, provision for taxes, bank overdraft, etc. Care should be taken to include in current liabilities all payments to be made against liabilities; suppose there is a loan outstanding and it is being repaid by instalments. The instalments falling due within one year will be treated as a current liability for the purpose of ratio analysis.

Current Ratio: It is the current ratio that really shows up the short-term financial position. It is computed as

$$\frac{\text{Current Assets}}{\text{Current Liabilities}}$$

Normally, the proper ratio is 2; in other words, current assets should be twice the current liabilities. The figure '2' indicates that current assets should yield funds sufficient-to-pay the liabilities when they fall due *and* leave a sufficient amount to pay the day-to-day expenses. This will not be so if the current assets are even equal to current liabilities (in other words the current ratio is only 1); in that case the funds yielded by current assets will be sufficient only to pay the amounts due to creditors; there will be nothing left to meet the expenses that are being incurred. If the ratio is less than one, the situation is full of risk since, in that case, the funds yielded by current assets will not be sufficient to pay the creditors; a continued situation like this, when creditors remain unpaid, will mean that the creditors may refuse to supply further goods to the concerned company.

Illustration: Tee Ltd gives you the following summarised Balance Sheet as at December 31, 1981:

Liabilities	Rs.	*Assets*		Rs.
Share Capital	25,00,000	Fixed Assets: Cost		85,00,000
Reserves	10,00,000	*Less* Depreciation		31,00,000
10% Debentures	15,00,000			
Term Loan from Bank	9,00,000			54,00,000
Creditors for goods and expenses	5,00,000	Inventories		5,50,000
Provision for Taxation	2,50,000	Sundry Debtors	6,50,000	
Proposed Dividend	1,50,000	*Less* Provision	50,000	6,00,000
		Bank Balance		60,000
		Advance: against Plant		60,000
		against materials		1,00,000
		Preliminary Expenses		30,000
	68,00,000			68,00,000

The term loan is repayable in 3 years by an annual instalment of Rs.3,00,000 falling due on 31st July each year. Comment on the short-term financial position of the company.

Solution :

The current assets and current lliabilities are the following:—

Current Liabilities	Rs.	*Current Assets*	Rs.
One-third of the term loan	3,00,000	Inventories	5,50,000
Creditors for goods	5,00,000	Sundry Debtors	6,00,000
Proposed Dividend	1,50,000	Bank Balance	60,000
Provision for Taxation	2,50,000	Advance against supply of materials	1,00,000
	12,00,000		13,10,000

The current ratio is : $\frac{13,10,000}{12,00,000}$ or 1.09

The ratio should be normally 2; 1.09 is very low, indicating a very tight financial position as far as the short period is concerned.

Quick Ratio or Acid Test: Another ratio, used to assess the immediate financial position, is worked out by considering the assets that can yield cash immediately or without much delay and the payments to creditors that are almost immediately due (or even current liabilities). The assets, called quick assets, that may be converted into cash without much delay are usually the following (besides cash and bank balances)

Sundry Debtors

Bills Receivable

Marketable Securities, *i.e.*, securities that can be and are meant to be sold whenever the need arises.

As regards liabilities, generally all current liabilities are considered —the only question is regarding bank overdraft. If the understanding with the bank is that the firm will be given good notice before it is to be adjusted, it should not be considered for calculating the Quick Ratio; if the bank is likely to ask for adjustment soon, it should be considered. The quick ratio or the acid test is computed as :

$$\frac{\text{Quick Current assets (i.e. Debtors, Bank Balance, Bills, receivable, Marketable Securities, etc.)}}{\text{Quick Current liabilities}}$$

If the ratio comes to 1, it is considered satisfactoy. A ratio of less than 1 indicates a difficult situation.

In the illustration given above, the quick assets total Rs.6,60,000 (that is sundry debtors and bank balance). Since payment of the term loan instalment is not immediately due and the proposed dividend also is not immediately payable, the current liabilities to be considered for the quick ratio total Rs.7,50,000. The quick ratio, therefore, is: $\frac{6,60,000}{7,50,000}$ or 0.89. This figure is less than 1; hence the immediate financial position is not comfortable.

Appraisal of Performance

The net result of operations of a firm, that is production and sale of goods or services, is profit or loss. The resources used by the firm consist both of equity (shareholders') funds and loan funds. The overall performance, therefore, can be judged by working out a ratio between the profit earned and the resources employed in operations.

Return on Investment. The ratio suggested above is called the Reutrn on Investment (R O I in short). The best way to compute the ratio is:

$$\frac{\text{Profit before interest and tax}}{\text{Capital Employed}}$$

Suppose a firm earns a profit after tax of Rs.3,50,000, the interest being Rs.1,50,000 and tax Rs.3,00,000. The profit before interest and tax will be Rs.8,00,000. If the capital employed is Rs.50,00,000, the Return on Investment is 16% *i.e.* $\frac{8,00,000 \times 100.}{50,00,000}$. The reason why the ratio is based on profit before interest and tax is that this figure shows the profit as far as operations are concerned—interest does not affect operations and tax depends upon many extraneous factors. To measure efficiency of operations, therefore, it is better to consider profit before interest and tax.

Capital employed will comprise both shareholders' funds and loan funds used in carrying out the operations of the firm—any amount invested in non-operating assets, *e.g.*, investments, or not represented by assets, *e.g.*, Preliminary Expenses, should be deducted from the total of the equity and loan funds. The figure of operating capital employed can be readily ascertained by adding net fixed assets (*i.e.*, after depreciation) and working capital (*i.e.*, current assets—current liabilites).

Consider the following summarised Balance Sheet of Y Ltd

Liabilities	Rs.	*Assets*	Rs.
Share Capital	10,00,000	Fixed Assets: Cost	35,00,000
Reserves	8,50,000	Depreciation	15,00,000
Loans @ 12%	10,00,000		
Current Liabilities			20,00,000
and Provisions	2,50,000	Investments @ 6%	1,00,000
		Current Assets	9,50,000
		Underwriting Commission	50,000
	31,00,000		31,00,000

The operating capital employed is Rs.27,00,000, calculated in two ways, as shown below:

				Rs.
(1)	Net fixed assets			20,00,000
	Working Capital:	Current Assets	9,50,000	
		Current Liabilities	2,50,000	7,00,000
				27,00,000
(2)	Share Capital			10,00,000
	Reserves			8,50,000
	Shareholders' Funds			18,50,000
	Loans			10,00,000
				28,50,000
	Less:	Non-operating asset—Investments	1,00,000	
		Fictitious asset— Underwriting Commission	50,000	1,50,000
				27,00,000

Suppose, continuing the example, the profit after tax @ 50%, is Rs.1,80,000. The profit before tax would be Rs. 3,60,000; to this should be added the interest paid which would be Rs.1,20,000 (since loans of Rs.10,00,000 carry interest @ 12%). The interest received, Rs.6,000, *i.e.* 6% on Rs.1,00,000 should be deducted. The operating profit before interest and tax would thus be Rs.4,74,000. The Return on Investment would be $\frac{4,74,000}{27,00,000} \times 100$ or 17.56%.

Notes : (1) Some people compute ROI on the basis of profits after tax but before interest. In that case the return on investment would be

$$\frac{2,94,000\ (i.e.,\ 1,80,000+1,20,000-6,000)}{27,00,000} \times 100 \text{ or } 10{\cdot}15\%$$

(2) Some people compute the return on the basis of the amount belonging to shareholders and the profit available for them. Shareholders' funds are Rs.18,00,000 in the above example, deducting Rs.50,000 for the underwriting commission; the profit after tax is Rs.1,80,000. The return is thus 10%.

The above two notes show that different meanings may be attached to the term "Return on Investment." Therefore, when it is to be computed, the meaning attached to profit and capital employed, both, should be made clear.

It is worth noting that the meanings given in the two notes are rather restrictive. The Return on Investment as ordinarily computed

$\left(\frac{\text{Profit before interest and tax}}{\text{Operating capital employed}}\right)$ not only measures the performance of the company concerned but *also* indicates how much extra profit may be earned if additional funds (whatever the source) are introduced and used as profitably as before.

Illustration: Zed Ltd. pays tax @ 60% of its profits; in 1980 it earned Rs.4,00,000 profit after tax. The following are the relevant items in the balance sheet.

	Rs.
13% Preference Share Capital	10,00,000
Equity Share Capital	30,00,000
Reserves	15,00,000
Loans @ 12%	25,00,000

In the beginning of 1981, 1,00,000 equity shares of Rs.10 each were issued at a premium of 30%. Assuming conditions in 1981 permitted additional funds to be used as profitably as in 1980, what is the profit expected per equity share in 1981 ?

Solution :

		Rs.
Return on Investment		
Profit after tax		4,00,000
Tax $4{,}00{,}000 \times \frac{60}{40}$		6,00,000
Interest		3,00,000
Profit before interest and tax		13,00,000
Capital employed : (Total of all the items given)		80,00,000
Reutrn on Investment $\frac{13{,}00{,}000}{80{,}00{,}000} \times 100$ or 16.25%		
Additional funds introduced in 1981		13,00,000
Total capital employed in 1981		93,00,000
Profit before interest and tax expected in 1981 @ 16.25%		15,21,750
Less : Interest		3,00,000
		12,21,750
Tax @ 60%		7,33,050
Profit after tax		4,88,600
Preference Dividend		1,30,000
Profit available for Equity Shareholders		3,58,600
Number of Equity Shares:	4,00,000	
Profit per Equity Share:	3,58,600÷4,00,000	0.896

Analysis of ROI. Profit (*i.e.*, profit before interest and tax) over capital (*i.e.*, operating capital employed) may also be expressed as $\frac{\text{Profit}}{\text{Sales}} \times \frac{\text{Sales}}{\text{Capital}}$. Profit/Sales is the margin on sales and Sales/Capital is the rate of turnover, *i.e.*, sales produced by each rupee of capital employed. The return on investment depends on these two factors jointly — one should optimise both the factors.

Margin on Sales, *also called Net Profit Ratio*, depends on the selling price and the operating expenses (*i.e.*, materials, labour, manufacturing expenses, administrative expenses and selling and distribution expenses). The ratio $\frac{\text{Operating expenses}}{\text{Sales}}$, called Operating Ratio indicates the proportion of sales that operating expenses absorb, the remaining proportion being the margin on sales. This ratio should be lowered as far as possible. The components of this ratio should also be worked out. These are :

Materials/Sales
Labour/Sales
Manufacturing Expenses/Sales
Administrative Expenses/Sales
Selling and Distribution Expenses/Sales

Comparison with 'other' firms in the same industry or with previous years for each of these ratios will indicate the room for improvement, if any. This will enable the firm to maximise its efficiency.

Sales/Capital may also be analysed further into :

(*i*) Sales/Fixed Assets,

(*ii*) Sales/Working Capital which, in turn, may be supplemented by :

(*a*) Sales/Average inventory
or
Cost of Sales/Average inventory; and

(*b*) Sales/Book Debts
or
Book Debts/Average daily sale (called the Debt Collection Period).

The Debt Collection Period should be on the low side but the other turnover ratios should be rather high but not very high—that will indicate over-trading. Suppose the average Sale/Working Capital for an industry is 3.5 and for a firm it is 3.9; it will indicate efficient management. But if, say, it is 5.0, it may mean that the firm is trying to do too much with too little. Similarly, if the ratio is low, say, only 2.0, it will indicate idleness of funds or under-trading.

It should be noted that low current ratio and very high turnover ratios will indicate over-trading. Similarly, high current ratio and low turnover ratios will probably be the result of under-trading.

Illustration: S. Ltd. gives you the following comparative figures for 1980 and 1981.

	1980 Rs.	1981 Rs.
Sales	50,00,000	60,00,000
Materials consumed	30,00,000	36,00,000
Labour	10,00,000	12,00,000
Production Expenses	4,00,000	5,00,000
Administrative and Selling Expenses	2,00,000	3,00,000
Interest	1,50,000	2,00,000
Total	47,50,000	58,00,000
Profit, subject to tax	2,50,000	2,00,000

The company also reported that :		
the net fixed assets used in the year were	20,00,000	25,00,000
and the working capital used on the operations of the company was	10,00,000	15,00,000

Comment on the performance of the company.

Solution :

	1980	1981
Return on Investment :		
Capital Employed	Rs.30,00,000	Rs.40,00,000
Profit before interest and tax	4,00,000	4,00,000
Return on Investment	13.33%	10%

Analysis :

Profit/Sales $\frac{4,00,000}{50,00,000} \times 100 = 8\%$ $\quad \frac{4,00,000}{60,00,000} \times 100 = 6.67\%$

Sale/Capital $\frac{50,00,000}{30,00,000} = 1.67$ $\quad \frac{60,00,000}{40,00,000} = 1.50$

ROI (as proof) $8.0\% \times 1.67 = 13.33\%$ $\quad 6.67\% \times 1.50 = 10\%$

This analysis shows that there was a decline in the profitability of the company from 13.33% in 1980 to 10% in 1981. The reason is that there has been a decline in both the margin on sales (from 8% to 6.67%) and in the rate of turnover (from 1.67 to 1.50).

Probably, the increase in capital employed has not yet resulted in the full increase in sales expected from it.

The reason for the decline in the margin on sales is apparent from the following ratio :

	1980	1981
Materials to Sales	$\frac{30,00,000}{50,00,000} \times 100 = 60.0\%$	$\frac{36,00,000}{60,00,000} \times 100 = 60.0\%$
Labour	$\frac{10,00,000}{50,00,000} \times 100 = 20.0\%$	$\frac{12,00,000}{50,00,000} \times 100 = 20.0\%$

Production Expenses $\dfrac{4,00,000}{50,00,000} \times 100 = 8.0\%$ $\dfrac{5,00,000}{60,00,000} \times 100 = 8.33\%$

Administrative and Selling Expenses $\dfrac{2,00,000}{50,00,000} \times 100 = 4.0\%$ $\dfrac{3,00,000}{60,00,000} \times 100 = 5.0\%$

It is clear that materials and labour costs have not risen but production expenses have risen, though slightly and administrative and selling expenses have risen quite substantially from 4% to 5%. It is worth noting that due to certain expenses, like salaries and rents, remaining unaffected when sales increase, the ratio of administrative expenses should have fallen when sales increase—on the contrary there has been an increase, which shows inefficiency or lack of control.

Gross Profit Ratio. The ratio of gross profit to sales is important; it shows up the relationship of sales with the direct cost involved such as purchases in the case of trading concerns and manufacturing costs in the case of industrial concerns. A decline in the gross profit ratio is a serious matter and the cause should be investigated. The cause may be any one or more of the following :—

(*i*) Increase in prices of materials or wages of workers without a corresponding increase in the selling price;
(*ii*) A fall in the selling price without a corresponding fall in the prices of materials or wages of workers;
(*iii*) A mistake in taking or valuing closing stock—if stock is under-valued (by mistake or otherwise), the gross profit and the gross profit ratio will fall;
(*iv*) Over-valuation of closing stock last year will mean higher opening stock this year—this will mean lower gross profit and gross profit ratio;
(*v*) Frauds and misappropriation whereby sales proceeds are not recorded or payment is made for goods not purchased ; and
(*vi*) Wastages of materials, time, *etc.*

These causes, in the reverse, may lead to higher gross profit and gross profit ratio.

Proprietory Ratio: The total of shareholders' funds or net worth to total assets is called "Proprietory Ratio". This ratio is better if it is on the high side indicating that there is a comfortable margin for outsiders. Suppose the Balance Sheets (liability side) show the following for two companies :

	A Rs.	B Rs.
Share Capital	20,00,000	15,00,000
Reserves	10,00,000	7,00,000
Loans	40,00,000	16,00,000
Current Liabilities	10,00,000	6,00,000
	80,00,000	44,00,000

The shareholders' funds are Rs.30,00,000 in A and Rs.22,00,000 in B. The proprietory ratio for the two companies is respectively 37.5% and 50%. The creditors of company B are safer than those of company A.

(*Note* : Sometimes the ratio $\frac{\text{Debt}}{\text{Total Assets}}$ is called the Solvency Ratio.

Debt/Total Assets in case of the two companies mentioned above will be 62.5 and 50%.)

Some other ratios, though hinted at above, are given below:—

(*i*) *Debtors ratio* : It is called the Debt Collection Period. It is calculated as :

$$\frac{\text{The amount of book debts including bills receivable}}{\text{Average daily sale}}$$

The resultant figure will indicate the number of days in which sale proceeds are actually collected on the average. Suppose at the end of a year, the amount of book debts is Rs.80,000, and the average daily sale (total sale ÷ 365) is 2,000. The debt collection period is 40 days.

The purposes (or advantages) of this ratio are the following :

(*a*) A comparison of this figure with the credit period actually allowed will indicate the efficiency or inefficiency of the debt collection work. If the firm, in the example given above, allows credit for 30 days, the actual period of 40 days will rather indicate inefficiency. For this purpose, however, the figure should be worked out only on the basis of credit sales since no collection work is involved in respect of cash sales.

(*b*) For estimating the amount of the required working capital, the figure is useful since it will show the period for which sales will remain outstanding before actual collection.

(*ii*) *Operating ratio* : The operating ratio measures the ratio of operating expenses (*i.e.*, the cost of production of goods, office and administrative expenses and selling and distributing expenses) to sales. Non-operating expenses like interest and income tax are excluded. Since, after meeting the expenses, the balance would be profit, the residue out of 100 after deducting the net operating ratio (expressed in terms of percentage) will indicate the net margin on sales or the ratio of net operating profit to sales. This figure will show the efficiency with which expenses and costs are being controlled. Lower the net operating ratio, the better it is since it will lead to higher profit and *vice versa*.

(*iii*) *Expenses ratio* : One can work out the ratio of each expense to sales. Broadly speaking, the various categories of expenses are as follow :

(*i*) Materials

(*ii*) Wages

(*iii*) Factory Expenses

(*iv*) Office and Administrative Expenses

(*v*) Selling and Distribution Expenses

A ratio of each one of these categories of expenses to sales will show whether there has been an increase or decline in the efficiency in respect of the expense concerned. The total will be equal to the Operating Ratio.

The total of the expenses and costs may be categorised as fixed and variable expenses. It will be fruitful to work out the ratio of both the categories separately. Normally, the ratio of variable expenses to sales should remain constant even if the sales fluctuate. But the ratio of fixed expenses to sales should decline if the sales increase; in the other case an increase in the ratio should be expected. It may also be noted here that if the ratio of variable expenses to sales is deducted from 100 (the ratio being expressed in terms of percentage), the residue is what is known as the "profit volume ratio", indicating the difference made to total profit by a change in the volume of sales.

(*iv*) *Inventory Turnover Ratio* : It may be calculated as

$$\frac{\text{Sales}}{\text{Average Inventory}} \text{ or } \frac{\text{Cost of Sales } (i.e., \text{ Sales minus gross profit})}{\text{Average Inventory}}$$

The average inventory is ascertained by adding opening and closing stocks and dividing by 2 *i.e.*, it is the mean of the opening and closing stocks.

This ratio shows better performance if it is higher—showing that more sales are being obtained from the capital used for holding inventories. At one time, it was the only turnover ratio that was worked out, that is why the turnover ratio at that time meant inventory turnover ratio. The ratio can help as certain some important figures. Suppose the inventory turnover ratio (based on cost of sales) is 6 and the average inventory is Rs. 5,00,000, then the cost of sales will be Rs. 30,00,000 *i.e.*, 5,00,000 × 6. If the gross profit ratio is 25% the sale will be Rs. 40,00,000 *i.e.*, 30,00,000 × 100/75.

Exercises

1. The following balance sheet is given to you :

	Rs.		Rs.
Equity Capital	1,00,000	Fixed Assets	2,00,000
General Reserve	20,000	Sundry Debtors	30,000
Secured Loans	80,000	Stock	30,000
Sundry Creditors	50,000	Bills Receivable	10,000
P. & L. A/c	30,000	Cash at Bank	30,000
Provision for Taxation	20,000		
	3,00,000		3,00,000

Calculate from the figures given above the following ratios :—

(*i*) Acid Test Ratio (*iii*) Debt-Equity Ratio

(*ii*) Current Ratio

(*B.Com.* (*Pass*), *Delhi*)

(1.0; 1.43; .67 or .40 *respectively*)

. From the following balance sheet of Tee Ltd. calculate ratios to indicate the financial postion of the company :

Balance Sheets

	Rs.		Rs.
11% Preference Capital	5,00,000	Fixed Assets : Cost	60,00,000
Equity Capital	10,00,000	Depreciation	20,00,000
Reserves	6,00,000		
10% Debentures	20,00,000		40,00,000
Public Deposits	4,00,000	Marketable securities	2,00,000
Sundry Creditors	6,00,000	Inventories	4,50,000
Provision for Taxation	2,00,000	Sundry Debtors	5,50,000
Proposed Dividend	1,50,000	Bank Balance	1,70,000
		Preliminary Expenses	80,000
	54,50,000		54,50,000

3. State which of the two companies has followed better financial policies :

	X Ltd. Rs.	Y Ltd. Rs.
Share Capital	20,00,000	15,00,000
Reserves	5,00,000	5,00,000
Loans from I.F.C.I.	10,00,000	20,00,000
Sundry Creditors and Provisions	10,00,000	8,00,000
Fixed Assets (net)	35,00,000	30,00,000

(*Note* : Ascertain current assets first).

4. The gross profit ratio of a company was 30% in 1980 but only 22% in 1981. Indicate the areas which you will investigate to ascertain the causes of the fall.

5. The totals of net fixed assets and working capital of a company during 1980 and 1981 were respectively Rs.50,00,000 and Rs.60,00,000. Its Profit and Loss Accounts could be summarised as follows :—

	1980 Rs.	1981 Rs.
Materials consumed	60,00,000	65,00,000
Labour	20,00,000	25,00,000
Manufacturing Expenses	10,00,000	11,00,000
Administrative Expenses	5,00,000	5,00,000
Selling and Distribution Expenses	6,00,000	6,30,000
Interest	5,00,000	6,00,000
Tax	3,00,000	3,70,000
Total	1,09,00,000	1,22,00,000
Profit	6,00,000	10,00,000
Sales, net	1,15,00,000	1,32,00,000

Comment on the performance of the company in 1981 as compared with that in 1980 and show the factors that have led to this change.

6. (*a*) The ratio of fixed assets to long ferm funds is 0·75 ; the working capital is Rs. 10,00 000. Ascertain the fixed assets and total long term fuuds. (*Rs. 30,00,000 and Rs. 40,00 000*)

(*b*) The ratio of net profit to sales is 6% and the total turnover vadio is 3·6. What is the ROI. (*21.6%*)

(*c*) The ROI in a company in 30% the total turnover ratio (Sales/Capital Employed) Is 6·0. What is the Operating Ratio ? (*95%*)

MISCELLANEOUS EXERCISES

1. Give the corrective journal entries in respect of the under-mentioned transactions in the books of a trader :

(*i*) The Discount Account was credited by Rs. 175 the amount representing the total of the Discount column of the debit side of the Cash Book.

(*ii*) The Sales Day Book was undercast by Rs. 100 ,

(*iii*) The sales proceeds of old furniture amounting to Rs. 1,500 were credited to the Sales Account;

(*iv*) A Bill Receivable for Rs. 350 was posted as Rs. 503 to the debit of the Acceptor's Account;

(*v*) Repairs to Motor Car Account—Rs. 750 were debited to the Motor Car Account as Rs. 570.

State how the above mentioned errors would affect the agreement of the Trial Balance and the Profit and Loss Account.

[*Trial Balance out by Rs. 423* (*excess debit*) *and profit increased by Rs. 2,500*]

2. The following mistakes were discovered when drawing up a Trial Balance as at 30th November, 1957. Show the entries required to rectify them and determine to what extent and Profit and Loss Account of the period in question was effected before rectification.

(*a*) A cheque for Rs. 160 received from A was returned dishonoured and was debited to General Charges Account.

(*b*) Goods sent out on approval were valued at Rs. 2,106. Out of this supply goods valued at Rs. 1,074 were returned as not approved and others retained. No entry has been passed for sending the goods on their return.

(*c*) A cheque for Rs. 1,000 received from an insurance company against a claim for loss of stock by fire was credited to Capital Account.

(*d*) A sum of Rs. 1,750 included in repairs cost was in respect of construction of a small factory shed.

(*e*) Discounts received were overcast by Rs. 100 and the debit total on Salary Account was undercast by Rs. 200.

(*Profit reduced by Rs. 3,642*)

(*Adapted from B. Com., Calcutta*)

3. On examining the Bank Pass Book of Nitram Ltd., it is found that the balance shown on 31st March, 1955, the close of the Company's financial year, differs from the Bank balance of Rs. 23,650 shown by the Cash Book on that date. From a detailed comparison of the entries it is found that :—

(*a*) Rs. 2,860 is entered in the Cash Book as paid into Bank on 31st March, 1955, but not credited by the Bank until the following day.

(*b*) Bank charges Rs. 70 on 31st March, 1955 are not entered in the Cash Book.

(*c*) A bill for Rs. 5,500 discounted with the Bank is entered in the Cash Book without recording the discount charge of Rs. 270.

(*d*) Cheques totalling Rs. 16,720 were issued by the company and duly recorded in the Cash Book before 31st March, 1955, but had not been presented at the Bank for payment until after that date.

(*e*) On 25th March, 1955, a debtor paid Rs. 1,000 into the Company's Bank in sttelement of his account in the Company's Sales Ledger but no entry was made in the Cash Book of the Company in respect of this.

(*f*) No entry has been made in the Cash Book to record the dishonour on the 15th March, 1955, of a cheque for Rs. 550 received from B. Khatar.

You are asked to show the necessary corrections in the Cash Book of Nitram Ltd. and to prepare a statement reconciling the Cash Book Balance as amended with the balance which should appear in the Bank Pass Book.

(*Cash Book Balance, Rs. 23,760; Bank Pass Book Balance, Rs. 40,480*)

(*B. Com., Calcutta*)

4. A draws a bill on B at 3 months' date for Rs. 4,000 on 1st June, and on acceptance discounts the Bill @ 5% per annum and sends half the proceeds to B. On the same date B draws a 3 months' Bill on A for Rs. 2,000 and remits half of the proceeds to A after discounting the Bill @ 6% per annum. B is declared as an insolvent on 31st August, and a first and final dividend of 20 P. in the rupee is received on 15th October.

Prepare B's Account in A's Ledger and A's Account in B's Ledger.

(*B. Com., Calcutta*)

5. (*a*) What is meant by Accommodation Bill ?

(*b*) X draws a bill for Rs. 1,500 and Y accepts the same for the mutual accommodation of both in the ratio of 2 : 1. X discounts the same for Rs. 1,410 and remits ⅓ of proceeds to Y. Before the due date Y draws another bill for Rs. 2,100 on X in order to provide funds to meet the first bill. The second bill is discounted for Rs. 2,400 by Y and a sum of Rs. 360 is remitted to X after meeting the first bill. The second bill is duly met. Show the accounts in the books of both X and Y

(*B. Com., Calcutta*)

6. The following information is obtained from the books of the concern for the month ended March 31, 1955 :—

(*i*) Opening Balances at the beginning of the month—A . Rs. 6,000; B : Rs. 9,000 ; C : Rs. 3,000 ; D : Rs. 5,000 ; P : Rs. 18,000 ; Q ; Rs. 22,000

(*ii*) Sales to A : Rs. 30,000; B : Rs. 28,000; C : Rs. 45,000 ; D : Rs. 37,000.

(*iii*) Payments received from A : Rs. 29,000 ; B : Rs. 32,000 ; C : Rs. 40,000; D : Rs. 38,000; P : Rs. 15,000; Q : Rs. 18,000.

(*iv*) Cheques received from the following parties, included in (*iii*) above, dishonoured C : Rs. 2,000; P : Rs. 1,000.

(*v*) The following discounts were allowed—A : Rs. 100; D : Rs. 200.

Draw up the General Ledger Adjustment Account as it would appear in the Debtor's Ledger.

[*Balance, Rs. 33,700 (Cr.)*]

(*B. Com., Calcutta*)

7. (*a*) What advantages are derived by a trader by keeping Ledgers under Self-balancing system ?

(*b*) Below are given particulars from the books of a trader for the month of January, 1956 :

				Rs.
January	1	1956	Opening Balance	30,000
„	31	„	Total Sales for the month	90,000
„	„	„	Sales Returns	500
„	„	„	Cash received from Debtors	40,000
„	„	„	Bills Receivable	15,000
„	„	„	Bills dishonoured	1,500
„	„	„	Discounts allowed to Debtors	400
„	„	„	Bad Debts	350
„	„	„	Transfers from Bought Ledger	750

He wants to maintain his books on Self-balancing system. You are asked to journalise the above transactions and raise relevant Adjustment accounts in the Sales Ledger and the General Ledger.

(*Balance, Rs. 64,500*)
(*Adapted from B. Com., Calcutta*)

8. (*a*) The following expenses are incurred during a year in respect of your College Building; state with reasons whether they should be treated in the books as Capital or Revenue expenditure :—

(*i*) Addition of a new wing to the Library Rs. 40,000;

(*ii*) Repairs to the Students' Common Room Rs. 500; and

(*iii*) White-washing the entire building Rs. 2,000.

(*b*) A trader intends to accept a consolidated bill to be drawn on the average due date to meet his total liability in respect of the following purchases :—

5th August Rs. 600 due 8th September.

15th September Rs. 400 due 8th October.

10th October Rs. 550 due 13th November.

5th November Rs. 800 due 8th December.

Ascertain the average due date. (*B. Com., Calcutta*)

9. It was decided to create a Maintenance Reserve Account by debiting a sum of Rs. 2,000 every year to Profit and Loss Account and adjusting from the said Reserve Account with actual repair and renewal charges which amounted to Rs. 1,500, Rs. 1,950 and Rs. 2,525 in successive years.

Show the Maintenance Reserve Account for three years.
(*B. Com., Calcutta*)

10. Misrilal keeps his books under the Single Entry system. The position of his business as on 1st January, 1958, was as under :—

Sundry Creditors Rs. 17,000 ; Freehold Premises Rs. 50,000 ; Stock Rs. 25,000; Sundry Debtors Rs. 20,000; Furniture Rs. 2,000. An abstract of the Cash Book is appended below :—

Receipts	Rs.	*Payments*	Rs.
Sundry Debtors	15,000	Overdrafts (1-1-58)	10,000
Cash Sales	80,000	Expenses	50,000
		Drawings	3,000
		Sundry Creditors	20,000
		Cash in hand	2,000
		Cash at Bank	10,000
	95,000		95,000

The following additional information is available :—

Closing Stock Rs. 30,000; Closing Debtors Rs. 25,000; Closing Creditors Rs. 12,000. No additions were made during the year to Premises and Furniture Account, but they are to be depreciated @ 10% and 15% respectively. A Bad Debts Provision of 5% is to be raised.

Prepare a Trading and Profit and Loss Account for the year ended 31st December, 1958 and a Balance Sheet as on that date.
(*Net Profit Rs. 33,450; Total of Balance Sheet, Rs. 1,12,4*[illegible]*)*
(*B. Com., Calcutta*)

11. On 1st January, 1958, A and B entered into a partnership, sharing profits and losses in the ratio of three-fifths and two-fifths respectively. They

did not keep proper books but the following information is ascertained from the records for the year ended 31st December, 1958 :—

(*a*) Deposits into the Bank as per Paying-in-slips were as follows :—

	Rs.
Capital introduced by A	56,000
Capital introduced by B	42,000
Balance of Cash Sales	70,000
Collections from Customers	1,36,000
Against Bills Receivable	12,000

(*b*) Payments from Bank as per Cheque-counterparts were as follows :—

To Creditors	2,12,660
For Staff Salary	17,500
Against Bills Payable	7,000
For Petty Cash	10,000
For Cost of Furniture	10,000
Drawings (A, Rs. 26,000; B, Rs. 14,000)	40,000

(*c*) A uniform rate of Gross Profit of 30% on Sales was earned.

(*d*) Discount allowed by Creditors Rs. 3,500, discount allowed to Customers Rs. 4,900 and Bad Debts written off Rs. 2,100.

(*e*) Bills Receivable received during the year Rs. 23,000 and Bills payable accepted during the year Rs. 14,000.

(*f*) On December 31, 1958, the amount owing to Creditors for goods supplied was Rs. 28,000, due by Debtors was Rs. 14,000.

(*g*) Expenses out of Petty Cash were—Postage Rs. 360, Stationery Rs. 1,325, Conveyance Rs. 1,620 and Rent Rs. 3,000, General Expenses, Rs. 1,860.

(*h*) Depreciate Furniture by 10%.

Prepare (*i*) a Trading and Profit and Loss Account for the year and (*ii*) a Balance Sheet as on 31st December, 1958.

(*Gross Profit, Rs. 75,000; Net Profit, Rs. 44,835; Total of Balance Sheet, Rs. 1,37,835*)

(*Adapted from B. Com,, Calcutta*)

12. (*a*) **State clearly the points of difference between a "Receipts and Payments Account" and an "Income and Expenditure Account".**

(*b*) **From the undermentioned Receipts and Payments Account for the year ended 31st December, 1954, prepare an Income and Expenditure Account for the same period and Balance Sheet as at the end of the year.**

		Rs.		Rs.
Opening Balance		25,000	Salaries and Wages	3,000
Subscription :			Telephone Expenses	350
1953	500		Postage and Stationery	975
1954	10,000		Purchase of Books	3,500
1955	575		Entertainment Exp.	1,500
	———	11,075	Purchase of $3\frac{1}{2}$% Treasury Savings Deposit Certificates (on 1-10-54)	8,000
Life Memberships		2,000	Miscellaneous Expenses	675
Sale Proceeds of waste paper		175	Closing Balances :	
Hall Rent		1,500	Cash in hand	350
Bank Interest		250	Cash at bank	23,650
Admission fees of new members (10% to be capitalised)		1,000		
		41,000		41,000

The following additional information is supplied :—

(*i*) Salaries and Wages outstanding Rs. 1,500, the figure on 31st December, 1953 being Rs. 1,100.

(*ii*) Miscellaneous and Entertainment Expenses Bill outstanding amount to Rs. 500 and 750 respectively.

(*iii*) Bank Interest receivable amounts to Rs. 350.

(*iv*) Subscriptions outstanding on 1st Jan., 1954 were Rs. 800 ; and subscriptions received in advance were Rs. 600. Subscriptions outstanding (in respect of 1954) at the end of the year were Rs. 600.

(*v*) On 1st January, 1954 there was furniture with a book value of Rs. 2,000 subject to depreciation of 10%.

(*Excess of income over expenditure, Rs. 7,095; Total of Balance Sheet, Rs. 38,620*)

13. Chhotamull of Calcutta, shipped in November 1955 to his agent, Badamull of Rangoon, 140 cases of goods, costing Chhotamull Rs. 1,29,000. Badamull was to sell the goods on account of the consignors and to receive a commission of 5% of the gross proceeds with a further 2% as *del credere* commission.

Chhotamull incurred the following charges in connection with the consignment :—

	Rs.
Carriage	500
Insurance and Freight	3,290
Loading Charges	210

Badamull sold 100 cases for an average Rs. 1,500 per case incurring Bad Debts of Rs. 4,310 and paid the following expenses :—

	Rs.
Landing Charges	500
Warehousing and Insurance	1,300
Packing and Selling Expenses	1,580

Raise the necessary accounts in the books of both parties to record the above transactions.

(*Profit on Consignment, Rs. 41,220; Net Profit for Badamull, Rs. 6,190*)

14. Jadu consigns to Madhu 40 cases of goods at a cost of Rs. 5,000 per case and incurs the following expenses in connection with the same, *viz.*—

Cartage, Rs. 940 ; Freight, 3,480 ; and Insurance, Rs. 12,500.

On arrival of the goods Madhu pays Clearing Charges, Rs. 3,120 ; Cartage, Rs. 960 to Godown; and Godown Rent, Rs. 200. Six cases are destroyed by fire and a sum of Rs. 30,000 is realised from the Insurance Company by way of compensation. Out of the remaining 34 cases, 24 are sold at a total price of Rs. 2,20,000.

Madhu is entitled to an Ordinary Commission of 5% and 2% *del credere* Commission on sales in addition to reimbursement for expenses incurred. He sends to Jadu an Account Sales together with a sight draft for the balance due to Jadu.

In the books of Jadu show the Consignment Account (indicating the profit or loss on consignment) and Madhu's Account.

(*Profit on Consignment, Rs. 71,800; Abnormal Loss, Rs. 3,150*)
(*B. Com., Calcutta University*)

15. Asoke and Bikas enter into a joint venture. They agree to share profits and losses as Asoke 75% and Bikas 25%. On 1st January, 1954, Asoke sends Rs. 50,000 to Bikas. The latter purchases several varieties of silk goods and sends them on to Asoke. The particulars of such purchases are given below :—

1,000 Ladies' garments @ Rs. 10 each Rs. 10,000; 2,000 Silk Shirts @ Rs. 15 each : Rs. 30,000; 500 Silk Punjabis @ Rs. 20 each : Rs. 10,000. The expenses incurred by Bikas amounted to Rs. 500. Asoke sells the first two varieties at double the price but in respect of the Punjabis he suffered a loss of Rs. 1,000. His expenses amounted to Rs. 2,000.

Prepare a joint venture account, ascertain the net profit, distribute the same between the venturers and close their accounts.

(Profit, Rs. 36,500)
(Adapted from B. Com., Calcutta)

16. Ananta, Ballav and Chapman entered into a joint venture and agreed to divide the profits as Ananta: 60%., Ballav: 30%, and Chapman : 10%. They purchased by auction 5 trucks for Rs. 50,000. A sum of Rs. 30,000 was spent on reconditioning. Ananta contributed Rs. 30,000, Ballav, Rs. 20,000 and Chapman, Rs. 10,000 for carrying on the transactions relating to the venture. A joint banking account was started. The venturers were successful in selling four trucks for Rs. 90,000; Ananta took the remaining truck at cost plus 10%. Ananta spent Rs. 2,450 and the two other venturers spent Rs. 1,250 each in connection with the venture.

You are asked to give the necessary entries to record the above transactions and close the accounts of the ventures. *(Profit Rs. 22,650)*

17. A and B enter into a joint venture for guaranteeing the subscription at par of 1,00,000 shares of Rs. 10 each of a Joint Stock Company. They agree to share profits and losses in the ratio of 2 : 3. The terms with the company are : $2\frac{1}{2}$% commission in cash and 2,500 shares of the company as fully paid up.

The public take up 88,000 of the shares and the balance shares of the guaranteed issue are taken up by A and B who provide cash equally.

The entire share-holding of the joint venture is then sold through brokers : 30% at a price of Rs. 9 : 50% at a price of Rs. 8.50; and the remaining 20% are taken over by A and B equally at Rs. 8 per share. The sale proceeds of the shares are taken by the partners equally.

Prepare a Joint Venture Account and the separate accounts of A and B in the books of B and A respectively showing the adjustment of the final balance between A and B. *(Profit, Rs. 28,975)*
(Adapted from B. Com., Calcutta)

18. (*a*) What is an Account Current ?

(*b*) ABC had the following transactions with PQR in 1960 :–

Jan. 1	Balance due to PQR — Rs. 600.
April 1	Sold goods to PQR — Rs. 1,600.
June 16	Received PQR's acceptance at 3 months' date — Rs. 800.
Oct. 1	Purchased goods from PQY — Rs. 1,400.
Oct. 4	Issued Acceptance at 4 months' for Rs. 400 in favour of PQR.
Dec. 6	Paid cash to PQR — Rs. 300.

Prepare and close PQR's Account in ABC's Ledger, calculating interest @ 6% per annum. *(Interest due to PQR, Rs. 20·08)*
(Adapted from B. Com., Calcutta)

19. X, Y and Z are partners in a firm sharing profits and losses (after interest on capital and salaries) as X, 80%, Y 10% and Z 10%, upto Rs. 40,000 the remaining profit being shared equally. The Profit and Loss Account of the firm for the year ended 31st March, 1958, before charging interest on Capital and Partnership salaries discloses a profit of Rs. 75,500. Interest at 6% p.a. is to be allowed to the partners the balance of whose Capital Accounts as on 1st April, 1957, stood as X, Rs. 50,000, Y, Rs. 25,000 and Z, Rs. 15,000. The Partnership salaries were to be allowed as X, Rs. 3,600, Y, Rs. 3,000 and Z Rs. 2,500 p.a.

You have been asked to give the Profit and Loss Appropriation Account of the partners for the year ended 31st March, 1958, and the Current Accounts of the partners incorporating therein the above transactions. (It is understood that the Capital Accounts of partners are fixed amounts.)

(*Besides Interest and Salary, X gets Rs. 39,000; Y and Z each get Rs. 11,000*)
(*Adapted from B. Com., Calcutta*)

20. Ram and Rahim are in partnership sharing profits and losses in the ratio of 3 : 2. As Ram, on account of his advancing age, feels he cannot work as hard as before, the Chief Clerk of the firm, Ratan, is admitted as a partner with effect from January 1, 1955, and becomes entitled to one-tenth of the net profits and nothing else, the mutual ratio between Ram and Rahim remaining unaltered.

Before becoming a partner Ratan was getting a salary of Rs. 500 per month together with a commission of 4% on the net profit after deducting his salary and the commission.

It is provided in the partnership deed that the share of Ratan's profits as a partner in excess of the amount to which he would have been entitled if he had continued as the Chief Clerk, should be taken out of Ram's share of profits.

The net profits for the year ended December 31, 1955, amounted to Rs. 1,10,000. Draw up the Ledger Account for the net profits showing the distribution amongst the partners.

(*Ram gets, Rs. 59,000; Rahim, Rs. 40,000; Rattan, Rs. 11,000*)
(*Calcutta University*)

21. A and B are partners in a firm sharing profits and losses as A 60% and B 40%. Their Trial Balance as on 31st December, 1955, is given below. You are asked to prepare the Trading and Profit and Loss Account and Profit and Loss Appropriation Account for the year ended 31st December, 1955, and the Balance Sheet as on that date.

	Rs.	Rs.
Opening Stock	80,000	
Freehold Premises	60,000	
Plant and Machinery	50,000	
Purchases and Sales	75,000	1,90,000
Discount	350	400
Sundry Debtors	40,000	
Sundry Creditors		25,000
Carriage In	750	
Carriage Out	1,200	
Furniture and Fixtures	5,000	
Wages	10,000	
Salaries	7,500	
Bad Debts	1,200	
Commission		2,500
Capital Accounts: A 50,000; B 40,000		90,000
Bills Receivable	20,000	
Bills Payable		5,000
A's Loan Account		50,000
Cash in hand	750	
Cash at Bank	5,250	
Trade Expenses	5,900	
	3,62,900	3,62,900

The following adjustments are required :—

(*i*) Closing stock amounted to Rs. 73,000, (*ii*) Plant and Machinery and Furniture and Fixtures are to be depreciated 6% and 20% respectively, (*iii*) Outstanding Liabilities to be provided for Wages Rs. 2,000 ; Salaries Rs. : 3,000. (*iv*) Partnership Salaries to be provided for : A, Rs. 5,000, B : Rs. 4000.

(*Gross Profit, Rs. 97,250 ; Net Profit, Rs. 65,000 : Total of Balance Sheet, Rs. 2,52,000*) (*Adapted fram B. Com., Calcutta*)

22. From the following list of balances, prepare Manufacturing, Trading Account and Profit and Loss Account for the year ended 31st December, 1959, and Balance Sheet as at that date :—

	Rs.		Rs.
Stock on 1-1-59 :		Advertisements	21,500
Raw Materials	30,000	Printing and Stationery	10,000
Work-in-Progress	20,000	Carriage Outwards	6,000
Finished Goods	1,50,000	Discount Allowed	10,000
Purchase of Materials	3,00,000	Cash in hand and at Bank	57,500
Carriage Inwards	11,000	Sundry Debtors	2,50,000
Wages	2,00,000	Plant and Machinery	2,00,000
Works Managers' Salary	56,000	Factory Land and Buildings	1,15,000
Factory Expenses	59,000	Sundry Creditors	3,26,000
Royalties (on Production)	12,000	Loan @ 9% (Cr.)	40,000
Sales	7,34,000	Drawings	61,000
Discount Received	11,000	Provision for Bad Debts	10,000
Office Salaries and Expenses	70,000	Capital Account	5,60,000
Office Rent and Insurance	42,000		

The following additional particulars are to be taken into consideration :—

(*a*) Stocks on 31-12-1959 :—

Raw Materials Rs. 40,000 ; Work-in-Progress Rs. 45,000 ; Finished Goods, Rs. 2,80,000.

(*b*) Outstanding Expenses :—

Wages, Rs. 6,000 ; Factory Expenses, Rs. 2,500 ; Office Salaries, Rs. 3,000.

(*c*) Depreciate Land and Buildings @ 2% and Plant and Machinery @ 7½%.

(*d*) Write off Rs. 5,000 as Bad Debts and provide a provision of 5% for Bad and Doubtful Debts.

(*Gross Profit, Rs. 2,35,200 ; Net Profit, Rs. 72,850 ; Total of Balance Sheet, Rs. 9,52,950*)

23. Below is given the Balance Sheet of Anusua and Priyambada as on 31st December, 1957. The partners share profits as Anusua, ¾ths and Priyambada, ¼th.

Balance Sheet

	Rs.	Rs.		Rs.
Sundry Creditors		30,000	Plant and Machinery	80,000
Reserve		20,000	Stock	30,000
Capital Accounts :			Sundry Debtors	25,000
Anusua	50,000		Cash at Bank	5,000
Priyambada	20,000			
		90,000		
		1,40,000		1,40,000

Sambida now joins them on condition that she should pay the partners Rs. 10,000 for ⅓rd share of the future profits. She introduces Rs. 25,000 as her capital. The partners have decided upon revaluation of the assets of the firm, before Sambida joins them, on the following terms :—

(*i*) Plant and Machinery is to be valued at Rs. 75,000 ; (*ii*) Stock is to be reduced by 10% ; (*iii*) A Provision is to be made against Sundry Debtors to the extent of 6% of the asset ; (*iv*) A liability of Rs. 1,500 included in Sundry Creditors is not likely to arise and hence is to be written back.

You are asked to journalise the above transactions in the books of the firm and give the resultant Balance Sheet on the admission of the new partner. What is the new profit sharing ratio ?

(*Capitals : Anusua Rs. 66,500 ; Priyambada Rs. 45,500 ; Total of Balance Sheet, Rs. 1,65,500*)

(*Adapted from B. Com., Calcutta*)

24. The Balance Sheet of Sridhar and Ghanashyam as on 31st December, 1959, is set out below ; they share profits or losses in the ratio of 2 : 1 :—

	Rs.		Rs.
Sridhar's Capital	39,000	Freehold Property	20,000
Ghanashyam's Capital	31,000	Furniture	6,000
General Reserve	24,000	Stock	12,000
Creditors	16,000	Debtors	60,000
		Cash	12,800
	1,10,800		1,10,800

They agree to admit Panchanan into the firm subject to the following terms and conditions :—

(*a*) Panchanan will bring in Rs. 9,000 as goodwill and pay in sufficient amount for proportionate capital ;

(*b*) He will be entitled to ¼ share of the profits of the firm ;

(*c*) 50% of the General Reserve is to remain as a Provision for Bad an Doubtful Debts ;

(*d*) Depreciation is to be provided on Furniture @ 5%

(*e*) Stock is to be revalued at Rs. 10,500.

(*f*) The capitals of all partners are to be in their profit sharing ratios.

Show journal entries, giving effect to the aforesaid arrangements (including cash transaction) and prepare the opening Balance Sheet of the new partnership.

(*Panchanan brings in Rs. 30,000 as Capital ; Total of Balance Sheet, Rs. 1,36,000*)

25. A, B and C were in partnership. On 1st January, 1950, A retired when the firm's Balance Sheet was as under :—

Liabilities	Rs.	*Assets*	Rs.
Capital Accounts :—		Land and Buildings	4,200
A	8,000	Plant and Machinery	6,980
B	6,800	Sundry Debtors	8,915
C	7,800	Investments	8,000
Creditors	6,928	Cash	1,433
	29,528		29,528

According to the Partnership Deed, assets were agreed to be revalued on A's retirement as under :—

Land and Buildings, Rs. 5,800 ; Plant and Machinery, Rs. 6,480 ; Investments, Rs. 8,400.

Besides, goodwill was then valued at Rs. 9.600. A accepted the investments at their revalued figure in part payment of his dues. B paid Rs. 4,000 as further Capital and A was paid off the balance of his account. Goodwill Account was not to be raised in books.

Prepare the revaluation Account, Partners' Capital Account and the revised Balance Sheet of B and C.

(*B : Capital, Rs. 9,700 ; C : Capital, Rs. 6,700 ; Total of Balance Sheet, Rs. 23,328*)

26. Rabi, Shashi and Tarak are in partnership sharing profits and losses in the proportions of 6 : 5 : 4. They take out a Joint Life Assurance Policy for Rs. 2,00,000 so that funds required to pay off the dues of a partner on his death may be available without presenting any financial difficulty to the firm. The annual premium on the policy is Rs. 7,500 and this is treated as a business expense. Accounts are closed annually on December 31, Shashi died on 31st March, 1956.

The partnership deed provides that the representatives of a deceased partner are entitled to (*i*) the deceased partner's capital as appearing in the last Balance Sheet ; (*ii*) interest on capital at 6% per annum to the date of his death ; (*iii*) his share of profits calculated till the date of his death on the average of the last three years' profits before inclusion of the policy premium as a business expense ; and (*iv*) share of goodwill calculated as two years' purchase on the average of the last three years' profits similarly calculated.

Shashi died on April 1, 1956. His drawings in 1956 amounted to Rs. 3,000. His Capital shown in the 1955 Balance Sheet was Rs. 80,000.

The profits for the years 1953, 1954, and 1955, after inclusion of the policy premium as a business expense, amounted to Rs. 65,000, Rs. 64,000 and Rs. 69,000 respectively.

Draw up Shashi's Account to show the amount due to his estate from the firm. Work to the nearest rupee. (*Rs. 1,99,992*)

(*Adapted from B. Com., Calcutta*)

27. Madhu, Radhu and Hadu are partners in the firm, sharing profits and losses as Madhu, 3/5th, Radhu, 1/5th and Hadu 1/5th. Balance Sheet of the firm as on the 31st December 1955 is as given below :—

Balance Sheet

		Rs.			Rs.
Capital Accounts :			Plant		35,000
Madhu	25,000		Stock		15,000
Radhu	20,000		Debtors	25,000	
Hadu	15,000		*Less* Provision for B.D.	1,000	
		60,000			24,000
Reserve		5,000			
Creditors		15,000	Cash at Bank		6,000
		80,000			80,000

The partners agree to sell the business to a private limited company which was incorporated with 50,000 shares of Rs. 10 each. The purchasing company agrees to take over the business for Rs. 80,000. The partners agreed to take 50% of the purchase price in cash and the balance is to be paid by issue of fully paid shares. The remaining shares were issued to the public and were paid for in full with the exception of one shareholder holding 100 shares who paid the application and the allotment monies of Rs. 3 and Rs. 2 respectively but failed to pay the call monies (Rs. 3 on the 1st Call and Rs. 2 on Final Call). You are asked to close the books of the firm and give Journal entries and the opening Balance Sheet of the new company on completion of the above transactions.

(*Profit on Realisation, Rs. 15,000 ; Total of Balance Sheet of the Company, Rs. 5,14,500*)

(*Calcutta University*)

28. J, G and M are partners, sharing profit in the proportions 2 : 2 : 1. They decided to dissolve the partnership on 31.12.58 and the Balance Sheet as on that date was as under :—

		Rs.			Rs.
Creditors		18,000	Freehold Property		8,000
Bank Overdraft (Guaranteed by J)		8,000	Plant and Machinery		14,400
Capital Accounts :			Stock		9,600
J	4,800		Debtors		2,400
G	6,000		Current Accounts :		
M	4,000		G	8,600	
		14,800	M	1,000	
					9,600
Current Account : J		3,200			
		44,000			44,000

The Freehold property realised Rs. 5,600 ; Plant and Machinery Rs. 10,800; Stock Rs. 6,000 ; and the Debtors Rs. 2,400. J paid off the Bank Overdraft. Expenses of realisation amount to Rs. 400. G became insolvent. In the estate of M there was a surplus of Rs. 2,600.

Draft the necessary Journal entries in the books of the partnership and close the Capital Accounts of the partners.

(*Loss on Realisation, Rs. 10,000 ; M pays Rs. 2,000 ; J receives Rs, 8,400*)

29. A, B and C were partners in a business and shared profits in the proportion of $\frac{1}{2} : \frac{3}{8} : \frac{1}{8}$ respectively. On 31st December, 1957, the Balance Sheet of their business was as under :

		Rs.		Rs.
Creditors		3,000	Goodwill	10,000
Capital Accounts			Sundry Assets	12,000
A	14,000		Cash at Bank	11,000
B	10,000			
C	6,000			
		30,000		
		33,000		33,000

On 1st January 1958 the following changes took place :—

(*i*) C retired from the business and his share valued at Rs. 8,000 was taken over by A and B who paid the former in their profit-sharing proportions from their personal resources.

(*ii*) S was then introduced in the business as a one-sixth partner on condition that a further sum of Rs. 6,000 was allowed to be credited to A and B in their respective proportions, and that he contributed such a sum as would make his capital equal to one-fourth of the total capital of A and B after all the above adjustments.

(*iii*) The new firm was converted into a limited company which took over the whole of the assets (except cash, for a consideration of Rs. 34,000, payable in fully paid shares of rupees ten each The shares are taken by the parties in their profit sharing ratio.

The Bank Balance of the firm was utilised in payment to creditors and the partners. You are required to show the Capital accounts of all the Partners, giving effect to the above transactions.

(Profit on Realisation, Rs. 6,000)
(Adapted from B. Com., Calcutta)

30. A, B and C are partners in a firm sharing Profits and losses @ 40%, 30% and 30% respectively. They decide to dissolve the firm and appoint B to realise the assets and distribute the proceeds. B is to receive 5% of the amount paid to other partners (before commission) as his remuneration and is to bear all the expenses of realisation.

The following is the Balance Sheet of the firm as on the date of the dissolution :—

Liabilities	Rs.	*Assets*		Rs.
Creditors	50,000	Cash at Bank		1,500
Capital Accounts :		Debtors	45,500	
A	20,000	*Less*		
B	20,000	Reserve	2,500	
				43,000
		Stock		60,000
		Capital Account :		
		C-Overdrawn		4,500
	1,09,000			1,09,000

B reports the result of realisation as follows :—

	Rs.
Debtors realise	35,000
Stock realise	40,500
Goodwill is sold for	2,000

Creditors are paid Rs. 57,000 in full settlement. In addition, Rs. 500 had to be paid for a discounted bill dishonoured.

The expenses of realisation came to Rs. 600, which is met personally.

A and B agree to receive from C Rs. 3,000 in full settlement of the firm's claim against him.

Show the Capital and Realisation Accounts of the firm.

(Loss on Realisation, Rs. 24,000; Commission due to B from A, Rs. 759)
(Adapted from B. Com., Calcutta)

31. PQR Ltd. issued 1,00,000 Equity Shares of Rs. 10 each payable @ Rs. 3 per share with application, Rs. 2 per share on allotment and the balanc @ Rs. 5 per share on first call. Full Payment was received except the call on 1,000 shares allotted to A. The directors pass a resolution forfeiting these 1000 shares and subsequently re-issue them to B as fully paid against cash payment of Rs. 7·50 per share. Make Journal and Cash Book entries and show how the Share Capital Account would appear in the Balance Sheet, according to the Companies' Act, 1956.
(Calcutta University)

32. A limited company issued 1,000 debenture bonds of Rs. 100 each at a premium of 10%, repayable at par at the end of the 10th year. The debenture bonds were issued at 25% on application, 35% on allotment (including the premium) and the balance on first and final call. All the monies were received by the company in due course

(*i*) You are asked to journalise the above transactions in the books of the company.

(*ii*) What provisions in your opinion should be made, if any for redemption of debentures ? (*Calcutta University*

33. New Enterprise Ltd, has a nominal capital of 1,50,000 ordinary shares of Rs. 10 each of which 1,00,000 shares have been in issue since the company commenced business. It was decided to issue the remaining shares at Rs. 15 each payable as follows :—

	Rs.
On Application	2·50
On Allotment (including premium)	7·50
1st Call (one month after allotment)	2·50
Final Call (two months after allotment)	2·50
	15·00

On 10th September, 1960, applications were received for 80,000 shares and on 29th September, 1960, the Directors allotted 50,000 shares, the application money being received on shares not allotted; amounts due on allotment were received on 10th October, 1960, and the first and final calls on their due dates with the exception of the final call on 500 shares. On 12th March, 1961, the 500 shares in default were declared forfeited by the Directors in accordance with the company's articles, such shares being re-issued on 16th April, 1961, at Rs. 10 each, the amount due being paid on the same day.

Give the necessary Journal entries to record the above transactions in the company's books. (*Calcutta University*)

34. From the following particulars prepare a Profit and Loss Account in respect of the year ended 30th September, 1962 and a Balance Sheet as at that date of Bright Traders Ltd. The Company has an authorised capital of Rs. 20,00,000 divided into 2,500 Preference shares of Rs 100 each and 1,75,000 Equity Shares of Rs. 10 each; 13,000 Preference and 50,000 Equity shares were issued and have been fully called up and paid.

	Rs.
Commission (Dr.)	11,000
Directors' Fees	2,000
Advance (Cr.)	10,000
Sales	37,09,846
Opening Stock :	
Raw Materials	1,14,114
Finished Goods	16,698
Sundry Creditors	87,000
Wages	61,414
Carriage Inwards	7,816
Carriage Outwards	2,000
Salary	86,606
Printing and Stationery	3,418
Postage and Telegrams	1,961
Rent, Rates and Taxes	4,800
Bank :	
Fixed Deposit	10,000
Current Account	94,462
Cash	1,720
Land	10,000
Buildings	1,11,130
Machinery and Plant	4,92,680
Furniture and Fittings	36,115
Vehicles	21,018
Book Debts	83,100
Purchase of Raw Materials	31,90,914
Profit and Loss Account (Dr.)	43,880

Value of Stock at end : Raw Materials Rs. 1,17,912 and Finished Goods Rs. 23,019; Liabilities for Salary Rs. 7,717, Rent Rs. 300 and Audit Fees Rs. 1,000; Interest on Fixed Deposit due Rs. 300; Depreciate Buildings @ 5%, Machinery and Plant @ 10%. Furniture and Fittings @ 6% and vehicles @ 20%. Create a Bad Debt Provision at 5% of the Book Debts. (Work to the nearer rupee).

(Profit Rs. 2,73,969: Total of Balance Sheet, Rs, 9,36,106)
(Adapted from B. Com., Calcutta)

35. Mafatlal (1962) Ltd. was formed to purchase the following assets of Mafatlal Ltd. (which company went in liquidation) which stood in the books of the latter company at the values stated :—

	Rs.
Goodwill	11,500
Freehold Premises	32,400
Stock	46,400
Book Debts	47,600
Patents	6,000

The Goodwill and Patents were of no value and took debts amounting to Rs. 2,400 were doubtful of recovery. The other assets appeared at correct value.

The purchase consideration was Rs. 1,20,000 to be paid as to Rs. 80,000 in cash and the balance in fully paid equity shares.

The company also allotted to the public, against cash payment, shares of the value of Rs. 56,000 and Debentures Rs. 60,000. It also raised a loan of Rs. 20,000 on mortgage.

Pass journal entries in the books of Mafatlal (1962) Ltd. to record the above transactions and prepare a Balance Sheet of the company.

36. A Ltd., was incorporated on 1st April, 1959, to take over as a going concern the partnership business of X and Y with effect from 1st January of the same year, from which date all profits of the business were to belong to the Company. The agreed purchase price was paid to the vendors on 30th April, 1959, with interest, which was due from 1st January to the date of payment.

The following is a list of items to be included in the Profit and Loss Account for the year to 31st December, 1959 :—

	Rs.		Rs.
Salaries	22,400	Interest paid to Vendors	1,220
General Expenses	3,684	Directors' Fees	2,675
Vendors' Salary	1,150	Depreciation of Motor Vans	460
Rent and Rates	764	Gross Profit	42,000
Commission on Sales	2,100		
Bad Debts (out of 1958 debts)	367		

The following additional information is available :—

(*a*) Sales during the year were—January to March Rs. 60,000; April to December Rs. 1,50,500.

(*b*) Salary paid to Vendors was for their services in managing the business upto 31st March, 1959.

(*c*) Two three-wheeler vans were taken over from the Vendors at an agreed value of Rs. 1,500 and a new one was purchased for Rs. 1,200 on 1st May, 1959. The rate of depreciation is 20% per annum.

Prepare the Profit and Loss Account of the company.

(Profit Rs. 4,999)

37. On January 10, 1940, a company issued at par Rs. 25,000 6% Redeemable Preference Shares of Rs. 10 each, to be redeemed at Rs. 12 per share on June 30, 1963. On January 1, 1942, Rs. 1,000 of the Preference Shares had

been forfeited for non-payment of the last call of Rs. 2·50 per share; 800 of these forfeited shares were subsequently re-issued on January 30, 1950, as fully paid for Rs. 5 per share.

On June 30, 1963, the credit balance of the Profit and Loss Account available for dividend was Rs. 2,00,000. Also to provide part of the funds required for the purpose of the redemption, 15,000 ordinary shares of Rs. 10 each were issued and allotted at a premium of Rs. 2 per share to the public on June 30, 1963 in consideration of full payment in cash. The redemption was carried out.

Show Cash Book entries and Ledger Accounts relating to the forfeiture of the Preference Shares and their re-issue, the issue of the Ordinary Shares and the Redemption of the Preference Shares.

(Adopted from B. Com., Calcutta)

38. The following is the Balance Sheet of Remfry & Co. Ltd. as on 31st December, 1961 :—

	Rs.		Rs.
Authorised Capital :		Goodwill	70,000
6,000 Shares of Rs. 100 each	6,00,000	Land and Buildings	80,000
		Plant and Machinery	1,50,000
Issued and Subscribed		Stock	50,000
Capital :		Sundry Debtors	43,000
2,000 Shares of Rs. 100 each		Cash at Bank	2,500
fully paid	2,00,000	Preliminary Expenses	4,500
200 5% Preference Shares		Profit and Loss A/c :	
of Rs. 1,000 each fully		Debit Balance	1,00,000
paid	2,00,000		
Sundry Creditors	50,000		
Bills Payable	5,000		
Bank Overdraft	45,000		
	5,00,000		5,00,000

The following scheme of reconstruction was duly approved and adopted :

(*a*) Without altering the number of shares in the Authorised Capital or issued and Subscribed Capital, the face value and the paid up value of each equity share be reduced to Rs. 50;

(*b*) The existing preference shares be converted into 100 7½% Debentures of Rs. 1,000 each fully paid ;

(*c*) Assets be revalued as under :—Land and Buildings Rs. 72,000; Plant and Machinery Rs. 1,40,000; Stock Rs. 45,000; Sundry Debtors subject to a Bad Debts provision of Rs. 2,500 ;

(*d*) Intangible and fictitious assets are to be written off :

Show journal entries in the books of the Company and also the Balance Sheet giving effect to the scheme of reconstruction.

39. The financial position of the Asian Patents Co. Ltd., as at 31st December, 1953, was as follows :—

Liabilities	Rs.	*Assets*	Rs.
Authorised and Issued		Preliminary Expenses	5,000
Share Capital :		Patent rights	1,50,000
15,000 shares of Rs. 10 each	1,50,000	Plant and Machiner	40,000
Sundry Creditors	1,40,000	Stock	20,000
		Debtors	60,000
		Cash	250
		Profit and Loss A/c	14,750
Total :	2,90,000		2,90,000

It was found necessary to reconstruct the company owing to shortage of working capital and depreciated value of the Patent Rights. The following scheme was submitted to the shareholders and creditors :—

1. The Company to be wound up voluntarily. All Assets and Liabilities being taken over by the Asiatic Patents Co. Ltd. formed with a nominal capital of Rs. 3,00,000 for the purpose.

2. The Preferential creditors amounting to Rs. 1,500 to be paid in full and as to the remainder Rs. 60,000 to receive eight annas in a rupee in full settlement and Rs. 78,500 to receive 6% Debentures to be issued at par as fully paid.

3. The shareholders of the old company to receive 15,000 shares of Rs. 10 each in the new company credited with Rs. 5 per share paid up. The balance of Rs. 5 per share being payable on allotment.

4. The liquidator's remuneration of Rs. 1,000 and his cost and expenses Rs. 960 to be paid by the new company as part of purchase consideration.

3. The remaining shares were issued to the public and were taken up and paid for. New Plant was purchased at a cost of Rs. 60,000.

Holders of Rs. 1,000 shares dissented and required their interest to be purchased. The price of Rs. 3·75 per share was agreed upon, which was duly realised by the liquidator by selling the said shares in the market, in return for the allotment of shares in the New Company.

Close the books of Asian Co., Ltd. and give the balance sheet of the Asiatic Patents Co. Ltd.

40. A New Company, C Ltd., is formed to take over two other existing companies A Ltd. and B Ltd., the Balance Sheets of which at the date of the taking over were as follows :—

	A	B		A	B
	Rs.	Rs.		Rs.	Rs.
Capital :			Freehold Premises	76,000	1,84,000
20,000 Ordinary Shares of Rs. 10 each	2,00,000		Furniture and fittings	12 000	8,000
25,000 Ordinary Shares of Rs. 10 each		2,50,000	Sundry Debtors	60,000	40,000
			Stock in hand	20,000	24,000
Sundry Creditors	10,000	20,000	Profit and Loss A/c (Dr.)	78,000	62,000
Bills Payable	16,000	18,000			
Bank Overdraft	20,000	3,000			
	2,46,000	3,18,0000		2,46 000	3,18,000

The Freehold Premises and the Furniture and Fittings are taken over at book values : Sundry Debtors at 80% and Stock at Rs. 16,000 and Rs. 18,000 respectively for A and B. The liabilities are to be taken over by C Ltd.

The appropriate purchase considerations are to be satisfied by fully paid shares of C Ltd.

Give the necessary Journal entries in the books of the three companies to give effect to the above taking over and draw up the opening Balance Sheet of C Ltd., which is floated with a nominal capital of 1,00,000 Ordinary Shares of Rs. 10 each of which 50,000 shares, fully paid, are issued in the first instance to satisfy the vendor companies as well as to arrange for working capital

(Total of Balance Sheet, Rs. 5,64,000)
(Adapted from B.Com., Calcutta)

41. The W. Company Ltd. is absorbed by the U. Company Ltd., the consideration being :—

(*i*) assumption of the liabilities,

(*ii*) discharge of the debenture debt at a premium of 5% by the issue of 6% debentures in the U Company Ltd.

(*iii*) payment in cash of Rs. 3 per share and exchange of three shares of Rs. one each in the U Company Ltd., at an agreed value of Rs. 1.50 P. per share for every share in the W. Company Ltd.

Below is given the Balance Sheet of the W. Company Ltd. as at the date of transfer.

Balance Sheet as at 31st March

	Rs.		Rs.
Share Capital : 60,000 shares of Rs. 5 each	3,00,000	Goodwill	25,000
		Land and Buildings	75.000
General Reserve	32.000	Plant and Machinery	2,20,000
Profit and Loss A/c (balance)	13,000	Patents	5,000
		Patterns and Drawings	2,500
Accident Insurance Fund	5,000	Stock-in-Trade	1,06,000
5% Debentures	1,50,000	Sundry Debtors	45,000
Sundry Creditors	20,000	Investments	5,000
		Cash at Bank and in hand	36,500
	5,20,000		5,20,000

Close the books of the Company by giving necessary Journal entries, assuming the costs of liquidation came to Rs. 5,000. Also record the transaction in the books of U Company Ltd. (*Profit on Realisation, Rs. 95,000*)
(*Adapted from B.Com., Calcutta*)

42. The Goa Ltd. is absorbed by India Ltd. on 31st December 1962 the consideration being, the assumption of liabilities, the discharge of the debenture debt at a premium of 5% by the issue of 5% debenture in India Ltd. and payment in each of Rs. 30 per share, and the exchange of three Rs. 10 shares, in India Ltd. at an agreed value of Rs. 15 per share, for every share in Goa Ltd.

The Balance Sheet of Goa Ltd. on the date of acquisition was as under :—

Balance Sheet as at 31st December 1962

	Rs.		Rs.
Share Capital : 60.000 Rs. 50 shares fully paid	30.00,000	Goodwill	2,50 000
		Land and Buildings	7,65,000
5% Debenture	15,00,000	Plant and Machinery	22,60,000
Sundry Creditors	2,00 000	Patents	50,000
Workmen's Profit Sharing Fund	1,00,000	Patterns and Drawings	25,000
Accident Compensation Fund	50.000	Work in progress and Stock	10,00,000
General Reserve A/c	3,20,000	Sundry Debtors	4,50,000
Profit and Loss A/c	30,000	Investments on Compensation Fund Account	50,000
		Cash at Bank	3,50,000
	52,00,000		52,00,000

You are asked to pass the journal entries to close the books of Goa Ltd. and the acquisition entries in the books of India Ltd.

(Profit on Realisation. 11,00,000)
(B.Com., Bombay)

43. A mine is taken on lease at a minimum rent of Rs. 10,000 per annum merging into a royalty of Re. 1 per ton of the ore raised, with a right to recoup short working during the two years following the one in which short-workings arose.

The raising for the first five years were : First year 2,000 tons ; Second year, 3,000 tons ; Third year, 15,000 tons ; Fourth year, 18,000 tons and Fifth year, 20,000 tons.

Write up the various ledger accounts including Dead Rent Account

44. H. Ltd., invoiced to their Northern Branch during the year goods at selling price (being 33⅓% added to cost) amounting to Rs. 74,000. The Credit sales of the branch were Rs. 31,000 and Cash Sales Rs. 17,000. The branch returns Rs. 2,000, stock at selling price and returns from customers, Rs. 1,000. The discount allowed to customers, by the branch amounted to Rs. 1,200. The branch remitted to Head Office Rs. 38,600, being the amount of cash sales and receipts from customers. The opening and closing stocks of the branch were Rs. 15,000 and Rs. 39,000 (both invoice value). The branch had debtors of Rs. 12,000 at the beginning. Loss through pilferage as ascertained to be Rs. 1,000 (cost Rs. 750).

Write up the necessary accounts to record the above in the Head Office books.

(Profit at branch, Rs. 9 800)

45. Ballygunge Chemical Ltd., has a branch office at Madras. On 1st April, 1955, the Head Office sent to Madras Branch goods costing Rs. 80,000 adding 20% to cost. On 30th June, 1955, it was found that the branch sold goods for cash amounting to Rs. 50,000. Goods of the value of Rs. 2,400 (invoice price) were returned to the Head Office. Cash received from Debtors by the 30th June amounted to Rs. 50,000, discounts allowed to them amounted to Rs. 250. The opening and closing balances of Stock and Debtors of the branch were : Stock Rs. 54,000 and Rs. 45,000 respectively (at invoice price) and Debtors Rs. 25,000 and Rs. 30,000 respectively. The expenses of the branch amounting to Rs. 10,000 were met by the Head Office by bank drafts.

You have been asked to record the above transactions in the book of the Head Office.

(Profit at branch, Rs. 9,500)
(Calcutta University)

46. Goods are invoiced by Head Office at cost plus 20% and branch sales are partly cash and partly credit. Good sold at the invoice price.

From the following particulars draw up accounts in the Head Office books to show profit or loss at the branch during 1960.

	Rs.
Stock of Goods at Branch at Jan. 1, 1960 (invoice price)	23,500
Goods sent to Branch (cost to H.O.)	2,75,000
Goods returned to Head Office (invoice price)	15,000
Cash Sale for the year	60,000
Credit Sales for the year	2,46,000
Returns from Customers	8,000
Discount and allowances to Customers	12,000
Bad Debts	1,000
Cash received from Customers	2,29,000
Sundry Debtors on Jan. 1, 1960	48,000
Establishment and Sundry other Branch Expenses	25,000

(Profit at Branch, Rs. 11,000)

Hint : Ascertain closing stock at the branch.

47. A sells an asset to B on January 1, 1960, on the Hire Purchase System. The total amount to be paid Rs. 50,000. The amount will be paid in four equal instalments at 6% per annum. The first instalments is paid on the delivery of the asset and subsequent instalment are paid on each anniversary of the date of delivery. The asset is to be depreciated at 10% per annum on the Reducing Instalment System.

Draw up the Vendors Account, Hire Charges Account and Asset Account in the the books of the Buyer. (The present value of Rupee one paid at the beginning of each year for four years is Rs. 36,730.

(Adapted from B. Com. Calcutta)

48. On 1st January, 1950, Messers X, Y, Z & Co., took delivery from Autocar Ltd., of 5 Motor Vans on a hire-purchase system, Rs. 2,000 being paid on delivery and the balance in five instalments of Rs. 3,000 each payable annually on 31st December. The Vendor Company charges 5% interest per annum on yearly balances. The cash-down value of the five vans was Rs. 15,000.

Show the Vendor's Account, Interest Account and the Motor Vans Account in the books of X, Y, Z & Co., for the five years, Provide depreciation at the rate of 20% on the diminishing balances. Adjust any difference in the fifth year's accounts. *(B. Com., Calcutta)*

49. (*a*) What are the main features of Double Account System of Book-keeping ?

(*b*) The undermentioned particulars have been collected from the books of Nabagram Electric Corporation Ltd. for the year ended 31st December, 1954 :—

	Rs.
50,000 Ordinary Shares of Rs. 10 each	5,00,000
20,000 Preference Shares of Rs. 100 each	20,00,000
Expended on Purchase of Land	10,00,000
" " Buildings	8,05,000
" " Mains and Service Pipes	75,000
" " Distributing Stations	50,000
" " Meters	30,000
" " Transformers	12,000
" " Public Lamps	20,000
" " Electrical Instruments	15,000
" " Preliminary Expenses	5,000

During the year 1955, the following further expenses were incurred: Buildings. Rs. 20,000, Meters, Rs. 10,000 Transformers, Rs. 12,000 and Public Lamps, Rs. 5,000.

You are asked to give the Capital Account for the year ended 31st December 1955. Prepare also a General Balance Sheet as on the 31st December, 1955, out of imaginary figures.

(*c*) How are Depreciation and Repairs and Renewals dealt with under Double Account System ? *(Calcutta University)*

50. A Gas Co. laid a main at a cost of Rs. 10,00,000 in 1940, materials constituting 60% and labour 40% of the cost in 1960, the main was replaced at a cost of Rs. 40,00,000. Between 1940 and 1960, material prices have doubled and labour rates have gone up 4 times. Journalise the entries on replacement.

51. Prepare a Statement of Affairs and Deficiency Account of Gujarat Good-luck Stores, who filed their petition on 31st December. 1952, Their books showed that they owed Rs. 40,100 of which creditors amounting to Rs. 6,500 held stock of the estimated value of Rs. 7,500 others amounting to Rs. 29,000 held stock of the estimated value of Rs. 15,000 and a mortgage on the property at Ahmedabad val d at Rs. 13.000, the Landlord being a preferential creditor for Rs. 100. Bill had been discounted amounting to Rs. 3,500 in respect of which it was estimated the firm would be liable for Rs. 500. The assets consisted of Book Debts: Good Rs. 1,500. Doubtful Rs. 600, estimated to produce Rs. 300; and Bad Rs. 700. Furniture and fittings Rs. 300, estimated to realise Rs. 150; Cash Rs. 50; B/R Rs. 350, Stock Rs. 1,600, estimated to produce Rs. 1,200. The firm commenced business on 1st January 1948 with a capital of Rs 25,000. After charging Rs. 1,000 a year for interest on capital, Rs. 1,300 a year for partners' salaries (which were credited to the Capital Account and not withdrawn), they made a profit in the first year of Rs. 2,700 but in the succeeding four years losses were incurred of Rs. 2,500, Rs. 3,200, Rs. 4.500 and Rs. 6,000 respectively. They drew out of cash at the rate of Rs. 1,200 a year. The property at Ahmedabad cost Rs. 22,000 and the stock mortgaged was subjected to a discount of 25 per cent.

(Deficiency Rs 1,550)
(B. Com., Bombay University)

Hint: Loss on stock is $\frac{25}{75}$ of the estimated realisable value.

52. Prepare the Balance Sheet of New India Bank Ltd. as at 31st December from the following particulars:

	Rs.
Authorised Capital	20,00,000
Issued and subscribed	8,00,000
Money at Call and Short Notice	5,00,000
Investments	30,00,000
Acceptances and endorsements for customers	2,00,000
Bills Receivable being bills for collection	4,00,000
Bills payable	5,00,000
Customers' Liability for Acceptances and Endorsements	2,00,000
Furniture and Fixtures	1,00,000
Land and Buildings	17,00,000
Loans	8,00,000
Cash Credits	3,00,000
Current Accounts	25,00,000
Fixed Deposits	14,00,000
Cash Certificates Issued	3,00,000
Profit for the year	4,00,000
Cash on Hand and at Bank	10,00,000
Savings Bank Accounts	7,00,000

The Reserve Fund is equal to Paid up Capital. The profit for the year is arrived at before making adjustment for unexpired discount of Rs. 5,000 on Bills discounted during the year but not matured on 31st December, 1954.

Investments include 5.000 shares of the face value of Rs. 100 each on which Rs. 50 is paid up. Claims against the Bank not acknowledged as debts amounted to Rs. 50,000).

(Total of Balance Sheet. Rs. 85.00.00

INDEX

OTHER IMPORTANT BOOKS ON COMMERCE AND MANAGEMENT

MODERN MARKETING (Principles and Practices)

R.S.N. Pillai & Bagavathi

This serviral and enlarged edition of the book is suitable for students of Marketing in college in India. The book consists of 38 chapters and is presented in a systematic manner.

CONTENTS: Market and Marketing • Modern Marketing Concept • Marketing System, Marketing Mix, Marketing Function • Buying, Assembling and Selling • Transportation • Storage and Warehouses • Standardisation and Grading • Marketing Finance • Marketing Risk • Marketing Information and Research • Marketing Management • Marketing Startegy & Planning • Product • Pricing • Branching and Packaging • Promotional Programme • Sales Promotion • Advertising • Personal Selling • Sales Organisation • Sales Forcast Management • Control of Sales Force • Sales Process • Remuneration to Salesmen • Consumer Behaviour • Consumerism • Law Relating to Sale of Goods • Channels of Distribution-I • Channels of Distribution-II • Marketing of Consumer Goods • Marketing of Industrial Goods • Marketing of Securities • Marketing of Agricultural Goods • Regulated Markets • Organised Markets • Co-operative Marketing • International Marketing • Marketing & Society.

07 301 ISBN : 81-219-1697-6 pp. 400

ISO 9000 — A MANUAL FOR TOTAL QUALITY MANAGEMENT

Suresh Dalela & Saurabh

The basic objective of the book is to provide the students of Engineering Discipline and Quality Professionals of business sectors, a survey of different Standards of Quality Assurance & Quality Management Systems.

CONTENTS: Introduction to Quality Concepts & ISO 9000 Series of Quality Systems • Quality Management System • Key Elements of ISO 9001 & Its Requirements (July 1994 version) • Defects Prevention & Quality Improvement Techniques • Documen-tation of Quality Management System • Quality Planning & Quality Programmes • Sample of a Quality Manual (form and Structure) • Assessment or Audit (Internal & External) • Implementing ISO 9000 Quality Systems & Certification • Quality Costs • Quality Management (Some relevant Topics) • Total Quality Control (Through Statistical Means) • Quality Awareness, Education & Training

07278 ISBN : 81-219-1483-3 (H.B.) pp. 448

HUMAN RESPONSE DEVELOPMENT

G.D. Maheshwari

Everybody is not a job hopper or a high jumper but even then he can reach the top of the ladder step by step. This book lays stress for creation of work environment in such a way that the individual is treated as an important component of the whole infrastructure and not just a cog in the wheel. This book describes even those who can never boast of a position or rank is their academic career, have acheived spectacular success in life.

CONTENTS: Time Management • Making meetings effecive • How to be a good boss? • Communication–The Key to Success • Motivation • Leadership How to Make a Mark as a Manager • Are you a Supervisor Stress Management • Conflict Management • Acheiving Improved Performances Towards Higher Administrative Efficiency • Delegation in Principle 'Yes' and in Practice? • The Art of Looking Busy and Doing Nothing Creativity and Brain Storming • Managing Success Successfully, Cutpieces • of TACT.

07 306 ISBN : 81-219-0431-5 pp. 742

PROFESSIONAL MANAGEMENT IN INDIA

Problems and Prospects

M.V. Pylee

K.C. Sankaranarayanan

The book, gives a detailed account of the Problems, that professional Management body in India faces with. these and related questions are dealt with in this volume which consists in all thirty-nine. Papers by Knowledge able persons, practising managers as well as management teachers.

07303 ISBN:81-219-1772-7 pp. 304

ENTREPRENEURIAL DEVELOPMENT

S.S. Khanka

The book has been written in a simple and self-learning style. Clarity has been given top priority throughtout the book. It is intended as an indepth knowledge source for an intending practitioner/entrepreneur in the field of entrepreneurship development.

CONTENTS : Entrepreneur • Women Entrepreneurship • Enterpreneurship• Factors Affecting Entrepreneurial Growth • Entrepreneurial Motivation Entrepreneurial Competencies • Entrepreneurial Mobility • Entrepreneurship Development Programmes (EDPs) •Small Enterprises: An Introductory Framework • Project Identification and Selection (PIS) • Project Formulation • Project Appraisal • Financing of Enterprise • Institutional Finance to Entrepreneurs • Lease Financing and Hire-Purchase • Institutional Support to Entrepreneurs • Taxation Benefits to Small-Scale Industry • Ownership Structures •
The Business: Its Nature and Scope • Fundamentals of Management • Working Capital Management • Inventory Management • Production and Operation Management • Marketing Management • Human Resource Management • Accounting for Small Enterprises • Growth Strategies in Small Business • Government Policy for Small-Scale Enterprises • Small Enterprises in International Business.

07 307 ISBN : 81-219-1801-4 pp. 330

प्रबंध लेखांकन

योगेन्द्र प्रसाद वर्मा, विजय बहादुर सिंह एवं अजेय वर्मा

प्रस्तुत पुस्तक में, विषय की प्रकृति को सही रूप में समझने से सम्बन्धित सभी बातों का समावेश तथा इसकी सरल भाषा में पूर्ण व्याख्या की गयी है। साथ ही इसमें प्रबंण लेखांकन का क्षेत्र क्यों और कैसे लेंखांकन के अन्य प्रारूपों से व्यापक है आदि का सविस्तार विश्लेषण किया गया है जो बी.कॉम (प्रतिष्ठा) और एम.कॉम के विद्यार्थियों के लिए उपयोगी सिद्ध होगी।

विषय सूची-प्रबंध लेखांकन: एक परिचय • वित्तीय विवरण : प्रकृति एवं महत्त्व • वित्तीय विवरणों का विश्लेषण एवं निर्वचन • तुलनात्मक एवं समानाकार विवरण • प्रवृत्ति विश्लेषण • अनुपात विश्लेषण • कोष प्रवाह विवरण • रोकड़ प्रवाह विवरण • स्कंध नियंत्रण • मुद्रा-स्फीति लेखांकन.

07311 ISBN:81-219-1854-5 pp. 504

PERSONNEL MANAGEMENT AND INDUSTRIAL RELATIONS

N.G. Nair

The book Consists of 23 chapters divided into five parts. Part I deals with development of perception and Part II deals with Acquistion and Absorption. Part III deals with Development Utilisation, Part IV deals with Maintenance with Motivation and Empowerment..

CONTENTS : H.R. DEVELOPMENT OF PRECEPTION • Introduction • Evelution And Environment • Theories of H.R.M. • ACQUISITION AND ABSORPTION • Human Resources Planning • Recruitment • Selection Placement, Induction and Socialisation • DEVELOPMENT AND UTILISATION • Theories of Training and Development • Employee Training • Management / Executive Development • Career Development • Promotion, Transfer and Separation • MAINTENANCE, AND RETENTION • Wages and Salaries Administration • Discipline and Grievances • Industrial and Labour Relations • Trade Unionism • Collective Bargaining • Rewards and Labour Welfare • Industrial Health and Safety • Performance Appraisal & Merit Rating • MOTIVATION AND EMPOWERMENT • Theories of Human Relation and Motivation • Vocational Guidance, Job Satisfaction and Morale • Steps to Promote Intrinsic Motivation • Organisation Structure Design and Development • Empowerment and Future of H.R.M.

07295 ISBN :81-219-1808-1 pp. 536

ACCOUNTING THEORY & MANAGEMENT ACCOUNTING

Sujit Kumar Roy & Sisir Kumar Bhattacharya

The book bears the testimony of being lucid in its expression and brevity in its expression and brevity in its exposition. Numerous problems of various nature have been worked out so that the users may find it useful to achieve their end and to have clear understinding of the subject.

07 270 ISBN : 81-219-1882-0 pp. 6

एडवान्स्ड एकाउन्ट्स – भाग-1

एम.सी. शुक्ला, टी.एस. ग्रेवाल, एम.पी. गुप्ता, बी.एम

प्रस्तुत पुस्तक के इस भाग में लेखांकन की आधारभूत विषय सामग्री की

इस पुस्तक में प्रत्येक

अध्याय की विषय-वस्तु का स्पष्ट परिचय कराते हुए, उसके आधारभूत नियमों की व्याख्या की गयी है तथा प्रत्येक अध्याय से चुने हुए विवेकपूर्ण क्रियात्मक प्रश्नों को पूर्ण हल सहित, क्रमवार प्रस्तुत किया गया है।

विषय-सूची: लेखांकन के नियम (जर्नल, लेजर, सहायक पुस्तकें तथा तलपट) • बिल सम्बन्धी व्यवहार • (बैंक सम्बन्धी लेनदेन तथा बैंक समाधान विवरण) • अशुद्धियों का संशोधन • लेखांकन अवधारणायें व प्रथायें • पूँजीगत तथा आयगत व्यय • माध्य भुगतान तिथि तथा चालू खाता विवरण • अन्तिम खाते • प्रेषण खाते • संयुक्त उपक्रम खाते • इकहरी प्रविष्ट प्रणाली • प्राप्ति-भुगतान व आय-व्यय खाते • स्वकीय संतुलन व वर्गीय संतुलन प्रणाली • जहाजी यात्रा सम्बन्धी खाते • पैकिंग सामान सम्बन्धी खाते • संचय कोष तथा आयोजन • ह्रास लेखांकन • साझेदारी खाते (*i*) साझेदार का प्रवेश (*ii*) साझेदार का अवकाश ग्रहण (*iii*) साझेदारी का समापन • अधिकार शुल्क खाते • विभागीय खाते • शाखा खाते • किराया क्रय तथा किस्त भुगतान पद्धति • दीवालिया सम्बन्धी खाते • विनियोग खाते • बीमा दावे।

07 219 ISBN-81-219-0450-1 pp. 1600

एडवान्स्ड एकाउन्ट्स – भाग-2 एम.सी. शुक्ला, टी.एस. ग्रेवाल, एम.पी. गुप्ता, बी.एम. अग्रवाल

प्रस्तुत पुस्तक के इस दूसरे भाग में लेखांकन की उच्चस्तरीय स्वरूपों की विवेचना की गयी है।

07 220 ISBN : 81-219-0451-X pp. 1100

INDUSTRIAL MANAGEMENT

I.K. Chopde, A.M. Seikh

The book is a beginning one year textbook in 'Industrial Management'. It will be useful for anyone desiring to learn management starting from the first principles without any prior preparation or initiation. It contains five parts. The first part of this book gives general introduction to the process and principles of introduction to the process and princples of management. It is not intended that the topics selected give an exhaustive treatment, but rather they are developed to the point that the beginner can understand and appreciate the like personnel, financial, marketing and materials management etc.

07 287 ISBN : 81-219-1480-9 pp. 336

MANAGEMENT ACCOUNTING

R.S.N. Pillai & V. Bagavati

The book has presented the subject in a simple languageand in a most systematic manner. The special feature of the book is that the concepts have been elaboratory explained step by step with minute details and suitable illustrations at the appropriate places. It contains a large number of theoretical questions and 234 practical problems.

CONTENTS : Management Accounting • Analysis and Interpretation of Financial

Statements • Accounting Ratios • Fund Flow Statements • Cash Flow Statement • Working Capital Management • Marginal Costing • Standard Costing I • Standard Costing II • Budget and Budgetary Control • Reporting to Management • Inflation Accounting

07 264 ISBN : 81-219-1062-5 pp. 570

BANKING LAW AND PRACTICE

K.P. Kandasami

This book has been designed to serve as a text-book for the students preparing for Banking Law and Practice paper of Commerce stream and other various Competitive examinations.

CONTENTS : Laws of Banking in India • Ralation between Banker and Customer • Customer's Accounts with Bankers • Special Types of Banker's Customers • Negotiable Instruments • Checks • Payment of Checks • Collection of Checks • Loans and Advances • Secured Advances— Types of Securities • Letters of Credit and qurantees.

07308 ISBN : 81 - 219-1781-6 pp.124

सांख्यिकी सिद्धान्त एवं व्यवहार

एस.पी. सिंह

प्रस्तुत पुस्तक के इस नवीन संस्करण में भारतीय सांख्यिकी नामक खण्ड के सभी अध्यायों को नए सिरे से संशोधित कर इसमें जनगणना 1991, CSO तथा NSSO की 1996-1997 तक की कार्य प्रगति, NSSO का 53वाँ दौर (जनवरी 1997 से दिसम्बर 1997), आर्थिक संगणना 1990, आदि नवीनतम विषयों का सविस्तार वर्णन किया गया है।

07 093 ISBN:81-219-0037-9 pp. 1220

[illegible] Accounting [illegible] Fund Flow Statements [illegible] Cash Flow Statement [illegible] Working Capital Management [illegible] Marginal Costing [illegible] Standard Costing [illegible] Uniform Costing [illegible] Budgets and Budgetary Control [illegible] Responsibility Accounting [illegible] Inflation Accounting [illegible]

[illegible] ISBN [illegible] [illegible]

BANKING LAW AND PRACTICE

K P M Sundaram

This book has been prepared to serve as a text book for the students preparing for Banking Law and Practice paper of Commerce stream and of various Competitive examinations

CONTENTS: Laws of Banking [illegible]

[illegible] ISBN [illegible]

[illegible]

[illegible] ISBN [illegible]